RETHINKING STATE AND BORDER FORMATION IN THE MIDDLE EAST

RETHINKING STATE AND BORDER FORMATION IN THE MIDDLE EAST

Turkish–Syrian–Iraqi Borderlands, 1921–1946

Jordi Tejel

EDINBURGH
University Press

Edinburgh University Press is one of the leading university presses in the UK. We publish academic books and journals in our selected subject areas across the humanities and social sciences, combining cutting-edge scholarship with high editorial and production values to produce academic works of lasting importance. For more information visit our website: edinburghuniversitypress.com

© Jordi Tejel 2023, 2024, under a Creative Commons Attribution-NonCommerical-NoDerivatives licence

Edinburgh University Press Ltd
13 Infirmary Street, Edinburgh, EH1 1LT

First published in hardback by Edinburgh University Press 2023

Typeset in 11/15 Adobe Garamond by
IDSUK (DataConnection) Ltd

A CIP record for this book is available from the British Library

ISBN 978 1 3995 0365 5 (hardback)
ISBN 978 1 3995 0366 2 (paperback)
ISBN 978 1 3995 0367 9 (webready PDF)
ISBN 978 1 3995 0368 6 (epub)

The right of Jordi Tejel to be identified as author of this work has been asserted in accordance with the Copyright, Designs and Patents Act 1988 and the Copyright and Related Rights Regulations 2003 (SI No. 2498).

CONTENTS

List of Figures — vi
Acknowledgements — vii

Introduction — 1
1 Networks of Violence in the Shatterzones of the Post-Ottoman Middle East — 35
2 Refugees, Borders and Identity Boundaries — 72
3 Cross-border Infringements: Smugglers, Criminals and Fugitives — 123
4 Interstate Cooperation against Diseases and Plagues and its Limits — 161
5 Railroads, Uneven Mobilities and Frail States — 200
6 Irredentism in a Context of Global Uncertainty — 239
7 De-bordering and Re-bordering Middle Eastern States — 277
Conclusion — 315

Bibliography — 328
Index — 368

FIGURES

I.1	Map of the Turkish–Syrian–Iraqi Borderlands and the Tri-Border Zone	8
1.1	Itineraries of the Commission in Mosul Contested Area, 1925	67
2.1	Illustration of the pillars erected along the Turkish–Iraqi border in 1927	82
2.2	Map of the Franco-British Convention of 1920 as interpreted by France and Britain	88
3.1	Border card or *passavant* used at the Turkish–Syrian border in the 1930s and 1940s	132
3.2	Map of smuggling routes from Syria and Iraq into Turkey, 1931	143
5.1	Map of the Baghdad Railway extension between 1936 and 1940	219
5.2	Passengers awaiting the arrival of the Taurus Express at Tel Kotchek, 1941	233

ACKNOWLEDGEMENTS

This book is the result of a larger research project undertaken at the University of Neuchâtel between 2017 and 2022, titled 'Towards a Decentred History of the Middle East: Transborder Spaces, Circulations, Frontier Effects and State Formation, 1920–46' (BORDER). This project as well as the publication of this book on open access is supported by the European Research Council (ERC) under the European Union's Horizon 2020 research and innovation approval Grant Agreement (No 725269). Therefore, I thank first the ERC for the grant that made both the research and the book possible.

Writing a book is often a long and tortuous adventure with ups and downs, and yet also a route coloured by countless encounters and discussions with a myriad of scholars and colleagues who, one way or another, leave their imprint upon the final manuscript and thus deserve public credit. I particularly thank the members of the research team gathered around the ERC project in Neuchâtel at the History department: Victoria Abrahamyan, César Jaquier and Laura Stocker (PhD students), and Ramazan Hakkı Öztan (post-doctoral Fellow). Together we convened for frequent reading seminars, talks, and two workshops that helped me refine my earlier views of the main topics analysed in this book. Together or separately, the team has also been instrumental in collecting thousands of digital pictures of records and newspaper articles from numerous public and private archives as well as at amazing libraries located around the world. Needless to say, should they have not drawn my attention to certain files retrieved from some of those collections, I would have certainly overlooked many of them. Beside their incalculable input, it has truly been a pleasure to work with them.

The two international workshops held in Neuchâtel in 2018 and 2019 were important events to kick start the project and, more importantly, meet and exchange with experts on issues that were central to my own research agenda: borders and borderlands, violence, refugees, cross-border mobility, state-formation processes and, more generally, the post-Ottoman Middle Eastern regional dynamics. Besides the members of the team, Seda Altuğ, Alexander E. Balistreri, Lauren Banko, Samuel Dolbee, Robert S. G. Fletcher, Ella Fratantuono, Peter Gatrell, Chris Gratien, Simon Jackson, Reşat Kasaba, Ayşenur Korkmaz, Katharina Lange, Norig Neveu, Orçun Can Okan, Maurus Reinkowski, Laura Robson, Davide Rodogno, Mehdi Sakatni, Aline Schlaepfer, Carl Shook, Nina Studer, Vahé Tachjian, Benjamin T. White and Adrien Zakar contributed to these workshops and enriched the discussions with their thoughts and ideas. Throughout the last five years I have also participated in a number of workshops and conferences held at the universities of Cambridge, Exeter, Geneva, Graz, Istanbul, Koya, Oxford, Torino, Vienna and Zakho, venues that provided me not only with additional opportunities to test my ideas, but also to learn from and discuss with savvy scholars. I am very grateful to all of them. Obviously, any flaws in the book are mine alone.

Léonard Schneider produced the maps and Claude Erard assisted me in creating the illustrations for the book. Daniela Livingstone was an early and enthusiastic reader. I also thank the Norwegian Museum of Science and Technology in Oslo for gracefully securing the rights to images.

Finally, I thank the two anonymous manuscript reviewers whose feedback helped shape this book. I owe a debt of gratitude to Emma House and Louise Hutton from the Edinburgh University Press for their support throughout the entire production process.

Jordi Tejel, Neuchâtel
July 2022

INTRODUCTION

On 27 August 1943, a Syrian citizen who had travelled to Viranşehir, in south-eastern Turkey, reported to the French Intelligence Services that all villages located on a strip of land 40–50 km north of the Turkish–Syrian border had been evacuated by the military authorities and several garrisons were erected in their stead. Despite the deployment of British troops in the Levant two years earlier to protect the region from Axis' activities, and although Turkey was a neutral country, political and military tensions between the Turks and the French seemed to be at their highest level along the common border zone. For one thing, Turkey had not recognised the authority of the Free French in Syria yet, and more importantly, since 1942 constant rumours fed by border dwellers and local Turkish authorities had themselves contributed to nourishing the idea that, all of a sudden, some dramatic developments were to take place.

Critically, while in Viranşehir, the Syrian informant was told that the local governor was soon to be appointed to Deir ez-Zor down south, which was supposed to become the new administrative centre of the region after the 'imminent' Turkish annexation of Northern Syria. Likewise, talking to a Christian notable from the same Turkish town, the Syrian traveller asked him why, unlike his brother who happened to be the *mukhtar* of Hasaka, he had not settled in Syria yet. The Christian notable answered that it did not make any sense to move to Syria since 'every now and then Turkish soldiers and civil servants tell everyone that very soon the Turks will enter into Syrian territory'.[1] Therefore, it was only a matter of time until he and his brother would be under the same jurisdiction again. The rumours about the potential Turkish annexation of Northern Syria that are central to this piece of intelligence were by no means new.[2] Their pervasiveness throughout more than two decades and the views expressed by borderlanders in this report must thus be read in light of a context marked by permanent uncertainty.[3]

This short piece of intelligence highlights three main themes that are dealt with in this book. First, the most obvious: more than twenty years after the signing of the post-war settlements, the newly-established system made up of nation states was still fragile in the Middle East and irredentism was a very real threat. In that regard, although the region was not one of the major battlegrounds of the Second World War, its borderlands and their populations were both witnesses of and contributors to the strains and dynamics of a conflict that unleashed far-reaching economic, political and social transformations across the region. In a sense, as in the early 1920s, Middle Eastern border zones found themselves at the heart of the many tensions of an international order that was coming to an end.

Indeed, the collapse of the Ottoman Empire paved the way for diverse projects of modern statecraft in the Levant and Mesopotamia under the French and British colonial oversight. However, the drawing of territorial and political boundaries that underpinned these new state configurations

---

[1] CADN, 1SL/1/V/2051. Special Services at Ras al-Ayn. Weekly bulletin, No. 36, 16 October 1943.

[2] For a comprehensive analysis about the circulation of rumours across the Turkish–Syrian border and their impact in the interwar years, see Ramazan Hakkı Öztan, 'Republic of Conspiracies: Cross-Border Plots and the Making of Modern Turkey, 1919–39', *Journal of Contemporary History*, Vol. 56, No. 1 (2021), pp. 55–76; Jordi Tejel, 'States of Rumors: Politics of Information along the Turkish-Syrian Border, 1925–45', *Journal of Borderlands Studies*, Vol. 37, No. 1 (2022), pp. 95–113.

[3] On the role of intelligence services in the area in those years, see Jean-David Mizrahi, *Genèse de l'Etat mandataire. Service des renseignements et bandes armées en Syrie et au Liban dans les années 1920* (Paris: Publications de la Sorbonne, 2003); Martin Thomas, *Empires of Intelligence: Security Services and Colonial Disorder after 1914* (Berkeley, CA: University of California Press, 2007).

quickly led to a period of fluidity, particularly in the border areas where colonial penetration was fiercely contested by a variety of state and non-state actors.[4] In Anatolia, the resistance movement used intense propaganda that promoted notions of Muslim solidarity in a bid to rally several tribal chiefs in a fight against the French and British troops. Because of their successive military victories, Mustafa Kemal and his followers forced the European powers to give up their imperial designs on Anatolia, dismiss the validity of the 1920 Treaty of Sèvres, and searched for a political compromise with an independent Turkey. By October 1921, Turkey and France had signed the Ankara Agreement, whereby both sides agreed that the boundary between Turkey and French-ruled Syria would in large part follow the tracks of the Baghdad Railway. In 1923, a more favourable Treaty of Lausanne replaced that of Sèvres. Even though Turkey was unable to regain the ex-Ottoman province of Mosul, the Ankara government secured significant economic advantages, notably over Mosul's oil. Meanwhile, France and Great Britain consolidated their position in Syria, Lebanon, Iraq, Palestine and Transjordan as mandatory powers on behalf of the newly-established League of Nations.[5] Despite the apparent stability of post-war settlements, the territorialisation process of Middle Eastern states was still an unfinished and contentious affair.

After all, Turkey had always considered the Syrian province of Alexandretta as part of her homeland – a portion of 'Turkish' territory that could be regained if political and diplomatic conditions were favourable to Ankara. In the same vein, a coalition of tribal forces constituted in Nejd (now in Saudi Arabia) around Wahhabism – an Islamic doctrine and religious movement

---

[4] Jean-David Mizrahi, 'Un "nationalisme de la frontière": Bandes armées et sociabilités politiques sur la frontière turco-syrienne au début des années 1920', *Vingtième Siècle Revue d'histoire*, Vol. 78 (2003), pp. 19–34; Michael Provence, *The Last Ottoman Generation and the Making of the Modern Middle East* (Cambridge: Cambridge University Press, 2017); Jonathan Wyrtzen, *Worldmaking in the Long Great War: How Local and Colonial Struggles Shaped the Modern Middle East* (New York: Columbia University Press, 2022).

[5] Erez Manela, *The Wilsonian Moment: Self-Determination and the International Origins of Anticolonial Nationalism* (Oxford: Oxford University Press, 2007); Susan Pedersen, *The Guardians. The League of Nations and the Crisis of Empire* (Oxford: Oxford University Press, 2015).

known as *Ikhwan* – challenged the eastern frontier of Transjordan as well as the south-western margins of the Iraqi state throughout the 1920s and early 1930s. Furthermore, despite the severe intervention of the French to crush the 'Syrian Kingdom' in Damascus in 1920, the dream of recreating Greater Syria as a political unit did not completely vanish in the interwar years. Finally, while most boundary accords were signed in the early 1920s, the delimitation of boundaries was a rather long and contingent path in which state representatives, League of Nations' experts and local populations interacted, all leaving their imprint on the final demarcation of nation state territorial markers, as late as the mid-1930s.

Yet, this was the time when Italian and Bulgarian revisionism in the eastern Mediterranean and the Balkans was met in turn with the re-awakening of Turkish irredentism over Syrian territories after the signing of the Franco-Syrian Treaty of 1936. Although France did not ratify the Treaty that projected an independent Syria, Turkey was quick in voicing her opposition to its terms.[6] Ankara saw in the ambiguities left by the accord on the future status of Alexandretta an opportunity to kill two birds with one stone: regain an ex-Ottoman province based on its alleged Turkish ethnic character, and secure Turkey's interests in the face of Italy's threat. After the annexation of Alexandretta – renamed Hatay – in 1939, and given the context of uncertainty and fluidity created by the Second World War, reports on Turkish territorial ambitions over northern Syria could only gain in credibility in the eyes of both French authorities and borderlanders.[7]

In that sense, border zones in the post-Ottoman Middle East must be seen as the very centres of influence, movements and tensions, ranging from irredentism and refugee issues to the demarcation of boundaries and customs policies, among many others, which transformed sovereignties into new forms throughout the 1920s and 1930s, in tandem with global and regional processes. As such, borders and borderlands should be framed as central to

---

[6] 'Antakya bizimdir', *Cumhuriyet*, 1 October 1936; Atatürk, *Atatürk'ün Söylev ve Demeçleri, I–III* (Ankara: Atatürk Araştırma Merkezi, 1997), p. 142.

[7] Sarah D. Shields, *Fezzes in the River: Identity Politics and European Diplomacy in the Middle East on the Eve of World War II* (Oxford: Oxford University Press, 2011). See also Amit Bein, *Kemalist Turkey and the Middle East: International Relations in the Interwar Period* (Cambridge: Cambridge University Press, 2017).

the making of the history of contemporary Middle East and consistently 'seen as charged sites, where identities are forged, policies take shape and interests clash'.[8] Traditionally kept off the radar of historians, a view from the borderlands might thus allow historians to both re-interpret the past and revise the well-established narratives about the state-formation processes throughout the two decades following the collapse of the Ottoman Empire.

Second, a view from the borderlands might also help us highlight borderlanders' agency and in particular their role in shaping the new 'regimes of mobility' that were in the making across the region.[9] In our initial story, the French officers did not provide any details about the identity of their 'informant', nor about the precise reasons that led the two brothers to remain separated on each side of the Turkish–Syrian boundary. Yet, the report reveals some of the facets that characterised the newly-established borders. On the one hand, the ability to cross a border freely depended on factors such as social status and the identity of the person crossing. In this case, the Syrian informant enjoyed a privileged status – i.e. connections with the French intelligence services, a valid passport, language skills and a valuable network of social relations in Turkey that allowed him to crisscross the international border with ease and 'prove' his value in the eyes of French officers. That was not, of course, the case for all borderlanders.

On the other hand, the social position of the two brothers – one, an urban notable in Viranşehir; the other a *mukhtar* in Hasaka, a small town created by the French in the mid-1920s – seems to suggest that establishing themselves in two different yet neighbouring countries was part of a family strategy. While moving southwards or northwards was still conceivable for them, they nevertheless opted for stasis, most likely to secure their social influence on both sides of the international border, despite growing diplomatic tensions between Turkey and French-ruled Syria. This was hardly

---

[8] Jordi Tejel and Ramazan Hakkı Öztan, 'Introduction', in Jordi Tejel and Ramazan Hakkı Öztan (eds), *Regimes of Mobility: Borders and State Formation in the Middle East, 1918–46* (Edinburgh: Edinburgh University Press, 2022), p. 8.

[9] On this notion, see Ronen Shamir, 'Without Borders? Notes on Globalization as a Mobility Regime', *Sociological Theory*, Vol. 23, No. 2 (2005), pp. 197–217; Nina Glick Schiller and Noel B. Salazar, 'Regimes of Mobility across the Globe', *Journal of Ethnic and Migration Studies*, Vol. 39, No. 2 (2013), pp. 183–200.

surprising. As suggested by Peter Sahlins in his seminal study of the Franco-Spanish frontier at the Cerdanya Valley, the establishment of modern borders and the subsequent limitations of cross-border mobility favoured the agency of individuals and groups who were able to either evade or respect them, depending on their own agendas.[10] In the Middle East, as elsewhere, while some borderlanders traded, worked, socialised and married as if the new boundaries did not exist,[11] others quickly 'viewed the international border for what it was – that is, the realm of separate sovereignties and hence an opportunity to benefit from disconnected jurisdictions.'[12] Thus, borders became a resource for a variety of individuals and groups such as smugglers, deserters, refugees, migrants and fugitives who helped both reconnect populations circumscribed by the borderlands and distinguish sovereignties as an experienced reality.

Finally, despite the prevalence of modernisation and dependency paradigms that tend to view the society as a passive recipient of state intervention in general, and within the process of state-formation, in particular, this piece of intelligence shows that there was not always a clear-cut boundary between 'state' and 'society'.[13] At times, borderlanders contacted border authorities as well as local officials in moments of personal need, requesting and (sometimes) receiving assistance regarding a variety of legal matters, in particular, disputes over citizenship and sovereignty in relation to cross-border crimes, marriages, inheritance, property and lost animals. Thus, while instances of violence – that is, forced displacement, repression of

---

[10] Peter Sahlins, *Boundaries: The Making of France and Spain in the Pyrenees* (Berkeley, CA: University of California Press, 1989). See also Oscar Jáquez Martínez, *Border People: Life and Society in the US-Mexico Borderlands* (Tucson: University of Arizona Press, 1994); David N. Gellner (ed.), *Borderland Lives in Northern South Asia* (London: Rowman & Littlefield, 2013); Mandy Sadan, *Being and Becoming Kachin: Histories Beyond the State in the Borderworlds of Burma* (Oxford: Oxford University Press, 2013).

[11] Hastings Donnan and Thomas M. Wilson (eds), *Borderlands. Ethnographic Approaches to Security, Power, and Identity* (London and New York: University Press of America, 2010), p. 9.

[12] Jordi Tejel and Ramazan Hakkı Öztan, 'Introduction', pp. 14–15.

[13] Philip Abrams, 'Notes on the Difficulty of Studying the State', *Journal of Historical Sociology*, Vol. 1, No. 1 (1988), pp. 63–4.

contraband, tribes and smugglers' raids against security forces – shaped state–society relations in the borderlands, their day-to-day interactions were context-specific and complex.[14] Ultimately, either by resisting state policies or by approaching state officials to solve their problems, local populations played a role in 'bringing the state back in'.[15]

All things considered, borderland (hi)stories help to highlight the liminality – i.e. a state of in-betweenness – of these spaces and their societies. The reason is that borderlands are not regions within nation states, but rather transnational spaces whose multicultural and multi-layered dimensions are underscored by the very same borders that seek to erase the liminal identity of borderlands populations.[16] That being the case, the liminality and ambivalence of borderlanders allow us to challenge some of the well-known '-isms' – such as nationalism, colonialism, modernism and structuralism – that historians and social scientists have used to study border-making and state-formation processes.[17]

Liminality, however, does not necessarily mean 'strangeness' with regard to current national, regional and global dynamics. As Hämäläinen and Truett suggest, the history of borderlands should not limit itself to a counter history; that is, a counter-narrative established by the 'centre'.[18] The study of borderlands requires, on the contrary, connecting local (hi)stories to broader spaces that are concomitantly historicised, and very often exceed national frameworks.[19]

---

[14] Timothy Mitchell, *Rule of Experts: Egypt, Techno-Politics, Modernity* (Berkeley, CA: University of California Press, 2002).

[15] Peter B. Evans, Dietrich Rueschemeyer and Theda Skocpol (eds), *Bringing the State Back in* (Cambridge: Cambridge University Press, 1985).

[16] Toufoul Abou-Hodeib, 'Sanctity across the border: pilgrimage routes and state control in Mandate Lebanon and Palestine', in Cyrus Schayegh and Andrew Arsan (eds), *The Routledge Handbook of the History of the Middle East Mandates* (London: Routledge, 2015), p. 383.

[17] For a seminal work on liminal identities in the borderlands, see Gloria Anzaldúa, *Borderlands/La Frontera: The New Mestiza* (San Francisco, CA: Aunt Lute Books, 1987). For a recent contribution, see Hiroko Matsuda, *Liminality of the Japanese Empire: Border Crossings from Okinawa to Colonial Taiwan* (Honolulu: University of Hawaii Press, 2018).

[18] Pekka Hämäläinen and Samuel Truett, 'On Borderlands', *Journal of American History*, Vol. 98, No. 2 (2011), pp. 357–8.

[19] Sanghamitra Misra, *Becoming a Borderland: The Politics of Space and Identity in Colonial Northeastern India* (New Delhi: Routledge, 2011).

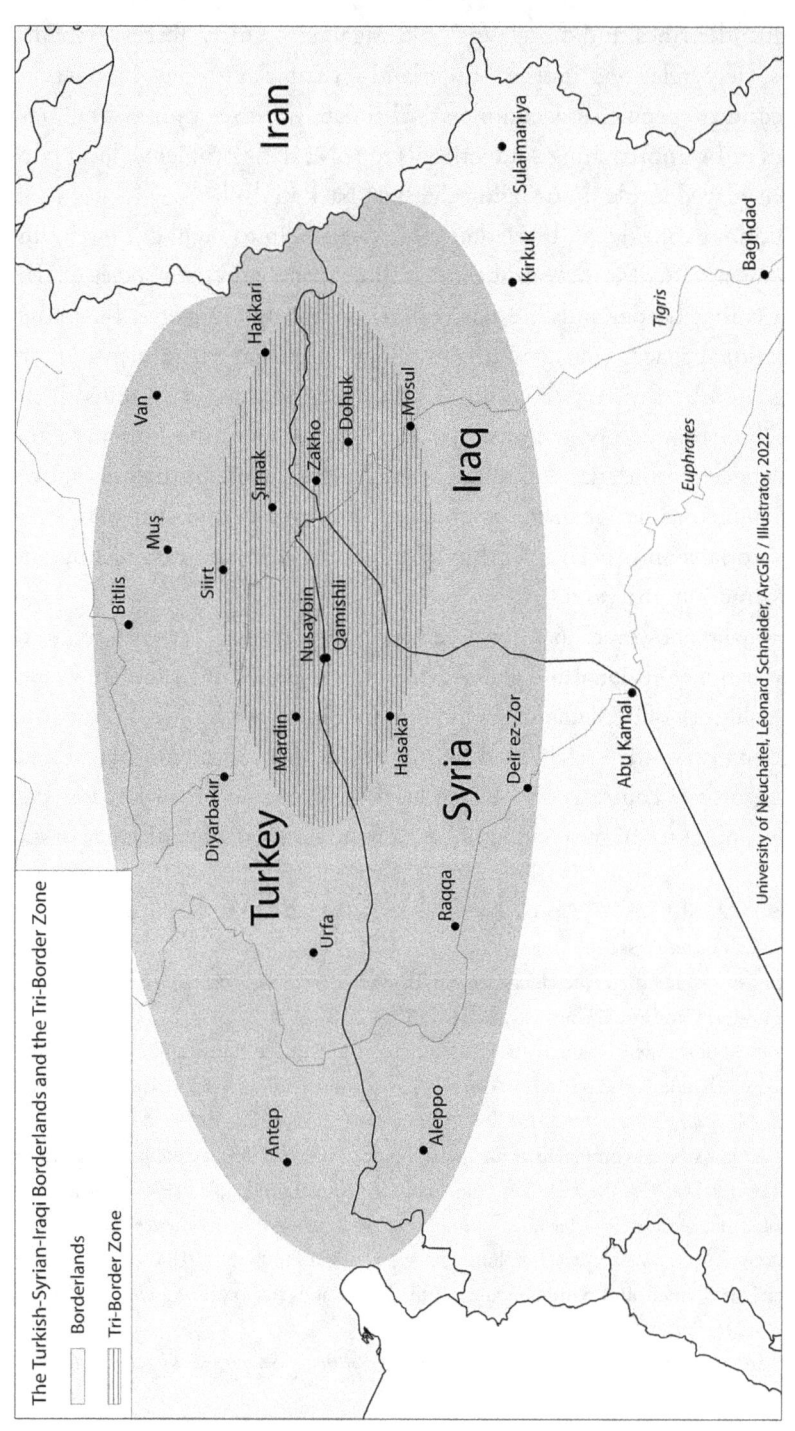

Figure I.1 Map of the Turkish–Syrian–Iraqi Borderlands and the Tri-Border Zone.

Because borderlands are spaces where place, identity and power relations intersect over time,[20] historians need to explore how the continuous entanglement and conflict between agency – individual and collective strategies – and the constraints imposed on it by embedded structures – globalisation, the territorial nation-state system, tribal and ethno-religious networks, among many others – has shaped the evolution of both borderlands and states in the post-Ottoman Middle East.[21]

State Formation in the Middle East: A Contentious Issue

The juxtaposition of unforeseen historic developments that unfolded in the last two decades, on the one hand, and old territorial disputes on the other, has strongly contributed to the revival of the debate – raging since the 1990s[22] – about the crisis of the nation state in the Middle East and the uncertain future of the international boundaries drawn by a series of international treaties signed in the interwar years. Of note is the emergence of new transnational actors – first al-Qaida, then the Islamic State in Iraq and the Levant (ISIS) – that have denounced the legitimacy of international borders 'imposed' by the colonial powers in the aftermath of the First World War – the so-called 'Sykes-Picot order';[23] the durability of conflicts revolving around the right to self-determination of the Palestinians and the Kurds as well as territorial disputes – i.e. Lebanon–Syria, Syria–Israel and Saudi Arabia–Yemen; and finally, the resilience of supra- and sub-national solidarities.

---

[20] Henri Lefebvre, *The Production of Space* (Trans. D. Nicholson-Smith, Oxford: Blackwell, 1991); Barney Warf and Arias Santa (eds), *The Spatial Turn: Interdisciplinary Perspectives* (London: Routledge, 2008).

[21] For a similar argument, see Randy William Widdis, 'Looking Through the Mirror: A Historical Geographical View of the Canadian-American Borderlands', *Journal of Borderlands Studies*, Vol. 30, No. 2 (2015), pp. 175–88 (here p. 181).

[22] Adeed Dawisha and William Zartman (eds), *Beyond Coercion. The Durability of the Arab State* (London: Croom Helm, 1988); Riccardo Bocco, ʻAsabiyât tribales et Etats au Moyen-Orient: Confrontations et connivences', *Maghreb-Machrek*, No. 147 (1995), pp. 3–12.

[23] Michael D. Berdine, *Redrawing the Middle East: Sir Mark Sykes, Imperialism and the Sykes–Picot Agreement* (London: I. B. Tauris, 2018); Ariel I. Ahram, *Break all the Borders: Separatism and the Reshaping of the Middle East* (Oxford: Oxford University Press, 2020).

The acceleration of the globalisation process needs to be added to these local and regional dynamics,[24] as it has affected all states without exception, contributing to the so-called 'international disorder' and the inevitable questioning of the Westphalian conception of territorial sovereignty.[25] The Middle East seems to embody the most encompassing socio-political trends of modern world development; namely, the emergence, ascendancy and subsequent crisis of what is best labelled 'territoriality'.[26] Against this background, two opposed strands of literature – traditional and revisionist – have sought to provide a historically informed perspective to either support or counter the notions such as 'failed', 'collapsed', 'fragile' and 'weak' states that have been widely used by observers and academics to 'explain' current developments in the Middle East.[27] Ultimately, however, the assessment of both the depth and the origins of the so-called 'crisis of the territorial state' in the region stems from conflicting views about the historicity of pre-modern political units as well as the nature of the nation state in the Middle East.

The first strand emphasises the artificiality of both the newly-established nation states in the Middle East and their respective international borders. This bulk of literature has consequently turned its attention to the series

---

[24] Kenichi Ohmae, *The Borderless World: Power and Strategy in the Interlinked Economy* (New York: Harper Business, 1990); Michael Shapiro and Hayward Alker (eds), *Challenging Boundaries: Global Flows, Territorial Identities* (Minneapolis: University of Minnesota Press, 1996).

[25] Bertrand Badie, *La fin des territoires. Essai sur le désordre international et sur l'utilité sociale du respect* (Paris: Fayard, 1995); Hartmut Behr, 'Deterritorialisation and the Transformation of Statehood: The Paradox of Globalisation', *Geopolitics*, Vol. 13, No. 2 (2008), pp. 359–82; Hans Vollaard, 'The Logic of Political Territoriality', *Geopolitics*, Vol. 14, No. 4 (2009), pp. 687–706.

[26] Charles S Maier, 'Consigning the Twentieth century to History: Alternative Narratives for the Modern Era', *The American Historical Review*, Vol. 105, No. 3 (2000), p. 807. For the questioning of territoriality as a marker of statehood in the contemporary world see Zygmunt Bauman, 'Reconnaissance Wars of the Planetary Frontierland', *Theory, Culture and Society* Vol. 19, No. 4 (2002), pp. 82–90.

[27] Peter Galbraith, *The End of Iraq: How American Incompetence Created a War Without End* (New York: Simon and Schuster, 2006); Noel Brehony, *Yemen Divided: The Story of a Failed State in South Arabia* (London: I. B. Tauris, 2013).

of secret contacts and accords – i.e. the Sykes-Picot Agreement (1916), the Balfour Declaration (1917), and the subsequent Anglo-French negotiations at the San Remo conference (1920) – that eventually brought the Middle East to its current territorial form.[28] Accordingly, Western powers created a new political framework for the region; a territorial sovereign state system fostered and secured by the mandates of the League of Nations, with the more or less voluntary cooperation of some local elites. The 'adaptation' to this new political system was uneven, though. Modern Turkey and Iran 'did better' because: they were the heirs of empires that lasted – i.e. Ottoman (1300–1922), Safavid (1501–1736) and Qajar (1789–1925) – they benefitted from stronger traditions of statehood,[29] shared one of the oldest frontiers in the region[30] and had been governed since the early 1920s by nationalist elites guided by a comprehensive top-down reform agenda.[31]

In Arab countries, by contrast, new nation states were 'artificial', for they lacked deep historical roots and, more importantly, were the products of Western colonial designs in the region. As a result, these new political entities were at odds with their own societies, characterised by high levels of religious and ethnic diversity, thereby precluding the emergence of a unified national consciousness. If new nation states were artificial, so were their borders. Thus, for instance, David Fromkin argued that the interwar period was an 'era in which Middle Eastern countries and frontiers were fabricated

---

[28] Yoav Alon, *The Making of Jordan: Tribes, Colonialism, and the Modern State* (London: I. B. Tauris, 2007); James Barr, *A Line in the Sand: Britain, France and the Struggle that Shaped the Middle East* (London: Simon and Schuster, 2011); T. G. Fraser, Andrew Mango and Robert McNamara, *The Makers of the Modern Middle East* (London: Gingko Library, 2011).

[29] Metin Heper, *The State Tradition in Turkey* (Hull: Eothen Press, 1985).

[30] For a comprehensive study on the contentious formation of this frontier, see Sabri Ateş, *The Ottoman–Iranian Borderlands. Making a Boundary, 1843–1914* (Cambridge: Cambridge University Press, 2013).

[31] Bernard Lewis, *The Emergence of Modern Turkey* (London: Oxford University Press, 1962); Erik J. Zürcher, *The Unionist Factor: The Role of the Committee of Union and Progress in the Turkish National Movement, 1905–26* (Leiden: Brill, 1984). For a comparative study of the reform movements led by Mustafa Kemal and Reza Khan in Turkey and Iran, respectively, see Touraj Atabaki and Erik J. Zürcher (eds), *Men of Order: Authoritarian Modernization under Atatürk and Reza Shah* (London: I. B. Tauris, 2004).

in Europe'.³² Not only did Europeans draw the borders of the Arab Middle East, but they also did it arbitrarily.³³

Furthermore, as Arab elites strove to implement their respective projects of state-building, these artificial borders presented a conundrum. Nationalism – itself an idea imported from the West – led to a contradiction between a non-territorial Arab nationalism that, in theory, sought to encompass all Arab states, and the actual state fragmentation of the Middle East resulting from the Western Mandates' order. In other words, the new state system challenged the region as 'the nationhood in its Western meaning was trapped between two poles: the infra-national belongings like the communitarian or tribal links, and the supra-national belongings, namely the *umma* – the Muslim community of believers – and pan-Arabism'.³⁴

Yet, the reality is much more complex than what the analyses of the so-called 'artificiality' of the nation-state system in the Middle East may suggest. In that regard, revisionist scholarship offers much more promising perspectives for a better understanding of the transition from the imperial framework towards the interwar state system. Crucially, Sara Pursley argues that the narrative on the artificiality of the Middle Eastern states, which emerged already in the 1920s, served to foster colonial claims in the region.³⁵ According to this narrative, because new nation states were devoid of any common identity and their provinces had no previous administrative ties, Middle Eastern societies

---

[32] David Fromkin, *A Peace to End all Peace: The Fall of the Ottoman Empire and the Creation of the Modern Middle East*, rev. ed. (New York: Henry Holt and Company, 2009, 1st edn. 1989), p. 9.

[33] For a comprehensive critique of this narrative, see Sara Pursley, 'Lines Drawn on an Empty Map: Iraq's Borders and the Legend of the Artificial State (Part I and II)', *Jadaliyya*, 2 June 2015, available at: https://www.jadaliyya.com/Details/32140 and https://www.jadaliyya.com/Details/32153; Louise Fawcett, 'States and Sovereignty in the Middle East: Myths and Realities', *International Affairs*, Vol. 93, No. 4 (2017), pp. 789–807.

[34] Ernest Gellner, 'Tribalism and state in the Middle East', in Philip S. Khoury and Joseph Kostiner (eds), *Tribes and State Formation in the Middle East* (London: I. B. Tauris, 1990), pp. 109–26; Daniel Meier, 'Introduction to the Special Issue: Bordering the Middle East', *Geopolitics*, Vol. 23, No. 3 (2018), p. 4.

[35] Sara Pursley, 'Lines Drawn on an Empty Map'.

were prone to un-governability.[36] Consequently, French and British presence in the region was deemed even more necessary in order to 'protect' ethnic and religious minorities from Arab nationalism, while preparing the elites of the future independent states for good governance.[37] Such discourse, however, deliberately overlooked local constitutional attempts, like the one elaborated by the representatives of the Syrian–Arab Congress (1920), to secure equality for all citizens regardless of their ethnic and religious backgrounds.[38]

This revisionist strand of the literature also points out that before nationalist doctrines were imported from Europe, 'patriotic' identities had already made their presence felt in many parts of the world, including the Middle East. While the *umma* and other religious affiliations, together with the sense of belonging to a particular place – i.e. village, steppe or city – continued to shape individual and collective identities in the early twentieth century, sources in local languages also reveal pre-modern 'traces of awareness of territorial consciousness' that marked a certain distinction between the proto-nations present in the region.[39] In that sense, the terms 'Syria', 'Bilad al-Sham' and 'al-Iraq', though they were never clearly defined or limited, had existed well before the establishment of the Mandates. Further, between the late nineteenth and early twentieth centuries, a cultural sense of Arabism was born, especially in Bilad al-Sham, which was 'soon picked up and amplified

---

[36] The discourse on the artificiality of non-Western borders was not only conveyed by civil servants and diplomats, but also by European social scientists who played a significant role in defining territorial and therefore political decision-making. See Camille Lefebvre, 'We Have Tailored Africa: French Colonialism and the "Artificiality" of Africa's Borders in the Interwar Period', *Journal of Historical Geography*, Vol. 37, No. 2 (2011), pp. 191–202.

[37] On the Mandates, see Nadine Méouchy (ed.), *France, Syrie et Liban, 1918–46: Les ambiguïtés et les dynamiques de la relation mandataire* (Damas: IFEAD, 2002); Nadine Méouchy and Peter Sluglett (eds), *The British and French Mandates in Comparative Perspectives* (Leiden: Brill, 2004); Cyrus Schayegh and Andrew Arsan (eds), *The Routledge Handbook of the History of the Middle East Mandates* (London: Routledge, 2015).

[38] Elizabeth F. Thompson, *How the West Stole Democracy from the Arabs: The Syrian Arab Congress of 1920 and the Destruction of its Historic Liberal-Islamic Alliance* (New York: Atlantic Monthly Press, 2020).

[39] Lorenzo Kamel, *The Middle East from Empire to Sealed Identities* (Edinburgh: Edinburgh University Press, 2019), pp. 184–5.

by emerging diaspora communities'.[40] Likewise, a closer observation of documents and maps predating the First World War shows that the separation of Baghdad and Basra provinces that was in place in 1914 and has been widely used to counter claims about the rootedness of local territorial entities dated back only to 1884.[41] In fact, for almost two centuries they had been governed as a single entity with Baghdad as the social and political centre of gravity.[42]

In sum, 'while it is necessary to reject any primordialist temptation – or the existence of communities that have been defining themselves on a territorial basis for a long time', it is equally important to highlight that countries such as 'Palestine, Iraq and Syria are not simply artificial creations'.[43]

Finally, although the San Remo Conference set the framework for the new territories under a mandatory oversight, their respective boundaries were drawn throughout the 1920s as the result of an 'arduous process of resolving competing claims to territory, often through war and always through the use of power'. In short, borders in the Middle East were formed 'in much the same way that nation-state borders everywhere have been formed'.[44]

Yet, beyond the binary nature of artificiality/historicity of Middle Eastern territorial nation states, there is another underlying key issue that informs the two approaches; that is, a radically different understanding of the 'true' nature of the newly-established states in the interwar Middle East. While the traditional strand of literature highlights the imported character of a Western

---

[40] Cyrus Schayegh, *The Middle East and the Making of the Modern World* (Cambridge, MA: Harvard University Press, 2017), p. 6. See also Andrew Arsan, *Interlopers of Empire: The Lebanese Diaspora in Colonial French West Africa* (London: Hurst, 2014); Stacy Fahrenthold, *Between the Ottomans and the Entente: The First World War in the Syrian and Lebanese Diaspora, 1908–25* (Oxford: Oxford University Press, 2019).

[41] Norwegian Institute for International Affairs Report, 'How a Post-Sectarian Strategy Can Change the Logic and Facilitate Sustainable Political Reform in Iraq', February 2009. Available at: http://english.nupi.no/content/download/8891/91333/file/Iraq%20Report%20%284%29.pdf. See also Dina Rizk Khoury, *State and Provincial Society in the Ottoman Empire: Mosul, 1540–1834* (Cambridge: Cambridge University Press, 1997).

[42] Reida Visser, 'Introduction', in Reida Visser and Gareth Stansfield (eds), *An Iraq of Its Regions: Cornerstones of a Federal Democracy?* (New York: Columbia University Press, 2008), p. 8.

[43] Lorenzo Kamel, *The Middle East from Empire to Sealed Identities*, p. 189.

[44] Sara Pursley, 'Lines Drawn on an Empty Map: Iraq's Borders and the Legend of the Artificial State (Part I and II)', *Jadaliyya*.

political idea – the Westphalian state – and its inadequacy regarding the Middle Eastern social fabric, the second one points to the hybrid character of the Middle Eastern state. The latter seems again more auspicious.

As Mohammad-Mahmoud Ould Mohamedou suggests, the model of the 'Westphalian state' has proven to be remarkably assertive, often regarded as the inevitable, near-sacralised point of reference. As a result, non-Western statehood is defined negatively; that is, 'given in relation not to what it is but to that which it is not'.[45] Yet, instead of choosing the story of Western state-making form as a point of departure and comparison to analyse state-formation processes elsewhere, scholars need to acknowledge that statehood in the Middle East followed a singular, yet multifaceted pattern.[46] Rephrasing Tassos Anastassiadis and Nathalie Clayer in relation to south-eastern Europe, one can argue that the process of state formation in the interwar Middle East was a complicated course that involved different institutional traditions – i.e. imperial, Westphalian, colonial – managing societies marked by varying degrees of political loyalty to the respective central powers, and coping with colonial intrusion embedded in the context of permanent uncertainty.[47] Henceforth, historians need to pay more attention to the socio-historical process of modern state formation; namely, how the modern national state was appropriated by and transformed into the local social fabric.

Furthermore, the way scholars approach 'the state' has significant consequences for how state–society relations are studied, and ultimately, doe the overall appraisal of state performances. Various schools of thought – from

---

[45] Mohammad-Mahmoud Ould Mohamedou, 'In Search of the Non-Western State: Historicising and De-Westphalianising Statehood', in Bertrand Badie, Dirk Berg-Scholsser and Leonardo Morlino (eds), *The SAGE Handbook of Political Science: A Global Perspective* (London: Sage, 2020), pp. 1335–48 (here p. 1336).

[46] Rifa'at 'Ali Abou-El-Haj, *Formation of the Modern State: The Ottoman Empire, Sixteenth to Eighteenth Centuries* (Albany: SUNY Press, 1991); Karen Barkey, *Bandits and Bureaucrats: The Ottoman Route to State Centralization* (Ithaca: Cornell University Press, 1994); Fatma Müge Göçek, *The Transformation of Turkey: Redefining State and Society from the Ottoman Empire to the Modern Era* (London: I. B. Tauris, 2011).

[47] Tassos Anastassiadis and Nathalie Clayer, 'Beyond the Incomplete or Failed Modernization Paradigm', in Tassos Anastassiadis and Nathalie Clayer (eds), *Society, Politics and State Formation in Southeastern Europe During the 19th Century* (Athens: Alpha Bank, 2011), pp. 11–32.

Weberianism to structuralism, Marxism, realism and neo-realism – have emphasised the study of the modern state as an autonomous organisation. By far the most popular has been the literature drawing upon Talcot Parsons' social-systems theory.[48] Parsons' approach subsumes both state and society in a broad conception of the so-called 'social system', whose various parts are bound together by an overarching and unified set of values. According to Parsons, it is this package of values that takes centre stage in the analysis of power, structure and change. Edward Shils, following Durkheim's notion of 'social morphology', further developed this approach by applying it to new states. Consistent with the 'centre–periphery' model, the state is located at the 'centre' of the system, whereas society, a passive recipient, is situated at the 'periphery'.[49] The 'centre' is characterised in this model by three aspects: a central value system comprised of the values and beliefs of the state; institutions that dominate the realm of action and exercise authority; and elites that possess ultimate authority. Critically, Shils explains that these three components are combined in a 'seamless wave'. Thus, the 'centre' is capable of enforcing decisions despite differing tendencies and preferences within society. Although Shils acknowledges that the 'centre' is not homogenous and more likely there is not a unique 'centre', in Shils' model the centre has always a positive meaning or force of attraction.[50]

This perspective parallels the modernisation and dependency literature wherein dualisms such as state/society, centre/periphery, modern/traditional have long dominated scholarship on state formation in the Middle East. In short, the 'failure' of the 'imported' Western state model in the region was attributed to the 'backwardness' of local societies and the inheritance of the corrupt Ottoman institutional and social order. So the argument goes that, with the exception of Kemalist Turkey where state elites introduced profound social reforms and thus broke with the Ottoman past,[51] state-building in the

---

[48] Talcot Parsons, *The Social System* (Glencoe, IL: Free Press, 1951).

[49] Edward Shils, *Center and Periphery: Essays in Macrosociology* (Chicago: University of Chicago Press, 1975).

[50] Massimo Rosati, *The Making of a Postsecular Society: A Durkheimian Approach to Memory, Pluralism and Religion in Turkey* (Farnham: Ashgate, 2015), p. 18.

[51] Daniel Lerner, *The Passing of Traditional Society: Modernizing the Middle East* (Glencoe, IL: Free Press, 1958).

interwar Middle East encountered insurmountable obstacles – the weight of social and religious traditions and the weakness of a 'centre' that was incapable of claiming authority, and the monopoly of violence, a constitutive element of statehood, according to the classical Weberian perspective.

Since the 1970s, however, post-colonial theory, including subaltern and gender studies, has challenged both Weberianism and the 'centre–periphery' model. Key to our discussion here is that while classical studies on state formation and modernisation processes view the state as a unitary, monolithic apparatus, new approaches have challenged this perspective by suggesting that, on the contrary, the state is a fragmented institution prone to 'flaws' and contradictions between its different 'segments'.[52] Accordingly, Joel S. Migdal has elaborated a theoretical approach – 'state-in-society' – wherein the state is defined as a 'field of power marked by the use and threat of violence and shaped by the image of a coherent, controlling organization in a territory, which is a representation of the people bounded by that territory, and the actual practices of its multiple parts.'[53] Similarly, Timothy Mitchell has conceptualised the state as a structural effect, 'a powerful metaphysical effect of practices that make such structures appear to exist.'[54] For both scholars thus, while the state projects to the outside an image of homogeneity and coherence, the actual practice or routine performance of state actors and agencies in various arenas often contradicts this image. Henceforth, in order to study state-formation processes, scholars need to observe the everyday practices of bureaucracies within the population, which might be contradictory to the discourse of the state.[55]

---

[52] While Georges Balandier highlights the 'flaws' of certain states, Joel S. Migdal underlines the contradictions within the state, on the one hand, and the interactions between the state and society, on the other. Georges Balandier, *Anthropologie politique* (Paris: PUF, 1967), pp. 167–8; Joel S. Migdal, *State in Society. Studying How States and Societies Transform and Constitute One Another* (Cambridge: Cambridge University Press, 2001).

[53] Joel S. Migdal, *State in Society*, p. 16.

[54] Timothy Mitchell, 'The Limits of the State: Beyond Statist Approaches and Their Critics', *American Political Science Review*, Vol. 85, No. 1 (1991), p. 94.

[55] Akhil Gupta, 'Blurred Boundaries: The Discourse of Corruption, the Culture of Politics, and the Imagined State', in Aradhana Sharma and Akhil Gupta (eds), *The Anthropology of the State: A Reader* (Malden, MA: Wiley–Blackwell, 2005), pp. 211–41.

Historians of the Ottoman Empire quickly tapped into this literature to challenge classical accounts on non-Western statehood and state–society relations. In his seminal work *A Moveable Empire,* Reşat Kasaba invites scholars 'to see the institutionalization of the Ottoman-Turkish state as a process unfolding in continuous relationship with other groups and elements of society and with counterparts in surrounding areas.'[56] Likewise, Janet Klein has explored how the state's attempts to monitor the margins of the Empire in the late nineteenth century led Ottoman authorities to establish Kurdish militias and give them the mission of placating a perceived Armenian threat. By doing so, however, the Ottoman state empowered Kurdish tribal leaders, which ran counter to its own previous endeavours.[57] The same argument is also advanced by Isa Blumi in his study on the transformation of the Ottoman Empire's institutions through the interactions with borderlanders in the Western Balkans, the Persian Gulf and Yemen.[58] Meanwhile, Karen Barkey has argued that while coercion was indeed a tool to impose state authority upon Ottoman subjects, mediation and negotiation were equally important in order to implement state policies and gain in legitimacy.[59] In parallel, historians have also observed how Islamic law changed throughout the nineteenth century with regard to the issues related to sexuality – i.e. age of marriage, rape, divorce or abortion, among many others, as a response to everyday interactions between state agents, religious courts and society.[60]

In the past few years, historians, political scientists and anthropologists have also revisited the Kemalist era (1923–46) to examine how social engineering policies were actually implemented, negotiated and/or subverted in Turkey's rural areas. Thus, contrary to traditional scholarship, which tends

---

[56] Reşat Kasaba, *A Moveable Empire: Ottomans, Nomads, Migrants, and Refugees* (Seattle and London: University of Washington Press, 2009), p. 8.

[57] Janet Klein, *The Margins of Empire: Kurdish Militias in the Ottoman Tribal Zone* (Stanford, CA: Stanford University Press, 2011).

[58] Isa Blumi, *Foundations of Modernity: Human Agency and the Imperial State* (London: Routledge, 2012).

[59] Karen Barkey, *Empire of Difference: The Ottomans in Comparative Perspective* (Cambridge: Cambridge University Press, 2008).

[60] Leslie P. Peirce, *Morality Tales: Law and Gender in the Ottoman Court of Aintab* (Berkeley, CA: University of California Press, 2003); Elyse Semerdjian, *'Off the Straight Path': Illicit Sex, Community and Law in Ottoman Aleppo* (Syracuse, NY: Syracuse University Press, 2008).

to overestimate the coherence and power of the Turkish state in the inter-war period, recent works underscore its internal contradictions as well as the blurred boundaries between state agents and rural populations.[61]

Building upon this literature, this book suggests that we recognise borders and borderlands as suitable sites for exploring the co-production and renegotiation of power, territorial, political and social loyalties in the modern Middle East. Because borders are social constructs around which power relations between state authorities and borderlanders unfold, they offer a unique standpoint to observe not only the everyday interactions between state and society, but also how these interactions inadvertently helped 'nationalise' an otherwise transnational space. In that regard, the virtual character of most Middle Eastern borders should not be seen as a sign of their 'artificiality' or even their 'failure'; rather, the idea of 'elusive borders' as much as 'elusive states' provides an entry point into the ideal of making the territorial nation-state an ongoing process.

Borders, Borderlands and State Formation

Contemporary developments – i.e. the refugee crisis, debates on migration, the construction of walls and fences in the border areas across the globe[62] – have certainly renewed scholars' interest in the study of borders, borderlands and cross-border mobility in the Middle East and beyond.[63] Yet, the variety

---

[61] Senem Aslan, 'Everyday Forms of State Power and the Kurds in the Early Turkish Republic', *International Journal of Middle East Studies*, Vol. 43, No. 1 (2011), pp. 75–93; Alexandros Lamprou, *Nation-Building in Modern Turkey: The People's Houses, the State and the Citizen* (London: I. B. Tauris, 2015); Hale Yılmaz, *Becoming Turkish: Nationalist Reforms and Cultural Negotiations in Early Republican Turkey 1923–45* (Syracuse, NY: Syracuse University Press, 2016).

[62] Gabriel Popescu, *Bordering and Ordering the Twenty-first Century* (Lanham: Rowman & Littlefield Publishers, 2011); Elia Pusterla and Francesca Piccin, 'The loss of sovereignty and the illusion of building walls', *Journal of Borderlands Studies*, Vol. 27, No. 2 (2012), pp. 121–38; Elisabeth Vallet (ed.), *Borders, Fences and Walls: State of Insecurity?* (Farnham: Ashgate, 2014).

[63] S. Latte Abdallah and C. Parizot (eds), *A l'ombre du mur. Israéliens et palestiniens entre séparation et occupation* (Arlès: Actes Sud/MMSH, 2011); Asher Kaufman, *Contested Frontiers in the Syria-Lebanon-Israel Region: Cartography, Sovereignty, and Conflict* (Washington, DC: Woodrow Wilson Center Press, 2014); Daniel Meier, *Shaping Lebanon's Borderlands*,

of objects and phenomena observed as well as the approaches adopted by scholars expose a rather fragmented field. Traditionally, borders have been analysed in terms of their geopolitical dimensions, namely as physical limits between two contiguous sovereign territorial systems.[64] Political scientists and geographers, on the other hand, underscored the centrality of power around borders,[65] which became the perfect symbolic and physical markers of 'the spatiality of self, identity, and state'.[66] In parallel, however, it appeared that the study of borders and cross-border dynamics required a clearer distinction between notions that had been used interchangeably. Nowadays, generally speaking, *borders* are conceived as political divides that are the result of state building,[67] whilst *boundaries* refer to the 'lines' on a political map.[68] Meanwhile, *frontiers* are associated with a 'remote, sparsely populated, and vaguely defined territory lying beyond the periphery of two or more core powers'.[69]

In parallel, from the 1990s onwards, practitioners of border studies began to pay less attention to political centres and the conditions that informed these outer lines of sovereignty. Instead, they turned their gaze towards the zones that constitute both sides of a border to observe the impact of international borders

---

(London: I. B. Tauris, 2016); Laura Robson, *States of Separation: Transfer, Partition, and the Making of the Modern Middle East* (Oakland, CA: University of California Press, 2017); Ramazan Aras, *The Wall: The Making and Unmaking of the Turkish-Syrian Border* (London: Palgrave Macmillan, 2020); Matthieu Cimino (ed.), *Syria: Borders, Boundaries, and the State* (London: Palgrave Macmillan, 2020).

[64] Michel Foucher, *Fronts et frontières: Un tour du monde géopolitique* (Paris: Fayard, 1991); Daniel Nordman, *Frontières de France. De l'espace au territoire XVIe–XIXe siècles* (Paris: Gallimard, 1999).

[65] David Newman, 'On Borders and Power: A Theoretical Framework', *Journal of Borderlands Studies*, Vol. 18, No. 1 (2003), pp. 13–25.

[66] Randy Widdis, 'New Directions at the Border: A Historical Geographical Perspective', *Journal of Borderlands Studies*, Vol. 36, No. 5 (2021), p. 854.

[67] Michiel Baud and Willem van Schendel, 'Toward a Comparative History of Borderlands', *Journal of World History*, Vol. 8, No. 2 (1997), pp. 214–5.

[68] John R.V. Prescott, *The Geography of Frontiers and Boundaries* (Chicago: Aldine Publishing Company, 1965), pp. 35–6.

[69] Sören Urbansky, *Beyond the Steppe Frontier: A History of the Sino-Russian Border* (Princeton, NJ: Princeton University Press, 2020), p. 4.

upon local populations.⁷⁰ Starting from the premise that the border is a social construct – i.e. not simply a rigid and material line of sovereignty – many studies sought to understand the ways in which border zones were subjectively experienced by 'border populations'; that is, not only as an area of instability and risk, but also as a potential resource for those living in its proximity.⁷¹

While this took many forms, scholars have by and large underscored the strategies and daily activities of individuals and/or groups seeking to transgress the border, such as cross-border marriages, smuggling and trafficking as well as criminal circuits and secessionist movements that thrived in border regions.⁷² After all, despite state efforts to monitor and limit cross-border mobility, older geographies and conceptions of time 'continued to make their presence known, even when reformulated in the presence of borders and states'.⁷³ As a result of such practices that may appear strange to citizens living at the 'centre' of the nation states, border regions would constitute a world apart,⁷⁴ and, at times, even a shelter for individuals and groups seeking to avoid the control of the modern state.⁷⁵

---

⁷⁰ Hastings Donnan and Thomas M. Wilson (eds), *Borderlands. Ethnographic Approaches to Security, Power, and Identity* (London and New York: University Press of America, 2010); See also Thomas M. Wilson and Hastings Donnan, 'Border and Border Studies', in Thomas M. Wilson and Hastings Donnan (eds), *A Companion to Border Studies* (Wiley–Blackwell, London, 2012), pp. 1–25.

⁷¹ Janet Roitman, 'The garrison-entrepôt: A mode of governing in the Chad Bassin', in Aihwa Ong and Stephen J. Collier (eds), *Global Assemblages. Technology, Politics and Ethics as Anthropological Problems* (London: Blackwell, 2005); Judith Schelle, *Smugglers and Saints of the Sahara. Regional Connectivity in the Twentieth Century* (Cambridge: Cambridge University Press, 2012).

⁷² Homi Bhabha, *The Location of Culture* (London and New York: Routledge, 1994); Alison Blunt, 'Cultural geographies of migration: Mobility, transnationalism and diaspora', *Progress in Human Geography*, Vol. 31, No. 5 (2007), pp. 684–94.

⁷³ Toufoul Abou-Hodeib, 'Involuntary history: writing Levantines into the nation', *Contemporary Levant*, Vol. 5, No. 1 (2020), p. 45. See also Ramazan Aras, 'Naqshandi Sufis and their conception of place, time and fear on the Turkish–Syrian border and borderland', *Middle Eastern Studies*, Vol. 34, No. 4 (2018), pp. 44–66.

⁷⁴ Clive H. Schofield (ed.), *Global Boundaries. World Boundaries, Vol. I* (London and New York: Routledge, 1994).

⁷⁵ James C. Scott, *The Art of Not Being Governed. An Anarchist History of Upland Southeast Asia* (New Haven and London: Yale University Press, 2009).

Framing border zones as spaces distinct from the national heartlands in many respects led to the rehabilitation of the notion of borderland. The latter was originally applied by American historians such as Frederick J. Turner and Herbert E. Bolton to refer to North America's 'colonial frontier'; that is, a zone of expansion of Euro-American pioneers.[76] Slowly, however, David J. Weber and other historians began embracing problems that transcended national borders and replaced the notion of the 'frontier' by that of 'borderlands', understood as zones of plural sovereignty, which by no means could be limited solely to the American experience.[77] In that regard, this notion gained new epistemological value, as it was used to study broader geographic areas from Asia to Europe and Africa.[78] Although there is no single definition of it, in its most basis sense, a *borderland* can be defined as an area that flanks both sides of an internationally recognised border that are of 'indefinite extent and thus cannot be measured in so many meters or miles'.[79] Adding a political dimension to it, James Anderson and Liam O'Dowd view borderlands as areas in the form of strip 'whose centres are physically and socially distant from that border'.[80] Because the two sides of the border constitute an organic whole that differs from the rest of a given national territory,[81] borderlands are liminal spaces that are unique in their geopolitical, socioeconomic, political and

---

[76] Herbert E. Bolton, *The Spanish Borderlands: A Chronicle of Old Florida and the Southwest* (New Haven: Yale University Press, 1921).

[77] David J. Weber, 'Turner, the Boltonians, and the Borderlands', *American Historical Review*, Vol. 91, No. 1 (1986), pp. 66–81; Jeremy Adelman and Stephen Aron, 'From Borderlands to Borders: Empires, Nation–States, and the Peoples in between in North American History', *The American Historical Review*, Vol. 104, No. 3 (1999), pp. 814–41. For a recent overview on the evolution of this notion in the writing of American History, see Brian Delay (ed.), *North American Borderlands* (London: Routledge, 2013).

[78] For a general overview of this concept and the historiography related to it, see Pekka Hämäläinen and Samuel Truett, 'On Borderlands'.

[79] Edward S. Casey, 'Border Versus Boundary at la Frontera', *Environment and Planning D: Society and Space* Vol. 29 (2011), pp. 384–98 (here p. 389).

[80] James Anderson and Liam O'Dowd, 'Borders, Border Regions and Territoriality: Contradictory Meanings, Changing Significance', *Regional Studies*, Vol. 33, No. 7 (1999), pp. 593–604 (here p. 595).

[81] Michiel Baud and Willem Van Schendel, 'Toward a Comparative History of Borderlands', *Journal of World History*, Vol. 8, No. 2 (1997), p. 216.

cultural environments.⁸² Yet, borderlands are not a given; rather, they are 'a physical, ideological, and geographical construct, a region of intersection that is sensitive to internal and external forces that both integrate and differentiate communities and areas on both sides of the boundary line.'⁸³

Given the multifaceted character of borderlands, many scholars readily acknowledged the concept's analytic potential to rethink the processes of border-making, state and identity formation for two interrelated reasons. On the one hand, historians and geographers have postulated that setting borderlands as a privileged unit of analysis would enable us to explore the process through which imperial and national borders are socially constructed, in particular by paying attention to their varying meanings – symbolic and material – across time and space.⁸⁴ In short, in order to deepen our understanding of the formation and consolidation of borders across historical periods, research should take into account local realities alongside political and diplomatic agendas.⁸⁵ Furthermore, because borderlands are established in areas of multiple sovereignties, involving continuous renegotiations of power among a myriad of local, national and transnational actors, they offer a unique site to observe the contradictions and dynamics at work within societies. Therefore, by examining social and political relations between 'state' and 'society' around specific borderlands, it would be possible to study the processes of formation and territorialisation of modern nation states.⁸⁶

---

[82] Pınar Şenoğuz, *Community, Change and Border Towns* (London: Routledge, 2018), p. 24. Gabriel Popescu, *Bordering and Ordering the Twenty-first Century*, p. 20.

[83] Randy Widdis, 'Migration, Borderlands, and National Identity', in John J. Bukowczy (ed.), *Permeable Border: The Great Lakes Basin as Transnational Region* (Pittsburgh: University of Pittsburgh Press, 2005), pp. 152–74 (here p. 154).

[84] Jeremy Adelman and Stephen Aron, 'From Borderlands to Borders', p. 815.

[85] Peter Sahlins, *Boundaries: The Making of France and Spain in the Pyrenees;* Sabine Dullin, 'L'invention d'une frontière de guerre froide à l'ouest de l'Union soviétique (1945–9)', *Vingtième Siècle Revue d'histoire*, No. 102 (2009), pp. 49–61; Isa Blumi, 'Agents of Post-Ottoman States: The Precariousness of the Berlin Congress Boundaries of Montenegro and how to Define/Confine People', in Hakan Yavuz and Peter Sluglett (eds), *War and Diplomacy: Russo-Turkish War and Berlin Treaty* (Salt Lake City: University of Utah, 2011), pp. 194–231.

[86] Joel S. Migdal (ed.), *Boundaries and Belonging. States and Societies in the Struggle to Shape Identities and Local Practices* (Cambridge: Cambridge University Press, 2004).

On the other hand, as I have argued elsewhere, 'borderlands are not just zones where actors compete and resist, locals negotiate, cultures intermingle, and identities transform, they are also a transnational space where individuals cross, commodities are exchanged, and diseases are spread;' as such, 'borders are not where mobilities come to an end.'[87] Rather, they are 'semipermeable membranes' allowing states to 'channel' – i.e. prevent, promote, re-direct – cross-border mobility,[88] while seeking to derive revenues, legitimacy and power from them.[89] Ultimately, 'borderlands are where "regimes of mobility" are re-cast and re-shuffled.'[90]

Taken together, scholarship on borders in the Middle East has reproduced the ambivalent view of this field on how and to what extent states – whether imperial or national – make their presence felt in the borderlands.[91] Indeed, from a borderland perspective, empires and nation states look simultaneously more fragile and violent in the periphery than in the political centre.[92] Thus, a significant number of works on borderlands in the region have emphasised how, from the nineteenth century onwards, centralising policies in the margins of empires and nation states involved, more often than not, the forced displacement of rebellious groups and undesirable populations, including massacres and genocide.[93] Likewise,

---

[87] Jordi Tejel and Ramazan Hakkı Öztan, 'Introduction', p. 13.

[88] For a discussion about the conceptualisation of borders as 'semipermeable membranes' in the late nineteenth century, see Valeska Huber, 'The Unification of the Globe by Disease? The International Sanitary Conferences on Cholera, 1851–94', *The Historical Journal*, Vol. 49, No. 2 (2006), pp. 453–76.

[89] Joel Quirk and Darshan Vigneswaran, 'Mobility Makes States', in Darshan Vigneswaran and Joel Quirk (eds) *Mobility Makes States: Migration and Power in Africa* (Philadelphia: University of Pennsylvania Press, 2015), pp. 6–8.

[90] Jordi Tejel and Ramazan Hakkı Öztan, 'Introduction', p. 13.

[91] For a critical assessment of borderlands history, see Pekka Hämäläinen and Samuel Truett, 'On Borderlands'.

[92] About imperial monitoring of the 'margins' through violent means, see Priya Satia, *Spies in Arabia: The Great War and the Cultural Foundations of Britain's Covert Empire in the Middle East* (Oxford: Oxford University Press, 2008).

[93] Donald Bloxham, *The Great Game of Genocide: Imperialism, Nationalism, and the Destruction of the Ottoman Armenians* (Oxford: Oxford University Press, 2005); Michael Reynolds, *Shattering Empires: The Clash and Collapse of the Ottoman and Russian Empires, 1908–18* (Cambridge: Cambridge University Press, 2011); Omer Bartov and Eric D. Weitz (eds),

researchers have highlighted the long-lasting negative effects of new borders upon border dwellers and nomadic populations; namely, how borders cut across pre-existing commercial and social networks causing the end of certain traditional ways of life, such as pastoralism.[94] Gradually, through a series of bureaucratic measures and monitoring techniques, modern states transformed the imperial borderlands into bordered lands.

Meanwhile, other scholars have framed borderlands as sites where state structures are less than fully articulated, and where the image of the state loses its clarity, developing more fluid forms of state control and presence, and thus allowing increasingly more room for borderlanders' manoeuvres.[95] In addition, because states' symbolic and physical presence in the border zones is elusive, Bedouins, smugglers, revolutionary groups and members of Sufi orders – among many others – transgress international borders on a regular basis, thereby subverting states' claims of exclusive sovereignty over their respective territories.[96]

Shatterzone of Empires: Coexistence and Violence in the German, Hapsburg, Russian, and Ottoman Borderlands (Bloomington: Indiana University Press, 2013).

[94] Anthony B. Toth, 'The Transformation of a Pastoral Economy: Bedouin and States in Northern Arabia, 1850–1950' (PhD Dissertation, Oxford: Oxford University, 2000).

[95] Janet Klein, *The Margins of Empire*; Uğur Ümit Üngör, 'Rethinking the Violence of Pacification: State Formation and Bandits in the Young Turk Era, 1914–37', *Comparative Studies in Society and History*, Vol. 54, No. 4 (2012), pp. 746–69.

[96] Isa Blumi, 'Illicit trade and the emergence of Albania and Yemen', in I. William Zartman (ed.), *Understanding Life in the Borderland: Boundaries in Depth and in Motion* (Athens GA: University of Georgia Press, 2010), pp. 58–84; Cyrus Schayegh, 'The Many Worlds of 'Abud Yasin; or, What Narcotics Trafficking in the Interwar Middle East Can Tell us about Territorialization', *The American Historical Review*, Vol. 116, No. 2 (2011), pp. 273–306; Metin Atmaca, 'Fragile Frontiers: Sayyid Taha II and the Role of Kurdish Religio-Political Leadership in the Ottoman East during the First World War', *Middle Eastern Studies*, Vol. 54, No. 3 (2018), pp. 361–81; Ramazan Hakkı Öztan and Alp Yenen (eds), *Age of Rogues: Revolutionaries and Racketeers at the Frontiers of Empires* (Edinburgh: Edinburgh University Press, 2021); See also the recent contributions of Ramazan Hakkı Öztan, 'The Last Ottoman Merchants: Regional Trade and Politics of Tariffs in Aleppo's Hinterland, 1921–9'; Robert S.G. Fletcher 'When Nomads Flee: 'raider', 'rebel' and 'refugee' in southern Iraq, 1917–30'; Laura Stocker, 'The Camel Dispute: Cross-border Mobility and Tribal Conflicts in the Northern Badiya, 1929–34' in Jordi Tejel and Ramazan Hakkı Öztan (eds), *Regimes of Mobility*, pp. 80–108, 286–318, 319–50, respectively.

Between these two apparently irreconcilable approaches, some authors suggest a more nuanced understanding of state–society relations in the borderlands, starting from the premise that there is not a single *typical* border or borderland in the Middle East.[97] In this region, as elsewhere, the implementation of borders was often patchy; state authority could thus be omnipresent in one instance, but absent in the next. Similarly, as Cyrus Schayegh points out, borders in the Middle East did not develop synchronously nor did their management develop linearly.[98] Admittedly, procrastination during diplomatic negotiations and boundary demarcation missions, local resistance and major events such as the Second World War had both delaying and reversing effects upon the evolution of Middle Eastern borders throughout the first half of the twentieth century.

In that regard, notions such as bordering, de-bordering and re-bordering seem to be the key to understanding border spaces, for they capture the changing nature of borders while taking into account 'all types of actors, institutions as well as companies, individuals and social groups involved in the conduct of border-work'.[99] Because these were both top-down and bottom-up processes – that is, at once shaped by states, international organisations, regional agencies and borderlanders – historians need to observe not only borderlands singular (hi)stories, interactions, border materiality and variations over time and space, but also how power was differently projected, negotiated and resisted in state margins.[100]

Moving Forward

In pursuing these inquiries, *Rethinking State and Border Formation in the Middle East* is engaged in conversation with three specific historiographies.

---

[97] Richard Schofield, 'International Boundaries and Borderlands in the Middle East: Balancing Context, Exceptionalism and Representation', *Geopolitics*, Vol. 23, No. 3 (2017), pp. 608 and 610.
[98] Cyrus Schayegh, 'Afterword', in Jordi Tejel and Ramazan (eds), *Regimes of* Mobility, p. 357.
[99] Daniel Meier, 'Introduction', *Bordering the Middle East*, p. 6.
[100] Richard Schofield, 'International Boundaries and Borderlands in the Middle East', p. 620. See also Inga Brandell (ed.), *State Frontiers: Borders and Boundaries in the Middle East* (London and New York: I. B. Tauris, 2006), pp. 18–19; Leïla Vignal (ed.), *The Transnational Middle East: People, Places, Borders* (London and New York: Routledge, 2017), p. 11.

First is the growing awareness among scholars about the potential benefits of combining certain strands of micro- and global history. Even though these two historiographies are very often seen as radically opposed to one another, both approaches problematise the familiar narratives and containers of national history and 'state-centrism',[101] and, more importantly, they are inclined towards the study of comparisons, networks and connections. In a bid to reconcile them, certain historians claim that 'spatial history' – that is, a history that emphasises space and connections that stretch across cultural boundaries[102] – offers promising perspectives in thinking about how historical processes are generated.[103] Because borderlands are 'transnational spaces' with social practices across singular yet connected places, they offer a means of writing a history of the modern Middle East in which the nation state does not occupy such a central position.[104]

To be sure, historians cannot underestimate the role played by states in many borderland contexts in the post-Ottoman Middle East, for the former made their presence increasingly felt among borderlanders in different ways – anti-smuggling measures, air strikes, quarantine buildings, among many others. Moreover, global debates on issues such as refugee settlements or trade flows and international campaigns against the spread of diseases or drug trafficking have also affected border zones. Likewise, scholars cannot dismiss the centrality of diplomacy and high-level geostrategic dynamics in the prevention and/or resolution of international conflicts. Yet, *Rethinking State and Border Formation in the Middle East* argues for the necessity of challenging

---

[101] Neil Brenner, 'Beyond State-centrism? Space, Territoriality, and Geographical Scale in Globalization Studies', *Theory and Society*, Vol. 28 (1999), pp. 39–78.

[102] Felix Driver and Raphael Samuel, 'Re-thinking the Idea of Place', *History Workshop Journal*, Vol. 39, No. 1 (1995), pp. v–vii; Richard White, 'What is Spatial History?', Stanford University Spatial History Lab Working Paper, 1 February 2010, pp. 1–6.

[103] For a comprehensive discussion on 'spatial history' as a means to reconcile micro- and global historians, see Christian G. de Vito, 'History without scale: the micro-spatial perspective', *Past and Present*, Supplement 14 (2019), pp. 348–72.

[104] Paul Readman, Cynthia Radding and Chad Bryant, *Borderlands in World History*, pp. 11–12; Matthew H. Ellis, 'Over the Borderline? Rethinking Territoriality at the Margins of Empire and Nation in the Middle East (Part I)', *History Compass*, Vol. 13, No. 8 (2015), p. 411.

the image of ontologically distinct scales of analysis, while also appreciating the roles played by non-state actors in these processes. By embracing borderlands as a point of departure, this book moves beyond the analytic categories of the global, regional, national and local and instead highlights the potential of studying trans-border geographies, circuits and networks to better capture the 'lived experience of territoriality' amidst the populations living in the borderlands stretching between Turkey, Syria and Iraq.[105]

Rethinking State and Border Formation in the Middle East is also informed by social history. As states attempted to sever smuggling networks, extradite criminals, keep diseases at bay, or remove the politically undesirable away from border zones, they gradually turned borders into complex social institutions around which power relations between state agents (border guards, local administration, soldiers) and borderlanders unfold.[106] Rather than focusing on territorial sovereignty, this book examines borderlanders' practices, strategies and attitudes towards state authorities and material institutions to rethink the transition from empires to nation states, while aiming to contribute to current debates about the place 'the state' should retain in border and borderland studies. Rephrasing Pekka Hämäläinen and Samuel Truett's critical assessment of borderlands history, one can argue that instead of merely asking what borderlanders in the Middle East did when the states struggled for power in the margins, researchers must ask how the former 'created the conditions for borderlands history rather than simply looking at how they acted within it'.[107]

Finally, *Rethinking State and Border Formation in the Middle East* is in conversation with environmental history. In the last few years, scholars have underlined how histories of disease and pests shed light on the social constructions of the past. Admittedly, it was a series of epidemics and locust infestations that compelled Turkey, French Syria and British Iraq to further cooperate and enact common policies on the shared borders by the late 1920s, thereby contributing to nourishing the fiction of international borders as containers of

---

[105] Matthew H. Ellis, *Desert Borderland: The Making of Modern Egypt and Libya* (Stanford, CA: Stanford University Press, 2018), p. 8.
[106] Jordi Tejel and Ramazan Hakkı Öztan, 'Introduction', p. 15.
[107] Pekka Hämäläinen and Samuel Truett, 'On Borderlands', p. 352.

separate national units.[108] It was these same microbes and insects that favoured the emergence of transnational networks of experts and the organisation of a series of global and interstate conferences wherein the sanitary measures to avoid disease and famine across the region were discussed. Yet, epidemics also enabled state authorities and nationalist elites to stigmatise certain groups and lifestyles, thus creating and shoring up existing internal social boundaries. By the same token, social interpretations of disease and pests helped 'nationalise' germs and insects, ultimately reaffirming identity boundaries between the Turks, Syrians and Iraqis. In examining the interactions between modern practices of territorial governance, environmental crises and discourses on epidemics and plagues, *Rethinking State and Border Formation in the Middle East* explores how non-human factors also became the driving forces of border-making and state-formation processes in the Middle East.[109]

Organisation of the Book and Sources

As Giovanni Levi points out, the observation of trans-border geographies cannot lead us to neglect locally grounded narratives, for even in a growing transnational world, 'the problem is to identify not only the uniformities but the specific answer produced in every political state and local situation'.[110] In that sense, and before presenting the main contents of the chapters included in this book, a few words seem necessary about their internal organisation as well as the archival materials that have contributed to my renewed reading of these contested areas.

Every chapter starts with a story, or a piece of intelligence drawn from reports elaborated by the authorities serving in the Turkish–Syrian–Iraqi borderlands. Even though these local events might appear banal or minor on first glance, the introduction to each chapter makes explicit how these developments had

---

[108] For a similar argument on the Ottoman period, see Sabri Ateş, 'Bones of Contention: Corpse Traffic and Ottoman-Iranian Rivalry in the Nineteenth-century Iraq', *Comparative Studies of South Asia, Africa and the Middle East*, Vol. 30, No. 3 (2010), pp. 512–32.

[109] See Samuel Dolbee, 'Borders, Disease, and Territoriality in the Post-Ottoman Middle East', in Jordi Tejel and Ramazan Hakkı Öztan (eds), *Regimes of Mobility*, pp. 205–27; Chris Gratien, *The Unsettled Plain: An Environmental History of the Late Ottoman Frontier* (Stanford, CA: Stanford University Press, 2022).

[110] Giovanni Levi, 'Frail Frontiers?', *Past and Present*, Supplement 14 (2019), p. 48.

wider socio-political reverberations. Then, I zoom out to provide a broader historical context about the main themes addressed throughout the book – violence, displacement, cross-border criminality, contraband and transport, among others. After that, I zoom in again upon the border zones to examine how these broader issues played out in the Turkish–Syrian–Iraqi borderlands by highlighting borderlanders' agency and interactions with the relevant 'centre' and/or other international actors. Finally, all chapters end with a thematic conclusion that also serves as a transition to the next. In other words, by observing different issues revolving around the border zones, the selected initial stories seek to showcase how locally lived experiences of territoriality became 'globalized in their patterns and impacts, and thus provide for a conversation across border research site'.[111]

Bringing the 'lived experiences of territoriality' amid borderlanders as well as trans-border dynamics to the fore through the lenses of official records presents, however, both methodological and epistemological challenges. It requires a careful reading of these sources, which are marked by official – state and imperial – views and priorities, and thus frequently leave aside borderlanders' perspectives and concerns.[112] Despite this potential trap, which, by the way, presents a danger for any historian, the breadth and depth of this documentation is rich enough, I argue, to offer new conceptual approaches to the history of the rise of the nation state in the Middle East, provided that scholars undertake, whenever possible, a double move: cross-checking and comparing official reports on the same topics picked up by different state and Mandate authorities on the one hand, and prioritising instances in which borderlanders contact state and border authorities in the first place, on the other. This does not mean, of course, that borderlanders' demands and voices are more important than states' views or concerns; rather, it is a call to acknowledge their value as historical sources that, even more importantly, can help us to better grasp how state-formation processes have been simultaneously adopted and re-shaped from below.

---

[111] Victor Konrad, 'New Directions at the Post-Globalization Border', *Journal of Borderlands Studies*, Vol. 36, No. 5 (2021), pp. 713–43 (here p. 722).

[112] Ann Laura Stoler, 'Colonial Archives and the Arts of Governance', *Archival Science*, Vol. 2, No. 1-2 (2002), pp. 87–109.

A final word on the sources analysed in this book: the reader will notice the overwhelming use of 'colonial sources', that is, French and British reports. There are two main reasons for this. On the one hand, French and British officers served at the border posts and peripheries of the Syrian and Iraqi states, because Mandate authorities were charged with the mission of 'protecting' the international borders of these two countries; they thus produced most of the relevant paperwork in the borderlands. On the other hand, the present security situation in Syria and Iraq prevents scholars from conducting thorough archival research in those countries for the time being. As for Turkey, even though I tried to use Turkish sources as much as possible throughout the chapters to balance Western views, anyone who has done research at the republican archives will agree that most files held in Ankara on Eastern Anatolia and border relations with neighbours are disappointing, for the 'decisions' that are accessible are devoid, in general, of the related background reports, correspondence and memos. This overall awkward situation has been partly compensated by relying on a wide variety of other primary sources – memoirs, diaries, travelogues, newspaper articles, private archival collections – and referring whenever possible to the original Turkish files that have been kept, in particular, at the French archives in Nantes. Furthermore, although most of the archival data presented and analysed in this book has been accessible to scholars for a while – with the exception of the Second World War period – it is hoped that the borderland perspective provides a new and refreshing reading of these sources.

The book is organised around seven thematic chapters. Chapter 1, 'Networks of Violence in the Shatterzones of the Post-Ottoman Middle East', examines the simultaneous and tumultuous delimitations of the Syrian–Turkish and Iraqi–Turkish borders between 1918 and 1925. Traditionally, however, these two border-drawing processes have been discussed in completely different sets of literature with narrow national focuses. In addition, they have been analysed from a top-down approach – namely, by favouring negotiations between states, including international organisations such as the League of Nations. By tracing the strategies and tactics of the most important local tribes, the chapter illustrates how borderlanders played a significant role in the actual resolution of these frontier disputes. Even though boundary agreements were the result of diplomatic discussions in distant places such as London, Paris and Geneva, the chapter showcases that the process through which Turkey, France and Great Britain came to abide by the new international borders cannot be fully apprehended without taking into account the interactions between local players and a variety of both state and non-state actors.

Chapter 2, 'Refugees, Borders and Identity Boundaries', argues that political negotiations are not the only tools states have used to create new realities on the ground. Peace agreements and diplomatic talks about boundary delimitation historically worked hand in hand with the emergence of another urgent international problem – i.e., the flood of refugees that originated from the sites of collapsing empires and massacres. Against this backdrop, the League of Nations responded by establishing a refugee regime where standardised paperwork and procedures were introduced, complete with a range of relief programmes designed to accommodate the displaced. Yet, while the League of Nations perceived refugeedom as an opportunity to minimise the prospects of ethno-religious conflict, state authorities exploited the refugee issue as a means of consolidating their colonial and national projects. Creating refugees and/or welcoming them – very often in the border zones – was a mutually constitutive process that reproduced discourses of governmentality and justified the modern territorial state, while redefining both the physical and metaphorical limits of belonging. The chapter thus explores the relationship between modern notions of territorial sovereignty, ethno-religious boundaries and refugeedom. Finally, it also scrutinises the extent to which refugees in these borderlands tapped into the League of Nations' jargon in advancing their own interests.

Chapters 3 and 4, 'Cross-border Infringements: Smugglers, Criminals and Fugitives' and 'Interstate Cooperation Against Diseases and Plagues and its Limits', examine how despite ongoing tensions between Turkey, France and Great Britain, interstate cooperation to deal with common challenges, such as cross-border mobility and the spread of epidemics and pests, has led to a standardisation of practices that aim at making the boundary a physical reality – border gates, posts, pillars – favouring the exchange of information, introducing common paperwork and facilitating the extradition of fugitive outlaws. Notwithstanding this, Chapter 3 emphasises that, because of the lack of human and material resources, borderland governance had to be accompanied by informal and extra-legal arrangements – a common practice which exposes the legacies of the imperial legal orders as well as the hybridisation of different legal traditions that prevailed in the new-born states throughout the interwar period.

In the same vein, Chapter 4 examines how political concerns have differed regarding diseases. For one, French and British authorities were less concerned with providing health care to Syrians and Iraqis than with the negative effects that the spread of diseases and infestations could have on their economic enterprises, regionally and globally. In contrast, the 'total war' against diseases and pests enabled Turkish officials to strengthen the representation of Turkey's southern border as a gateway for 'foreign invaders' and enemies. Hence, social interpretations of diseases and locust infestations helped enact the principle of territoriality in Turkish border zones. Finally, both chapters explore the extent to which borderlanders resisted against and adapted to inter-state cooperation aiming at controlling human and non-human mobility.

Chapter 5, 'Railroads, Uneven Mobilities and Frail States', suggests that a view from the borderlands also helps problematise the linear, and sometimes celebratory terms by which globalisation in the modern Middle East has been presented. While it has become a truism that railway infrastructure development is a fundamental project of both nation-state making and global connectedness, it is less widely acknowledged that the impact of roads and railways are both 'heightened and complicated in borderland regions'.[113] In that sense, the tumultuous completion of the Baghdad Railway in 1940 – a transport project initiated in the late Ottoman period, interrupted during the First World War, and thought to accelerate the speed of movement and increase the economic relations between Europe and the Middle East – is a case in point. The chapter thus explores the factors that either favoured or prevented the completion of a long-awaited transport project. It also analyses how and to what extent the Baghdad Railway increased the connectedness across these borderlands, thereby re-creating economic and social links that pre-dated the newly-established borders in the region.

---

[113] Galen Murton, 'Nobody Stops and Stays Anymore: Motor roads, Uneven Mobilities, and Conceptualizing Borderland Modernity in Highland Nepal', in Alexander Horstmann, Martin Saxer, and Alessandro Rippa (eds), *Routledge Handbook of Asian Borderlands* (London and New York: Routledge, 2018), pp. 315–24 (here p. 318).

Chapters 6 and 7 address the ambivalent impacts – re-bordering and de-bordering processes – of the Second World War upon Middle Eastern borders. By analysing the diplomatic correspondence exchanged between Turkey and Great Britain, Chapter 6, 'Irredentism in a Context of Global Uncertainty', examines Ankara's attempts to obtain territorial gains at the post-war negotiating table. Irredentism, however, did not emerge solely among states in the region. The chapter then turns its attention to irredentist claims advanced by secessionist movements – i.e. Armenian and Kurdish committees – who proved to be extremely active across the region and beyond.

Chapter 7, 'De-bordering and Re-bordering Middle Eastern States', observes the efforts deployed by the Middle East Supply Centre (MESC) to boost wheat and meat production – i.e. the import of tractors, water pumps, anti-locust campaigns and veterinary control – within the context of the Second World War, marked by important shortages of food supplies. As a result, MESC's policies contributed to fostering regional connectivity and dependency, whilst protecting Middle Eastern borders from the Axis' economic influence with some nevertheless unexpected outcomes; namely, that borders and border dwellers regained a political, social and economic centrality that has been by and large overlooked by scholarship on the Second World War. In addition, the chapter discusses the emergence of informal rules, networks and regimes in order to compensate for the shortage of basic foodstuffs during the war.

Given that each chapter ends with its own thematic conclusion, the final 'Conclusion', while first connecting the past and present developments in the Turkish–Syrian–Iraqi borderlands, provides an assessment of the broader questions the monograph raises on territoriality, borders, trans-border mobility, borderlanders' agency and state formation. It also delineates the outlines of a synthetic analytical framework and innovative methodology that allows for a more holistic, yet finely grained understanding of the formation of the territorial state in the interwar Middle East.

1

NETWORKS OF VIOLENCE IN THE SHATTERZONES OF THE POST-OTTOMAN MIDDLE EAST

In March 1919, several letters originating from the Committee of Union and Progress (CUP) branch of Jazirat ibn Umar – considered by the British as a hub for 'Turkish propaganda' in Eastern Anatolia – were funnelled to the Turkish-Iraqi armistice line area urging the expulsion of 'foreigners' (the British) while asking local tribes to support the Ottoman government.[1] The actual instruments of anti-British propaganda were the Goyan, a Kurdish tribe situated for the most part just outside British administrative area, to the north of Zakho. In return, the British established an intelligence centre around this small town to gather information about the 'enemy' and sent pro-British agents to spread propaganda within the Turkish territory.[2]

Propaganda quickly gave way to widespread violence. Between 1919 and 1921, British authorities detected anti-Christian massacres in the Goyan country, because the local Nestorians and Assyrian Levies had come to be seen as the allies of 'foreign-infidels'.[3] Encouraged by Turkish agents in the

---

[1] TNA, FO 371/7782. Iraq Intelligence report, Colonial Office, 5 December 1922. For a detailed account on the role of main Eastern cities and towns within the 'National movement liberation' see Oktay Bozan, *Millî Mücadele Döneminde Diyarbakır, 1918–23* (Konya: Çizgi Kitabevi, 2016), pp. 255–312.
[2] Enes Demir, *Yeni Belgeler Işığında. Vazgeçilmeyen Topraklar Mîsak-ı Millî* (Istanbul: Post, 2017), pp. 344–60.
[3] TNA, FO 608/95. Telegram, Political Officer, Baghdad, to Foreign Office, 7 April 1919.

area, the Christian villages of the Amadiya district were systematically raided by Kurdish tribal groups. Even though the loss of life was small, crops and sheep were subject to theft and destruction. In return, British aeroplanes bombed the rebellious tribes, including unarmed residents of the villages and towns.[4] Despite the end of anti-Christian attacks by early 1922, the British authorities considered that frequent air raids against frontier tribes were a necessary policy to obtain a 'marked effect' on the Kurds – that is, to hamper any attempt on the part of the Turks to open direct communication between Rowanduz (northern Iraq) and Jazirat ibn Umar (Turkey).[5]

Further west, diverse Arab and Kurdish tribes fought the French troops along the provisional armistice line between Turkey and Syria in the name of Islam and Ottoman solidarity. As Mustafa Kemal and other ex-Ottoman officers obtained a series of significant military victories in the Caucasus, French Cilicia, Antep, Maraş and Urfa provinces, the resistance movement made its territorial ambitions clear through what was called the 'National Pact', which laid claim over Mosul Province as well as northern Syria, including Alexandretta and Aleppo.[6] The pact of January 1920 rejected any division of territories populated by those Ottoman Muslims who were allegedly united in religion, culture, and aim and, consequently, served as basis for cooperation between different anti-colonial fronts in which borderlanders played a relevant, albeit sometimes contradictory, role.

This chapter thus examines the unofficial war that developed along the provisional frontiers between Turkey, Syria and Iraq between 1918 and 1925.[7] For

---

[4] TNA, AIR 5/202. Appendix III to Major General Fraser's Report on British Forces in Iraq, 8 April–30 September 1922.

[5] See Jafna L. Cox, 'A Splendid Training Ground: The Importance of the Royal Air Force in its Role in Iraq, 1919–32', *Journal of Imperial and Commonwealth History*, Vol. 13 (1985), pp. 157–84; David E. Omissi, *Air Power and Colonial Control: The Royal Air Force 1919–39* (Manchester: Manchester University Press, 1990); Priya Satia, *Spies in Arabia: The Great War and the Foundations of Britain's Covert Empire in the Middle East* (Oxford: Oxford University Press, 2008), pp. 239–62.

[6] See Cosima Flateau, 'La sortie de guerre de l'Empire ottoman', *Les Cahiers Sirice*, No. 17 (2016), pp. 29–45.

[7] For a British account of the 'unofficial war' between Britain and Turkey along the Anatolian front, see Alfred Rawilson, *Adventures in the Near East, 1918–22* (London: Jonathan Cape, 1923). For a Turkish version of this conflict in the Turkish–Iraqi and Turkish–Syrian frontier

one, although the First World War formally ended on 11 November 1918, it left behind several zones of post-war violence, as the collapse of empires – from the Balkans to the Caucasus and the Middle East – created spaces without order or a definite state authority.[8] Admittedly, violence in the former imperial borderlands could hardly be considered a new phenomenon. In the eastern margins of the Ottoman Empire, as many historians have shown, a geography of endemic violence had emerged at least since the nineteenth century when the Sublime Porte managed to dismantle the diverse semi-autonomous Kurdish emirates. The end of these polities brought about the replacement of traditional ruling families by tribal chieftains and religious leaders who nevertheless sealed alliances with the Ottoman state in exchange for certain social and economic privileges.[9] As a result, however, theft of flocks, robbery and vendettas became part of daily life on the eastern fringes of the Empire.

Yet, while this violence was largely 'linked to social structures in which tribal affiliation and clans were important' and connected to a fierce competition for resources between sedentary agriculturalists and nomadic pastoralists,[10] from the

---

areas, see Ahmet H. Saral, *Türk İstiklal Harbi cilt IV: Güney Cephesi: İngiliz ve Fransızların Güney-Doğu Anadolu'yu işgal etmeleri Milli Mücadele hareketleri, bu bölgede yapılan muharebeler ve Revandiz Harekatı* (Ankara: Genelkurmay Başkanlığı Harp Tarihi Dairesi, 1966).

[8] Gerwarth, Robert and John Horne (eds), *War in Peace: Paramilitary Violence in Europe after the Great War* (Oxford: Oxford University Press, 2012); Eyal Ginio, *Ottoman Culture of Defeat: The Balkan Wars and their Aftermath* (Oxford: Oxford University Press, 2015). On the Middle Eastern experience at war, see Mustafa Aksakal, *The Ottoman Road to War in 1914: The Ottoman Empire and the First World War* (Cambridge: Cambridge University Press, 2008); Kristian Coaster Ulrichsen, *The First World War in the Middle East* (London: Hurst, 2014); Leila T. Fawaz, *A Land of Aching Hearts: The Middle East in the Great War* (Cambridge, MA: Harvard University Press, 2014); Eugene Rogan, *The Fall of the Ottomans: The Great War in the Middle East* (New York: Basic Books, 2015); Ian Rutledge, *Enemy on the Euphrates: The Battle for Iraq, 1914–21* (London: Saqi Books, 2014); Rob Johnson, *The Great War and the Middle East* (Oxford: Oxford University Press, 2016).

[9] Janet Klein, *The Margins of Empire: Kurdish Militias in the Ottoman Tribal Zone* (Stanford, CA: Stanford University Press, 2011). See also A. C. S Peacock (ed.) *The Frontiers of the Ottoman World* (Oxford: Oxford University Press, 2009); Ali Yaycioglu, *Partners of the Empire: The Crisis of the Ottoman Order in the Age of Revolutions* (Stanford, CA: Stanford University Press, 2016).

[10] Erik Jan Zürcher, 'Postscript', in Ramazan Hakkı Öztan and Alp Yenen (eds), *Age of Rogues: Revolutionaries and Racketeers at the Frontiers of Empires* (Edinburgh: Edinburgh University Press, 2021), pp. 383–9 (here p. 385).

late nineteenth century onwards killings and plundering became increasingly coloured by political factors. Nationalism, Islamism and socialism – at times intermingled – were the main ideological strands that came to interplay with old conflicts in the later stages of the Ottoman and Qajar empires.[11] Unsurprisingly, the Great War expanded the room for manoeuvre for 'transgressive actors'[12] – bandits, revolutionaries and rogues – within the context of generalised violence across the region.[13] Critically, insecurity in the borderlands of the disintegrating Ottoman Empire persisted after the armistice, as France and Britain strove to impose their colonial presence in the Middle East, under a new form – the mandate system under the aegis of the League of Nations.[14] While an increasing number of historians have studied these episodes of low-intensity warfare in non-European theatres in order to examine the Great War 'within a frame that is both longer (temporally) and wider (spatially)' than generally admitted,[15] the former are also important for other interrelated reasons.

First, most of these 'shatterzones'[16] would form the international borders of the newly-established states in the Middle East. Hence, the pervasive

---

[11] Houri Berberian, *Roving Revolutionaries: Armenians and the Connected Revolutions in the Russian, Iranian, and Ottoman Worlds* (Oakland, CA: University of California Press, 2019).

[12] Ramazan Hakkı Öztan and Alp Yenen, 'Age of Rogues: Transgressive Politics at the Frontiers of the Ottoman Empire', in Ramazan Hakkı Öztan and Alp Yenen (eds), *Age of Rogues*, pp. 3–52.

[13] Ryan Gingeras, *Fall of the Sultanate: The Great War and the End of the Ottoman Empire, 1908–22* (Oxford: Oxford University Press, 2016); Yigit Akin, *When the War Came Home: The Ottoman's Great War and the Devastation of an Empire* (Stanford, CA: Stanford University Press, 2018).

[14] For three comprehensive studies of the Mandates in the Middle East, see Peter Sluglett and Nadine Méouchy (eds), *The British and French Mandates in Comparative Perspective* (Leiden: Brill, 2004); Cyrus Schayegh and Andrew Arsan (eds), *The Routledge Handbook of the History of the Middle East Mandates* (London: Routledge, 2015); and, Susan Pedersen, *The Guardians: The League of Nations and the Crisis of Empire* (Oxford: Oxford University Press, 2015).

[15] Robert Gerwarth and Erez Manela (eds), *Empires at War, 1911–23* (Oxford: Oxford University Press, 2014), p. 2. See also Julie d'Andurain and Cloé Drieu, 'Introduction to the Special Issue: Par-delà le théâtre européen de 14–18. L'autre Grande Guerre dans le monde musulman', *Revue des Mondes Musulmans et de la Méditerranée*, Vol. 141 (2017), pp. 11–33.

[16] Omer Bartov and Eric D. Weitz (eds), *Shatterzone of Empires: Coexistence and Violence in the German, Habsburg, Russian, and Ottoman Borderlands* (Bloomington: Indiana University Press, 2013). See also Alfred J. Rieber, *The Struggle for the Eurasian Borderlands: From the Rise of Early Modern Empires to the End of the First World War* (Cambridge: Cambridge University Press, 2014).

violence in these zones is key to our understanding of both the conditions and the processes through which new expressions of nationalism,[17] new states, notions of 'territoriality' and indeed new borderlands emerged in the early 1920s.[18] In the Middle East, as elsewhere, 'the main episodes of boundary formation ... followed major wars and the breakdown of empires'.[19] Yet, while scholars such as Charles Tilly highlight the coercive face of the state in this process,[20] many of the actors involved in armed struggle in the borderlands of the former Ottoman Empire could hardly be considered *state* actors. Taking advantage of a power vacuum, colonial powers, quasi-states (Turkish agents acting on behalf the Ankara government since 1920) and non-state actors interacted at times through violence, at other times through volatile alliances thereby playing a formative role in the emergence of the modern Middle East.[21]

Second, observing the endemic violence in the old and new border zones in the Middle Eastern region allows us to call attention to continuities between the Ottoman and post-Ottoman eras. As in the late nineteenth and

---

[17] Erik J. Zürcher, *The Unionist Factor: The Role of the Committee of Union and Progress in the Turkish National Movement, 1905–26* (Leiden: Brill, 1984); Ryan Gingeras, *Sorrowful Shores: Violence, Ethnicity, and the End of the Ottoman Empire, 1912–23* (Oxford: Oxford University Press, 2009); Caner Yelbasi, *The Circassians of Turkey: War, Violence and Nationalism from the Ottomans to Atatürk* (London: I. B. Tauris, 2019).

[18] According to Richard Schofield, there are few examples of historical borderlands in the Middle East in the classical sense of the term; that is 'zonal states or imperial margins that have served as a frontier'; the Ottoman-Persian frontier would in that sense constitute classic historical borderlands. Richard Schofield, 'Foreword', in Gilbert E. Hubbard, *From the Gulf to Ararat: Imperial Boundary Making in the Late Ottoman Empire* (London: I. B. Tauris, 2016), p. xiii.

[19] Jonathan Goodhand, 'Epilogue: The View from the Border', in Benedikt Korf and Timothy Raeymaekers (eds), *Violence on the Margins: States, Conflict, and Borderlands* (New York: Palgrave Macmillan, 2013), pp. 247–64 (here p. 252).

[20] Charles Tilly, *Coercion, Capital and European States, AD 990–1990* (Cambridge: Blackwell, 1990). See also, Anthony Giddens, *The Nation-State and Violence* (Cambridge: Cambridge University Press, 1985).

[21] Non-state actors can be defined as 'largely or entirely autonomous ... from political impulses beyond state control and direction'. Critically, they operate as or participate in networks, which extend across boundaries of two or more in order to affect political outcomes. See Daphné Josselin and William Wallace, 'Non-state Actors in World Politics: A Framework', in Daphné Josselin and William Wallace (eds), *Non-state Actors in World Politics* (New York: Palgrave Macmillan, 2002), pp. 3–4.

early twentieth centuries, armed struggle and revolts around the armistice line were conducted by a conglomerate of diverse – local-yet-connected – actors such as ex-Ottoman officers, tribal chieftains and irregular bands. Critically, anti-colonial resistance did not take place in isolation; rather, these different sites formed part of a broader struggle that nonetheless harboured diverse discourses and influences. In that regard, the borderland stretching between south-eastern Anatolia, the Syrian Upper Jazira and the northern margins of the former Mosul Vilayet was a case in point. Here, much as in other shatterzones, anti-colonial warfare and discourses on self-determination reactivated old conflicts – in particular tribal struggles for power, tax collection and related land issues,[22] as well as the dynamics of violence and revenge between Nestorian and Kurdish tribes.[23]

Finally, the new international visions of territoriality 'were subverted by indigenous actors who populated it with local notions, creating a hybrid political order.'[24] Thus, throughout the 1920s and 1930s, Western notions, such as the sovereign state having a defined territory, mingled with Islamic

---

[22] Under the 1858 Ottoman Land Law, the usufructs of state lands were granted sometimes to the peasants, though more often to the tribal chieftains, city merchants and notables, for an appropriate fee. On the eastern margins of the Empire, the destruction of the Kurdish emirates allowed big landowners (*aghas*), local chieftains, and religious families (*shaykhs*) to increase their land properties at the expense of Christian peasants. In addition, Kurdish and Nestorian tribes entered in conflict over land use in the Hakkari region. See Gökhan Çetinsaya, 'Challenges of a Frontier Region: The Case of Ottoman Iraq in the Nineteenth Century', in A. C. S. Peacock (ed.), *The Frontiers of the Ottoman World* (Oxford: Oxford University Press, 2009), pp. 271–87. See also Nadir Özbek, 'The Politics of Taxation and the "Armenian Question" during the Late Ottoman Empire, 1876–1908', *Comparative Studies in Society and History*, Vol. 54, No. 4 (2012), pp. 770–97.

[23] On the Armenian genocide, see Donald Bloxham, *The Great Game of Genocide: Imperialism, Nationalism, and the Destruction of the Ottoman Armenians* (Oxford and New York: Oxford University Press, 2005); Ronald Grigor Suny, *'They Can Live in the Desert but Nowhere Else': A History of the Armenian Genocide* (Princeton, NJ: Princeton University Press, 2015). On Kurdish–Nestorian tensions, see Sema Yasar Baraç, 'Nestorians, Kurds, and the State: The Struggle to Survive in the Frontier in the Late Ottoman Period, 1839–1908' (MA Thesis, Istanbul: Bogaziçi University, 2015).

[24] Benjamin D. Hopkins, 'The Bounds of Identity: The Goldsmith Mission and the Delineation of the Perso-Afghan Border in the Nineteenth Century', *Journal of Global History*, Vol. 2, No. 2 (2007), pp. 233–54 (here p. 234).

legal principles of territoriality, together with local models based on relational power around the so-called paramount leaders – tribal and religious chieftains – rather than on a strict territorial control. Consequently, from north-western Syria to the Ottoman–Persian border, diverse paramount shaykhs attempted to create new polities that reflected the emerging hybrid political order, half-way between traditional tribal chiefdoms and semi-autonomous polities. Although these statelets were short-lived, some of these experiences laid the foundations for nascent territorial nationalisms inspired by the increasingly hegemonic notions of statehood promoted by the new international system.

Challenging Post-War Settlements

With the Armistice of Mudros on 30 October 1918, most of the Arab provinces of the Ottoman Empire were placed under the control of the British army. In Iraq, the British introduced first a military government and then a civil administration. In Syria, the establishment of an Arab administration supported by a proto-Arab army led by Sharifian officers who had joined the Arab revolt during the Great War did not meet any British resistance. In parallel, British and French forces occupied Constantinople, while Greek and Italian forces landed on the Aegean coast.[25] Under such conditions, the sultan's government agreed to all post-armistice peace settlements.

Critically, the mandates for Syria and Lebanon were awarded to France, while that of Iraq was conferred to Great Britain at the San Remo Conference of 25 April 1920. In addition, the Treaty of Sèvres, signed on 10 August 1920, adopted the Wilsonian programme – including the right of self-determination for non-Turkish 'nationalities' under the Ottoman rule – to the Allied forces' advantage, thereby projecting the formation in Eastern Anatolia of both an Armenian and a Kurdish state (Article 62). Further, the Kurdish districts of Mosul Vilayet were to be permitted to join this autonomous state, if they wished to do so upon a series of conditions (Article 64).[26] Yet, by the time the Treaty of Sèvres was signed, multiple signs indicated that the implementation

---

[25] On the Allied management of occupied Constantinople, see Daniel-Joseph MacArthur-Seal, 'Resurrecting Legal Extraterritoriality in Occupied Istanbul, 1918–23', *Middle Eastern Studies*, Vol. 54, No. 5 (2018), pp. 769–87.

[26] 'Treaty of Peace with Turkey'. Signed at Sèvres, August 10, 1920. Presented to the Parliament by Command of His Majesty.

of these international agreements was to be more complex than British and French officials had expected.

Indeed, the Committee of Union and Progress (CUP) leaders had managed to flee the Ottoman capital to exile in Germany to avoid a martial trial on crimes committed during the Great War, in particular the Armenian genocide. However, before their departure, Talat Pasha – the former Grand Vizir – held secret meetings with lower ranks of the Committee to organise the CUP's underground and paramilitary branches, endowed with the mission of fighting against the conditions of the armistice.[27] Subsequently, local CUP branches established diverse Defence of National Right Societies (*Müdâfaa-i Hukuk Cemiyetleri*) across Anatolia. Meanwhile, Enver Pasha – former Minister of War – enjoined his followers in the army to keep alive the *Teşkilat-ı Mahsusa*'s paramilitary and propaganda activities against the Allies throughout the Muslim world, particularly in North Africa, the Caucasus and Central Asia.[28] Indeed, paramilitary activities found a fertile ground in Anatolia, especially in the regions where ethno-religious conflicts had arisen in earlier stages. Thus, following the French occupation of Cilicia, paramilitary operations targeted the remaining Armenian population in this area. In Western Anatolia, CUP-associated local guerrillas launched attacks against the Greek population, too.[29]

Taken together, these initiatives were thought to lay the foundations for an underground power that would eventually emerge as a legitimate one after the foreign occupation had been overcome. Yet, while at first the CUP's leadership played a crucial role in organising the resistance movement, its momentum was ephemeral. Due to the organisational autonomy of the diverse CUP underground branches, autonomous local and key military commanders of the Ottoman army, such as Mustafa Kemal, Rauf Pasha, Kazim Karabekir and Ali Fuad Pasha, slowly took over the direction of the 'National Struggle' (*Millî*

---

[27] For a comprehensive and critical biography of Talat Pasha, see Hans-Lukas Kieser, *Talaat Pasha: Father of Modern Turkey, Architect of Genocide* (Princeton, NJ: Princeton University Press, 2018).

[28] Alp Yenen, 'Elusive Forces in Illusive Eyes: British Officialdom's Perception of the Anatolian Resistance Movement', *Middle Eastern Studies*, Vol. 54, No. 5 (2018), pp. 788–810 (here p. 793).

[29] Ibid.

Mücadele) or the 'War of Independence' (*İstiklâl Harbi* or *Kurtuluş Savaşı*), thereby defying Talat and Enver Pasha's leadership.[30]

Reinvigorated by a series of military victories in the Caucasus and southeastern Anatolia, the resistance movement made its territorial ambitions clear through a series of documents. Thus, the Amasya Protocol of July 1919 vowed to fight to secure the 'integrity of the Ottoman fatherland, the assurance of our nation's independence, and the inviolability of the sultanate and caliphate'.[31] Seemingly, the congress held at Erzurum between July and August 1919 rejected all post-war settlements signed by the Sultan and vetoed granting any special rights to Christian minorities, specifically the Greeks and Armenians. A month later, at the Sivas Congress, delegates of the resistance movement discussed effective strategies for securing the unity and integrity of the fatherland – including the choice between a potential international mandate over Turkey and full independence. After the delegates of the Eastern committees chose the latter option, the definition of the nation and its borders became more pressing.

On 28 January 1920, the Ottoman Parliament echoed the deliberations made at the Sivas and Erzurum congresses, thereby taking a set of decisions concerning Turkey's independence and its territorial boundaries in what was to be known as the *Misak-ı Millî* or National Pact. Specifically, the pact's first article refers to the ceasefire line of 30 October 1918 as a potential border, but continues by claiming that

> all the territories, whether *inside* or *outside* this ceasefire line, which are inhabited by a majority of Ottoman Muslims united in religion, culture, and aim, (and) filled with a feeling of mutual respect and solidarity constitute a *de facto* and *de jure* whole whose division is unacceptable for any reason.[32]

---

[30] Salahi R. Sonyel, 'Mustafa Kemal and Enver in Conflict, 1919–22', *Middle Eastern Studies*, Vol. 25, No. 4 (1989), pp. 506–15.

[31] Burna Turnaoğlu, *The Formation of Turkish Republicanism* (Princeton, NJ: Princeton University Press, 2017), p. 198.

[32] Alexander E. Balistreri, 'Revisiting Millî: Borders and the Making of the Turkish Nation State', in Jordi Tejel and Ramazan Hakkı Öztan (eds), *Regimes of Mobility: Borders and State Formation in the Middle East, 1918–46* (Edinburgh: Edinburgh University Press, 2022), pp. 29–58 (here p. 29).

In parallel, however, the National Pact acknowledged the right of self-determination for the peoples inhabiting Western Thrace and the Arab-majority provinces in present Syria and Iraq.

At the new parliament, the Grand National Assembly (*Büyük Millet Meclisi*), formed on 23 April 1920, Mustafa Kemal addressed this issue again – the eastern border included the districts of Kars, Ardahan and Batum, while the western border passed through Edirne. Southwards, the border started from the south of Iskenderun, thereby constituting a line towards Aleppo, Katima and Jarablus up to the eastern part of the province of Mosul, including the surroundings of Kirkuk and Sulaimaniya.[33]

The extent to which Turkey's 'national borders' (*hudud-ı milliye* or *millî hudut*) were inviolable and non-negotiable still remains a bone of contention. Turkish historiography tends to depict Turkish nationalism in the early 1920s as above all territorial in nature, free of irredentist ambitions, while reifying the indivisibility of the Turkish state and its nation and the irreversibility of its borders.[34] Contrary to these accounts, Alexander E. Balistreri argues that the borders envisioned by the National Pact were 'both pragmatic and open to change'. Thus, Turkey's borders could be subject to change throughout history and determined by Turkish national leadership, depending on the context and opportunities.[35] In that regard, he quotes Mustafa Kemal in a discourse in the parliament in 1921: 'What is our national border? . . . Our national border is that national border which enables us to live happily and independently, and whichever border we can draw to best optimise our interests will be our national border. [There is] after all [no] clearly delineated boundary'.[36]

---

[33] Mustafa Kemal Atatürk, *Atatürk'ün Söylev ve Demeçleri, I–III* (Ankara: Divan Yayıncılık, 2006), p. 24.

[34] Ayşe Kadıoğlu, 'The Twin Motives of Turkish Nationalism', in Ayşe Kadıoğlu and E. Fuat Keyman (eds), *Symbiotic Antagonisms: Competing Nationalisms in Turkey* (Salt Lake City: University of Utah Press, 2011), p. 48. See also Ali Kazancıgil 'The Ottoman-Turkish State and Kemalism' in Ali Kazancıgil and Ergun Özbudun (eds), *Atatürk: Founder of a Modern State* (London: Hurst, 1981), p. 51; Ugur Kaya, 'Frontière et territorialité dans la perception selon l'Etat turc', *Confluence Méditerranée*, Vol. 101, No. 2 (2017), pp. 13–25.

[35] On the same idea, see Amit Bein, *Kemalist Turkey and the Middle East: International Relations in the Interwar Period* (Cambridge: Cambridge University Press, 2017), p. 10.

[36] TBMMZC, 16 October 1921, p. 355. Quoted in Alexander E. Balistrieri, 'Revisiting Millî', p. 33.

There was thus a contradiction between the commitment of the leaders of the rebellious government in Ankara vowing to defend all Ottoman territory outside the ceasefire line, and the promise to allow populations living in such territories to decide their political future through a plebiscite. Such contradictions and ambiguities that reflected the fragile compromise between 'pragmatic' and 'utopian' nationalist factions unfolded even more dramatically as the resistance movement grew regionally. Crucially, when the Syrian mandate was attributed to France on 25 April 1920, relations between different Arab armed bands and the Ankara leadership were reinvigorated in order to weaken French military presence in the Aleppo area. However, when these organisations and their contentious activities forced the French to overstretch their military presence in the region,[37] the irregular forces operating in the southern front campaign (*Güney Cephesi*) soon lost their utility as Ankara neared a victory vis-à-vis the Greeks in western Anatolia. Hence, when the potential of a diplomatic settlement appeared on the horizon, Mustafa Kemal opted to sever his links with the armed groups active in north-western Syria that he had formerly supported.[38]

On 20 October 1921, Turkey and France signed the Ankara Agreement, also known as the Franklin-Bouillon Agreement, which allowed for the end of the armed conflict between the two countries and the settlement of a provisional frontier. In particular, the agreement defined the frontier line as starting at a point south of Payas, Meydan Ekbez, and then passing eastwards to join the Baghdad Railway at the station of Çobanbey. From there the line would follow the railway, 'of which the track as far as Nusaybin will remain on Turkish territory; thence it will follow the old road between

---

[37] Cosima Flateau, 'La sortie de guerre de l'Empire ottoman: Grande Guerre, guerre nationale, guerre coloniale à la frontière syro-turque, 1918–23', *Les Cahiers Sirice*, Vol. 17, No. 3 (2016), pp. 29–45.

[38] Mizrahi, Jean-David, 'La répression du banditisme sur les confins de la Syrie mandataire: nouveaux Etats et nouvelles frontières dans le Moyen-Orient des années 1920', *Relations Internationales*, No. 114 (2003), pp. 173–87; Mizrahi, Jean-David, 'Le nationalisme de la frontière turco-syrienne au début des années 1920', *Vingtième siècle. Revue d'histoire*, No. 78 (2003), pp. 19–34. Support for Mustafa Kemal did not only come from Muslim Sunnis; some Alawi communities in today's Syria also fought alongside the Kemalist forces. See Stefan Winter, *A History of the Alawis: From Medieval Aleppo to the Turkish Republic* (Princeton and Oxford: Princeton University Press, 2016), pp. 9, 219, and pp. 247–9.

Nusaybin and Jazirat ibn Umar' (Art. 8). The same article set up the conditions for the precise delimitation of the boundary 'within a period of one month from the signature of the present agreement'. Although the establishment of the mixed commission comprising delegates of the two parties did not materialise until September 1925, the Ankara Agreement meant both the de facto French recognition of the 'new' Turkey and the growing political isolation of Britain, which was increasingly challenged by the Kemalist activities in the Mosul Vilayet.

Indeed, as negotiations with France progressed, all eyes turned towards the so-called 'Mosul Affair'. Mustafa Kemal, for instance, stated at Grand National Assembly that Turkey would never compromise over the issue of the Mosul Vilayet.[39] Diverse deputies were even more vocal on this issue, highlighting that Mosul Province was a part of the motherland, while encouraging the new Turkish authorities to follow the principles of the National Pact: 'Raise our flag on the frontier of Mosul, and put it like bayonets on the British flag and into their throat!'[40] Tension in the Grand National Assembly rose to the point where moderate deputies were side-lined after the resignation in June 1921 of Foreign Minister Bakir Sami, who was deemed favourable to the settlement of the 'Mosul Affair' through diplomatic negotiations. In addition, Mustafa Kemal and his followers were actively seeking to destabilise the region by encouraging anti-British unrest in Mesopotamia.[41] Such developments and manoeuvres, combined with mounting concerns over the financial costs of the Mandate led British officials in London to agree with the High Commissioner in Baghdad, who argued that stability could only be achieved through the inclusion of Kurdish districts in Iraq.

This was in line with the British policy that was largely spelled out at the Cairo Conference in March 1921. The main object of the conference was

---

[39] Atatürk, *Atatürk'ün Söylev ve Demeçleri*, V (Ankara: Türk İnkilap Tarihi Enstitüsü, 1972), p. 74.

[40] TBMMZC, Ikinci Celse, 21 December 1921. Quoted in Othman Ali, 'The Career of Ozdemir: A Turkish Bid for Northern Iraq, 1921–3', *Middle Eastern Studies*, Vol. 53, No. 6 (2017), p. 968.

[41] A.L. Macfie, 'British Intelligence and the Causes of Unrest in Mesopotamia, 1919–21', *Middle Eastern Studies*, Vol. 35, No. 1 (1999), pp. 165–77. For a comprehensive study on Turkish activities in Iraq, see Izzet Al-Jumaily, *Irak ve Kemalizm Hareketi, 1919–23* (Ankara: Atatürk Araştırma Merkezi, 1999).

'to maintain firm British control as cheaply as possible'.[42] In that sense, the Royal Air Force was to play a central role in the maintenance of order in Iraq.[43] Besides, Faysal's candidature to the kingdom of Iraq, together with the fate of the Kurdish-majority districts were also widely discussed.[44] In the face of the Turkish threat and in order to secure Iraq's frontier against Turkish claims over Mosul Vilayet, some concrete – albeit contradictory – measures were implemented. On the one hand, in a rather 'opportunistic manner',[45] the British fostered Kurdish nationalism in northern Iraq in order to counter Turkey's pan-Islamic appeals to the Kurdish population. On the other hand, however, the British government attempted to reconcile the aspirations of Kurdish nationalists with the objectives of British policy in Iraq: the consolidation of King Faysal's government in Baghdad and the maintenance of the territorial integrity of Iraq so that it would become a viable state.[46]

The second step was taken at the Lausanne Peace Conference, which began on 20 November 1922. While the new treaty negotiated in Lausanne annulled that of Sèvres, the former left the future status of Mosul Vilayet open for negotiation between Turkey and Britain. It was clear from the onset, however, that Turkish and British positions were irreconcilable. The Turkish view on Mosul Vilayet advanced several ethnic, economic and legal arguments:

a) Turks and Kurds – racially inseparable – were a majority in the province;
b) local populations had been economically oriented towards Anatolia for centuries;
c) the occupation of the Vilayet after the armistice was illegal; and
d) the inhabitants of the province wanted to live with their peers in Anatolia.

---

[42] Peter Sluglett, *Britain in Iraq: Contriving King and Country* (New York: Columbia University Press, 2007), p. 40.
[43] Toby Dodge, *Inventing Iraq: The Failure of Nation Building and a History Denied* (New York: Columbia University Press, 2003).
[44] For an account on the opposing British views expressed in Cairo, see Saad Eskander, 'Southern Kurdistan under Britain's Mesopotamian Mandate: From Separation to Incorporation, 1920–3', *Middle Eastern* Studies, Vol. 37, No. 2 (2001), pp. 153–6.
[45] Liora Lukitz, *A Quest in the Middle East: Gertrude Bell and the Making of Modern Iraq* (London: I. B. Tauris, 2006), p. 174.
[46] Othman Ali, 'The Career of Ozdemir', p. 966.

The British position claimed quite the contrary:

a) the Kurds were racially different from the Turks;[47]
b) most local trade was with the rest of Iraq;
c) legally, the British government had been entrusted with the mandate over Iraq by the League of Nations;
d) frequent Kurdish revolts first against the Sultan and then against the Ankara government – in particular, the Koçgirî revolt in Dersim area – contradicted Turkish claims on Turkish-Kurdish brotherhood.[48]

Against this backdrop on 4 February 1923, Turkey and the Allied representatives in Lausanne agreed to temporarily exclude the 'Mosul Affair' from the conference agenda. Notwithstanding incompatible views on Mosul, different factors helped to unwind relations between Turkey and Britain. Firstly, the electoral victory of the Conservative Prime Minister Andrew Bonar Law in November 1922 opened the door to an appeasement of Turkey, particularly as Britain began to show signs of abandoning its previous pro-Greek policies and limiting its support to Assyrian and Kurdish claims in northern Iraq. In return for these concessions, Turkey joined the League of Nations and by doing so helped Britain and France to further isolate Bolshevik Russia with whom Turkey had constructed a working relationship in the early 1920s.

The second factor that eased the tensions between Turkey and Britain was the conviction of the Turkish delegate İsmet Pasha that the British would do everything in their power to avoid an open war against Turkey, because Britain's main concern in Iraq was oil, not the implementation of the Treaty

---

[47] Although Turkey and Britain exploited statistical data relating to Mosul's population in the absence of a plebiscite to determine the wishes of the vilayet's population, Great Britain's Mandate in Iraq allowed the British representatives a pervasive use of updated statistical data on Mosul's population – ethnicity, distribution and religion – to support 'scientifically' its political and military interests throughout the negotiations between 1922 and 1925. Fuat Dündar, 'StatisQuo: British Use of Statistics in the Iraqi Kurdish question, 1919–32', Crown Paper (Brandeis University), No. 7 (2012), pp. 1–63.

[48] *Lausanne Conference on Near Eastern Affairs, 1922–3: Records of Proceedings and Draft Terms of Peace* (London: HMSO, 1923), pp. 262–4 and 366–7, 369–70.

of Sèvres.[49] This is a view shared by the historian Peter Sluglett, who argues that although the British had advanced security concerns to justify the establishment of a strategic frontier in the mountainous areas between Turkey and Iraq, British and Iraqi priorities over Mosul Vilayet were determined by 'the desire to ensure that the oilfields remained on the Iraqi side of the *de facto* frontier, and secondly to maintain the integrity of the Iraqi state as British and Iraqi politicians envisaged it in the 1920s'.[50]

Notwithstanding this, Ankara renewed anti-British propaganda efforts in the Rowanduz area,[51] while Turkish deputies in the Grand National Assembly pressed Mustafa Kemal to 'regain' Mosul Vilayet.[52] Against this background, Mustafa Kemal asked the Turkish Assembly to make a choice between war and the postponement of the Mosul question. In a conciliatory move, he explained that 'the postponement of this issue did not necessarily mean abandoning the Mosul Vilayet, but perhaps only deferring it until Turkey was in a stronger position'.[53]

As a matter of fact, by May 1924 the negotiations had proved to be unsuccessful. Subsequently, Turkey and Great Britain agreed to send the dispute to the League of Nations, thereby implicitly acknowledging that the strategies carried out by both sides since 1919 had resulted in a deadlock. The issue started to be discussed in Geneva on 20 September 1924, where the debates focused only on the demarcation of the Turkish–Iraqi border, the so-called 'Brussels Line'.[54]

---

[49] Bilal Şimşir, *Lozan Telgrafları I* (Ankara: Atatürk Kültür Dil ve Tarih Yüksek Kurumu, 1990). No. 25, 40, 59, 25–30 November 1922. İsmet Pasha to Rauf Bey. For a general description of the views and perception of the conference amid the Turkish representatives and journalists, see Mustafa Özyürek, *Akşam Gazetesi Basyazarı Necmeddin Sadık Bey'in Lozan Mektupları* (Ankara: Gece Akademi, 2019).

[50] Peter Sluglett, *Britain in Iraq*, p. 76.

[51] Murat Güztoklusu, *Elcezire ve Özdemir Harekatı* (Istanbul: Ümit Yayınları, 2006), pp. 148–9.

[52] TBMMZC, Cilt 3, 23 March 1923, p. 163.

[53] Sevtap Demirci, 'Turco–British diplomatic manoeuvres on the Mosul Question in the Lausanne Conference, 1922–3', *British Journal of Middle Eastern Studies*, Vol. 3, No. 1 (2010), pp. 57–71 (here p. 64).

[54] TNA, FO/371/10826. 'Minutes of the Third Meeting of the League of Nations Council'. 31st session, 29 October 1924, p. 1.

In this context, Britain encouraged France to advance the position of its military posts on the eastern limits of the future Turkish–Syrian border; that is, in the 'Duck's Bill'. The reason was that Britain feared that Ankara could use the Upper Jazira as a second front against its troops deployed in Mosul Province in the event of an open conflict between Turkey and Britain.[55] In turn, the French were also interested in consolidating their presence in this tri-border area for three reasons. First, France had anticipated the establishment of agricultural colonies in the Upper Jazira to boost the Syrian economy and thus decrease the financial burden that the Mandates involved. Beyond these economic considerations, France aimed to control a strategic zone that could ensure various means of communication with the Mosul Vilayet, and further east with Persia. Finally, some French officers considered it of strategic military importance to maintain a position close to the Kurdish districts of Iraq, a region going through a very volatile period.[56]

As a result of French interference, the Turkish government complained of incessant trans-border raids on Turkish villages and patrols, carried out partly by tribesmen from the Syrian side, but partly also by irregular bands, which the French had allegedly fomented.[57] In turn, however, the French accused the Turkish government of doing exactly the same on the Syrian side of the still-provisional boundary line. Even more worrisome, pending the League of Nation's decision on the 'Mosul Affair', French Intelligence Services reported a series of meetings reuniting Turkish officers with tribal chieftains in diverse southern Anatolian towns, wherein a potential war against France and the subsequent annexation of Northern Syria and Mosul Province were discussed.[58]

Rumours of a potential Turkish intervention in the Mosul Vilayet were also detected by the British, who discussed preparing against this eventuality: air action, bringing reinforcements from India and enrolling Kurdish tribes

---

[55] CADN, 1SL/1/V/549. 'Incidents on the Syrian–Turkish Frontier'. The French High Commissioner (Beirut) to the Ministry of Foreign Affairs (Paris). Beirut, 28 April 1927, p. 5.

[56] David McDowall, *A Modern History of the Kurds* (London, I. B. Tauris, 1996), pp. 151–71.

[57] Yücel Güçlü, 'The Controversy over the Delimitation of the Turco-Syrian Frontier in the Period between the Two World Wars', *Middle Eastern Studies*, Vol. 42, No. 4 (2006), pp. 641–57 (here p. 645).

[58] SHAT, 4H 91. Service de Renseignements. Bulletin No. 289. Aleppo, 10 December 1925.

in Iraqi and Turkish territories to attack the Turkish lines of communications in the rear. Ultimately, a Defence Committee was established to ponder all possible actions against Turkey, should it reject a contrary decision taken in Geneva regarding the Turco-Iraqi frontier.[59] As expected by sceptical deputies in Ankara and the Turkish press,[60] the League eventually ceded Mosul Vilayet to Mandate Iraq in December 1925, a decision that was nevertheless accepted by the Turkish government.

Yet, while this brief description of the main political and diplomatic dynamics unfolding between 1920 and 1925 seems to suggest that the fate of the emerging borderlands between Turkey, Syria and Iraq was sealed because of a series of transactions between diplomats and officials, the following sections introduce two important nuances to such an incomplete view. First, the process through which Turkey, France and Britain came to abide by the post-Ottoman boundary agreements can only be fully grasped if we consider the interactions between local players and a variety of both state and non-state actors. Second, because these relations – including networks of violence – exceeded the respective national frameworks, it is even more necessary to study them as a whole.

Merging Discourses on Identity and Territoriality Along the Borderlands

Michael Reynolds argues that 'the affirmation of the nation-state by the great powers as the normative unit of global politics exerted a tremendous impact upon local politics already in turmoil'. On the one hand, the language and programme of nationalism became essential in the realm of modern politics, thereby facilitating the spread of nationalist ideologies worldwide. On the other hand, 'the structure of the global order and interstate system provided powerful incentives to adopt nationalist ideologies by tying control of the state and its territory to claims made on behalf of the nation'.[61] Likewise, Erez Manela points out that the 'Wilsonian moment' (1919–20) allowed anti-colonial movements to search for new allies, languages and methods to help their quest to challenge imperialism. Yet Wilson's rhetoric of self-determination in the colonial

---

[59] TNA, FO/371/10826. Foreign Office to London, 11 December 1925.
[60] 'Karardan Sonra', *Yeni Adana*, 21 December 1925.
[61] Michael A. Reynolds, *Shattering Empires: The Clash and Collapse of the Ottoman and Russian Empires, 1908–18* (Cambridge: Cambridge University Press, 2011), p. 18.

world was not only defined by the intention of its author, but by the perceptions, goals and contexts of its, often, unintended audiences.⁶² As new 'national identities' – such as Turkish, Arab or Kurdish – were not yet fixed, the 'cultural system' of nationalism could have been the vehicle for different and shifting aspirations, open to disparate influences. The shifting context, along with the fluid character of 'national identities' in the early 1920s, was thus reflected in the diversity of political projects and discourses advanced by borderlanders, ranging from Ottoman Muslim solidarity to tribal and local bonds, as well as to ethnic nationalism.

By the time of the Sivas Congress of September 1919, the French and the British had signed an agreement providing for the total withdrawal of British forces from Cilicia and the coastal regions of Syria, and their subsequent replacement by a French military administration. Thereupon, the French occupied Maraş, Antep and Urfa in southern Anatolia, leaving the inner districts of Greater Syria as areas for the future Iraqi state. According to Eliezer Tauber, it was precisely the Anglo-French agreement that prompted several ex-Ottoman Arab officers, together with certain local tribes of the Jazira area, to revolt against British rule in Iraq and seek Mustafa Kemal's support.⁶³ Meanwhile, Damascus was to remain the headquarters of the rebellious movement that aimed to place Iraq under the political influence of an Arab kingdom.⁶⁴

---

⁶² Erez Manela, *The Wilsonian Moment: Self-Determination and the International Origins of Anticolonial Nationalism* (Oxford: Oxford University Press, 2007).

⁶³ Eliezer Tauber, 'The Struggle for Dayr al-Zur: The Determination of Borders between Syria and Iraq', *International Journal of Middle East Studies*, Vol. 23, No. 3 (1991), pp. 361–85 (here p. 366). For a recent and comprehensive study of the anti-British revolt in the Jazira region, see Rebecca Irvine, 'Anticolonial Resistance in the Post-Ottoman Mashriq: Examining the Iraqi Jazirah' (MA Thesis, Lunds: Lunds University, 2018).

⁶⁴ Diverse Arab nationalist societies such as *Al-Ahd* operated in Syria and Iraq before the Great War. After the armistice, the Iraqi branch of *al-Ahd* that was to play an important role in the anti-British revolt moved to Syria to escape from the British radar. Jafar al Askari (trans. by Mustafa Tariq al Askari), *A Soldier's Story: From Ottoman Rule to Independent Iraq. The Memoirs of Jafar al Askari* (London: Arabian Publishing, 2003). See also Abbas Kadhim, *Reclaiming Iraq: The 1920 Revolution and the Founding of the Modern State* (Austin: University of Texas Press, 2012).

On 15 December 1919, Lieutenant Colonel Şakir Nimet, a former Ottoman officer who was at the head of the national resistance organisation in Aleppo, sent a cable to Mustafa Kemal's headquarters calling for close military cooperation to establish an independent Syrian state (including Syria, Lebanon and Palestine), which would keep some form of ties with the Sultan Caliphate and Anatolia.[65] Mustafa Kemal's response was affirmative. The French withdrawal from Maraş in February 1920 opened the door for further military moves southwards, and thus connected Southern Anatolia to the southwest of Aleppo, where the rebellious movement led by Ibrahim Hananu proved to be particularly active.[66] In return, Ibrahim Hananu and other rebel leaders tapped into moral and material support from Ankara through the intermediary of Polat Bey, a 'Circassian Chief of Turkish *çetes* (bandits)'.[67]

On 24 July 1920, however, the Arab forces lost the battle of Khan Maysalun against the French, thereby bringing an end to the Arab Syrian kingdom proclaimed in Damascus on 8 March of the same year. Although Faysal and some of his supporters were repatriated, and eventually became part of the ruling establishment in Iraq (that is, Nuri al-Said and Jafar al-Askari), the underground cooperation between some Arab guerrilla bands and Mustafa Kemal continued well beyond the end of Faysal's government in the name of Muslim solidarity.[68]

Indeed, in an analogous manner to the exact meaning of the 'national borders' envisioned by the National Pact, the central term *'millî'* (national)

---

[65] Sina Akşin, 'Turkish-Syrian Relations in the Time of Faisal (1918–20)', *The Turkish Yearbook of International Relations*, Vol. 20, No. 1 (1980), pp. 1–17 (here p. 7).

[66] James L. Gelvin, *Divided Loyalties: Nationalism and Mass Politics in Syria at the Close of Empire* (Berkeley, CA: University of California Press, 1998), pp. 133–4; Watenpaugh, Keith David, *Being Modern in the Middle East: Revolution, Nationalism, Colonialism and the Arab Middle Class* (Princeton, NJ: Princeton University Press, 2006), p. 125.

[67] NARA, RG165, box 723, 2044–51. Quoted in Fred H. Lawson, 'The Northern Syrian Revolts of 1919–21 and the Sharifian regime: Congruence or Conflict of Interests and Ideologies?', in Thomas Philipp and Christof Schumann (eds), *From the Syrian Land to the States of Syria and Lebanon* (Beirut: Orient-Institut der DMG Beirut, 2004), pp. 257–74 (here p. 259).

[68] James L. Gelvin, *Divided Loyalties*, p. 85.

used by the resistance movement's propaganda also requires some clarification. While traditional studies of both the Anatolian resistance movement and the popular uprisings in the Arab provinces depict these rebellions as expressions of Turkish and Arab nationalism respectively,[69] another strand of scholarship suggests a different reading of these revolts and their ideological motivations. Erik J. Zürcher, for instance, argues that the terminology employed by the leadership of this movement was eminently religious – that of the 'Ottoman Muslims'.[70] The invocation of Islam and a shared Ottoman past presented not only a system of powerful political and cultural symbols, but also constituted a legitimate discourse that could be readily recognised and understood by all. Thus, in several calls and proclamations, Kemal denounced the enemies as 'crusaders' (*ehl-i salib*), and appealed to religious sentiments:

> Since the beginning of the assaults to which the Caliphate and the Sultanate have been exposed, the Ottoman nationalist forces, having observed with determination the gravity of the situation and being confident about the sentiments and the resistance of the Muslim world against the crusaders, are convinced that they can count on the divine aid and assistance in the struggle they have undertaken.[71]

Oral propaganda was equally important. In that regard, military commanders in eastern Anatolia were instructed to contact tribal chieftains and, more generally, Muslim notables in Iraq, Syria and the Caucasus to ask them for assistance in the name of Ottoman brotherhood and a shared history.[72] To Erik J. Zürcher and other historians, it was only after the Republic of Turkey was proclaimed in 1923 that Mustafa Kemal and his followers came to terms with Ottoman references to impose Turkish nationalism as an

---

[69] Philip S. Khoury, *Syria and the French Mandate: The Politics of Arab Nationalism, 1920–45* (Princeton, NJ: Princeton University Press, 1987), p. 106; Abdul-Karim Rafeq, 'Arabism, Society and Economy in Syria, 1918–20', in Youssef M. Choueiri (ed.), *State and Society in Syria and Lebanon* (New York: St. Martin's Press, 1993), p. 18.

[70] Erik J. Zürcher, 'The Vocabulary of Muslim nationalism', *International Journal of the Sociology of Language*, Vol. 137 (1999), pp. 81–92.

[71] CADN, 36PO/1/201. Proclamation by Mustafa Kemal, 19 March 1920.

[72] Burna Turnaoğlu, *The Formation of Turkish Republicanism*, p. 216.

official ideology.⁷³ Thus, in most cases, ex-Ottoman officers, rural notables, tribal and religious leaders of different ethnic backgrounds were mobilised against the armistice clauses attracted by an explicit religious idiom rather than nationalism, be it Turkish or Arab.⁷⁴

Notwithstanding this, the rebels' motives were extremely mixed, and it is indeed difficult to disentangle the various strands of anti-French, pro-Kemalist and Muslim sentiments as drivers of armed resistance. To Nadine Méouchy, for instance, 'the fundamental motive of *işaba* (small units of rebels) mobilisation was rather to protect a style of life and a set of cultural values, increasingly undermined by rapid economic change and French interference'.⁷⁵ Thus, primordial and local solidarities interacted with a more institutionalised and articulated level – i.e. Islam – helping to guide rebellious activities.

Yet Islam and the Wilsonian principles of self-determination also interplayed with local notions of power – particularly, tribal chiefdoms – and territoriality to bring about a number of statelets or state-like polities in the early 1920s, taking advantage of an absence of effective state control. As in other shatterzones, emerging political leaders in these statelets consisted of individuals and groups with divergent aims and motivations: autonomy from any state authority, inter- and intra-tribal rivalries, the struggle for resources and certain doses of idealism.

In the Syrian Jazira, as Faysal's kingdom collapsed in July 1920, Shaykh Hajim ibn Muhayd of the Fidan Wuld, together with a group of ex-Sharifian officials, proclaimed an independent state – 'Dawlat Hajim' – with Raqqa

---

[73] Erik J. Zürcher, 'The Vocabulary of Muslim nationalism', p. 90. See also Gavin D. Brockett, *How Happy to Call Oneself a Turk: Provincial Newspapers and the Negotiation of a Muslim National Identity* (Austin: University of Texas Press, 2011), pp. 39–40. For Behlül Özkan, however, the shift occurs already by 1921, Behlül Özkan, *From the Abode of Islam to the Turkish Vatan: The Search for a National Homeland in Turkey* (New Haven, Conn: Yale University Press, 2012), pp. 94–5.

[74] James L. Gelvin, *Divided Loyalties*, pp. 133–4; Fred H. Lawson, 'The Northern Syrian Revolts of 1919–21 and the Sharifian regime', pp. 257–74.

[75] Nadine Méouchy, 'Rural Resistance and the Introduction of Modern Forms of Consciousness in the Syrian Countryside, 1918–26', in Thomas Philipp and Christof Schumann (eds), *From the Syrian Land to the States of Syria and Lebanon*, p. 286.

as its capital. Meanwhile, following a rather usual tribal strategy aiming at securing tribe's influence, Hajim's cousin, Mujhim, sided with the French. Thereafter, a coalition of tribal chiefs and representatives of the nationalist *effendiyya* joined their efforts in order to defend their own, sometimes contradictory, interests, while harbouring symbols – Faysal's kingdom flag – and a discourse attuned to nationalism:

> The Arab nation struggled beside the allies during the war, relying on the promises which they had given to the Sharif of Mecca, at the time Sharif Husayn. When the war came to an end the allies divided up the country and occupied it without legal justification. Now they have entered Damascus after a battle with the people and the army. . . We, the assembled representatives of this region, have chosen to proclaim the Amir Hajim bin Muhayd as its head, with the title of leader of the National Movement.[76]

As in other rebel zones, the shaykh and his 'nationalist' entourage maintained secret contact with Mustafa Kemal between 1920 and 1921, as the latter saw Raqqa as a potential strategic location placed at the crossroads between Aleppo to the west and Deir ez-Zor to the east. After securing Kemal's support, Shaykh Hajim attempted to expand his territorial stronghold westwards, where Ibrahim Hananu had succeeded in bringing the French military advance to a standstill. Despite Ankara's promises, the Turkish reinforcements did not arrive in due time, leaving Hajim's fighters at the mercy of heavy French attacks both on the ground and from the air.

Immediately afterwards, Shaykh Hajim negotiated his surrender with the mandatory power under certain conditions – namely, his leadership in a semi-autonomous emirate comprising the districts of Urfa and Raqqa, under French aegis.[77] Following French refusal, he pursued his secret contacts with the Anatolian resistance movement, while his loyal henchmen continued to cause trouble to the French around Raqqa throughout the summer of 1921. Against this backdrop, the French considered that the only way of severing

---

[76] Norman N. Lewis, *Nomads and Settlers in Syria and Jordan, 1800–1980* (Cambridge: Cambridge University Press, 1987), p. 151.
[77] Ibid. pp. 152–3.

Turkish-Arab cooperation, as well as consolidating security on the northern fringes of the Syrian state, was to find a diplomatic deal with the Ankara government. As already mentioned, on 20 October 1921, Paris and Ankara signed an agreement to end hostilities and define the frontier between Turkey and French-mandated Syria; the Jazira south of the Baghdad Railway – from Raqqa to Deir ez-Zor – was to fall within Syria, leaving the district of Urfa in Turkish territory. Without external support, Hajim's statelet eventually collapsed. After moving across the provisional Turkish–Syrian frontier for some months, he returned to the Jazira and accepted an official submission to the French in July 1922, making his cousin the uncontested Shaykh of the Fidan Wuld.

According to Norman N. Lewis, Hajim's trajectory between 1920 and 1921 was not extraordinary. Rather, it tended to conform to a traditional pattern already observed in the Jazira regions as well as in other areas of Arabia:

> [A] shaykh establishes himself as the strongest leader in his own tribal group and then extends his influence over other tribes and over the settled people of his vicinity. He thus becomes head of a chiefdom, that is of a particular geographical area and of its people, over which he exerts a varying blend of rule and influence.[78]

Contrary to Western notions of state territoriality and sovereignty, Bedouin shaykhs did not necessarily seek to exercise a tight control over the territory they claimed. Instead, clannish loyalty enforced through either voluntary alliances or violence was the traditional tool used by paramount tribal leaders to build their legitimate authority.[79] Arguably, Hajim's strategy in the Jazira can also be read through the lenses of an older rivalry between his own tribe and

---

[78] Ibid. p. 148.

[79] From the mid-nineteenth century onwards, some sheep herding tribes established themselves in the Badia (a semi-arid steppe in Central Syria) and paid taxes to the Ottoman state in order to protect their interests. Others, like the Fid'an, saw themselves as free. Those tribes controlling a main military district were granted 'control' of these areas against a payment to the Sultan as well as rights to levy taxes on passing traffic. Dawn Chatty, 'The Bedouin in Contemporary Syria: The Persistence of Tribal Authority and Control', *Middle East Journal*, Vol. 64, No. 1 (2010), pp. 30–31.

a stronger and more extensive chiefdom to the north – that is, the Milli tribal confederation led by Ibrahim Pasha and comprising several Muslim Kurdish clans together with a few Arab and Yazidi tribes.[80]

Ibrahim Pasha had consolidated his position thanks to Milli's raids of other tribes and collecting dues from caravans on the Urfa–Mardin route. Strategically, he established his headquarters at Viranşehir, which lay midway between the two cities. His importance across south-eastern Anatolia was confirmed in 1890 when he was empowered by Sultan Abdülhamid II to form one of the *Hamidiye* regiments, a tribal cavalry militia modelled on the Cossacks to serve the Sultan at need, and was given the rank of Brigadier General and the title of Pasha.[81] For almost two decades, Ibrahim Pasha administered a 'little empire of his own',[82] threatening the influence of other tribal confederations north, south, and eastwards.[83]

During the Young Turk revolution of 1908, at the height of his power,[84] he again sided with the Sultan, and mobilised his militias in support of Abdülhamid II to Aleppo where they waited for instructions from the Sultan before heading to the Hijaz. However, the new power sent troops to stop his advance and after some weeks of chasing him, Ibrahim Pasha eventually succumbed to dysentery on 27 September 1908.[85] From 1912 onwards, Mahmud Beg ibn Ibrahim Pasha took over the confederation while maintaining good relations with the Ottoman state until the British occupation of Cilicia, Syria and Iraq.[86]

---

[80] For an overview of Milli's earlier years, see Stefan Winter, 'Les Kurdes du Nord-Ouest syrien et l'Etat ottoman, 1690–1750', in Mohammad Afifi et al. (eds), *La société rurale à l'époque ottomane* (Cairo: IFAO, 2005), pp. 243–58.

[81] The *Hamidiye* regiments were established with the main task of subduing a perceived Armenian threat in the eastern provinces of the Ottoman Empire. Although the tribal militias failed in suppressing Armenian revolutionaries, their violent activities – i.e., plundering and killings – against both Christian and Muslim settlers left a lasting impact on the region, announcing later events such as the Armenian genocide. See Janet Klein, *The Margins of Empire*.

[82] TNA, FO 424/202. General Report on the Vilayet of Aleppo. Aleppo, 13 May 1901.

[83] Mark Sykes, 'Kurdish Tribes of the Ottoman Empire', *The Journal of the Royal Anthropological Institute of Great Britain and Ireland*, Vol. 38 (1908), pp. 451–86 (here p. 470).

[84] TNA, FO 195/2283. Head to Barclay. Diyarbakır, 4 June 1908.

[85] TNA, FO 195/2284. Heard to Lowther. Diyarbakır, 13 October 1908.

[86] Azad Ahmad Ali, 'Le rôle politique des tribus kurdes Milli et de la famille d'Ibrahim Pacha à l'ouest du Kurdistan et au nord du Bilad al-Cham (1878–1908)', in Jean-Claude David

This was the time when Mahmud Beg was considered one of the serious candidates to lead a Kurdish state under British rule, as per the clauses of the Treaty of Sèvres.[87] Following the withdrawal of the British troops from the Cilicia and Urfa regions, Mahmud Beg sided with the French, hoping to recreate a sort of semi-autonomous chiefdom around Viranşehir. However, after the French defeat in Urfa, Mahmud and his loyal Milli sections settled in Ras al-Ayn, south of the Baghdad Railway. Taking advantage of the Milli's difficulties, Shaykh Hajim's bid for 'Arab nationalism' cannot thus be disentangled from the defence of his own interests and his competition with other tribal confederations such as the Milli. As it turned out, neither of these two shaykhs became the chief of a lasting territorial polity. Yet Mahmud Beg of the Milli and Shaykh Muhjim of the Fidan did secure privileged links with the French authorities throughout the 1920s and 1930s, most notably becoming deputies in the Syrian Parliament.[88]

'Southern Kurdistan'

Further east, another statelet born out of the political fluidity left behind by the armistice was to have more lasting effects – the so-called 'Southern Kurdistan' – a semi-autonomous entity established by the British in November 1918. Although by 1921 the British civil administration promoted Kurdish incorporation into Iraq, the contradictory signals sent by Britain's policy with regard to the fate of the Kurdish districts in Iraq and the activities of Kemalist agents in the Mosul Province created favourable conditions for anti-British uprisings and widespread insecurity along the uncertain frontier that separated Turkey from Iraq until 1926.[89]

and Thierry Boissière (eds) *Alep et ses territoires: Fabrique et politique d'une ville, 1868–2011* (Beirut/Damascus: Ifpo, 2014), pp. 67–79 (here p. 77).

[87] TNA, WO 106/64. Report by Captain C.L. Woolley on his recent mission to Viranşehir from 11–18 May 1918; See also TNA, FO 371/91479/E44/91479/3050. Captain C.L. Woolley, 1919.

[88] Myriam Ababsa al-Husseini, 'Mise en valeur agricole et contrôle politique de la vallée de l'Euphrate (1865–1946): Etude des relations Etat, nomades et citadins dans le caza de Raqqa', *Bulletin d'études orientales*, Vol. 53/54 (2001–2), pp. 459–88 (here p. 477). Stefan Winter, 'The Other Nahdah: The Bedirxan, the Millis and the Tribal Roots of Kurdish Nationalism in Syria', *Oriente Moderno*, Vol. 86, No. 3 (2006), pp. 461–74.

[89] For a comprehensive analysis of border dynamics between Turkey and Iraq, see Jordi Tejel, 'Making Borders from Below: The Emergence of the Turkish-Iraqi Frontier, 1918–25', *Middle Eastern Studies*, Vol. 54, No. 5 (2018), pp. 811–26.

The Mosul Vilayet covered the districts of Mosul, Sulaimaniya and Kirkuk, including a heterogeneous population of Kurds, Arabs, Turkmen, Chaldeans, Assyrians, Jews and Armenians. Yet, the districts of Zakho, Amadiya, Aqra and Rowanduz were essentially inhabited by Kurds and Assyrians. Following the partial British occupation of the Mosul Vilayet, the consolidation of the armistice line between the Ottoman and British forces became an urgent issue. To the dismay of the British, however, the scarcity of British units, combined with the rugged geography of the region, made the military occupation of the entire area difficult. In this context, the British opted for establishing a buffer Kurdish state under a semi-independent ruler.

Therefore, Major Edward W.C. Noel, the Acting Civil Commissioner, appointed Shaykh Mahmud Berzinji (1882–1956), a religious figure with strong tribal connections in Sulaimaniya and its surroundings, Governor or *hukumdar* of 'Southern Kurdistan'; the term defining the area between the Great Zab and the Diyala rivers. For each of these minor sub-divisions, Kurdish officials were assigned to work under the supervision of the British political officers. The remaining districts of the Mosul Vilayet, however, were placed under nominal British control.

In parallel, British colonial goals in Iraq also involved other local communities, particularly the displaced Assyrian populations (i.e. Nestorians) who originally hailed from the Hakkari region. The latter had sought refuge in Iran during the First World War to escape from Ottoman and Kurdish massacres. As the Great War entered its final stage, a group of Assyrians fought back against the Ottomans alongside the British army and local Armenian militia. Following their defeat, these regiments, together with their families, were evacuated under British protection to the Baqubah refugee camp, north of Baghdad.[90]

The British interest in Assyrians as a potential supplementary military force was not halted by the end of the war.[91] Although some Assyrian leaders

---

[90] See Laura Robson, 'Refugee Camps and the Spatialization of Assyrian Nationalism in Iraq', in Sasha R. Goldstein-Sabbah and Heleen L. Murre-van den Berg (eds), *Modernity, Minority, and the Public Sphere: Jews and Christians in the Middle East* (Leiden: Brill, 2016), pp. 237–56.

[91] As Laura Robson argues, British endeavours to recruit Assyrians into the Levies fit into a much longer and broader history of coercing marginal ethno-national groups to serve the colonial state, often under the justification that such groups constituted martial 'races' prone to display their 'natural' capacities. Laura Robson, 'Peripheries of Belonging: Military

asked the British for permission to return to Hakkari, the irresolution of the border dispute as well as pressure from the British convinced most of them to stay in Iraq pending a final territorial settlement. While Assyrian representatives petitioned in Paris and Geneva in favour of an autonomous Assyrian homeland,[92] hundreds of Assyrians were hired as policemen in mobile units to monitor the provisional Turkish–Iraqi border and keep tribal unrest in check.[93]

British policies in the region were far from unchallenged, however. Anti-British propagandists, such as Commander Özdemir Pasha (Ali Shafiq)[94] had a significant success in Rowanduz area. The propaganda around Muslim solidarity was also effective among different local chieftains and notables further south. Specifically, the vali of Van, Qadri Effendi was in contact with the tribal chiefs of the Hamawand, Hawraman, Mariwan and Jaf, as well as the urban notables in Arbil and Kirkuk.[95] According to Rafiq Hilmi, Shaykh Mahmud's secretary in 1919, the latter sealed an agreement with Özdemir, resulting in the expulsion of all British collaborators from Sulaimaniya in the name of the 'Kurdish-Turkish friendship' on the grounds of a shared Muslim bond, association that lasted several years, thereby allowing the Turks to press the British until the resolution of the Mosul Affair.[96]

Recruitment and the Making of a Minority in Wartime Iraq', *First World War Studies*, Vol. 7, No. 1 (2016), p. 27.

[92] TNA, FO/608/274. Memo presented by the Assyrian National Associations of America, 29 March 1919; CADN, Fonds Ankara, 36 PO/1/128. Memo presented by the Assyrian representatives in Paris, 1920.

[93] TNA, FO 371/7780. Sir Percy Cox (Baghdad) to Winston Churchill, Colonial Secretary, 9 December 1921.

[94] Beside propaganda activities, he was also instrumental in organising concentrations of troops in the frontier area, trade embargoes and frontier blockades. For a comprehensive account on Özdemir's role in the area, see Othman Ali, 'The Career of Özdemir', p. 968.

[95] TNA, CO 730/40. Intelligence Report. Secretariat of the High Commissioner for Iraq. Baghdad, 18 September 1924.

[96] Rafiq Hilmi, *Yaddaşt* (London: New Hope, 2007), pp. 163–7. See also TNA, CO 730/40. Intelligence Report. Secretariat of the High Commissioner for Iraq. Baghdad, 1 June 1923; TNA, AIR 23/317. Special Service Officer (Sulaimaniya) to the Administrative Inspector (Kirkuk), 27 February 1925. For a letter exchanged with Ankara asking for money, doctors and ammunition, see BCA.030.18.1.1.15.54.8, 24 August 1925, p. 15.

This Muslim tone was not only present in the documents and letters exchanged with the Turkish agents in the region, but also between local actors. Tribal chiefs such as Mahmud Khan Dizli (Hawraman), for instance, wrote a series of letters to Kurdish leaders intermingling religious and patriotic terms. In one such letter, Mahmud Khan Dizli refers to Shaykh Mahmud as 'Jihad Shaykh Mahmud' who 'for the honour of our religion turned the English out of Sulaimaniya and Halabja and from among the Kurds'.[97] More tellingly, Shaykh Mahmud himself sent a dispatch to the Arab commander of the National Movements in Al Jazira and Iraq in which he justified his actions to 'frustrate the evil intentions of the British against the Islamic world and to upset the effects of their policy which is to sever the people of South Kurdistan (either by threats or persuasion) from the Great Government of Turkey'.[98]

Yet, the discourse around 'Muslim solidarity' was paired with that of the right of the Kurdish people to self-determination. Shaykh Mahmud himself encouraged the spread of Kurdish nationalism in Sulaimaniya,[99] just as Shaykh Hajim ibn Muhayd had done in Raqqa.[100] Indeed, Kurdish nationalism had become a source of Shaykh Mahmud's legitimacy, particularly as he engaged with the British authorities in 1918. He was not alone, though. He surrounded himself with the local intelligentsia, which included civil servants, teachers, journalists and ex-officers of the Ottoman army.[101] Tellingly, the first

---

[97] TNA, CO 730/19. Sir Percy Cox (Baghdad) to Winston Churchill, Colonial Secretary, 20 January 1922.

[98] TNA; FO 371/9005/E6695. Air Ministry to Baghdad. 'Turkish Activities in Kurdistan', 27 June 1923.

[99] In 1925, the Sulaimaniya population was about 10,000 people, of whom 9,000 were Muslim Kurds, 750 Jews and 129 Assyrians. Cecil J. Edmonds, *Kurds, Turks and Arabs* (London: Oxford University Press, 1957), p. 80.

[100] In local historiography, both leaders are depicted as purely nationalists (Kurdish and Arab, respectively). On Shaykh Mahmud's nationalist credentials, see Ahmed Khawaja, *Çim Dît: Şoreşakanî Sheikh Mahmud-i Mezin* (Arbil: Dar Aras, 2013); Kamal Nuri, Maruf, *Yaddaştakanî Sheikh Latif-i Hafid Lasar Şoreşakanî Sheikh Mahmud-i Hafid* (Pirmam: Cultural Centre of Kurdistan Democratic Party, 1995). On Shaykh Hajim ibn Muhayd, see 'Abd es-Salam al-'Ujaily', *Sawt al-Rafiqa*, No. 15 and 16, October-November 1998. Quoted in Ababsa, Myriam, 'Mise en valeur agricole et contrôle politique de la vallée de l'Euphrate (1865–1946)', p. 467.

[101] TNA; AIR 23/324. Special Service Office (Sulaimaniya) to Air Staff Intelligence (Baghdad), 30 June 1927.

government of Shaykh Mahmud created a Kurdish 'national' flag[102] and the urban intelligentsia of Sulaimaniya helped to forge the first experience of the autonomous Kurdish administration.

By early 1919, Shaykh Mahmud attempted to expand his political as well as economic influence – that is, levying taxes – beyond Southern Kurdistan's administrative boundaries by exploiting his religious and tribal networks, including his cross-border Persian connections. Notwithstanding this, Shaykh Mahmud's conception of power and influence were not primarily embedded within modern notions of state sovereignty and tight control over 'Southern Kurdistan' territory. Much like Shaykh Hajim ibn Muhayd, Shaykh Mahmud counted on both traditional loyalties and new alliances established with tribal and religious leaders to exert authority across 'his' chiefdom. Such manoeuvres, however, threatened British policies in the entire Vilayet, thus prompting a quick response; Political Officer E. B. Soane replaced Major Edward W. C. Noel, deemed too 'pro-Kurdish'.[103] Relations between the two men grew difficult and in May 1919 Shaykh Mahmud imprisoned all British soldiers in office at Sulaimaniya, and proclaimed the independence of Kurdistan. However, without any significant assistance from his 'allies', the British captured Shaykh Mahmud by June 1919. In Baghdad, the latter was sentenced to death by a military court, but his sentence was commuted to exile in India.[104]

Sulaimaniya did not, however, experience a long period of stability. Threatened by the advance of rebellious Kurdish tribes and Turkish *çetes*, the British evacuated the town on 1 September 1922. The High Commissioner in Baghdad suddenly decided to re-instate Shaykh Mahmud as Governor of Kurdistan. In December 1922, Shaykh Mahmud proclaimed himself the 'King of Kurdistan' and again encouraged the diffusion of nationalism among urban and tribal elements through the restoration of the Kurdish flag, the publication of Kurdish newspapers, the printing of Kurdish postal stamps and the organisation of military parades – with the collaboration of Sulaimaniya's leading intellectuals and poets. In one of the celebratory

---

[102] The flag designed in 1919 was green with a red circle and a white crescent inside the circle.
[103] Stephen H. Longrigg, *Iraq, 1900 to 1950. A Political, Social and Economic History* (Oxford: Oxford University Press, 1953), p. 104.
[104] Political Officer in Baghdad to Secretary of State for India, 23 August 1919, TNA, FO/248/1248; Political Officer in Baghdad to FO, 23 August 1919, TNA, FO/371/4192.

articles published right after the reinstatement of Shaykh Mahmud, one could read:

> No one in this country or among the Kurds desires to be under foreign rule, no one has any desire other than to live as a free and independent nation. This is the era of nationalism and every people is looking for its independence and liberty.[105]

Interactions Between Borderlanders and States' Discourses and Strategies

Borderlanders' discourses in Mosul Province, however, did not merely play into Turkish and British strategies. As local actors became increasingly involved in the Mosul dispute, it appeared that Turkish and British discourses were neither completely independent from each other's (enemies and borderlanders) classification and strategies, nor unchangeable. On the one hand, Kurdish tribal chieftains asked the Kemalist resistance for a decree issued by the Caliph himself in order to join the rebel forces.[106] In other words, the spread of pro-Turkish Muslim rhetoric among tribal areas was not simply a top-down strategy. It was also the result of local constraints and demands in order to join the anti-British movement in northern Iraq. On the other hand, while the 'defence of Islam' became the main expression of resistance against the foreign occupiers from 1919 to 1921, this language shifted to that of nationalism and minority rights, in particular, during the Lausanne Peace Conference.

Accordingly, Britain and Turkey were obliged to readjust their claims over Mosul by taking into account this new reality. In Ankara, Turkish officials both at the Grand National Assembly and in Lausanne emphasised the idea of Turkish–Kurdish unity. In the border area, Özdemir Pasha acknowledged Shaykh Mahmud's position as the President of the Committee of Representatives of Kurdistan, and by 1922 Turkish propaganda conveyed the idea that the Turks, unlike the British, were ready to give full autonomy to the Kurds under the protection of a 'Muslim Government'.[107] In turn, Britain issued a joint Anglo-Iraqi statement of intent recognising the right of the Kurds

---

[105] *Roji Kurdistan*, 'A Claim for Our Just Rights', No. 8, 10 January 1923.
[106] CADN, 36 PO/1/202. Telegram sent by Colonel Rafet, 15 February 1921.
[107] TNA, CO 730/19. Intelligence Report. Secretariat of the High Commissioner for Iraq. Baghdad, 15 January 1922.

in Iraq to set up a Kurdish government.[108] In spite of such half-promises, a feeling of distrust seemed to prevail between all the players concerned. To the British, Shaykh Mahmud was not trustworthy because of his 'treachery'. Likewise, Özdemir Pasha suspected Shaykh Mahmud of being a tool of the British and depicted him as a 'cunning man'.[109]

Adaptations of official discourses did not stop after the Lausanne Conference. The repression of 1925 Kurdish rebellion led by Shaykh Said[110] in Turkey – notably involving the execution of a number of Kurdish personalities and the forced displacement of thousands of Kurds[111] – seemed to cast doubt upon 'Kurdish-Turkish brotherhood' in the eyes of the Commission. Thereafter, the Turkish government emphasised the predominantly Sunni character of the Mosul population, which better linked the latter to Turkey. In addition, the significant Shia constituency in southern Iraq made the attachment of Mosul Vilayet to Turkey all the more urgent.[112]

Crucially, the internationalisation of the 'Mosul affair' provided borderlanders with a new opportunity to voice their concerns. Although their views were not explicitly included in the final decision taken by the League in December 1925, their actions and statements had an indirect effect on the definitive resolution of the dispute. The Council of the League of Nations discussed the matter on 30 August 1924. Contrary to British expectations, however, it decided to send a commission made up of three delegates to the Mosul Vilayet to determine whether the locals wanted to be part of the new Republic of Turkey or preferred British mandatory Iraq. At a meeting in Brussels, the Swedish prime minister and rapporteur of the commission, Hjalmar Branting, suggested that a temporary demarcation line be drawn

---

[108] TNA, FO 371/9004/E1019. J.E. Shuckburgh to Mr Osborne. 'Kurdish situation', 25 January 1923.

[109] TNA, FO 371/9004/E3620. Colonial Office to Foreign Office, 9 April 1923.

[110] For a comprehensive study of this revolt, see Robert Olson, *The Emergence of Kurdish Nationalism and the Sheikh Said Rebellion, 1880–1925* (Austin: University of Texas Press, 1989). For a detailed account on the evolution of this revolt drawing from Turkish records, see *Genelkurmay belgelerinde Kürt Isyanları, Cilt 1* (Ankara: Kaynak Yayınları, 1992).

[111] See Uğur Ü. Üngör, *The Making of Modern Turkey: Nation and State in Eastern Anatolia, 1913–50* (Oxford: Oxford University Press, 2011), pp. 55–170.

[112] Fuat Dündar, 'Statisquo', p. 23.

somewhere between the British and Turkish lines, taking into consideration natural formations, such as mountain crests and rivers.[113]

From the start, Britain perceived the presence of the commission as a potential threat to their continuing authority over Mosul. In that sense, British 'support' for the League project was not a proof of self-confidence, but a strategy to 'minimise the possible threats to its own rule'.[114] The mandate authorities even went so far as to try to restrict the movement of the representatives assigned by Ankara to accompany the commission.[115] As a result, the commissioners refused to begin their work until the British and Iraqi authorities allowed all representatives, including the Turkish delegation, to accomplish their mission. The autonomy of the commission from British interests became even more explicit as the Swedish delegate carried out an active foreign policy based on solidarity with and support from the League of Nations, thereby creating additional worries amongst the mandate's officials.[116]

The League's initiative and its potential destabilising effect on the northern districts of Iraq had an immediate impact on the mandatory power. Thus, before the arrival of the commission in February 1925, 'the Iraqi Minister of Interior Affairs toured Mosul Vilayet and promised that the Kurds' national rights would be respected if they decided to stay within Iraq'.[117] A meeting in Arbil along the same lines followed suit, while pro-Iraqi agents were sent into Turkey to fuel unrest.[118] In turn, pro-Turkey secret societies in the cities of Arbil and Kirkuk proved to also be especially active.[119]

Critically, borderlanders' agency unleashed a violent state reaction on both sides of the provisional frontier. On the one hand, Iraqi border leaders

---

[113] John Rogers, 'The Foreign Policy of Small States: Sweden and the Mosul Crisis, 1924–5', *Contemporary European History*, Vol. 16, No. 3 (2007), pp. 349–69.

[114] Sarah D. Shields, 'Mosul, the Ottoman Legacy and the League of Nations', *International Journal of Contemporary Iraqi Studies*, Vol. 3, No. 2 (2009), pp. 217–30 (here p. 221).

[115] BCA.030.10.7.40.33, 26 January 1925, p. 2.

[116] John Rogers, 'The Foreign Policy of Small States', pp. 349–69.

[117] Othman Ali, 'The Kurdish Factor in the Struggle for Vilayet Mosul, 1921–5', *Journal of Kurdish Studies*, Vol. 4 (2001–2), pp. 31–48 (here p. 41).

[118] BCA.030.10.112.756.20, 9 May 1925.

[119] See Güldem B. Büyüksaraç, 'Trans-border Minority Activism and Kin-state Politics: The Case of Iraqi Turkmen and Turkish Interventionism', *Anthropological Quarterly*, Vol. 90, No. 1 (2017), pp. 17–54.

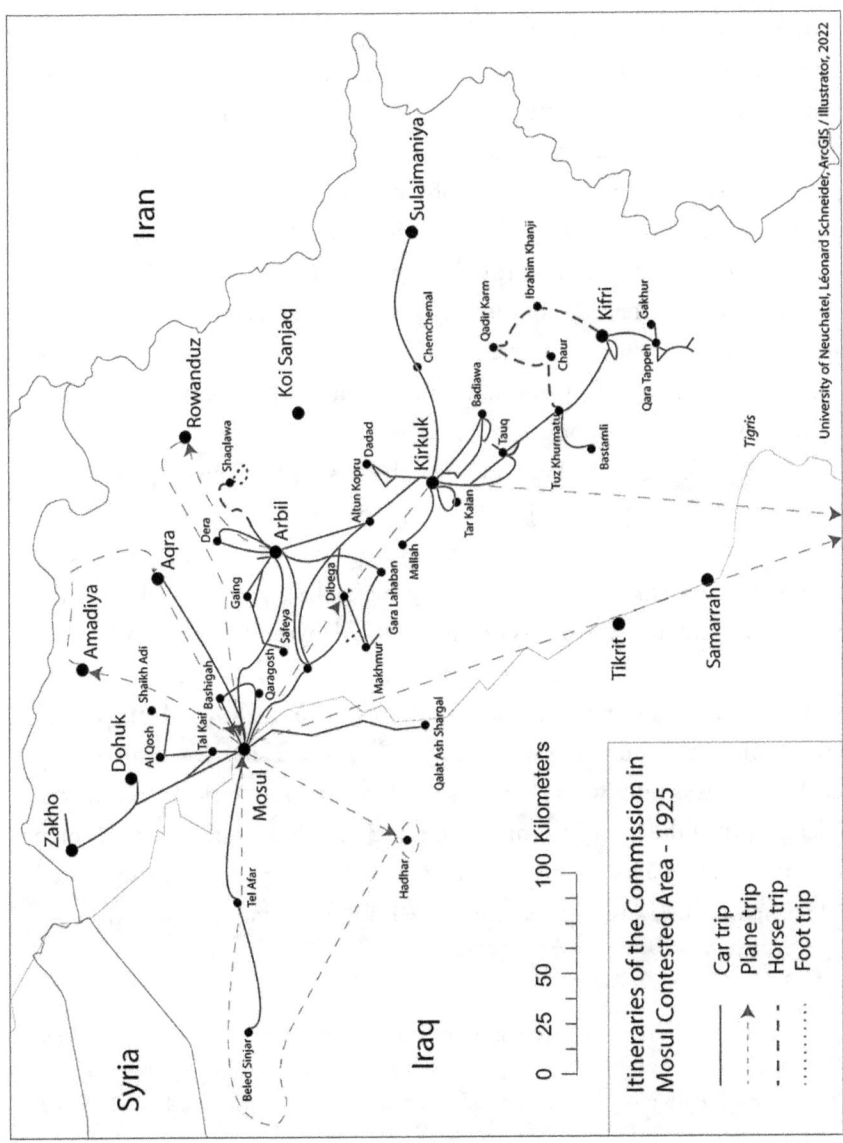

Figure 1.1 Itineraries of the Commission in Mosul Contested Area, 1925.

Source: TNA, AIR 5/611.

who had manifested their loyalty to Turkey were either killed, imprisoned or banished, while some villages located in the border area were bombarded from the air or burned down by the Assyrian Levies.[120] Significantly, the coercive campaign reached such intense levels that some border tribes situated on the Iraqi side threatened to migrate to Turkey if the reprisal campaign did not stop immediately.[121] On the other hand, the Turkish authorities similarly threatened Kurdish chieftains whose lands were in the border region: 'If you support the Iraqi government, you will become an ally with the Arabs and the unbelievers. Regret will be no use.'[122] Further, a regiment of Turkish soldiers attacked some Assyrian and Kurdish villages in the Goyan district because their leaders had expressed their desire to be included in Iraq to the Frontier Commission. According to different accounts over 2,000 Assyrian refugees fled to Zakho and Mosul, while all their flocks and stocks of grain were confiscated by the Turkish troops.[123]

The massacres against Assyrians nevertheless had certain repercussions for Western public opinion and the secretariat of the League of Nations, as the events were revealed to the press by an American journalist working for the *Chicago Tribune*, who happened to be in the region reporting on the works of the League's Commission in Mosul Vilayet.[124] Additionally, local actors such as Mgr. Thimothee Magdaci, the Bishop of Zakho and Dohuk, also played a role in drawing the attention of the League towards the fate of this community. Although news of the massacres was already circulating by June 1925, it was only when the League's Commission decided to tour the border areas that the Iraqi government and the Mandate authorities gave some resonance to Magdaci's claims. Crucially, the British government requested the Council of the League of Nations to send representatives to the frontier.

---

[120] According to Turkish reports, Sefer Agha, chief of the Doski, and his son were assassinated in May 1925. After their killing, the police authorities in Zakho informed the population that all pro-Turkish proxy elements would follow the same fate. BCA.030.10.258.737.10, 30 May 1925.

[121] TNA, FO 371/10837. Telegram No. 305, Lindsay to Chamberlain, 15 April 1925.

[122] TNA, AIR 23/308. Translated leaflet, undated.

[123] Ibid.

[124] Ibid.

The Commission arrived in Mosul on 30 October 1925, and drafted a final report in which the British charges were found to be substantiated. In addition, the text confirmed that Turkish soldiers had occupied all the villages and had deported Assyrians en masse, some of whom fell ill and were abandoned, while others died of starvation and cold.[125]

Finally, local tribes also tried to voice their uneasy position when asked about their 'national' preference. Confidential British reports reveal that borderlanders pledged before the Commission for an 'open border solution' which would guarantee them free mobility across the Turkish–Iraqi frontier in order to access their summer grazing lands situated in Turkish territory.[126] Borderlanders' claims, in fact, also echoed the views expressed in Geneva. In 1924, for instance, the League had already acknowledged that:

> If the disputed territory is assigned to Iraq, its inhabitants should be given full freedom of trade with Turkey and Syria, and moreover, facilities should be afforded to the Turkish frontier towns to use the Mosul route for exporting their produce and importing manufactured articles.[127]

Alarmed by these reports, British authorities encouraged Kurdish notables to write petitions in support of British claims, whereby they argued that Mosul Vilayet was economically connected to Baghdad rather than to Anatolia, and that only a 'natural' boundary delimited by the mountainous region running from Zakho to Rowanduz would secure Iraqi safety and progress.[128] The impact of borderlanders' views on the border regime as envisioned by the Frontier Commission and the League of Nations cannot be overstated. Yet, it is interesting to highlight that while Turkey and Britain stated that Mosul

---

[125] LON, C.783.1925.VII. 'Question de la frontière entre la Turquie et l'Irak'. Report prepared by General J. Laidoner. Geneva, 9 December 1925.

[126] MEC, Edmonds Collection, GB165–0095/1/2B. Administrative Inspector Mosul to Baghdad. Mosul, 4 February 1925.

[127] LON, C.400.M.147.1925.VII. 'Question of the Frontier between Turkey and Iraq: Report Submitted to the Council by the Commission Instituted by the Council Resolution of September 30th, 1924'.

[128] MEC, Edmonds Collection, GB165–0095/1/2B. Special Service Officer. Sulaimaniya, 28 February 1925.

Vilayet was economically oriented to Anatolia and Baghdad, respectively, borderlanders' practices and views fitted better with the liberal approach the League was eager to develop in the interwar period.[129]

Despite the de facto recognition of the Ankara government by the French in 1921 and the delimitation of a provisional frontier between Turkey and French Syria, the ideas of self-determination and territorial sovereignty continued to nourish previous tensions, while providing borderlanders with a new range of discourses and opportunities. Thus, throughout the frontier disputes between Turkey and French Syria, on the one hand, and between Turkey and Britain, on the other, borderland representatives advanced different claims and aspirations depending on the context and the targeted audience, thereby allowing them to play off Turkish, French and British agents against each other and, by doing so, gain brokerage.

Admittedly, borderlanders did not constitute a homogenous group, but were rather an assemblage of networks and individuals with different and sometimes conflicting personalities, interests and ambitions. Yet, whether they were opportunistic or full-hearted anti-imperialists or both, local actors, through their shifting alliances, pushed British, French and Turkish authorities to the conclusion that separate permanent agreements on their respective common borders were the best solution for all parties. Neither the Turks nor the mandatory powers in Syria and Iraq were capable of coping with local revolts and changing strategies along a restless, moving frontier.

Borderlanders' contradictory strategies and attitudes need to be interpreted in two complementary ways. First, like other post-Ottoman communities, frontier dwellers simultaneously had multiple group identities, and could be classified according to location, faith, clan or occupation. Yet, because of the League of Nations' endeavours to determine borderlanders' 'national' identity, as well as which state could claim sovereignty over Mosul Province, the liminal character of borderlanders became even more noticeable. As the League of Nations delegates arrived in the province of Mosul

---

[129] See also Nicholas Danforth, 'Nomads, No Problem: Rethinking Border Regimes in the Post-Ottoman Middle East', http://www.midafternoonmap.com/2017/01/the-myth-of-myth-of-borders.html, accessed 3 October 2022.

in 1925, local populations provided a complex and nuanced response to the commission's survey. Arguably, the political preference of the people of Mosul could only be conditional upon a variety of criteria, such as the identity of the ruler, the potential economic impact, or the survival of previous social networks.[130]

Second, far from being a signal of their incapacity to adapt to the new world order, historians should analyse such attitudes and opinions as a striking example of the capacity for local agency; that is, the capacity of individuals and groups to develop strategies to pursue or safeguard their own interests. Obviously, agency does not avert unforeseen consequences.[131] Thus, while local revolts, transborder mobility and shifting alliances with Turkish, French and British representatives had allowed local players to gain autonomy from all state actors and extend their spheres of influence, it was at least partly borderlanders' agency that led central governments to search for a permanent solution based on the principle of territorial sovereignty within a modern international system of nation states. In so doing, local actors inadvertently contributed to the emergence of new national boundaries embedded within new power relations, while transforming older ones. In that regard, refugees and forced displacement were both the result of the violence unleashed in the border zones and a powerful driver of state and identity formation, as we shall see in the next chapter.

---

[130] Sarah D. Shields, 'Mosul, the Ottoman Legacy and the League of Nations', pp. 217–30.
[131] On this idea, see also Pekka Hämäläinen, *The Comanche Empire* (New Haven and London: Yale University Press, 2011), p. 14.

2

REFUGEES, BORDERS AND IDENTITY BOUNDARIES

On 27 March 1934, Mr Silver, head of the Alliance Israélite School in Damascus, travelled to Qamishli, a border town established by the French in the Syrian Jazira in 1926 as a military post just next to the Turkish city of Nusaybin. By 1927, however, this frontier post had become home to hundreds of Christian refugees – Armenians and Syriacs – and to the almost entire Jewish community from Nusaybin, which was either escaping from forced conscription or was motivated by the pervasive rumours about Ankara's plans to expel all non-Muslim groups from Turkey's borderlands.[1] Subsequently, Muslim Kurds also settled in Qamishli, thereby reinforcing its singularity; an ex-nihilo border town emerged, numbering as many as 15,000 inhabitants by 1934, constituted by a majority of Christian, Jewish and Kurdish refugees and migrants originating mainly from Turkey.

The official purpose of this visit was to inquire about the willingness of Jews in Qamishli – an 'unknown' community of 2,000 souls – to attend a school of the Alliance wherein they would 'learn the language of their benefactors – the

---

[1] See Ahmet Kütük, 'Tairihi Süreç İçerisinde Nusaybin Yahudiler', *Islâmî Ilimler Dergisi*, Vol. 10, No. 2 (2015), pp. 93–115; Michael Menachem Laskier, 'Syria and Lebanon', in Reeva Spector Simon, Michale Menachem Laskier and Sara Reguer (eds), *The Jews of the Middle East and North Africa in Modern Times* (New York: Columbia University Press, 2002), pp. 316–34 (here p. 323).

French'.[2] Upon his return to Damascus, the head of the Alliance school also reported his views about Qamishli and its dwellers. Like many other urban Western-educated visitors, Mr Silver highlighted the most exotic characteristics of the Upper Jazira – a peripheral rural region idly connected to the Syrian capital and apparently alien to modernity. Culturally and socially, Qamishli's Jews – called 'Ibri' by their Muslim and Christian neighbours – embodied an image contrary to what the Alliance hoped for: illiteracy within the community was widespread, the 'Ibri' lived in houses made of mud and straw and wore oriental clothes, just like the local Bedouins. Likewise, more than a decade after the Syrian Mandate, the Jews and the borderlanders trading at Qamishli's bazars continued to use the Ottoman currency – a silver coin called 'Mecid', after the Sultan Abdul Mecid (1823–61) – instead of the Syrian lira. Equally surprising for the visitor was the fact that most Jews in Qamishli didn't speak Hebrew at all, but a combination of Arabic, Kurdish and Turkish.

Notwithstanding this, Mr Silver noted that the Jews from Qamishli were not entirely isolated from the other Jewish populations. On the one hand, the annual pilgrimage to Rabbi Judah ben Bathyra's tomb located on the nearby hills allowed local Jews to meet the remainder of the Jewish communities from Eastern Anatolia[3] – mainly in neighbouring Nusaybin and Diyarbakır up north – and in the Iraqi towns of Aqra and Amadiya, thereby keeping their religious networks alive in spite of the newly-established international borders.[4] On the other hand, once a year, a few Jewish merchants from this border town travelled to British Palestine to purchase some products that were rare in the Syrian Jazira. This annual trip was also a first-hand opportunity to gather relevant information about the current developments in the mandatory territory and thus better evaluate the advantages and disadvantages of staying

---

[2] 'Les Juifs de Kamechlié', *Paix et Droit*, Vol. 14, No. 4 (1934), p. 10.

[3] Rabbi Judah ben Bathyra, who lived in today's Nusaybin before the destruction of the Second Temple of Jerusalem, that is, before 70 BCE, is considered one of the prominent authors of the Mishna – a written collection of Jewish oral traditions. The pilgrimage to Bathyra's tomb took place every year, four days before Shavuot.

[4] By 1934, the Jewish community in these two towns numbered 150 and 300, respectively. 'Neighbours fail to assimilate Diarbekir Jews', *Jewish Daily Bulletin*, Vol. XL, No. 2913 (1934), p. 5.

in Syria, rather than moving into the Yishuv, the Jewish 'national home', which was still in the making.[5]

Alliance Israélite representative's visit to Qamishli in 1934 was not entirely coincidental, though. Between 1930 and 1934, a series of developments had turned the north-eastern fringes of the Syrian territory into the focus of national, regional and global attention. Firstly, growing French interventionism in Jabal Sinjar, a mountainous area traversed by the provisional frontier between Syria and Iraq, raised British concerns about either the potential immigration of 'their' Yazidi tribes to the Upper Jazira, or the Sinjari leaders' request to the League of Nations to have Syria administer the Jabal. Both options were being openly encouraged by the French in 1931 given the frontier dispute between French Syria and British Iraq while the tensions between certain Yazidi leaders and the Iraqi government were on the rise.[6] Prompted by these fears, and pressed by the upcoming expiration of the Mandate over Iraq in 1932, the British increased their political contacts with the Sinjari leaders to secure their loyalty to the Iraqi state and sever any ties between them and the Syrian Jazira. Although few Yazidis did eventually move to Syria, this border dispute greatly affected Yazidi tribal affairs throughout the 1930s.[7]

Secondly, the French's veiled propaganda about France's protection of 'minorities' and the economic prospects which the Upper Jazira offered to 'hard-working' settlers also attracted Iraqi Assyrians' interest. After supporting the British army in the north-western Persian front against the Ottoman army, most of the Assyrian evacuees followed the British forces and settled in the Baqubah refugee camp, north of Baghdad. Following the closure of the camp in 1921, however, hundreds of Assyrians were recruited into the

---

[5] As a result of the 1929 Great Depression and its ensuing impact on the Syrian economy, some Jewish families hailing from Qamishli migrated to Palestine, where the economic prospects looked more promising.

[6] By the time of this report, Yazidis were concentrated mainly in the Balad Sinjar and Shaykh Adi districts in northern Iraq. Outside Iraq, Yazidis were also present in Syria (north of Aleppo and Jazira), Turkey (Mardin province) and the Caucasus (Georgia and Armenia). Yazidis are mostly Kurdish speakers, but their religion is considered a mélange of pre-Muslim paganism, Islam and Christian influences. See Birgül Açıkyıldız, *The Yezidis: The History of a Community, Culture and Religion* (London: I. B. Tauris, 2014); Sebastian Maisel, *Yezidis in Syria: Identity Building among a Double Minority* (Lanham: Lexington Books, 2016).

[7] Nelida Fuccaro, *The Other Kurds: Yazidis in Colonial Iraq* (London: I. B. Tauris, 1998), p. 113.

Levies – a police force under British guidance – to secure peace and stability along the northern borders against both foreign and domestic threats, namely, Turkish penetration beyond the armistice line, as well as anti-British uprisings among local Arab and Kurdish populations. Yet, after more than a decade of unabated cooperation with the British, and only a year after the official independence of the Iraqi state, some dozens of armed Assyrians crossed over to the Syrian Jazira in August 1933.

The ex-Assyrian Levies hoped that the French would grant them lands and protection, just as they had done earlier with the refugees originating from Turkey. Indeed, between 1930 and 1933, the Assyrian tribal and religious leaders voiced their disappointment as the British authorities, the League of Nations and the Baghdad government had dismissed all their demands for either local autonomy in Iraq or repatriation toward Turkey. Thus, even though the British had contributed to fostering Assyrian ethnic separateness in the early 1920s, now the former invited the latter to fully integrate into the unitary Iraqi nation-state. Against all expectations, the French authorities rejected their request and deported the Assyrian contingent back to Iraq. Upon their return, skirmishes occurred between the Assyrian trespassers and the Iraqi army, resulting in some casualties. Subsequently, Iraqi army units together with Arab and Kurdish armed bands attacked several Assyrian villages, killing hundreds of their unarmed inhabitants. Although the massacres came to a halt, the fate of the Assyrian community in Iraq seemed henceforth jeopardised.

Finally, the Syrian Jazira became a focus of attention for the Zionist movement in the face of the dramatic events unfolding in Germany in early 1933. Indeed, the Zionist movement envisaged alternative venues for the transfer of Europe's Jewish communities to the Middle East, as it considered that British Palestine could not accommodate all the Jews who were striving to settle there. One of the potential sites for the establishment of a 'Jewish colony' was precisely the Syrian Jazira.[8] Thus, in December 1933, Nassim Tajer, son of the former Rabin of Damascus, travelled to this region along with Leo

---

[8] This project was not entirely new. In 1926, the Zionist movement and the French High Commissioner Henri de Jouvenel negotiated the establishment of a Jewish colony in Syria. While the former preferred southern Syria as a location for the settlement of European Jews, the latter offered the Jazira instead. Yitzhak Gil-Har, 'French policy in Syria and Zionism: Proposal for a Zionist Settlement', *Middle Eastern Studies*, Vol. 30, No. 1 (1994), pp. 155–65.

Winz – journalist and member of the Zionist movement in Tel Aviv – and a German 'capitalist' who was considering financing the creation of Jewish agricultural settlements across the Khabur Basin. In Damascus, the three men informed the Zionist representatives about the prospects of such project, as well as of the existence of a Jewish community in Qamishli.[9]

Crucially, the context surrounding the 'discovery' of the 'unknown' Jewish community of Qamishli by the Alliance Israélite and the Zionist movement, highlights a series of related topics that this chapter seeks to explore – the intertwined relationship between modern notions of territorial sovereignty, the consolidation of ethno-religious boundaries and refugeedom. As we have seen in the previous chapter, the low-intensity war along the borderlands between the newly-established states of Turkey, Syria and Iraq aimed at obtaining substantial territorial gains that could secure an advantageous position to the three parties at the different negotiating tables where the delineation of the future international boundaries was to be discussed. The perspective from the borderlands, however, reveals that warfare, massacres and subsequent frontier disputes overlapped with the emergence of another urgent and related international problem: the flood of refugees that originated from the sites of collapsing empires and emerging nation states.

Although the frontier disputes in the contiguous border zones of Turkey, Syria and Iraq did not provoke population movements comparable to those of the late Ottoman period, the formative years of these states led thousands of Jews, Christians of different denominations, Muslim and Yazidi Kurds to seek refuge in the northern edges of Syria and Iraq, paralleling the dynamics unfolding in the Balkans and Eastern Europe in the same years.[10] In addition, the final destination for the survivors of the Armenian genocide of 1915–16 was not set yet. Against this backdrop, the League of Nations responded by establishing a refugee regime with standardised paperwork and procedures, completed with a range of relief programmes designed to

---

[9] CADN, 1SL/1/V/616. 'Projet d'installation de Juifs allemands en Syrie'. Beirut, 23 December 1933.
[10] Claudena Skran, *Refugees in Interwar Europe: The Emergence of a Regime* (Oxford: Clarendon Press, 1995).

accommodate the displaced. Certainly, this was not a first in the Middle Eastern region.[11]

By the late 1850s, the Ottoman Empire was flooded with the influx of Muslim refugees running away from violence and warfare that spread along the Ottoman–Russian frontier. Thereafter, each successive cycle of warfare only repeated this pattern of displacement, as the Ottoman Empire not only continued to welcome, but also began to generate refugees of its own. Within this context, the *Muhacirin Komisyonu* (Migrants Commission) – an Ottoman institution created in 1860 – undertook a series of new policies with an emphasis on the practices of refugee aid, programmes of resettlement,[12] and corresponding transformation of legal categories.[13] These institutional endeavours formed an evolving bureaucratic script of Ottoman governance that eventually informed the imperial practices of demographic engineering as well as the processes of internal colonisation across the empire.[14]

In the aftermath of the First World War, however, new nation states and international bodies, such as the League of Nations, readjusted Ottoman as well as European imperial practices to the demands of the interwar context. Among these practices, one can mention the settlement of refugees and migrants in new agricultural colonies in the border zones, the creation of border towns populated by refugee populations, the recruitment of refugees in separate police forces to protect the border, and the use of displaced populations to alter the ethno-religious demographic balance in the borderlands.[15]

---

[11] On the origins of modern humanitarianism in the Middle East, see Keith D. Watenpaugh, *Bread from Stones: The Middle East and the Making of Modern Humanitarianism* (Oakland, CA: University of California Press, 2015).

[12] Vladimir Hamed-Troyansky, 'Circassian Refugees and the Making of Amman, 1878–1914', *International Journal of Middle East Studies*, Vol. 49, No. 4 (2017), pp. 605–23.

[13] David Cuthell, 'The Muhacirin Komisyonu: An Agent in the Transformation of Ottoman Anatolia, 1860–6' (PhD dissertation, New York: Columbia University, 2005); Başak Kale, 'Transforming an Empire: The Ottoman Empire's Immigration and Settlement Policies in the Nineteenth and Early Twentieth Centuries', *Middle Eastern Studies*, Vol. 50, No. 2 (2014), pp. 252–71.

[14] Ella Fratantuono, 'Producing Ottomans: Internal Colonization and Social Engineering in Ottoman Immigrant Settlement', *Journal of Genocide Research*, Vol. 21, No. 1 (2019), pp. 1–24.

[15] See Dawn Chatty, 'Refugees, Exiles, and other Forced Migrants in the Late Ottoman Empire', *Refugee Survey Quarterly*, Vol. 32, No. 2 (2013), pp. 35–52.

In other words, refugees' presence in the borderlands helped the states exercise their power over the margins of their national territories, while transforming border zones into a safe haven wherein the former could find protection and new opportunities. In return, states expected these refugee communities be loyal to their 'benefactors', in Alliance Israélite representative's terms.

Yet, refugees' close relationship with the British and the French mandatory powers, together with their disproportionate presence in the border zones, also involved some risks. For one thing, the process of border-making in these borderlands went hand in hand with that of 'ordering' – land and people – and 'othering' – that is, rejecting and erecting otherness.[16] Refugees and 'unwanted' populations were thus the 'natural' outcome of a non-written consensus between mandatory powers, nationalist ruling elites and the League of Nations. Although the minorities treaties and the international refugee regime designed by the League of Nations attempted to provide minority groups and refugees with special protections, population transfer and the generation of refugees were also seen not only as an opportunity to minimise the prospects of future ethno-religious conflicts, but also as a means for consolidating the nation state in the region. In sum, 'creating refugees and welcoming them was a mutually constitutive process that reproduced discourses of governmentality and justified modern territorial state' in the era of new internationalism, 'while redefining the limits of belonging'.[17]

Bordering the Middle East

By the early 1920s, the post-war settlement had introduced a precise territorial order to the region with a new set of international boundaries. After a decade of bilateral negotiations and the establishment of the respective frontier commissions, all shared borders between Turkey, Syria and Iraq were drawn on maps,

[16] Henk Van Houtum and Ton Van Naerssen, 'Bordering, Ordering and Othering', *Tijdschrift voor Economische en Sociale Geografie*, Vol. 93, No. 2 (2002), pp. 125–36.

[17] Mark Mazower, *No Enchanted Palace: The End of Empire and the Ideological Origins of the United Nations* (Princeton, NJ: Princeton University Press, 2009), pp. 104–48; Glenda Sluga, *Internationalism in the Age of Nationalism* (Philadelphia: University of Pennsylvania Press, 2013). See also Jordi Tejel and Ramazan Hakkı Öztan, 'Towards Connected Histories of Refugeedom in the Middle East', *Journal of Migration History*, Vol. 6, No. 1 (2020), pp. 1–15 (here p. 2).

boundary markers were laid down on the ground, and the three states agreed to introduce procedures to solve common border issues such as cross-border mobility, the exchange of criminals or fighting against human and animal diseases through a series of bilateral accords.

Nevertheless, this perceptible diplomatic rapprochement did not wipe out imperial Franco-British rivalries nor mutual distrust between independent Turkey and its southern neighbours – French Syria and British Iraq. By 1928, for instance, the French Intelligence Services still reported about sustained links between Ankara and diverse Syrian tribes in order to weaken French military presence in northern Syria. The same year, the British acknowledged Turkish manoeuvres to mobilise Iraqi tribes against the mandatory power to 'regain' the Mosul Province.[18] In turn, Turkish informants cabled numerous reports to Ankara, stressing French and British support to Turkey's enemies – that is, ex-Ottoman Armenians, Kurdish nationalists and Assyrians settled along Turkey's southern borders.[19]

This tension was especially perceptible where territorial uncertainties remained: notably, the eastern edges of the Turkish–Syrian–Iraqi tri-border area, also known as 'Bec de Canard' (or 'Duck's Bill'), and the Jabal Sinjar on the provisional Syrian–Iraqi frontier. In these sections, the lack of determination of territorial sovereignty opened the door to a diplomatic trade-off accompanied by divergent interpretations of the existing maps, as well as which boundaries constituted the most 'natural' borders. Crucially, while the League of Nations and the relevant state authorities established the corresponding boundary commissions to 'scientifically' delineate the borders in the region, borderlanders were involved in the boundary-making process in different ways such as petitioning the League or providing topographical information to the boundary delegates surveying the area.

---

[18] CADN, 1SL/1/V/549. Captain Bonnot to the High Commissioner. Deir ez-Zor, 10 June 1928; TNA, FO 371/13043. 'Turkish Activities against Iraq'. Colonial Office to the High Commissioner. London, 21 September 1928.

[19] See BCA.030.10.113.771.1 (4 April 1929) on the establishment of the Khoybun League, a Kurdish-Armenian committee based in Syria and Lebanon seeking to establish a Kurdish and Armenian states in Eastern Anatolia; on the alleged British support to Assyrian tribes against Turkish national security, see BCA.030.10.230.548.8, 24 July 1930.

The first boundary delineation procedure that highlighted all these complexities was the Turkish–Iraqi border. Geographer Richard Schofield considers that overall 'Iraq's territorial definition was essentially a consequence of its position at the edge of several discrete imperial episodes in which Britain was centrally involved'.[20] Hence, the imperial strategic imperative of maintaining the Persian Gulf under British control and securing a land corridor through today's Iraq not only dictated how territorial limits were forged, 'but also often resulted in boundaries drawn for very particular reasons'.[21] Consequently, the work of the successive boundary commissions operated with closely defined parameters and their flexibility for territorial revision was generally limited, for 'the contextual strategic die had been cast at a much earlier stage'.[22] Such was the case, according to Schofield with the Iraq–Turkey boundary, which had been identified as a strategic frontier by the British as early as 1915, in accordance with the recommendations advanced by the de Bunsen Committee;[23] that is, safeguarding a mountainous, 'natural' boundary running to the north of Mosul's Ottoman provincial limits, as well as putting together the latter with two other Ottoman provinces, namely, Baghdad and Basra. Overall, 'despite many twists and turns in strategic thinking in the years that followed, the de Bunsen commission had drawn a blueprint' for the Turkish–Iraqi boundary that the Mosul Commission simply confirmed in 1925.[24]

While the ubiquity of British imperial visions in the Middle Eastern region in the post-war period is undeniable, the resulting Turkish–Iraqi boundary was not merely the 'natural' outcome of the former. As seen in the previous chapter, between 1919 and 1922, the Anatolian resistance movement threatened British control over the northern fringes of the Mosul Province through its alliances with local tribal leaders, resulting in a series of British military

---

[20] Richard N. Schofield, 'Laying it Down in Stone: Delimiting and Demarcating Iraq's Boundaries by Mixed International Commission', *Journal of Historical Geography*, Vol. 34, No. 3 (2008), pp. 397–421 (here p. 398).

[21] Ibid.

[22] Ibid.

[23] For a comprehensive analysis of the British cartographic work on the Middle Easter region until the early 1920s, see Daniel Foliard, *Dislocating the Orient: British Maps and the Making of the Middle East* (Chicago: University of Chicago Press, 2017).

[24] Richard N. Schofield, 'Laying it Down in Stone', p. 398.

setbacks and the subsequent withdrawal of British positions southwards. Crucially, without an active policy combining RAF aerial intervention, the co-optation of 'loyal' Kurdish tribes, the settlement of Assyrian refugees in the Kurdish districts of Dohuk, Zakho and Aqra in 1921, and the recruitment of Assyrians into the Levies, by the time the Mosul Commission toured the region, the security context and thus its final decision would have been radically different.

Yet, once all obstacles had been overcome, the boundary delimitation process went extremely fast, by all standards. From November 1924 to March 1925, a special three-member sub-commission, appointed by the League, investigated the boundary problem. Its recommendation, the following July, was that the 'Brussels Line' be accepted as the international boundary between Turkey and Iraq. The dispute was then referred to the Permanent Court of International Justice at The Hague for advisory opinion, and, by November, the Court recommended awarding the former Mosul Vilayet to Iraq. Subsequently, the Ankara Treaty signed on 5 June 1926 between the United Kingdom, Iraq and Turkey, instituted that the Iraq–Turkey boundary was to follow the 'Brussels Line'. Demarcation of the boundary was to be undertaken as soon as possible and a permanent Frontier Commission was established to meet at least once every six months to address all the relevant frontier issues. In addition, a frontier zone was set up, 75km wide (45 miles) on either side of the boundary, within which each country would seek to ensure that no raids and other hostile acts took place across the border.

Turkish and British sources coincide in depicting the delimitation works as having gone smoothly,[25] despite some practical problems such as the difficulties due to the mountainous terrain[26] and the long meetings 'devoted to correcting the names for the map'.[27] The Turkish-Iraq Frontier Delimitation Commission started work on 20 March 1927 and finished by signing the report on 23 September of the same year. During this period, fifty-eight meetings were held and ninety-nine boundary stones erected. They decided to place the Turkish crescent cut in the stone on the one side, and the

---

[25] *Akşam*, 28 May 1928.
[26] TNA, CO 730/113/3. L. Nalder, Frontier Delimitation Commissioner. Beduh, 20 June 1927.
[27] TNA, CO 730/113/3. L. Nalder, Frontier Delimitation Commissioner. Gerana, 9 August 1927.

82 | RETHINKING STATE AND BORDER FORMATION

seven-pointed Iraqi star on the opposite side, while the number of the pillar (in Arabic numerals) was to be cut into the remaining two sides.[28] During the delimitation procedures, few rectifications were made, except for the area south of the Turkish villages of Aluman and Ashuta, which were allocated to Turkey, as a favour, in order to include in Turkish territory a road connecting these two points.[29] While the border post at Zakho would become the main gateway for trade between Turkey and Iraq after 1924, a series of administrative buildings, border posts and checkpoints completed the web of border infrastructures that regulated cross-border mobility thereafter.[30]

The resolution of the Mosul Affair paved the way for the ensuing delimitation of the Turkish–Syrian boundary. Indeed, as soon as the League of Nations allocated Mosul to mandatory Iraq, France accelerated its diplomatic contacts with Turkey to sign a 'Good Neighborhood Treaty' on 30 May 1926,

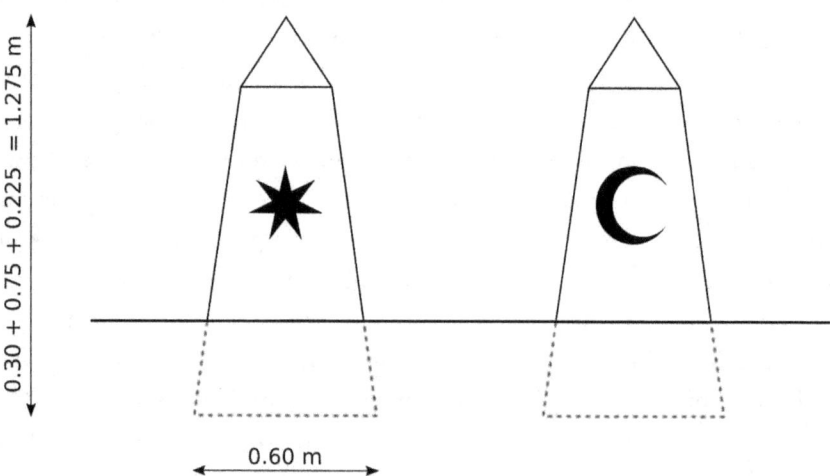

Figure 2.1 Illustration of the pillars erected along the Turkish–Iraqi border in 1927.

Source: Redrawn by the author, TNA, CO 730/113/4.

[29] TNA, CO 730/113/3. L. Nalder, Frontier Delimitation Commissioner. Beduh, 20 June 1927.
[30] LON, R58/1/17502/44571. 'Report to the League of Nations on the Administration of Iraq, April 1923–4', p. 64.
[28] TNA, CO 730/113/3. L. Nalder, Frontier Delimitation Commissioner. Robozak, 20 May 1927.

only six days before the latter signed the Treaty of Ankara with Great Britain on Mosul.[31] Yet, the Turkish–Syrian boundary-making process proved to be rather complex. The Ankara Treaty or Franklin-Boullion Agreement of 20 October 1921 had established a provisional borderline running in the west across the coastal town of Payas and extending eastward, passing to the south of Kilis and arriving directly at the train station of Çobanbey. Thence, it followed the Baghdad Railway until Nusaybin station. From there, it went along the 'old road' to Jazirat ibn Umar, where it rejoined the Tigris River. The areas of Jazirat ibn Umar and Nusaybin remained in Turkey, but the two governments had the same rights of access to this road. In addition, France obtained the Sanjaq of Alexandretta on condition it granted the latter a form of autonomy to protect the minority rights of the Turkish population, as well as some financial concessions upon the Baghdad Railway and mineral mines. Finally, the treaty foresaw the establishment of a Franco-Turkish Commission to demarcate the international boundary.

At the Lausanne Conference of 1923, however, both sides seemed to evaluate new thoughts about the frontier. On the one hand, Foreign Minister İsmet İnönü received a telegram from Ankara in which he was pressed to claim a boundary lying much further south when compared to the 1921 treaty.[32] On the other hand, when the Turkish delegation requested that the borderline foreseen by the Ankara Accord be included in the Treaty of Lausanne, the French initially rejected the demand.[33] Although the Treaty of Lausanne did eventually retain the provisional frontier as per the Ankara Accord, such diplomatic moves announced further tensions. Despite resuming the frontier negotiations with France in April 1925, the Turks erected several military posts on the stretch between Nusaybin and Jazirat ibn Umar, that is, beyond the provisional frontier. In doing so, they hoped to impede the advance of French troops towards the Tigris.

---

[31] See Müzehher Yamaç, 'Fransız Diplomatik Belgerinde Türkiye-Suriye Sınır Sorunu, 1918–40', *Belleten*, Vol. 82 (2018), p. 1159.

[32] Seha L. Meray, *Lozan Barış Konferansı, Tutanaklar, Belgeler*, Volume 2 (Istanbul: Yapı Kredi Yayınları, 2011), p. 343.

[33] İsmet İnönü, *Hatıralar* (Ankara: Bilgi Yayınevi, 2014), p. 117.

Although cross-border infringements represented a cause for concern for both parties, it was the developments unfolding elsewhere that provided the incentive to attend to these problems. On the one hand, the eruption of the Shaykh Said rebellion in early 1925 reminded Ankara of the significance of cooperating with the French vis-à-vis cross-border circuits that could easily get out of control.[34] In that regard, the definitive annexation of the Mosul Province by Iraq meant the loss of a predominantly Kurdish territory which Turkey could not effectively monitor. Similarly, the arrival of thousands of Kurdish refugees in this Syrian region was viewed by Turkey as a dangerous development, because from that moment onwards, new Kurdish populations 'feeling nothing but hate' for the Turks would evade Ankara's authority.[35] On the other hand, the outbreak of the Great Syrian Revolt in the summer of 1925 in Hauran made the French grasp 'the danger of allowing this Turco-French controversy to drag on while the internal crisis in the French-mandated territory continued unabated'.[36]

Within this context, Turkey and Syria signed the 'Convention of Friendship and Good Neighbourly Relations' on 30 May 1926. It provided for arbitration of disputes, disposal of the goods of the absent, quarantine, railway, customs and frontier matters.[37] In its Article 16, the convention foresaw the call for a mediator to solve the frontier issue. This convention divided the boundary into three sectors: from the locality of Payas to Çobanbey; from Çobanbey to Nusaybin; and, finally, from Nusaybin to Jazirat ibn Umar. Rapid progress was made in sectors one and two. The third sector, however, remained an issue of contention as the Turkish and French delegations held different interpretations about the precise track of the 'old road' between Nusaybin and Jazirat ibn Umar, where it was to join the Tigris.

---

[34] TNA, FO 424/538, 'Turkey: Annual Report, 1925', p. 11.

[35] CADN, 1SL/1/V/549. The High Commissioner to His Excellency the Minister of Foreign Affairs. Beirut, 28 April 1927.

[36] Yücel Güçlü, 'The Controversy Over the Delimitation of the Turco-Syrian Frontier in the Period between the Two World Wars', *Middle Eastern Studies*, Vol. 42, No. 4 (2006), pp. 641–57 (here p. 645).

[37] Ibid.

For the French, this road was indeed the 'old Roman road' starting at Sevran and connecting directly Nusaybin to Jazirat ibn Umar. For the Turks, however, there was not one 'Old Road', but several 'old roads', thereby suggesting as a boundary the one that crossed the area further south.[38] If accepted, the proposed borderline would give Turkey a post on the right bank of the river affording direct contact with Iraqi territory – a scenario that, in turn, raised British concerns. From a military point of view, Turkish territorial gains in the Syrian wedge would certainly lead the French to abandon the entire Upper Jazira, providing the Turks with an accessible route for their army in case of an open conflict with Britain.[39] From an administrative perspective, the British High Commission also considered that the 'Duck's Bill' should be Syrian, for if the Turkish proposal were to be implemented, 'it would be more difficult even than it is at present to obtain satisfaction in the case of trans-frontier raids, as the Turkish and Syrian governments respectively would naturally throw the blame on each other in doubtful cases'.[40]

Given the lack of consensus on certain stretches, a mixed international commission led by Danish General Ernst started its work in March 1927. When the commission asked borderlanders about the precise location of the 'Old Road', the latter confirmed that there were indeed two roads to be taken into consideration: '*Darb al-Antik*' (Old Road) – as per the French proposal and '*Darb al-Sultani*' (Sultan's Road) – according to the Turkish version.[41] Against this backdrop, the Turkish delegation suggested a third track as a boundary between the two countries, making Demir Kapu a tri-border nexus. Nonetheless, the

---

[38] CADN, 36/PO/1/149. Turkish Delegation (Jemal Bey). Nusaybin, 22 November 1927.
[39] TNA, FO 371/ 11454. 'Turkish attack on Khanik'. Colonial Office (London), 18 January 1926; TNA, FO 371/12305. The British High Commissioner in Baghdad (H. Dobbs) to Foreign Office (London). Baghdad, 4 April 1927.
[40] TNA, CO 732/31/4. The British High Commissioner in Baghdad (H. Dobbs) to Colonial Office (London). Baghdad, 19 September 1928.
[41] See Soheila Mameli-Ghaderi, 'Le tracé de la frontière entre la Syrie et la Turquie (1921–9)', *Guerres mondiales et conflits contemporains*, Vol. 207, No. 3 (2002), p. 133. Both delegations claimed that the other contentious party had put pressure on Bedouins, Yazidis and peasants in order to support their respective allegations before the International Frontier Commission. CADN, 36/PO/1/149. Turkish Delegation (Jemal Bey). Nusaybin, 22 November 1927.

French rejected this alternative for it took away from Syria one of the most watered and potentially productive areas of the Upper Jazira. As General Ernst backed the French version, the Turkish delegation withdrew and asked for bilateral negotiations to commence immediately. Meanwhile, Turkish newspapers rejected the proposed boundary for two main reasons: the prevailing insecurity along the borderline since the establishment of the French Mandate in Syria, and its 'inequitable' character, in particular on the west.[42]

Following multiple consultations, the two countries signed a protocol on 22 June 1929, elaborating in detail the boundary demarcation between Nusaybin and Jazirat ibn Umar. According to this protocol, in which many of the previously granted Turkish demands were taken back, the boundary was declared to follow the 'old Roman road', which, in turn, was to fully fall into Turkish territory. With regard to the Mersin–Adana–Tarsus railroad, the French maintained their right to management of the line between Bozanti to Nusaybin and thence of the eventual extension to Mosul.

The works of the bilateral Commission of Delimitation in the 'third section' ended in 1930. During the process, Turkish and French border authorities agreed to use white stones for marking the borderline. Ultimately, the French 'recovered' Çobanbey and a territorial strip of 800km^2 comprising 101 villages, including the third sector. In exchange for eighty Kurdish villages conceded to Turkey, France obtained the incorporation of eighty-five villages with access to the Tigris. To the French officer Louis Dillemann, the agreement with Turkey was not a diplomatic victory but, mainly, a return to 'the old system of reciprocal concessions.'[43]

The delimitation of the Turkish–Syrian boundary, together with the pending termination of the British Mandate over Iraq, accelerated in turn the delimitation of the Syrian–Iraqi border. Prior to the French occupation of Damascus in July 1920, King Faysal and Sir Percy Cox, British High Commissioner in Iraq, signed the so-called Leachman Accord on the

---

[42] See 'Türkiye ve Suriye', *Cumhuriyet*, 7 January 1928, p. 1. On 10 October 1928, *Milliyet* denounced Franco-Kurdish cooperation in the Upper Jazira, thereby provoking insecurity and anarchy in the Duck's Bill area.

[43] Louis Dillemann, 'Les Français en Haute Djézireh', *Revue Française d'Histoire d'Outre-Mer*, t. LXVI (1979), p. 54.

provisional frontier between Syrian and Iraq, which would constitute the basis for the Franco-Convention of 23 December 1920. According to the latter, the

> boundaries between the territories under the French Mandate of Syria and Lebanon on the one hand and the British Mandates of Mesopotamia and Palestine on the other are determined as follows: on the east, the Tigris from Jazirat ibn Umar to the boundaries of the former Vilayets of Diyarbakır and Mosul.

On the south-east and south, 'the aforesaid boundary of the former vilayets southwards as far as Roumelan Kewi thence a line leaving in the territory under the French Mandate the entire basin of the western Khabur and passing in a straight line towards the Euphrates which it crosses at Abu Kamal.'[44]

At the time of the Franco-British accord, both mandatory powers were satisfied with a rather vague designation of their mutual zones of influence in the region; the precise delimitation of the common frontier was considered as worthless, for 'no Government will exercise effective control over the Syrian desert . . . governments are concerned only with the administration of settled districts'.[45] Against this backdrop, a sort of division of labour regarding the maintenance of security and policing of the region gave this responsibility to the British for the population on both sides, putting de facto Jabal Sinjar under British administration.[46] Furthermore, the French admitted no restriction on their sovereignty, except a reciprocal renunciation of the right to create permanent military posts.[47] By 1929, however, French appraisal of the situation in this borderland shifted as France's presence in the Jazira was by

---

[44] Richard N. Schofield (ed.) *Arabian Boundary Disputes* (Farham Common: Archive Editions, 1992), p. 355.

[45] Comments quoted in Note by India Office titled 'Settlement of Turkey and Arabian Peninsula', 30 November 1918, reproduced in Richard N. Schofield (ed.) *Arabian Boundary Disputes*, p. 355.

[46] Inga Brandell, *State Frontiers: Borders and Boundaries in the Middle East* (London and New York: I. B. Tauris, 2006), p. 14.

[47] TNA, FO 371/12304/E1678/162/89. 'Franco-Syrian Right of Entry into *de facto* Iraq Zone'. London, 9 April 1927.

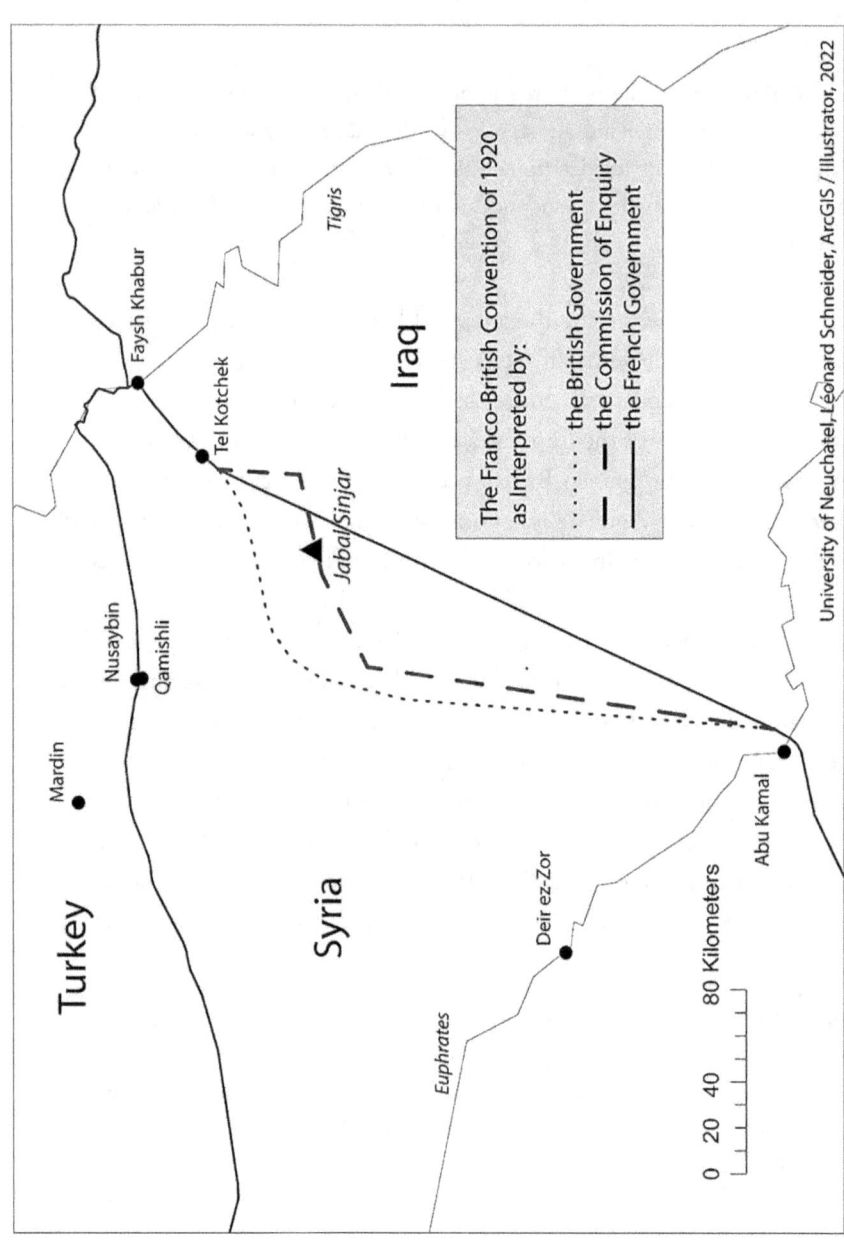

Figure 2.2 Map of the Franco-British Convention of 1920 as interpreted by France and Britain.

Source: TNA, FO 925/17215.

then consolidated. Thus, although in the past France had not pressed her full claim in practice over the provisional frontier, the French High Commissioner requested now a 'just' frontier treaty between France and Britain.

At first, the British rejected French claims over the Sinjar, for they considered that securing the unity of the Yazidi Mountain would ease its administrative management.[48] Yet, it appeared from the start that the French High Commissioner was ready to cede western Sinjar to British Iraq only on condition of a favourable global settlement of the Syro–Iraqi and Syro–Transjordanian border – especially in the Yamurk Valley – under the egis of the League of Nations.[49] In addition, the indication that west Sinjar might have oil resources led the French mandatory power to adopt a firm position on the Jabal within the context of the ongoing Franco-British rivalry in the region.[50] Given a prolonged exchange of dispatches addressing procedural problems and the subsequent lack of agreement, the Syrian–Iraqi frontier dispute was eventually submitted to the League of Nations. Thereafter, the League appointed a special commission to tour the area to clarify the course of the Iraq-Syria boundary.

The commission started work in February 1932. As expected, the delimitation of the northern portions of the Syrian–Iraqi boundary along the Jabal Sinjar was the most contentious part. In the Ottoman times, the area southwest of Tel Rumailan belonged to either Baghdad or Mosul Provinces. According to the Franco-British convention of 1920, a provisional boundary-line ran from Abu Kamal to Tel Rumailan. Yet, while on the maps in use at the time such a line gave the whole of the Jabal to Iraq, it soon appeared that it actually cut Jabal Sinjar in two and crisscrossed the city of Abu Kamal on the Euphrates. Yet, to facilitate the circulation and management of the frontier in this area, the 1920 definition was shifted westwards at Jabal Sinjar and eastwards at Abu Kamal. Thereafter, the commission was entrusted with the mission of delineating the most 'natural' boundary that would have a less negative impact on borderlanders' economic and social relations.

---

[48] CADN, 1SL/1/V/1518. Residency (Baghdad) to the French High Commissioner (Beirut). Baghdad, 31 January 1929.
[49] CADN, 1SL/1/V/1518. French High Commissioner (Beirut) to the British Residency (Baghdad). Beirut, 31 March 1923.
[50] CADN, 1SL/1/V/1529. 'Le Sindjar'. Intelligence Report, Euphrates Region, 14 August 1929.

Within this context, French and British mandatory powers advanced opposing arguments – mainly of a topographical and economic tenor – to claim their sovereignty over Jabal Sinjar, while encouraging local dwellers to support their respective views. Records from the border authorities show that these endeavours had started earlier, though. By December 1929, French interference in the western portions of the Jabal Sinjar – mainly propaganda activities and collecting taxes among borderlanders – were already lamented by the British for 'these intrigues are causing considerable uneasiness in the Jabal and as the Yazidis are an excitable people may lead to serious events'.[51] Such activities were nonetheless reinforced by early 1931 when the French sent some agents to the Jabal Sinjar to spread rumours among the local Yazidis about the upcoming military occupation of the mountain.[52] A few months later, French activities apparently bore some results, as an increasing number of Yazidis believed that 'it had been finally decided that the Balad Sinjar would be included in French Syria'.[53]

In turn, the British encouraged Yazidi leaders to claim their Iraqi loyalty to the League of Nations. In 1932, several Yazidi representatives sent a petition to the Frontier Commission where they declared that 'we are Iraqis by nationality' and 'since our childhood and up to the present times, we have never had any trading business with the Syrians'.[54] Consequently, Sinjari traders voiced their desire for the inclusion of the Jabal in Iraq on the grounds of their traditional economic interests tightly connected to Mosul.[55] The British mandatory authorities advanced other concerns, such as the survival of religious networks in order to press for the indivisibility of Jabal Sinjar. To the British, the division of the Yazidi Mountain would involve a serious interference into the religious lives of the local population, as the major Yazidi pilgrimage centres were located in Iraqi territory. Meanwhile, the assessors for the commission completed their investigation of the borderlands between

---

[51] TNA, AIR 23/94. Memorandum from the Administrative Inspector at Mosul liwa. Mosul, 16 January 1930.
[52] TNA, AIR 23/94. Intelligence report. Mosul, 28 February 1931.
[53] TNA, AIR 23/95. Intelligence report. Mosul, 27 August 1931.
[54] TNA, AIR 23/95. Fortnightly report. Mosul, 22 April 1932.
[55] TNA, AIR 23/95. Fortnightly report. Mosul, 7 May 1932.

March and May 1932, to study the area, visit the villages and question the local dwellers.

Fearing a potential diplomatic setback, the Iraqi authorities also intervened in the dispute by reassuring the League of Nations of their intention to fulfil the aspirations of the Iraqi 'minority groups', including the local Yazidi population. These same anxieties led the British to seek a bilateral accord with France aside from the League of Nations' final deliberation. Thus, although the recommendation of the Frontier Commission eventually supported British arguments in its report presented to the League Council in October 1932, France and Britain made a territorial arrangement in parallel, by which Jabal Sinjar was incorporated into Iraq, while Abu Kamal and the entire basin of the river Khabur were included in Syria.[56]

On 14 February 1933, the Council in Geneva appointed Swiss Colonel Frédéric Iselin as president of the Frontier Commission to demarcate the borderline. A month later, the commission commenced its works and by April 12, it had demarcated the line west of the Euphrates, that is, from Leachman's Pillar, Abu Kamal, to Jabal Tanf. Yet, when the commission arrived in the Duck's Bill, the tasks were undertaken in an atmosphere of mutual recrimination and mistrust to the extent that Sabih Beg – the Iraqi representative – withdrew from the commission and Colonel Iselin retired to Syria. According to British accounts, Colonel Iselin was accused of partiality towards the French, 'with the result that on his ruling the Iraqis lost territory of potential value west of the Euphrates and of considerable value in the Jabal Sinjar'. In addition, the President of the Commission instructued the Iraqi delegation that the final sector of the frontier on the Duck's Bill, between Rumeilan Kewi and Faysh Khabur, should run in a straight line, without any regard for local topographical considerations.[57]

When Colonel Iselin telegraphed Geneva asking to be recalled, the French informed the British that, should the president give up his mission, the French government would consider the whole frontier question 'reopened'. In these circumstances, the British advisers in Baghdad proposed

---

[56] Nelida Fuccaro, *The Other Kurds*, pp. 148–9.
[57] TNA, WO 181/1. British Embassy in Baghdad, 24 May 1933.

that the Iraqi government accept the President's ruling despite its 'defects'.[58] Following the erection of boundary pillars, except for a small section in the extreme north – that is, between Faysh Khabur and the Jabal Sinjar – the two countries concluded a Franco-Iraqi agreement on 3 July 1933.[59] As foreseen by the British advisors, in later negotiations the Iraqi government obtained further readjustments on this section in exchange for concessions southwards between the Jabal Sinjar and Abu Kemal.[60] Although the French mandatory power delayed the signature of the 'Convention of Friendship and Good Neighbourly Relations' with the Iraqi government for three years, its ultimate signature in 1937, together with the rise of the National Bloc's political influence in Damascus, were celebrated by the Arab nationalist newspapers on both sides of the border as a preliminary step to achieve political and economic unity between the two countries, bound by a shared struggle against European colonialism.[61]

Southwards, in contrast, the process of boundary delimitation went smoothly and, as César Jaquier argues, a 'mobile' border made up of several border posts and checkpoints erected across the Syrian Desert throughout the 1920s and early 1930s accompanied, or even preceded the demarcation of the border itself. Indeed, as French and British authorities attempted to control and manage cross-border mobility along the trans-desert route between Damascus and Baghdad, several customs and border posts on both the Syrian and Iraqi side of the provisional border emerged further upstream, constituting the early infrastructure of the future Syrian–Iraqi border. Moreover, as this author shows, too, French and British authorities had to adapt the location of their checkpoints and customs posts to the car circuits crossing the Syrian Desert, rather than the other way round. In other words, trans-desert routes and practices of mobility determined the organisation and infrastructure of the Syrian–Iraqi border,[62] a dynamic that supports two interrelated arguments

---

[58] Ibid.
[59] LON, C.413.1933.VI. 'Frontier between Iraq and Syria. Work of the Demarcation Commission'. Geneva, 3 July 1933.
[60] TNA, WO 181/1. Completion of the demarcation of the Syrian boundary. Baghdad, 29 May 1933.
[61] See the summaries of articles on this agreement published in several Syrian and Iraqi newspapers in CADN, 1SL/1/V/637.
[62] César Jaquier, 'Motor Cars and Transdesert Traffic: Channelling Mobilities between Iraq and Syria, 1923–30', in Jordi Tejel and Ramazan Hakkı Öztan (eds), *Regimes of Mobility:*

advanced by borderlands scholars. First, borders are not just territorial borderlines, but rather social and political institutions that evolve over time. As such, borders are always in motion.[63]

Ordering and 'Othering' Borderlands and Beyond

Scholars have long pointed to the strong contingent relationship between the emergence of the nation state with its 'national borders' and the generation of large-scale refugee movements,[64] to the extent that in the modern era, refugees are created in the interaction of displaced people and borders and are indeed otherwise hard to understand.[65] In that regard, state- and border-making processes convey a paradoxical effect: on the one hand, 'borders are erected to erase territorial ambiguity and ambivalent identities in order to shape a unique and cohesive order'; on the other, they 'create new or reproduce latently existing differences in space and identity'.[66] Against this backdrop, scholars such as Paolo Novak and Robert Sack argue that it is important to explore how territoriality reveals itself through the inscription of state-centred discourses and practices[67] – in other words, how 'boundaries actively order space' and consequently the populations bound up with them.[68] Houtum and Naerssen, however, point out that 'ordering' people and lands also entails an 'othering' process. Historically, the interwar years constitute in that sense a key period in the Middle East, for, as elsewhere, 'defining the

Borders and State Formation in the Middle East, 1918–46 (Edinburgh: Edinburgh University Press, 2022), pp. 228–55.

[63] Victor Konrad, 'Toward a Theory of Borders in Motion', *Journal of Borderlands Studies*, Vol. 30, No. 1 (2015), pp. 1–17.

[64] Aristide Zolberg et al., 'International Factors in the Formation of Refugee Movements', *International Migration Review*, Vol. 20, No. 2 (1986), pp. 151–69.

[65] Randall Hansen, 'State controls: Borders, Refugees, and Citizenship', in Elena Fiddina Qasmiyeh et al. (eds), *The Oxford Handbook of Refugee and Forced Migration Studies* (Oxford: Oxford University Press, 2014), pp. 1–2.

[66] Henk van Houtum and Ton Van Naerssen, 'Bordering, Ordering and Othering', p. 126.

[67] Robert Sack defines territoriality as the 'attempt by an individual or social group (in this case, the state) to affect, influence and control people, phenomena and relationships by delimiting and asserting control over a geographical area (here, the national territory)'. Robert David Sack, *Human Territoriality: Its Theory and History* (Cambridge: Cambridge University Press, 1986), p. 1.

[68] Paolo Novak, 'The Flexible Territoriality of Borders', *Geopolitics*, Vol. 16, No. 4 (2011), p. 743.

boundaries of the new "nation-states" was the best way to demonstrate who belonged to them and who was excluded from them'.[69]

Refugees were, however, not the only by-product of the emerging international system. Victorious powers at the peace conference of 1919 embraced nationality politics and imposed a series of treaties or declarations to the new nation states created in Central and Eastern Europe after the disintegration of the defeated empires, with special provisions for the protection of 'minorities'.[70] This top-down approach, however, made things worse, for 'East European leaders rushed to strengthen their claims to the territory by forcing out members of different groups whom they did not wish to include in their new nation-states'.[71] In so doing, by the early 1920s, the 'minority' and 'refugee' issues had thus become tightly connected within the international system promoted by the League of Nations.

Admittedly, post-Ottoman nation states became a powerful instrument in generating statelessness, refugees and 'minorities', who, in some cases – for example, Armenians and Assyrians in Syria and Iraq – were the same communities. On the one hand, nationalist elites passed laws to avoid the return of the displaced and elaborated a political discourse that tended to make non-core groups 'alien' to the emerging national identity.[72] On the other hand, statelessness, refugees and minority regimes constituted the very raison d'être of post-war mechanisms of international authority, such as the League of Nations and the mandates in the Middle East. In other words, the spirit of the mandate system, as framed by the founders of the League in 1920, 'was the reformulation of essentially imperial ideas about race, civilization, and sovereignty' – already present in the Berlin Act

---

[69] Asher Kaufman, *Contested Frontiers in the Syria-Lebanon-Israel Region* (Washington, DC: Woodrow Wilson Center Press, 2014), p. 34.

[70] Fifteen agreements on minority protection were concluded in Paris paralleling the spirit of the Minority Treaty between the Principal Allied and Associated Powers and Poland, signed on 28 June 1919. See Carole Fink, 'The League of Nations and the Minority Question', *World Affairs*, Vol. 157, No. 4 (1995), pp. 197–205.

[71] Mark Mazower, *Governing the World: The History of an Idea* (London: Penguin Books, 2012), p. 156.

[72] Harris Mylonas, *The Politics of Nation-Building: Making Co-Nationals, Refugees, and Minorities* (Cambridge: Cambridge University Press, 2012), p. xx.

of 1885 – 'into an emerging discourse of international law that purported to be essentially non (though not anti-) imperial'.[73]

In independent Turkey, much like prior to the First World War, the warfare which was going on in Anatolia, along with the Western occupation of certain portions of the collapsing Ottoman Empire, fostered a perception among Turkish nationalists of non-Muslim populations as potential fifth columns in the hands of imperialist powers. For one thing, by supporting the British and French armies on frontlines such as Western and Southern Anatolia, ex-Ottoman Christians were identified as a threat to Anatolian territorial independence.[74] Once the Greek and Armenian supplementary forces withdrew from Anatolia between 1921 and 1922, the remaining non-Muslim populations constituted the last obstacle to achieving national homogeneity, increasingly associated with the ruling Turkish-Muslim core-group.[75]

The first move towards national homogenisation led to the population transfer of about 1,350,000 Greeks from the Aegean region. Further, the Treaty of Lausanne, signed a year later, authorised the forced transfer of Greeks and Turks to places other than Istanbul and Eastern Thrace.[76] Thereafter, thousands of Greeks, Armenians and Jews were compelled to leave Turkey. The fate of the properties left behind by these people, both during the war and immediately after it, became a key issue in the early days of the new Turkish Parliament. Tellingly, the first laws and regulations that appeared in the republican period primarily dealt with legal aspects of the abandoned Armenian and Greek properties seized in 1915. In addition, new regulations were passed to impede the return of all non-Muslims found abroad and to limit internal travel. A law signed on 5 September 1923 explicitly targeted Armenians, Assyrians

---

[73] Laura Robson, *The Politics of Mass Violence in the Middle East* (Oxford: Oxford University Press, 2020), p. 57.

[74] Ryan Gingeras, *Sorrowful Shores: Violence, Ethnicity, and the End of the Ottoman Empire, 1912–23* (Oxford: Oxford University Press, 2009).

[75] Soner Cagaptay, *Islam, Secularism, and Nationalism in Modern Turkey: Who is a Turk?* (London and New York: Routledge, 2006).

[76] Onur Yıldırım, *Diplomacy and Displacement: Reconsidering the Turco-Greek Exchange of Populations, 1922–34* (New York: Routledge, 2006).

and Greeks: 'those cooperating with the enemy who flee or emigrate from our country or went with a foreign passport or laissez-passer, and Ottoman Greeks subject to population exchange cannot return'.[77]

Unsurprisingly, the new Turkish Parliament reacted against the actions of the League of Nations to secure the protection of 'minority groups' on the grounds that its proposals were part of an imperialist project, which was in neat contradiction to the Turkish political elite's vision of having a homeland 'without debts, without minorities, with complete sovereignty'.[78] The solution to Turkey's challenges was not granting privileges to otherwise disloyal Ottoman subjects, but rather achieving homogeneity inside the national boundaries through either assimilation or expulsion of all non-Muslims elements.[79]

Even though most scholars highlight that the Treaty of Lausanne and its minority rights clauses had an impact on the subsequent laws issued by the Turkish government to deter Christians living abroad from returning to their homeland, the *de facto* recognition of Turkey's provisional frontiers with Syria and Iraq provoked further concrete effects – namely, an unofficial campaign to free the border zones from 'unwanted' populations. By late 1923, the Armenians from Urfa and its surrounding villages were expelled from their houses and lands, which were subsequently confiscated by the government under the pretext that the owners had abandoned them. In the process, wealthy landowners and tribal chiefs were rewarded for their involvement in the Independence Movement and for their loyalty to the new regime by receiving the 'abandoned properties'.[80]

Furthermore, although the Treaty of Lausanne provided non-Muslims with a rather restrictive interpretation of minority clauses – notably, religious freedom – the treaty was an issue of concern for the Turkish Parliament, for

---

[77] Ümit Kurt, 'Revising the Legal Infrastructure for the Confiscation of Armenian and Greek Wealth: An Analysis of the CUP Years and the Early Modern Republic', *Middle Eastern Studies*, Vol. 53, No. 5 (2017), pp. 700–23 (here p. 710).

[78] TBMM 3.11.1338/1922, p. 372. Cited in Yeşim Bayar, 'The League of Nations, Minorities, and Post-Imperial Turkey', *Journal of Historical Sociology*, Vol. 33, No. 1 (2020), pp. 172–83 (here p. 178).

[79] TBMM 4.1.1339/1923. Cited in Ibid. p. 180.

[80] Müslüm Akalın, *Cumhuriyet Halk Fırkası Urfa Heyet-i Ideresi Mukarrerat Defteri, 1924–6* (Urfa: Şurkav, 1999).

it opened the door to individual repatriation for non-Muslim refugees. In this environment, the Grand National Assembly hotly debated the new Turkish Constitution and the precise definition of 'Turkish citizenship'. While some deputies argued for an ethnic definition of Turkishness as 'possessing Turkish culture', eventually Article 88 of the 1924 Constitution coined a rather vague definition of Turkish citizenship in order to comply with Article 39 of the Treaty of Lausanne and minority clauses. According to this definition, 'the people of Turkey, regardless of their religion and race would, in terms of citizenship, be called "Turk"'.[81] Nevertheless, ensuing laws secured a further restrictive understanding of Turkish citizenship and imposed new limitations to the right of return to Turkey. In that regard, the 1927 Denaturalisation Law established that 'those Ottoman subjects who had stayed outside Turkey and did not participate in the National Resistance during the War of Independence . . . and had not returned since then would lose their citizenship'.[82]

Paradoxically, even though Turkish deputies perceived the minority clauses as an obstacle towards complete sovereignty, the Ankara government soon realised that the League of Nations' principles on nationality and state sovereignty indirectly supported its internal policies geared towards non-Muslim groups. By legitimising the 'population exchange' solution between Greece and Turkey, as well as the primacy of sovereignty while dealing with independent states such as Turkey, the League 'facilitated Turkification as a means to forge the kind of ethno-national state that was to fit into the global community of states.'[83]

Meanwhile, new priorities emerged. In the aftermath of the Shaykh Said rebellion, the Ankara government devised radical measures to 'solve' the Kurdish problem altogether. Although recent scholarship has shown that the revolt was the result of a combination of different factors – notably, a reaction

---

[81] Lerna Ekmekçioğlu, 'Republic of Paradox: The League of Nations Minority Protection Regime and the New Turkey's Step-citizens', *International Journal of Middle East Studies*, Vol. 46, No. 4 (2014), pp. 657–79 (here p. 670).

[82] Law No. 1041 cited in Lerna Ekmekçioğlu, 'Republic of Paradox', p. 671.

[83] Carolin Liebisch-Gümüş, 'Embedded Turkification: Nation Building and Violence within the Framework of the League of Nations, 1919–37', *International Journal of Middle East Studies*, Vol. 52, No. 2 (2020), pp. 229–44 (here p. 243).

against the abolition of the Caliphate as well as the growing Turkish nationalist tendencies in the Turkish Parliament – the Ankara government depicted the uprising as being purely religiously motivated.[84] More importantly, some Turkish ruling elites believed that the Kurds were incapable of embracing modernity and the principles of the new republic. In this context, forced displacement was seen as a legitimate tool to advance towards the formation of a new national identity based on two basic pillars: Islam and Turkishness.

While the deportation scheme was not fully implemented, the repression of the 1925 revolt and the subsequent instability in the region opened the door to the removal of certain Kurdish families from the Eastern provinces to central Anatolia, as well as to new episodes of violence against the 'unwanted' elements in the southern Turkish borderlands.[85] Hence, in April 1926, on the grounds of a new Kurdish uprising that erupted in the Mardin area, the Ankara government punished Christians along with the Kurds and Yazidis from that region. As a result, by mid-April, thousands of Kurds and Yazidis crossed the border into Iraq on the Nusaybin–Sinjar road and settled in towns located as far as Mosul.

In addition to forced displacement and the destruction of villages in the Eastern provinces, the Independence Tribunals that were established to prosecute Shaykh Said and his comrades in 1925 continued to work until 1927, while expanding their mission; that is, of prosecuting opponents in Turkey.[86] Notwithstanding this, the Ankara government considered that a permanent structure was needed in order to secure stability across the territory. Hence, drawing on the Ottoman institutional experience of securing the borderlands of Thrace and Eastern Anatolia in the early twentieth century, on 26 June 1927, the Turkish government created the General Inspectorate for the Eastern provinces – an autonomous institution entrusted by the ministry of Interior with the mission of overseeing the economic, social and, in particular, security

---

[84] Hakan Özoğlu, 'Exaggerating and Exploiting the Shaykh Said Rebellion of 1925 for Political Gains' *New Perspectives on Turkey*, Vol. 41 (2009), pp. 181–210.

[85] CADN, Fonds Ankara, 104. French Embassy (Ankara) to the Ministry of Foreign Affairs (Paris). Ankara, 30 November 1927.

[86] See Mahmut Akyürekli, *Şark İstiklal Mahkemesi, 1925–7* (Istanbul: Tarih Kulübü Yayınları, 2013); Ergün Aybars, *İstiklal Mahkemleri, 1920–7* (Izmir: Eylül University, 1988).

developments of the predominantly Kurdish provinces.[87] Even though the new authorities had planned to establish this institution by 1922, the Shaykh Said rebellion gave a definitive push for its creation.[88]

Admittedly, violence and removal of populations in the Eastern European and Middle Eastern borderlands were widely decried by Western powers and their respective public opinions. Yet, prominent states within the League of Nations – notably, France and Britain – also saw the potential advantages of such policies. For one, the 'ordering' of land and populations within Turkey created income refugees and migrants that could be used in French-Syria and British-Iraq for their own interests in the region: legitimising their presence in the Arab provinces of the ex-Ottoman Empire by 'protecting' existing refugee populations, increasing the proportion of 'minority groups' – non-Arab and/or non-Muslim elements – in the mandatory territories to gain leverage against Arab nationalists, and using them to consolidate state presence in the border zones.

It was in the name of the principle of nationality that France first decided to separate Lebanon from Syria and transform it into a Christian-dominated nation-state.[89] It was in the name of the protection of local ethno-religious groups that France also divided Syria into distinct statelets – Aleppo and Damascus for the Sunni population, and distinct administrative units for the Shia Alawites and Druzes in the early 1920s.[90] Britain, however, promoted the creation of a de facto autonomous region in the Sulaimaniya area between 1919 and 1925, while playing off Sunni and Shia Arab Muslims against each other to avoid the formation of a transversal Iraqi movement against British rule.[91] Finally, it was for the sake of refugee protection that France and

---

[87] See Celim Koçak, *Umumî Müfettişlikler, 1927–52* (Istanbul: İletişim, 2010), p. 57 and 76; Ercan çağlayan, *Cumhuriyet'in Diyarbakır'da Kimlik İnşası* (Istanbul: İletişim, 2014).

[88] Abidin Özmen, 'Genel Müfettişlikler Hakkında Bir Düşünce', *Idâre Dergisi*, Vol. 184 (1947), pp. 237–8.

[89] Asher Kaufman, *Reviving Phoenicia: The Search for Identity in Lebanon* (London: I. B. Tauris, 2004).

[90] Philip Khoury, *Syria and the French Mandate: The Politics of Arab Nationalism, 1920–45* (Princeton, NJ: Princeton University Press, 1987), pp. 127–48.

[91] Toby Dodge, *Inventing Iraq: The Failure of Nation Building and a History Denied* (New York: Columbia University Press, 2003), pp. 43–100.

Britain helped shape identity boundaries throughout the mandate period by encouraging 'communal survival' among Armenians and Assyrians in Syria and Iraq, respectively.

Refugees, Relief and Colonialism: A Complex Relationship

Diverse historians have explored how interwar humanitarianism in the Middle East was guided by a combination of colonialist interests, prevailing cultural norms, moral economies and modern forms of humanitarianism.[92] In that regard, Keith D. Watenpaugh argues that the League of Nation's approach to Armenian refugees settled in Syria and Lebanon encapsulates the main characteristics of 'modern humanitarianism'; that is, evolving conceptions of human dignity and shared humanity 'subordinated to the demands of twentieth-century nationalism and the persistence of late colonialism'.[93] Following the failure of the project of establishing an Armenian state supported by the victors of the First World War, the League of Nations developed a special form of humanitarianism on behalf of the Armenians, which combined two complementary aims: asserting the national rights of the Armenians, on the one hand, and 'saving' the 'Armenian nation' from cultural assimilation through diverse collective and individual welfare instruments, i.e. refugee camps, education, employment, distribution of lands, on the other.

Yet, the interplay between humanitarianism, state- and boundary-making in the interwar Middle East has received less attention. Between 1915 and 1930, around 100,000 Armenians immigrated to Syria. As historians have observed, the settlement of most Ottoman Armenians in cities such as Aleppo, Damascus and Beirut in the early 1920s had an enormous impact upon the host country with an Arab majority; notably, an increasing competition for

---

[92] Davide Rodogno shows, however, that this was already the case in the nineteenth century, when European 'humanitarian interventions' in the Middle East held a putative humanitarian motivation on condition that they served their immediate interests. Davide Rodogno, *Against Massacre: Humanitarian Interventions in the Ottoman Empire, 1815–1914* (Princeton, NJ: Princeton University Press, 2011); See also Keith D. Watenpaugh. 'The League of Nations' Rescue of Armenian Genocide Survivor and the Making of Modern Humanitarianism, 1920–7', *American Historical Review*, Vol. 115, No. 5 (2010), pp. 1320–21.

[93] Keith D. Watenpaugh, *Bread from Stones*, p. 161.

limited jobs in these urban settings and the development of new neighbourhoods for the displaced.[94] Although numerically less important, the impact of incoming Armenian, Assyrian and Kurdish refugees located in the northern fringes of French Syria in the host country was equally significant when it comes to the evolution of frontier disputes, discourses over national identity and territoriality in the interwar period. Their role was, however, contingent on other factors, such as the weak presence of the state in the borderlands.

This was especially the case in the Upper Jazira where, despite the Ankara Accord of 1921, the Turkish government encouraged anti-French propaganda and cross-border raids to hinder the advance of French troops into the region well into the mid-1920s.[95] Ankara's activities strengthened indirectly the positions of various unions, opposition parties and anti-colonial committees in France that raised concerns about the financial viability of maintaining the mandatory rule in the Levant.[96] It is within this context, marked by both external and internal constraints, that the French High Commissioner saw the launching of a profitable economic programme in Syria as a tool which could serve to justify its 'civilising' mission in the Levant.[97] This vision was particularly significant for the Syrian Jazira, where the French hoped to settle nomadic tribes.[98] The agricultural development of the region as such would

---

[94] Vahé Tatchjian, 'Des camps de réfugiés aux quartiers urbains: processus et enjeux', in Reymond Kévorkian et al. (eds), *Les Arméniens, 1917–39: La quête d'un refuge* (Beirut: Presses de l'Université Saint-Joseph, 2006), pp. 112–45.

[95] Altuğ, Seda and Benjamin T. White, 'Frontière et pouvoir d'Etat: La frontière turco-syrienne dans les années 1920 et 1930', *Vingtième Siècle. Revue d'histoire*, Vol. 103 (2009), pp. 91–104.

[96] Paul Huvelin, *Que vaut la Syrie?* (Marseille: Chambre de Commerce de Marseille, 1919); Alice Poulleau, *À Damas sous les bombes: journal d'une Française pendant la révolution syrienne, 1924–6* (Yvetot: Imprimerie Bretteville, s.d.); Pierre Bonnardi, *L'Imbroglio syrien* (Paris: Rieder, 1927).

[97] Christian Velud, 'La politique mandataire française à l'égard des tribus et des zones de steppe en Syrie: L'exemple de la Djézireh', in Riccardo Bocco, Ronald Jaubert and Françoise Métral (eds), *Steppes d'Arabie. Etats, pasteurs, agriculteurs et commerçants: le devenir des zones sèches* (Paris: PUF, 1993), pp. 70–1.

[98] This was a developmentalist vision that existed for the Jazira since the late Ottoman times. See Samuel Dolbee, 'The Locust and the Starling: People, Insects, and Disease in the Late Ottoman Jazira and After, 1860–1940' (PhD dissertation, New York University, 2017), pp. 104–65.

not only serve the French imperial interests, but also help counter Ankara's manoeuvres to extend its influence into this region. Yet, it soon became clear to the French that the existing Kurdish and Arab nomadic communities were neither sufficiently large, nor very willing to transition to a settled life. The French High Commissioner's solution was to settle the incoming waves of Christian migrants and refugees from Turkey in the area, most notably the Armenians and Syriacs, and resettle there thousands of Armenian refugees who had until-then populated the refugee camps established around cities such as Beirut and Aleppo.[99] In legal terms, the distribution of land to these refugees meant turning uncultivated (*mawât*) plots of land, which belonged to no one, into cultivable ones (*miri*), the latter belonging to the state and thus susceptible to being awarded to new owners upon condition of exploiting the land for at least ten years.

By 1925, the French authorities decided to expand this policy and include Kurdish refugees who had been fleeing repression from the Turkish government after the collapse of the Shaykh Said rebellion, while keeping an eye on Turkish policies against the remnant Christian populations along Turkey's southern borderlands. Thus, between 1929 and 1930, as new measures were taken against Armenian villagers in the Diyarbakır region, 8,000–9,000 Armenian refugees were allowed to settle in the Upper Jazira with the assistance of the League of Nations, the Armenian General Benevolent Union, Armenian Unions and wealthy Armenians from the diaspora.[100] Taken as a whole, the settlement of these refugees was intended to serve two complementary goals: stabilising the frontier and increasing the agricultural production of the Upper Jazira. Finally, in order to protect refugees and their harvests, the French also granted significant plots of land to the main Bedouin shaykhs of the Jazira; if they did not want to cultivate themselves, they could hire Christian and Kurdish refugees to do so instead.

Unsurprisingly, French 'altruism' was severely criticised in Turkey. As the numbers of Kurdish tribal chiefs seeking refuge in both Syria and Iraq increased, so did the risk of forming dangerous pockets of different groups of

---

[99] Vahé Tatchijan, *La France en Cilicie et en Haute-Mésopotamie. Aux confins de la Turquie, de la Syrie et de l'Irak* (Paris: Karthala, 2004).

[100] CADN, 1SL/1/V/2544. Letter No. 375. Beirut, 22 December 1929.

Kurdish opponents along Turkey's southern borders. In such circumstances, the First General Inspectorate published on 23 May 1928 the terms of an amnesty addressed to Kurdish leaders who had participated in revolts against the republic. Although this amnesty officially applied to the Kurds living in Turkey, several tribal leaders and exiled intellectuals based in Syria and Iraq obtained permission to return to their homes. In that setting, Kurdish refugees became subject to a strong competition between Turkey and French-Syria. For the latter, Kurdish chiefs had become key actors in stabilising the Turkish–Syrian border as well as in encouraging the settlement of thousands of Kurdish peasants – a necessary condition for increasing the exploitation of Jazira's soil. French authorities reacted by granting salaries to some paramount leaders as well as encouraging Kurdish nationalist leaders based in the Levant to spread propaganda among Kurdish tribes against the Ankara proclamation.[101] Against this backdrop, the editor of *Milliyet* and deputy for Siirt, Mahmud Bey, accused the French administration in Syria of perverting every effort to prevent the Kurdish refugees from returning to Turkey.[102]

In the face of Turkish critiques for settling 'unwanted' populations along the Turkish–Syrian border, the French sometimes advanced humanitarian reasons, and at other times practical factors such as the proximity to their homelands and 'natural' environment: 'if some Armenians have settled in the Khabur Basin and around Qamishli, it is just because these locations were closer to Urfa and Mardin regions where they used to live'.[103] Without denying truly humanitarian motivations, foreign diplomats and observers also highlighted the potential benefits of providing aid to refugees. Thus, even though the French complained in official circles about the financial burden these refugees represented for the mandatory power, the American consul in Aleppo noted that '. . . the French may not be entirely averse to the settlement

---

[101] CADN, 1SL/1/V/549. Intelligence Services, Euphrates Region, 12 June 1928. On the ambiguous relationship between the Khoybun League and the French authorities in Syria, see Jordi Tejel, *Le mouvement kurde de Turquie en exil: Continuités et discontinuités du nationalisme kurde sous le mandat français en Syrie et au Liban, 1925–46* (Bern: Peter Lang, 2007).
[102] NARA, RG84, Box 415. Review of the Turkish Press for the period May 14–27, 1928, p. 5.
[103] CADN, 36/PO/1/139. French High Commissioner to the Ministry of Foreign Affairs. Beirut, 28 April 1933.

on wasteland in northern Syria of these Christians, and possibly pro-French population'.[104]

Refugees not only became agricultural settlers across the Upper Jazira, but also played a role as founders of new towns such as Hasaka (1922) (the administrative centre of the Sanjaq of Jazira), Amuda, Derbessia, Qamishli (1926), Ayn Diwar (1929) and Derik (1930), as well as drivers for economic development in already existing ones, such as Ras al-Ayn. The evolution of these urban centres was uneven, though.[105] While Qamishli soon became a lively centre of trade and agricultural production in the region, the other towns suffered from a combination of negative factors: a less favourable geographical location, British and Turkish endeavours in order to halt contraband networks connecting the Syrian Jazira with Turkey and Iraq, the effects of the 1929 global crisis on trade, and the decrease in the numbers of displaced refugees in Syria by the early 1930s.[106] Nevertheless, none of these towns was fully deserted by their inhabitants during the French Mandate.[107]

Finally, building upon their imperial experiences,[108] French and British mandatory powers recruited thousands of refugees into supplementary forces aimed at protecting the border zones where incidentally refugee and 'minority' populations constituted a majority.[109] In Iraq, for instance, while in 1919

---

[104] NARA, RG84, Reel 5. 'New Armenian Emigration from Turkey into Syria'. American Consulate General (Beirut) to the Secretary of State (Washington, DC). Beirut, 23 January 1930.

[105] See Christian Velud, 'L'émergence et l'organisation sociales des petites villes de Jézireh, en Syrie, sous le Mandat français', *URBAMA*, 16–17 (1986), pp. 85–103.

[106] SHAT, 7N 4173, Dossier 1. 'Situation des Minorités en Djézireh sous Mandat français: répercussions sur les minorités des pays voisins'. Special Services, 3 October 1933, pp. 1–2.

[107] According to French statistics, by 1938, the number of inhabitants in the Upper Jaziran towns was as follows: Hasaka (5,708), Ras al-Ayn (1,781), Derbessia (1,912), Amuda (3,540), Qamishli (18,490), Derik (1,730). SAULCHOIR, Haute Djézireh, D 45, Vol. 1. 'Rapport Général de reconnaissance foncière de la Djézireh (1939–40)', p. 12.

[108] James Onley, 'The Raj Reconsidered: British India's Informal Empire and Spheres of influence in Asia and Africa', *Asian Affairs*, Vol. 40, No. 1 (2009), pp. 44–62.

[109] During the military campaign in Cilicia, France already enlisted the aid of Armenians, Senegalese and Algerian troops. After the French withdrawal from south-eastern Anatolia, some of these former Armenian fighters were recruited again in Syria.

the Levies encompassed mainly local Arab and Kurdish elements, by the late 1920s, the Levies became entirely Assyrian.[110] During these years, the Assyrian Levies, while officially acting under British command in campaigns to crush uprisings led by unruly Kurdish chiefs such as Shaykh Mahmud of Sulaimaniya, also acted independently in clashes with the Turkish forces as well as local Kurdish tribes in the frontier zone.[111] Likewise, the French also created Christian battalions entrusted with the mission of monitoring both the border zone with Turkey and the Arab-Muslim rural areas to prevent any anti-French uprising.[112] The French thus opened the door of the 'Troupes Spéciales' to Armenian refugees, although, unlike the Assyrians in Iraq, the latter never constituted a majority within these units.[113]

Interestingly, Turkish views about Assyrian settlements in the border zone evolved over time, as new challenges and priorities emerged in the eyes of the Ankara government. By 1931, as the echoes of a new Kurdish uprising that erupted across the Agri-Dagh region still resonated through Eastern Anatolia and new flows of Armenian refugees settled in the border towns in the Syrian Jazira, the Turkish government urged the Iraqi Primer Minister Nuri Said to do what he could to prevent the Assyrians settled in Iraq near the Turkish frontier from emigrating to Syria. The reasons for such a shift in Turkish views were twofold. First, the Assyrian Levies could be used in Iraq to keep their Kurdish neighbours in check. Second, Turkey did not wish for Assyrians to increase the size of the non-Muslim minorities already established in Syria close to the Turkish frontier.[114]

Regardless of states' vested interests and priorities, refugee populations and leaders proved to be less accommodating than expected. Indeed, British

---

[110] Laura Robson, 'Peripheries of Belonging: Military Recruitment and the Making of a 'Minority' in Wartime Iraq', *First World War Studies*, Vol. 7, No. 1 (2016), pp. 23–42 (here p. 23). See also David Omissi, 'Britain, the Assyrians and the Iraq Levies, 1919–32', *The Journal of Imperial and Commonwealth History*, Vol. 17, No. 3 (1989), pp. 301–22.

[111] Solomon Solomon, *The Assyrian Levies* (Chicago: Atour, 2006), pp. 5–6.

[112] TNA, AIR 23/90. Mosul, 18 October 1926.

[113] N. E. Bou-Nacklie, 'Les Troupes Spéciales: Religious and Ethnic Recruitment, 1916–46', *International Journal of Middle East Studies*, Vol. 25, No. 4 (1993), pp. 645–60 (here p. 653).

[114] TNA, FO 371/16037. British Embassy (Ankara) to Foreign Office (London). Ankara, 4 January 1932.

and French attempts to create buffer zones along their shared borders with Turkey were both facilitated and frustrated by the agency of refugees and immigrants themselves, by way of testing the limits of colonial rule and taking the opportunities provided by both the mandatory framework and the indeterminacy of territorial boundaries.[115] In that regard, a view from the borderlands supports Keith D. Watenpaugh's call to change the basic terms of the conversation on imperialism and 'to unravel the ways different ethnic groups and social classes' – along with refugee and migrant communities I would add – 'interacted with colonialism in the interwar period in a manner that recovers the plurality to it' and contributes to exceed binary categories such as collaborator-resistant.[116]

Structurally, the presence of the colonial state and the increasing role assumed by the League of Nations in Iraqi and Syrian affairs 'offered many groups new models and opportunities of mobilization based on ethnic and religious identities either against or for the respective mandatory powers'.[117] In Iraq, in particular, the League of Nations played a key role in promoting the idea of communal identification as the most important criterion for reclaiming collective rights – religious, linguistic, self-determination – as well as for determining territorial belonging not only during the Mosul dispute (1923–25), but also through the activities of the boundary commissions which toured the area in 1925 and in 1932 for the delimitation of the Turkish-Iraqi and Syrian–Iraqi boundaries, respectively.

In that sense, the League, while acting as referee within the frontier commissions established for the fixing of the provisional northern and western borders of Iraq, 'contributed to strengthening (sic) the idea that there existed a direct relation between group specificity and territory'.[118] Obviously, ethnic

---

[115] Lauren Banko, 'Refugees, Displaced Migrants, and Territorialization in Interwar Palestine', *Mashriq & Mahjar*, Vol. 5, No. 2 (2018), pp. 19–48.

[116] Keith D. Watenpaugh, 'Towards a New Category of Colonial Theory: Colonial Cooperation and the Survivors' Bargain–The Case of the Post-genocide Armenian Community of Syria Ynder French Mandate', in Nadine Méouchy and Peter Sluglett (eds), *The British and French Mandates in Comparative Perspectives* (Leiden: Brill, 2004), pp. 597–622 (here p. 600).

[117] Nelida Fuccaro, 'Minorities and Ethnic Mobilization: The Kurds in Northern Iraq and Syria', in Nadine Méouchy and Peter Sluglett (eds), *The British and French Mandates in Comparative Perspectives*, pp. 579–95.

[118] Nelida Fuccaro, *The Other Kurds*, p. 151.

and religious solidarities and networks existed prior to the League's interventions in the borderlands. In some cases, nationalist committees – Kurdish, Armenian, Assyrian – lobbied for full independence at the Peace Conference of 1919 before the creation of the League of Nations and the emergence of the ensuing minority and refugee regimes. During what Erez Manela calls the 'Wilsonian moment' (1919–20), nationalist and anti-colonial movements accepted the affirmation of the nation state as the normative unit of global politics.[119] Henceforth, former Ottoman subjects had to 'talk the same language' as the founders of the new international system made up of nation states by resorting to the use of historical arguments as well as topographical maps backing their 'national' claims.

Yet, the boundary delimitation procedure, along with the minority treaties and the uncertainties created by the upcoming termination of the mandates, combined to awaken and even extend ethno-religious solidarities to portions of the border populations that had until then remained alien to ethno-religious mobilisation. Kurds, Christians and Yazidis – from the Upper Jazira to the Iraq–Iran border and the Jabal Sinjar – asked for special rights and opposed administrative centralisation. Like the Peace Conference of 1919, the League of Nations, along with the Permanent Mandates Commission, created a favourable framework for local populations to send petitions to Geneva adopting the League founders' language on 'nationality', 'self-determination' and 'minority rights'.[120]

This was also the case with refugees. Tapping into the League's and mandatory powers' discourse on refugees – the latter being depicted at times as victims, at others as a resource for economic development – refugees' representatives and individuals also harboured ambivalent discourses on their condition. Thus, for example, while Armenian relief organisations and individuals asked the League to help the 'dispossessed', in other instances, Armenian committees exploited French economic plans in the Syrian Jazira by requesting the mandatory authorities to establish refugee newcomers in 'vacant places along the coast of the Khabur and Euphrates Rivers, which

---

[119] Erez Manela, *The Wilsonian Moment: Self-Determination and the International Origins of Anticolonial Nationalism* (Oxford: Oxford University Press, 2007).

[120] Susan Pedersen, *The Guardians: The League of Nations and the Crisis of Empire* (Oxford: Oxford University Press, 2015).

places were considered as the most fertile regions of the world during Roman supremacy in the past'.[121] Hand in hand with the French, Armenian refugees would contribute to the *mise en valeur* (economic development) of areas where local dwellers, notably, Arab Bedouins, had failed to do so for many centuries.[122] By the mid-1930s, former refugees could take pride in highlighting their accomplishments in the region, as opposed to the recent past where the Jazira was just a 'desert' left to 'Bedouin raids' and 'brigands'.[123] Such petitions and discourse in a remarkably racist and 'civilising' tone were not simply the result of refugees' views about host societies, but rather the outcome of an already existing structure. In other words, refugees' claims and strategies in Syria and Iraq were 'shaped by the social, cultural and administrative context, within which' they emerged.[124] Consequently, it is essential for historians to pay attention to these different contexts to better understand the ways in which refugees framed their claims.

The relationship established between the Assyrian tribes and the British authorities in Iraq is a case in point. The construction of an Assyrian identity based on nationality rather than religion was largely the result of the nineteenth century encounters between British and American Protestant missions as well as Western archaeologists, on the one hand, and some Assyrian religious and lay representatives, on the other.[125] Like other indigenous Christian communities in the Middle East, the Assyrians became the object of romanticised visions about the 'original' Christians who had allegedly kept their

---

[121] 'Armenian Immigrants from Turkey: Relief and Settling of Armenians in Syria', *Aztag*, 21 January 1930. Translated from Armenian. NARA, RG84, Reel 5. American Consulate General (Beirut) to the Secretary of State (Washington, DC). Beirut, 23 January 1930.

[122] See Simon Jackson, 'What is Syria Worth? The Huvelin Mission, Economic Expertise and the French Project in the Eastern Mediterranean, 1918–22', *Monde(s)*, No. 4 (2013), pp. 83–103.

[123] CHEAM, No. 212.078, Anonymous, 'La vérité sur les événements de la Djézireh', 1936, pp. 10–11.

[124] Peter Gatrell et al. 'Reckoning with Refugeedom: Refugee Voices in Modern History', *Social History*, Vol. 46, No. 1 (2021), pp. 70–95 (here p. 78).

[125] Shawn Malley, 'Layard Enterprise: Victorian Archaeology and Informal Imperialism in Mesopotamia', *International Journal of Middle East Studies*, Vol. 40, No. 4 (2008), pp. 623–46.

traditions almost 'untouched' throughout and by history. Crucially, archaeological findings such as the ruins of Nineveh and Babylon provided the 'Assyrian nation' with 'scientific' arguments to 'prove' their affiliation with the pre-Islamic Assyrian golden age.[126] When the Ottoman Empire attempted to increase its control over the Hakkari region in the late nineteenth century, local Assyrian leaders 'saw their association with Western missionaries and archaeologists as potentially beneficial and began to adopt a mission-derived language of national independence for their own purposes'.[127]

Within the context of the First World War, British officials assessed the possibility of establishing a military alliance with this 'Christian nation' against the Ottomans. As a matter of fact, diverse Assyrian tribes hailing from the Hakkari region engaged in a military campaign against the Ottoman army in the final stages of the war. Being obliged to withdraw toward Western Persia, about 40,000 Assyrians and Armenians arrived for settlement at the Baqubah refugee camp between 1919 and 1920. While the Mar Shimun – a paramount religious family – had been traditionally influent within the community, following the sudden death of the Patriarch Mar Shimun Palos in May 1920, the religious leadership became increasingly challenged by the commanding officer of the Assyrian forces, General Agha Petros, who fought with the British army during the First World War. Upon his arrival in Iraq, Agha Petros succeeded in gaining both tribal and British support, thanks to his key role in the recruitment of thousands of Assyrians previously hosted in the Baqubah camp in the Levies, thereby claiming to represent the interests of the Assyrian nation.[128]

In the meantime, however, ideas of Christian self-determination that had been promoted by the Assyrian National Council during the Peace Conference in Paris, led mainly by individuals from the diaspora, were updated by local Assyrian representatives in the mid-1920s.[129] The latter hoped to obtain British

---

[126] John Joseph, *The Modern Assyrians of the Middle East: Encounters with Christian Missions, Archeologists, and Colonial Powers* (Leiden: Brill, 2000).

[127] Laura Robson, *States of Separation: Transfer, Partition, and the Making of the Modern Middle East* (Oakland, CA: University of California Press, 2017), p. 39.

[128] Nelida Fuccaro, *The Other Kurds*, p. 152.

[129] See the Assyrian memorandum sent to the British delegation in 1919. FO 608/82/17144.

support for the Assyrian autonomy scheme for two main reasons. First, Assyrians considered British support for an 'Assyrian homeland' as a due on the basis of their alliance with Great Britain in the First World War and their role in monitoring Iraq's northern borders and its populations since 1922. Secondly, they were aware of the activities of a pro-Assyrian lobby in England, in particular those of the Archbishop of Canterbury and other Anglican clerics.[130] Subsequently, several Assyrian leaders petitioned the British High Commissioner on 14 February 1926 to either obtain lands in Iraq where Assyrian would be autonomous, or transfer them to any of the British Colonies.[131] Although these initiatives remained unsuccessful, by the end of the Mandate, and fearing the consequences of Britain's withdrawal from the country, some Assyrian lay leaders shifted their strategy and started promoting the idea of an enlarged Christian nation which included all the non-Muslim 'minorities' in northern Iraq: Christians (Nestorians and Chaldeans), the Yazidis and the Jews.[132]

When the Assyrian leaders learned that the draft version of the British-Iraqi treaty of alliance, which was concluded in 1930 in preparation for the termination of the mandate regime in Iraq in October 1932, did not contain clauses for minority protection, pro-Assyrian lobbies in England and Iraq sent petitions to the League of Nations[133]. As a result, in May 1932, the Iraqi government was constrained to give a declaration of guarantees before the Council of the League of Nations.[134] Despite this gesture of good will, Patriarch Mar Shimun sent new petitions to Geneva in which he stated that it was impossible for his community to live in Iraq without British protection

---

[130] The Patriarch Mar Shimun had been educated under the protection of the Archbishop of Canterbury.

[131] See some comprehensive passages in Müller-Sommerfeld, pp. 273–4.

[132] Nelida Fuccaro, *The Other Kurds*, p. 154.

[133] Hormuzd Rassam, who had been Agha Petros' supporter in the early 1920s, and Matthew Cope, a British citizen who arrived in Iraq at the beginning of 1930 for a commercial venture, established in July 1930 the Iraq Minorities (non-Muslim) Rescue Committee, which was based in London, with the main purpose of raising funds for the relief of the Assyrians in northern Iraq. This Committee was particularly vocal in requesting protection for Assyrians in Iraq. Nelida Fuccaro, *The Other Kurds*, p. 164.

[134] LON, A.17.1932.VII, Official Journal, July 1932, pp. 1347–50.

and asked for resettlement of Assyrian Christians outside Iraq. In addition, the Assyrian Levies started a mutiny and announced that the termination of their military service for Great Britain would begin on 1 July 1932. The British Mandate ended without meeting any of these demands. It is within this context that, as we have seen, some ex-Levies fighters started looking towards Syria as a potential location for their resettlement and protection under the aegis of the League of Nation treaties.

Muslim refugee leaders had an advantageous position compared to Armenians and Assyrians, as they could negotiate their 'loyalty' to the three neighbouring states with a Muslim majority. This was the case of Hajo Agha of the Heverkan, a tribal confederation comprised of Muslim Kurds, Christians and Yazidis, whose influence stretched between Mardin, Tur Abdin (Turkey) and Jabal Sinjar (Iraq). Alien to the anti-Christian massacres during the First World War, Hajo Agha was nevertheless pressed to assist the Ankara government in keeping the French troops away from the Nusaybin-Jazirat ibn Umar area. In exchange for his cooperation, the Kurdish chieftain received weapons and ammunitions.[135] In June 1923, Hajo and his tribesmen attacked a French regiment at Behandur, inflicting important casualties among the latter and bringing French advance in the 'Duck's Bill' area to a standstill for two years.

While Hajo continued his correspondence with the Turkish authorities after this episode, he also met with the Yazidi leaders from Jabal Sinjar to organise an uprising against the Ankara government. The revolt in Tur Abdin started in March 1926, and lasted only ten days. Once it became evident that he had to either surrender or settle abroad, Hajo first contacted the British authorities in Iraq. As the latter refused Hajo's terms of submission, he then turned to the French authorities in Syria. Despite his key role in the Behandur events three years earlier, the French pardoned him. In exchange for weapons, protection and a number of villages, Hajo and his 400 tribesmen cooperated with the French by warding off attempts by Turkish forces to penetrate the eastern fringes of Turkish–Syrian frontier.[136]

---

[135] CADN, Fonds Ankara, Ambassade 104. Le général Billote, Représentat du Haut Commissaire à Alep à Damas. Aleppo, 21 September 1926.
[136] CADN, 1SL/1/V/549. Report of Lieutenant Terrier. Qamishli, 11 August 1926.

Involved in local affairs, he also participated in the establishment of the Khoybun League in 1927 – a Kurdish nationalist committee – wherein he played a relevant role in spreading the nationalist message among Kurdish tribes, not only in the Syrian Jazira,[137] but also in the Jabal Sinjar.[138] More important, perhaps, is the fact that between 1936 and 1938, Hajo became one of the leaders of the Jazira autonomist movement, along with diverse Christian notables of Hasaka and Qamishli. The main demands of the autonomist movement can be summarised as follows: a special status with guarantees from the League of Nations comparable to that of the Alawites and the Druzes; the support of French troops to guarantee their security; and the nomination of a French governor under the control of the League of Nations. In exchange for this special status, Jazira's dwellers would agree 'to be Syrian citizens', to contribute to the development of the country and to defend 'Syria's frontiers with all their might'.[139]

Like Assyrians in Iraq, the autonomist leaders also received external support, notably from the French Services Spéciaux (SS). Indeed, the announcement of a Franco-Syrian Treaty in 1936 and the clauses that it contained – i.e. termination of the mandate – constituted a threat to their autonomy of action in the margins of the Syrian territory. Against this backdrop, some officers attempted to prevent, or at least delay, the ratification by the French Parliament of the Franco-Syrian Treaty of 1936.[140] Consequently, they encouraged the regionalist movement in Jazira to send petitions to the French High Commission and the League of Nations. Although the Christian-Kurdish alliance collapsed by 1938, Hajo maintained his privileged position until he passed, thanks to his unabated cooperation with the mandatory power.[141]

---

[137] The Khoybun League was created in October 1927 in Lebanon. The committee brought together representatives from several Kurdish organisations as well as tribal chiefs around these goals: to fight the Turks in order to create a Kurdish entity; to collaborate with the Armenians; to have friendly relations with the USSR, Persia and Iraq; and to seek support from a Western power. CADN, 1SL/1/V/1055. Intelligence Report. Aleppo, 19 November 1927.

[138] Nelida Fuccaro, *The Other Kurds*, pp. 127–30.

[139] SAULCHOIR, Haute-Djézireh, D-45, Vol. II, 'Le Manifeste de la Djézireh'. April 1938, p. 3.

[140] CADN, 1SL/1/V/505. Note No. 918, Cabinet Politique. Damascus, 13 June 1939.

[141] Hajo received subsidies from the mandatory power until he passed in 1940. CADN, Fonds Beyrouth, BD 237. 'Dossier concernant le relèvement de la subvention d'Hajo Agha'. Damascus, 22 January 1940.

Costs of Refugees' Agency

While aligning their voices with mandatory powers' visions and policies allowed some refugee individuals and groups to upgrade their status in Syria and Iraq, refugee communities as a whole became more exposed, too. In this light, while analysing the French policy of divide and rule with regard to the Armenians and other communities in Syria, the American Consulate in Beirut predicted the dramatic events that were to unfold throughout the 1930s in the region:

> Playing off one against the other is a dangerous method which may eventually prove to be a weapon sharpened against themselves. Their policy towards the Armenians . . . tends to increase Muslim suspicion, as well as to intensify their hatred of the Armenian people.[142]

Admittedly, refugees and minority groups came to be seen as 'colonial collaborators', thereby becoming the objects of different strategies that took, nevertheless, a highly sectarian form. First, national authorities and newspapers promoted an aggressive discourse against minorities and, more particularly, against individuals and groups that had been hosted as 'refugees'. Second, Syrian and Iraqi officials considered the removal of the refugee communities from the border zones and even resorted to mass violence as a means of deterring minority and refugee groups from challenging their respective nation-building projects.

Although some Assyrian groups sided with the Iraqi government in a clear move towards full integration, the Mar Shimun initiatives for territorial autonomy in Iraq along with the transformation of the Levies into fully Assyrian troops fostered sectarian divisions and hatred.[143] In that regard, as the termination of the British Mandate approached, the Iraqi representative at the League of Nations Nuri al-Said used precisely this issue as an argument to reject Assyrian aspirations for local autonomy:

> The Rapporteur to the Mandates Commission himself points out that the adoption of such a solution [Assyrian autonomy in northern Iraq] would

---

[142] NARA, RG84, Reel 5. 'Armenian Settlement in Syria', American Consulate General. Beirut, 26 February 1931.

[143] Laura Robson, 'Peripheries of belonging', p. 32.

imperil the unity of the Iraqi state, and could not but perpetuate the antipathy with which Assyrians believe themselves to be viewed by the other elements of the nation in the midst of which they are destined to live.[144]

Unsurprisingly, right after the termination of the mandate, Iraqi army units were sent to the northern borderlands of Iraw to proceed with the disarmament of the ex-Levies battalions. Against this background, some of the ex-Levies crossed the Syrian border seeking (unsuccessfully) French protection. Although the Assyrian fighters were defeated upon their return to Iraq, the former were accused of having mutilated the bodies of some Iraqi soldiers.[145] Subsequently, the Iraqi army, together with Kurdish and Bedouin irregulars, opened fire on Assyrian civilians in the small town of Simele and surrounding villages in the Dohuk district, even though local dwellers had not been associated with the earlier developments. Newspapers in Baghdad reported that the Iraqi army in its first important intervention following Iraq's independence had crushed an Assyrian separatist revolt in the borderlands adjacent to Syria and Turkey. Significantly, when general Bakr Sidqi, who had guided the military operations against the Assyrians, returned to Baghdad there were celebratory parades held in his honour.[146]

Both in Baghdad and Geneva, the conclusion that domestic stability and nation-building projects could only be accomplished through ethnic homogenisation and forced or voluntary emigration came to the surface, again. Some weeks after the massacres, the League of Nations established a special committee to propose different scenarios of an 'unavoidable' transfer of the remaining ex-Assyrian refugees towards a third country,[147] while evaluating the 'financial burden' of such a transfer and how it was to be shared.[148]

---

[144] 'Questions of Assyrians', *Iraq Herald*, 17 December 1932.

[145] Sami Zubaida, 'Contested Nations: Iraq and the Assyrians', *Nations and Nationalism*, Vol. 6, No. 3 (2000), p. 368.

[146] Keith D. Watenpaugh, *Bread from Stones*, p. 195.

[147] Greece, Australia, Brazil, British Guiana, French West Africa and South Africa were some of the potential host countries that were suggested in the negotiations to receive the incoming Assyrian refugees. LON, C.1530 20A/80619/18766. 'Settlement of the Assyrians of Iraq'. Geneva, 24 October 1933.

[148] TNA, FO 371/17834. Committee for the Settlement of the Assyrians. Note by the Secretary-General. Geneva, 18 January 1934.

When the League of Nations, the Iraqi central government and France eventually reached an agreement in 1937 according to which most of the Assyrians were allowed to resettle on the Khabur River, the latter had already created a de facto colony in the Upper Jazira with French consent.[149]

Interestingly, anti-refugee discourses in Iraq and Syria had an unexpected effect; namely, they became the drivers of state formation that conceived new territorialities. In that regard, Benjamin T. White has aptly shown the ways in which the arrival of Armenian and Kurdish refugees in the French Mandate of Syria triggered nation-wide debates by raising the stakes of the necessity to define Syria in terms of both its geography and national identity.[150] For one, while the citizenship and voting rights granted to Armenians by the French mandatory power in the 1920s had already raised concerns among Arab nationalist committees about refugees' 'privileges', the demands for autonomy in the Upper Jazira advanced by Kurdish and Christian local notables in the mid-1930s pointed to another key issue: the relationship between identity and territoriality. Thus, in reaction to such demands, nationalists in Damascus responded by affirming the importance of this region for the Arab nation: 'The Jazira was the cradle of Arabness'. Consequently, the Arabs were ready to fight to protect 'an essential part' of their 'fatherland' in the face of senseless demands based on the existence of a handful of 'Kurdish villages in the north of the Jazira'.[151]

In the same vein, Seda Altuğ has exposed how the arrival of additional numbers of Kurdish, Armenian and Assyrian refugees between 1929 and 1933 in the Upper Jazira caused extreme alarm and anxiety among Arab nationalist circles in the Syrian capital; an unease 'expressed in a new framework: harmful strangers versus outraged Syrians'.[152] Slowly, the Syrian nation and its sacred

---

[149] Between 1933 and 1935, hundreds of Assyrians crossed the border illegally to establish themselves in the Syrian Upper Jazira.

[150] Benjamin T. White, 'Refugees and the Definition of Syria, 1920–39', *Past & Present*, Vol. 235, No. 1 (2017), pp. 141–78.

[151] Cited in Benjamin T. White, *The Emergence of Minorities in the Middle East: The Politics of Community in French Mandate Syria* (Edinburgh: Edinburgh University Press, 2011), p. 119.

[152] Seda Altuğ, 'Syrian-Armenian Memory and the Refugee Issue in Syria under the French Mandate, 1921–46', *The Armenian Weekly*, 2012, https://armenianweekly.com/2012/07/05/syrian-armenian-memory-and-the-refugee-issue-in-syria-under-the-french-mandate-1921-46 (last accessed 1 March 2022).

territory materialised in the Arab nationalist discourse as an organic body that was being 'violated' by constant waves of 'infiltrators'.[153] As the Jazira autonomist movement proved to be more active between 1936 and 1938, the tone of Arab newspapers' articles became even more aggressive against the 'refugees'. While 'loyal' Jazira dwellers were depicted as 'locals' and the true 'owners' of the country,[154] autonomist leaders and their followers were labelled as thankless 'refugees' who, in addition, sought to steal the lands of the Arab nation.[155]

While building upon this scholarship, Victoria Abrahamyan demonstrates that the discourse about the 'otherness' of Armenian refugees was not only the result of a top-down process; rather, it was the outcome of a complex, dynamic and interactive process in which diverse nationalist committees, diaspora organisations and the French mandatory authorities became involved throughout the mandate. Crucially, Armenian political parties, churches and related media outlets harboured different discourses about how Armenianness could accommodate to the emerging Syrian national identity, ranging from full integration into the Syrian fabric, to separateness in order to avoid assimilation; from pledging their loyalty to the new Syrian state, to highlighting their debt towards France – their main protector.[156] Either way, however, most Armenian voices pledged their right to stay in Syria for, much like the Arabs in northern Syria, they were ex-Ottoman citizens who had inhabited the former Aleppo Vilayet for centuries. In other words, Armenians were not strangers to the Syrian land.[157]

By the same token, in the face of Arab nationalist attacks against the 'refugees' and 'foreigners' that founded the Jazira autonomist movement in the mid-1930s, its leaders responded by reaffirming their 'rights' over Jazira's lands and their identity specificities. In short, they didn't consider themselves 'refugees'; rather, they were the true creators of modern Jazira.[158] It was thanks to their arrival, hard work and French protection that the Upper Jazira

[153] 'Suriyya allatti la Hurmata Laha', *al-Shaab*, 13 November 1935.
[154] 'Iskân al-arman fi Suriyya', *al-Shaab*, 21 June 1928.
[155] 'Wataniyya al-Fikra wa Masaria al-Sahra', *al-Qabas*, 5 February 1938.
[156] Victoria Abrahamyan, 'Citizen Strangers: Identity labelling and Discourse in the French Mandatory Syria, 1920–32', *Journal of Migration History*, Vol. 6, No. 1 (2020), pp. 40–61.
[157] *Yeprat*, 23 April 1928. Cited in Victoria Abrahamyan, 'Citizen Strangers', p. 50.
[158] 'La Voix de la Djézireh', *Le Courrier de Syrie*, 21 April 1936.

had been transformed from a desert-like territory into a fertile land: 'They believed that they had consequently the right to self-rule'.[159]

Obviously, arguments and counterarguments exposed by both Arab nationalists and autonomists in Syria were not alien to the broader context of the interwar Middle East. On the one hand, the reaction of Syrian nationalists against Armenian refugees and the Jazira autonomist movement was partly determined by fears of the Syrian elites sensing the formation of a settler entity similar to the Yishuv in British Palestine, on their land. The 'Zionist' reference as a potential threat for the young Arab states awoke suspicions with regard to the 'autochthone' minority groups, too. Thus, for instance, in one of the rare travelogues written in Arabic on 'Southern Kurdistan' (Northern Iraq) in the early 1930s, Ali Saydu Gurani, secretary to the Jordanian Legislative Council, explains that, while resting in a café in Mosul, he heard a discussion between some local merchants in which they compared the Kurds of Iraq with the Zionist settlers in Palestine.[160] Evidently, the comparison of the Kurdish movement in Iraq with the Zionist one was not on its settler dimension, but rather the fact that Kurdish demands for local autonomy could ultimately open the door to the 'loss' of what Arab elites and 'ordinary' people considered as a portion of the Iraqi (Arab) land.[161]

On the other hand, the autonomist demands in the Jazira were also the product of the anxieties of non-Muslim and non-Arab populations who feared that the emergence of an independent Arab nation state would open the door to aggressive policies towards Syrian minority groups, as had happened in Turkey and Iraq. The 1933 massacres of Assyrians in Iraq, in particular, only confirmed the anxieties of these communities.[162] This scenario could not have

---

[159] Vahé Tatchjian, *La France en Cilicie et en Haute-Mésopotamie*, pp. 424–5.
[160] Ali Saydu Gurani, *Min Amman Ila al-Imadiyya Aw Jawla fi Kurdistan al-Janubiyya* (Cairo: al-Sa'adaa, 1939), p. 146. I thank César Jaquier for drawing my attention to this travelogue.
[161] After the main terms of the Anglo-Iraqi Treaty were published on 1 July 1930, local notables from Sulaimaniya submitted a number of petitions to the League of Nations demanding the formation of a Kurdish autonomous region in northern Iraq under the supervision of the League. Jordi Tejel, 'Urban Mobilization in Iraqi Kurdistan during the British Mandate: Sulaimaniya, 1918–30', *Middle Eastern Studies*, Vol. 44, No. 4 (2008), pp. 542–3.
[162] CADN, 1SL/1/V/494. Délégué Général du Haut-Commissaire au Ministre des Affaires Etrangères. Beirut, 24 April 1936, pp. 4–5.

been completely excluded. On 18 November 1931, upon his return from a tour across diverse Syrian regions among which the Jazira, Muhammad Kurd Ali, Minister of Education, elaborated a memorandum addressed to the Syrian government where the removal of the Kurdish populations from north-eastern Syria – locals and refugees – came under consideration:

> In my opinion, they [the Kurds] need to settle far from the borders of Kurdistan, otherwise it will sooner or later become a political problem, which could lead to the separation of the Jazira from Syria's body . . . it will suffice to claim their rights and nationalism as it can be said with regard the Turks in Alexandretta, who have created problems for the Syrians.[163]

In the face of such prospects, Kurd Ali suggested granting lands to the Kurds and Armenians in the provinces of Aleppo and Homs, where one could hope that they would be assimilated into the local Arab culture.

Abroad, refugees were also the targets of diplomatic and public pressure. Turkey, in particular, observed with anxiety the formation of enclaves constituted by undesirable elements along its southern border. Hajo Agha, for instance, became the focus of frequent Turkish complaints to the Frontier Commission established in 1926 and Turkish newspapers. On 6 November 1928, for instance, *Milliyet* carried an article attacking the French authorities in Syria who were accused not only of extending protection to Agha Hajo, but also of turning over to him the 'administration' of a portion of the frontier. In that sense, the newspaper sarcastically underlined that 'this is the first time that diplomatic annals record the case of a bandit entrusted with such a mission'.[164] A few days later, an editorial in *Cumhuriyet* regretted that, in the light of such policies, Turkey was 'bound to consider France not only as danger to the peace of the world, but as an avowed enemy of Turkey'.[165]

Even more worrisome was Hajo's involvement in the Khoybun League, which had collaborated with the Armenian Dashnak Party.[166] Subsequently,

---

[163] Muhammad Kurd Ali, *Al-Mudhakkirat*, Vol. II (Riyadh: Adwa al-Salaf, 2010), p. 440.
[164] NARA, RG84, Box 415. Review of Turkish Press for the period November 1–14, 1928, p. 31.
[165] NARA, RG84, Box 415. Review of Turkish Press for the period November 15–28, 1928, p. 22.
[166] See BCA.030.10.113.771.1; BCA.030.10.113.771.2; BCA.030.10.113.771.3; BCA.030.10.113.771.4; BCA.030.10.113.771.7; BCA.030.10.113.771.9.

the Turkish delegation at the bilateral Frontier Commission denounced the presence of Kurdish and Armenian cells along the border on regular basis.[167] At first, the French did not undertake any drastic measures against the two committees. However, after the failure of a Khoybun leaders' armed operation in July 1930, the Mandate authorities took a more negative stance towards both organisations.[168] French authorities hence expelled some Khoybun members from the border zone and imposed house arrests to others. Likewise, although the Dashnak Party did not participate in this military intervention, some Dashnak members were resettled in other cities, and others, who happened to be abroad, were not allowed to return to Syria.[169]

Seemingly, the settlement of Kurdish and Assyrian refugees in Iraq became a permanent bone of contention during the meetings of the Turkish-Iraqi Frontier Commission.[170] Although Assyrian settlers in the Zakho and Amadiya districts were not enrolled in the Levies working for the British, the former were accused not only of frontier infringements, raids and crimes committed against Turkish troops and subjects, but also of attacking the material symbols of Turkish state power and sovereignty: the boundary pillars.[171]

Such allegations need to be analysed within a broader context. Worried about refugee communities escaping from its control and, perhaps more importantly, their potential collaboration with France and Britain, Turkey resorted to all diplomatic means and kinds of arguments to ensure a say on Syrian and Iraqi affairs. As Seda Altuğ puts it, the Turkish state 'creatively exploited the

---

[167] BCA.030.10.230.549.4, 24 May 1931.

[168] In 1930, as the Turkish army surrounded the Kurdish rebels in Mount Ararat, the Khoybun leadership in Syria organised a raid in Turkey to divert Turkish attention from the Ararat area. However, the lack of support among the Kurdish populations in Turkey led the raiders to return to Syria immediately. CADN, 1SL/1/V/1055. Sûreté Générale. Beirut, 9 August 1930.

[169] TNA, AIR 23/243. Mosul, 9 September 1930; MAE, Quai d'Orsay, Série Levant 1918–40, sous-série Syrie-Liban, 466. Report by Lieutenant Mortier (Intelligence Services). Beirut, 23 August 1930.

[170] TNA, AIR 23/374. 8th Meeting of the Permanent Frontier Commission, held at Mardin on 6 July 1930.

[171] TNA, AIR 23/374. 2nd Session. 7th Meeting of the Permanent Frontier Commission, held at Mosul on 18 October 1929; TNA, AIR 23/374. 4th Session. 8th Meeting of the Permanent Frontier Commission, held at Mardin on 20 June 1930.

cross-border reality to solidify its own claim to rule, both domestically and cross-border wise'. In addition, the constant exposure of the threats coming from Turkey's southern borders both in the Turkish media outlets and parliamentary debates had an inner function: the 'southern border' (*cenup hududu*) term was 'a necessary metaphor and a space for the symbolic dominance of the Turkish state in the society'.[172] Because Turkey's southern borders were threatened by a coalition of imperialist powers and 'undesirable' populations, the Turkish state was 'obliged' to transform these borders into a fortress, as well as to claim full sovereignty over Turkey's territory and its population.

Building upon the long nineteenth-century tradition of humanitarian intervention, the post-First World War practices and discourses of humanitarianism still shared the same civilisational hierarchies, drawing to the Middle East a range of non-state actors and organisations with humanitarian agendas driven by a quasi-colonial mindset.[173] As humanitarian conduct continued to comprise part of the ideological underpinning that legitimised, if not facilitated, the mandatory rule in the Middle East, the British and French policies of ethno-religious division targeted the region's refugee communities, such as Armenians, Jews and Assyrians, as a way of consolidating their own colonial authority.[174] Indeed, refugees and migrants in Syria and Iraq contributed to the ordering of borderlands as well as to the co-production of new territories, in particular, by populating new settlements in the border zones and protecting them from foreign intervention. In that regard, as British historian Peter Gatrell points out, 'while refugees are the product of state-led practices, they also help to constitute the modern nation-state'.[175]

Yet, as this chapter has shown, the effects of 'colonial humanitarianism' in Syria and Iraq were severely felt throughout the 1920s and 1930s, as Kurdish, Armenian and Assyrian refugees who settled in Syria and Iraq became the target

---

[172] Seda Altuğ, 'The Turkish–Syrian Border and Politics of Difference in Turkey and Syria, 1921–39' in Matthieu Cimino (ed.), *Syria: Borders, Boundaries, and the State* (London: Palgrave, 2020), p. 57.

[173] Davide Rodogno, 'Non-State Actors' Humanitarian Operations in the Aftermath of the First World War: The Case of the Near East Relief', in Fabian Klose (ed.), *The Emergence of Humanitarian Intervention: Ideas and Practice from the Nineteenth Century to the Present* (Cambridge: Cambridge University Press, 2015), pp. 185–207.

[174] Laura Robson, *States of Separation*, pp. 7–34.

[175] Peter Gatrell, *The Making of the Modern Refugee* (Oxford: Oxford University Press, 2013), p. x.

of frequent complaints by Turkish, Syrian and Iraqi nationalist elites – the latter accusing the former of working for foreign interests and threatening the security of the nation's borders. Crucially, the drawing of new boundaries had long-term consequences for these refugee groups. Indeed, 'undesirable' communities hailing from the borderlands were divided by the new political boundaries and thus became 'minorities', for they did not belong to the ruling elite's core group in those states. Nonetheless, this chapter has provided some necessary nuances about the relationship between international boundary-making processes, on the one hand, and the ordering and othering policies implemented in the interwar years by Turkey, Syria and Iraq, on the other.

First, the formal recognition of 'minority rights' for such groups varied according to their identity and the state's interests over time. Thus, while Christian groups were granted some religious rights in Turkey, Syria and Iraq, Muslim Kurds were not recognised as 'minorities' either in Turkey or in Syria – the latter being nevertheless granted limited 'cultural' rights in Iraq.[176] Likewise, the consequences of settling in a neighbouring country also differed depending on the trespassers' identity. Whereas Armenians and Assyrians were granted the refugee status in Syria and Iraq as per the League of Nations' refugee regime, Muslim and Yazidi Kurds were not – the latter being considered as migrants from an international legal viewpoint. Even so, informal arrangements implemented by colonial officials could nevertheless pair the former with the latter – Muslim and Yazidi Kurds, therefore, received lands and protection in many instances, both in Syria and Iraq. On the other hand, Muslims Kurds who had settled in Northern Syria and Iraq throughout the 1920s were allowed to return to Turkey under certain conditions, whereas Armenians and Assyrians became 'undesirable', risking legal action against them should they be captured on Turkish territory.

Second, we should be careful not to amalgamate all Middle Eastern states. Turkey, as an independent state, looked at her borders mainly as would-be walls meant to protect the country from her neighbours' conspiracies. For France and Britain, meanwhile, Syrian and Iraqi borders delimited zones of influence within larger imperial frameworks running from northern Africa to

---

[176] The protection of racial, religious and linguistic minorities was implemented in Iraq with the legal system under constitutional law in 1925, and again confirmed by the Iraqi Declaration of Guarantees to the Council of the League of Nations from May 1932.

India. Likewise, not only did Middle Eastern borders not develop synchronously, but also the material and discursive dimensions of borders were not similar.[177] Thus, while British mandatory authorities erected physical barriers such as barbed wire fences and watchtowers along Palestine's boundaries to better monitor cross-border mobility, 'crossing' the border between Turkey and Syria or between Syria and Iraq was hardly a difficult act. These borders were not physical barriers so much as symbolic and jurisdictional ones.[178] In other words, 'territorialisation in the interwar Middle East occurred on multiple levels, including state prohibition of, or permission for, certain activities at and across borders, and the government's use of immigration regulations to control movement'.[179] Part of this regulation involved the classification and categorisation of immigrants, refugees and citizens in the post-Ottoman states.

Finally, refugees and 'minority groups' were not just passive subjects of international, colonial and national elites' designs and discourses. This chapter has explored how territorial indeterminacy provided them with some room for manoeuvre. Indeed, itinerancy rather than fixity was a common feature in the borderlands, for not only was the boundary yet to be fixed, but also the 'nationality' of their populations.[180] When conditions were favourable, certain borderlands' groups and individuals were able to act as 'courtiers of nationality' – that is, measuring the 'comparative advantages between diverse offers of nationality'.[181] All in all, nationality did matter to borderlanders, but not in the manner that states envisioned it.

---

[177] Cyrus Schayegh, 'Afterword', in Jordi Tejel and Ramazan Hakkı Öztan (eds), *Regimes of Mobility*, p. 352.

[178] Benjamin T. White, *The Emergence of Minorities in the Middle East*, p. 102.

[179] Lauren Banko, 'Border Transgressions, Border Controls: Mobility along Palestine's Northern Frontier, 1930–46', in Jordi Tejel and Ramazan Hakkı Öztan (eds), *Regimes of Mobility*, pp. 256–85.

[180] For instance, as many as 60 per cent of the local dwellers in the Tigris district had not been registered at the Civil Office in 1939. It appeared thus impossible for the French and Syrian authorities to know when refugees and migrants had settled in Syria, as well as whether they had crossed the border several times or not. CADN, 1SL/1/V/505. 'Note pour Monsieur le Lt. Colonel, Inspecteur Délégué'. Hasaka, 8 February 1939.

[181] On this idea, see Mohammad Oualdi, 'Nationality in the Arab World, 1830–1960: Negotiating Belonging and the Law', *Revue des Mondes Musulmans et de la Méditerranée*, No. 137 (2015), p. 8.

3

CROSS-BORDER INFRINGEMENTS: SMUGGLERS, CRIMINALS AND FUGITIVES

On 12 June 1938, two unknown men paid a visit to the Presbyterian mission led by Reverend Roger C. Cumberland in Dohuk, a small town located in north-western Iraq.[1] After exchanging words of greeting, one guest fired several shots, first at Cumberland and then at his servant, who tried to help the missionary. Although Cumberland's British contacts in the region arranged to fly them to a hospital in Mosul, both victims of the attack eventually succumbed to their wounds. As soon as the news spread across the Dohuk area, the murder of the American missionary was associated with the turmoil caused by the tragic events witnessed in the Syrian–Iraqi borderlands in 1933, along with Cumberland's relentless fifteen-year-long endeavours to convert Kurdish Muslims and Yazidis. For one thing, despite being a critical voice against the Assyrian leadership who asked the League of Nations for 'special rights', Rev. Cumberland had denounced the Iraqi Army for the 1933 anti-Assyrian pogroms perpetrated in the village of Semel and, more decisively, allowed the survivors of the massacre to find shelter in the Presbyterian mission. While Cumberland secured his position in Dohuk after the pogroms, he nevertheless received numerous threats, which he fatally

---

[1] Born in 1894, Rev. Cumberland arrived in Iraq in 1923 to begin his work as Presbyterian missionary. On Cumberland's activities in Dohuk, see NARA, RG89, Box 2, Folder 6. 'Memorial Minute, Rev. Roger Craig Cumberland'. Presbyterian Historical Society, 13 June 1938.

dismissed. Against this backdrop, Iraqi officials were quick to attribute the murder to local 'religious fanaticism'.[2]

In spite of a serious investigation led by local authorities and different government representatives to bring the perpetrators to justice, it turns out that they were never apprehended. Admittedly, both the American Legation and the British Embassy in Baghdad urged the Iraqi authorities to do everything possible to find the assassins, which resulted in Cumberland's criminal investigation being made a priority for more than a year.[3] While the initial investigation revealed the identity of the murderers,[4] the failure to hold a trial opened the door to numerous theories and speculations about the specific motivations of the killers, from mental instability to political goals,[5] as well as their whereabouts. After some months of intensive search in the rugged mountainous region, the Iraqi authorities informed the American Legation that the two outlaws had crossed the Turkish-Iraqi border and sought asylum among their relatives close to the border, in the Hakkari province of Turkey.

Even though the Iraqi authorities sent an extradition request to their Turkish counterparts,[6] the former also exhorted the American Legation to show patience and understanding given the complexity of the case, not only because the murderers found refuge on the Turkish side of the border but also because 'the inhabitants of those regions are connected by tribal ties and feelings in a conspicuous manner'. Hence, borderlanders 'do not much care to assist the governmental authorities in the chase and pursuits'.[7] In addition, 'the tribes

[2] See Joe P. Dunn, 'A Death in Dohuk: Roger C. Cumberland, Mission and Politics among the Kurds in Northern Iraq, 1923–38', *Journal of Third World Studies*, Vol. 32, No. 1 (2015), pp. 245–71.

[3] NARA, RG84, UD 2752, Box 3. 'Memorandum: Representations in the Roger C. Cumberland case'. The American Legation. Baghdad, 3 September 1938.

[4] Before being transferred to Mosul, Cumberland was able to provide his wife with a description of the identity of the murderers. See Joe P. Dunn, 'A Death in Dohuk', pp. 245–71.

[5] NARA, RG84, UD 2752, Box 3. 'Assassination of the Rev Roger C. Cumberland'. The American Legation, Baghdad, 16 June 1938; NARA, RG84, UD 2752, Box 3. 'Memorandum Concerning the Murder of the Late R.C. Cumberland'. The American Legation. Baghdad, 21 October 1938.

[6] NARA, RG84, UD 2752, Box 4. Confidential. The American Legation. Baghdad, 6 February 1939.

[7] NARA, RG84, UD 2752, Box 3. Confidential. The American Legation. Baghdad, 4 August 1938.

consider the capture of a criminal a sport and go to any length to hide and conceal him' – an attitude that had been already decried at the Iraqi Parliament on several occasions.[8] Bringing the two fugitives to justice could be a long and uncertain road. Indeed, as it turned out, the Turkish gendarmes were by no means more successful than the Iraqi police, leaving the case forever unsolved.

More importantly for our purposes, the flight of Cumberland's murderers to Turkey, the ensuing extradition process and the failure to apprehend the outlaws highlight three interrelated issues that are key to the understanding of boundary- and state-formation processes, on the one hand, and the frontier effects, on the other (that is, the consequences regarding spatial and social organisation that the boundaries drawn in the Middle East generated throughout the interwar years).

First, a significant body of literature on borders and borderlands has examined the ways in which the post-Ottoman settlements fractured the socio-demographic dynamics in what were in other circumstances multi-ethnic border regions: borders not only disrupted older circuits of mobility – whether economic, social or religious – but also separated social groups from one another, even breaking up simple family units in the process.[9] Seemingly, scholars focusing on minority groups and nationalism in the interwar Middle East have underscored how borders created minorities and, in some cases, became conducive to violent forms of government.[10] Taken as a whole, these strands of literature highlight the negative effects of the post-Ottoman borders upon the populations located at the margins of the newly-established states in the region.

---

[8] NARA, RG84, UD 2752, Box 3. 'Memorandum: Representations in the Roger C. Cumberland case'. The American Legation. Baghdad, 3 September 1938.

[9] Martin Thomas, 'Bedouin Tribes and the Imperial Intelligence Services in Syria, Iraq and Transjordan in the 1920s', *Journal of Contemporary History*, Vol. 38, No. 4 (2003), pp. 539–61; Anthony B Toth, 'Tribes and Tribulations: Bedouin Losses in the Saudi and Iraqi Struggles Over Kuwait's Frontiers, 1921–43', *British Journal of Middle Eastern Studies*, Vol. 32, No. 2 (2005), pp. 145–67.

[10] Mesut Yeğen, 'The Turkish State Discourse and the Exclusion of Kurdish Identity', *Middle Eastern Studies*, Vol. 32, No. 2 (1996), pp. 216–29; Mark Levene, 'Creating a Modern Zone of Genocide: The Impact of Nation- and State-Formation on Eastern Anatolia, 1878–1923', *Holocaust and Genocide Studies*, Vol. 12, No. 3 (1998), pp. 393–433; Uğur Ü. Üngör, 'Rethinking the Violence of Pacification: State Formation and Bandits in Turkey, 1914–37', *Comparative Studies in Society and History*, Vol. 54, No. 4 (2012), pp. 746–69.

Seemingly, this body of scholarship underscores by and large local resistance to the imposition of 'unnatural' borders through either overt means (armed revolts, assaults on caravans and border posts) or through everyday practices (such as cross-border marriages, continued mobility and smuggling).[11] By doing so, it reflects the grids of analyses of an important bulk of academic research on state-formation and border-making processes in other geographical sets; namely, as new state authorities intend to impose their power and control over the frontier zones, borderlanders develop different strategies of (political) resistance to those attempts. Thus, for instance, James C. Scott sees the transgression of boundaries by traders, smugglers and labourers in the south-eastern Asian region as a part of the repertoire of political resistance displayed by individuals and societies confronted by states seeking to dominate border and peripheral populations.[12] Meanwhile, Reece Jones prefers to conceptualise these practices through the notion of a 'space of refusal' – that is, everyday actions that disregard the state-imposed rules and classification (legal/illegal, national/alien, and so on), but which do not necessarily constitute politically motivated resistance to the state sovereignty in the area which is not firmly administered.[13] The notion of a 'space of refusal', however, slots into a long-standing debate on political intentionality, or the absence of it, of individuals engaged in daily activities; it also opens a debate on the definition of the concept of the 'political' as such.[14] Moreover, Jones tends to reify the dichotomy between 'resistance' and 'non-resistance', between 'political' and 'apolitical', thereby neglecting the 'local ambivalence' of both individuals and groups.[15]

Critically, social practices such as smuggling can harbour political connotations in some contexts where political and non-political networks cross

---

[11] Ramazan Aras, *The Wall: The Making and Unmaking of the Turkish–Syrian Border* (New York: Palgrave Macmillan, 2020), p. 3.

[12] James C. Scott, *The Art of Not Being Governed. An Anarchist History of Upland Southeast Asia* (New Haven and London: Yale University Press, 2009).

[13] Reece Jones, 'Spaces of Refusal: Rethinking Sovereign Power and Resistance at the Border', *Annals of the Association of American Geographers*, Vol. 102, No. 3 (2012), pp. 685–99 (here p. 687).

[14] Michel de Certeau, *L'invention du quotidien Vol. I* (Paris: Gallimard, 1990); Jacques Lagroye (ed.), *La politisation* (Paris: Belin, 2003); Asef Bayat, *Life as Politics: How Ordinary People Change the Middle East* (Stanford: Stanford University Press, 2010).

[15] Shaherzad R. Ahmadi, 'Local Ambivalence in the Arabistan-Basra Frontier, 1881–1925', *British Journal of Middle Eastern Studies*, Vol. 48, No. 3 (2021), pp. 436–54.

or overlap, even though they are *a priori* independent from each other.[16] Furthermore, at times, borderlands are inhabited by 'local people who trade, work, socialise and marry as if the line between countries was not there'.[17] In other words, although the locals are apparently facing the same reality, their attitudes and perceptions may vary.[18] Therefore, the overall context does not necessarily determine the choices, actions or attitudes of individuals. In other words, because neither borderlands nor borderlanders are monolithic, the 'frontier effects' induced by the emergence and consolidation of borders should not therefore be simply examined in light of their relation to time and space; rather, scholars should also consider individual and collective perceptions, acts and strategies. In other words, over time, borders change not only physically (i.e., by redrawing sections of a given border, or introducing border markers) and institutionally (i.e. by modifying boundary regimes), but through the variance of their practical and symbolic meanings depending on borderlanders' individual and collective resources and their relationship to the border.[19] Ultimately, a multiplicity of borders may coexist in time and space, 'simultaneously experienced by those inhabiting them'.[20]

In that regard, and contrary to top-down approaches to the emergence and consolidation of borders in post-colonial countries, ethnographic studies in the borderlands of Africa and Asia show that cross-border activities such as contraband may contribute to the co-production and consolidation of state borders.[21] In addition, while border zones may be seen as areas of instability and risk, they may become potential resources for people living

---

[16] William Zartman (ed.), *Understanding Life in the Borderlands. Boundaries in Depth and in Motion* (Athens and London: University of Georgia Press, 2010), pp. 10–11.

[17] Thomas M. Wilson and Hastings Donnan (eds), *Border Identities. Nation and State at International Frontiers* (Cambridge: Cambridge University Press, 1998), p. 9.

[18] David Newman, 'On Borders and Power: A Theoretical Framework', *Journal of Borderlands Studies*, Vol. 18, No. 1 (2003), pp. 19–20.

[19] See, for instance, Adrian Little, 'The Complex Temporality of Borders: Contingency and Normativity', *European Journal of Political Theory*, Vol. 14, No. 4 (2015), pp. 429–47.

[20] Benjamin D. Hopkins and Magnus Marsden, *Fragments of the Afghan Frontier* (London: Hurst, 2011), p. 4.

[21] Paul Nugent, *Smugglers, Secessionists and Loyal Citizens: The Life of the Borderlands since 1914* (Oxford: James Currey, 2002); Janet Roitman, 'A Successful Life in the Illegal Realm', in Peter Geschiere, Birgit Meyer and Peter Pels (eds), *Readings in Modernity in Africa* (Bloomington: Indiana University Press, 2008), pp. 214–20.

in its proximity, too.²² Hence, borderlanders do not always resist the creation of state borders – on the contrary, they may cope or even benefit from them. Seemingly, international borders do not necessarily pose a threat to the communities living on the frontier. Building upon his fieldwork in the West African sub-region, Paul Nugent argues that post-colonial borders in this area did not disrupt 'old trading networks'; rather, their collapse was a consequence of the 'deeper penetration of European merchant capital'. On the other hand, he contests the 'popular belief' according to which cross-border trade, including contraband, necessarily implies inter-communal harmony. Actually, smugglers and traffickers rely upon 'their own networks of close kinsmen and fellow villagers, whereas more remote contacts could not always be trusted'.²³ Consequently, the interactions between the state, borderlanders and the border may trigger social and communal boundaries, thereby (re-)producing hierarchies and the division among border dwellers.

Against this background, a new generation of historians has suggested the necessity of studying the 'lived experience of territoriality' in the borderlands in order to explore how borderlanders, taken in their plurality of interests and identities, at once adapted to, if not shaped, the social and economic dynamics that were borne out of the newly-established boundaries.²⁴ It is thus by observing how different sets of borderlanders act and interact with each other as well as with the border that we can better grasp the different meanings and temporalities of Middle Eastern borders. This chapter thus delves into the cross-border infringements of three different groups of borderlanders: smugglers, outlaws and fugitive women, each of whom assumed the forms of the Westphalian states with delineated borders, but did so in pursuit of their own goals.

Cumberland's unsolved murder points to a second important issue in this chapter – the importance of trans-border networks and the resilience

---

[22] Judith Schelle, *Smugglers and Saints of the Sahara. Regional Connectivity in the Twentieth Century* (Cambridge: Cambridge University Press, 2012).

[23] Paul Nugent and A.I. Asiwaju (eds), *African Boundaries: Barriers, Conduits and Opportunities* (London: Cassell/Pinter, 1996), pp. 55 and 59.

[24] Matthew H. Ellis, *Desert Borderland: The Making of Modern Egypt and Libya* (Stanford, CA: Stanford University Press, 2018), p. 8.

of multiple sovereignties in the borderlands. After all, local patterns of mobility, kinship and justice (raids, blood feuds) that had prevailed for decades in the late Ottoman period, did not disappear overnight. Quite to the contrary, they remained resilient in many ways and, in some instances, were reformulated as new boundaries were drawn.[25] Middle Eastern states sought to cope with this difficult equation by using different means, such as violence, high-level diplomatic manoeuvres, security cooperation and formal, as well as informal, agreements between low-level officials. As a result, 'the proximity of multiple, often conflicting judicial authorities' together with the adaptation, if not reinforcement, of older practices made the border zones 'a particular space differentiated from nearby areas in terms of the rules that were applied or suspended there'.[26] Consequently, observing frontier crime regulations, along with informal extradition systems between Turkey, Syria and Iraq, allows us to highlight the resilience of the Ottoman's 'legal pluralism' and layered sovereignties in contrast to master narratives, particularly in Turkey's historiography, that tend to overemphasise the state's capacity and willingness to impose a unique legal system across a given national territory.[27]

Finally, Cumberland's criminal investigation, along with the extradition procedures related to it underscores an additional question key to understanding the consolidation of borders and thus of state institutions in the modern Middle East. Taken as a whole, borderlanders' actions (crimes, licit and illicit trade, cross-border marriage alliances and splitting the tribes over different national territories) as well as mobility strategies (migration flows, nomadic circuits and travel) provoked a paradoxical effect on the transformation of borders and boundary regimes in the interwar period. On the one hand, borders helped connect some populations living in the border areas; smugglers, petty criminals, tribes, families and fugitives relied on networks

---

[25] Toufoul Abou-Hodeib, 'Involuntary History: Writing Levantines into the Nation', *Contemporary Levant*, Vol. 5, No. 1 (2020), pp. 44–53.
[26] Eric Lewis Beverley, 'Frontier as Resource: Law, Crime, and Sovereignty on the Margins of Empire', *Comparative Studies in Society and History*, Vol. 55, No. 2 (2013), pp. 243–4.
[27] Bernard Lewis, *The Emergence of Modern Turkey* (Oxford: Oxford University Press, 1961); Paul Dumont, *Mustafa Kemal invente la Turquie moderne* (Brussels: Complexe, 1997).

of trust, which were reinvigorated, or at least kept alive despite, or rather because of, the delineation of new borders.

On the other hand, the introduction of anti-smuggling measures and extradition systems gradually turned borders into social institutions, with concrete frontier effects, as power relations began to unfold between state agents and borderlanders.[28] As in the late Ottoman era, official awareness of contraband flows and daily cross-border mobility served not only as a catalyst for institution formation and the expansion of state power, but also as trigger for increasingly blurred boundaries between state representatives and borderlands populations.[29] In addition, despite the ongoing diplomatic tensions between Turkey, France and Britain, cooperation and exchange of information to fight border infringements constituted alternate ways for these states to interact among themselves, too.[30] This chapter thus shows that interstate cooperation to track smugglers, outlaws and fugitive women led to the 'normalisation' of both the border and the state in the borderlands.

Boundary Management in the Tri-border Area

In the Middle East, as elsewhere, newly-established boundaries created a 'legal fiction'; that is, the idea of a social and political authority – a sovereign state over a given territory and its population – on the ground.[31] Moreover, 'the legal claims created by border demarcation created a demand among

---

[28] Toufoul Abou-Hodeib, 'Sanctity Across the Border: Pilgrimage Routes and State Control in Mandate Lebanon and Palestine', in Cyrus Schayegh and Andrew Arsan (eds), *The Routledge Handbook of the History of the Middle East Mandates* (London: Routledge, 2015), p. 383.

[29] Nadir Özbek, 'Policing the Countryside: Gendarmes of the Late 19th-Century Ottoman Empire (1876–1908)', *International Journal of Middle East Studies*, Vol. 40, No. 1 (2008), pp. 47–67 (here p. 48); Ramazan Hakkı Öztan, 'Tools of Revolution: Global Military Surplus, Arms Dealers and Smugglers in the Late Ottoman Balkans, 1878–1908', *Past & Present*, Vol. 237, No. 1 (2017), pp. 167–95.

[30] Robert Fletcher, *British Imperialism and the Tribal Question* (Oxford: Oxford University Press, 2015); Cyrus Schayegh, *The Middle East and the Making of the Modern World* (Cambridge, MA: Harvard University Press, 2017), pp. 9–10.

[31] On this idea, see Friedrich Kratochwil, 'Of Systems, Boundaries, and Territoriality: An Inquiry into the Formation of the State System', *World Politics*, Vol. 39, No. 1 (1986), pp. 27–52.

state-builders to make the nation-state *actual* in places where local authority failed to map onto state capacity'.[32] Admittedly, whether closely monitored or loosely surveyed 'boundary regimes' quickly became integral parts of the social and political fabric of borderlands in the interwar Middle East.[33]

As we saw in the previous chapter, the resolution of the Mosul Affair in December 1925 facilitated the ensuing delimitation of the Turkish–Syrian boundary, together with the signature of a 'Good Neighbourhood Treaty' with Turkey on 30 May 1926. Crucially, the Convention of 1926 laid the foundations for a boundary regime along the Turkish–Syrian border, signalling a push for bilateral cooperation in order to decide which movements were 'benign, regulated, observed, allowed, and taxed and movements that (were) threatening, illicit, unseen, unapproved, and untaxed'.[34] In this regard, Turkey and France sought not only to facilitate borderlanders' mobility and animal husbandry activities, but also to contain diseases and prevent 'evil movements', such as illicit circuits of cross-border trade.[35]

Article 6, for instance, reads that both countries committed to the 'suppression of acts of brigandage and smuggling in the frontier region'; that is, a zone 50 kilometres in breadth on either side of the frontier.[36] In line with the proliferation of identification documents and bureaucratic techniques for administering the boundaries of the nation in both territorial and

---

[32] Jonathan Obert, 'Policing the Boundary and Bounding the Police: Fictious Borders and the Making of Gendarmeries in North America', *Journal of Borderlands Studies*, Vol. 36, No. 2 (2021), p. 302.

[33] George Gavrilis defines 'boundary regimes' as locally cooperative methods of border control. George Gavrilis, *The Dynamics of Interstate Boundaries* (Cambridge: Cambridge University Press, 2008), pp. 14–15.

[34] Reece Jones, *Violent Borders: Refugees and the Right to Move* (London: Verso, 2016), p. 166.

[35] Some of these practices, however, dated back to the late nineteenth century. Will Smiley, 'The Burdens of Subjecthood: The Ottoman State, Russian Fugitives, and Interimperial Law, 1774–1869', *International Journal of Middle East Studies*, Vol. 46, No. 1 (2014), pp. 73–93; David Gutman, 'Travel Documents, Mobility Control, and the Ottoman State in the Age of Global Migration, 1880–1915', *Journal of Ottoman and Turkish Studies Association*, Vol. 3, No. 2 (2016), pp. 347–68.

[36] League of Nations (1926–7). Convention of Friendship and Good Neighbourly Relations, with Procès-Verbal of Signature. Signed in Angora, 30 May 1926. Treaty Series No. 1285, Vol. 54, pp. 195–229 (here p. 201).

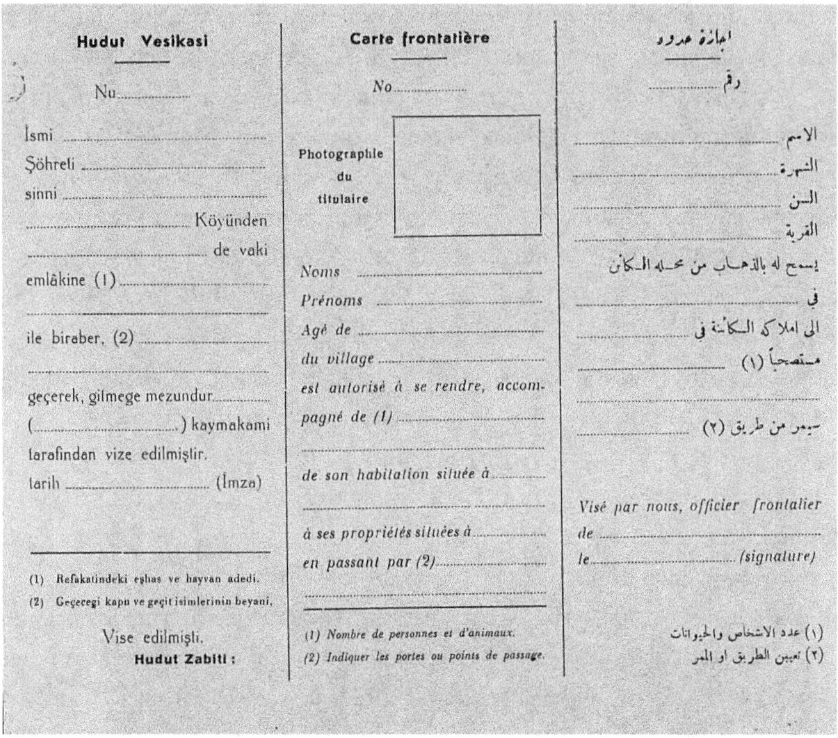

Hudut Vesikasi

Nu

İsmi

Şöhreti

sinni

Köyünden

de vaki

emlâkine (1)

ile biraber, (2)

geçerek, gilmege mezundur

( ) kaymakami

tarafindan vize edilmiştir.

tarih (İmza)

(1) Refakatindeki eşhas ve hayvan adedi.

(2) Geçeceği kapu ve geçit isimlerinin beyani,

Vise edilmişti.

Hudut Zabiti :

Carte frontalière

No

Photographie du titulaire

Noms

Prénoms

Agé de

du village

est autorisé à se rendre, accom-pagné de (1)

de son habitation située à

à ses propriétés situées à

en passant par (2)

(1) Nombre de personnes et d'animaux.

(2) Indiquer les portes ou points de passage.

اجازة حدود

رقم

الاسم

الشهرة

السن

القرية

يسمح له بالذهاب من محله الكائن

في

الى املاكه الكائنة في

مستصحباً (١)

سيمر من طريق (٢)

Visé par nous, officier frontalier

de

le (signature)

(١) عدد الاشخاص والحيوانات

(٢) تعيين الطريق او الممر

Figure 3.1 Border card or *passavant* used at the Turkish–Syrian border in the 1930s and 1940s.

Source: CADN, 1SL/1/V/2149.

membership terms,[37] Article 9 allowed for cross-border mobility for persons residing within five kilometres on either side of the border and for an annual border card or *passavant*[38] issued to the borderlanders involved in farming and commerce – landowners, their families, as well as their labourers. Although many borderlanders (and clandestine foreigners) continued to crisscross the

[37] John Torpey, *The Invention of the Passport: Surveillance, Citizenship and the State* (Cambridge: Cambridge University Press, 1999); Gérard Noiriel, *La tyrannie du National: Le droit d'asile en Europe, 1793–1993* (Paris, Calmann-Lévy, 1991).

[38] Between 1930 and 1939, French and Turkish border authorities delivered more than 5,000 border cards. CADN, 1SL/1/V/2126. The Adjunct to the High Commissioner (Aleppo) to the Turkish Vali (Antep). Aleppo, 31 July 1939.

border without any papers, cross-border cooperation and shared bureaucratic techniques served to make border populations more visible to the state.

Protocol III dealt with frontier surveillance and was also key to this convention; on the one hand, the competent authorities were requested to 'warn each other as promptly as possible of any act of pillage or brigandage that may be committed in their territory' and display 'every means in their power to prevent the offenders from crossing the frontier' (Article 3).[39] On the other hand,

> should one or more armed persons, after committing a crime or offence in the neighbouring frontier zone, succeed in taking refuge in the other frontier zone, the authorities of the latter zone shall be bound to arrest such persons and to place them, in accordance with the law, at the disposal of the judicial authorities, together with their booty and arms (Article 4).[40]

In Article 7, the Convention defined the competent authorities responsible for the application of these measures. Hence, the Military Frontier Commission on the Turkish side, and the General Commanding from the Aleppo district on the French side, were central for the general collaboration. In parallel, within each respective section of the border, the Turkish structure involved local *kaymakams*, *mudirs*, officers commanding the Gendarmerie and Valis. On the French side, intelligence officers (Service de Renseignements), officers from the Armée du Levant and the Gendarmerie (including the mobile units) participated in border control. Article 8 encouraged both sides to establish police stations as frontier gates.[41] Finally, Article 9 permitted cross-border mobility for Syrian and Turkish tribes possessing customary rights of pasture on the other side of their respective 'national borders', under certain conditions.[42]

Despite this legal breakthrough, the 1926 Convention remained an issue of contention, particularly in Turkey, where some deputies to the parliament and border authorities saw in the *passavant* regime a gateway for contraband

---

[39] League of Nations (1926–7). Convention of Friendship and Good Neighbourly Relations, p. 217.
[40] Ibid.
[41] Ibid. p. 219.
[42] Ibid. p. 220.

and attacks against Turkish sovereignty.[43] Precisely because smugglers, Bedouins and criminals continued to trespass the border without being seriously inconvenienced, on 29 June 1929, a new Franco-Turkish Protocol was signed to improve the surveillance along the Turkish–Syrian frontier.[44] The new agreement also intended to accelerate the extradition system, thereby giving a more significant role to the competent local authorities. The passport regime for travellers and foreigners in general was also adapted to follow the recommendations of the International Passport Conference of May 1926, which abolished visas for Turkish and Syrian nationals returning to their respective territories.

Interestingly, both states acknowledged the impossibility of thoroughly monitoring all sections of the shared border, thus opening the door to recruiting borderlanders of 'good repute' to improve the security in the border zone, just as the Ottoman Empire had done before.[45] The 1929 Protocol also paved the way for the establishment of a permanent border commission, which began to work on the definitive delineation of the Syrian–Turkish boundary at its eastern section, that is, between Nusaybin and Jazirat ibn Umar.[46] Thereafter, the work of this Commission resulted in a dramatic increase in the number of border posts and guards.[47]

Overall, the 1926 Franco-Turkish Convention and the additional 1929 Protocol were important landmarks, for they established a model for inter-state cooperation in subsequent border agreements. Indeed, although the sections of the Ankara Treaty of 5 June 1926 about neighbourly relations and extradition

---

[43] Ömer Osman Umar, *Türkiye-Suriye İlişkileri, 1918–40* (Ortadoğu Araştırmaları Yayınları: Elazığ, 2003), pp. 272–81; Tahir Ögut and Erhan Akkaş, 'Suriye Toprak Reformunun Türkiye'ye Yansımaları: Pasavan Rejimi Krizi', *Journal of Social Policy Conferences*, Vol. 71, No. 2 (2016), pp. 127–63.

[44] For the full text, see CADN, 1SL/1/V/2136, 'Protocole', 29 June 1929.

[45] CADN, 1SL/1/V/2136. Protocol, Chapter I, Article 5, 29 June 1929.

[46] CADN, 1SL/1/V/1482. 'Protocole d'abornement de la frontière turco-syrienne signé à Angora le 22 juin 1929'.

[47] In 1930, for instance, 138 posts were created along the border to be used by borderlanders holding *passavants*, while 14 other border gates were established for travellers. CADN, 1SL/1/V/2152, The Adjunct to the High Commissioner (Aleppo) to Services Spéciaux (Azaz and Jarablus), Aleppo, 23 July 1930.

procedures between Turkey and Iraq was less developed than in the Franco-Turkish Convention, the former tapped into some articles included in the latter. Thus, for instance, Articles 8 and 9 foresaw the exchange of information and extradition of criminals between the two countries in a similar fashion.[48] There were, nevertheless, some variations. According to Article 10, the frontier zone was 75km wide, instead of 50, on either side of the border. Likewise, the competent authorities differed on the Iraqi side. The Ankara Treaty of 1926 stipulated that, on the Turkish side, the military commandant of the frontier was responsible for general cooperation and the measures to be taken, whereas the *Mutasarrifs* of Mosul and Arbil were on the Iraqi side. With regard to the exchange of local information and urgent communications, the Turkish Valis were left free to appoint the relevant authorities, while the *Qaymmaqams* of Zakho, Amadiya, Zibar and Rowanduz were explicitly appointed, on the Iraqi side.[49]

Likewise, the Franco-Turkish agreements also served as a negotiation basis for both the renegotiation of the extradition system between Turkey and Iraq in the early 1930s,[50] and the 'Good Neighbourly' agreement signed by Syria and Iraq in April 1937. Thus, for instance, cross-border circuits of nomadism were permitted for tribes holding customary rights of pasture on either side of the boundary, without paying any customs duties or any dues at the border posts. Similarly, peasants and villagers, holders of a border card, who were property owners in the frontier zone (stretching 5km on either side of the international border) were allowed to crisscross the borderline to continue farming their lands. From an organisational perspective, the general cooperation and responsibility for the implementation of the provisional border regime was secured by the Adjunct Delegate to the French High Commissioner, on the Syrian side, and the *Mutasarrif* of the Mosul Liwa, on the Iraqi side. As for the exchange of local information and urgent

---

[48] 'Treaty Between the United Kingdom and Iraq and Turkey Regarding the Settlement of the Frontier Between Turkey and Iraq with Notes Exchanged', *The American Journal of International Law*, Vol. 21, No. 4 (1927), pp. 136–43 (here p. 139).

[49] Ibid.

[50] TNA, AIR 23/374, 8th Meeting of the Permanent Frontier Commission. From Mutasarrif (Mosul) to the Ministry of Interior (Baghdad). Mosul, 6 July 1930.

communications, the section abutting the Syrian Jazira and north-western Iraq gathered together the Intelligence Services (renamed Services Spéciaux in 1931) at Ayn diwar, Hasaka and Deir ez-Zor, on the Syrian side, and the local Qaymmaqam of Zakho, Sindjar and Tel Afar, on the Iraqi side.[51]

The 'legal fiction' created by new boundaries in the interwar Middle East has been an object of critical inquiry for geographers and historians who highlight that the effects of international accords and emerging boundary regimes on the ground were not immediate. According to Cyrus Schayegh, for instance, 'borders did not create quick *fait accomplis*' across the Bilad al-Sham, for the numbers of 'customs officials, gendarmes, policemen, and soldiers were kept to a minimum'.[52]F Likewise, Clive Schofield dismisses the consequences of the establishment of new borders and related boundary regimes in the region.[53] While examining the Turkish–Syrian border throughout the interwar era, Benjamin T. White argues that 'the term "crossing the border" was literally meaningless: the border had no material presence, nor was its location agreed by the two jurisdictions it was supposed to separate'.[54]

Rather than dismissing or over-stating the local and regional consequences of the newly-established borders in the interwar Middle East, the remaining sections in this chapter explore how the increased encroachments of smugglers, criminals and fugitives from the late 1920s onwards allow us to not only test the viability of the existing boundary regimes in the Turkish–Syrian–Iraqi borderlands, but also to underscore the ways borderlanders negotiated, contested, shaped and re-shaped state borders, thereby paving the way for different and sometimes contradicting understandings of territoriality.

---

[51] CADN, 1SL/1/V/637. Minutes of the Meeting between the Mutasarrif of Mosul and the Adjunct Delegate to the High Commissioner. Deir ez-Zor, 23 June 1933.

[52] Cyrus Schayegh, 'The Many Worlds of 'Abud Yasin; Or, What Narcotics Trafficking in the Interwar Middle East Can Tell Us About Territorialization', *American Historical Review*, Vol. 116, No. 2 (2011), pp. 273–306 (here p. 278).

[53] Clive Schofield, 'Elusive Security: The Military and Political Geography of South Lebanon', *GeoJournal*, Vol. 31, No. 2 (1993), pp. 149–61 (here p. 153).

[54] Benjamin T. White, *The Emergence of Minorities in the Middle East: The Politics of Community in French Mandate Syria* (Edinburgh: Edinburgh University Press, 2011), pp. 102 and 104–5.

Smugglers and the Consolidation of Border Governance

Because a borderland is a place of contact marked by continuous fluidity, its realities on the ground are not simply outcomes either of national policies on each side, nor of inter-state cooperation. Except in highly surveyed frontier zones, borderland communities continue to be active border crossers regardless of provisions introduced by international boundary regimes, thereby posing challenges to state authorities and their policies. Furthermore, despite the apparent symmetry between neighbouring states bounded by international conventions and protocols, reality is much more complex. After all, states are not equal in the face of borderlanders' activities; on the contrary, borderlands dynamics reveal the '(inter)national asymmetries of power, capabilities and resources' that eventually 'shape the structure of border contact and governance'.[55] Consequently, as Yuk Wah Chan puts it, 'border regions often form a frontier thermometer that detects changing inter-state relations' as well as, I would add, state capacities to cope with those very changes. In that regard, the creation of new national economies and the subsequent crafting of different systems of laws, taxes and fiscal management between Turkey, French Syria and British Iraq had an immediate translation along the shared boundaries where new barriers to the large movement of goods developed in the interwar years.

When the Turkish Republic was established in 1923, the economic challenges were enormous. On the one hand, the prolonged warfare brought about the disruption of existing patterns of trade, along with the massive loss of human lives. On the other hand, economic resources and local industry were largely under foreign control.[56] Because the Turkish elites were inspired by the ideological principles of the Unionist committees – nationalism, modernisation and the westernisation of state structures – the Ankara government saw in the economic policies a means to advance towards both state- and nation-building. Consequently, the republic's leadership strove to create a

---

[55] Yuk Wah Chan and Brantly Womack, 'Not Merely a Border: Borderland Governance, Development and Transborder Relations in Asia', *Asian Anthropology*, Vol. 15, No. 2 (2016), pp. 95–103 (here p. 96).

[56] By 1924, Turkey's population did not exceed 13,000,000 – that is, a decrease of about 25 per cent from a decade before – about 80% of which was rural in character.

national economy within the new borders through the development of transport infrastructures and the nationalisation of the economy.

To reach these goals, however, the Ankara government had to first renegotiate the economic clauses imposed by the victorious powers in the aftermath of the First World War. In that regard, the Treaty of Lausanne turned out to be a landmark for the new Republic in three complementary directions: first, the commercial and legal privileges of European citizens and companies – i.e. the capitulations – were abolished; second, the Ottoman debt was renegotiated and distributed between successor states in the region such as Syria and Iraq; finally, it was agreed that the tariff system and the restrictions against quotas would be revised in 1929. After that date, Turkey would once more be able to freely decide upon its own commercial policies.[57]

Despite a significant recovery in the Turkish economy up to 1929, the Great Depression brought about a decline in the volume of imports and, perhaps more importantly, the rise of the debt burden for countries like Turkey, which had become net borrowers before 1929.[58] In addition, Turkey and other Middle Eastern countries saw the prices of their primary exports fall between 1929 and 1932, as a consequence of the decline in demand on the international markets. As Owen and Pamuk point out, further problems came for the states whose currencies were directly tied to British sterling (Turkey and Iraq), or the franc (Syria), 'both of which were subject to drastic devaluation in the 1930s'.[59] The effects of these economic dynamics were quickly felt, thereby causing increasing discontent with the regime, in particular in the agricultural and export-oriented sectors.

Against this backdrop, the Ankara government responded in two complementary directions. First, the Turkish government adopted new customs tariffs in June 1929 to protect its national market against any possible invasion of foreign goods. Subsequently, by 1931 the Turkish government began to apply a quota system in foreign commerce to stop or decrease the import of goods that could be produced in Turkey. Second, the Ankara government

---

[57] Roger Owen and Şevket Pamuk, *A History of Middle East Economies in the Twentieth Century* (London: I. B. Tauris, 1999), p. 13.
[58] Ibid. p. 6.
[59] Ibid. p. 7.

announced in 1932 the beginning of a new strategy, etatism (*devletçilik*) or state-led import-substituting industrialisation.[60] As a result of the combination of both strategies, by the late 1930s, state economic enterprises such as Sümerbank and Etibank emerged as central producers in a number of key sectors such as iron and steel, textiles, sugar, cement and mining.[61]

While the Turkish response to the 1929 crisis generated positive developments for Turkey's economy, it also created new problems with its southern neighbours, particularly with French Syria. Building up the traditional colonial interests among the Lyonnais silk industry and the chamber of commerce of Marseille,[62] pro-Mandate economic lobbies in France aspired to take over Syrian commerce to 'restore imperial and regional prosperity'.[63] Within this context, the economies of the newly-established mandatory territories were submitted to a quasi-colonial form of economic management according to which Syria and Iraq were obliged to provide most favoured nation treatment – also known as an 'open-door policy' – to the members of the League of Nations as well as the US, thereby tempering 'the Mandate powers' ability to raise tariffs effectively'.[64] Furthermore, France and Britain shared a view about their role as economic actors in Syria and Iraq, respectively; that is, the need to balance the budget, along with giving priority to political over economic considerations.[65] The combination of both principles had an enormous impact upon the mandatory territories in

---

[60] Dilek Barlas, *Etatism and Diplomacy in Turkey: Economic and Foreign Policy Strategies in an Uncertain World, 1929–39* (Leiden: Brill, 1998).

[61] Şevket Pamuk, *Uneven Centuries: Economic Development of Turkey Since 1820* (Princeton, NJ: Princeton University Press, 2018), p. 177.

[62] Dominique Chevallier, 'Lyon et la Syrie en 1919: les bases d'une intervention', *Revue historique*, No. 1 (1960), pp. 275–320. See also, Hubert Bonin et al. (eds), *L'esprit économique impérial (1830–1970): groupes de pression et réseaux du patronat colonial en France et dans l'Empire* (Paris, Publications de la SFHOM, 2008).

[63] Simon Jackson, 'What is Syria Worth? The Huvelin Mission, Economic Expertise and the French Project in the Eastern Mediterranean, 1918–22', *Monde(s)*, No. 4 (2013), pp. 83–103 (here p. 94).

[64] Cyrus Schayegh, *The Making of the Modern Middle East*, p. 204.

[65] Roger Owen and Şevket Pamuk, *A History of Middle East Economies in the Twentieth Century*, p. 53.

the 1920s since little was done to aid the development of internal security, education, health or infrastructure.

Although France and Britain attempted to bring the mandatory economies closer by establishing a customs union between Syria, Lebanon and Palestine, their economic policies differed, while customs duties and external tariffs remained central.[66] By the late 1920s, however, the two mandatory powers chose opposite policies. While Britain remained loyal to 'official penny-pinching' until the end of the Mandate in 1932,[67] France deviated from budgetary balance in the Levant due to the increasing pressure exerted by well-organised Syrian and Lebanese interest groups, as well as the negative effects of the 1929 crisis. First, the French raised the rates on imports such as silk thread and cement, while opening the doors to cheap Japanese textiles, which were all the more necessary for the peasantry impoverished by the global recession. Second, from 1934 onwards, France allowed a considerable increase in the public works budget – new roads, ports and railroads slowly transformed the mandatory territories into more connected economies both at home and abroad.

It was the first decision, however, that had further serious repercussions for Turkey. Back in the early 1920s, when the discrepancy in tariff regimes between Turkey and Syria was too low to encourage wide-scale smuggling, the illegal exchange of goods was largely limited to those that were produced under a state monopoly: tobacco, matches, sugar, salt and gas. In 1928, the Siirt deputy Mahmut Bey already called attention to this phenomenon:

> The smuggling, which is being carried out on this border on a large scale, deserves particular attention. [French] Frontier guards openly protect smugglers . . . The merchandise which in, one way or another, is being clandestinely smuggled into our country is sold at low prices. Our honest businessmen, being unable to meet such competition on account of expenses incurred through the payment of [C]ustoms duties, suffer great loss as a result of this state of affairs.[68]

---

[66] TNA, CO 733/22. 'Report on Administration for Period July 1920–December 1921'.
[67] Peter Sluglett, *Britain in Iraq: Contriving King and Country* (London: I. B. Tauris), p. 87.
[68] 'Cenup Hududu Dair', *Milliyet*, 16 October 1928.

During the Great Depression, Turkey became increasingly protectionist while French Syria continued to adhere to the practices of free trade, keeping its tariffs low, in line with the mandatory open-door policies.[69] As Ramazan Hakkı Öztan has shown, the corresponding tariff variances led to the expansion of the illicit economy along their shared border, where smuggling the goods subject to the highest tariff rates in Turkey – cheap Japanese textiles, for instance – was particularly profitable for Syrian borderlanders.[70] According to diplomatic records, this contraband took different forms. In order to transport the goods, smugglers used a wide range of means of transportation, such as border couriers (men carrying the goods on their backs), donkeys, camels, and, from the 1930s onwards, private cars owned by tribal chiefs. In the villages near the Tigris, smugglers also passed their goods on inflatable boards.[71] Meanwhile, newspapers reported that contraband was carried out by either small groups of individuals or large bands involving as many as one hundred smugglers at a time.[72]

In 1931, Şükrü Kaya, the Turkish Minister of Interior Affairs, underscored the gravity of the problem in a comprehensive report, in which he highlighted the efforts made by the Ankara government to integrate Turkey's southern borderlands into its national economy since the mid-1920s; namely, the promotion of the port of Mersin and the extension of the railroads towards Diyarbakır.[73] To Ankara's dismay, however, the prosperous contraband activities in the area reversed the situation, for Aleppo was once again becoming the centre of trade across the region.[74] In parallel, such developments had

---

[69] See Norman Burns, *The Tariff of Syria, 1919–32* (Beirut: American Press, 1933), pp. 52–66.

[70] Ramazan Hakkı Öztan, 'The Great Depression and the Making of Turkish–Syrian Border, 1921–39', *International Journal of Middle East Studies*, Vol. 52, No. 2 (2020), pp. 311–26.

[71] CADN, 1SL/1/V/33. Service politique du Levant. Bureau de Deir ez-Zor, 7 September 1944.

[72] *Yeni Mersin*, for instance, reported about the activities of a band of a hundred smugglers from the Elbistan region who crossed the Turkish–Syrian border. On their way back, however, the Turkish authorities captured thirty smugglers, killing another three. TNA, FO 371/17958/E593/256/44. 'Capture of Smugglers Near Aintab', 25 January 1934.

[73] BCA.30.10.0.0.180.244.6, 5 December 1931.

[74] For an analysis of the struggle between Turkey and France over the hinterland of Aleppo, see Ramazan Hakkı Öztan, 'The Last Ottoman Merchants: Regional Trade and Politics of Tariffs in Aleppo's Hinterland, 1921–9' in Jordi Tejel and Ramazan Hakkı Öztan (eds), *Regimes of Mobility: Borders and State Formation on the Middle East, 1918–46* (Edinburgh: Edinburgh University Press, 2022), pp. 80–108.

immediate consequences for Ankara's reserves. In a public speech, İsmet İnönü 'estimated the loss caused to the state by smuggling at Turkish lira 20 to 25 million a year, apart from the prejudice caused to local industry by the illicit introduction of non-taxed foreign goods', most notably coming into the country via Syria.[75]

Against this backdrop, in 1932 the Ministry of Justice established specialised courts (*İhtisas Mahkemesi*) in areas where smuggling activities were particularly widespread.[76] Thereafter, the Antep and Adana Special Courts proved to be tremendously vigorous. Thus, in 1934, these courts reportedly ruled on 4,250 cases in Antep alone.[77] A year later, 620 prosecutions took place before the Adana Special Court, and judgement was pronounced in 505 cases. Prison sentences given to borderlanders were accompanied by heavy pecuniary fines, together with additional measures geared towards seizing foreign commodities on the spot.[78] As border guards increased their presence along the frontier, though incidents against border authorities on both sides of the international border also increased.[79]

Yet the battle against contraband required a certain degree of international cooperation. In line with the bilateral conventions signed between 1926 and 1929, Turkish authorities thus pressed their French counterparts for urgent and thorough intervention in order to dismantle the contraband networks acting from the Syrian side of the border.[80] According to Turkish

---

[75] TNA, FO 371/15381/E6375, 'Prevention of Smuggling on Frontiers of Turkey', Ankara, 28 December 1931.

[76] 'Askeri ve İhtisas Mahkemeleri Hakkında Kararname', *Resmi Gazete*, 26 January 1932.

[77] Murat Metinsoy, 'Rural Crimes as Everyday Peasant Politics: Tax Delinquency, Smuggling, Theft and Banditry in Modern Turkey', in Stephanie Cronin (ed.), *Crime, Poverty and Survival in the Middle East and North Africa: The 'Dangerous Classes' Since 1800* (London: I. B. Tauris, 2019), pp. 135–54 (here p. 144).

[78] CADN, 1SL/1/V/2145, Sûreté Générale, Aleppo, 6 June 1935.

[79] These incidents were regularly reported by the Turkish and Syrian newspapers. See, for instance, *Cumhuriyet*, 17 November 1931; *al-Qabas*, 1 February 1931; *al-Qabas*, 4 April 1932; *al-Shaab*, 6 May 1934.

[80] See for instance a list of shops and their estimated value prepared by the governor of Urfa in 1938. CADN, 1SL/1/V/2145, 'Kazim Demirer (Vali d'Urfa) au Adjoint du Haut-Commissaire pour le Mohafazat d'Alep', Urfa, 3 September 1938.

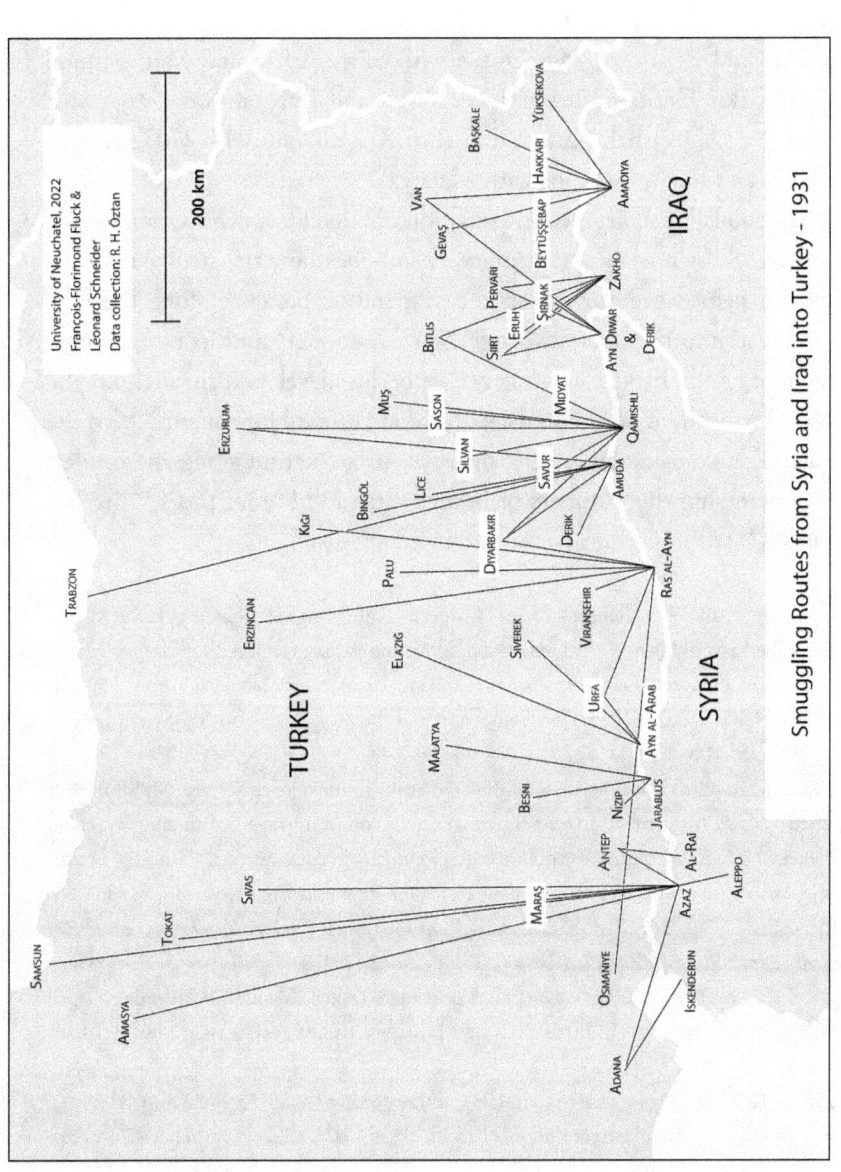

Figure 3.2 Map of smuggling routes from Syria and Iraq into Turkey, 1931.

Source: Data collected by Ramazan Hakkı Öztan from diverse files, namely in TNA, FO 371/16975 and BCA, 030.10.180.244.6. I thank Öztan for allowing me to publish his unpublished map.

sources, contraband routes connected Syrian border towns to Turkish towns and cities, sometimes as far as Erzurum and Trabzon, the latter located on the shores of the Black Sea: Qamishli with Mydiat, Bitlis, Sasoon, Muş, Silvan, Diyarbakır and Erzurum; Ayn Diwar with Siirt, Şırnak and Van; Amuda with Diyarbakır, Derik, Erzurum, Lice, Bingöl and Trabzon; Ras al-Ayn with Erzincan, Palu, Diyarbakır and Viranşehir; Ayn al-Arab with Urfa, Siverek and Elazığ; and finally, Jarablus with Malatya.[81]

Conspicuously, the detailed information obtained from the Syrian side of the border, whilst not always accurate, exemplifies how the struggle against contraband helped the Turkish state to expand its presence along the border zones and improve its 'knowledge' on the periphery and its populations. On the one hand, Turkish intelligence gathering developed throughout the 1930s in the southern borderlands, with the aid of local informants.[82] On the other hand, Ankara expanded the material infrastructure along the border; namely, increasing the numbers of border gates and border posts,[83] mechanised units,[84] telegraph lines,[85] and mounted guards.[86]

---

[81] See Adnan Çelik, 'Challenging State Borders: Smuggling as Kurdish Infra-Politics during "The Years of Silence"', in Lucie Drechselova and Adnan Çelik (eds), *Kurds in Turkey: Ethnographies of Heterogeneous Experiences* (Lanham: Lexington Books, 2019), pp. 159–84; Ramazan Hakkı Öztan, 'The Great Depression and the Making of Turkish–Syrian border, 1921–39', pp. 311–26.

[82] In 1927, the Ankara government established the Turkish Intelligence Service 'Millî Emniyet Hizmeti' (MAH) to combat diverse 'threats', such as communism, Kurdish and Armenian nationalism as well as to monitor political developments in Alexandretta. Crucially, to officials in Ankara, many of the potential dangers for the Republic originated from its southern borders. Eray Göç, 'Türk İstihbaratının Tarihsel Gelişimi', *Çankırı Karatekin Üniversitesi İktisadi ve İdari Bilimler Fakültesi Dergisi*, Vol. 3, No. 2 (2013), p. 100.

[83] CADN, 1SL/1/V/2145, 'Création de postes douaniers à Akçe-Koyounli, Muslimie', 3 April 1938. On the construction of further customs posts, see also BCA.030.18.1.2.86.21.14, 11 March 1939.

[84] BCA.030.18.1.2.26.16.11, 13 March 1932; BCA.030.18.1.2.88.72.2, 22 July 1933. In early 1938, the General Directorate of Turkish Customs decided to purchase European motorbikes together with armoured cars and trucks to better monitor the Turkish–Syrian border. CADN, 1SL/1/V/2145, 'Répression de la contrebande en Turquie. Sûreté Générale des territoires Syrie Nord, Muslimie', 11 May 1938.

[85] BCA.030.18.1.2.26.20.11, 31 March 1932; BCA.030.18.1.2.41.86.9, 4 December 1933.

[86] CADN, 1SL/1/V/2145, 'Répression de la contrebande en Turquie'. Sûreté Générale. Jarablus, 1 April 1938.

Material efforts were accompanied by government and public opinion campaigns against smugglers, in which the latter were vilified as traitors to the 'homeland' (*vatan*) and the 'nation' (*ulus*).[87] Although all ethnic groups living in the frontier zone were involved in smuggling activities, Turkish reports and letters sent to the French pointed specifically to 'anti-Turkish elements', that is, Armenians and Kurds. In other words, the involvement of Kurdish and Armenian smugglers in the illicit economy not only harmed Turkey's economy but the regime's stability altogether.[88] Anti-smugglers measures could also be felt in other domains. Thus, throughout the 1930s, the Ankara government modified the Turkish penal code by introducing tougher punishments, in particular with regard to offences that threatened the 'nation' and 'state security', such as smuggling and forging money.[89]

In parallel, by November 1932, the local power of *valis* and *kaymakams* serving along Turkey's southern frontier could issue arrest orders without any judicial warrant. Likewise, some governors, such as the one at Mardin, took direct command over the mounted units committed to border surveillance.[90] The consequence of the tighter contraband control revealed itself in the statistics of the killed and wounded smugglers at the Turkish–Syrian border. According to the memoirs of a Turkish army general, the numbers of smugglers arrested, killed and wounded between 1932 and 1936 amounted 87,000: 86, 600 simply arrested, 207 killed and 130 wounded.[91] Two years later, an official report lowered these figures to 40,000 smugglers arrested, and nearly 300 killed in border clashes between 1931 and 1938. Notwithstanding this, the recorded amounts demonstrated the net increase of border incidents during that decade.[92]

---

[87] See, for instance, 'Kaçak ve Kaçakcılık', *Yenilik*, 5 June 1936; 'Kaçakçılara Öğüt: Kaçakçılar Vatana Düşmandır', *Yenilik*, 30 June 1936; 'Kaçak İşi Önemli bir Yurt ve Ulus İşidir!', *Yenilik*, 3 July 1936.

[88] BCA, 490.01.998.856.1, p. 22.

[89] See Ruth A. Miller, *Legislating Authority. Sin and Crime in the Ottoman Empire and Turkey* (New York and London: Routledge, 2005), pp. 107–14.

[90] Sabri Cigerli and Didier Le Saout, *Les Kurdes. L'émergence du nationalisme kurde (1874–1945) dans les archives diplomatiques françaises* (Paris: L'Harmattan, 2019), pp. 317–18.

[91] Bülent Varlık, *Umumî Müfettişler Toplantı Tutanakları, 1936* (Ankara: Dipnot Yayınları, 2010), p. 202.

[92] BCA, 490.1.0.0.1455.38.1, July 1938, p. 40.

Despite the progress made in limiting contraband activities along the Turkish–Syrian border, a number of obstacles continued to preclude Turkey's efforts. Firstly, too many Turkish officials and soldiers in the frontier zone were not fully 'committed' to fighting smuggling activities. In 1930, for instance, the First Inspector General İbrahim Tali complained that the gendarmes who were stationed in the east for more than three years 'were exhausted and burned out'. Consequently, they 'did not embrace their duties with the necessary seriousness'.[93]

Another obstacle to the effective struggle against contraband was the collusion of borderlanders with smugglers and outlaws, as already mentioned in Cumberland's criminal investigation. Protection of smugglers could take different forms, from hiding them from the state authorities to providing false information to the police or even attacking the frontier mobile units to help the smugglers evade. On 8 June 1936, for instance, as two Syrian gendarmes were running after three smugglers who intended to return to Turkey, the Syrian patrol was attacked with stones and sticks by a crowd of 150 labourers who were working in the fields on the Turkish side of the borderline. Ultimately, the three men ran away, while one of the gendarmes was lightly wounded.[94]

A careful reading of security reports shows, however, that the relationship between smugglers and borderlanders was not always so harmonious. For one thing, villagers occasionally robbed small groups of smugglers, as the former also wanted to benefit from the ongoing illicit activities in the border zone. That was the case in the Jarablus area where, ironically, Turkish smugglers even complained to the French gendarmerie about this situation, claiming that 'malefactors' from both sides of the border were encouraged to do so by the Turkish border authorities as a means of fighting against contraband more efficiently. According to other accounts, however, the reason for such attacks was instead the extreme poverty that affected local dwellers in the Jarablus area.[95] At times, the French mobile guard units intervened not to protect the smugglers

---

[93] BCA, 030.10.69.454.36, 4 January 1930.

[94] CADN, 1SL/1/V/2195. 'Incident entre contrebandiers et gendarmes'. Gendarmerie Mohafazat of Aleppo, 12 June 1936.

[95] CADN, 1SL/1/V/2145. Inspection générale du vilayet d'Alep. Aleppo, 26 November 1933.

but 'to avoid that armed individuals move across the border zone freely'.[96] In other words, contraband dynamics created a symbiotic and complex relationship between borderlanders, smugglers and state officials through which the boundaries between the state and society, on the one hand, and between licit and illicit practices, on the other, became increasingly blurred.

When compared to the cross-border networks of illicit trade between Turkey and Syria, throughout the 1920s and 1930s the Turkish–Iraqi border and the northern section of the Syrian–Iraqi border were indeed less significant gateways for long-distance circuits of contraband. Thus, while illicit trade – mainly sheep, sugar, tobacco and textiles – was also a widespread feature in the Turkish–Iraqi borderlands, it remained a rather local affair. The reason for this seems to be twofold. On the one hand, the geography of the frontier zone and the absence of roads made the transport of an important number of goods difficult across this border.[97] On the other hand, the low density of the population on both sides of the border did not encourage the emergence of border towns, which could become hubs for exchange across the region, thereby diminishing the potential profit on these routes.

The situation was slightly different in the Jabal Sinjar area, though. The very presence of the provisional frontier between Syria and Iraq eventually led to a diversification of Sinjar commercial networks; namely, between the markets of Mosul and Hasaka in the Syrian Upper Jazira, without mentioning contraband activities developed across the frontier.[98] As a result, Mosul strengthened its position as the intermediary market centre between Sinjar and Syria, since many Sinjari goods were first sent to Mosul and thereafter distributed to the Syrian Jazira.[99] The importance of contraband activities between Hasaka and the Jabal was confirmed by the British efforts to hamper

---

[96] CADN, 1SL/1/V/2145. Services Spéciaux. 'Des contrebandiers dévalisés'. Arab Punar, 16 December 1933.
[97] For a detailed description of the existing routes connecting Turkey to Iraq and the planned construction of land roads by 1940, see diverse files in FO 195/2467.
[98] The main gateways for contraband along the Syrian–Iraqi border were the small towns of Abu Kamal, Tel Kotchek and Hasaka.
[99] Nelida Fuccaro, *The Other Kurds: Yazidis in Colonial Iraq* (London: I. B. Tauris, 1998), p. 75.

trade between the former and the latter by levying high import duties on goods crossing the border.[100]

Criminals and the Dynamics of Legal Pluralism

Smugglers' cross-border activity was not the only pressing issue that tested the solidity of the emerging boundary regimes in the region. As I have argued elsewhere, legal pluralism on the border provided structures that enabled some individuals and groups to outwit the law, and others to call it into play.[101] After all, as in most border regions, once fugitives trespassed the international boundaries, their status and the laws that applied to them changed.[102] Unsurprisingly then, much of the communication exchanged between the border authorities was concerned with cross-border criminality and subsequent extradition requests, although the types of crimes gathered by both administrations varied, as well as their social and economic significance. They ranged from the theft of an animal to cross-border raids committed by armed bands stealing up to hundreds of cattle, looting jewellery, to instances of rape, kidnapping and murder.[103]

The 1926 Turkish–Syrian convention which, as mentioned earlier, served as a model for ensuing agreements in the area, foresaw that extradition

---

[100] CADN, 1SL/1/V/1528. 'Note au sujet des relations commerciales entre les commerçants de Hassetché et les populations du Djebel Sindjar'. Hasaka, 2 May 1932.

[101] Jordi Tejel and Ramazan Hakkı Öztan, 'Borders of Mobility? Crime and Punishment along the Syrian-Turkish Border, 1921–39', in Kate Fleet and Ebru Boyar (eds), *Borders, Boundaries and Belonging in Post-Ottoman Space in the Interwar Period* (Leiden: Brill, 2023), pp. 204–24.

[102] The role of borders as a realm of freedom and protection for fugitives – political refugees, outlaws, and lovers – has been celebrated by Kurdish folk songs. See Wendelmoet Hamelink and Hanifi Baris, 'Dengbêjs on Borderlands: Borders and the State as Seen Through the Eyes of Kurdish Singer-poets', *Kurdish Studies*, Vol. 2, No. 1 (2014), pp. 34–60.

[103] For some examples, see BCA, 30.10.0.0.128.922.14, 4 July 1932; CADN, 1SL/1/V/2126, 'Services Spéciaux (Alep) au Qaymmaqam de Birecik', Arab Pounar, 23 April 1938; CADN, 1SL/1/V/2145, 'Procès-verbal de la réunion entre les autorités frontalières de premier degré à Jerablus', 11 October 1938; CADN, 1SL/1/V/2145, 'Deux citoyens turcs tués', Alexandretta, 21 December 1938; CADN, 1SL/1/V/2155, 'Statistiques sur les activités transfrontalières (1.1.1938–30.6.1939)'; TNA, AIR 23/374, 'Second Session of the Frontier Commission', 22 October 1927; CADN, 1SL/1/V/2051, Weekly Report. Qamishli, 14–18 April 1943.

requests be submitted through the ordinary diplomatic channels, together with all the legal documents describing the exact nature of the crime or offence.[104] Despite these dispositions, it took three years for the relevant authorities – the governors of the Turkish border provinces of Antep, Urfa and Mardin, as well as the French Adjunct Delegates of Latakia, Aleppo and Deir ez-Zor – to meet for the first time within the framework of the Permanent Commission. Thereafter, the commission gathered every six months to discuss all ongoing border-related issues, including the extradition of criminals, the exchange of booty and the disarmament of tribes in the border zone.[105] In addition, meetings between low-level officials took place on a regular basis.

As cooperation between the two countries increased, they frequently updated the 1929 Frontier Protocol to improve the monitoring of the Turkish–Syrian border. In 1935, for instance, new regulations extended the power of border authorities to arrest offenders, as well as to implement measures in order to compensate for any damages in the border area.[106] Only a year later, the Turkish consulate in Beirut submitted to the French High Commissioner an official request for further collaboration between Turkish and French Mandate security services on three issues: judicial affairs (inquiries on suspected outlaws and, if relevant, their arrest); trafficking, forgery and international crime; and, the combat against communist organisations.[107] After the Turkish annexation of Alexandretta in 1939, the two countries signed a new Convention of Friendship and Good Neighbourly Relations, which supposedly served to solve all territorial issues. In addition, the new document introduced some adjustments to earlier versions to better deal with cross-border criminality and the political manoeuvres against the respective governments led by opposition movements abroad.[108]

---

[104] A year later, the 'Regulations for the Extradition of Criminals arrested on the Iraqi–Turkish Frontiers' was signed.
[105] BCA, 30.10.0.0.230.549.3, 22 December 1929.
[106] CADN, 36PO/1/153, 'Echange de lettres relatif à la remise des criminels dans la zone frontalière turco-syrienne'. Istanbul, 11 April 1935.
[107] BCA, 30.18.1.2.61.7.20, 11 April 1936.
[108] CADN, 1SL/1/V/2136, 'Convention syro-turque d'amitié et de bon voisinage', Beirut, 25 April 1940.

Incidentally, border cooperation against cross-border criminality also allowed for the improvement of criminal investigation methods in the borderlands. Because joint inquiries sought to find out who was responsible for the border incidents and thus for the compensation procedure, it became central to determining the identities of the offenders and, even more importantly, their points of origin. In that regard, it was also vital by the late 1930s to resort to forensic science including diverse identification systems such as Bertillonage,[109] photography, dactyloscopy (finger and footprints) as well as ballistic analyses, in documenting cross-border crimes.[110]

Yet a number of factors complicated the full application of regulations. Firstly, an important number of borderlanders were bi-nationals. As such, they could cross the border without being harassed, while exploiting their dual citizenship either to hide in one of the two countries, or to pursue illicit activities.[111] Against this background, the new 1940 Convention of Friendship and Good Neighbourly Relations between French Syria and Turkey established that 'any acquisition of nationality, in any circumstances, if it is prior to an offence for which extradition of an individual is requested, will not be used as an obstacle to the delivery of offenders'.[112] By the early 1940s, however, many borderlanders could still play off the system of existing legal pluralism in the border zone, particularly in the Upper Jazira which suffered from the poor quality of civil registers. As it turned out, during the Second World War, thousands of dwellers in the Syrian *caza* (district) of

---

[109] Alphonse Bertillon (1853–1914) developed in France an anthropometric system of identification. Anthropometrics used the measurements and descriptions of parts of the body to identify individuals. The Bertillon card included two photographs, one full-face and one profile. On the transmission of Bertillonage between the late nineteenth and early twentieth centuries across the world, see Simon A. Cole, *Suspect Identities: A History of Fingerprinting and Criminal Identification* (Cambridge, MA: Harvard University Press, 2002); Pierre Piazza, *Un œil sur le crime. Naissance de la police scientifique. Alphonse Bertillon de A à Z* (Bayeux: Orep Editions, 2016).

[110] For some examples of joint criminal investigations using forensic techniques between 1938 and 1940, see CADN, 1SL/1/V/2131.

[111] CADN, 1SL/1/V/2145, 'Répression de la contrebande en Syrie. Services Spéciaux du Levant', Afrin, 22 October 1940.

[112] Ibid.

Tigris were not registered at all, and in other cases they had obtained Syrian citizenship while keeping their Turkish passports.[113]

More generally, as with smugglers, connivance of border authorities with raiders was another obstacle to the implementation of border protocols. The British, for instance, could write:

> I am convinced that in practically every raid against Iraq territory, the Turkish Gendarmerie is involved, either actively or in connivance. Reasons for this are the dilatory methods of Turkish Pay Masters and Supply Department, and the troops are often forced to steal to live.[114]

Border officials also encouraged cross-border raids as a means of pressuring the neighbouring authorities into rapid action to either extradite requested criminals, or to undertake a swift investigation. In some instances, local officials could even amass certain amounts of money from the cross-border raids in dubious ways. On 14 July 1930, for instance, Bozan Shahin, chief of the Barazi tribe from the caza of Jarablus, sent a letter to the French authorities explaining that six members of the Jess tribe, Turkish nationals, had robbed him of fifty-four camels and attacked his tribesmen. Following the lack of action by the French officers at the Arab Pounar post, Bozan Shahin sent a band of four men into Turkey to inquire about the fate of the above-mentioned animals. As it turned out, the camels were still in possession of the Jess tribe. The Barazi tribesmen then formally asked the Jess chiefs to return the animals, but the latter refused and asked for eighty Turkish pounds in gold to be paid to the Urfa governor as a 'gift'. Against this background, Bozan Shahin asked higher French authorities to intervene and mediate – should the French authorities fail to help him, his tribesmen would enter the Turkish territory again to seize the camels on their own.[115]

---

[113] CADN, 1SL/1/V/2195, 'Sur les relations frontalières', Lt. Lannurien (Services Spéciaux à Ayn Diwar) au Délégué Adjoint du Haut-Commissaire (Alep), Ayn Diwar, 9 April 1941.

[114] TNA, AIR 23/374. Administrative Inspector Mosul Liwa to the Adviser, Ministry of Interior (Baghdad). Mosul, 10 July 1928.

[115] CADN, 1SL/1/V/2160. Letter from Bozan Shahin to the Délégué Adjoint du Haut Commissaire. Aleppo, 14 July 1930.

Outlaws and raiders' room for manoeuvre was not unlimited, though. Despite mutual accusations of 'disloyalty', in particular between Turkey and French Syria, cooperation rather than conflict had prevailed in the frontier zones from 1929 onwards. Furthermore, the content of letters exchanged between diverse border administrations demonstrates the need for historians and scholars in general to go beyond formal diplomatic channels to better understand how the newly-established borders – understood as social institutions – created their own dynamics. Hence, according to some available statistics, between 1929 and 1935, the French had delivered, through informal channels, 348 people out of 976 requests presented by Turkish authorities. In turn, Turkey had released 114 outlaws out of 461 requests to their French counterparts. A similar trend remained with regard to official extradition procedures: while Turkey had delivered only one individual out of 25 demands, French authorities had extradited seven people out of 52 regular requests.[116]

Overall, these statistics expose that informal arrangements were more frequent than official extradition procedures. Everyday practices at the borders were thus deeply informed by ground-level customary cooperation between low-level officials who could tailor informal arrangements to ease border relations, at times at odds with the prevailing relations at a diplomatic level.[117] In Turkey, although the First General Inspectorate and provincial governors were, in theory, the key to monitoring the security situation in the provinces adjacent to the Turkish–Syrian and Turkish–Iraqi borders,[118] in practice, the border officials on both sides were granted final authority in solving issues related to the exchange of outlaws and criminals. A rationale that, in fact, mirrored similar dispositions undertaken on the Syrian and Iraqi sides of the border. Thus, for instance, extradition procedures were deemed unnecessary for individuals having committed crimes in the frontier zone and having escaped to the corresponding zone. Therefore, the suspected criminals

---

[116] CADN, 1SL/1/V/2144, 'Extradition d'individus par les autorités turques et syriennes', Le Haut-Commissaire de la France à Basri Riza bey, Consul général de la Turquie à Beyrouth, Beirut, 15 February 1935.

[117] For a list of cases 'solved' on the spot thanks to informal extraditions of criminals and fugitives, see for instance CADN, 1SL/1/V/2134, 'Rapport mensuel sur l'application des accords frontaliers', Services Spéciaux, Arab Pounar, 1 February 1938.

[118] Cemil Koçak, *Umumî Müfettişlikler, 1927–52* (Istanbul: İletişim, 2003), pp. 72–81.

were simply returned with their loot and arms to their country of origin. In other words, the three governments accepted the principle that 'minor frontier questions could be settled on the spot' without producing excessive paperwork.[119]

The method adopted regarding returning the criminals without extradition procedure was as follows: a) the *Qaymmaqam*s of the frontier *caza*s of each government informed the frontier authorities of the corresponding side of such criminals. Upon receiving the information, the corresponding side immediately arrested the person wanted by either government; b) after the above action was carried out, the criminals were returned upon demand by the Frontier *vali* on the Turkish side, by the Service de Renseignements (later Services Spéciaux) of the *mohafazat* on the Syrian side, and by the Special Officer along with the Inspector of the Mutasarrif on the Iraqi side; c) the surrender into custody was to be carried out only upon demand by the said high authorities in this manner, and such demands had to contain information about the description of the criminal, nature, date and place of the crime and other similar particulars.[120]

Finally, frontier officials often mediated between borderlanders to avoid endless rounds of cross-border tribal raids. By doing so, however, they agreed to dispense 'justice' according to customary law. Moreover, as the British had done in Iraq, at the insistence of the French officials, a provision for a separate tribal jurisdiction was included in the French Mandate's legal regime. Henceforth, crimes committed between tribes were not brought before civil courts; only offenses perpetrated between sedentary populations or by tribes against settlers were submitted to regular tribunals.[121] Either individually or collectively perpetrated, a crime committed against another tribe affected the whole clan. As such, tribal chieftains played a central part in the resolution

---

[119] TNA, AIR 23/374. Despatch from British Embassy (Constantinople) to the High Commissioner (Baghdad). Constantinople, 17 February 1927.

[120] See TNA, AIR 23/374, 'Procès-Verbal of the 8th Permanent Frontier Commission held at Mardin', Air Headquarters (Hinaidi) to Special Service Officer (Arbil and Mosul), Hinaidi, 27 November 1930.

[121] CADN, 1SL/1/V/988, 'Législation bédouine', Beirut, 11 July 1929. For the criminal disputes regulation in Iraq, see TNA, FO 371/15360. 'Tribal Criminal and Civil Disputes Regulation'. Baghdad printed at the Government Press, 1926.

(or not) of a given conflict.[122] In the process, however, chieftains' position was reinforced by border authorities which, first and foremost, wished to secure peace and stability along the shared borders, on the one hand, and find a solid mediator between the state and the tribesmen, on the other.[123] In some instances, though, the aim of state representatives' intervention in the Bedouin areas was geared towards (re-)establishing a certain equilibrium between tribes, rather than rendering justice. In other words, mediation meetings between chieftains and border authorities after a series of cross-border raids served to discuss general issues such as the use of certain grazing zones; the restoration of the stolen animals could be even left out from the final settlements.[124]

When tribesmen were killed by other members of a tribe, whether from the same or a neighbouring country, tribal customary law – 'blood money' or *diya/diyet* – was used in order to compensate the assaulted tribe. In doing so, *diya* became a trans-border legal practice implemented by French Syria and British Iraq to keep peace in the shared borderlands.[125] Crucially, however, informal arrangements also served to solve crimes committed against state officials in the frontier zone. Hence, although the Turkish state claimed the absolute prominence of the civil and penal codes over customary laws across the country, joint border governance with Iraq also led Turkish local governors and border authorities to accommodate 'legal pluralism' prevailing in Iraq.[126]

---

[122] Eveline van der Steen, *Near Eastern Tribal Societies during the Nineteenth Century. Economy, Society and Politics between the Tent and Town* (London: Routledge, 2014), p. 117.

[123] See Christian Velud, 'La politique mandataire française à l'égard des tribus et des zones de steppe en Syrie: L'exemple de la Djézireh', in Riccardo Bocco, Ronald Jaubert and Françoise Métral (eds), *Steppes d'Arabie. Etats, pasteurs, agriculteurs et commerçants: le devenir des zones sèches* (Paris: PUF, 1993), pp. 61–86. For a similar argument with regard to British Iraq, see Toby Dodge, *Inventing Iraq: The Failure of Nation Building and a Future Denied* (New York: Columbia University Press, 2003), pp. 83–100.

[124] CADN, 36PO/153. Seventh session of the Permanent Frontier Commission. Damascus, 29 June 1935.

[125] TNA, AIR 23/156. SSO (Mosul) to Air Headquarters (Hinaidi). 'Hasaka Conference'. Mosul, 16 March 1929.

[126] The notion of 'legal pluralism' in Syria and Iraq has traditionally been used to define the socio-economic boundaries established by the French and the British by dividing the countries between the steppe or *badiya* and the agricultural areas or *mamura*. In each of these zones, the judicial system varied to 'adapt' laws to 'local traditions'. In fact, the separation

Because keeping stability along the border zone and/or good relations with local chieftains was crucial for frontier officials, the latter accepted tribal customs as the new 'normal'. Thus, for instance, whenever Turkish or Iraqi soldiers and police officers were killed by tribesmen at the Turkish–Iraqi border, both states despatched *diya* for the murdered men, in accordance to tribal customary law.[127] In addition, and in order to maintain good relations between the two countries, the clan of the offenders was removed as a whole from the frontier zone.[128] By doing so, however, Turkish and Iraqi authorities contributed to further blurring the boundaries between different existing legal systems (that is, tribal, national and transnational) and, ultimately, to creating and endorsing hybrid forms of sovereignty in the borderlands.

Gender Contours of Legal Pluralism

While border authorities saw in the so-called 'local traditions' the best tool to prevent tribal unrest in the borderlands, such practices became increasingly contested both by local political elites and even mandatory officials, who lamented the negative impact of customary law on local populations – in particular, upon women.[129] Indeed, reports from the border zones and local

---

of Bedouin and settlers was mainly used for political purposes; that is, avoiding intense relations between nationalist movements in cities with Bedouin tribes. See Daniel Neep, 'Policing the Desert: Coercion, Consent and the Colonial Order', in Laleh Khalili and Jillian Schwedler (eds), *Policing and Prisons in the Middle East: Formations of Coercion* (London: Hurst, 2010), pp. 41–56.

[127] By 1930, the amount of *diya* for a murdered Turkish soldier by Iraqi tribesmen was 2,500 Turkish pounds. TNA, AIR 23/374. 8th Meeting of the Permanent Frontier Commission. Mardin, 20 June 1930.

[128] TNA, AIR 23/374. 6th Meeting of the Permanent Frontier Commission. 3rd Session. Mardin, 31 May 1929.

[129] Noga Efrati argues that tribal customs were increasingly critiqued both by some British officials and Iraqi lawmakers. Nevertheless, they remained in force until 1958. Noga Efrati, 'The First World War and its Legacy for Women in Iraq', T. G. Fraser (ed.), *The First World War and its Aftermath: The Shaping of the Middle East* (London: Cingko, 2015), pp. 82–4. For a critical appraisal of rights granted to women and their 'subaltern' status in Syria during the French Mandate, see Elizabeth Thompson, *Colonial Citizens: Republican Rights, Paternal Privilege, and Gender in French Syria and Lebanon* (New York: Columbia University Press, 1999).

newspapers are riddled with examples in which groups of tribesmen illegally crossed the boundary to abduct cattle and women, in order to claim justice and compensation.[130] According to these regulations, in the settlement of blood feuds, tribes required the guilty party, in addition to paying *diyas*, to hand over one or more women from his clan to the family of the victim for the purpose of marriage.[131]

Importantly, the woman in question 'continued to belong to her own kin group even though she lived in the tribe of her husband'.[132] By borrowing pre-existing Ottoman legal frameworks under the pretext of tradition – albeit adapting it to new purposes – Turkish, British and French authorities encouraged practices that, paradoxically, not only entailed further (female/clannish) cross-border mobility, but also helped (re)-connect older geographies despite the establishment of new borders.[133]

On the other hand, women living in the borderlands were not simply passive victims of tribal and frontier regulations. Whenever possible, they attempted to mobilise border resources and took risks to evade both customary laws and state control of borders. Like smugglers and outlaws, fugitive women seeking refuge on the other side of the border took advantage of the disruption of sovereignties, while also relying on networks of trust. This was the case, for instance, for Nassiba, a female Turkish citizen who was caught in Syrian territory and condemned to a month-long prison sentence for having crossed the border illegally. While waiting in her cell to be extradited to Turkey, Nassiba wrote a letter where she begged the French for 'mercy' – should she be delivered to her family, she would be killed by her own brothers who wanted to 'save their lost honour' soiled by 'unfounded' rumours about Nassiba's promiscuous sexual behaviour. In the light of this, she requested to

---

[130] 'Suriye'ye Kadın Kaçıran Haydutlar', *Akşam*, 20 August 1929; On the common practice of abducting women in exchange for cattle, see CADN, 1SL/1/V/2051, Weekly Report, Ras al-Ayn, 4 January 1943.

[131] Noga Efrati, *Women in Iraq: Past Meets Present* (New York: Columbia University Press, 2012), p. 23.

[132] Eveline van der Steen, *Near Eastern Tribal Societies during the Nineteenth Century*, p. 218.

[133] Iraqi Criminal Law was an amalgamation of Ottoman law with Anglo-Sudanese-Egyptian law. Sara Pursley, *Familiar Futures: Time, Selfhood, and Sovereignty in Iraq* (Stanford, CA: Stanford University Press, 2019), p. 47.

be freed and thus allowed to settle in her relatives' house in Aleppo, as she had planned while in Turkey.[134]

Nassiba's story was not unique. Dozens of women escaping from 'honour killings' found shelter in the house of a male relative – often that of a brother, a cousin, or an uncle – on the other side of the border.[135] Likewise, some women wishing to remarry or have a new start in the neighbouring country sought refuge in their relatives' households. In that regard, women developed different strategies. They could arrange their own abduction by their lovers and marry them after crossing the international boundary. In other instances, they carefully prepared their departure:

> [Received] arrest and delivery warrants for Zeyneb ... from Ziyaret [Urfa, Turkey], who has allegedly deserted her husband together with her daughter, while taking with her jewellery and the titles of house property. She had hidden in her parents' house in Alishar [Ayn al-Arab, Syria] where she had allegedly been married to another man illegally.[136]

Although trespassing the border was not a difficult act, the extradition system rendered these acts hazardous. While some 'fugitive' women returned to their marital home due to either the mediation of relatives or the intervention of border authorities, elopement could also lead to subsequent acts of retaliation from the 'deserted' groom or husband's clan.[137] At times, though, accusations of elopement against women could also function to conceal local dynamics such as competition for resources or revenge strategies. Thus, for instance, the *mukhtar* of Borjilat (on the Turkish side of the Turkish–Iraqi border)

---

[134] CADN, 1SL/1/V/2144, Le Délégué Adjoint du Haut Commissaire à Alep à Selim Feyzi Gönen, Consul général de la Turquie à Alep, Aleppo, 12 December 1940.

[135] CADN, 1SL/1/V/2161, Le Délégué Adjoint du Haut Commissaire à Alep au Lieutenant des Services Spéciaux à Arab Pounar, Aleppo, 2 August 1937. On 'honour killing' reports see, for instance, CADN, 1SL/1/V/2134, 'Rapport mensuel sur les relations frontalières', Arab Pounar, 3 June 1938.

[136] CADN, 1SL/1/V/2134, Le Lieutenant Doumeyrou (Services Spéciaux) au Délégué Adjoint du Haut Commissaire à Alep. Ayn al-Arab, 1 August 1939.

[137] See Lale Yalçin-Heckmann, *Tribe and Kinship among the Kurds* (Frankfurt: Peter Lang, 1991), pp. 247–53.

provided false information about a young woman who was allegedly abducted from that village into Iraq. As it turned out, however, the young woman was married with the approval of her relatives and by her own consent to an Iraqi citizen. In addition, she had already reached the age of puberty and it was attested that she also had Iraqi citizenship. Ultimately, the investigation revealed that the *mukhtar*'s claims targeted first and foremost her brother, who was a shepherd working for him. Crucially, the latter had abandoned the cattle to accompany his sister to Iraq, thereby harming the *mukhtar*'s economic interests.[138]

Far from being alien to the new legal and international developments in the region, women living in the borderlands also took advantage of their citizenship status. By late 1939, for instance, a woman named Rabia, recently married to a Turkish citizen, abandoned her marital home. As the marriage had not been consummated and since she had been registered as Syrian national in 1922, Rabia left her husband and moved to Syria, where she had some relatives. Despite her husbands' manoeuvres and Turkish requests for 'extradition', legally Rabia could not be delivered to the Turkish border authorities.[139] Indeed, 'desertion' of the conjugal domicile was not included in the different conventions signed by both countries as a valid reason for extradition. Therefore, the official response to such claims depended, to a certain extent, on border authorities' willingness to cooperate or not in this kind of issue.

Admittedly, the ongoing border relations and personal views rather than transnational law could have an impact on officials' decisions, ultimately based on their 'discretionary power'.[140] This is perfectly illustrated by the correspondence exchanged between different French officials serving in the northern borderlands. Thus, while by 1937 the Adjunct Delegate to the French High

---

[138] TNA, AIR 23/374. 8th Meeting of the Permanent Frontier Commission. 5th session. Mardin, 22 June 1930.

[139] CADN, 1SL/1/V/2161, Services Spéciaux, Ayn al-Arab, 16 February 1940.

[140] On the notion of 'discretionary power', see Michael Lipsky, *Street-Level Bureaucracy: Dilemmas of the Individual in Public Services* (New York: Russel Sage Foundation, 1980). On a recent contribution applied to the role of *mukhtars* in relation to the everyday interactions/mediation between state and society, see Elise Massicard, *Street-Level Governing: Negotiating the State in Urban Turkey* (Stanford, CA: Stanford University Press, 2022).

Commissioner in the Aleppo province consented to hand over the 'fugitive' women seeking shelter in Syrian territory for they were perceived as 'guilty' of marital desertion,[141] three years later the newly appointed Adjunct Delegate in Aleppo opposed this practice on two grounds. Firstly, there was no legal obligation resulting from the accords sealed with Turkey to follow such a policy. Secondly, the French official did not view 'marital desertion' as a crime or an act of brigandage. Therefore, the restitution of women was not compulsory 'unless we apply the same regime to women that we do for cattle'.[142]

Finally, women's infringements on the frontier zone were also linked to other dynamics, such as their participation in illicit economic activities, including contraband. Whether holders of a *passavant* or mingling with groups of labourers crossing the border, women carried smuggled goods hidden in their traditional loose clothes and headdresses. For this matter, they were able to take advantage of a certain restraint among border guards while examining female border crossers. Women's role in smuggling activities was important enough to draw the attention of Turkish journalists who toured the region seeking 'exotic' features of Turkey's borderlands.[143]

After an initial period of low intensity guerrilla warfare in the Turkish/Syrian/Iraqi borderlands, regional and domestic developments dictated the delimitation of the Turkish–Syrian and Turkish–Iraqi boundaries, thereby initiating a long-winded process that would ultimately result in the emergence of transnational border governance. As such, the authorities on each side of the newly-established borders committed themselves to settling border issues through bilateral commissions, which would feature the participation of local administrators, too. The willingness of the French, British and Turkish authorities to cooperate in monitoring the border, however, encountered serious challenges, particularly after the

---

[141] CADN, 1SL/1/V/2161, Le Délégué Adjoint du Haut Commissaire à Alep au Lieutenant (Services Spéciaux) à Arab Pounar, Aleppo, 2 August 1937.

[142] CADN, 1SL/1/V/2144, Le Délégué Adjoint du Haut Commissaire à Alep au Lieutenant de la Gendarmerie Légion à Azaz, Aleppo, 7 February 1940. See also Jordi Tejel, 'Des femmes contre des moutons: franchissements féminins de la frontière turco-syrienne (1929–44)', *20&21. Revue d'histoire*, Vol. 145 (2020), pp. 35–48.

[143] 'Cenup Hududu Hain', *Tan*, 1 January 1937; 'Kaçakçı Kadına randevu var', *Tan*, 20 January 1937.

Global Depression in 1929 – an important watershed that reshuffled the existing commodity, labour and capital flows.

In particular, the developments across the Turkish–Syrian border soon began to reflect some of these globally rooted changes, as borderlanders became involved in the consolidation of increasingly profitable illicit networks that crisscrossed the border zone. Eager to contain these illegal connections, the Ankara government reacted by passing anti-smuggling legislations and militarising the border through the deployment of growing numbers of border posts, gates, mechanised and cavalry units. Unilateral policies were obviously worthless due to the transnational nature of smuggling activities. Against this background, Turkish authorities sought to cooperate more directly with their French, and to a lesser extent, British counterparts over the years.

Transnational governance was, however, challenged by other groups and individuals inhabiting the borderlands, including fugitive women and a variety of criminals and outlaws who saw in borders a resource that could serve their own agendas. To be sure, the Paris Peace Conference paved the way for the emergence of new modern states in the Middle East, whether as mandatory or fully independent states, by granting them sovereign powers within new 'national' territories. Paradoxically, then, as in other borderlands, 'the same sovereignty that empowered states also undermined them by limiting the reach of their authority in a world in which people crossed borders, with much more dexterity than law'.[144] Within this context, states not only strengthened their legal and security cooperation, but also resorted to older practices and informal arrangements, leading to the hybridisation of different legal traditions as well as the intensification of state and society relations in the borderlands.

Yet illicit human mobility was not the only driver of increased international coordination and the necessary readjustment of older policies and practices at the border; national and international endeavours to keep pests and diseases at bay in the borderlands became another central instrument of state formation process in the interwar years.

---

[144] Bradley Miller, *Borderline Crime: Fugitive Criminals and the Challenge of the Border, 1819–1914* (Toronto: University of Toronto Press, 2016), p. 6.

4

INTERSTATE COOPERATION AGAINST DISEASES AND PLAGUES AND ITS LIMITS

On 21 September 1935, Shaykh Ahmad Khaznawi (1887–1950), head of an influential Naqshbandi *tariqa* (order) with influence in southeast Turkey and northern Syria, submitted a petition to the French High Commissioner in which, for the umpteenth time, he requested the right to return to Khazna – his village of origin, situated in the Sanjaq of Jazira – and thus leave Tel Maruf where he and his family had been 'exiled' by the French some years earlier.[1] In the same letter, Khaznawi contested Turkish allegations about his involvement in 'anti-Republican' activities. On the contrary, the Sufi shaykh highlighted his relentless efforts to spread religious teachings attuned to 'modern sciences' among borderlanders. As was the case in the past, however, Khaznawi's endeavours remained unsuccessful.

Turkish accusations against Khaznawi were not new, though. Ahmad Khaznawi was the son of Mela Murat, a local imam. As such, he was trained first by his father and then in several Naqshbandi religious centres in Eastern Anatolia, including Silvan, Hizan and Norshin. Just before the First World War, Khaznawi became one of the *khalifas* (appointed deputy) of Shaykh Diyaeddin Norshini, before returning to his native Khazna.[2] According to

---

[1] CADN, 1SL/1/V/567. Request from Shaykh Ahmad Khaznawi. Deir ez-Zor, 30 October 1935.
[2] Kutbeddin Akyüz, *Ahmed el-Haznevî ve Hazneviyye Tarikatı* (MA Thesis, Yalova: Üniversitesi, 2015); M. Şerif Korkusuz. *Nehri'den Hazne'ye Meşayih-i Nakşibendî* (Istanbul: Kilim Matbaacılık, 2010).

some hagiographic accounts, during the 'war of liberation' against the British and French presence in Anatolia and the Bilad al-Sham, French military forces deployed in the region allegedly asked him to call on his disciples (*murids*) to fight against Mustafa Kemal and his followers. Because Khaznawi refused to combat his 'Muslim brothers', French officials adopted a negative stance against him thereafter.[3]

Despite this initial setback, after the Ankara government banned all Sufi orders in 1925, Khaznawi's safe haven in Syria allowed him to attract large numbers of *murids* from Turkey as well as local Qadiri shaykhs, thereby exercising a 'virtually unrivalled influence in north-eastern Syria, both among the Arabs and the Kurds.'[4] Nonetheless, Khaznawi's ascent on both sides of the Turkish–Syrian borderline raised serious concerns among Turkish officials who protested against his presence in the border zone. According to Turkish reports, Shaykh Ahmad Khaznawi pretended to be a messiah, thus exploiting 'people's ignorance' for his own benefit and, ultimately, becoming a potential challenger to Turkey's Republican values garnered with the ideas of science, modernity and progress. Moreover, because folk medicine and superstitions were widespread among borderlands dwellers, increasing numbers of *murids* from Turkey crisscrossed the border to pay a visit to Khaznawi asking for his blessing and 'miracles' to cure a variety of health issues – from infertility to severe blindness due to trachoma.[5] By doing so, however, Khaznawi's disciples were potential transmitters of infectious diseases as they returned home.[6] For all these reasons, Turkish officials pressed the French to expel Khaznawi from the border zone; the French, in order to ease neighbourly relations with

---

[3] Şeyh Alâaddin Haznevî, *Hazret ve Şah-ı Hazne* (edited by Abdullah Demiray) (Istanbul: Semerkand Yayınları, 2012), p. 93.

[4] Martin van Bruinessen, *Agha, Shaikh and the State: The Social and Political Structures of Kurdistan* (London: Zed Books, 1992), p. 338.

[5] Caused by the bacterium *Chlamydia trachomatis*, this contagious eye disease develops in adverse conditions that lack basic sanitation or adequate water supply. Trachoma's most distinctive symptom is the formation of granulated eyelids. In some cases, it can lead to irreversible blindness. Katherine Schlosser, *Trachoma Through History* (New York: International Trachoma Initiative, 2020), pp. 1–9.

[6] BCA.030.10.177.220.14, March 1930.

Turkey, eventually forced the Sufi shaykh to move first to Deir ez-Zor and then to Tel Maruf, north-east of Hasaka.

By the mid-1930s, however, regional and global developments offered a chance to Shaykh Khaznawi to extend his influence, while improving his relations with the French. For one, the Mandates in the Middle East reinforced the encroachment of European imperialism on Muslim territories, leading France and Britain to regulate the Hajj for thousands of pilgrims travelling from Syria, Iraq, Lebanon, Transjordan and Palestine to Mecca.[7] Yet, as in the past, sanitary and political considerations were key issues to explain France's management of the Hajj.[8] In that sense, French officials aimed to keep pilgrims from the Maghreb separated from those of the Levant to avoid 'contamination' of *hajjis* with anti-French propaganda.[9] Therefore, in the early years of the French Mandate in the Levant, and despite petitions submitted by urban entrepreneurs from Damascus and Aleppo asking for the establishment of bus lines between Syria and Saudi Arabia, French authorities favoured the maritime road to Mecca. Notwithstanding this, two complementary developments brought about a dramatic shift on this matter.

On the one hand, Iraq opened new land routes to facilitate the Hajj to Mecca in 1934. On the other hand, two years later, protests in Syria against the French monopoly on the Hajj gained in strength, while illegal caravans

---

[7] Luc Chantre, *Pèlerinages d'empire: Une histoire européenne du pèlerinage à La Mecque* (Paris: Editions de la Sorbonne, 2018). Eric Tagliacozzo, *The Longest Journey: Southeast Asians and the Pilgrimage to Mecca* (Oxford: Oxford University Press, 2013); John Slight, *The British Empire and the Hajj, 1865–1956* (Cambridge, MA: Harvard University Press, 2015).

[8] Sylvia Chiffoleau, 'Entre bienfaisance, contrôle des populations et agenda international: la politique sanitaire du mandat français en Syrie et au Liban', *Canadian Bulletin of Medical History*, Vol. 30, No. 2 (2013), pp. 91–111. See also Michael C. Low, 'Empire and the Hajj: Pilgrims, Plagues,, and Pan-Islam under British Surveillance, 1865–1908', *International Journal of Middle East Studies*, Vol. 40, No. 2 (2008), pp. 269–90.

[9] The fear of political contamination was also extended to Muslim pilgrims coming from India via Iraq, thereby prompting Franco-British cooperation, despite the traditional rivalry between the two European powers in the Middle East. See James Casey, 'Sacred Surveillance: Indian Muslims, Waqf, and the Evolution of State Power in French Mandate Syria', in James R. Fichter (ed.), *British and French Colonialism in Africa, Asia and the Middle East: Connected Empires across the Eighteenth to the Twentieth Centuries* (London: Palgrave Macmillan, 2019), pp. 89–110.

of pilgrims from different Syrian locations proliferated. Against this background, the French High Commission allowed pilgrims coming from Iraq or departing from Syria to use land routes towards Mecca.[10] Subsequently, the already existing trans-desert route connecting Baghdad to Damascus via Deir ez-Zor was open to pilgrims,[11] thereby introducing the coexistence of different forms of mobility as well as the multiplication of local actors involved in this religious, economic, social and political venture.[12]

It is within this context that Khaznawi's influence in northern Syria attracted French attention – they chose him as an agent and contact to organise the Hajj in the Jazira region. Thereafter, Khaznawi collected all the applications from individual pilgrims – some of them from Turkey – and made the travel arrangements for them to gather in Damascus. From there, *hajjis* continued their long journey to Mecca.[13] Unsurprisingly, Khaznawi's prestige grew even stronger across the region; he had become not only a trans-border spiritual figure, but also a nodal actor of 'one of the largest gatherings of human beings on the planet'.[14] Furthermore, the role of overland routes and borderlanders in facilitating the flows of pilgrims increased during the Second World War as the maritime routes became unsafe and the pilgrims turned into privileged targets of political propaganda. Against this backdrop, French authorities in Syria favoured the reverse course: Syrian pilgrims were channelled towards Iraq

---

[10] For a comprehensive report on trans-desert routes and transport companies in the Middle East in the interwar period, see TNA, CO 732/65/5. 'Nair Transport Company', British Consulate (Damascus) to the Secretary of State for Foreign Affairs. Damascus, 29 January 1934.

[11] John M. Munro, *The Nairn Way: Desert Bus to Baghdad* (Delmar: Caravan Books, 1980).

[12] César Jaquier, 'Motor Cars and Transdesert Traffic: Channelling Mobilities between Iraq and Syria', in Jordi Tejel and Ramazan Hakkı Öztan (eds), *Regimes of Mobility: Borders and State Formation in the Middle East, 1918–1946* (Edinburgh: Edinburgh University Press, 2022), pp. 228–55; Philippe Pétriat, 'The Uneven Age of Speed: Caravans, Technology, and Mobility in the Late Ottoman and post-Ottoman Middle East', *International Journal of Middle East Studies*, Vol. 53, No. 2 (2021), pp. 273–90.

[13] CADN, 1SL/1/V/1085–6. French High Commissioner to the Adjunct Delegate at Deir ez-Zor, 6 December 1941.

[14] Eric Tagliacozzo and Shawkat M. Toorawa, 'Introduction', in Eric Tagliacozzo and Shawkat M. Toorawa (eds), *The Hajj: Pilgrimage in Islam* (Cambridge: Cambridge University Press, 2015), pp. 1–9 (here p. 1).

before travelling under British surveillance to Mecca.[15] Khaznawi's role in the Hajj did not last long, though. Upon the closure of the French Mandate in 1944, Syrian state officials replaced Khaznawi in the organisation of the Hajj in the Jazira.[16] Nonetheless, Shaykh Ahmad Khaznawi and his sons succeeded in consolidating a religious and cultural landscape that continued – and still continues – to ignore international borderlines.[17] Beyond Khaznawi's individual and collective trajectory during the French Mandate, his story sheds light on three key issues in relation to the management of pests and diseases in the borderlands as well as the role of human and non-human actors in the emergence and consolidation of new borders in the aftermath of the First World War.

First, just as cross-border criminality prompted neighbouring states to work together more closely and catalysed the creation of institutions, germs and insects also became drivers for increasing interstate cooperation and border control. This process, however, was by no means self-evident. Informed by environmental history, this chapter thus argues that non-human actors such as germs and insects played an ambivalent role in the state- and border-making processes in the aftermath of the First World War.[18] On the one hand, the spread of diseases, locusts, and other pests across the border zones strained even more the already-tense relations between Turkish, French and British authorities. Each state accused the other of not making serious efforts to prevent infectious diseases and pests from 'crossing' into their respective 'national' territories, thereby jeopardising the economic and social life of neighbouring countries. Hence, diseases and locust plagues nourished

---

[15] MAE, Vichy, série E, Correspondance Politique, No. 166. Report from the Office internationale de l'Hygiène Publique. Paris, 8 June 1942.

[16] CADN, 1SL/1/V/1128. Sûreté aux Armées (Deir ez-Zor) to the Director of Sûreté Générale (Damascus). Deir ez-Zor, 30 October 1944.

[17] Ramazan Aras, 'Naqshbandi Sufis and their Conception of Place, Time and Fear on the Turkish–Syrian Border and Borderland', *Middle Eastern Studies*, Vol. 55, No. 1 (2019), pp. 44–59.

[18] For a comprehensive appraisal of this booming field, see John R. Mc Neill, José Augusto Padua, and Mahesh Rangarajan (eds), *Environmental History as if Nature Existed* (Oxford: Oxford University Press, 2010); Andrew C. Isenberg (ed.), *The Oxford Handbook of Environmental History* (Oxford: Oxford University Press, 2014); Marco Armiero and Richard Tucker (eds), *Environmental History of Modern Migrations* (London and New York: Routledge, 2017).

mutual suspicion as well as nationalist fantasies in the face of 'foreign invaders' and 'enemies'. On the other hand, because state officials and experts soon realised that, separately, each state was unable to eradicate epidemics and insect infestations, interstate cooperation was, despite all the odds, necessary to deal with common threats and challenges.

In that regard, the exploitation of health issues by Turkey in order to force the expulsion of potential challengers, such as Ahmad Khaznawi, from the frontier zone as well as the vision of diseases and pests as 'foreign invaders' – largely shared by state officials – all point to a second, yet connected theme: domestically, social interpretations of diseases and locust infestations helped 'nationalise' germs and animals, and ultimately enacted the principle of territoriality in the border zones. After all, demarcating and consolidating borders 'seemed to be the indispensable condition for the birth or rebirth of nations'.[19] In parallel, however, as the example of Khaznawi and his Sufi order shows it, discourses on public health also contributed to the formation of internal boundaries between 'good' and 'bad' citizens; between partisans of 'progress' and devotees of superstitions and 'backwardness'.[20] Although less radical than in Turkey, state officials together with experts' discourses on diseases in Syria and Iraq also stigmatised certain groups and walks of life – in particular, pilgrims and Bedouins, viewed as disease carriers, utterly reluctant to embrace the demands of modern life and hygiene. Furthermore, state officials' visions of local societies and their immediate environment also reinforced spatial and socio-cultural boundaries: in Turkey, between the East and the West, and in Syria and Iraq, between the 'civilised' or productive areas inhabited by settler populations and the wastelands populated by 'primitive' nomadic tribes.

Thirdly, and finally, the survival of social practices and religious circuits performed by Khaznawi's disciples reminds us that the perception of cross-border mobility of both human and non-human agents as a problem or a

---

[19] Patrik Zylberman, 'Civilizing the State: Borders, Weak States and International Health in Modern Europe', in Alison Bashford (ed.), *Medicine at the Border: Disease, Globalization and Security, 1850 to the Present* (Palgrave/Macmillan: New York, 2007), pp. 21–40 (here p. 21).

[20] Kyle T. Evered and Emine Ö. Evered, 'State, Peasant, Mosquito: The Biopolitics of Public Health Education and Malaria in Early Republican Turkey', *Political Geography*, Vol. 31 (2012), pp. 311–23.

threat is a state-centric narrative, which is obviously neither unique nor hegemonic. In Turkey, despite the new state elites' aspirations to impose a sole space of reference, diverse grassroots actors in the borderlands continued to promote the networks that were linked with their own needs and temporalities, thereby contributing to the cultivation of alternative understandings of cross-border regions, social and religious groups in the Turkish–Syrian–Iraqi borderlands. In other words, the religious and cultural landscape of Sufi orders such as Khaznawi's, was cadenced by other perceptions 'of place, time and fear which ... transcended political borders for decades, contradicting official cartographic imagination and the modern-secular understanding of place and time'.[21] Likewise, archival sources show that the arsenal of practices developed by borderlanders for either resisting or subverting state sanitary policies was rich and diverse: from the smuggling of cattle (thus escaping sanitary controls), to the avoidance of vaccination campaigns, among many others. Needless to say, microbes and insects continued to ignore borders, although agencies of Middle Eastern states, as elsewhere, unreasonably expected them not to.[22]

Yet, borderlanders did not always resist states' endeavours to control pests and diseases. As we shall see, borderlanders' attitude could only be conditional upon a variety of criteria, such as the potential economic impact of sanitary measures or the survival of previous social networks. Critically, the complex and sometimes conflicting relationship that unfolded between borderlanders, animals, state officials, international experts, insects and germs in the borderlands produced new outcomes as well as new ways of conceiving health issues and the territorial state in the post-Ottoman Middle East.

Towards Increasing Interstate and Transnational Cooperation

In the nineteenth century, the global cholera pandemic that struck Europe in the 1830s, alongside a series of cholera outbreaks that erupted in the Ottoman Empire between 1846 and 1851, transformed the Middle Eastern

---

[21] Ramazan Aras, 'Naqshbandi Sufis and Their Conception of Place, Time and Fear on the Turkish–Syrian Border and Borderland', p. 44.

[22] See Sören Urbansky, *Beyond the Steppe Frontier: A History of the Sino–Russian Border* (Princeton, NJ: Princeton University Press, 2020), p. 81.

region into a space that nourished both European anxieties and discourses about European superiority or 'epidemiological Orientalism' in the face of 'backward' societies and weak states 'incapable' of containing the spread of cholera.[23] During the Paris International Sanitary Conference held in 1851, European states and the Ottoman Empire focused their efforts on the standardisation of quarantine measures in Europe and the Ottoman Empire.[24] Even though the participants to the conference failed to agree on common quarantine regulations, the Ottoman Empire slowly transformed its 'health borders' into territorial ones. Indeed, increasing surveillance of Ottoman borders to prevent the spread of cholera was only possible after the demarcation and delimitation of the frontiers and by marking the limits of Ottoman and Qajar sovereignties.[25] Maintaining the '*cordons sanitaires*' at the border areas therefore served two complementary goals: containing diseases and consolidating the state presence in the periphery of the Ottoman Empire.[26]

At the Constantinople Conference of 1866, plans were crafted to manage the annual Muslim pilgrimage to Mecca, which 'European powers understood to be the conduit for cholera to Europe'.[27] The main issue of contention between European powers and the Ottoman Empire was the increasingly different attitudes toward infectious diseases. While European states slowly opted for a strategy of disease prevention, taking into consideration local

---

[23] Notably, 'epidemiological Orientalism' in the mid-nineteenth century was a manifestation of a pre-existing narrative conflated by old tropes such as 'Oriental backwardness' and 'Asiatic despotism', whose roots went back to the Plague of Marseille (1720). Nükhet Varlık, '"Oriental Plague" or "Epidemiological Orientalism?"' in Nükhet Varlık (ed.), *Plague and Contagion in the Islamic Mediterranean* (Kalamazoo, MI: Arc Humanities Press, 2017), pp. 57–87.

[24] Isacar A. Bolaños, 'The Ottomans During the Global Crises of Cholera and Plague: The View from Iraq and the Gulf', *International Journal of Middle East Studies*, Vol. 51, No. 4 (2019), pp. 603–20 (here p. 608).

[25] Sabri Ateş, 'Bones of Contention: Corpse Traffic and Ottoman-Iranian Rivalry in Nineteenth-Century Iraq', *Comparative Studies of South Asia, Africa and the Middle East*, Vol. 30, No. 3 (2010), pp. 512–32 (here p. 524).

[26] Daniel Panzac, 'Politique sanitaire et fixation des frontières: l'exemple ottoman (XVIIIe–XIXe siècles)', *Turcica*, No. 31 (1999), pp. 87–108 (here p. 100).

[27] Alison Bashford, 'Global Biopolitics and the History of World Health', *History of the Human Sciences*, Vol. 19, No. 1 (2006), pp. 67–88 (here pp. 70–71).

ecological and sanitary conditions, the Ottoman Empire still privileged the containment of the movement of people and animals through the creation of quarantine posts at its frontiers.[28] Within this context, the mounting initiatives to fight infectious diseases globally became a tool in the hands of European powers to intervene in Ottoman Empire's internal affairs, thereby adding new facets and layers to the 'Eastern Question'.[29]

By the 1890s, however, Ottoman experts aligned with their European counterparts by gradually adopting the 'infectionist' view. Specifically, the first International Sanitary Convention dealing exclusively with cholera was signed in 1892. According to Valeska Huber, although the concrete effects of the convention were rather modest, the convention provided a growing 'shared scientific and legal vocabulary around germs and infections' – conditions that were essential for the advent of a global consensus on international sanitary and quarantine measures.[30] Thereafter, the Ottoman authorities continued expanding quarantine stations along their frontiers with Russia and Persia, while simultaneously adopting health measures informed by local ecological realities, particularly in the Iraqi provinces where the passage of Muslim pilgrims travelling to Mecca or the Shia religious centres such as Najaf and Karbala made this region particularly susceptible to the propagation of infectious diseases. These interventions also extended to the management of livestock circulating across the Ottoman frontiers by establishing veterinary police. Likewise, in 1912, the Ottoman government passed a Provisional Locust Act which established structures in the provinces in coordination with the Ministry of Agriculture.[31]

Despite the Ottoman endeavours to 'catch up' with the demands of an increasingly connected world, European countries still lamented the failure of

---

[28] The Quarantine Commission was created in 1838. The first quarantine stations were established three years later at Erzurum and Trabzon.

[29] Nermin Ersoy, Yuksel Gungor and Alishan Akpinar, 'International Sanitary Conferences from the Ottoman Perspective, 1851–1938', *Hygiea Internationalis: An Interdisciplinary Journal for the History of Public Health*, Vol. 10, No. 1 (2011), pp. 53–79.

[30] Valeska Huber, 'The Unification of the Globe by Disease? The International Sanitary Conferences on Cholera, 1851–94', *The Historical Journal*, Vol. 49, No. 2 (2006), pp. 453–76 (here p. 454).

[31] Ertan Gökmen, 'Batı Anadolu'da çekirge felâketi, 1850–1915', *Belleten. Türk Tarihi Kurumu*, 74/269 (2010), pp. 127–80.

the Sublime Porte to effectively control the spread of diseases in its territory. Moreover, the Great War had an even more negative effect on the Ottoman's attempts to build an efficient state apparatus at its borders and beyond. In particular, a devastating locust plague affected the Bilad al-Sham region in 1915, which when combined with drought and the economic blockade imposed by Britain and France produced famine and an impressive death toll in diverse Ottoman provinces, including Mount Lebanon.[32]

After the creation of the League of Nations and the establishment of the Mandates at the Conference of San Remo in 1920, public health and other social issues in the Middle East became an even more international affair.[33] In particular, 'the health policies of the French Mandate in Syria and Lebanon provide an illustration of how scientific interest for the colonial world was channelled more specifically to the mandates, as a consequence of international supervision'.[34] Hence, the League alongside private international institutions sent experts to the mandatory territories to elaborate surveys and reports on sanitary conditions in order to map out the state of public health, globally.

By the same token, the League bodies and non-state actors became increasingly entangled in different fields. In that sense, like scientific experts, voluntary organisations managed to assert themselves as meaningful actors on both the national and international arenas by reporting 'independent' data and pressuring public authorities. Thus, for instance, in 1920, a report intended for the Mutual Life Insurance Company issued a report on the sanitary situation in Aleppo and its hinterland. According to the report, 'malaria is undoubtedly an unseen member of nearly every household during the summer and autumn'.

---

[32] Zachary J. Foster, 'The 1915 Locust Attack in Syria and Palestine and its Role in the Famine During the First World War', *Middle Eastern Studies*, Vol. 51, No. 3 (2015), pp. 370–94 (here p. 370).

[33] Magaly Rodriguez Garcia, Davide Rodogno, and Liat Kozma, 'Introduction', in Magaly Rodriguez Garcia, Davide Rodogno, and Liat Kozma (eds), *The League of Nations, Work on Social Issues* (Geneva: UN Publications, 2016), p. 14.

[34] Philippe Bourmaud, 'Internationalizing Perspectives: Re-reading Mandate History through a Health Policy Lens', *Canadian Bulletin of Medical History*, Vol. 30, No. 2 (2013), pp. 9–21 (here p. 19). See also Sylvia Chiffoleau, *Genèse de la santé publique internationale. De la peste d'Orient à l'OMS* (Rennes: Presses Universitaires de Rennes, 2012).

Besides malaria, other infectious diseases proliferated in the area such as trachoma and a singular epidemic disorder called the Aleppo boil or oriental sore, transmitted by sand flies and mosquitoes.[35] In 1923, an international medical committee of the League visited Syria and prepared a comprehensive report on the sanitary conditions which were found to exist in this country, while advancing some general proposals to be adopted by the French mandatory authorities.[36] A year later, the Rockefeller Foundation sent a team to Iraq to elaborate a report on blindness linked to infectious diseases in this country.[37]

Unsurprisingly, Turkey did not wish for the League – dominated by France and Britain – nor its southern neighbours, who happened to be under the rule of the same countries, to be allowed to use sanitary issues to interfere in Turkish domestic affairs, just as European powers had done with the Ottoman Empire throughout the nineteenth century. Decisively, the Treaty of Lausanne of 1923 had secured Turkish sovereignty over Anatolia and, as we saw in Chapter 2, deputies as well as officials in Ankara observed the rising role of the League in both international and national matters – notably through the minority and refugee protection clauses – with apprehension, for it could become an obstacle to the consolidation of their nation state project in Turkey.

In that regard, the pretext of human and non-human diseases allowed Turkish officials to contest and renegotiate aspects of international accords as well as cross-border practices that were perceived as being averse to Turkey's interests. Concretely, Article 13 of the Ankara Accord of 1921 between France and Turkey specified that 'sedentary and semi-nomadic inhabitants having the use of pastures or having properties on one or the other side of the line' of the border 'will continue as in the past to exercise these rights'. Within this context, denouncing the alleged outbreaks of animal diseases such as rinderpest in Syria and Iraq became a tool to prevent nomadic groups from entering

---

[35] NARA, RG59, Reel 14. Health and sanitation in Aleppo. American Consulate. Damascus, 18 August 1920.

[36] NARA, RG59, Reel 14. Public Health Statistics. American Consulate. Damascus, 29 February 1924.

[37] According to this report, in the three main cities of this country (Baghdad, Mosul and Basra) there were 25,000 blind people living 'all in miserable condition'. NARA, RG 84, Box 83. Royal Hospital (Baghdad) to American Consulate (Baghdad), 22 July 1926.

into Turkey.[38] Subsequently, as Samuel Dolbee has shown, Turkish officials in several instances denied Syrian tribes access to Turkish pastures under the pretext of rinderpest flare-ups, even though French counterparts 'insisted that the allegation of bovine plague decimating the Syrian herds [was] baseless'.[39] Whether real or not, bovine plague's menace on Turkish herds 'served the purpose of turning the border from an illusion that might be crossed by nomads or landholders into a reality that restricted this kind of movement'.[40]

In turn, Syrian veterinary authorities claimed that Turkey did not inform them when outbreaks of rinderpest and other epizootic diseases occurred in the frontier zone.[41] For one thing, after the signature of the 'Good Neighbourhood' convention of May 1926, French authorities published a monthly report on the sanitary conditions in Syria, which was shared with the governors of Antep, Urfa and Mardin, in addition to the Turkish Consul in Beirut. Likewise, while the authorities in Palestine, Transjordan and Iraq made the sanitary situation public in their countries, 'the Turks [did] not provide any information' about the situation in Turkey. Faced with the lack of reciprocity, the French decided to stop sending the monthly report to the Turkish authorities which by the way 'do not take into account our reports'.[42] Rather, officials in Ankara preferred to collect the data from the Turkish veterinary officials at the border zone and take unilateral decisions, which in addition to being contrary to the boundary accords signed by the two countries, were merely of a vexatious nature.[43]

The Turkish attitude towards Iraqi nomadic and border dwellers was virtually the same. British officials complained about frequent frontier

[38] BOA.HR.IM. 109–76, 5 July 1924.
[39] Samuel Dolbee, 'Borders, Disease, and Territoriality in the Post-Ottoman Middle East', in Jordi Tejel and Ramazan Hakkı Öztan (eds), *Regimes of Mobility: Borders and State Formation in the Middle East, 1918–46* (Edinburgh: Edinburgh University Press, 2022), pp. 205–27 (here p. 215).
[40] Ibid. p. 217.
[41] CADN, 1SL/1/V/2149. Veterinary Inspector to the Sanitary Police. Aleppo, 7 June 1930.
[42] CADN, 1SL/1/V/2149. Adjunct Delegate (Aleppo) to the Veterinary Major at Aleppo, 18 January 1927.
[43] CADN, 1SL/1/V/2149. Principal Veterinary (Aleppo) to the High Commissioner (Beirut). Aleppo, 28 August 1926.

incidents in relation to Iraqi nomads being refused entrance into Turkish territory and the confiscation of their flocks.[44] Like the French, however, British officials had a different opinion on how rinderpest infected 'Iraqi' cattle. From a British perspective, the great difficulty in combating bovine plague lay in the fact that many of the big sheep tribes were nomadic and spent most of the year, generally the summer, outside Iraqi territory. On their way back, they frequently introduced infection into Iraq and epidemics followed.[45]

Notwithstanding the mutual distrust, between 1929 and 1931, a series of interrelated dynamics eased regional cooperation. On the one hand, the signature of the 1929 Frontier Protocol brought about an appeasement between France and Turkey. Thereafter, the Turkish government committed to exchange information about its domestic sanitary situation.[46] On the other hand, the outbreak of cholera that affected Iraq in 1931 resulted again in a regional push for further coordination in order to avoid the spread of the disease, while guaranteeing mobility across the adjacent borders; concretely, every individual originating from Iraq and wishing to enter Syria and/or Turkey had to hold a certificate of double vaccination along with the standard visa from the 'hosting' country. Additionally, vaccination was also rendered compulsory for borderlanders as well as for villages located along the main motor road between Baghdad and Damascus.[47]

Encouraged by this momentum, the Ankara government proposed to convene a veterinary conference between Iraq, Turkey, Syria and Persia in 1931. Although Turkey and Iraq had drafted a veterinary convention in 1927, the text had not been ratified by either of the two contracting states; therefore, all the preventive measures to be adopted on the Turkish–Iraqi border were

---

[44] NARA, RG 84, Vol. 116. Office of the Director of Civil Veterinary Department. Baghdad, 26 September 1925.
[45] TNA, AIR 23/374. 5th Meeting of the Permanent Frontier Commission. Mosul, 5 December 1928.
[46] CADN, 1SL/1/V/2149. 'Monthly report about infectious diseases among domestic animals'. Ankara, Yeni Gün matbaasi, 1931.
[47] CADN, 36 PO/1/411. 'Cholera Epidemic'. General Delegate to the High Commissioner (Beirut) to the French Ambassador (Ankara). Beirut, 28 August 1931.

virtual.[48] Having 'normalised' its relations with the neighbouring countries by the late 1920s, Turkey now felt confident about its sovereignty and proved to be open to consolidating regional cooperation on sanitary issues. Even though this initiative failed, a new draft of the convention was submitted to the Turkish, Iraqi, Syrian and Iranian authorities, which was signed at the conference held in Baghdad in 1938.[49]

In parallel, in 1935 Turkey and Iraq ratified an international convention for the campaign against contagious diseases of animals in Geneva.[50] Indeed, bilateral, regional and international cooperation and conventions increased dramatically and also nourished one another. After all, epidemic diseases affecting animals were harmful to everyone. In the borderlands, rinderpest impoverished the sheep-breeding tribes, thereby provoking border disorder. In addition, bovine plague could deal a heavy blow to the wool and tanning trades, which provided two of the chief exports for Turkey and Iraq.[51] Concerns over rinderpest and its impact on wool exports also had a global dimension: 'The question of the existence of this disease in this region of Turkey [southeast] is of importance to American wool importers since a large share of the wool shipped from Aleppo originates in this region'.[52]

Finally, the obsession with preventing infectious diseases also made the pilgrimage to Mecca a sensitive issue in the years following the First World War. As in the past, Western experts shared the conviction that the pilgrims were generally careless concerning health matters.[53] Yet, after the First World

---

[48] The convention provided for a frontier zone 30 kilometres wide, under the special supervision of the two Veterinary Services. In this zone, two permanent veterinary posts were to be established by each government. All animals exported for slaughter or for trade had to cross the frontier via one of the posts in each country. Finally, veterinary certificates were to prove that the exported cattle were not infected with any contagious disease. In case of an epizootic outbreak, the frontier was to be closed.

[49] BCA.030.18.1.2.83.38.18, 18 November 1937; BCA.030.18.1.2.2, 28 February 1938.

[50] The Department of State Bulletin, Vol. IV, Nos. 80–105, 4 January–28 June 1941, p. 520.

[51] LON, R2320/6A/38719/655. Report on the Administration of Iraq, 1931, p. 202.

[52] NARA, RG 84, Vol. 116. 'Spread of Rinderpest in the District'. American Consulate. Aleppo, 4 January 1926.

[53] LON, Health 12B, R848, 25546. Note by Dr Lutrario on Pilgrimages to the Holy Places. 27 November 1922.

War, new developments came to complicate the international sanitary regime, as the number of states involved in the management of the Hajj increased after the demise of the Ottoman Empire, each protecting its own interests. In that regard, 'the different international sanitary conventions and conferences on the issue of the pilgrimage' show not only how 'pressing the subject was for contemporaries, but also how difficult it was to come to an agreement in a charged political climate'.[54] Hence, despite new hegemonic discourses on prevention, local states and colonial powers favoured strategies of disease containment through surveillance systems and emergency responses, along with new transborder regulations.

The Role of Experts in the Sanitary Transnational Networks

As in the past, the role of experts in the growing transnational sphere was ambivalent. On the one hand, they were instrumental in 'translating' and 'bringing' foreign notions and measures to address sanitary issues into their respective nation states, thereby contributing to the domestic implementation of new policies and approaches. In that sense, transnational endeavours to tackle health issues connected the dots between the national and the global. Thus, while the quarantine and sanitary conferences held throughout the nineteenth century 'allowed for the consolidation of Westphalian systems in practice', the new internationalism that appeared in the era following the First World War 'created national public health measures'.[55]

On the other hand, the emergence of a transnational arena alongside diverse networks of experts in different fields did not preclude the pervasiveness of national and colonial interests from being present in the management of global challenges. As transnational historians have shown, internationalism went hand in hand with the consolidation of nation-state projects and imperial designs throughout the interwar period.[56] Hence, conferences and congresses

---

[54] Valeska Huber, 'International Bodies: The Pilgrimage to Mecca and International Health Regulation', in Eric Tagliacozzo and Shawkat M. Toorawa (eds), *The Hajj: Pilgrimage in Islam*, p. 187.

[55] Alison Bashford, 'The Age of Universal Contagion': History, Disease and Globalization', p. 3.

[56] Davide Rodogno, Bernhard Struck and Jakob Vogel (eds), *Shaping the Transnational Sphere: Experts, Networks and Issues from the 1840s to the 1930s* (New York: Berghahn, 2014).

on global issues 'provided specific platforms of competition and identity formation, especially between representatives of different nations'.[57] Likewise, while certain experts established personal and intellectual linkages, regardless of the evolution of inter-state relations, the former never lost sight of the national (and sometimes private) interests. The transnational endeavours to deal with epidemics and pests were not an exception regarding this ambivalence; nor were the borderlands exempted from its contradictory effects.

Indeed, infectious diseases affecting human beings encouraged Middle Eastern states to enter into the transnational arena on health issues. Turkey, for instance, joined numerous international organisations dealing with diverse maladies. Significantly, in 1937 the executive committee of the international organisation against trachoma proposed that Turkey join the former as being among 'the most trachomatous' zones, alongside other countries such as Egypt and India. The ramifications of this involvement were in turn felt domestically. In 1929, for instance, Dr Vekif Bulat together with Dr Niyazi Gözcü attended an ophthalmological congress in Amsterdam. Upon their return, the two experts worked on the elaboration of a nationwide report on trachoma in Turkey.[58] Incidentally, Turkish doctors trained abroad were appointed to regions severely affected by trachoma such as Adıyaman and Urfa.[59] Yet, amongst the Turkish experts in the international health arena, Dr Nuri Fehmi Ayberk proved to be the most active; he travelled to Syria, Palestine, Egypt, Tunisia, Greece and Poland, among many other countries, to observe health policies used to combat trachoma. Subsequently, he submitted to the Turkish government a series of measures designed to eradicate this disease.[60] Turkish experts also attended numerous international

---

[57] Valeska Huber, 'The Unification of the Globe by Disease?', p. 458.
[58] Sevilay Özer, 'Türkiye'de Trahomla Mücadele (1925–45)', *Ankara Üniversitesi Türk İnkılâp Tarihi Enstitüsü Atatürk Yolu Dergisi*, No. 54 (2014), p. 127.
[59] NARA, RG84, Box 436. Consular Istanbul. 'Digest from the Turkish Press' (11–24 June 1931).
[60] Nuri Fehmi Ayberk. 'Dünya Trahom Mücadelesi', *Türk Oftalmoloji Gazetesi*, Vol. 1, No. 11–12 (1931), pp. 688–710. Some decades later, Ayberk admitted that the 'combat' against trachoma failed in the 1930s, despite official statements declaring the opposite. Nuri Fehmi Ayberk, 'Türkiye Trahom Mücadelesi Tarihçesine ait Hatıralarım', *Göz Kliniği*, Vol. 10 (1961), p. 134.

workshops convened by the League of Nations on other widespread diseases in Turkey, such as malaria.[61]

Beyond the global arena there were, however, other original initiatives geared towards establishing a regional arena of knowledge and cooperation beyond colonial oversight. In that regard, as Liat Kozma has shown, the Egyptian Medical Association played an essential role in re-Egyptianizing the medical profession as well as in creating a regional network of 'Arab' doctors.[62] Beginning from 1931, the annual conference of the Egyptian Medical Association was held, usually alternating between Egypt and a neighbouring Arab city – 1931 in Beirut, 1933 in Jerusalem, 1935 in Damascus and 1938 in Baghdad. Crucially, the last one was labelled the eighteenth 'Arab medical conference, thus Arabising all previous conferences in retrospect'.[63]

Nonetheless, it is perhaps within the framework of the regional struggle against locust infestations that the ambiguities of this era, marked both by its internationalism and its rising nationalism, become more evident. The necessity for common action between states against insect pests had already been acknowledged in early international conferences and conventions; notably, the International Conference on Phytopathology in 1914, and the Convention on the Fight against Locusts in October 1920. In June 1923, an International Congress of Phytopathology and Entomology held in Amsterdam gathered together different delegations from Middle Eastern countries, including independent Turkey.

Yet, it was the presence of locust swarms in northern Syria in 1924 that prompted the Ankara government to summon its southern neighbour to take its responsibilities at the frontier zone, and to ask for coordination to eradicate this problem.[64] Between January and July 1925, two regional conferences on locusts held in Aleppo and Damascus laid the foundations for the establishment of the

---

[61] BCA.030.18.01.02.31.69.8, 1932; BCA.030.18.01.02.34.18.3, 1933.
[62] Liat Kozma, 'Doctors Crossing Borders: The Formation of a Regional Profession in the Interwar Middle East', in Ebru Boyar and Kate Fleet (eds), *Middle Eastern and North African Societies in the Interwar Period* (Leiden: Brill, 2018), pp. 136–7.
[63] Ibid. p. 138.
[64] CADN, 36/PO/1/139. Ministry of Foreign Affairs of Turkey to the representative of the French Republic in Turkey in Constantinople. Ankara, 10 August 1924.

International Locust Bureau in Damascus on 20 May 1926.[65] According to its statutes, this bureau's main function was to collect and distribute information with a view to concerted action in the contracting states (Palestine, Transjordan, Iraq, Syria, and Turkey). Actual coordination, however, remained in the hands of local and border authorities. The expenses of the new organisation were covered by contributions from the five governments, each of which was represented on the council. The official language of the bureau was French, but communications made to the bureau by each of the various contracting states could be submitted in the official language of the state of origin. Although there was no rule on this issue, the technical advisers who represented the contracting states on the committee of the bureau were officials working for the respective ministries of agriculture.[66]

The enforcement of international cooperation between the contracting states was neither linear nor without obstacles. By late 1927, the bureau was still inactive, and some key members had not paid their fees. Likewise, in 1928, the Iraqi representative reported that, while the cooperation with Syria had been 'close and effective', it had not proved possible 'to get in touch with the Turkish anti-locust officials on the Turco-Iraq frontier'. Although the British delegation had hoped to arrange this cooperation at the International Conference in Damascus, 'unfortunately no representative from Turkey was present nor was any letter sent explaining to whom Turkey had confided its representation'.[67] Ironically, a few months earlier, the Turkish government had asked the Iraq authorities to take measures to deal with locust pests on the Turkish–Iraqi frontier, for Turkish efforts on their side of the frontier could only be successful if emulated by the Iraqi authorities on the other side.[68] Similar accusations were advanced by the Syrian experts vis-à-vis the

---

[65] Sevilay Özer, *Anadolu'da Görülen Çekirge İstilaları ve Halk Üzerindendeki Etkisi, 1914–45* (Ankara: Türk Tarih Kurumu Yayınları, 2016), p. 49.

[66] CADN, 36/PO/1/139. 'Office international de renseignements sur les sauterelles'. Beirut, 26 June 1926.

[67] TNA, CO 730/128/5. Memorandum by the Inspector-General of Agriculture. Baghdad, 19 March 1928.

[68] TNA, FO 371/12256/E982/81/65. Turkish Ambassador (London) to Foreign Office (London), 25 February 1927.

Turkish border authorities in 1931; that is, five years after the establishment of the Locust Bureau.[69]

Meanwhile, Anglo–French rivalries in the Middle East also affected coordination in the interstate fight against locusts. Significantly, the French High Commission had little sympathy for the bureau, as they viewed it as being too much under British influence. Against this background, 'the main preoccupation of the [French] mandatory power is not so much the vigorous prosecution of anti-locust research as the attachment of the Bureau to its own orbit'.[70] With this object in view, the French delegate proposed increasing French representation on the board.[71] In addition, the French pledged for a key role of the bureau in the Middle East, a claim supported by 'objective' reasons; that is, the 'central geographic position' of Syria within the group of contracting states and its 'considerable role . . . in fighting against locusts'.[72] Nevertheless, French pretentions were curtailed by the election of Subhi bey Hassibi, a Syrian expert with Arab nationalist leans, backed by Great Britain and the other pro-British contracting states. Henceforth, from time to time, the pro-French Syrian representative threatened withdrawal.[73]

French concerns were not groundless. The British position in the anti-locust research worldwide had been reinforced after the arrival of the Russian émigré Boris P. Uvarov (1889–1970) at the Imperial Bureau of Entomology in London, where he remained between 1920 and 1945. His position in London allowed him to work on the identification of the insects from all parts of the Commonwealth and complete his book *Locusts and Grasshoppers* in 1928, which increased his influence in the field as well as his transnational

---

[69] CADN, 36/PO/1/139. The High Commissioner (Beirut) to the French Embassy in Turkey (Istanbul). Beirut, 23 June 1931.

[70] TNA, FO 684/5. 'Bureau International de Renseignements sur les sauterelles'. Consul E.C. Hole (Damascus) to Arthur Henderson (London). Damascus, 14 January 1931.

[71] TNA, FO 684/5. 'Réunion du Bureau International de Renseignements sur les sauterelles'. Damascus, 18 January 1928.

[72] Ibid.

[73] TNA, FO 684/5. 'Bureau International de Renseignements sur les sauterelles'. Consul E.C. Hole (Damascus) to Arthur Henderson (London). Damascus, 14 January 1931.

network among experts.⁷⁴ A year later, Uvarov was appointed head of the Anti-Locust Research Centre, tasked with the mission of defending colonial agriculture against locust invasions.⁷⁵ Crucially, he toured for research purposes 'the great locust area which comprises the south-eastern vilayets of the Turkish Republic, the northern provinces of Syria and northern Iraq' between 1931 and 1932, thereby consolidating his personal relations with entomologists in these three countries.⁷⁶

In particular, the correspondence exchanged between Uvarov and Mehmet Süreyya Bey, the Turkish representative at the bureau and its president by 1932, reveals a long and friendly relationship between the two men, despite undergoing diplomatic tensions. As entomologists, they exchanged information about locusts and results from their respective research in the field. Yet, a careful reading of this correspondence shows that Uvarov also used this relationship to defend his and Britain's interests. Thus, for instance, in one of the letters exchanged in 1932, Uvarov insisted on limiting the works of the bureau on the Moroccan locust as well as in including a representative of the Imperial Institute of Entomology into the bureau.⁷⁷ Moreover, since the establishment of the bureau in Damascus, Uvarov lobbied for moving its headquarters to Palestine or Iraq, the latter option being seen as 'absolutely necessary for the success of the scheme that Persia should join'.⁷⁸

Although Persia joined the bureau in March 1931, frictions between the two imperial rivals did not disappear altogether. On the contrary, Palestinian

---

⁷⁴ Boris P. Uvarov, *Locusts and Grasshoppers: A Handbook for their Study and Control* (London: The Imperial Bureau of Entomology, 1928). On Uvarov's 'phase theory' to explain the origin and decline of locust plague, see for instance, Arnold van Huis, Keith Cressman and Joyce I. Magor, 'Preventing Desert Locust Plagues: Optimizing Management Interventions', *Entomologia Experimentalis et Applicata*, Vol. 122 (2007), pp. 191–214 (here p. 191).

⁷⁵ Vincent B. Wigglesworth, 'Boris Petrovitch Uvarov', *Biographical Memoirs of Fellows of the Royal Society*, Vol. 17 (1971), pp. 713–40.

⁷⁶ Boris P. Uvarov, 'Ecological Studies on the Moroccan Locust in Western Anatolia', *Bulletin of Entomological Research*, Vol. 23, No. 2 (1932), pp. 273–87; 'Preliminary Report on Locust Investigations in the Middle East in May–June 1932' (Manuscript); 'Ecology of the Moroccan Locust in Iraq and Syria and the Prevention of its Outbreaks', *Bulletin of Entomological Research*, Vol. 24, No. 3 (1933), pp. 407–18 (here p. 407).

⁷⁷ TNA, AY 11/56. B.P. Uvarov to Süreyya Bey. 13 January 1932.

⁷⁸ TNA, CO 730/128/5. 'Locusts'. Baghdad, 28 March 1928.

and Transjordanian representatives considered that, since the international clearing house for locust information was in London at the Office of the Committee on Locust Control, the usefulness of the Damascus Bureau would seem to have ceased. Moreover, the Damascus Bureau 'is concerned primarily with the Moroccan locust, an insect which is a menace neither to Palestine or Transjordan but which intimately concerns Syria, Turkey and Iraq'.[79] As of 31 December 1933, Palestine and Transjordan quit the bureau, officially for financial reasons.[80]

Britain won the battle for prestige in the anti-locust field in the global arena, too. During the First International Locust Conference held in Rome in 1931, it was agreed that the Imperial Institute of Entomology in London should be recognised as the international centre for biological and systematic research on locusts.[81] Tellingly, by 1935, Moscow contacted the British Embassy to notify its willingness to collaborate in the international investigation of the locust problem. In turn, the British invited the USSR to send a representation to the fourth international locust conference held in Egypt in 1936.[82] Although the USSR eventually declined the invitation, these bilateral contacts again showcased the centrality of the British Empire in this field to the expense of France.[83]

Bringing 'Civilisation' to the Borderlands

As a result of increasing international cooperation, by the early 1930s, state officials and experts shared an increasing understanding of 'global challenges'. Hygiene was one such new concern that became hegemonic throughout these years, as Turkey, Britain and France echoed this approach in their respective territories.[84] In Iraq, for instance, the British considered that 'education is

---

[79] TNA, FO 371/16855. E. Ballard (Jerusalem). 15 November 1932.

[80] TNA, FO 371/16855. A.G. Wauchope (High Commissioner for Palestine and Transjordan) to Philip Cunliffe-Lister (Secretary of State for the Colonies). Jerusalem, 17 December 1932.

[81] TNA, FO 371/16855/E4260/401/65. 'Locust Control in the Middle East'. Ogilvie-Forbes (Baghdad) to Foreign Office (London). Baghdad, 2 August 1933.

[82] TNA, FO 370/473/L1785/63/405. 'International Cooperation in Anti-locust Research Work'. Lord Chilston (Moscow) to Foreign Office (London). 20 March 1935.

[83] Etienne Forestier-Peyrat, 'Fighting Locusts Together: Pest Control, and the Birth of Soviet Development Aid, 1920–39', *Global Environment*, Vol. 7, No. 2 (2014), pp. 536–71 (here p. 566).

[84] Alison Bashford, 'Global biopolitics and the history of world health', pp. 76–7.

the best means of combating' preventable diseases. Hence, 'special lectures on health and hygiene are being given in the schools, and illustrated charts with an explanatory text have been prepared by the Health Directorate for exhibition in class rooms'.[85] Likewise, French experts in Syria advised French troops and officials to privilege hygiene and prevention rather than healing maladies.[86] In Turkey, the state established itself as 'an educator on topics of wellness and disease'. For this purpose, the republic's representatives 'sermonized about modern medicine and condemned societal traditions that were deemed ineffective, unscientific, or simply superstitious' – a pedagogical effort that, while seeking to consolidate the Kemalist project, was 'profoundly consistent with contemporary public health concerns observable in the West over hygiene, sanitation, and civilization, as well'.[87]

Nonetheless, although apparently inspired by identical principles and understandings of public health, sanitary policies varied considerably from one territory to another, especially as they depended on different powers with different ideological views and colonial practices.[88] And yet, French, British and Turkish sanitary policies in their shared borderlands bore some similarities, with unsurprisingly analogous effects. Although a comprehensive study of state officials' cultural and ideological background in French Syria, British Iraq and Republican Turkey during this period is beyond the scope of this chapter, it is indeed important to recall that elites and officials' imaginary about local societies, particularly in the margins of their respective states, had significant consequences for how global health issues and sanitary approaches were implemented locally.

At the time of the Great War, British and French colonial officials held an ambivalent image of the Orient. On the one hand, the Levant and Mesopotamia conveyed the image of the 'fertile crescent, the everlastingly prolific river valley, the very cradle of civilization'.[89] Conversely, the Syrian

---

[85] LON, R59/1/17502/56968. Report on the Administration of Iraq for the year 1926, p. 52.
[86] CADN, 1SL/1/V/2190. Notions of Hygiene. Lecture by Dr. Laroque. Intelligence Services.
[87] Kyle T. Evered and Emine Ö. Evered, 'State, Peasant, Mosquito', p. 312.
[88] Philippe Bourmaud, 'Internationalizing Perspectives', p. 16.
[89] Priya Satia, 'A Rebellion of Technology: Development, Policing, and the British Arabian Imaginary', in Diana K. Davis and Edmund Burke III (eds), *Environmental Imaginaries of the Middle East and North Africa* (Athens: Ohio University Press, 2011), pp. 23–59 (here p. 23).

Desert[90] – encompassing portions of Syrian, Iraqi, Jordanian and Saudi Arabian lands – represented 'the archetypical wasteland, a barren desert of glaring sun and bleak horizons testifying at once to man's and nature's cruelty'.[91] When Britain and France took over the mandatory territories in the region in the early 1920s, the idea of 'restoring' and expanding the Fertile Crescent at the expenses of wastelands came to the surface. While protecting minorities and refugees in the ex-Ottoman Arab provinces served as a tool to justify the Mandates in Geneva, transforming the landscape through agricultural settlements, the domestication of the desert and the education of local populations were also seen as important means to reaffirm Western supremacy and oversight in these territories.[92] In sum, the Mandates in Iraq and Syria could also be used as a decisive instrument to rebuild civilization, 'after many years of anarchy and desolation'.[93]

In both countries, Bedouin and nomadic populations were seen as a problem for at least two reasons. First, nomads and their livestock were portrayed as particularly destructive and were blamed for widespread deforestation and subsequent aridification of the once Fertile Crescent.[94] As in Algeria, French officials in Syria conveyed negative stereotypes on the Bedouins and their environmental impact on the Levant. Therefore, the French Mandate was to promote sedentary life in order to attain a higher form of civilisation and restore the 'grandeur' of the region under France's guidance.[95] Such views were translated into concrete policies and initiatives, such as the introduction of 'Tree Festivals' across the country in which school children planted new trees

---

[90] For a geographical definition of the Syrian Desert, see Christina Phelps Grant, *The Syrian Desert: Caravans, Travel and Exploration* (New York: Macmillan, 1936), pp. 6–10.

[91] Priya Satia, 'A Rebellion of Technology', p. 23.

[92] Robert S. Fletcher, 'Decolonization and the Arid World', in Martin Thomas and Andrew S. Thompson (eds), *The Oxford Handbook of the Ends of Empire* (Oxford: online publication), pp. 374–5.

[93] Priya Satia, 'A Rebellion of Technology', p. 31.

[94] The image of wasteland went back to the nineteenth century, though. In 1847, German botanist Matthias Schleiden wrote of the deforestation and aridification of the Levant, Mesopotamia, Egypt and Persia. In France, diverse botanists also wrote about the climate benefits of reforestation. Diane K. Davis, *The Arid Lands: History, Power, Knowledge* (Cambridge, MA: MIT Press, 2016), pp. 89–91.

[95] Andrea E. Duffy, 'Civilizing through Cork: Conservationism and *la Mission Civilisatrice* in French Colonial Algeria', *Environmental History*, Vol. 23 (2018), pp. 278–9.

to be made aware of the importance of forests and trees in a civilised world.[96] A measure that was also introduced some years later in Turkey by Mustafa Kemal to whom a 'land without tree and forest [was] not acceptable to be country'.[97]

More importantly, French authorities divided the country into two supposedly distinct regions. The eastern part of Syria, including the Jazira, was considered a 'nomadic zone' or *badiya*; that is, the domain of Bedouin pastoralists and, as such, a territory that required a specific form of administration: the Contrôle Bedouin. By contrast, the western part of the country was the 'sedentary zone' or *mamura*, which required protection from Bedouin depredations.[98] While this division had a clear political rationale – i.e. avoiding the possibility that nationalist effervescence contaminate Bedouin Arabs – it also responded to the ecological imaginary in colonial rulers' minds. This internal boundary was thought to prevent sheep and goats from harming the existing forests and to limit deforestation in the 'sedentary zone'.[99] It was only after establishing order in the steppe and demarcating these two distinct zones that the French would be able to launch developing plans in the region and ultimately 'bring civilization back' to the Jazira, in particular.[100]

---

[96] LON, R22.4284.47053. Rapport sur l'administration dans les territoires de la Syrie et le Liban, 1924, p. 55.

[97] Zöhre Polat, 'The Presidents Perspective on Landscape: Sample of the First President Mustafa Kemal Atatürk in Turkey', *Türk Bilimsel Derlemeler Dergisi*, Vol. 6, No. 2 (2013), pp. 158–62 (here p. 161).

[98] In fact, Bedouins Arabs did not represent a separate world in a country divided by a clear socio-economic boundary between settler and nomadic areas or between cultivated and arid lands. Nomadic tribes in Syria, like in Iraq, had strong ties with urban merchants and established a sort of mutually dependent relationship whereby the former purchased food and grain while selling their livestock and products in the urban markets. Sarah D. Shields, *Mosul before Iraq: Like Bees Making Five-Sided Cells* (Albany: SUNY Press, 2000); Mehdi Sakatni, 'From Camel to Truck? Automobiles and the Pastoralist Nomadism of Syrian Tribes during the French Mandate (1920–46)', *Comparative Studies of South Asia, Africa and the Middle East*, Vol. 39, No. 1 (2019), pp. 159–69.

[99] LON, R22.4284.47053. Rapport sur l'administration dans les territoires de la Syrie et le Liban, 1924, p. 55.

[100] Christian Velud, 'La politique mandataire française à l'égard des tribus et des zones de steppe en Syrie: L'exemple de la Djézireh', in Riccardo Bocco, Ronald Jaubert and Françoise Métral (eds), *Steppes d'Arabie. Etats, pasteurs, agriculteurs et commerçants: le devenir des zones sèches* (Paris: PUF, 1993), p. 64.

As we saw in Chapter 2, the economic development of the steppe could only be achieved, according to French officials, by encouraging the immigration of settler populations from Turkey and the sedentarisation of semi-nomadic tribes who potentially could become 'good farmers'. Like in Algeria, French officials and publicists saw themselves the heirs of the Roman Empire in the Orient. Hence, like the Romans, the French could use migrants and refugees to protect the margins of the French Empire in the Levant.[101] Henceforth, the French encouraged tribal chiefs to appropriate vast tracts of land which could be cultivated by tenant farmers from outside the tribe, usually Kurds or Christians.[102] As a result of this process, by the late 1920s the Upper Jazira was treated as a 'sedentary zone' whereas the rest of the Jazira continued to be considered as a 'nomadic zone', thereby creating new socio-economic, and ultimately identity boundaries in the Jazira region. For one, while Kurdish and Christian farmers were associated with the economic development of the Jazira, nomadic Arab lifestyle remained concomitant to disorder and 'backwardness'.[103]

By and large, urban elites in Damascus shared French views on the negative effects of nomadic life in the Jazira. Thus, through a careful reading of Damascene newspapers, Samuel Dolbee shows that the former denounced the present situation in the area. While in Ancient times, this region was called 'the cradle of civilization for Greeks, Assyrians, Chaldeans, Persians, and Arabs', enjoying a fertility that no one 'no matter his eloquence or power of expression would be able to describe', now contemporary Jazira consisted of 'desolate wastelands' and 'Arab and Kurdish tent-dwellers'. Moreover, suffering from 'backwardness' in both 'civilization and science', nomadic and semi-nomadic populations did little to exploit the agricultural potentiality of its fertile soils and transform this region into a new granary for the Middle East and beyond.[104]

In Iraq, as in Syria, 'it was the urban-rural divide, identified by the British, that structured their understanding of the emerging polity and determined the

---

[101] Ibid. p. 76.
[102] Ibid. p. 75.
[103] Jordi Tejel, 'Un territoire de marge en Haute Djézireh syrienne (1921–40)', *Etudes rurales*, No. 186 (2010), pp. 61–76.
[104] *Al-Qabas*, 31 May 1929; *Al-Qabas*, 11 September 1928. Quoted in Samuel Dolbee, 'The Locust and the Starling: People, Insects, and Disease in the Late Ottoman Jazira and After, 1860–1940' (PhD dissertation, New York University, 2017), p. 312.

individual-collective tensions that emerged'.[105] As in Syria, 'this anti-urbanism can be partly explained by the fact that Baghdad was the main centre of nationalism'. Yet, British distaste for the cities and their population in the initial stages of the Mandate was also due to the influence of 'ruralism' among the British colonial officers in Iraq. In this sense, Toby Dodge has shown how different British officials maintained a romantic view of tribal chiefs, be they nomadic or sedentary; that is, as individuals 'untouched' by modernity, and as holders of tradition and 'authentic' values such as honour and bravery.[106]

The historical references differed, as well. While the French longed to emulate the Roman Empire in the Levant, the British in Iraq referred instead to the mythical Babylonia and ancient Mesopotamia. For Priya Satia, '[r]estoring Arabia was part of the larger project of restoring the Old World after its orgy of self-destruction'.[107] This mission nevertheless encountered numerous obstacles, such as anti-British resistance, including in the rural areas, and harsh environmental conditions. Indeed, it encountered an 'unhealthy climate, subject to the ravage of practically every known form of infectious disease in an endemic and epidemic form'.[108]

Despite these minor differences, both mandatory administrations shared financial constraints that ultimately jeopardised their developmental projects in the region, as well as their health policies. In Syria, the High Commission created the Inspection générale des Services de Santé, Hygiène, Assistance publique, Oeuvres sociales et Services quarantenaires to control both the private and public health services across the country. In parallel, each 'state' possessed a public health service. Yet, the High Commission did not invest in health infrastructures, leaving the initiative in this field to private hospitals and dispensaries, usually run by missionaries and located almost exclusively in the main cities. In this way, the French authorities imposed a health system

---

[105] Toby Dodge, *Inventing Iraq: The Failure of Nation Building and a History Denied* (New York: Columbia University Press, 2003), p. 69.

[106] Ibid.

[107] Priya Satia, *Spies in Arabia: The Great War and the Cultural Foundations of Britain's Covert Empire in the Middle East* (Oxford: Oxford University Press, 2008), p. 174.

[108] Omar Dewachi, *Ungovernable Life: Mandatory Medicine and Statecraft in Iraq* (Stanford, CA: Stanford University Press, 2017), p. 13.

based on charity efforts; 'that is, a medicine that heals diseases, yet without any real social project'.[109]

The effects of this policy were felt heavily in the peripheral areas, according to the rare sources left by local dwellers and doctors serving in the borderlands. This was the case for Ahmad Nafiz (1902–68), a Kurdish doctor hailing from Maden, Turkey, who sought refuge in Damascus in the late 1920s.[110] Wishing to improve health conditions in the Upper Jazira, Dr Nafiz requested the French to let him serve in the Turkish–Syrian–Iraqi borderlands. Although at first the French rejected his demand, the shortfall of medical personnel willing to take up office in this peripheral region led the authorities to accept his petition and appoint him as the forensic doctor at Ayn Diwar, a border town. Thanks to his good relations with a French officer, Dr Nafiz was able to obtain significant amounts of quinine and neosalvarsan, key drugs for treating malaria and syphilis, respectively. By 1935, he moved to Qamishli, where he opened a private dispensary two years later while touring the surrounding villages to treat infectious diseases and thus filling the void left by French and Syrian health policies in the borderlands.[111] His treatment of diseases on the spot was accompanied by a pedagogical effort through the publication of some articles in the newspaper *Hawar* on frequent health problems, in particular amid rural populations.[112]

By the late 1930s, Nafiz's individual efforts were complemented by the opening of a dispensary run by the Dominican friars in Derbessia, and another by Franciscans in Ras al-Ayn.[113] Nevertheless, during the Second

---

[109] Sylvia Chiffoleau, 'Entre la bienfaisance, contrôle des populations et agenda international', p. 99.

[110] Imprisoned in Diyarbakır between 1925 and 1928 for his alleged support of the Shaykh Said rebellion, he took refuge in Aleppo and resumed his medical career in Damascus by 1930. Konê Reş, 'Doktor û welatparêzê ku nayê ji bîrkirin Dr. Ehmed Nafiz Zaza', *Armanc*, No. 148 (1994), p. 5.

[111] See the memoirs written by Nafiz's brother, Noureddine Zaza, *Ma vie de Kurde* (Lausanne: Les éditions du Tigre, 2021), pp. 111–25.

[112] The first contribution in *Hawar* was published in 1932. Dr. Ehmed Nafiz, 'Ta, Tawî û Tabir', *Hawar*, No. 2 (1932), pp. 3–4.

[113] On the poor sanitary conditions in the area, see also the memoirs of Ekrem Cemil Paşa, *Muhtasar Hayatım* (Brussels: Kurdish Institute of Brussels, 1991), pp. 88–9.

World War the situation worsened due to the general drug shortage.[114] As in Hasaka, malaria affected up to 70% of the population in Qamishli by 1943; since quinine was not found at the public dispensary or at the French garrison in that town, it provoked a significant rise in prices.[115] As a result, 'only wealthy dwellers can afford this product. The rest ... *Allah Karim!* (It's God's will)'.[116] The poor situation of health infrastructures in the rural areas was partially compensated by the creation of mobile units that toured deserted and semi-deserted areas in the Syrian borderlands.[117] Yet, according to Robert Blecher, these units were a 'performance', rather than a consistent attempt to cure Bedouins; 'desert medicine' was a tool to win Bedouins loyalty, 'prove ethnographic accounts, confirm the categories of colonial knowledge, and justify the need for the French presence'.[118]

In Iraq, unlike in Syria, British doctors emphasised state welfare logics and the centralisation of health-care infrastructure, and they called on the Iraqi government to focus on disease prevention and cutting down on economic waste. In that regard, the British saw centralising Iraq's health-care administration as necessary to the vitality of the new state and for governance under the rapid modernisation of national infrastructure.[119] Nonetheless, the earlier attempts to create an Iraqi Ministry of Health failed due to the lack of finances and the High Commission's unwillingness to hand over public health matters to local doctors. Instead, a team of British and Iraqi physicians ran a modest Directorate of Health under the auspices of the Iraqi Ministry of the Interior that was, more or less, under British control. Although the directorate was charged with expanding Iraq's health services and infrastructure, collecting and producing vital statistics, and reporting developments in the country's health care to the British Civil Administration, its work was often challenged by the lack of resources.[120] In the northern borderlands, like

---

[115] CADN, 1SL/1/V/2051. Weekly Report. Qamishli, 28 November–4 December 1943.

[116] CADN, 1SL/1/V/2051. Weekly Report. Qamishli, 27 June–17 July 1943.

[117] LON, R2307.6A.536.4361. Rapport sur l'administration dans les territoires de la Syrie et le Liban, 1927, p. 72.

[118] Robert Blecher, 'Desert Medicine, Ethnography, and the Colonial Encounter in Mandatory Syria', in Nadine Méouchy and Peter Sluglett (eds), *The British and French Mandates in Comparative Perspectives* (Leiden: Brill, 2004), pp. 267–8.

[119] Omar Dewachi, *Ungovernable Life*, p. 15.

[120] LON, R2315.6A.22103.655. Report on Administration for 1929, p. 61.

in Syria, rural dwellers could only resort to traditional healers and a few dispensaries run by Christian missionaries in provincial towns, such as Dohuk.

While sanitary policies in Turkey have very often been studied separately because Turkish elites instilled a highly ideological direction on state policies, and the country enjoyed full independence, there were at least two common features when compared to French Syria and British Iraq: namely, the formation of a symbolic boundary between two distinct territories (Western and Eastern Anatolia), and the lack of financial resources in Ankara's struggle against human and animal diseases.

As we have seen, Turkish officials cultivated the imaginary of Turkey's southern border as a gateway for 'foreign invaders' and enemies. In that sense, the discourse around 'foreign' diseases and pests provided Turkey with an additional argument to exert diplomatic pressure on her southern neighbours and, more importantly, lay claims of political dominance on both sides of her shared borders. Domestically, however, the fight against diseases was used to inculcate Turkish nationalism and spread republican values among Turkey's citizens. Part of this discourse was the idea that the Ottoman Empire had done nothing to improve the sanitary conditions in the rural areas whose 'nature was narrated as something to be modernized or depicted as the scene of a disastrous Ottoman past'.[121] As such, health policies were used as an additional tool to mark the rupture between the two eras.[122] In that regard, the so-called 'Village Laws' included articles that were geared towards making rural space healthier and cleaner, and summoned villagers to change their lifestyle to avoid the spread of infectious diseases.[123] More decisively, the public health law on dealing with infectious diseases from 24 April 1930 became a landmark in the early republican years. The law heralded 'public health as essential to the republic's survival and prosperity, while defining Turkey's biological and societal adversaries'.[124] Moreover, the 1930 law expanded the powers of the

---

[121] Eda Acara, 'From Imperial Frontier to National Heartland: Environmental History of Turkey's Nation–building in its European Province of Thrace, 1920–40', in Onur Inal and Ethemcan Turhan (eds), *Transforming Socio-Natures in Turkey: Landscapes, State and Environmental Movements* (London and New York: Routledge, 2020), pp. 52–70 (here p. 55).
[122] Rükneddin Fethi, *Doğu Köylerinde* (Istanbul: Çığır Kitabevi, 1938), pp. 18–19 and 41.
[123] Ibid. p. 46.
[124] Kyle T. Evered and Emine Ö. Evered, 'State, Peasant, Mosquito', p. 313.

state and its officials.¹²⁵ Yet neither the moment chosen, nor the spirit given, to this bill by lawmakers in Ankara were entirely coincidental.

During the early years of the republic, the Eastern provinces had become the scenes of the two most important Kurdish rebellions – that of Shaykh Said (1925) and Ararat or Agri-Dagh (1927–31) – against the Turkish government. Within this context, the range of exceptional measures implemented against thousands of Kurds, whether or not they were directly implicated in the uprisings, contributed to the delimitation of a symbolic socio-political boundary separating the West from the East, which from then on was portrayed as a distinct region, possessing a homogeneity that did not really exist. The 'East' became a territory of refuge for an intrinsically counter-revolutionary popular culture. After the eradication of the 'Armenian threat', Kurdish identity (the language, social structures, attachment to the religious orders) was held forth as a symbol of otherness, so the 'East' and its 'Kurdishness' began to symbolise what the Turkish elites deemed 'anti-Republican', or even worse 'illegal'.¹²⁶

In parallel, the physical environment and material life of Easterners embodied exactly the opposite of what the republican elites hoped for the Turkish nation. For one, the 'regions of trachoma' and other infectious diseases transmitted due to the flaws associated with insufficient hygiene overlapped with the East; that is, the most backward provinces in Turkey.¹²⁷ Trachoma was seen as evidence of Eastener's backwardness and as justification for paternalistic policies enacted towards rural populations. In addition, Turkey's southern borders had become a nest for smugglers and agents working for foreign imperialist forces. In addition, by 1930, southern Anatolia was infested by locust swarms originating from Syria and provoking important damage to Turkish agriculture. It was these circumstances that prompted Turkish officials, politicians and publicists to elaborate the

---

¹²⁵ Yücel Yanikdağ, *Healing the Nation: Prisoners of War, Medicine and Nationalism in Turkey* (Edinburgh: Edinburgh University Press, 2013), p. 153.

¹²⁶ Jordi Tejel, 'The Shared Political Construction of the East as a Resistant Territory and Cultural Sphere in the Kemalist Era, 1923–38', *European Journal of Turkish Studies*, No. 10 (2009), http://ejts.revues.org/index4064.html (last accessed 5 October 2022).

¹²⁷ Sevilay Özer, 'Türkiye'de Trahomla Mücadele (1925–45)', *Ankara Üniversitesi Türk İnkılâp Tarihi Enstitüsü Atatürk Yolu Dergisi*, No. 54 (2014), pp. 121–52.

discourse about the 'East', as a separate region where social and physical ills converged in different ways.[128]

Thus, for instance, Turkish officials explained the spread of smallpox in the Mardin province in 1930 through the constant cross-border infringements of 'bandits' and 'brigands' (*çapulcular*) between Syria and Turkey, facilitated by the passivity of the French border authorities.[129] Accordingly, as the most important clashes between the Kurdish rebels and Turkish army around the Agri-Dagh region took place in summer of 1930, Turkish newspapers published caricatures and used expressions – i.e. '*çekirgelere İlân Harp*' (Declaration of War on locusts), 'enraged enemies', 'bands of locusts', 'creatures' (*mahlûklar*), 'insects', 'cleansing' (*temizlik*) – in which the combat against Kurdish fighters and locusts became explicitly amalgamated.[130] As a result, Kurdish opponents, just as during the Shaykh Said revolt, were dehumanised and assimilated to animals and germs that had to be crushed for the sake of the Turkish Republic.[131] Turkish journalist Esat Mahmut Bey toured the Agri-Dagh region in 1930 and provided some descriptions of how 'Easterners' lived and behaved. In order to catch Westernised Turkish readers, he drew comparisons between Turkey's borderlands and the American frontier, highlighting that 'the type of people' who lived there resembled 'the savage American Indians we see in the cinema'.[132]

More generally, the inhabitants of the 'East' were perceived by the Kemalist cadres and state officials on the ground through a double prism: on the one hand, Kurds were stigmatised as 'backward,' having remained on the side-lines

---

[128] The idea of Eastern Anatolia as a frontier zone between civilisation and backwardness was not completely new. In the same vein, to the Ottoman authorities, the Jazira also constituted an ecological boundary between the regions of 'greenery', inhabited by settlers, and the 'desert' (*çöl*), the domain of nomadic and semi-nomadic populations. Samuel Dolbee, 'The Locust and the Starling', pp. 168–9.

[129] BCA. 030.10.00.00.177.220.14, 1930.

[130] For a comprehensive study of this amalgamation, see Nevcihan Özbilge, *Çekirgeler, Kürtler ve Devlet: Erken Cumhuriyet Dönemine Yeniden Bakmak* (Istanbul: Tarih Vakfı Yurt Yayınları, 2020), pp. 107–25.

[131] See Bariş Erdoğan, 'L'Etat, la presse et la violence déployée contre les Kurdes de Turquie', *The Journal of Kurdish Studies*, Vol. IV (2001–2), pp. 49–56.

[132] 'Tenkil harekti ileriyor', *Akşam*, 3 July 1930.

of civilisation; on the other hand, they were also seen as 'Turkish' citizens who, with a bit of help, could re-join the path of progress. Thus, People's Houses (*Halkevleri*) were given the mission to 'make Turkish' the inhabitants of the Eastern provinces and improve 'people's health and social knowledge' by organising public conferences and screening educational films.[133] In this battle, however, People's Houses were not alone. Doctors and vets were also seen as soldiers of the republic:

> Today young active and idealist Turkish doctors are committed in every Eastern district trying to close the wounds of this region, marked by suffering and deprivation . . . Let the people of the East and villagers awake from their long and lasting era of resignation to listen to the good news brought [by the republic].[134]

In sum, by curing physical diseases such as trachoma, which was 'decimating the East', doctors and officials could attract these provinces towards the republic and its values.[135]

State Flaws and Local Attitudes

As mentioned in the introduction to this chapter, regarding the cross-border movement of nomadic tribes, pilgrims, livestock and borderlanders as a 'problem' formed part of a state-centric narrative that, obviously, was not shared by these trespassers. Nor was the view of these borderlands as a hostile physical and cultural landscape that had to be domesticated, or indeed civilised. To be sure, locust infestations, smallpox, typhus, trachoma or malaria provoked suffering and significant human and economic losses among borderlanders. Child mortality, for instance, was extremely high in the borderlands and rural areas, in general. Likewise, the after-effects of infectious diseases could be severe in some cases in both children and adults.

While superstitions and folk medicine were still influential, borderlanders' resistance or reluctance to accept modern notions of health and the use of

---

[133] BCA. 490.01.1211.22.1.38, p. 25.
[134] Rükneddin Fethi, *Doğu Köylerinde*, pp. 86–7.
[135] Saygi Öztürk, *İsmet Paşa'nın*, pp. 20–1, 80–1, 122–3; İsmet İnönü, *Defterler (1919–73) Vol. I*, edited by Ahmet Demirel (Istanbul: YKY, 2008), pp. 164–5.

new technologies to deal with diseases and pests uncritically can be explained by other factors, too. First, for nomadic tribes, extended families, and Sufi orders, such as Khaznawi's, cross-border networks were central to their very survival. New international borders were not, by definition, a problem for these populations, unless they prevented the latter to keep their mental and physical geographies alive, which did not necessarily coincide with those of the state(s) involved. Long and short-distance pilgrimages, transborder marriages and cross-border forms of pastoralism were thus social practices that, with or without the states' consent, were to be maintained for the sake of these groups' very interests. Within this context, transmission of human and animal diseases as a result of these practices was deemed a lesser evil. In addition, Bedouins developed other strategies for avoiding locust pests, which did not entail the use of poison and were more in line with their immediate environment and practices; they simply moved from one place to another.

Second, socio-economic factors were also at stake here, for the efforts to turn 'unhealthy areas' into 'healthy' ones clashed with locals' economic interests. This was the case, for instance, with rice production in northern Iraq. Even though growing rice was particularly favourable to the breeding of mosquitoes, it was so profitable (when compared to other harvests) that the peasants factored in the risks of malaria.[136] Likewise, the contraband of sheep and cross-border raids in the borderlands were also important means for the survival of the local economy in a peripheral region, despite the risks that these practices could entail. Notably, smugglers and raiders could perish during armed clashes with either border guards or other tribesmen. In addition, by 'exporting' or 'importing' cattle off the states' radar and thus evading quarantine policies, smugglers and tribes could provoke flare-ups of livestock diseases unintentionally, thereby further jeopardising their livelihoods.

By the same token, while smuggling sheep was a particularly profitable economic activity favoured by the establishment of international borders, cross-border raiding was first and foremost a tool for restoring an economic and power balance between borderlands tribes and livestock owners.[137] Concretely,

---

[136] LON, R2319/6A/30847/655. Report on Administration for 1930, p. 57.
[137] Nora Barakat, 'An Empty Land? Nomads and Property Administration in Hamidian Syria' (PhD dissertation, Berkeley: University of California, 2015), pp. 122–32.

by 'raiding an opponent, a social group – whether a whole tribe or a fraction of it – could ensure its survival as well as contest the domination of a rival group'.[138] The centrality of livestock for both settlers and semi-nomadic and nomadic Bedouins in the borderlands can be easily explained: for farmers, livestock was both capital and workforce.[139] For Bedouins, 'breeding animals was an important source of income, and collective identity was often defined not only by the territories they inhabited but also by the species of animal they bred'.[140]

Third, while colonial officials and urban 'modern' classes pointed to popular religious visions and 'primitive' practices such as eating roasted locusts as a persistent obstacle to attaining state goals in the anti-locust struggle,[141] such assumptions call for some nuances. From a state perspective, the dramatic consequences of locust infestations on agricultural production and the subsequent financial burden on the governments justified warfare-like campaigns against these 'armies of destruction', regardless of what the potential consequences might be.[142] Ironically, as in Ottoman times, expanding agricultural settlements and 'bringing civilization' into wastelands to gain legitimacy and levy taxes facilitated, in turn, the reproduction of locust swarms. Yet, in the

---

[138] Mehdi Sakatni, 'From Camel to Truck', p. 164. See also Robert S. Fletcher, 'Running the Corridor: Nomadic Societies and Imperial Rule in the Inter-War Syrian Desert', *Past and Present*, Vol. 220, No. 1 (2013), pp. 185–215.

[139] On the centrality of animals as forms of property in the Ottoman period, see, for instance, Alan Mikhail, *Under Ottoman's Tree: The Ottoman Empire, Egypt, and Environmental History* (Chicago: University of Chicago Press, 2017), pp. 111–30.

[140] Efrat Gilad, 'Meat in the Heat: A History of Tel Aviv under the British Mandate for Palestine, 1920s–1940s' (PhD dissertation, Geneva: The Graduate Institute of International and Development Studies, 2021), p. 113.

[141] The Syrian newspaper *al-Qabas*, for example, reported that some rural populations refused to participate in the anti–locust campaigns on religious grounds, 'describing the locust as a soldier of God (*jundi allah*), meaning fighting the locust was tantamount to fighting divine power'. *al-Qabas*, 29 May 1930. In other instances, local residents avoided providing information about the locations of eggs. Quoted in Samuel Dolbee, 'The Locust and the Starling', pp. 365–6.

[142] Anthony Clyne, 'Man's immemorial enemy: New Anti-Locust Campaign in Africa and the Middle East', *The African World*, 1943, p. 97.

era of modern technology, states were convinced that they would win the battle against locusts.[143]

In that regard, British Iraq took the lead in eradicating locust infestations. On the one hand, the air control scheme developed by the Royal Air Force (RAF)[144] – i.e. aerial bombing campaigns, armoured cars and local levies, and intelligence collection – was adapted to the management of locust swarms; aircrafts and armoured cars were thus deployed in the fight against locusts, while Special Officers gathered information to efficiently organise massive operations. On the other hand, London-based experts, such as P. Uvarov, encouraged the development of chemical methods by creating a special Insecticides Research Section at the Anti-Locust Research Centre to test the effects of poison on locusts.[145] Thereafter, resorting to spraying chemicals – such as sodium arsenite – from trucks became a widespread practice encouraged by the British authorities along the Syrian–Iraqi borderland which took advantage of the fuzziness of the international boundary.

In spite of the growing use of chemical pesticides to fight locusts, the results were not always convincing. In addition, the toxic effects of poison on both the flocks and the humans paved the way for rumours around chemicals and protests among locals, in particular among the semi-nomadic and nomadic tribes who were obliged to change their migration routes to escape the risk of losses. In that regard, as Samuel Dolbee puts it, 'tribal migration was nothing new, but migration in response to government pesticide treatments for locusts rather than in response to the locusts themselves presented a stark change indeed'.[146] In other cases, tribes hid their flocks to avoid paying taxes, but also as a protest against chemical pesticides.

---

[143] See Edmund Russell, *War and Nature: Fighting Humans and Insects with Chemicals from World War I to Silent Spring* (Cambridge: Cambridge University Press, 2001).

[144] David E. Omissi, *Air Power and Colonial Control: The Royal Air Force, 1919–39* (Manchester: Manchester University Press, 1990); Scot Robertson, *The Development of RAF Strategic Bombing Doctrine, 1919–39* (Wesport: Praeger, 1995); Cameron A. Cerbus, 'The Legacy of Air Control: A Reassessment of the "Splendid Training Ground" of Mandate Iraq' (MA Thesis, Beirut: American University of Beirut, 2021).

[145] TNA, CO 730/128/5. Ministry of Irrigation and Agriculture to High Commissioner for Iraq. Baghdad, 28 April 1928.

[146] Samuel Dolbee, 'The Locust and the Starling', p. 369.

Admittedly, while the use of chemicals was, in principle, limited to 'unpopulated' areas, and landmarks were supposedly displayed to notify the locals about poisoned areas, Bedouins and shepherds frequently lamented the loss of goats and camels due to the lack of appropriate information:

> In the Hasaka region, an important number of cattle have died while grazing where the Agriculture Services had sprayed pesticides last spring . . . The population strongly protests against this service that was supposed to take all necessary precautions.[147]

Whether resulting from their 'negligence' or the 'flaws' in how the information was conveyed, state authorities invariably blamed borderlanders for such 'incidents'.[148]

Borderlanders' attitudes towards anti-locust policies were problematic for another reason. Local authorities hired hundreds and, at times, thousands of locals to collect locusts and put them into sacks that were emptied into digs and immediately buried.[149] Alternatively, when local manpower was not sufficient, the use of flame-throwers replaced the former. Yet, international experts apprehensively observed the role played by the locals in the fight against locust swarms: 'Above all, the minor administrative officials must be absolutely eliminated from the control organisation, since it is notorious that anti-locust campaigns in those countries are regarded by them as a source of income owing to the practice of conscripting labour'.[150] No wonder, then, that for entomologists borderlanders were not seen as completely interested in eradicating this 'necessary enemy'.

Finally, the discourse, which was particularly virulent in Turkey, against traditional healers and superstitions as being real obstacles to the control and eradication of infectious diseases also concealed a central – albeit unspoken – reality of this period. State officials' idealism was also curtailed by financial

---

[147] CADN, 1SL/1/V/2128. Weekly report. Hasaka, 11–17, December 1944.
[148] LON, R2314.6A.6774.655. British Mandate for Iraq. Report on Administration, 1929.
[149] The important 1930 locust pest mobilised thousands of locals in the Turkish–Syrian–Iraqi borderlands. In Turkey, authorities evaluated at 100,000 the total number of villagers combatting locusts that year. BCA.030.10.185.277.11, 25 August 1930.
[150] Boris P. Uvarov, *Locusts and Grasshoppers*, p. 261.

constraints. As Ebru Boyar has shown, in Turkey, 'apart from the problem of personnel, the fight against disease was an expensive venture, particularly since the majority of medical equipment and drugs were imported'.[151] To make things worse, the international market of essential drugs such as quinine and neosalvarsan was particularly disrupted during the Second World War. Hence, much like in Syria, prices skyrocketed to the extent that 'even money did not remedy the scarcity of drugs'.[152] Against this background, Aziz Uras, a deputy from the Mardin province, requested that the Ankara government furnish the medicine to the poorest families free of charge.[153] The lack of responsiveness from Ankara, however, led locals to keep using traditional medicine or, alternatively, favouring the contraband of drugs to compensate for the lack of dispensaries and remedies to cure diseases.[154]

Crucially, faith in 'modern' medicine also had to be tested by experience. In 1930, for instance, a child who had been vaccinated against smallpox perished in the *caza* of Nusaybin. This tragic event had further consequences as his father killed the doctor who had administered the vaccine. Meanwhile, rumours about the deadly qualities of drugs distributed by the Turkish state quickly spread across the region. As a result, when mobile units arrived in other villages for vaccination purposes, villagers ran away to the nearest mountains.[155] Although trust was re-established over the years,[156] faith in medicine was tested by other incidents; as in other peripheral areas, the shortage of medical personnel in the borderlands facilitated the appearance of dubious individuals who

---

[151] Ebru Boyar, 'Taking Health to the Village: Early Turkish Republican Health Propaganda in the Countryside', in Ebru Boyar and Kate Fleet (eds), *Middle Eastern and North African Societies in the Interwar Period* (Leiden: Brill, 2019), pp. 166–7.

[152] Ibid. p. 168.

[153] BCA. 030.10.00.00.8.50.16, 3 April 1945.

[154] Contraband of quinine and other drugs thus became a widespread and profitable activity along Turkey's southern border, in both directions, depending on the price oscillations. See CADN, 1SL/1/V/33. Border Post at Ayn Diwar, 28 July 1944; BCA.490.01.512.2055.1, 14 February 1944.

[155] BCA.030.10.177.220.14, 1930.

[156] BCA.030.10.177.223.16, 28 November 1942. In north-eastern Syria as well, medical authorities expressed their satisfaction as the general vaccination of both settlers and nomads was implemented without any significant incidents. CADN, 1SL/1/V/2149. General Doctor Martin (Aleppo) to General Delegate (Beirut). Aleppo, 17 June 1937.

pretended to be doctors, at times with dramatic consequences. In his memoirs, Noureddine Zaza (1919–88), Dr Nafiz's brother, recalls how in the mid-1930s an Armenian charlatan, 'Boghos the bather', opened a dispensary in Qamishli where town dwellers and villagers were treated without any real precautions. When a local landowner died after having received a treatment in his dispensary, suspicion towards chemical remedies resurfaced.[157]

Finally, discontent at the periphery was not necessarily a signal of opposition amongst borderlanders to 'modernity' and 'science'. In actual fact, town dwellers often protested against the poor management of garbage handling by municipalities, which fatally facilitated the spread of infectious diseases across the region.[158] These instances thus suggest that the issue of contention among settlers, unlike the Bedouin, was not necessarily the increasing presence of the state in the borderlands, but its incompetence in dealing with health and environmental challenges.

In the Middle Eastern border zones, as elsewhere, sanitary international cooperation meant an increasing state presence through policies such as vaccination campaigns, (re)introduction of certificates for humans and livestock, as well as the erection of quarantine buildings and additional border gates. Much like in the nineteenth century, public health in the interwar period was therefore 'in part a spatial form of governance'.[159] Borders were supposed to function as barriers or '*cordons sanitaires*' aiming at regulating the circulation of people and animals to avoid both the spread of infectious diseases and the 'invasion' of undesirable insects such as locusts. Border inspections of people and animals – including their bodies, identities and documents –thus became key elements in the construction of both the international health regime and the increasingly bureaucratised administrative government over 'nationals' and 'foreigners'. Even though health documents pre-dated the formation of new states in the post-Ottoman Middle East, the widespread use of passports and other identity documents from the 1920s

[157] Noureddine Zaza, *Ma vie de Kurde*, pp. 125–6.
[158] CADN, 1SL/1/V/2128. Weekly report. Hasaka, 28 April–4 May 1945; CADN, 1SL/1/V/2051. Weekly report. Ras al-Ayn, 19 September–2 October 1943; CADN, 1SL/1/V/2051. Weekly report. Qamishli, 28 November–4 December 1943.
[159] Alison Bashford, *Imperial Hygiene*, p. 1. See also Valeska Huber, 'The Unification of the Globe by Disease?', pp. 453–76.

onwards made jurisdictional borders meaningful; rather than 'abstract lines on maps', they transformed borders into 'a set of practice on the ground'.[160]

In parallel, the expansion of agricultural projects provided governments with an opportunity to reinforce the process of state territorialisation in peripheral areas as well as additional sources of income. Likewise, conducting surveys on diseases and mapping out the evolution of locust swarms across the area helped states to advance in the process of 'nationalising' microbes and insects as well as integrating those zones as genuine portions of their respective territorial nation states.

While there were real instance of resistance against state policies to deal with pests and diseases in the frontier zones, borderlanders' attitudes and stakes regarding national and international endeavours varied and need to be contextualised. Settlers, in particular, often complained about authorities' negligence with regard to locust infestations and the management of prevailing sanitary conditions in the borderlands. In other words, for many border dwellers, states intervened too late and/or idly in the periphery, thereby endangering their crops and livelihood.

Ultimately, the shortage of both financial and human resources, together with the willingness of states to expand their presence in the frontier zones, created favourable conditions for a constant – albeit, at times conflicting – negotiation between state agents, international bodies and borderlanders; that is, between different, yet increasingly connected understandings of the spiritual and material ecology in the borderlands. Therefore, following Timothy Mitchell's approach, one can argue that, rather than considering germs and insects whose actions upon the borderlands exist separately from humans, historians should analyse their very existence and actions as dependent upon a series of interrelationships between human and non-human actors[161] – interdependences that went hand-in-hand with another important development; namely, the reshuffling and adaptation of prevailing borderland mobilities, as we shall see in the next chapter.

---

[160] Alison Bashford, 'The Age of Universal Contagion', p. 7.

[161] Timothy Mitchell, *Rule of Experts: Egypt, Techno-Politics, Modernity* (Berkeley and Los Angeles: University of California Press, 2002). See also Samuel Dolbee, 'The Desert at the End of Empire: An Environmental History of the Armenian Genocide', *Past and Present*, Vol. 247, No. 1 (2020), pp. 197–233; Chris Gratien, *The Unsettled Plain: An Environmental History of the Late Ottoman Frontier* (Stanford, CA: Stanford University Press, 2022).

5

RAILROADS, UNEVEN MOBILITIES AND FRAIL STATES

On 24 July 1938, the Station Master at Tel Kotchek – a small town located at the junction of the Syrian–Iraqi border – sent a series of telegrams to the office of Services Spéciaux in Qamishli in which he exhorted them to urgently dispatch French units to protect the Baghdad Railway facility from an imminent Bedouin attack. Given that Tel Kotchek only had two guards, failure to send the requested security forces would entail the departure of the personnel along with their families, thereby leaving the post without surveillance. The immediate reason for such alarming wires was that the corpse of a Bedouin related to an Iraqi tribe had been found next to the railway station. As soon as a small group of Bedouins arrived in town the same day, rumours surrounding the inevitable attack of Iraqi Bedouins to revenge the killing of their tribesman began spreading rapidly, thereby provoking a collective panic reaction. When the first French unit arrived at Tel Kotchek, its commandant found locals and railway employees assembled in front of the station, completely 'demoralized' and 'ready to quit the town by train'.[1]

The ensuing investigation report, however, considered that the Station Master's moves had been 'unnecessary', 'irresponsible' and prompted by 'false news'. Admittedly, the Iraqi tribesmen never attacked Tel Kotchek, and although the identity of the four Bedouins who arrived at the station on 24 July

---

[1] CADN, 1SL/1/V/706. Telegram No. 2. Qamishli, 24 July 1938.

could not be ascertained, the author of the report reckoned that they were more likely to be Syrian nationals. After all, local Bedouins frequently stopped by Tel Kotchek to purchase food supplies at the station buffet, just like the workers employed on the extension of the Baghdad Railway on the Iraqi side of the border.[2] Despite the lack of evidence of any real threat, the Services Spéciaux sent three additional divisions to reassure the personnel and the population of Tel Kotchek. In addition, French and Iraqi border authorities agreed to coordinate their efforts in order to guarantee the safety of the town dwellers and, even more importantly, prevent them from deserting a post that was 'worth millions' of Syrian pounds.[3] Finally, the piece of intelligence suggested the necessary replacement of the station manager along with his close collaborators by agents endowed with 'stronger character', for the security and economic stakes in Tel Kotchek were too high to be left to 'unreliable employees'.[4]

Even though no Iraqi Bedouins actually assaulted Tel Kotchek, the French appraisal of the employees' attitude was somewhat unfair. Throughout the interwar period, much as with camel caravans in the Ottoman times,[5] automobile services connecting Damascus and Baghdad became the target of frequent Bedouin attacks to the extent that French and British authorities were obliged to coordinate their police forces to secure the viability of the trans-desert route. Arguably, as the number of users of this motor road increased, the former also attracted the attention of the Bedouins, Druze rebels and outlaws.[6] Consequently, highway

---

[2] CADN, 1SL/1/V/706. Ch. Valadier to the French High Commissioner. Baghdad, 26 July 1938.
[3] CADN, 1SL/1/V/706. Report from Lieutenant-Colonel Marchand on the situation in Tel Kotchek. Deir ez-Zor, 4 August 1938.
[4] CADN, 1SL/1/V/706. The Adjunct Delegate to the High Commissioner (Aleppo) to the Director of the D.H.P. Railway Company. Aleppo, 29 July 1938.
[5] Fulya Özkan, 'Gravediggers of the Modern State: Highway Robbers on the Trabzon-Bayezid Road, 1850–1910s' *Journal of Persianate Studies*, Vol. 7, No. 2 (2014), pp. 219–50; Philippe Pétriat, 'Caravan Trade in the Late Ottoman Empire: The Aqil Network and the Institutionalization of Overland Trade', *Journal of Economic and Social History of the Orient*, Vol. 63, No. 1–2 (2019), pp. 38–72.
[6] The anti-French revolt of 1925 left behind several zones where Syrian rebels continued to attack French forces and interests, among which the road networks. Michael Provence, *The Great Syrian Revolt and the Rise of Arab Nationalism* (Austin: University of Texas Press, 2005). On the post-1925 rebel activities, see Laila Parsons, *The Commander: Fawzi Al-Qawuqji and the Fight for Arab Independence, 1914–48* (London: Saqi, 2018).

robbery, armed attacks and even the murder of passengers and automobile drivers became the toll for mounting trans-border mobility across the Syrian Desert. In that regard, in 1925, the most important hold-up occurred when brigands seized a consignment of 15,000 Turkish gold pounds that was being transferred to the Imperial Bank of Persia.[7] The same year, a convoy carrying the French Consul in Baghdad and his family from the Iraqi capital to Damascus was attacked by 'highway bandits'. During the incident, the consul's wife was murdered.[8] As a result of these events, automobile traffic was temporally redirected towards the Baghdad–Amman route.[9] Even though armoured cars escorting motor convoys during the so-called 'protected days' provided for the consolidation of the trans-desert route by the late 1920s, insecurity in the Syrian–Iraqi borderlands did not disappear overnight.[10]

Further north, by the mid-1930s, the Shammar – a Syrian–Iraqi tribal confederation – still illegally levied taxes on camel caravans passing through their region.[11] In addition, convoys using the alternative motor route that connected Mosul to Deir ez-Zor were also the object of raids and plunder.[12] More decisively for our story, in 1937, Daham al-Hadi – a paramount chieftain of a Shammar clan in Syria[13] – and his tribesmen occupied a construction site

[7] César Jaquier, 'Motor Cars and Trans-desert Traffic: Channelling Mobilities between Iraq and Syria, 1923–30', in Jordi Tejel and Ramazan Hakkı Öztan (eds), *Regimes of Mobility: Borders and State Formation in the Middle East, 1918–46* (Edinburgh: Edinburgh University Press, 2022), p. 240.

[8] TNA, AIR 5/408. RAF Headquarters to Air Ministry, 13 March 1925; LON, R59/1/17502/51544, Report by His Britannic Majesty's Government on the Administration of Iraq, 1925, p. 43.

[9] TNA, AIR 5/408. High Commissioner (Baghdad) to the Secretary of State for the Colonies (London). Baghdad, 1 September 1925.

[10] See TNA, CO 732/33/5. 'Trans-desert Routes'. Economic report, No. 105, 31 March 1928; TNA, FO 371/13745/E3771/191/65. 'Trans-desert routes in Near East'. London, 27 July 1929.

[11] NARA, RG59, Reel 3, 'Political Events'. American Legation. Baghdad, 17 May 1934.

[12] César Jaquier, 'Motor Cars and Transdesert Traffic: Channelling Mobilities between Iraq and Syria, 1923–30', pp. 228–55.

[13] The Shammar tribal confederation, the most important trans-border Bedouin tribe in the area stretching between Deir ez-Zor and Mosul. On Daham al-Hadi and his ambiguous relations with both the French authorities and the Syrian nationalists, see Philip S. Khoury, 'The tribal shaykh, French tribal policy, and the nationalist movement in Syria between two world wars', *Middle Eastern Studies*, Vol. 18, No. 2 (1982), pp. 180–93.

adjacent to Tel Kotchek, advancing different claims such as ownership of the land and the purported exclusivity of hiring his tribesmen as construction labourers.[14] Within this context, foreign engineers decided to temporally evacuate the site, remove all valuable materials and hence stop all activities until the situation was deemed safe.[15] Although there were no casualties during the occupation, the memory of this incident was certainly still present only a year later in the minds of the railway personnel in Tel Kotchek and its inhabitants.

A view from the borderlands thus helps problematise the linear and sometimes celebratory terms in which, according to some authors,[16] the first wave of globalisation, which spanned between 1880 and 1940 in the Middle East, has been presented.[17] To be sure, in the early twentieth century, non-Western areas witnessed significant shifts in technologies of global communication and transportation, such as the railway and telegraph, resulting in an important new round of 'time-space compression' or the accelerated 'shrinking of the world,' thus making the world smaller, the time shorter, and life faster.[18] Nevertheless, historians of globalisation also underline that this process was neither linear nor consistent across the region.

One the one hand, while the Middle Eastern region witnessed an unprecedented intensification of the movement of people, goods, and ideas, the

---

[14] CADN, 1SL/1/V/706. Telegram Director Régie Générale de Chemins de Fer (Paris) to Post Office Adviser (Beirut). Paris, 17 August 1937.

[15] CADN, 1SL/1/V/706. Colonel Sarrade (Deir ez-Zor) to the High Commissioner. Deir ez-Zor, 14 September 1937.

[16] James L. Gelvin and Nile Green (eds), *Global Muslims in the Age of Steam and Print* (Oakland, CA: University of California Press, 2014); Liat Kozma, Cyrus Schayegh and Avner Wishnitzer (eds), *A Global Middle East: Mobility, Materiality and Culture in the Modern Age, 1880–1940* (London: I. B. Tauris, 2015).

[17] Peter Mentzel, *Transportation Technology and Imperialism in the Ottoman Empire, 1800–1923* (Washington, DC: American Historical Association, 2006); Michael B. Miller, 'Pilgrims' Progress: The Business of the Hajj', *Past and Present*, Vol. 191, No. 1 (2006), pp. 189–228; Roland Wenzlhuemer, *Connecting the Nineteenth-Century World: The Telegraph and Globalization* (Cambridge: Cambridge University Press, 2015); On Barak, *Powering Empire: How Coal Made the Middle East and Sparked Global Carbonization* (Berkeley, CA: University of California Press, 2020).

[18] Houri Berberian, *Roving Revolutionaries: Armenians and the Connected Revolutions in the Russian, Iranian, and Ottoman Worlds* (Oakland, CA: University of California Press, 2019), pp. 41–2.

new states that emerged out of the Ottoman Empire developed more or less effective techniques for monitoring and controlling their borders in order to limit such movements, and, more importantly, their negative consequences.[19] As elsewhere at this time, new states sought to both facilitate and prevent the mobility through different 'channelling processes'.[20] Moreover, in the Turkish–Syrian–Iraqi borderlands, the distrust between Turkey and French Syria, on the one hand, and the traditional imperial rivalry between France and Britain on the other, hampered the pace of developing a more interconnected Middle East, in spite of the completion of the Berlin–Baghdad Railway by 1940 – a transportation project initiated in the late Ottoman period deemed to accelerate the speed of movement and improve economic relations between Europe and the Middle East.

On the other hand, as the reports on Tel Kotchek show, observation of particular locations allows us to add nuance to the narratives that tend to emphasise mobility and integration, while neglecting the 'limitations and tenuousness of global exchange' in the interwar years.[21] Actually, the acceleration of speed and time compression, which characterised incipient modern globalisation, spread in a rather uneven manner through the Middle East;[22] that is, 'interruptions, reversals, and processes of deglobalisation' were also a part of it.[23] As such, individuals and groups experienced the tensions between

---

[19] Liat Kozma, Cyrus Schayegh and Avner Wishnitzer, 'Introduction', in *A Global Middle East, 1880–1940*, p. 1.

[20] Valeska Huber, *Channelling Mobilities: Migration and Globalisation in the Suez Canal Region and Beyond, 1869–1914* (Cambridge: Cambridge University Press, 2013).

[21] Nile Green, 'Fordist Connections: The Automotive Integration of the United States and Iran', *Comparative Studies in Society and History*, Vol. 58, No. 2 (2016), pp. 290–321 (here p. 292).

[22] Jordi Tejel, 'The Last Ottoman Rogues: The Kurdish-Armenian Alliance in Syria and the New State System in the Interwar Middle East', in Ramazan Hakkı Öztan and Alp Yenen (eds), *Age of Rogues: Rebels, Revolutionaries and Racketeers at the Frontiers of Empires* (Edinburgh: Edinburgh University Press, 2021), pp. 371–5; See also Philippe Pétriat, 'The Uneven Age of Speed: Caravans, Technology, and Mobility in the Late Ottoman and Post-Ottoman Middle East', *International Journal of Middle East Studies*, Vol. 53, No. 2 (2021), pp. 273–90.

[23] Caroline Douki and Philippe Minard, 'Histoire globale, histoires connectées: un changement d'échelle historiographique ?', *Revue d'histoire moderne contemporaine*, Vol. 54–5, No. 5 (2007), p. 11.

acceleration and deceleration processes during their journeys across a region in motion.[24]

A view from the borderlands also allows us to explore how processes of globalisation, deglobalisation and modernity – i.e. 'an uneven experience [of men and women to get a grip on the modern world] punctuated by shifting moments of order and chaos, categorization and fragmentation, . . . legibility and disunity'[25] – unfolded on the periphery in the interwar period. Admittedly, states, banks and railway companies were key actors in the Baghdad Railway tribulations from start to finish. Yet, in the face of the constant hesitations and concerns raised by policymakers in London, Paris, Damascus, Baghdad and Ankara about the economic and geo-strategic benefits they could obtain from the construction of this railroad, local actors became both subjects as well as objects of modernisation projects in two complementary ways. First, local merchants and notables in cities such as Aleppo and Mosul lobbied for the completion of the Baghdad Railway in a bid to boost their respective economies and re-invigorate social and commercial networks that pre-dated the newly-established borders in the region.

Second, besides merchants, borderlanders in general were not alien to these developments; rather, they maintained a multifaceted relationship with these new means of transportation. As the story at the outset of this chapter reveals, the assaults against motor caravans and railway facilities in the borderlands left their imprint by both slowing down the construction plans and redirecting the movement of people and goods. In short, borderlanders frustrated the national and imperial ambitions of the Mandatory powers to a certain extent. Conversely, they also contributed to making the transportation facilities real by either providing workforce or securing complementary means to preserve local, regional and global connectivity, pending railroad termination. Hence, in the Turkish–Syrian–Iraqi borderlands, as in many

---

[24] On this idea, see Huber Valeska, *Channelling Mobilities*.
[25] Galen Murton, 'Nobody Stops and Stays Anymore: Motor Roads, Uneven Mobilities, and Conceptualizing Borderland Modernity in highland Nepal', in Alexander Horstmann, Martin Saxer and Alessandro Rippa (eds), *Routledge Handbook of Asian Borderlands* (London and New York: Routledge, 2018), p. 317. Definition based on Marshall Berman, *All That is Solid Melts into Air: The Experience of Modernity* (London: Verso, 1983).

other places in the Middle East, there were multiple and interdependent forms of mobility that were nevertheless shaped by grassroots agencies.

This chapter thus posits that, while the expansion of the railway and motor road networks was key to the process of territorialisation of the respective states in the periphery, this process was also the result of everyday interactions between officials and railway representatives, travellers and borderlanders, along with old and new technologies and subsequent experiences of mobility.[26] Moreover, as the railroad prompted further flows of people and goods, and therefore an increased police control on the trains running across the borderlands, the border between Turkey and Syria, on the one hand, and between Syria and Iraq, on the other, was altered in many respects. While the borderlines were kept untouched and maintained their primary functions, borders as institutions around which power relations unfold were also introduced in other locations; namely, on the trains, railway and bus stations, thus becoming 'mobile borders'.[27]

In that regard, by observing the multi-layered constructions of borders through mobility, who travelled and for what purpose, as well as the local 'appropriation' of the Baghdad Railway in the tri-border area, this chapter argues that such processes and experiences provided for the conditions of a sort of 'borderland modernity'.[28] Although 'borderland modernity' in the steppe certainly differed from the modernity in urban centres and seaports in the interwar period,[29] this concept undoubtedly helps us to connect the social, economic and political transformations across Middle Eastern borderlands to the so-called 'age of speed'.

The Tumultuous Completion of the Berlin–Baghdad Railway

When on 8 January 1939 the first international train arrived in Mosul, the pro-railway lobby in France and the Levant celebrated this 'historical event'

---

[26] See also Matthew Ellis, 'Over the Borderline? Rethinking Territoriality at the Margins of Empire and Nation in the Modern Middle East (Part I)', *History Compass*, Vol. 13, No. 8 (2015), pp. 411–22.

[27] See Anne-Laure Amilhat Szary and Frédéric Giraut, *Borderities and the Politics of Contemporary Mobile Borders* (London: Palgrave Macmillan, 2015).

[28] Galen Murton, 'Nobody Stops and Stays Anymore', pp. 315–24.

[29] Keith D. Watenpaugh, *Being Modern in the Middle East: Revolution, Nationalism, Colonialism and the Arab Middle Class* (Princeton, NJ: Princeton University Press, 2012); Liat Kozma, *Global Women, Colonial Ports: Prostitution in the Interwar Middle East* (Albany: SUNY Press, 2017).

as the definite proof that the era of railroads was not over, contrary to the 'false prophesies' about the decline of railway transportation advanced by the pro-automobile sectors.[30] Despite the 'Anglo-Saxon interested propaganda' favouring cars and trucks, trains were still faster, safer and economically more advantageous compared to automobile services, for trains could carry tons of merchandise at once.[31] Consequently, railroads were to remain central elements of progress and prosperity in the modern world. Despite French publicists' enthusiasm, however, when the first convoy left Baghdad for Istanbul on the night of 17 July 1940– thereby bringing to fruition the five-decade transportation project – the Iraqi cabinet decided not to celebrate the occasion by an opening ceremony in Mosul in view of the international context.

Firstly, as a contemporary observer pointed out, 'constructed primarily for peaceful commerce', the line nevertheless acquired high military value during the Second World War.[32] Indeed, two months before its inauguration, the Germans suspended the Paris–Milan section of the Simplon-Orient Express. Furthermore, from 1941 onwards, the Baghdad Railway became a key instrument in transporting the material and food supplies for the Allied forces and their Middle Eastern allies. During the war, although the Taurus Express – the Asiatic extension of the Simplon-Orient Express – continued to run twice a week in each direction between Istanbul and Baghdad, the passage of Axis agents between Europe and the Allied-controlled territories was rendered difficult by strict security measures. Within this overall context, no wonder its touristic mission in the Middle East virtually ended.[33]

Secondly, as the British pointed out, cars and lorries competed on many of the routes provided for by the river and rail across the region, for the former gave a speedier service for passengers and some types of goods than the

---

[30] *Le Commerce du Levant*, 20 January 1939, p. 1.
[31] In 1935, strikes led by car and bus drivers in the main Syrian cities against French transport policies were depicted as initiatives encouraged by 'Anglo-Saxon' interests, for almost all automobiles in the Levant were made in America. See CADN, 1SL/1/V/701. 'Car and Railway Transports', 10 April 1935.
[32] Philip Willard Ireland, 'Berlin to Baghdad up-to-date', *Foreign Affairs*, Vol. 19, No. 3 (1941), p. 665.
[33] Amit Bein, *Kemalist Turkey and the Middle East: International Relations in the Interwar Period* (Cambridge: Cambridge University Press, 2017), p. 214.

locals could afford to pay for. As a result, automobile services deprived 'other forms of transport of revenue which would enable rates to be economically lowered'.[34] Moreover, the construction of motor roads was cheaper than that of rail tracks, as the latter required at times important engineering work, intense human and animal workforce, as well as the transportation of heavy construction materials.[35] Tellingly, by the late 1930s, the number of cars and trucks imported into countries such as Syria, Lebanon and Iraq indicated that 'this was a flourishing market, denoting increased social demand for vehicles'.[36] By the time the Second World War began, car and bus services had become real competitors for railroad projects in the Middle East.

Notwithstanding this, a closer look at how the transportation schemes expanded in the first half of the twentieth century in the region calls for two important nuances. On the one hand, as different scholars have pointed out, one cannot systematically oppose the development of railways and motor roads. As we shall see in this section, they were rather interdependent, for local car and bus services maintained the nexus first between Tel Ziwan and Mosul, and later between Tel Kotchek and Mosul. On the other hand, even though the eastern sections of the Baghdad Railway never became the popular venture that railway companies and the tourist industry hoped for, both the Taurus Express and the 'mixed' trains – half passenger and half goods – running through Turkish–Syrian–Iraqi borderlands carried other types of passengers – pilgrims, students, state employees, soldiers, peasants, smugglers and merchants – who benefited from this railroad for different purposes and were increasingly connected. Tellingly, by late 1936, wagons carrying wheat from Mosul to Aleppo were put on hold at Tel Kotchek and replaced by passenger coaches to meet the unexpected demand for travelling in the

[34] TNA, CO 730/162/5. 'Memorandum by the Director of Railways Regarding Road and Railway Competition in Iraq'. Baghdad, 28 January 1930.

[35] Already by 1923, the French High Commissioner enthusiastically noted that the Baghdad–Damascus motor road was becoming the safest, the quickest and the least expensive route that would soon be connecting Europe to Persia. CADC, 48CPCOM42. Letter from General Weygan. Beirut, 1 December 1923.

[36] Mehdi Sakatni, 'From Camel to Truck? Automobiles and the Pastoralist Nomadism of Syrian Tribes during the French Mandate, 1920–46', *Comparative Studies of South Asia, Africa and the Middle East*, Vol. 39, No. 1 (2019), pp. 159–69 (here p. 160).

borderlands. A month later, supplementary trains were introduced to prevent Iraqi wheat from rotting at Tel Kotchek.[37] In short, the decline of the Berlin–Baghdad Railway as an international means of transportation at the end of the Second World War was thus the result of the combination of complex local, regional and global dynamics, rather than the 'natural' outcome of an obsolete project.

The origins of the Berlin–Baghdad Railway project dated back to 1888, when two important German banks created a syndicate and obtained a concession from the Ottoman authorities to extend the Istanbul–Ankara line to Baghdad via Adana, Aleppo, Nusaybin and Mosul. Yet, the actual construction of the railway began in 1904 with a concession granted to Germany by Sultan Abdulhamid II in 1902.[38] However, as soon as the scheduled scheme became public, concerns emerged in Russia, France and Britain regarding the implications of the German-Ottoman deal. Crucially, European competitors feared direct German access to the Persian Gulf, thereby threatening British oilfields as well as securing a closer position in relation to the Suez Canal, Asia and Germany's colonies in Africa.[39] Despite many ups and downs in the construction process, by 1915, the single-track railroad ended some 80km east of Diyarbakır. Another section heading east from Aleppo ended at Nusaybin. A third spur originating in Baghdad went north to Tikrit and south to Kut. Just before the armistice, the railroad reached Nusaybin, a small town situated at the crossroads between south-eastern Anatolia and the Jazira.

On a diplomatic level, the 1919 Treaty of Versailles cancelled all German rights to the Baghdad Railway.[40] According to Article IV, the Anatolian Railway

---

[37] CADN, 1SL/1/V/706. Bureau diplomatique. Beirut, 20 January 1937.

[38] On the origins and development of the Baghdad Railway between 1888 and 1914, see Murat Özyüksel, *The Berlin-Baghdad Railway and the Ottoman Empire: Industrialization, Imperial Germany and the Middle East* (London: I. B. Tauris, 2016). See also William I. Shorrock, 'The Origin of the French Mandate in Syria and Lebanon: The Railroad Question, 1901–14', *International Journal of Middle East Studies*, Vol. 1, No. 2 (1970), pp. 133–53; Sean McMeekin, *The Berlin-Baghdad Express: The Ottoman Empire and Germany's Bid for World Power* (Cambridge, MA: Harvard University Press, 2010).

[39] Volkan S. Ediger and John V. Bowlus, 'Greasing the Wheels: The Berlin-Baghdad Railways and Ottoman Oil, 1888–1907', *Middle Eastern Studies*, Vol. 56, No. 2 (2020), pp. 193–206.

[40] Nevertheless, the Deutsche Bank transferred its holdings to a Swiss bank and thus continued to be involved in this international venture.

and those parts of the Baghdad Railway lying within Turkish territory were to be operated by a company whose capital would be subscribed to by the British, French and Italian financial interests. In addition, the DHP (Damascus, Hama and Extensions) obtained from the French government the right to provisionally exploit the Baghdad Railway from Konya to Nusaybin. Critically, as mentioned in Chapter 2, the ensuing 1921 Treaty of Ankara established the provisional Syrian–Turkish border as running along the railway tracks from çobanbey in the west to Nusaybin in the east, with the border on the Syrian side of the tracks, leaving the tracks in Turkish territory (Article VIII). Further west, the Treaty set the border immediately north of the town and railway station of Meydan Ekbez. As a result, 'the railroad-cum-border practically divided the Ottoman province of Aleppo into two, separating the commercial hub that the city of Aleppo was from its southern Anatolian hinterland', with enduring consequences for regional commerce.[41] Eight years later, Selim Jambart, the head of the Aleppo Chamber of Commerce, stated in a rather dramatic tone: 'The old commercial centre Aleppo (*sic*), once the crossroads of caravans linking Orient and Occident, has died'.[42]

Once completed, the three-day journey from Istanbul to Baghdad was not straightforward either. Passengers from Europe had to transfer in Istanbul by taking the ferry across the Bosporus to Haydar Pasha railway station, while in Baghdad they were requested to change from the standard-gauge line to the Baghdad–Basra metre-gauge line. This state of affairs was even more damaging for commerce; the difference of gauge line required transhipment of goods, which involved considerable time and expense.

The management of the line along the borderlands also became a complex issue. Between Meydan Ekbez on the Turkish–Syrian border, and Tel Kotchek, three different companies operated the railroad crossing the borderlands. While the Turkish State Railways secured the train connection from Haydar Pasha to Syria, the company La Société française du chemin de

---

[41] Ramazan Hakkı Öztan, 'The Last Ottoman Merchants: Regional Trade and Politics of Tariffs in Aleppo's Hinterland', in Jordi Tejel and Ramazan Hakkı Öztan (eds), *Regimes of Mobility*, pp. 80–108 (here p. 81).

[42] Quoted in Cyrus Schayegh, *The Middle East and the Making of the Modern World* (Cambridge, MA: Harvard University Press, 2017), p. 177.

fer Bozanti–Alep–Nisibin et prolongements (BANP) ran the section from Meydan Ekbez to Aleppo and back to the Turkish frontier at Çobanbey, where the private railway company *Cenub Demiryollari* (Southern Lines or CD) operated it up to Nusaybin. Thence, the BANP took over again as far as Tel Kotchek, on the Syrian–Iraqi border. From that point, the Iraqi Railways managed the section to Baghdad and also the metre-gauge line from Baghdad to Basra.[43]

This complicated configuration was also amplified until the mid-1930s by the tense relations between Turkey and its southern neighbours, in particular French Syria. In the aftermath of the First World War, delays in the exploitation of the Baghdad Railway were due to the partial destruction of diverse bridges and rails during the combat between the pro-Turkish and pro-French armed bands in 1921 at different sections around Jarablus, and from Tel Abyad to Nusaybin. It was only in 1924 that the line was repaired.[44] Although France allowed the Ankara government to use the tracks on the Syrian side of the border to carry thousands of Turkish soldiers deployed in eastern Anatolia to repress the Shaykh Said rebellion in 1925, some months after crushing the Kurdish uprising, the Turks denied the use of the line by the French not only for civilian but also for military purposes.[45]

After negotiations with Ankara, the Compagnie internationale des Wagons-Lits, which had operated the Orient Express since 1883, launched a service between Istanbul, Aleppo and Tripoli in 1927, known as the Taurus Express. However, the completion and subsequent management of the eastern section of the Baghdad Railway remained a bone of contention. In parallel, in Syria, neither the French High Commission nor the Damascene elites wished to pay for this costly infrastructure, leaving the question of who would take responsibility for the loans unresolved.[46] Within this context, France and Turkey disregarded its conclusion until the early 1930s.

---

[43] Philip Willard Ireland, 'Berlin to Baghdad Up-to-date', p. 665.
[44] NARA, RG59, Reel 16. American Consulate. Aleppo, 27 October 1924.
[45] NARA, RG59, Reel 16. 'Clash between the Turks and the French Over the Use of the Eastern Branch of the Baghdad Railroad'. American Consulate. Aleppo, 21 December 1925.
[46] NARA, RG59, Reel 5. 'Contemplated French Loan to Syria and Lebanon'. American Consulate. Beirut, 24 January 1930.

Instead, Turkey prioritised the densification of her domestic railway network. Republican elites' appraisal of the situation prevailing by 1923 was appalling. The system inherited from the old Ottoman Empire left more than half of the country without any rapid form of transportation.[47] Only the western regions were connected by a system of railway lines. Moreover, nearly half of the ex-Ottoman railroads fell outside Turkey's borders as of 1923. Against this background, the new authorities gave themselves the mission of reversing the situation, for they considered that the exploitation of the natural wealth of the country, its progress and its economic balance closely depended upon the expansion of Turkish railroads. Moreover, the key role played by the Baghdad Railway in transporting Turkish units to suppress the Shaykh Said rebellion in the spring of 1925 revealed another central dimension of railroads. From that moment on, the development of transportation facilities across the whole country was to secure the political and military stability throughout Turkey's most peripheral regions by bringing closer the western and eastern provinces. Ultimately, railways and motor roads were to become essential tools in cementing the expected loyalty towards the state and national unity.[48]

Yet, two important obstacles curtailed Turkish ambitions throughout the 1920s. On the one hand, in the aftermath of the First World War, foreign companies and trustees owned most railway lines in Turkey, the former holding their own views and interests regarding which lines could be more profitable and under which conditions.[49] On the other hand, the Lausanne

---

[47] Ilhan Tekeli and Selim Ilkin, 'Cumhuriyetin Demiryolu Politikalarının Olusumu ve Uygulanması', *Cumhuriyetin Harcı Modernitenin Altyapısı*, Vol. III (Istanbul: Bilgi Üniversitesi Yayınları, 2010), p. 274.

[48] Ismail Yıldırım, 'Atatürk Dönemi Demiryolu Politikasına Bir Bakış', *Atatürk Araştırma Merkezi Dergisi*, Vol. 12, No. 35 (1996), pp. 387–96.

[49] In 1923, for instance, the American Chester Company intended to construct a railroad linking eastern Anatolia and the Mosul region to the Black Sea and the Mediterranean. In return, the American company would have the right to exploit the oil in the Mosul area for a period of 99 years. Even though the Turkish Parliament accepted these conditions, the Chester Company did not sign the deal, for Mosul Province escaped from effective Turkish control. See Selim Ilkin, *A Foreign Capital Investment Enterprise in Turkey in the Years 1922–3: The Chester Railway Project* (Istanbul: Türkiye İş Bankası, 1981).

Treaty imposed some key financial conditions on Turkey. First, the Republic of Turkey could not increase customs duties until 1928, thereby limiting Ankara's capacity to launch comprehensive policies gearing towards boosting Turkey's economic development. Second, Turkey accepted the foreign debts of the Ottoman Empire, whose payments became a burden on the state budget. Against this setting, Turkey prioritised repairing the old railway lines damaged during the First World War and the early 1920s and the nationalisation of the same, while increasing the links between Ankara and other urban markets in Western and Central Anatolia.

With the end of Lausanne's conditions in 1929, along with the effects of the Great Depression, the Turkish government opted for a radical shift in Turkey's economic policies. As we saw in Chapter 3, Ankara slowly developed *etatism*; that is, an economic policy that put the state in a central position both as the owner of key infrastructures and the producer of essential products, while also allowing the private sector to flourish. Within this context, the government launched new transportation projects and continued to nationalise the existing lines.[50] While security considerations were still prominent among Ankara's policymakers in the 1930s, the latter also saw in the expansion of the railroad network a way of fighting unemployment and boosting national economy altogether.[51] In short, according to both President Mustafa Kemal and Prime Minister İsmet İnönü, enhancing the railway network was a 'national need', regardless of the negative impacts upon Turkey's public debt.[52]

The expansion of Turkish railroads in the border zones was nevertheless a much more sensitive issue. Indeed, while it has become a truism that railway infrastructure development is a fundamental project of both nation-state making and global connectedness, it is less widely acknowledged that the impact of roads and railways is 'both heightened and complicated in borderland regions'.[53] Because the expansion of the Turkish railway network in the

---

[50] On the nationalisation of railroads, see Sena Bayraktaroğlu, 'Development of Railways in the Ottoman Empire and Turkey' (MA dissertation, Istanbul: Boğaziçi University, 1995), pp. 69–71.

[51] Evren Güngör, 'Les transports en Turquie: problèmes et points de vue sur les solutions'. *Anatolia moderna*, T. 5 (1994), p. 155.

[52] *Demiryollar Mecmuası*, Vol. 6, No. 66–70 (1930), pp. 272–3; *Ulus*, 29 December 1937.

[53] Galen Murton, 'Nobody Stops and Stays Anymore', p. 318.

early years of the republic was seen first and foremost as an important tool in building the Turkish state, this key infrastructure had to be kept away, as much as possible, from the influence of Turkey's southern neighbours. Much as with other border issues, Franco-Turkish accords and declarations on the subject of the Baghdad Railway did not erase the conflicts between border authorities. The signature of the frontier protocol on 22 June 1929, which was thought to ease Franco-Syrian relations around the common border, included a limited extension of the Nusaybin section of the Baghdad Railway into Syrian territory; it enabled passengers of the 'Taurus Express' to carry their luggage from Nusaybin (Turkey) to Tel Ziwan (Syria), before getting on a bus or a car that would drive them to Mosul and Baghdad.[54] Notwithstanding this, almost a year later Turkey still opposed its implementation, for Ankara considered that French border authorities had done little to control the contraband activities on the Syrian side of the border.[55] Likewise, while Turkish nationals were allowed to enter Syrian territory upon presentation of a border card, Turkish guards created obstacles to Syrian nationals at border gates such as Qamishli/Nusaybin. Hence, taxi drivers providing the connection between Qamishli and Nusaybin's railway station, complained that Turkish authorities requested them to present a passport as well as pay a customs tax for every entry into Turkey.[56]

Distrust was not limited to Franco-Turkish relations; the old imperial rivalry between France and Britain also had an impact on the turbulent construction process of the Baghdad Railway. At the time of signing the Treaty of Ankara in 1921, France did not hide her ultimate plans with regard to the completion of the Baghdad Railway; that is, connecting the eastern Mediterranean ports – Alexandretta, in particular – to Persia through railway and motor routes. Against this backdrop, the British considered that the Baghdad Railway scheme would mainly benefit French Syria, with foreseen prejudices for Iraq, for the Syrian railways have 'everything to gain and nothing to lose by quoting low rates'.

---

[54] Until then, passengers of the 'Taurus Express' needed to carry their luggage using handcars from Nusaybin to Mahmaqiyye.

[55] CADN, 1SL/1/V/706. 'Dérangement du trafic sur le BANP'. Beirut, 19 March 1930.

[56] CADN, 1SL/1/V/706. 'Interdiction aux syriens de l'accès de la gare de Nusaybin'. Aleppo, 29 June 1932.

Moreover, 'the whole tendency of the connection also would be to favour trade with Mediterranean ports to the detriment of that from more distant ports and the East'.[57] In other words, the British Empire's zone of influence stretching between the Persian Gulf and India could be, from an economic viewpoint, endangered by the success of the Baghdad Railway.

British Iraq was thus hardly interested in accelerating the completion of the Baghdad Railway in the 1920s. Instead, the British strove to secure an alternative connection between Baghdad and the Mediterranean – that is, the Baghdad–Haifa scheme. While this project was already in preparation in the 1920s, it became a priority among certain British officials in the Middle East and London, as the Tehran government decided to divert Iranian trade with Europe from Iraqi routes to a domestic port in the Gulf, thereby curtailing Iraq's transit trade. Against this backdrop, the proponents of this project envisioned a parallel construction of the Haifa–Baghdad railway, along with the proposed Iraq–Mediterranean pipeline. The spot chosen as the future terminus for the railway and pipeline was the port of Haifa, which was formally opened in October of 1933.[58] Hence, between 1933 and 1936, the partisans of the Baghdad–Haifa railway became more vocal, resulting in further Franco-British competition in the Levant which was also reflected in the border relations between French Syria and Iraq by way of minor incidents. In 1935, for instance, the Iraqi Department of Foreign Affairs sent an official letter to the French Legation in Baghdad complaining about the violation of Iraq's territory. According to Iraqi allegations, the engineers working on the extension of the Baghdad Railway to Tel Kotchek together with their teams had crossed the boundary pillars carrying with them construction materials well beyond Syrian territory. Hence, the competent French authorities in Syria were requested to intervene immediately in order to remove the 'adverse disturbs inflicted onto the Iraqi border'.[59]

Franco-British antagonism in the Middle East was not the only reason for British and Iraqi reluctance in the face of French plans, though. Certain

---

[57] TNA, CO 730/133/18. 'Baghdad Railway extension through Iraq', 19 April 1928.
[58] Morton B., Stratton, 'British Railways and Motor Roads in the Middle East, 1930–40', *Economic Geography*, Vol. 20, No. 3 (1944), pp. 190–91.
[59] CADC, 50CPCOM459. Ministry of Foreign Affairs. Baghdad, 5 February 1935.

British officials feared the economic and ultimately, political consequences of finalising the Baghdad Railway for Iraq, thereby holding ambivalent views about the prospects of such projects. Director General of Iraq Railways, Ramsay Tainsh, for instance, elaborated an internal report in 1928 highlighting the economic potential of extending the Aleppo–Mosul route both as a trade and tourist course. On the one hand, 'the present bad condition of trade in the eastern Mediterranean Sea has led to a cutting of sea freights and both the shipping companies and the Syrian railways are looking for and willing to encourage any new routes that offer possibilities of increased trade'.[60] On the other hand, the dire conditions of trade in Mosul made any cheaper and quicker route naturally appealing to the merchants there. In addition, owing to the extraordinarily high shipping rates from Basra to Europe and America, Persian carpets entering/loaded at Khaniqin could be sent via Mosul to Alexandretta, and onwards by sea, at no greater cost, and to some places, at a lower cost.[61]

Nevertheless, as France and Turkey moved forward in that direction, Ramsay Tainsh view changed altogether; Ramsay Tainsh's point was that if Mosul secured an outlet to the Mediterranean at Alexandretta, Mosul would then 'become independent from Baghdad'[62] economically. In a comprehensive letter submitted to the British Embassy in Baghdad, Tainsh developed his argument further: 'Mosul will not be indebted to Baghdad for anything [since] all her supplies will come directly from the west and at lower freight rates than could be expected via Basra and Baghdad'. Anticipating further consequences, Tainsh drew British officials' attention towards the East: 'With this rail connection from the Mediterranean to Mosul and a motor lorry service from Mosul to Erbil and through the Rowanduz road to Iran, the cheap products of Europe will compete with the goods from the East that are imported via Bandar Shahpur' in the Persian Gulf.[63]

---

[60] TNA, AIR 23/1023. 'Trade and Tourist Route from Nisibin to Mosul'. Ramsay Tainsh, Director of Railways. Baghdad, 7 November 1928.
[61] Ibid.
[62] TNA, FO 624/3/96/53/35. 'Railways, Part II'. G. H. Bateman (London), 21 August 1935.
[63] TNA, FO 371/18922/3/7/35. Ramsay Tainsh to British Ambassador Sir Archibald Clark Kerr. Baghdad, 18 June 1935.

In order to avoid such harmful consequences, Tainsh lobbied for delaying as much as possible the railroad section from Tel Kotchek to Mosul and putting the Baghdad–Baiji line out of use; in other words, keeping a narrow-gauge line from Mosul to Baghdad. Alternatively, he argued for building a broad-gauge railway from Mosul to Haifa via Baiji, Tikrit and Hit, before the connection of Mosul to the Mediterranean by rail through Syria became an accomplished fact. This delaying strategy was also shared by the British Ambassador to Iraq and former British High Commissioner, Francis H. Humphrys.[64] He also considered that the completion of the Baghdad Railway, as originally conceived by the Germans, would make Alexandretta the seaport on the Mediterranean for Iraq. As a result, the centre of gravity would tend to shift 'from Baghdad to Mosul and, in my opinion, political consequences would follow which would constitute a grave threat to the unity and stability of this country'.[65]

It was thus against all odds that the interest in finishing the Baghdad Railway was renewed by the mid-1930s due to a combination of a number of global, regional and local dynamics.[66] First, in the face of the British interest in opening the Baghdad–Haifa route at the expense of the Baghdad Railway, French Syria and Turkey initiated a slow process of cooperation on transportation along the shared border. In October 1932, a joint Franco-Turkish declaration relative to an accord on the future control of the Baghdad Railway included the prolongation of that railway beyond Nusaybin;[67] that is, crossing one of the sections of the Turkish–Syrian border that had created most tension between the two countries throughout the 1920s. Furthermore, acting under pressure from French banks and private business interests, French High Commissioner in the Levant decided to extend the railroad track from Tel

---

[64] British Consul at Aleppo A. Monck-Mason, on the contrary, lobbied for the extension of the Nusaybin-Mosul section. TNA, FO 371/24595/E477/55/65. Consul Monck-Mason. Aleppo, 19 January 1931.

[65] TNA, FO 371/18922/E1287/528/65. Sir Francis Humphrys to Sir John Simon. Baghdad, 23 February 1935.

[66] For a detailed account on the construction progress of the Baghdad Railway in the sections connecting Turkey, Syria and Iraq, see Shereen Khairallah, *Railways in the Middle East, 1856–1948* (Beirut: Libraire du Liban, 1991), pp. 123–47.

[67] BCA.030.10.152.7.8.29, Protocol of 1932.

Ziwan – the terminus of the Taurus Express inaugurated in 1930 – to Tel Kotchek, on the Syrian–Iraqi border. From there, Ford automobiles took passengers to Kirkuk via Mosul. Beginning on this date, too, the Taurus Express ran via Ankara instead of Konya.

Second, French interest in securing an overland route that would connect Syria to Persia combined with increasing Turkish and British anxieties in the face of the rising fascist bloc in Europe and, in particular, Italian revisionism in the eastern Mediterranean, including the colonial expansion into Abyssinia.[68] Against the eventuality of a maritime blockade, overland routes in the Middle East, such as the Baghdad Railway, appeared as serious alternatives to secure a safe connection between Turkey and the French and British spheres of influence in the region.[69]

In parallel, new domestic dynamics unfolded in Iraq and Syria. On the one hand, Iraq became a nominally sovereign and independent state in 1932. Furthermore, under the terms of the Railway Agreement of 31 March 1936, the Iraqi Railways passed from British ownership to the Government of Iraq, with a subsequent change at its head. On 29 October 1936, a coup d'état brought a new coalition of nationalist leaders to the new Iraqi cabinet; notably, Prime Minister Hikmat Sulaiman and General Bakr Sidqi as Chief of Staff, both having a strong affinity with Kemalist Turkey and aiming at freeing Iraq from British patronage.[70] Significantly, only a few days after seizing power, the new government approved the completion of the Baghdad Railway project. The construction began in November 1936 from Tel Kotchek to Mosul, and on 31 March 1939, the first Taurus Express reached Mosul.[71]

On the other hand, the emergence of a nationalist government in Syria in early 1936 also helped the Iraqi authorities commit themselves to building the missing link on the old Baghdad Railway by joining the railhead at Baiji to the

---

[68] See Macgregor Knox, *Mussolini Unleashed, 1939–41: Politics and Strategy in Fascist Italy's Last War* (Cambridge: Cambridge University Press, 1982), pp. 3–42.

[69] In the early 1930s, France elaborated comprehensive reports to better evaluate the commercial and tourist benefits of extending the Baghdad Railway up to Persia. See, for instance, CADN, 1SL/1/V/704. Pierre Watteau to Mr de Lassus Saint-Geniès. Beirut, 2 July 1934.

[70] Charles Tripp, *A History of Iraq* (Cambridge: Cambridge University Press, 2000), pp. 84–94.

[71] 'Calais to Baghdad by Rail', *Times*, 20 November 1936.

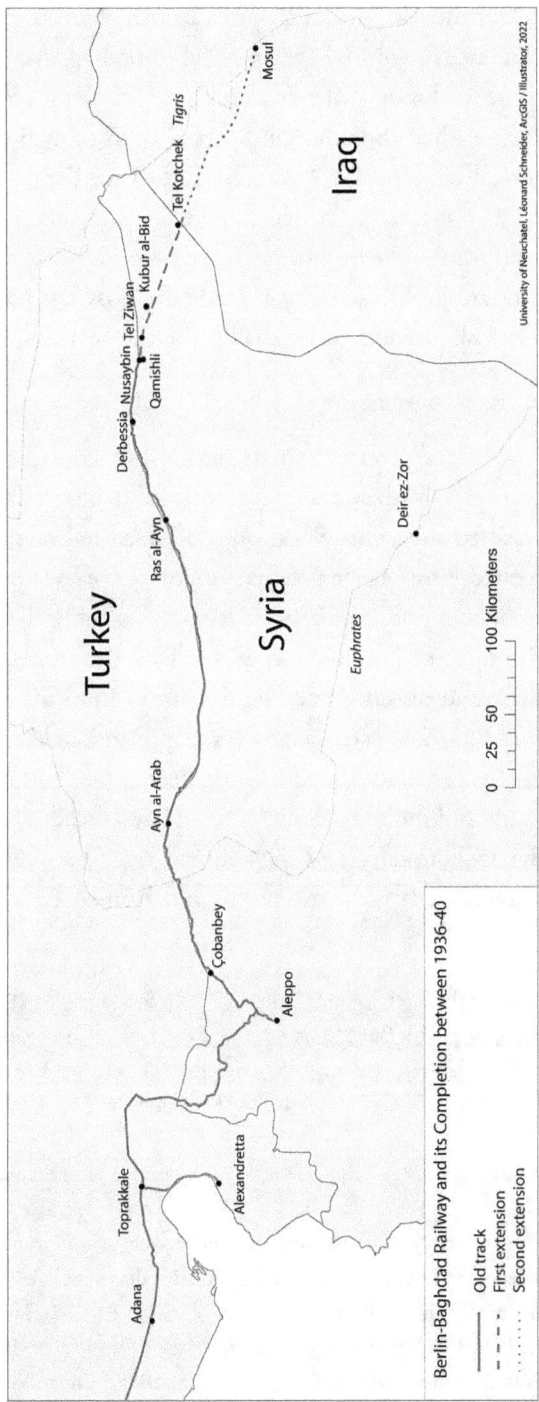

Figure 5.1 Map of the Baghdad Railway extension between 1936 and 1940.
Source: CADN, 1SL/500/163.

Syrian railhead at Tel Kotchek.[72] According to a British observer, the National Bloc victory in Damascus 'removed the Iraqi inhibition against making the connexion with Europe through Aleppo', and gave 'the Iraqi government a direct incentive to join their "brethren" in Syria'.[73] Even though the Franco-Turkish convention of 23 June 1939 granted Turkey the Sanjaq of Alexandretta with the railway and the port which were supposed to serve Aleppo, the Upper Jazira and Mosul, the beginning of the Second World War and the subsequent blockade in the Mediterranean made this 'loss' less important for French, Iraqi and British interests, as we shall see in the next chapters.

Local Agency and its Repercussions

In November 1937, at the ceremony inaugurating the construction of the projected railway from Diyarbakır to the Iranian and Iraqi borders, Turkish officials underscored the tight relationship between railways, modernity and progress, while recalling Mustafa Kemal's dictum expressed in the course of a speech at the opening of the Grand National Assembly the same year: 'railways bring with them civilisation and prosperity'.[74] Ironically, while state officials and publicists advanced modernist discourses to justify the need to finalise the Baghdad Railway to start a new era, engineers, archaeologists and policy-makers' designs for the region had long been part of an ancient history of trade caravans and mobility flows.[75] As we have already seen, sections of the Turkish–Syrian boundary and the railroad track between Çobanbey and Nusaybin followed to a great extent the old Roman Road. Likewise,

---

[72] For a detailed account on the ascent of the National Bloc in Syria between 1936 and 1937, see Philip S. Khoury, *Syria and the French Mandate: The Politics of Arab Nationalism, 1920–45* (Princeton, NJ: Princeton University Press, 1987), pp. 457–93.

[73] TNA, FO 371/20853/E1262/83/44. 'Turkish Railway Development'. Sir P. Loraine (Istanbul), 2 March 1937.

[74] TNA, FO 371/20853/E6979/83/44. 'Turkish Railway Development'. Sir P. Loraine (Ankara), 26 November 1937.

[75] As the Germans were studying the best route for the stretch of the proposed Baghdad Railway between Aleppo and Mosul, Max von Oppenheim discovered Tel Halaf site and did his best to convince German investors to bring the railroad to Tel Halaf in order to facilitate the access. Lionel Gossman, *The Passion of Max von Oppenheim: Archaeology and Intrigue in the Middle East from Wilhelm II to Hitler* (Cambridge: Open Book Publishers, 2013), pp. 107–15.

the Nusaybin–Mosul trail, as envisioned by the French and Iraqi authorities, overlapped with the Iraqi section of the ancient Abbasid Road as well as with the route used by the caravans of pilgrims throughout the nineteenth century to travel from Mosul to Mecca, by way of Nusaybin, Aleppo and Damascus.[76] More generally, in the Ottoman times, Mosul had an important transit trade in animals, particularly sheep, passing to and fro across the areas now belonging to the Syrian and Turkish borderlands, and beyond.[77]

Thus, the borderlanders did not expect the Baghdad Railway to create a new reality; rather, it was meant to reconnect social and economic links that had been severed by the newly-established borders, while increasing both the speed and the amount of goods transported from one point to another. Unsurprisingly, merchants constituted the most important lobby for the resumption of traditional commercial networks between Aleppo, Diyarbakır and Mosul in order to recover the 'grandeur' of these provinces dating back to the Ottoman era. In particular, given that the development of the railway web in Turkey was a 'national priority' and that the French – unlike the British – had been keen on completing this old project since the late 1920s, it was in Mosul that the local supporters of the railroad became more vocal.

As of the late 1920s, the Mosul Chamber of Commerce lamented that the volume of exports to Turkey had decreased about 90 per cent since the war. The main reason was that the Turkish provinces bordering Iraq now obtained such goods mostly via Syrian ports due to the better transportation and customs facilities provided by the Nusaybin Railway and the Syrian-Turkish Customs Agreement. To regain their warehouse trade with Jazira, Mosul merchants had to deliver their goods to Nusaybin at a cost not greater than that of goods shipped to Alexandretta and transported by rail from there. In this context, Mosul merchants recommended that the Iraq Railway be extended to Mosul as soon as possible, thus offering them cheap transportation through Iraq for their goods imported via Basra. In the meantime, the Chamber of Commerce requested the construction of good motor roads to

---

[76] J. M. Fiey, 'The Iraqi Section of the Abbasid Road Mosul-Nisibin', *Iraq*, Vol. 26, No. 2 (1964), pp. 106–17.

[77] Sarah D. Shields, *Mosul before Iraq: Like Bees Making Five-Sided Cells* (Albany: SUNY Press, 2000), pp. 95–121. See also Hala Fattah, *The Politics of Regional Trade* (Albany: SUNY Press, 1997), pp. 1–61.

the border.[78] Concretely, the expected export traffic from the Mosul Province would be wool, skins and gallnuts, while the import would be piece goods, cotton and silk, and other valuable commodities.[79]

Despite British reluctance to complete the Baghdad Railway, as Iraq became a nominally independent state, local merchants and newspapers renewed their pressure on the Iraqi authorities concerning this matter, 'on the grounds both of economic advantage and pan-Arab sentiment.'[80] Mosul merchants frequently complained about the high rates imposed at the port of Basra on their products. In addition, the Mosul Chamber of Commerce submitted a letter to the Iraqi deputies representing Mosul at the Iraqi Parliament where the former stated that the extension of the railroad towards Syria was 'relentlessly debated' in their province. It also recalled that before the inauguration of the Suez Canal, Mosul held an important position from a commercial viewpoint; indeed, it was a nodal point between the East and the West. Unfortunately, Mosul's status went from bad to worse during the First World War and the Great Depression, rendering the city and its markets marginal. In order to reverse the economic situation, the Chamber of Commerce supported connecting Mosul and Aleppo and thence the Mediterranean.[81]

Significantly, during King Ghazi's visit to Mosul, merchants and notables attempted to convey this message via the Mutasarrif of Mosul.[82] Yet, faced with little reaction to their desiderata, Mosul's merchants declared that from then on, they would employ new methods and means to make their voice heard. Subsequently, Muhammad Habib al-Obaidi, mufti of Mosul with his political sights on the local Mosul Chamber, protested against the Iraqi government as 'still in the hands of the British', and stood against the Baghdad–Haifa railway scheme.[83] Likewise, the Iraqi newspaper *Fata al-Iraq* harshly denounced the government's attitude, for it ignored the local demands in this

---

[78] Iraqi Administration Report for 1927, p. 54.

[79] TNA, AIR 23/1023. 'Trade and Tourist Route from Nisibin to Mosul'. Ramsay Tainsh, Director of Railways. Baghdad, 7 November 1928.

[80] TNA, FO 371/18922/E1287/528/65. Sir F. Humphrys to Sir John Simon. Baghdad, 23 February 1935.

[81] *Sawt al-Arab*, 17 March 1934.

[82] *Al-Tariq*, 14 June 1934; *Ikha al-Watani*, 26 June 1934.

[83] CADN, 1SL/1/V/706. Mr. Darche (Mosul Consulate) to French High Commissioner Comte de Martel. Mosul, 19 November 1934.

affair and lamented the 'deadly isolation' of Mosul and its inhabitants whose 'pockets' were 'empty'.[84]

The inauguration of the extension of the Aleppo–Nusaybin Railway from its former terminus at Tel Ziwan to the new terminus at Tel Kotchek on 4 May 1935 offered a new occasion for Syrian and Iraqi newspapers to highlight the potential of this line and its necessary completion.[85] The Iraqi paper *al-Islah*, for instance, wrote that after the French move towards Iraq, the government in Baghdad would render 'a great service to the country in extending the railway system to the north, and it is believed that it should do it forthwith, disregarding any obstacles which it might encounter on the way'.[86]

Expectations among local merchants were so high at that time that as soon as the Tel Kotchek station became operational, and even in the absence of a railroad linking Tel Kotchek–Mosul–Baghdad, this group tested the possibilities of the northern railway connection. Hence, for instance, the growing export trade in poultry and eggs from northern Iraq to Palestine was being carried almost exclusively by rail from Tel Kotchek.[87] Likewise, the value of the Tel Kotchek route to merchants was proved in January 1936, when a number of Baghdadi traders experimentally imported some 50 tons of mixed merchandise – wood for matches, leather, cheese, chocolates – a savings of ID [Iraqi dinars] 2,000 to ID 2,200 per ton, compared to the Rutbah route freights.[88] Furthermore, the extension of the Aleppo–Nusaybin railway to Tel Kotchek allowed Mosul to import European as well as cheaper goods, such as Rumanian petrol and kerosene, wood, cement and other building materials.[89]

---

[84] *Fata al-Iraq*, 27 October 1934, and *Fata al-Iraq*, 14 November 1934, respectively. See other articles on the same topic published by the same newspaper in the issues of 3 and 7 November 1934.

[85] TNA, FO 371/18922/E3074/528/65. Consul-General Havard to Sir John Simon. Beirut, 8 May 1935.

[86] *al-Islah*, 1 June 1935. Quoted in NARA, RG59, Reel 3. 'Current Events'. Legation of the United States of America. Baghdad, 26 June 1935.

[87] Between December 1935 and January 1936, some 6,660,000 eggs were exported through this route. TNA, FO 371/19981/E1423/518/65. Sir Archibald Clark Kerr to Mr Eden. Baghdad, 16 March 1936.

[88] TNA, FO 371/19981/E1423/518/65. Sir Archibald Clark Kerr to Mr Eden. Baghdad, 16 March 1936.

[89] TNA, FO 371/18922/E4086/528/65. Sir Archibald Clark Kerr to Sir Samuel Hoare. Baghdad, 2 July 1935.

Predictably, when the works on the Tel Kotchek–Baiji section started, local newspapers celebrated what was considered an important landmark for the economic and political relations between Syria and Iraq. The pro-French outlet *La Syrie* stated that 'the completion of the Baghdad Railway is the triumph of good sense, and we are happy to add, of French good sense'.[90] The Syrian newspaper *Fata al-Arab* considered that this was an important step which would allow Syria to connect further with neighbouring countries and thus strengthen a relationship that 'had been interrupted for already fourteen years'.[91] Very quickly, however, credit for this regional leap became a bone of contention among local actors, too. While Syrian nationalists celebrated the extension of the line as an 'Arab victory', regionalist leaders in the Upper Jazira highlighted that Tel Kotchek and its economic success was the fruit of both French and Upper Jazira populations' efforts (mainly Christians and Kurdish refugees and migrants), instead:

> Tel Kotchek, the last stop of the railway line, has become an important point for transit trade. In 1936–7, at certain days 100 trucks of wheat had arrived from Mosul to be transported to the inner Syrian towns ... The exported wheat in 1936 only by the railway exceeded 55,000 tons against 1,000 in 1927 ... The testimony of High Commissioner Jacquot shows that without the Jaziran crops, Syria would suffer from famine in the 1936–7 winter.[92]

In any event, by the onset of the Second World War, local, regional and global hopes around this transportation facility were at its peak. In 1939 alone, 33,000 tons of goods – mainly grain, raisins, wool and sheep – were carried from Mosul to Aleppo, while 8,000 tons – construction materials, sugar and manufactured products – went the other way round.[93] By the same

---

[90] *La Syrie*, 16 February 1937.
[91] *Fata al-Arab*, 23 March 1936.
[92] Comité général de la défense de la Haute Djézireh, La question syrienne. La vérité sur les événements de la Djézireh. Aperçu historique par un témoin oculaire (Beirut: Imprimerie Catholique, 1937). Quoted in Seda Altuğ, 'Sectarianism in the Syrian Jazira: Community, Land and Violence in the Memories of World War I and the French Mandate, 1915–39' (PhD dissertation, Utrecht: University of Utrecht, 2011), p. 294.
[93] Eleuthère Eleftériadès, *Les chemins de fer en Syrie et au Liban: Etude historique, financière et économique* (Beirut: Impr. Catholique, 1944), p. 286.

token, a report elaborated in 1939 foreshadowed a considerable expansion of Iraqi trade with Europe as a result of the Baiji–Tel Kotchek extension. Despite the outbreak of the Second World War and the subsequent interruption of shipping services in the Mediterranean, freight lost on this account would be 'more than compensated by inward and outward traffic to Turkey, Egypt and Palestine, which had been diverted to Basra . . .'[94]

The local impact of the Baghdad Railway was not only significant for merchants in cities such as Aleppo and Mosul. As the different sections of the railroad expanded, so did the networks of motor companies along the rail track. By 1930, for instance, Compagnie Auto-Routière du Levant, a motor company whose quarters were in Beirut, operated between Aleppo and Mosul via Deir ez-Zor.[95] Sleeping accommodation 'simple though clean' was available at Deir ez-Zor, and there was a 'passable restaurant kept by a Russian'.[96] The automobile company was also important in launching a promising overland trade route; in 1937, for instance, its trucks carried more than 6,000 tons of Iranian grain to Tel Kotchek, before being transported by train to Alexandretta.[97]

The complementarity of railroad and automobile facilities, as for instance along the trans-desert route, provided for an entangled relationship between motors and railroads. After all, local drivers and mechanics became key actors in guaranteeing the connectivity both between the Baghdad Railway and urban centres in Iraq as well as between towns in the periphery of Turkey, Syria and Iraq. As the railroad project was resumed in the early 1930s, much work was done on the Aleppo–Deir ez-Zor road, which, in 1932, was for the first time passable throughout the winter. Thence, car services allowed passengers to reach Qamishli and other towns, such as Amuda and Hasaka. On the Turkish side of the border, hotels, garages and restaurants flourished

[94] TNA, FO 371/27109/E3025/3025/93. Sir K. Cornwallis, British Embassy. Baghdad, 16 April 1941.
[95] The cars were similar to those used on the Beirut–Tripoli–Lattaquie–Aleppo line, which carried twelve passengers in the front of the vehicle and two and a half tons of merchandise at the back.
[96] TNA, FO 371/13745/E6564/191/65. Consul Monck Mason (Aleppo) to Foreign Office (London), 17 December 1929.
[97] CADN, 1SL/1/V/706. 'Railway Traffic via Tel Kotchek'. Beirut, 27 October 1937.

between Diyarbakır and Nusaybin.⁹⁸ Finally, on the main roads in northern Iraq connecting Mosul to Tel Kotchek, Zakho and Amadiya, despite their unsuitability during the rainy season, businesses were also developed around motorcars. A growing web of car services that was also connected to the first private initiatives to develop the tourist industry sprouted up in northern Iraq. By 1934, for instance, the small town of Rowanduz was being used as a resort for foreigners and Arabs wishing to escape during the summer months from the heat of Baghdad and other cities.⁹⁹

Likewise, the expansion of railway traffic also helped border towns along the Turkish–Syrian boundary to consolidate their development in relation to the rails: 'There is a wayside station, on the average, every twenty miles along the line . . .', so that 'along the 300-odd miles of track on the frontier, you step out one door into Turkey and out of the opposite door into Syria'.¹⁰⁰ Critically, some border towns and villages such as Jarablus, Ayn al-Arab, Tel Abyad, Ras al-Ayn, Derbessia, Tel Ziwan, Tel Kotchek or Kubur al-Bid owed their very existence to a station nearby, built either in the late Ottoman period or during the Mandates.¹⁰¹ Other border towns such as Qamishli, although not completely dependent upon the extension of the Baghdad Railway, nevertheless became important urban centres partly thanks to their railway stations.

By 1939, Qamishli, with over 20,000 residents, attracted all kinds of people, including some from Aleppo, who tried to make a living.¹⁰² In that

---

⁹⁸ As in Syria and Iraq, cars for hire in Turkey were mainly American brands: Ford and Chevrolet. For a detailed list of hotels and garages where travellers could hire a car between Diyarbakır and the Syrian/Iraqi border, see FO 371/25014. 'Road Report' Reconnaissance of the various routes connecting Durnakh (Iraq) and Diyarbakır (Turkey). Ankara, 6 December 1940.

⁹⁹ Lindfield Soane, 'A Recent Journey in Kurdistan', *Journal of the Royal Central Asian Society*, Vol. 22, No. 3 (1935), pp. 403–17 (here p. 412).

¹⁰⁰ Richard Pearse, *Three Years in the Levant* (London: Macmillan & Co. Ltd, 1949), p. 102.

¹⁰¹ On the symbiotic relationship between formation of the Turkish–Syrian border and the Baghdad Railway, see Matthieu Rey, 'Drawing a Line on the Sand? Another (Hi)story of Borders', in Matthieu Cimino (ed.), *Syria: Borders, Boundaries, and the State* (London: Palgrave Macmillan, 2020), pp. 27–46.

¹⁰² Decree No. 1080 (1937) placed Qamishli in the sixth position among Syrian cities, after Damascus, Aleppo, Homs, Hama and Lattaquie, in terms of population and annual budget.

regard, the Baghdad Railway contributed to bringing socio-economic features of the urban and modern life into the borderlands. Like most Middle Eastern cities, from a spatial perspective, the town expanded into quarters organised along religious lines: Jews, Muslims and Christians. In the same vein, like other cities, Qamishli also had two mixed quarters: Christian-Jewish and Christian-Muslim. In addition to the community-based bazaars for each neighbourhood, the inauguration of the central marketplace made of metallic structures in 1936, along with the installation of a power generator, constituted the symbols of 'modernity' in Qamishli.[103] During the Second World War, a casino as well as a series of hotels and cafes became popular venues for merchants, notables, state employees, soldiers and foreigners residing in or visiting Qamishli, thereby allowing for the emergence of a small 'cosmopolitan cosmos' in the tri-border region.

As small towns with state buildings appeared or expanded along the railroad, and motor tracks were improved to connect distant places, so did the railroad help reorganise space and undertake the process of territorialisation in the borderlands. In Syria, in particular, it offered the French an opportunity to support two of the most important initiatives they launched in the interwar period in the northern margins: namely, the settlement of refugees originating from Turkey along the Turkish–Syrian border, and the subsequent agricultural and urban development of the Jazira. By doing so, however, the reorganisation of space brought about some side-effects in the borderlands.

On the one hand, as Samuel Dolbee has shown, locusts maintained an almost symbiotic relationship with trains crossing the Turkish–Syrian–Iraqi borderlands. Through a careful reading of a newspaper report about the journey between Aleppo and Nusaybin published in *Cumhuriyet*, he explains how despite the heat during the summer of 1928, the Turkish columnist deemed it 'necessary to close the train-car windows', with which the black flying insects 'by the thousands' collided 'incessantly' throughout the ride.[104] Ironically, therefore, the search for speedier forms of transportation had a paradoxical effect: locusts could travel more rapidly across the borderlands than in the

---

[103] CADN, 1SL/1/V/981. 'Etude sur la ville de Kamechlie'. Beirut, 21 March 1936.

[104] Samuel Dolbee, 'The Locust and the Starling: People, Insects, and Disease in the Late Ottoman Jazira and After, 1860–1940' (PhD dissertation, New York University, 2017), p. 343.

past thanks to the railroad, thereby curtailing state attempts to combat insect infestations and their negative effects upon harvests. By the same token, diseases such as typhoid and cholera also crossed the borders with relative ease thanks to passengers who became privileged human carriers for viruses.[105]

On the other hand, because Turkey and Syria, unlike Iraq, used steam locomotives powered by coal, trains crossing the Turkish–Syrian borderland produced fire sparks as they passed. Against this setting, crop fires during the dry seasons became frequent, prompting protests among landowners who put forward financial disclaims against the railway companies operating along the Baghdad Railway. Even though authorities tended to put the blame on the landowners and peasants for cultivating along the tracks and not cleaning up the adjacent surfaces to the railroad,[106] inquiries revealed that accidents were often due to the negligence of railway personnel:

> Numerous fires have broken out throughout this week, among which around 800 metres north of the town of Ras al-Ayn . . . The fire broke out after the passage of a mixed train on 27 June 1943, as the mechanist voided the locomotive fireplace in three different points, thereby spreading fire in a 4-km² surface. The officers of the Services Spéciaux have already received several written claims on behalf of some farmers and landowners who intend to submit a complaint against the railway company.[107]

Much like with locusts and diseases, fires were also an issue of concern for border authorities in a bid to keep the 'bonne entente' between neighbouring countries: 'On 16 June a fire was declared in Turkish territory around the village of Jurb-Jurb . . . The authorities being alerted, several firemen teams were sent there to avoid the flames advancing into Syrian territory . . .'[108] Failure to prevent the flames from crossing the frontier could entail a lawsuit and thus financial responsibilities against the state where the fire first broke out.[109] As

---

[105] CADN, 36 PO/1/411. Telegram from High Commission to the French Embassy in Turkey. Beirut, 16 September 1931.
[106] CADN, 1SL/1/V/2051. Weekly Report, No. 17, Ras al-Ayn, 23–29 May 1943.
[107] CADN, 1SL/1/V/2051. Weekly Report, No. 22, Ras al-Ayn, 27 June–3 July 1943.
[108] CADN, 1SL/1/V/2051. Weekly Report, No. 20, Ras al-Ayn, 13–19 June 1943.
[109] CADN, 1SL/1/V/706. 'Fire between Demir-Kapou and Tel Kotchek'. French High Commissioner (Beirut) to French Ambassador (Baghdad). Beirut, 19 November 1938.

with other natural disasters, managing crop fires became at once both a driver for border cooperation and for tension, helping along the states to further the process of territorialisation in the border zones.

Local Appropriations of the Baghdad Railway

Borderlanders were not just passive witnesses of further connectivity and regional trade facilitated by the expansion of both railway and road transportation facilities throughout the 1920s and 1930s. They also adjusted their traditional networks and practices to new engines, while shaping the pace at which railways developed in the region.[110] Unfortunately, public records provide little information about who worked on the extension of the railroad from 1930 onwards, or about who travelled through the borderlands and for what purposes. Likewise, novels and travelogues written by Western visitors mainly mention European travellers, spies and tourists as the main passengers using the Orient and Taurus Express.[111] Notwithstanding this, incidents recorded by border authorities together with some rare memoirs written by borderlanders, archaeologists and officers serving on the Baghdad Railway offer some interesting insights into the local experiences of mobility and indigenous appropriation of this means of transportation, revealing a much more colourful picture.

First, as the initial story tells it, Syrian borderlanders were commonly hired as construction workers to build the extension of the Baghdad Railway, while also putting forward their demands, if necessary. Likewise, some records mention that Christian and Kurdish residents from Qamishli and the surrounding villages worked on the extension of the track between the former and Tel Kotchek, while the Iraqi section of the Shammar tribe was said to provide as many as 2,000 builder labourers to the Baghdad government to speed up the completion of the railroad.[112] Second, train and car services not only combined

---

[110] For a similar argument, see Robert Fletcher, 'Running the corridor: Nomadic societies and imperial rule in the inter-war Syrian Desert', *Past and Present*, Vol. 220, No. 1 (2012), pp. 197–8.

[111] See, for instance, Agatha Christie, *Murder on the Orient Express* (London: Collins Crime Club, 1934).

[112] CADN, 1SL/1/V/706. Sûreté Générale. Beirut, 9 March 1937.

to make the journeys possible, but they provided alternatives, depending on climate conditions and the identity of passengers. During the rainy season, for instance, when the soft alluvial clay was reduced to very sticky mud, motor tracks in the steppe became impassable for weeks. Hence, travellers might opt for the railroad instead. In other words, the profile of passengers using automobile and railway services was not necessarily different.

Conversely, because identity controls were frequent on the train between Çobanbey and Nusaybin, borderlanders allegedly involved in anti-Kemalist political activists in northern Syria – mainly Armenians and Kurds – or simply illegal manoeuvres could resort to motor and bus services for the transportation of animals without being bothered by the border authorities. Such was the case, for example, for Yashar Khanum, who, by late 1928, left western Turkey on a rather long and perilous journey to join her husband, Ihsan Nuri, on the Turkish–Iranian border, where he was leading a Kurdish rebellion against the Turkish government. Drawing on Khanum's memoirs, Kumru Toktamis reports that she travelled first by train up to Izmir; from there, she took a boat to Mersin and then another train to Aleppo. After spending some months in diverse houses of Kurdish activists supporting the rebellious movement there, and thus being under Turkish surveillance, she travelled several times from Aleppo to Ayn al-Arab, and vice-versa, on carriages. When the rainy season ceased, she decided to leave Syria using the motor route towards Mosul and Baghdad via Deir ez-Zor to avoid Turkish identity controls on the train.[113]

Such identity controls became even tighter during the Second World War, thereby irremediably provoking delays and frequent complaints from simple passengers, including foreign and local tourists, pilgrims and soldiers using the Taurus Express, who ultimately preferred the dusty motor tracks.[114] British officer Richard Pearse, who worked on the security of the Taurus Express, described

---

[113] Kumru Toktamis, 'Yashar Khanum: The Woman for Whom the War never Ended', in Tomasz Pudlocki and Kamil Ruszala (eds), *Intellectuals and World War I: A Central European Perspective* (Krakow: Jagiellonian University Press, 2018), p. 299.

[114] Shereen Khairallah, 'Railway Networks of the Middle East to 1948', in Thomas Philipp and Birgit Schaebler (eds), *The Syrian Land: Processes of Integration and* Fragmentation (Franz Steiner Verlag: Stuttgart, 1998), p. 92.

this awkward situation with a rather sarcastic tone: 'with no less than seven Allied and Turkish control points between Ankara and Baghdad, the Taurus ceased to be very express'.[115]

Public records and memoirs agree that soldiers and state employees represented the most important Turkish contingent of passengers on the Taurus Express between Aleppo and Nusaybin.[116] In his diary, German archaeologist Max von Oppenheim, for instance, highlights the significant presence of Turkish soldiers and officers using the Baghdad Railway during his journey from Aleppo to Ras al-Ayn: 'A Turkish company with several officers boarded our train. The Turkish troops, who pass through French territory to travel from Cilicia to Turkish Mesopotamia, are not allowed to get off in Aleppo, but have a station building, in Muslemiyeh', though.[117] Two years later, on his way to Mardin, Oppenheim referred to this feature again:

> A number of Turkish officers were on the train, including Ekram Bey, who spoke good German. The first class was fully occupied by officers. We had to sleep in the second class. The railroad goes to the foot of the Mardin Mountains. From here we continue our journey to the city by car.[118]

British officer Richard Pearse provided a much more detailed description of its users – albeit one attuned to his colonial and Victorian mindset. First, Pearse informs us that because the Taurus Express became a crowded transportation facility where different kinds of individuals – first-class to third-class passengers of all ethnic and social backgrounds, men and women – met for some hours creating a particular atmosphere, it received an unofficial title, the 'bordel ambulant' (travelling/moving brothel or chaos/mess). Concretely, 'going westwards into Europe on business were travellers from Chungking, Kabul, Bombay, Baghdad, and Tehran'. Among them, 'there were engineers,

---

[115] Richard Pearse, *Three Years in the Levant*, p. 103.
[116] Tensions between French and Turkish soldiers on this line were not rare. See correspondence on these affairs in CADN, 1SL/1/V/2155.
[117] SRWK, Abt. 601, Max von Oppenheim, No. 260. Spring journey 1927, Journey from Aleppo to Ras al-Ayn.
[118] SRWK, Abt. 601, Max von Oppenheim, No. 261. Aleppo, 7 June 1929.

diplomats, students, journalists and others about whom one never knew enough'. Interestingly, Pearse's accounts also make female passengers visible: 'Women of all classes, whether travelling first, second or third, made a habit of feeding their infants, taking for granted that no one objected.'[119] Finally, this small world gathered on the Taurus Express was also a mirror of the existing socio-economic disparities:

> The clean sheets and polished woodwork, the immaculate uniforms of the attendants in the luxury end of the train inhabited by Primer Ministers, diplomats, engineers, Arab princes, Turkish princesses, Egyptian professors, mystery men and beautiful blondes . . . contrasted strongly with the hard-seated third-class coaches occupied by sturdy Kurdish mountaineers, dirty Arabs and lice-carrying Turks.[120]

Borderlanders, however, could use other types of trains running on the Baghdad Railway: that is, the 'mixed' trains that circulated between Adana, in Turkey, and Tel Kotchek, on the frontier of Iraq, a journey of nearly 1,100 kilometres. In his memoirs, Noureddine Zaza, for instance, recalls that the 'Kurds, Syriacs, Armenians, Arabs and Jews' he met on the train during the journey from Aleppo to Nusaybin were not alien to him, for they hailed from Qamishli where he had sought refuge. He also provides some details about the nature of the regional trade that was rendered possible thanks to this transportation facility: 'some merchants travelled to Aleppo to sell their produce and sheep there, and others to generate stocks in textiles, tea, coffee, sugar and soap for their shops'.[121]

According to Richard Pearse, the passenger coaches of the 'mixed' trains 'were like travelling villages', for 'they were always overcrowded with Arab, Turkish and Kurdish peasants who, as soon as the train set out from Aleppo in its long trek across the steppes to Iraq, settled down the sociable picnics and jovial intercourse'.[122] A borderland sociability that also allowed passengers

---

[119] Richard Pearse, *Three Years in the Levant*, p. 109.
[120] Ibid. p. 107.
[121] Noureddine Zaza, *Ma vie de Kurde* (Lausanne: Les éditions du Tigre, 2021), p. 142.
[122] Richard Pearse, *Three Years in the Levant*, p. 109.

Figure 5.2 Passengers awaiting the arrival of the Taurus Express at Tel Kotchek, 1941.
Credit: ©Bergan, Finn/DEXTRA Photo/The Norwegian Museum of Science and Technology.

to exchange information about the ongoing developments on both sides of the border, spread rumours and forge views about the economic and political prospects of the region, which in turn could also determine mobility strategies such as migration. The potential impact of borderland intercourse was a sensitive issue in the frontier zone to the extent that in 1942, Turkey considered having separate wagons for Turkish and non-Turkish citizens along the tracks running through Turkish territory to avoid the 'contamination' of Turkish passengers with dangerous ideas such as communism and Kurdish nationalism.[123]

The Baghdad Railway also attracted smugglers' attention. Even though authorities improved the surveillance methods on the trains, the illicit transfer of commodities (gold, drugs) and merchandise, including living animals,

[123] BCA.030.10.99.641.27, 28 October 1945.

remained an issue of concern for border authorities as different legislations on customs, for instance, prevailed.[124] Richard Pearse's accounts are again very valuable, for they provide a detailed description of smuggled goods as well as the strategies developed by smugglers to hide them: 'Turkish travellers ran profitable smuggling rackets in silk stockings, Swiss watches, gold and mail'.[125] Wrist watches and alcoholic beverages brought into Iraq at lower prices were particularly profitable for smugglers on the Taurus Express, together with other traditionally lucrative commodities such as drugs and jewels. Obviously, within the context of the Second World War, the contraband of light weapons also became a delicate issue. Further, the scarcity of trained soldiers on these matters, the complicity of the railway personnel with smugglers as well as the sheer number of wagons, made the fight against contraband activities a difficult task: 'Likely places were the huge lamps on the front of the engine, oil-boxes, cracks and slits in the woodwork of trucks, and amongst bales of cotton and sacks of wheat'.[126]

During the Second World War, the Baghdad Railway also became an important gateway for human trafficking, affecting in particular Iraqi and European Jews.[127] In Baghdad, an agency smuggled the Jews destined for Palestine. Although British authorities were not sure about how illegal Jewish

---

[124] The relationship between new means of transportation and the traffic of gold was by no means a new problem in these borderlands. Already in 1923, French Consul in Baghdad pointed to the responsibility of automobile drivers crossing the steppe in the contraband of gold between Syria and Iraq. Moneylenders and merchants in Aleppo encouraged such activities. In addition, camel caravans also transported smuggled gold between Syria and Iraq. CADN, 1SL/1/V/854. 'Gold contraband'. French Consulate (Baghdad) to French High Commission (Beirut). Baghdad, 15 December 1923.

[125] Richard Pearse, *Three Years in the Levant*, p. 107.

[126] Ibid. p. 111.

[127] Following the short Iraqi–British war and the subsequent collapse of the Rashid Ali government, a wave of anti-Jewish violence broke out in Baghdad between 1 and 2 June 1941. From that moment, increasing numbers of Iraqi Jews considered migrating to Palestine. In addition, as British Mandate authorities in Palestine limited Jewish migration into this territory, Iran and Iraq became important gateways for illegal Jewish immigration. See correspondence on this issue in TNA, FO 624/290015. On Iraqi Jews, see Orit Bashkin, *New Babylonians: A History of Jews in Modern Iraq* (Stanford, CA: Stanford University Press, 2012). For an Iraqi viewpoint on the Iraqi–British war, see Mahmud al-Durah, *al-Harb al-Iraqiyya al-Britaniyya 1941* (Beirut: Dar al-Taliah, 1973).

immigrants reached Palestine, it became clear that the smugglers used either the Nusaybin-Tel Kotchek railroad, or the related motor tracks to channel Jewish migrants. According to British sources, the Baghdad manager of the agency railed Jews to Kirkuk, whence they were motored to Mosul, then the Mosul manager got them up to the Syrian frontier near Tel Kotchek, where they walked over the border to a village accompanied by a local guide. Thence, the journey of smuggled Jews was at times a complicated affair: 'Seventeen of these emigrants were caught in Qamishli the other day, by the Forces Spéciales people, and they were returned to Iraq'.[128]

The railroad was also used to smuggle impoverished Kurds from Turkey into Syria and thence to Lebanon. The economic underdevelopment of the eastern provinces in Turkey had led thousands of Kurds to migrate to large towns, such as Baghdad and Beirut, since the 1920s, where they worked as dock and builders' labourers.[129] As the economic situation worsened after the Great Depression and again during the Second World War, the flow of migrants from Turkey towards the southern neighbours remained unchecked. Nevertheless, within the context of the war, human cross-border mobility became a sensitive issue – identity controls increased and problems at the border arose accordingly, for most of these Kurdish migrants were smuggled by gangs with false documents:

> Every week scores of them passed through my hands. They did not know they were the victims of a smuggling traffic in human labour. They were too dull-witted and ignorant to realise they provided a handsome slave trade for Levantine labour merchants – most of whom were Christians –, who bought and sold them as they would buy and sell mules and camels. Kurds were more obedient than mules, and were cheaper to feed.[130]

Bedouin and Kurdish nomadic tribes also took the benefit of the Baghdad Railway in other, unexpected ways. On the Turkish side of the border, for

---

[128] TNA, FO 624/29. 'Palestine: Immigration'. British Consulate (Mosul), 5 March 1942.
[129] On the political causes of economic underdevelopment in the eastern provinces of Turkey, see Veli Yadirgi, *The Political Economy of the Kurds of Turkey: From the Ottoman Empire to the Turkish Republic* (Cambridge: Cambridge University Press, 2017).
[130] Richard Pearse, *Three Years in the Levant*, p. 118.

instance, they frequently carried off railway material for their own purposes, without being seriously punished by the Turkish authorities until the late 1920s.[131] Likewise, as thousands of sheep were transported from Mosul to Tel Kotchek by train before being redirected to Deir ez-Zor, borderland tribes saw in the concentration of important amounts of livestock an easy target for raiding, at the expense of merchants.[132] Finally, trains crossing the borderlands were also the focus of attacks perpetrated by 'bandits' who used horses and cars to assault the wagons and steal basic food, such as sugar.[133]

In turn, however, since Bedouin raiders, bandits as well as smugglers used automobiles, trucks or indeed the train to do their business and move faster, border authorities adapted their means and strategies accordingly. By 1938, Turkish customs authorities at the Turkish–Syrian border employed motorbikes, trucks and blinded vehicles to chase smugglers along the railway/boundary track.[134] More generally, while smugglers and Bedouins benefited from the increasing reconnectedness between ex-Ottoman urban markets thanks to the expansion of modern forms of transportation, the completion of the railroad went hand in hand with the establishment of growing economic control over the periphery and international boundaries.

Obviously, customs formalities could become even more painstaking depending on the ongoing relations between states. Thus, for instance, by 1931, the French seemed 'to be difficult in connection with customs formalities, holding up convoys at Demir Kapu, Kubur al-Bid and Qamishli for examination of passengers' baggage'. The reason was that the French High Commissioner had suggested to the British that the port of Alexandretta should be added to the new schedule of the Iraq-Syrian transit trade agreement, so that it would become 'the natural port for goods consigned for Aleppo by sea and therefore for Iraq goods in transit to Syria by the Mosul-Nusaybin route'.[135] So long as the Iraqi government procrastinated in its response, the French pursued the customs formalities with great zeal.

---

[131] TNA, AIR 2/1023. Consul Monck-Mason to Lord Cushendun. Aleppo, 30 October 1928.
[132] CADN, 1SL/1/V/2051. Hasaka, Weekly Report, No. 4, 20–26 January 1943.
[133] CADN, 1SL/1/V/2051. Ras al-Ayn. Weekly Report, No. 5, 23–30 January 1943.
[134] CADN, 1SL/1/V/2145. Sûreté Générale. Muslimiyye, 11 May 1938.
[135] TNA, FO 371/15281/E477/55/65. 'Mosul–Aleppo trade route via Nusaybin'. Consul Monck-Mason. Aleppo, 29 January 1931.

In addition to the increasing control over individuals and commodities circulating through the Baghdad Railway, the consolidation of the latter as a means of transportation had further consequences in the borderlands – modest buildings for customs, quarters for the railway employees, and rooms for the storage of confiscated and dutiable goods slowly became a new reality of the border landscape, thereby marking the expansion of state presence and its growing interference in borderlanders' everyday life.[136] In other words, by the 1930s, border regimes, transportation networks such as railroads and motor roads along with tax systems became tools by which Turkey, French Syria and Iraq sought to effectively territorialise the periphery and create increasingly legible citizen subjects in the borderlands.[137]

Historians have made significant contributions to the study of the Baghdad Railway, mainly pointing to the geopolitical and economic dimensions of a project that became a symbol of both rising European power and declining Ottoman fortunes between 1888 and 1914. Nevertheless, scholars have so far neglected the final stages of the construction of this railway facility. Admittedly, the rather tumultuous completion of this railroad can help us explain the reasons behind this gap in scholarship. In addition, historians interested in globalisation have argued that because the Baghdad Railway zigzagged at different points along the Turkish–Syrian borderline before heading to Iraq, it failed to become a real driver for global commerce and communication. Yet, the narrative on the 'natural failure' of the Baghdad Railway both as a catalyser of world economy in the Middle East as well as a connector between the West and the East needs some nuance.

While in its first section this chapter examined how the double function of the Baghdad Railway tracks, international borders, and travel facilities, in fact hindered the rapid and effective fulfilment of this transportation project, it has also demonstrated that despite Turkish and British initial reluctance, by the mid-1930s, local, regional and global factors intersected to give a definitive push to its completion. By changing the scale of analysis, the chapter has

---

[136] TNA, AIR 2/1023. Consul Monck-Mason. Aleppo, 28 November 1930.
[137] On state endeavours to make borderlanders 'more legible', see James C. Scott, *The Arts of not Being Governed: An Anarchist History of Upland Southeast Asia* (New Haven: Yale University Press, 2009).

shown in its second section that when the railway reached Tel Kotchek in 1936, the economic and social impacts were almost immediate, fuelling high hopes amidst urban merchants and borderland populations.

Train commerce increased, old and new towns around railway stations developed and a sense of trans-border connectedness emerged among borderlanders. Nevertheless, the intensification of movement of people and goods went hand in hand with growing control and a variety of techniques to limit it. As a result of these two seemingly contradictory processes, the development of the Baghdad Railway contributed to shaping new configurations of mobility and containment in the Turkish–Syrian–Iraqi borderlands, which were, after all, a characteristic of the modern world. In that regard, frequent controls of passengers' identity and goods circulating on the Taurus Express running between Meydan Ekbez-Aleppo and Mosul, in both directions, are indeed a reminder that borders, as already argued in Chapter 3, are always subject to change.[138] Borders thus do not limit themselves to the (sometimes) visible and institutionalised lines and fences erected by states on the edges of 'national' territory; rather, they can be altered over time and space by new forms of mobility facilitated, for example, by the introduction of cross-border travel services and remote security systems. The subtle transformation of borders in the region – for instance, from fixity to multi-location – was even more evident within the highly sensitive context of the Second World War, as we shall see in detail in the next two chapters.

---

[138] Victor Konrad, 'Toward a Theory of Borders in Motion', *Journal of Borderlands Studies*, Vol. 30, No. 1 (2015), pp. 1–17.

6

IRREDENTISM IN A CONTEXT OF GLOBAL UNCERTAINTY

In early 1941, the French Intelligence services at Azaz, north of Aleppo, gathered a number of reports on Turkish soldiers and officials spreading rumours about the imminent Turkish annexation of northern Syria. According to one such report, state employees at Kilis informed a Turkish national who had a land dispute with a Syrian citizen that it was not worth going to Syria to solve that issue, for 'in ten days Turkey is going to occupy Syria'. Anxious about the effects that such rumours could have upon the Syrian borderlanders, French border authorities asked their Turkish counterparts for an urgent meeting to halt the circulation of similar 'false reports'.[1] Some months later, questioned about the pervasiveness of these rumours, Ahmet Umar, Turkish Consul at Damascus, declared to a British political officer that Turkey did not desire the annexation of Aleppo and its surroundings. In fact, 'Pan-Turanians' like himself 'looked Eastwards and North Eastwards to the Turks in Azerbaijan and the Caucasus'. For this reason, Turkey only wished for minor boundary rectifications with Bulgaria after the war, while the change that the Turks aspired to along the Syrian–Turkish border was one that would 'bring the whole of the railway from Ankara to Tel Kotchek into Turkish territory'.[2] Even though the Turkish Consul did not elaborate on how Turkey would secure the control

---

[1] CADN, 1SL/1/V/2144. Captain Terras to the Turkish *kaymakam* of Kilis. Azaz, 24 June 1941.
[2] TNA, FO 226/236. British Legation. Beirut, 13 August 1942.

of the railway, such a move nevertheless entailed two significant vicissitudes. First, Turkey needed to build a new railroad to bypass Aleppo and its northern vicinity. Second, managing the Baghdad Railway from Ankara to Tel Kotchek, located at the Syrian–Iraqi border, meant de facto seizing some portions of the Syrian Jazira.

Northwards, diplomatic relations between Turkey and the Soviet Union worsened rapidly with the commencement of the Second World War, after almost two decades of relatively *bon voisinage* association. Crucially, on 19 March 1945, Soviet Foreign Minister Vyacheslav Molotov informed Turkey's ambassador to Moscow that his government had withdrawn from the 1925 Non-Aggression Pact, unilaterally. The conditions for the renegotiation of the pact required, on the one hand, the establishment of Soviet military bases in the Straits and the 'return' to the USSR of the Eastern districts of Kars, Artvin and Ardahan, ceded to Turkey in 1921, as per the Treaty of Moscow, on the other.[3]

Yet, revisionist and irredentist tendencies in the Middle East did not emerge solely among state actors during the world conflict. Indeed, the Second World War seemed to provide new opportunities to 'the small nations' who considered that they had been 'betrayed' by the Western powers in the aftermath of the First World War – namely, the abandonment of the Treaty of Sèvres, which provided for the formation of an Armenian and Kurdish state in Eastern Anatolia – and now observed closely the developments across the globe and the Middle East.

Critically, after the fall of France in 1940 and the alignment of French authorities in Syria and Lebanon with the new Vichy government, pro-Nazi propaganda rapidly spread in the Levant, including along the border zones. In that regard, Werner Otto von Hentig – chief of the Near East Department of the German Foreign Office – toured the Upper Jazira and met Khalil ibn Ibrahim Pasha, the Kurdish leader of the Milli tribe at Ras al-Ayn, carrying letters from Max von Oppenheim, archaeologist, Near East advisor and 'old friend' of the Ibrahim Pasha family, with a political message: the Ibrahim Pasha were

---

[3] For a Soviet perspective on this crisis, see Vahram Ter-Matevosyan, *Turkey, Kemalism and the Soviet Union* (London: Palgrave Macmillan, 2019). For a Turkish perspective, see Onur Isçi, *Turkey and the Soviet Union during World War II* (London: I. B. Tauris, 2019).

to play an important political role in the new Middle East resulting from Germany's victory.[4] Although after the First World War Ibrahim Pasha had been considered by the British as a potential leader of an autonomous Kurdish entity, by 1940 the Germans viewed his son Khalil Beg as 'completely nationalist oriented', that is, anti-French and close to the Syrian Arab nationalists in Damascus.[5] In parallel, however, German projects for the region also included mobilising 'the small nations' against the Allies. Concretely, German plans required a renewed coalition between the Kurds and the Armenians in order to organise a military revolt in the Eastern provinces of neutral Turkey, further to which Germany would back Kurdish and Armenian aspirations for independence. As a result of these contacts, the Khoybun League and the Armenian Dashnak Party were allegedly converted to the German cause by early 1941.[6] Similar plans concerned the Kurds in Iraq, in particular supporting the old Kurdish leader, Shaykh Mahmud Barzanji, and the Pizhdar tribe against the British, in return for some form of autonomy in northern Iraq.[7]

Views on who the best ally was for their national cause varied among nationalist figures, though, depending on both interpersonal relations and the evolution of the conflict. Thus, after a series of military battles had been won by the Allies, it was reported that the Armenians and Kurds in Syria had stopped seeing the German as the 'invincible soldier' and started betting on the Allies' final victory. Interestingly, the same intelligence piece highlighted the high hopes certain Kurdish leaders held about the future formation of a Kurdish autonomous state with the support of one of the great powers involved in the war. As proof of such excitement, a Free French officer related that Bozan Shaheen Beg, along with a group of local notables

---

[4] FONDS RONDOT, 'Syrian Kurds'. Captain Aziz, Muhafazat of Jazira. Hasaka, 5 February 1941.

[5] R. L. Melka, 'Max Freiherr von Oppenheim: Sixty Years of Scholarship and Political Intrigue in the Middle East', *Middle Eastern Studies*, Vol. 9, No. 1 (1973), pp. 81–93 (here p. 91).

[6] SHAT, 4H 387/3. Special Services. Aleppo, 1 August 1942.

[7] Operation MAMMUT designed by the Germans was mainly concerned with sabotage actions geared towards seizing and holding the Kirkuk oilfields until German troops arrived in Northern Iraq. The plan, however, was never realised. Adrian O'Sullivan, *The Baghdad Set: Iraq through the Eyes of British Intelligence, 1941–5* (London: Palgrave Macmillan, 2019), pp. 187–9.

from the Jarablus area, performed a 'Kurdish national dance' before him – the one that they would dance when Diyarbakır (in south-eastern Anatolia) becomes 'the capital of their Great nation [Kurdistan]'.[8]

Meanwhile, a revolt led by Mullah Mustafa Barzani erupted in September 1943, near the Turkish–Iraqi border.[9] While at first British officials considered that 'economic difficulties rather than thwarted nationalism' were the cause of the rebellion, 'unwise' Iraqi police actions against the rebels, together with persistent food shortages in the borderlands, prompted the reawakening of Kurdish demands for local autonomy in Iraq.[10] Further east, by 1944, the centre of Kurdish turbulence in Iran was situated around the town of Mahabad, where Qazi Muhammad, a notable from that area, was leading a movement for local autonomy, backed by nationalist committees and receiving some material support from the Soviet troops deployed in Iran three years earlier.[11] Following the gradual deterioration of the relations with the central government, Qazi Muhammad proclaimed the Kurdish Republic of Mahabad in January 1946, which was celebrated among Kurdish nationalist circles in Iraq and Syria, and largely decried by Turkish authorities.[12]

As Soviet–Turkish tensions were at their height by late 1945, a significant number of Turkish units left the Turkish–Syrian border zone to be redeployed along the Soviet–Turkish frontier. Within this context, the French newspaper *Le Monde* reported that in Turkey 'a certain agitation reveals that the time when revolutionary Armenian and Kurdish committees will swing into action is approaching'. Relying on reports provided by Turkish officials, the article further suggested that 'Soviet influence' was not alien to this excitement.[13]

---

[8] CADN, 1SL/1/V/1097. Sûreté Générale. Ayn al-Arab, 31 January 1942.

[9] Mullah Mustafa Barzani, a younger brother of the Kurdish Shaykh Ahmad Barzan who led an uprising against the Iraqi authorities between 1931 and 1932, was exiled to Sulaimaniya after the failure of the revolt. By July 1943, Mustafa Barzani left Sulaimaniya and moved towards Barzan, his traditional stronghold near the Turkish border.

[10] TNA, FO 195/2596/E2782/104/34. Eastern Department to Foreign Office. Ankara, 2 April 1946.

[11] See Archie Jr Roosevelt, 'The Kurdish Republic of Mahabad', *Middle East Journal*, Vol. 1, No. 3 (1947), pp. 247–69; William Eagleton, *The Kurdish Republic of 1946* (London: Oxford University Press, 1963).

[12] CADN, 1SL/1/V/802. Ministre Plénipotentiaire de la France au Levant (Beirut) to the Ministry of Foreign Affairs (Paris), 15 April 1946.

[13] 'Les minorités arméniennes et kurdes s'agitent en Turquie', *Le Monde*, 29 December 1945.

A few weeks later, a Turkish official in Damascus warned the Syrian Prime Minister, Saadallah Jabri, that the Kurdish-Armenian coalition movement was ready to take up arms in northern Syria in coordination with their brethren from Iraq and Iran. Further, the revolt was to erupt in case the United Nations Security Council did not meet the Kurdish national claims, while debating the Kurdish issue.[14]

Despite this rather tumultuous context, by and large War History and Middle East scholarship have paid little attention to how the Second World War unfolded in the Middle Eastern region.[15] This omission can be explained by different factors. First, as it happened, neither did Turkey obtain any territorial gains in northern Syria nor did the USSR 'recover' Kars and Ardahan from Turkey in the aftermath of the Second World War. Likewise, the Kurds and Armenians failed to create an independent entity with the support of one of the great powers. Much like after the First World War, all belligerents courted the Kurds, but none of them envisaged satisfying their territorial and political demands. As the deputy director of British military intelligence in Cairo wrote in 1942:

> The Kurdish question bristles with difficulties. I cannot see an independent Kurdish state existing. It sprawls over so much country, and the Kurds in Kurdistan are as mixed up with Persian, Lurs, Armenians, Azerbaijanis, and Turks that the ethnological problem would be enormous.[16]

As for Armenians, 'the United States and Britain never considered Armenian national aspirations in their policy deliberations', for it 'was quickly learned that there were few Armenians left in the disputed territories in Turkey.'[17] Meanwhile, after hinting at some political support for Armenian territorial

[14] CADN, 1SL/1/V/815. Sûreté aux Armées. Beirut, 13 January 1946.
[15] For some exceptions, see Kirk George, *The Middle East in the War* (Oxford: Oxford University Press, 1952); Selim Deringil, *Turkish Foreign Policy during the Second World War: An 'Active' Neutrality* (Cambridge: Cambridge University Press, 1989); Robert Lyman, *First Victory: Britain's Forgotten Struggle in the Middle East, 1941* (London: Little, Brown, 2006); Ashley Jackson, *Persian Gulf Command: A History of the Second World War in Iran and Iraq* (New Haven: Yale University Press, 2018); Onur Isçi, *Turkey and Soviet Union*.
[16] Quoted in Adrian O'Sullivan, *The Baghdad Set*, p. 140.
[17] Ronald Grigor Suny, *Looking Toward Ararat: Armenia in Modern History* (Bloomington: Indiana University Press, 1993), p. 171.

claims, Moscow began to elide the question of Armenian territories in Turkey by early 1946. From Moscow's perspective, what really mattered was to reach an agreement with Turkey regarding the Straits. Hence, the Armenians in Turkey and the diaspora, like the Kurds and Azeris in Iran, were only useful tools to advance the most vital Soviet interests.

Second, the Middle East has generally been seen as a peripheral theatre of an otherwise global war.[18] Christian Destremeau, for instance, contends that 'Arab populations in the Middle East did not have, by and large, a direct experience of the war' besides the heavy presence of the Allied forces deployed throughout the region. Therefore, Middle Eastern populations followed the war mainly 'from the distance, via the newspapers, rumours and above all the radio'.[19] Likewise, Cyrus Schayegh considers that overall 'WWII was not catastrophic in the Middle East', for two chief reasons. On the one hand, open warfare in the Middle East lasted only three years and, perhaps more importantly, it was mostly limited to North Africa and the southern Mediterranean Sea. On the other hand, unlike between 1915–16, a severe famine did not repeat itself during the second world conflict.[20]

While largely accurate, it appears necessary to introduce some nuance to this reading to propose a much more comprehensive understanding of what the Second World War meant for the Middle East and its role during the war. To begin with, as we shall see in the first section of this chapter, the rapid progress of Italian and German armies between 1939 and 1941 opened up a phase of critical instability for Middle Eastern governments – particularly in Iran, Syria, Lebanon and Iraq –, which in turn threatened not only the Franco-British front in the Eastern Mediterranean, but also the solidity of the British Empire altogether. As Ashley Jackson puts it:

> It might be argued that the focus on the British Empire's defence of Egypt rather misses the point that this was primarily intended to protect what lay

---

[18] Lloyd E. Lee, *The War Years: A Global History of the Second World War* (London: Routledge, 1989).

[19] Christian Destremau, *Le Moyen-Orient pendant la seconde guerre mondiale* (Paris: Perrin, 2011), p. 575.

[20] Cyrus Schayegh, *The Middle East and the Making of the Modern World* (Cambridge, MA: Harvard University Press, 2017), pp. 272–3.

beyond it – the oil of Iran and Iraq – as well as the vital Suez Canal, which itself was prized . . . as an artery through which Iranian oil could flow.[21]

Iran and Iraq were thus two key pieces of the imperial puzzle, for the British needed unrestricted access to the region's oil and to its lines of communication. Furthermore, the German–Soviet Nonaggression Pact signed on 23 August 1939 meant that pro-German sympathies in Iran and Iraq posed a serious international threat. Likewise, Palestine was central for air communication to India, the overland route to Iraq, and a potential staging post for military reinforcement from India to Egypt.[22] In sum, the Middle East and Mediterranean 'formed a massive theatre of diverse conflicts, most of them with roots in Britain's imperial past and imperial strategic predilections'.[23]

Second, as the above-mentioned reports collected from the border areas by different intelligence services and officials reveal, the instability did not only originate from the political centres of the Middle Eastern states, but also from their margins. Hence, the borderlands became a constant issue of concern for both local governments and the Allied forces. In that regard, this chapter argues in its second section for a reassessment of the 'peripheral' status of, at least, some Middle Eastern borderlands during the conflict. After all, borderlanders not only witnessed the presence of foreign troops in the border zones; they also observed and interacted with intelligence agents and saboteurs, as well as with thousands of incoming refugees, migrants, deserters and smugglers who ushered thousands of weapons into the region, leading to further insecurity along the Middle Eastern borders.

Furthermore, because the Baghdad Railway simultaneously marked the border between Turkey and Syria for over 350km and became *de facto* the only land link between Europe and the Allied-controlled territory, its role was unique when it comes to counterintelligence and espionage activities during the Second World War for at least two interrelated reasons. First, the Taurus Express running through the Baghdad Railway carried passengers into or out

---

[21] Ashley Jackson, *Persian Gulf Command*, p. 2.
[22] Daphna Sharfman, *Palestine in the Second World War: Strategies and Dilemmas* (Eastbourne: Sussex Academic Press, 2014), p. 5.
[23] Ashley Jackson, *The British Empire and the Second World War* (London: Hambledon Continuum, 2006), p. 97.

of an otherwise closed Europe. Second, as a British officer pointed out, during the war there were only four frontiers between the Allied-held territory and neutral countries, excluding the Far East: United Kingdom/Ireland, Soviet Union/Turkey, Iraq/Turkey and Syria/Turkey. Of those, however, 'the Taurus Express made the Turco-Syrian Frontier by far the most important'.[24] It was only when Turkey broke off diplomatic relations with Germany in August 1944 that the gateway between Europe and the Middle East was effectively closed for Axis agents.

Finally, the chapter will showcase how the prospects of redrawing the borders of the Middle East in the post-war era regionally awoke irredentist claims. For one, high-level diplomatic exchanges, together with war propaganda, espionage and rumours paved the way for the emergence of new subjectivities and indeed expectations among significant numbers of local actors, including state authorities, political activists and mere individuals, leading at times to concrete actions and, ultimately, to actual consequences.

Mounting Instability in the Middle East

At the outbreak of the Second World War, Turkey, Syria and Iraq were at a difficult juncture. In Turkey, the annexation of Alexandretta was widely celebrated as a victory, indeed, as the reparation of a historical injustice. This diplomatic triumph was nevertheless tarnished by two developments. On the one hand, the direction of both Turkey's domestic and international politics after the death of Mustafa Kemal was still unclear. Pro-Nazi and pan-Turanian political currents lobbied for a radical shift of Turkey's position within a fast-moving international context.[25] On the other hand, while Italy and Turkey had maintained a friendly relationship between 1928 and 1932, thereafter, Benito Mussolini started challenging the post-First World War order in the Mediterranean with a series of diplomatic moves;[26] notably, the Italian fortification of the Dodecanese

---

[24] Richard Pearse, *Three Years in the Levant* (London: Macmillan & Co. Ltd, 1949), p. 103.
[25] On a general overview of Turkish politics during İsmet İnönü's office, see Cemil Koçak, *Türkiye'de Milli Şef Dönemi, 1938–45* (Istanbul: İletişim Yayınları, 1996); Osman Akandere, *Milli Şef Dönemi, 1938–45* (Istanbul: İz Yayınları, 1998).
[26] Dilek Barlas, 'Friends or Foes? Diplomatic Relations between Italy and Turkey, 1923–36', *International Journal of Middle East Studies* 36, No. 2 (2004), pp. 231–52.

Islands as well as the invasion of Abyssinia in October 1935.[27] Following the Italian invasion of Albania in April 1939, Mussolini's revisionism in the Eastern Mediterranean had become a real threat for Turkey. Subsequently, Britain and Turkey signed a joint declaration on 12 May 1939 announcing their political will to stand against an eventual aggression in the Mediterranean. The bilateral agreement was followed by a tripartite agreement among Turkey, Britain and France on 19 October 1939.[28]

In Syria, as Philip S. Khoury puts it, the world conflict 'found the nationalist leadership exhausted and politically bankrupt'.[29] Indeed, the Franco-Syrian Treaty of 1936, which provided for Syrian independence, had not been ratified in Paris, and the Syrian nationalist circles were more divided along personal lines than ever.[30] As Germany declared the war against France and Britain, martial law was proclaimed in the Levant, thus further reducing the political field for the National Bloc.

Meanwhile, Prime Minister Nuri Said and his cabinet dreamt of making Iraq the centre of a large pan-Arab federation, including Syria. At the same time, Iraq feared that after regaining Alexandretta, Turkey would advance territorial claims over the Jazira, and eventually over the former Ottoman Vilayet of Mosul. Domestically, pan-Arab and pro-Axis tendencies within the army asserted themselves, mainly but not exclusively, to rid Iraq of British control.[31] After all, the Italian and German legations in Baghdad had been centres of anti-British propaganda since the 1930s. Furthermore, Rashid Ali al-Gaylani, Iraqi Prime Minister, was influenced by Amin Al-Husseini, the

---

[27] For a comprehensive report on the Turkish assessment of the rapid changes in the Mediterranean, see BCA.30.10.219.476.5, 18 November 1935.

[28] Dilek Barlas and Seçkin Barış Gülmez, 'Turkish-British Relations in the 1930s: From Ambivalence to Partnership', *Middle Eastern Studies* Vol. 54, No. 5 (2018), pp. 827–40 (here p. 835).

[29] Philip S. Khoury, *Syria and the French Mandate: The Politics of Arab Nationalism, 1920–45* (Princeton, NJ: Princeton University Press, 1987), p. 584.

[30] See Dhuqan Qarqut, *Tatawor al-Haraka al-Wataniyya fi Suriyya, 1920–39* (Beirut: Dar al-Taliah, 1975); Sami M. Moubayed, *The Politics of Damascus, 1920–46: Urban Notables and the French Mandate* (Damascus: Tlass House, 1999).

[31] Eric Davis, *Memories of State: Politics, History, and Collective Identity in Modern Iraq* (Berkeley, CA: University of California Press, 2005), p. 69.

grand mufti of Jerusalem, who was exiled from Palestine for his anti-British activities first in Lebanon and then in Iraq. By 1940, Rashid Ali encouraged the formation of a small circle of army generals, known as 'the Golden Square', to organise a *coup d'état* against the royal family and all the pro-British elements in the Iraqi government when conditions became favourable.[32] Overall, the war seemed to create at once new opportunities and threats for the local political elites who, as the war became global, were put under growing pressure to choose one of the belligerent camps.

After the fall of France in 1940, the French authorities in Syria and Lebanon aligned themselves with the new Vichy government with significant consequences. In parallel, German propaganda in the Levant and Iraq disseminated rapidly. According to David Motadel, Muslims became relevant in the eyes of Nazi's leadership in two contexts. Geographically, as the European war turned increasingly into a world war, Muslim areas became war zones – from the Caucasus to the Maghreb, the Balkans and the Middle East. Strategically, Germany's attempts to mobilise Muslims against their enemies can be seen as part of a general shift toward strategic pragmatism and the logic of total mobilisation. Creating zones of unrest behind enemy lines was thus the most important objective of Muslim propaganda endeavours in the Middle East.[33] In that regard, German propaganda was widely disseminated by the press, films, radio and records across the region. The latter was considered by the Allies as especially dangerous, for 'satiric songs and slogans had an enormous success, and they are repeated all day long thereafter' among the poor and workers in the Levant.[34]

Against this backdrop, plans to occupy Syria and Lebanon were drafted – encountering little enthusiasm among Britain's potential allies. Even though Charles de Gaulle had been keen on such a move, he and the Free French suspected the British of seeking to replace France as a mandatory power in the

---

[32] Youssef Aboul-Enein and Basil Aboul-Enein, *The Secret War for the Middle East: The Influence of Axis and Allied Intelligence Operations during World War II* (Annapolis: Naval Institute Press, 2013), p. 49.

[33] David Motadel, *Islam and Nazi Germany's War* (Cambridge, MA: Harvard University Press, 2014), p. 3.

[34] CHEAM, No. 200000046/19. 'L'action allemande en Syrie', 5 December 1941, p. 4.

Levant. On the other hand, the Turkish foreign minister, Şükrü Saraçoğlu, conveyed to Britain that his government could not accept any Allied proposal to occupy northern Syria, as this might involve it in war with France and, possibly, Germany.[35] Notwithstanding this, Vichy France allowed Germany and Italy full landing and provisioning rights in Syria as well as the permission to establish an airbase at Aleppo. By early May 1941, the pro-Vichy French High Commissioner approved the shipment of French arms and munitions from Syria to assist the Germans and Iraqi rebels via Tel Kotchek. Subsequently, three trains left Aleppo for Tel Kotchek carrying arms and munitions as well as artillery supplies. When the material fell into British hands, the War Office had definite proof of the pro-Vichy High Commissioner's collusion with Nazi Germany.[36]

The Allied invasion, including a multi-national coalition made up of Free French, British, Jordanian and Indian troops, began on 7 June 1941. After six weeks of violent combat, Vichy envoys arrived to negotiate the armistice, which was signed at Acre on July 14, bringing Syria into the Allied fold and thus shifting the balance of power in the region. For one, Britain was now in control of Iraq, Palestine, Transjordan and Egypt. In addition, Britain launched a third major military campaign in the Middle East in 1941, this time invading Iran. This campaign was the final act by which the area between the Mediterranean and the western frontier of India was cleared of Axis interference and intrigue.[37]

Within this more favourable context, on 1 June 1941, the Regent Abdul-Ilah returned to Baghdad and a pro-British cabinet was entrusted with the task of moving Iraq away from the German sphere of influence. In the Levant, the de Gaulle-Lyttelton Agreement of 25 July 1941 ceded authority over all military matters in the Levant to the British Middle East command, while territorial command in Syria and Lebanon – comprising civil administration as well as public security – was to be fulfilled by the French. However, due to

---

[35] Youssef Aboul-Enein and Basil Aboul-Enein, *The Secret War for the Middle East*, pp. 90–95.
[36] TNA, FO 624/25/517. American Consul General to British Embassy. Baghdad, 31 October 1941.
[37] Ashley Jackson, *The British Empire and the Second World War*, p. 156.

their military weakness as well as the lack of financial and administrative backing from Paris, the Free French position in the Levant was weak. This uneven partnership became even more evident as the British appointed Edward Spears to the official function of serving as liaison between the Free French forces, on the one hand, and the British army command and the minister of state in Cairo, on the other.[38]

Indeed, it rapidly became apparent that Spears had established a British 'shadow administration' in Syria and Lebanon to the dissatisfaction of the Free French.[39] Thereafter, Franco-British tension revealed itself around many themes, among which was the conflict of competence between the Allies on the northern frontier. To the French, all matters of public administration and security, including border control, were their prerogative as long as no military action took place in the area. In contrast, the British considered that, in wartime, efficient control of the Syrian–Turkish border was a matter not just of public order but also of military security. From their point of view, frontier zones had to be considered potential zones of military operations and therefore fell within the British realm.[40]

When the War Came to the Borderlands

Undoubtedly, the Spears mission, together with the second British occupation of Iraq and the Anglo-Soviet military penetration in Iran, contributed to freeing the Middle Eastern region from direct Axis interference. Notwithstanding this tour de force, both the external and internal borders of the Allied sphere of influence were not fully impermeable against wartime challenges such as the dramatic increase of weapons circulating across and along the border zones as well as the infiltration of pro-Axis agents and enemy spies into Allied-occupied territories.

Indeed, as the pro-Vichy forces surrendered to the British, they were said to have distributed arms in certain Armenian and Kurdish villages along the

---

[38] Aviel Roshwald, 'The Spears Mission in the Levant 1941–4', *The Historical Journal*, Vol. 29, No. 4 (1986), pp. 897–919 (here p. 900).

[39] Charles de Gaulle, *Mémoires de guerre* (Paris: Plon, 1999).

[40] Katharina Lange, 'Peripheral Experiences: Everyday Life in the Kurd Dagh during the Allied Occupation in the Second World War' in Heike Liebau et al. (eds), *World in World Wars* (Leiden: Brill, 2010), pp. 401–28 (here p. 406).

Turkish–Syrian border as well as among Bedouin tribes.[41] As a result, between 1941 and 1942, insecurity across significant portions of Syrian territory became an issue of concern.[42] For one thing, Bedouins armed with machine guns perpetrated frequent raids causing more casualties than ever before.[43] As an Aleppo merchant put it, 'in the Ottoman times, a cavalry unit composed of six soldiers sufficed to drive under escort a powerful tribal chieftain'. Since the occupation of Syria by the Allied forces in 1941, however, Bedouin chiefs had seen no limits to their actions:

> Possessing arms and ammunitions stolen to pro-Vichy forces or abandoned on purpose, rich of subsidies, cereals and dates provided by the occupying authorities, spoiled by the Officers charged with the Bedouin affairs, the tribal chieftains see themselves in a very privileged situation that they seek to exploit in their own interest.[44]

Hidden or sold to tribesmen in the Syrian–Iraqi borderlands,[45] the contraband of weapons was made to a large scale in the Jazira for different reasons. First, since the outbreak of the Second World War, tribes and individuals alike had sought to collect as many weapons as possible for security reasons. Second, in the aftermath of the Iraqi revolt in 1941 important amounts of arms were seized by the population, while Italians and Germans also delivered weapons to local tribes in the event of a general uprising against the British. Finally, when the Anglo-Soviet troops occupied Iran, between 27,000 and 30,000 Iranian soldiers found refuge in Turkey. Even though most of these troops were disarmed by the Turkish border authorities, hundreds of the former sold their weapons on the black market. In turn, numerous Turkish soldiers also sold the guns seized at the border to make a living. It is within this context that hundreds of rifles made in Germany, yet

---

[41] TNA, FO 371/27332. Military Attaché (Ankara) to the War Office, 17 August 1941.
[42] According to the Turkish authorities, Armenians also acquired weapons and led armed attacks in the tri-border area in summer 1941. See Ankara's protests in TNA, WO 201/967A. Middle East to Military Palestine, 28 July 1941.
[43] SHAT, 431/1. Sûreté Générale. Aleppo, 1 June 1942.
[44] SHAT, 431/1. Sûreté Générale. Aleppo, 20 May 1942.
[45] SHAT, 307/4. Sûreté Générale. Deir ez-Zor, 29 December 1941.

with an Iranian stamp, crossed the Turco–Syrian border to be sold in Syria, particularly among tribes both in the Upper Jazira and the Syrian Desert, wherein the Tay along with the Syrian and Iraqi Shammar clans were found to be among the most prominent buyers.[46]

Unsurprisingly, Tel Kotchek, being located at the crossroads between Syria and Iraq, became a hotspot of arms contraband and took advantage of the chaotic context in the region. Damascene merchants with pro-Axis tendencies moved to the border zone to facilitate the smuggling of weapons between Syria and Iraq.[47] Subsequently, these weapons were to play a key role during the latest stages of the French Mandate in Syria; between June and July 1945, Kurdish and Arab tribes attacked Christian populations and French troops in the Jazira, with the complicity of the British forces based at Derbessia since 1941, who wished to force the end of the French Mandate in the face of Free French hesitations.[48]

The situation was hardly different in the northern Iraqi borderlands. British Ambassador Cornwallis in Baghdad, for instance, informed London that Iraqi Kurds, seeing what was happening in Iran, where tribal and irregular groups rose up against state forces following the Anglo-Soviet occupation of 1941, 'followed suit by taking every Persian army and police post along the whole length of the frontier'.[49] Cornwallis referred to the alarming dispatches sent by the British Consulate in Kermanshah who, as early as 1941, informed that 'Kurdish tribal unrest' in the border zones separating Iran from Turkey and Iraq could take on a new character within the war context, for he 'suspected that the Kurds . . . were being encouraged by the Soviet Russian authorities to resist the Iranian military forces'.[50] In addition, unlike in the past, borderlanders on both sides of the Iranian–Iraqi boundary

---

[46] SHAT, 307/4. Free French Delegation at Deir ez-Zor, 3 January 1942.

[47] SHAT, 307/4. Military Cabinet to Mohafazat of Euphrates and Jazira. Beirut, 14 January 1942.

[48] For a comprehensive, yet anti-British report on the attacks upon Christians and Free France forces in the Upper Jazira in the summer 1945, see SAULCHOIR, D61, Dominican Mission in the Upper Jazira. 'British Activity in the Upper Jazira'. Beirut, 21 July 1945, pp. 1–12.

[49] Fieldhouse (ed.), *Kurds, Arabs and Britons: The Memoir of Wallace Lyon in Iraq, 1918–44* (London: I. B. Tauris, 2002), p. 220.

[50] TNA, FO 248/1405. British Consul (Kermanshah) to British Legation (Tehran), 8 October 1941.

possessed modern weapons: 'For them it was a real bonanza: crates of Czech rifles and ammunitions, some of them still packed in grease, were the prizes of war'.[51] As a result, as in the Syrian–Iraqi borderlands, 'the use of coveted Brno rifles as currency meant that hijackings, sheep stealing and cross-border raids increased'.[52]

In addition to the dramatic rise in smuggled weapons and subsequent surge of violent actions along the borderlands, increasing human mobility became another issue of concern during the war. While by mid-1941, the Syrian–Turkish border had been a gateway for the pro-Axis combatants who had fought the Allies in Iraq and Syria to escape into neutral Turkey, in the face of both Turkey's fragile neutrality and the first important Allied victories, hundreds of Turkish soldiers deserted the army and crossed the border southwards. At first, Turkish deserters were welcomed as an important source of information for the Allies; these deserters were thoroughly questioned by the French authorities to make sense of the Turkish military moves along the common boundary or, more generally, about Turkish politics.[53] After being interrogated, deserters were gathered together in a camp away from the frontier zone. As the numbers of deserters grew, Free French authorities preferred to free them discretely so that they could return to Turkey. If they were arrested again in Syria, however, they were delivered to the competent Turkish civil authorities, namely the local *kaymakam*.[54] However, while to begin with the French authorities seemed to be satisfied with this unexpected source of information, they gradually realised that the news provided by the deserters were often irrelevant; rather than first-hand intelligence information, their reports turned out to be rumours at best, or were counter-intelligence efforts borne out of the Turkish espionage strategies, at worst.[55]

In that regard, the Baghdad Railway was to play a crucial role. From 1940 onwards, the Taurus Express ran on the Baghdad Railway, linking Turkey, Syria and Iraq, operating twice a week and, more importantly, providing a

[51] Fieldhouse (ed.), *Kurds, Arabs and Britons*, p. 220.
[52] Ashley Jackson, *Persian Gulf Command*, p. 197.
[53] See dozens of files in interrogatories of Turkish deserters in CADN, 1SL/1/V/2145.
[54] CADN, 1SL/1/V/2145. Délégation française Mohafazat of Aleppo, 4 November 1943.
[55] CADN, 1SL/1/V/816. 'Turkish deserters'. General Caillault to Mr Puaux, French High Commissioner in Syria and Lebanon. Damascus, 29 February 1940.

direct means of communication between the Germans and their agents in Iraq. As a matter of fact, a number of sleeping-car attendants worked for the Nazi regime, whereas many of the passengers acted as international couriers. As a British officer put it, 'it was well known that the Taurus Express had already carried in its luxury sleeping- and restaurant-cars more international agents and spies than any other train in the world'.[56] Against this backdrop, rigorous control of both travellers and staff was necessary:

> There were days when travellers had to be closely interrogated, their luggage pulled to pieces, their papers and letters thoroughly examined and all their clothing removed. Many unsuspecting agents were surprised to find themselves removed from the train and taken to destinations they least desired to see.[57]

In Syria, the frontier zone was divided into three sectors: Jarablus, Afrin and Idlib. The French elements in charge of border surveillance were the Light Cavalry units, the Mobile Guards, the Syrian Gendarmes, the customs units and the Sûreté Générale. In addition, the border control was reinforced by the Transjordanian troops, the Field Security Section (FSS) active in the surveillance of the train, and the British Security Mission (BSM) in Aleppo. In September 1941, a security control officer (SCO) was first stationed at Tel Kotchek. His task was to cooperate with the Franco-Syrian authorities in seeing that the orders regarding entry into and exit from Syria were complied with, and to carry out passenger checks on trains running between Tel Kotchek and Tel Ziwan. These controls worked fairly well, with the defence Security Office receiving weekly entrance and exit lists from the SCO that provided them with all relevant information about the Taurus Express passengers' passports and visas.

Nevertheless, the control system was less effective when it came to merchandise and luggage, due to the limited number of personnel employed in the searches.[58] In that regard, we can only appreciate the importance of this task if we bear in mind that on the Meydan Ekbez line alone, 'every

---

[56] Richard Pearse, *Three Years in the Levant*, p. 103.

[57] Ibid. pp. 103–4.

[58] SHAT, 4H 318/1. 'Rapport du comité convoqué pour l'examen du contrôle de la frontière turco-syrienne'. Aleppo, 13-15 February 1943.

week and in both directions, there are two Taurus Express, two mixed trains and between 8 and 12 trains only for merchandises'.[59] Another problem was associated with the searching of sleeping cars at Tel Kotchek, which provoked Syrian and French anxiety because the attendants were neutral Turkish nationals. The French felt that any unpleasant incident during the searches of Turkish couriers and other diplomatic personnel might result in the limitation of the special privileges they enjoyed on the Turkish section of the railway between Aleppo and Nusaybin. Likewise, the British were concerned by Turkish reprisal: 'It should be realized that approximately 25 British couriers travel through Turkish territory in comparison with 5 Turkish couriers travelling through British controlled territory. Should the Turks decide to retaliate, we would be very much the losers.'[60]

Yet, although British officers agreed that all precautions had to be taken not to upset Turkish personnel, the former considered that overall security concerns were more important than the extreme sensitivity of the Turkish. On the one hand, legally, only the crossed diplomatic bags were exempt from search. As a courtesy, diplomatic officials were not searched, but consular officials and couriers did not benefit from the same treatment. On the other hand, searches in the past had revealed its importance, for 'uncensored mail – in many cases directed to addresses of enemy nationality in enemy or enemy-occupied countries – [was] carried by couriers and others with diplomatic passports', which was 'not only a breach of the regulations, but . . . a grave danger'.[61]

In the face of a dramatic increase of the numbers of travellers using the Taurus Express between Aleppo and Baghdad – 2,000 per month by 1943 – an Anglo-French control centre (Centre d'examination des voyageurs) was established in Aleppo. All passengers travelling to Iraq (or Iran) were required to submit their passports on the Taurus Express after crossing the Turkish–Syrian border, disembark, endure examination, and get on the train again, which then remained sealed until it reached Iraqi territory.[62] It was only when Turkey broke off diplomatic relations with Germany on 2 August 1944

---

[59] SHAT, 4H 332/1. Sûreté Générale to Chief of the Military Cabinet. Beirut, 8 April 1943.
[60] TNA, FO 195/2473/6. General Headquarters. Middle East Forces, 8 September 1942.
[61] TNA, FO 195/2473/6. Patrick Coghill (BSM) to General Spears (Beirut), 18 October 1942.
[62] Adrian O'Sullivan, *The Baghdad Set*, p. 155.

that the connection between Berlin and Baghdad was vigorously affected.⁶³ Further, this diplomatic breakthrough opened the door for additional cooperation between Turkey and the Allies. Thus, for instance, the Baghdad Railway was used to send both Allied war material and British officers into Turkey.⁶⁴

German espionage and counterintelligence plans in the borderlands were not limited to the Taurus Express, though. In particular, following the Soviet victory at Stalingrad, since it appeared more clearly that Germany could not win the war, Nazi intelligence services attempted desperately to mobilise any Muslim groups behind Allies' lines. In early 1943, for instance, the presence of pro-Axis agents in the Mardin-Nusaybin region seeking to establish contacts with the Kurdish nationalist movement in Syria was reported by the French intelligence services.⁶⁵ More importantly, in June 1943, three German parachutists accompanied by a Kurdish interpreter landed 25km north of Mosul, carrying with them wireless equipment, a supply of explosives and written propaganda in favour of Kurdish independence. Later questionings in Baghdad revealed that the group of German agents had landed there by mistake – the initial intention having been to drop them near the point where the frontiers of Iraq, Iran and Turkey meet, and thence blow-up different key infrastructures in Iraq, such as oil pipelines and bridges. Although the three parachutists were arrested fourteen days after being dropped from an aircraft, British authorities were quite disturbed by the fact that the Iraqi officials responsible for the area in question did not make the arrests until they had been threatened with prosecution if the would-be saboteurs were not brought in. In other words, two years after the Iraqi-British war of May 1941, the British felt that the lack of willingness to arrest the three German agents showcased that Allies' enemies 'still found themselves among friends' in Iraq and were thus worried about the police connivance with pro-Nazi elements.⁶⁶

In parallel, the movement of unidentified aircraft over the Iraqi northern borderlands between 16 and 19 June of the same year was reported by British

---

⁶³ SHAT, 4H 443/1. Free French Forces, 3° Bureau, 24 October 1944.
⁶⁴ SHAT, 4H 430/2. Free France Forces, 2° Bureau, 31 August 1944.
⁶⁵ CADN, 1SL/1/V/2051. Weekly Report, 24–30 January 1943. Special Services. Qamishli, 30 January 1943.
⁶⁶ NARA, RG84, UD 2752, Box 10. Telegram sent to the Secretary of State (Washington), 5 July 1943; NARA, RG84, UD 2752, Box 10. 'German Parachutists Land Near Mosul', Baghdad, 9 July 1943.

officers deployed in the area: Tel Kaif, Faysh Khabur (both at the Syrian–Iraqi border), Barzan (Turkish–Iraqi border), Rowanduz (Iraqi–Iranian border) and Mosul.[67] Even though from a military viewpoint such a move had no real repercussions, the psychological effects were nevertheless immediate among Kurdish nationalist circles. The news of the parachutists' landing in Iraq soon became public and gave rise to rumours exaggerating the strength of the party and their intentions, as well as a renewal of Kurdish political activities in important urban centres in the north, such as Sulaimaniya. Under these circumstances, the local *Mutasarrif* ordered the arrest of some political figures in that city on the grounds that their detention was in the interest of public security.[68] Yet, towards the middle of the Second World War, the potential winds of change in the Turkish–Syrian–Iraqi borderlands did not come from Berlin, but from Ankara.

Renewed Turkish Irredentism

The outbreak of the Second World War precipitated dramatic changes in the Middle East, with profound consequences for French-ruled Syria and its relations with Turkey. The background of the rapid deterioration of relations between the two parties goes back to the mid-1930s, though. More notably, Italian and Bulgarian revisionism was met with the awakening of Turkish irredentism over Syrian territories after the signing of the Franco-Syrian Treaty of 1936, which allowed for complete Syrian independence. Although France did not ultimately ratify the Treaty, Turkey voiced her opposition to its terms. In addition, in the ambiguities left by the accord on the future status of Alexandretta, Turkey saw an opportunity to kill two birds with one stone: regain an ex-Ottoman province on the basis of its ethnic character, as per the National Pact of 1920, and secure Turkish interests in the face of threat from Italy.[69]

---

[67] NARA, RG84, UD 2752, Box 10. Special Security Report. Baghdad, 4 July 1943.

[68] NARA, RG84, UD 2752, Box 10. Defence Security Office. American Legation. Baghdad, 29 July 1943.

[69] In his opening speech at the Grand National Assembly in Ankara in December 1937, Mustafa Kemal underlined the importance of Alexandretta for the Turkish Republic. Atatürk, *Atatürk'ün Söylev ve Demeçleri, I-III* (Ankara: Atatürk Araştırma Merkezi, 1997), p. 142. In addition, both the press inside Turkey and the Sanjaq's own Turkish-language press, together with local committees, launched a series of campaigns in favour of the annexation of this territory into Turkey. See, for instance, 'Antakya bizimdir', *Cumhuriyet*, 1 October 1936; 'Suriye Başvekili Büyük Şefe takdim edildi', *Ulus Sesi*, 24 December 1937.

As Alexandretta, now renamed Hatay, officially became a Turkish territory in 1939, the question for France was whether Turkey would advance new claims over Syrian territory or not. Echoing the German annexation of Austria and Czechoslovakia between 1938 and 1939, together with that of Alexandretta in mind, the French Advisor to the High Commissioner considered 'that this country [Turkey] has never given up his ambitions over a region [the Syrian Jazira] that is so close and whose oil potential cannot but awake its interest'. Therefore, the French official predicted the next Turkish steps:

> Using the pan-German style, it will suffice that a number of Jazira villages suddenly deploy Turkish flags so that the Ankara government, arguing that it was a spontaneous move from local populations, put again the question of the Jazira on the table using all kinds of arguments, including the military ones, . . . to consolidate its position.[70]

Turkish geo-strategic position in the Mediterranean and the Middle East was bolstered by the British and French need to attract Turkey into their sphere of influence in the face of the Nazi-Soviet Pact, as well as German and Italian advances in Central Europe and the Balkans.[71] Within this context, France and Britain adopted a policy of 'appeasement' towards the would-be Turkish ally, which included allowing Turkey to retake Alexandretta and tightening the border control in the shape of border posts and mobile units on the Syrian side to thoroughly combat the contraband along the Turkish–Syrian frontier.[72] In parallel, Mussolini's attack on Albania on 7 April 1939 precipitated Turkish negotiations with Britain and France and definitely marked a point of separation from the Axis camp.[73]

Officially, however, Turkish newspapers and authorities denied any territorial ambitions in Aleppo and the Jazira; Turkey was 'committed' to the *bon*

---

[70] CADN, 1SL/1/V/505. The Embassy Advisor to the High Commissioner to Mr. Puaux, French High Commissioner in Syria and Lebanon. Damascus, 13 June 1939.

[71] Dilek Barlas and Seçkin Barış Gülmez, 'Turkish-British Relations in the 1930s', pp. 827–40.

[72] CADN, FA, 36PO/1/153. 'On Frontier relations'. The Adjunct Delegate at Aleppo to the High Commissioner. Aleppo, 16 November 1938.

[73] George Lenczowski, *The Middle East in World Affairs* (Ithaca: Cornell University Press, 1952), pp. 139–40.

voisinage accords signed with French Syria and, more importantly, Ankara acknowledged Syrian aspirations to full independence and territorial integrity.[74] Despite official assurances, intelligence reports provided a different picture. In June 1938, for instance, the French reported the establishment of pro-Turkish propaganda offices at Hasaka, Qamishli and Deir ez-Zor, receiving instructions from a central committee based at Mardin. As a result of these activities, on 17 January 1939, the Turkish Consul in Damascus met in different instances with a group of Kurdish notables originating from the Upper Jazira. During the discussions, the Consul highlighted the ties between the Kurds and Turks, based on religion, as opposed to the French, who allegedly intended to settle all Syrian Christians in the Jazira. The Turks, on the contrary, would never let them down.[75]

With the outbreak of the Second World War and despite the potential threat of the Axis camp, in addition to being almost surrounded by countries dominated by German political influence, Ankara favoured neutrality as a means of securing the survival of Turkey as a sovereign independent state,[76] a position that was viewed as 'justified' in great part by some Allied officials, such as the British Ambassador in Ankara.[77] It was precisely the refusal of any form of adventurism that led Ankara to decline British encouragements to seize Aleppo as plans to occupy Syria were drafted by the War Office by early 1941.

The British territorial offer to Turkey was the result of two considerations. First, the British were aware that Turkey aspired to control the whole Baghdad Railway between Ankara and Tel Kotchek. Second, they hoped that their territorial bargain would prevent Turkey from aligning itself with Germany. In that regard, on 25 March, the Chancery at Ankara reported, 'what is undoubtedly a fact is that the Axis have been offering neighbouring territories to Ankara';

---

[74] See a series of articles in that regard in *Yeni Sabah*, 21 February 1939; *Ikdam*, 24 February 1939; *Türk Sözü*, 17 October 1940.

[75] CADN, 36PO/1/155. High Commissioner to Ministry of Foreign Affairs. Beirut, 25 February 1939.

[76] Selim Deringil, *Turkish Foreign Policy During the Second World War*, pp. 1–3.

[77] This issue is raised in several instances in the memoirs written by the British Ambassador who served in Ankara between 1939 and 1944. See Sir Hughe Knatchbull-Hugessen, *Diplomat in Peace and War* (London: John Murray, 1949).

namely, Aleppo and some of the Greek islands.[78] The evidence from the German side seems to confirm their suspicions. On 14 July 1941, the German ambassador in Ankara, Franz von Papen, wrote to Joachim von Ribbentrop, Minister of Foreign Affairs, that in order for Turkey to join Germany her territorial ambitions in northern Syria had to be met.[79]

Against this setting, the British even gauged the annexation of Northern Syria as a whole by Turkey, despite the expected subsequent negative reactions from the French and the Arabs: 'we would excite violent animosity against ourselves in Iraq if we were to promise northern Syria to Turkey ... but on the other hand, the Egyptians would probably not mind so much, especially as their thoughts are taken up at present with the Italian menace'.[80] To the disappointment of the British, Turkey rejected their encouragements at that time, fearing that this move would simultaneously provoke immediate French and German attacks on Turkish territory.

When the Free French and British troops ousted the pro-Vichy authorities from Syria and Lebanon, the territorial question seemed to be definitely solved. By late 1941, however, Turkey requested British support for a rectification of the Syrian frontier sufficient to allow her to assure the effective control and defence of the Baghdad Railway.[81] The desiderata of the Turkish government, though not formally specific, evidently included not only the Upper Jazira, but also Aleppo itself, as well as a strip of Syria parallel to the frontier and broad enough for the reasonable protection of the line.[82] In fact, the Turkish position was surrounded by ambiguity:

---

[78] TNA, FO 195/2470/81/V. 'Turkish Government's Attitude to Syria'. London, 6 December 1941.

[79] Selim Deringil, *Turkish Foreign Policy during the Second World War*, pp. 141–2.

[80] TNA, FO 371/24594. War Cabinet Secret Memorandum by C. Baxter 'The Sacrifice of North Syria to Turkey', 1 November 1940.

[81] By Article 10 of the Franco-Turkish Agreement of 20 October 1921, Turkey had recognised the transfer of the line to a French group, and by Article 5 of the Franco-Turkish Agreement of 1932, she undertook not to buy the section which lies in Turkey (Çobanbey-Nusaybin) till 1947, but she would then, it was understood, proceed to expropriate it.

[82] TNA, FO 371/44188/R9943/9943/44. Foreign Office Research Department to Mr Clutton, 24 June 1944.

At an interview in Cyprus on March 18th [1941], the Turkish Minister of Foreign Affairs said that he had recently made clear to the French Ambassador that while Turkey had no territorial ambitions as regards Syria it was essential for her to be able, in peace and war, to use the section of the Mosul-Nusaybin railway running through Syria.

On 28 March, an article appeared in the semi-official newspaper *Ulus* claiming: 'the sole aim of the Turkish government in respect of Syria is that the territorial integrity and security of that country should remain inviolate'.[83] Early in April, the Turkish Minister of Foreign Affairs informed the British that he had confirmed to the French Ambassador that the French were under an obligation to allow the Turks the free use of the frontier railway. Should the French refuse, Turkey would take steps to secure her communications; that is, gaining control of the railway, including Aleppo.[84]

In response to Turkish pretensions, the Foreign Office informed its Turkish counterpart that it was most important to emphasise that, if the Turkish government undertook such action, it was understood that the move had to be of temporary nature and that their action in no way could prejudice the future status of the occupied area. Against British reluctance to the durable occupation of Syria, Turkish Minister of Foreign Affairs, Şükrü Saraçoğlu, intimated that there was some 'injustice' in the settlement of the territorial issues after the First World War which Turkey had always desired to see repaired at an appropriate time.[85] Diplomatic exchanges throughout 1941 did not produce any kind of agreement or secret accord on the Turkish–Syrian border. Yet, by early 1942, Britain was ready to revise her conditions, as the War Office considered that the construction of a railroad connecting Turkey directly to Iraq was necessary from a military viewpoint:

> When the question of the possible cession of Syrian territory to Turkey first came up ... we turned it down quite flat, principally because it was not ours to give, ... and because in any case we did not want to start carving up

---

[83] TNA, FO 195/2470/81/V. 'Turkish Government's Attitude to Syria'. London, 6 December 1941.
[84] Ibid.
[85] Ibid.

the Middle East in anticipation of the peace conference. Subsequently we had reluctantly to reconsider the matter because the military considered the construction of the link between Arada and Diyarbakır vital to their strategic plans ... A territorial as well as a financial bribe seemed to us the only possible means of overcoming [Ankara's] delays which we put down to Turkey's fear of provoking Germany.[86]

As Turkey agreed to the construction of the railway on the understanding that it should obtain a territorial rectification of the Syrian borderline, Britain meanwhile played a waiting game, leaving the initiative to the Turks while secretly hoping that the evolution of the conflict would not require giving the Turks any sort of assurance on the annexation of Aleppo and the Jazira. Eventually, the British strategy proved to be successful as a result of the developments in the Middle and Far East. Both the War Office and the Foreign Office concluded that the construction of the railway was no longer of vital strategic urgency, and that the railway, if constructed in the present circumstance, might prove of more assistance to the enemy than to the Allies.[87] When the British informed Turkey that their territorial offer was no longer valid, Turkish Foreign Minister did not show any disappointment, leading the British to believe that this issue was solved.

Beyond official statements, however, Turkish officials did not give up on Turkey's claims over northern Syria, given the potential favourable conditions that an international context marked by uncertainty and moving alliances seemed to offer. Hence, Turkish officials deployed additional means to gain leverage in the area. On the one hand, Turkish agents attempted to co-opt Bedouin tribes from the Syrian borderlands as well as urban elements in cities such as Aleppo by conveying the idea that they would be better off under Turkey's sovereignty, rather than in French Syria. In that regard, in an intercepted letter written on 9 September 1942 by the Persian Consul-General in Beirut and addressed to the Iranian Minister of Foreign Affairs, the former reported that the Turkish government had established relations with tribal chiefs in northern Syria to

---

[86] TNA, FO 195/2473/154. Foreign Office (London) to British Embassy (Ankara), 12 May 1942.
[87] Ibid.

whom Ankara had provided financial support. In return, Bedouin chiefs were expected to spread pro-Turkish propaganda among their tribesmen.[88]

On the other hand, by mid-1943, it seemed that Ankara was playing another card; that is, favouring the settlement of Turkish citizens in the Jazira to claim its historical 'Turkish' character. While the British were unsure about the reasons for the sudden and massive migration of Turkish citizens into the Jazira, its effects were nevertheless real. Syrian officials claimed that in the summer of 1943, some 14,000 Turkish nationals, mostly Kurds but also Arabs, Turks and Christians, came over to the Jazira without visas or other formalities. With the Alexandretta question still present in the minds of Syrian officials, the Syrian government denounced an organised campaign to support Turkey's irredentist ambitions in Syria.[89] Likewise, French authorities reckoned that the presence of an important number of 'Turkish citizens' could be exploited to advance Turkish territorial ambitions in northern Syria.[90] Consequently, the Syrian government ordered the expulsion of a number of migrants who had illegally penetrated into the Jazira.[91] Expulsions were not thoroughly carried out, however, for the British advised the Syrian government not to provoke serious disturbances among the Kurds, which would certainly erupt, should the governmental plans be fully implemented.[92]

Aware of such activities, British experts in Iraq suggested again avoiding any commitment vis-à-vis Turkey on northern Syria, for 'to give them Aleppo would undoubtedly also lead to a demand for Mosul'. In the long-term, Turkish authorities 'want direct rail communication with Iraq not crossing Syrian territory on the way', and 'they want the present Turco-Syrian railway to be well within Turkish territory for strategic reasons'. Since the solution offered by the British – bypassing Aleppo and giving ownership of the Turco-Syrian

---

[88] TNA, FO 226/236. British Security Mission, 19 September 1942.
[89] TNA, FO 195/2478/224. Office of the Political Officer (Damascus) to the British Legation (Beirut), 20 August 1943.
[90] CADN, 1SL/1/V/2202. General Security. Qamishli, 1 April 1943.
[91] TNA, FO 195/2478/224. British Legation (Beirut) to British Embassy (Ankara), 23 August 1943.
[92] TNA, FO 195/2478/224. British Legation (Beirut) to British Consulate (Damascus), 12 August 1943.

railway to Turkey – did not meet the case, Saraçoğlu's suggestion for a modification of the Turco-Syrian boundary was once more turned down by the British ambassador in Ankara.[93] If the Baghdad Railway had a strategic value for Turkey, it also did for the British, in particular with regard to the Allied endeavours to coordinate supply policies in the Middle East:

> The railway from Aleppo to Nusaybin is of essential strategic importance in the Middle East as it is the only railway link with Iraq. It is also of special importance to Syria . . . for the distribution of cereals. In the circumstances it seems best that any request for assistance on the part of the Turkish authorities should be treated sympathetically though in fact nothing would be done to facilitate the supply of the railway material required. This attitude is however subject to the proviso that there is no danger of the introduction of German experts either in the survey of the proposed lines or in the actual work of construction.[94]

By early 1945, Turkey was alone among the neighbouring powers in not having recognised the independence of the Levantine states. The reason for this was Syria's refusal to make any formal acknowledgement of the Turkish title to the Hatay, which the Turkish government was anxious to obtain in return for recognising Syrian independence. Occasional interpellations in the Syrian Chamber, press articles, pamphlets and even demonstrations in favour of the return of the Hatay kept the question alive. Notwithstanding this, in the face of Soviet threats upon Turkey's northern frontiers, the Ankara government 'felt an increasing urgency to establish amicable relations with their southern neighbour'.[95] The relationship with Syria was nevertheless clouded by another old question; that is, the presence of Armenian and Kurdish refugee populations in the frontier zone as well as in the main cities of the Levant, from where nationalist organisations saw in wartime context an encouraging environment for revisionist activities.

---

[93] TNA, FO 371/37527. 'Turco-Syrian Frontier'. Eastern Department, 30 July 1943.

[94] TNA, FO 195/2478/389. Foreign Office (London) to British Embassy (Ankara), 3 December 1943.

[95] TNA, FO 371/52909. G. Young (Beirut) to the Secretary of State for Foreign Affairs, 28 August 1946.

Revisionism among the 'Small Nations'

Following the failure of the Ararat revolt in 1931, the strategic alliance between the Armenian Dashnak Party and the Kurdish Khoybun League in the Levant ceased to exist. While personal contacts between leading figures of both committees persisted, the re-edition of a politico-military coalition was put aside, pending more favourable conditions. Crucially, Dashnak and Khoybun privileged the integration of their respective communities into Syrian society, while striving to avoid their cultural assimilation. In that sense, the exiled Kurdish intellectuals originating from Turkey launched a renaissance cultural movement through the publication of cultural journals, textbooks and educational initiatives in the Kurdish language. This option also had the support of the French authorities, which in the early 1930s did not wish to provoke a diplomatic conflict with Turkey.[96]

Yet, the outbreak of the Second World War seemed to open new horizons for both nationalist movements. In Iraq, the signature of the Eastern Pact of Saadabad in 1937 between Turkey, Persia, Afghanistan and Iraq prompted the first signs of an awakening of the Kurdish movement, especially among a new generation of activists made up of students and urban intelligentsia who established 'shadow' societies in Baghdad, Erbil, Kirkuk and Sulaimaniya.[97] The Iraqi Kurds felt that this regional security pact targeted, in fact, 'internal threats' such as the Kurdish movement and therefore sent protest letters to the British, French, Italian and German ambassadors serving in Baghdad.[98] Just a few months before the official start of the Second World War, a very concise British note drafted on the opportunity of exploiting the Kurdish question during a potential world conflict stated that, although some Kurdish claims were reasonable, Kurdish nationalism fitted in nowhere with the British policy in regards to Iraq, Palestine, or any other Arab country in the Middle East: 'We have sponsored the pan-Arabist ideal, and, having placed a

---

[96] CADN, 1SL/1/V/1055. Damascus, 28 December 1932.
[97] TNA, AIR 23/671. Air Liaison Officer (Sulaimaniya) to Air Headquarters (Dhibban), 23 February 1938.
[98] TNA, AIR 23/671. Air Liaison Officer (Sulaimaniya) to Air Headquarters (Dhibban), 29 April 1938.

great deal of reliance (possibly unwisely) on Arab friendship, we are unlikely to re-orient our present viewpoint'.[99]

Meanwhile, according to French reports, Kurdish notables from Damascus entered in contact with the former Italian Consul in Beirut by 1940. The latter would have promised financial support if Kurdish tribes in the Jazira launched an anti-French uprising. Being informed of these initiatives, the British representatives in Damascus asked Kurdish notables to sever their relations with the Italians. In return, the British would generously 'reward these efforts'.[100] In spite of this, pro-Axis propaganda seemed to be highly appealing at that time. Concretely, German propagandists argued that since Turkey had signed a treaty with Britain and France, the Kurds could not expect from them any support for Kurdish territorial projects.

After the fall of France in June 1940, the German Mission in Syria led by Werner Otto von Hentig paid a visit to Khalil ibn Ibrahim Pasha. The German Mission also met Khoybun leaders to whom it was emphasised that German support was conditional on a renewal of the Kurdo-Armenian alliance against Turkey; that is, between the Khoybun and the Dashnak Party.[101] According to diverse French security reports, members of the Khoybun and Dashnak held several meetings between 1941 and 1942 both in Beirut and the Upper Jazira in order to organise a military revolt in Turkey.[102] For British Colonel Elphinstone, Kurdish (and Armenian) agitation was understandable:

> The Kurds in general, and even more the refugee leaders here and their youngest followers, are convinced that they are going through a unique moment of their history, from which they have to take advantage. If they do not jump on this opportunity, they think that they will miss it for ever . . . it is unreasonable to expect that they will remain passive for an indefinite period of time.[103]

---

[99] TNA, AIR 23/671. Extract from Air Liaison Officer on 'Kurdish Nationalism', 26 April 1939.

[100] CADN, 1SL/1/V/571. Troupes du Levant. Damascus, 26 November 1940.

[101] Although there was no official position from the Dashnak Party on Nazi Germany, a sector, especially the members based in Europe, sealed an agreement with the Third Reich, brought to the public later on in 1943. Ronald Grigor Suny, *Looking toward Ararat*, p. 224.

[102] See for instance, CADN, 1SL/1/V/572. Lebanese Police. Beirut, 15 May 1941; CADN, 1SL/1/V/72. Sûreté Générale, Qamishli, 22 June 1942.

[103] CADN, 1SL/1/V/802. Colonel Elphinstone to British Legation in Damascus, 4 September 1942.

German propaganda was, however, adaptable. While the idea of supporting Kurdish and Armenian independence was vaguely advanced during secret contacts with the two committees in Damascus, pro-Muslim propaganda targeted Kurdish and Arab tribal leaders in Northern Syria. Thus, according to a Dominican priest based in the Upper Jazira,

> the Kurd and the Bedouin have been worked by the German propaganda ... To them, the Allies represent the Christian element, the hated religion, while the Nazi embody the man without religion, thus the potential ally against the Christian.[104]

The success of German propaganda among Kurdish and Armenian parties in the early stages of the Second World War needs, however, to be read in a wider context. Like the Arab nationalist committees, some Kurds and Armenians looked at Germany as a potential ally to reach their irredentist political objectives. In fact, like the Arab and Turkish elites of the time, the Kurdish movement held multifaceted perceptions of Nazi Germany as well as of the Allied forces.[105] At first, Nazi Germany appeared as a successful nationalist regime, a country led by a strong and charismatic leader who had returned pride and strength to a nation that had been severely punished after the First World War.[106] Like in Lebanon, Palestine or Iraq, Christian and Kurdish youth organisations similar to the European Fascist youth movements emerged in towns of the Upper Jazira such as Hasaka and Amuda in the late 1930s.[107] In the event of a radical shift in the area, Kurdish youngsters had to be ready to prove their patriotic feelings and discipline. Yet, much as in those countries, Nazism as an ideology had little impact, particularly because both Armenians and Kurds were simultaneously in contact with other powers, too, and because German ascendency in the Middle East declined from 1941 onwards.

---

[104] SAULCHOIR, Upper Jazira, D8. Father de Rudder (Derbessia) to Mgr Cardinal Tisserant (Rome), 18 March 1942.

[105] Peter Wien, *Iraqi Arab Nationalism: Authoritarian, Totalitarian, and pro-Fascist Inclinations, 1932–41* (London: Routledge, 2006), pp. 113–16.

[106] On the necessary search for a strong leader for the Kurdish nation, see 'Mileté bêserî', *Hawar*, No. 32 (1941); 'Dermanê nezaniyê', *Hawar*, No. 32 (1941).

[107] CADN, 1SL/1/V/504. Weekly Bulletin. Hasaka, 22 December 1938. See also the memoirs of Cigerwxîn, *Jînenigariya min* (Spanga: Apec, 1995), p. 228.

As the British troops entered Syria and Lebanon, a section of the Dashnak Party immediately rallied the Allied camp.[108] Likewise, a French report of January 1942 highlighted that a series of Allied victories had had an enormous impact. As a result, 'to Armenian and Kurdish eyes, the German does not appear anymore as the invincible soldier or Hitler as the all-powerful Genius.'[109] A British officer serving at Qamishli expressed the same idea:

> The general impression I have gathered is that the leading lights are now definitely convinced that the Allies will win this war and that they are adopting their line of policy accordingly. They see that hostility to Turkey does not fit in with the general scheme of things.[110]

Allied victories, however, were not the only factor that led to this dramatic shift in minorities' perceptions and strategies. Free French and British counter-propaganda efforts were also crucial, in that regard. In a short secret note, the French Special Services in the Levant evaluated the results of Allied endeavours regarding the Kurds. It stated that the British and the Free French launched by early 1941 a 'pro-Kurdish policy seeking to make the Kurdish population pro-Allied'. British expert on Kurdish affairs in Iraq, C.J. Edmonds, was one of the supporters of satisfying Kurdish grievances provided that a 'Kurdish policy' did not preclude British interests:

> If the Germans manage to force their way into the Caucasus . . . they can hardly fail to try to rouse the Kurds with promises of independence . . . Kurdish unrest would carry the encirclement of Turkey still further round to the East and South, and would prepare the way for action towards Iraq.[111]

By early 1942, pro-Kurdish policy had already produced some concrete results; notably the publication of pro-Allied propaganda in the Kurdish newspapers published both in Syria and Iraq; the revelation of the identity of pro-Axis

---

[108] CADN, 1SL/1/V/1097. Délégation Générale de la France au Levant. Beirut, 28 July 1942.
[109] CADN, 1SL/1/V/1097. Sûreté Générale. Ayn al-Arab, 31 January 1942.
[110] TNA, FO 195/2477. Commanding British Security Mission, 13 January 1943.
[111] MEC, Edmonds Collection, Box 3/2. C.J. Edmonds to Sir Kinahan Cornwallis, 26 June 1941.

elements among the Kurdish political parties; and the Kurdish commitment to fighting alongside the French and British if Turkey joined the Axis. Given these first promising fruits, the French Special Services suggested strengthening the ties with the 'loyal elements'.[112] Hence, new pro-Allied magazines such as *Ronahî* (1942–5), *Roja Nû* (1943–6), and *Stêr* (1943–5) appeared in Damascus and Beirut, whereas *Dengî Gêtî Taze* was first published in Iraq in 1943. The Levantine Kurds still availed themselves of other means of expression during the Second World War. Radio programmes aired from Beirut in Kurdish began on 5 March 1941 and consisted of thirty-minute broadcasts twice a week. Although the broadcasts were not very long, news read in Kurmanji dialect reached Turkey, giving both real and symbolic importance to Kurdish language programmes from Radio Levant.[113]

Supporting Kurdish cultural activities did not mean encouraging irredentist claims altogether. Immediately after the British intervention in Iraq in 1941, Shaykh Mahmud submitted a memorandum where moderate grievances were put forward: 1) implementation of the decisions of the League of Nations – local autonomy and education in Kurdish – in their entirety, and their execution on the northern liwas; 2) the maintenance of order and security and the internal administration of the government offices of the liwa of Sulaimaniya should be in Kurdish hands; 3) branches of the agricultural bank should be opened in all the northern liwas.[114] The British response was not enthusiastic, to say the least. In Edmonds' view: 'The Kurds have many grievances, particularly in respect of education and social services ... but administrative autonomy is a different thing'.[115]

Yet British cautiousness with regard to Kurdish claims had further consequences as the world conflict evolved. Mullah Mustafa Barzani escaped from detention in Sulaimaniya and launched a series of attacks against Iraqi police posts.[116] Although the situation in Persian Kurdistan was particularly

---

[112] CADN, BD 237. 'Note on the Kurdish Question', 21 August 1942.
[113] CADN, 1SL/1/V/802. Sûreté aux Armées. Beirut, 28 January 1946.
[114] MEC, Edmonds Collection, Box 3/2. C.J. Edmonds to Sir Kinahan Cornwallis, 25 June 1941.
[115] MEC, Edmonds Collection, Box 3/2. C.J. Edmonds to V. Holt, 16 June 1941.
[116] Stefanie K. Wichhart, 'A New Deal for the Kurds: Britain's Policy in Iraq, 1941–5', *The Journal of Imperial and Commonwealth History*, Vol. 39, No. 5 (2011), pp. 815–31 (here p. 816).

tumultuous after the 1941 Anglo-Soviet occupation of Iran, and British officials in Baghdad were perpetually worried that this instability, and with it Soviet influence, would spread into Iraq, the British wanted to avoid direct intervention in the Kurdish crisis. Alternatively, the embassy urged the Iraqi government to address some Kurdish grievances by appointing more Kurdish officials, providing supplies to Kurdish areas, and developing infrastructure – a Kurdish 'New Deal' in Wichhart's words – in the north. The Iraqi government did make some concessions to the Kurds in 1945, including the Barzan Amnesty Law and the proposal to redraw the administrative boundaries of northern Iraq to better address Kurdish grievances. However, by the summer of 1945, it became clear that the Kurdish 'New Deal' had failed due to the lack of government will, a shift in British priorities with the end of the war and the renewed insurgent activities of Mullah Mustafa.[117]

In Syria, while most of the Khoybun leaders seemed to sided with the British by 1942,[118] after having allegedly received some vague promises about British support for the formation of a Kurdish state,[119] it soon appeared that Britain did not wish to commit to the Kurdish question.[120] Consequently, British hesitation served to discredit its latest promises and alienated a large number of Kurdish leaders in Syria, who were also being courted by Moscow. Indeed, Turkey's relations with the USSR were increasingly strained: Turkey feared Soviet revisionism in the Straits, and the USSR resented, first, Turkey's alliance with the Western powers, and then, after the Nazi invasion, Turkey's neutrality.[121]

As Turkish–Soviet relations worsened by 1944, Moscow revisited its former 'minority policy' in the Middle East. As Taline Ter Minassian has shown, in the early 1920s, the Comintern supported minority networks – mainly Armenians and Jews – to expand the communist presence in the region. Yet, in the 1930s, an 'Arabisation' policy of local cadres was launched

---

[117] Ibid. p. 827.
[118] TNA, FO 195/2477. Political Officer (Damascus) to Beirut Chancery, 14 March 1943.
[119] CADN, 1SL/1/V/802. Colonel Elphinstone to Hamilton. Damascus, 4 September 1942.
[120] CADN, 1SL/1/V/802. Direction Générale de la France Libre au Levant. Beirut, 13 June 1942.
[121] Georges Lenczowski, *The Middle East in World Affairs*, pp. 146–7. Likewise, Mustafa Aydın considers that the main source of apprehension to Turkey during the war was the Soviet Union. Mustafa Aydın, 'Turkish Foreign Policy in the Chaos of War, 1939–45', *Journal of Balkan and Near East Studies*, Vol. 23, No. 6 (2021), pp. 854–71.

in order to gain influence among the 'Arab masses' and establish good relations with the anti-British Arab committees. However, during the Second World War, Moscow sought again to exploit minorities in the Middle East in order to advance its interests in the region. Between 1943 and 1944, the Soviet Union opened two new legations in the Middle East, one in Cairo and the other in Beirut. In addition, Moscow established an Anti-fascist Jewish committee, which was to produce and spread anti-Nazi propaganda.

It is within this context that Soviet propaganda targeting the Kurds and Armenians intensified from 1944 onwards. Slogans proclaiming the Soviet Union as a protector of the oppressed national minorities and the future liberator of the Kurds and Armenians became more and more frequent in the Levant.[122] Behind these activities was the Service for Kurdish-Armenian Affairs, based in Beirut and led by the Consul Rouben Aharonov and two other officials originating from the Soviet Republic of Armenia.[123] In Soviet advocacy of Kurdish nationalism, the accent was on the work done by the Soviet Republic among its own Kurds in reviving the Kurdish language and culture.

Kurdish nationalist sympathy for the USSR in Syria grew considerably as a result of the contacts established with Soviet representatives at the beginning of 1945. Two delegations of Kurdish intellectual and notables from the Upper Jazira paid a visit to Daniel Solod, the Soviet Envoy to Damascus, to whom the Kurdish delegates submitted memorandums and letters.[124] According to French intelligence reports, the main result of these initiatives was a political document endorsed by Molotov, who was committed, in the name of his government, to diplomatic support for any Kurdish nationalist movement tending towards the resuscitation of the 'old Independent State of Kurdistan'.[125] However, this support was subject to certain conditions, notably, the military involvement of the Kurds in Turkey. The Kurdish delegates, conscious of the lack of a clandestine organisation in Turkey capable of organising a revolt, failed

---

[122] CADN, 1SL/1/V/825. Sûreté aux Armées. Beirut, 10 June 1944; CADN, 1SL/1/V/1135. Sûreté aux Armées. Beirut, 9 October 1944.

[123] Taline Ter Minassian, *Colporteurs du Komintern. L'Union Soviétique et les minorités au Moyen-Orient* (Paris: Sciences Po, 1997), p. 291.

[124] CADN, 1SL/1/V/802. Délégation Générale de la France au Levant. Beirut, 8 May 1945.

[125] CADN, 1SL/1/V/802. Délégation Générale de la France au Levant. Beirut, 5 September 1945.

to give a clear response to the Soviet legation, preferring instead to wait for more precise details from Moscow.[126]

Soviet–British competition for leverage among the Kurds was invariably met with an increase of Kurdish activism. First, contact with agents from the USSR left its mark on both the Kurdish nationalist movement and Kurdish nationalism itself. There is de facto evidence of a changing paradigm, which translates as a division between the 'old' and 'new' generations of Kurdish nationalists. Whereas the former can be considered as Westernised elites, the latter, following the example of the new generation of Syrian nationalists, were influenced by populism mingled with certain socialist references and the rhetoric of national liberation movements. In the border town of Amuda, for instance, the 'young' elements established the 'Friends of the USSR' committee in early 1945.[127] In addition, the Kurdish nationalists created a new association, the Kurdish League (Yekbûn û Azadî, 'Unity and Freedom'), to replace the Khoybun. More importantly, Soviet propaganda led Kurdish committees in Iran, Iraq and Syria to establish more direct relations. If these relations existed already by 1944,[128] the establishment of the Kurdish Republic of Mahabad in Iran in early 1946 only reinforced these transborder links.

Second, the Atlantic Charter of August 1941 came to be seen as a commitment of the United States and Great Britain to respecting the right of self-determination of stateless nations such as the Kurds.[129] Prompted by this new development, the Levantine Kurds submitted a memorandum to General De Gaulle and Colonel Elphinstone in September 1942. This document also laid the foundations for a subsequent memorandum submitted to the Allied forces on 30 August 1943.[130] The latter gave a concise review of Kurdish history,

---

[126] Ibid.

[127] CADN, 1SL/1/V/802. Délégation Générale de la France au Levant. Beirut, 7 May 1945.

[128] See correspondence between the two committees in Kadri Cemil Paşa, *Doza Kurdistan. Kürdistan Davası. Kürt Milletinin 60 Yıllık Esaretten Kurtuluş Savaşı Hatıraları* (Ankara: Öz-Ge Yayınları, 1991), p. 159.

[129] Stefanie K. Wichhart, 'Selling Democracy During the Second British Occupation of Iraq, 1941–5', *Journal of Contemporary History*, Vol. 48, No. 3 (2013), pp. 509–36 (here p. 529). On political debates on 'liberal democracy' among Arab circles in Iraq, see Orit Bashkin, *The Other Iraq: Pluralism and Culture in Hashemite Iraq* (Stanford: Stanford University Press, 2008).

[130] SHAT 4H 319/3. 'The Kurds'. Beirut, 19 January 1943.

ethnic boundaries, population, race, language, religion and so on. In the English version, the Allies were reminded of the Wilsonian principles in accordance with which the Treaty of Sèvres of 1920 had provided for the creation of a Kurdish state.[131] Likewise, by late 1943, Kurds in Iraq addressed a similar petition to the United States, a great power seen at once as a guarantor of the Atlantic Charter and as having fewer imperialistic ambitions in the Middle Eastern region than either Britain and France:

> What can the Americans do for the Kurds? They can help to create a new nation out of the present boundaries of the Kurdish speaking section of Turkey, Iran, Syria and Iraq. Isolationism is now dead . . . We do not think that America will leave the weak nations alone as she did after the last war.[132]

Meanwhile, once the issue of Armenian irredentism in Turkey was raised, political organisations in the Armenian diaspora mobilised in support of the Soviet demands. The Armenian National Council of the United States addressed an appeal to the San Francisco Conference for the unification of the lands of Turkish and Soviet Armenia and the return of Armenians to their motherland. Further, the new head of the Catholicos, Gevorg VI, sent a letter to Stalin calling for repatriation of Armenians and the return of Armenian lands in Turkey. Even the major Armenian political party in the diaspora, the Dashnak, long opposed to the Soviet domination of Armenia, seemed now to be willing to help the Soviet authorities to restore and rebuild the homeland.[133]

Thus, during the Second World War numerous Kurdish and Armenian petitions and memos originating from both the Middle East and the diaspora were submitted to all great powers. Taken together, these memos reiterated

---

[133] Ronald Grigor Suny, *Looking toward the Ararat*, p. 169.

[131] For a detailed analysis of territorial claims put forward in Kurdish maps during the Second World War, see Maria O'Shea, *Trapped Between the Map and Reality: Geography and Perceptions of Kurdistan* (London: Routledge, 2004), pp. 172–9. For the complete list of these memos and summaries of their contents, see Wadie Jwaideh, *The Kurdish Nationalist Movement: Its Origins and Development* (Syracuse, NY: Syracuse University Press, 2006), 272–6.

[132] NARA, RG84, UD 2752, Box 13. 'Memorandum'. American Legation (Baghdad), 1 December 1943.

Kurdish and Armenian grievances expressed after the First World War and requested that the great powers accepted the right of peoples to independence. A second important theme in these documents was the 'demonstration' of the importance of Kurdistan and Armenia for the stability of the entire region. Finally, letters and memos were at times accompanied by maps, whose most fundamental function was to bring their territorial claims into view as well as to produce geopolitical visions.[134] Greater Kurdistan and Greater Armenia presented the ethnic and historical boundaries of the respective groups as objective. Yet in both cases they were too irredentist to be taken as serious political proposals by the great powers. In fact, as O'Shea points out, these maps presented elements of a 'persuasive cartography'; that is, a cartography that seeks to change or influence the reader's opinion rather than illustrating a social reality.[135]

Despite all these endeavours, the Kurdish and Armenian committees failed to obtain diplomatic and military support from the great powers. While the British maintained their cautious approach to the Kurdish question, by early 1946, the Soviet government had made it clear to the Allies that what Moscow pursued was an agreement with Turkey regarding the Straits. Although Ankara rejected all Soviet conditions, Turkish authorities could from then on count on a strong ally: on 21 October 1946, the US State Department drafted a memorandum making the case for providing moral, diplomatic, economic and military aid to Turkey against any foreign threats. The foundations were laid for the strengthening of US–Turkish relations in the aftermath of the Second World War as well as for the Cold War.

As we have seen in the previous chapters, the delimitation of the three borders connecting the Turkish–Syrian–Iraqi borderlands throughout the 1920s and 1930s was accompanied by the emergence of a new 'regime of mobility'

---

[134] Judith Tyner, *Principles of Map Design* (New York: The Guilford Press, 2010), p. 37; Gertjan Dijkink, *National Identity and Geopolitical Visions: Maps of Pride and Pain* (London: Routledge, 1996), p. 11.

[135] Maria O'Shea, *Trapped Between the Map and Reality*, pp. 172–9; On this concept, see Judith Tyner, 'Persuasive Cartography', *Journal of Geography*, Vol. 81, No. 4 (1982), pp. 140–4.

along Middle Eastern borders that was the result of both socio-political contestations and negotiations between multiple state and non-state actors, such as peasants, Bedouins, pilgrims, smugglers, travellers, merchants and travel companies. Yet, much as in other parts of the world, the emerging regime of mobility was contingent on international changes.[136]

In that regard, the outbreak of the war had a notorious impact on the international regulatory and surveillance administration system in place, and ultimately upon individual and collective mobility. The strict measures applied to the Baghdad Railway, which served both as international border and as the sole land link between Europe, Syria and Iraq, in order to render the crossing of the Turkish–Syrian border by Axis agents difficult, is perhaps the example that best illustrates this dramatic shift. In a sense, further strict control of travellers' identity and activities on the Taurus Express during the world conflict showcased the multi-layered constructions of borders through mobility – the control of cross-border mobility was not limited to the territorial Turkish–Syrian–Iraqi borderlines; rather, it could also be conducted beyond the international borders – Aleppo, Tel Ziwan, Mosul, Baghdad – and on the move.[137] Although not all border posts were controlled as thoroughly as some train stations along the Baghdad Railway and the Taurus Express itself, state authorities and Allied representatives in the region considered Middle Eastern borderlands as their Achilles' heel.

First, they represented vast areas where state presence was elusive, thus providing a privileged arena for counterintelligence and sabotage activities as well as contraband. Even on the closely monitored Taurus Express and related border posts, the lack of personnel made the system only partially effective. Second, borderlanders maintained transborder contacts that could be exploited at once for the sake of states' own interests, but also against them by foreign powers. Much as in the period between 1918 and 1925, borderlanders developed multiple strategies with regard to different state actors, depending

---

[136] Nina Glick Schiller and Noel B. Salazar, 'Regimes of Mobility across the Globe', *Journal of Ethnic and Migration Studies*, Vol. 39, No. 2 (2013), pp. 188–9.
[137] See Jussi P. Laine, 'The Multiscalar Production of Borders', *Geopolitics*, Vol. 21, No. 3 (2016), pp. 465–82.

on their interests and the evolution of the conflict, including competitors' alliances. Finally, although all major border issues had been settled between Turkey, Iraq and Syria by the 1930s, with the exception of Alexandretta, the context of the war released irredentist claims again.

By analysing the diplomatic correspondence exchanged between Turkey and Great Britain, as well as pointing to other means such as the spread of rumours and the contacts established between Turkish officials and borderland tribal chiefs, this chapter has shown that contrary to traditional accounts of Turkey's commitment to diplomatic settlements after the First World War,[138] the Ankara government deployed significant efforts to obtain territorial gains at the post-war negotiating table. Finally, the chapter has turned its attention to the diplomatic moves deployed by the Armenian and Kurdish nationalist committees, which had remained dormant in Syria and Iraq since the early 1930s, in order to secure the political, financial and/or military support from any of the great powers which would guarantee their territorial independence. Despite some vague promises, neither the Kurds nor the Armenians succeeded in gaining any effective support from the big players involved in the conflict. The chapter has demonstrated that Great Britain's position, in particular, was central in maintaining the international status quo notwithstanding pressing claims advanced by both Turkey and the above-mentioned nationalist committees.

---

[138] Selim Deringil, *Turkish Foreign Policy during the Second World War*; Ahmad, Feroz, *Turkey: The Quest for Identity* (Oxford: Oneworld, 2003).

7

DE-BORDERING AND RE-BORDERING MIDDLE EASTERN STATES

In August 1941, a Free French officer serving at the border post of Tel Kotchek drafted a short, yet telling report on the flaws in the French authorities' system to prevent wheat contraband in the northern fringes of the Syrian–Iraqi border zone.[1] Within the context of food shortages created by the war, Free French and British forces sought to control the production and distribution of basic foodstuffs, such as wheat and barley, in the Allied-occupied territories in the Middle East. As it happened, however, the contraband of food supplies and the speculation on their price became widespread practices across the region during the conflict.[2] The situation in 1941 was especially critical in Syria, where the seasonal harvest of wheat coalesced with the fall of the pro-Vichy government in July, thus paving the way to lose control of Syria's borders, and other illegal cross-border activities. The above-mentioned report, however, pointed to additional factors that

---

[1] SHAT, 4H 297-2. Tel Kotchek Section, 18 August 1941.
[2] In August 1942, for instance, the American Legation at Baghdad reported that 4,000 tons of barley had mysteriously 'disappeared' from the town of Ramadi on the Syrian border. Likewise, a shipment of 6,000 sacks (600 tons) of rice had reportedly been slipped across the frontier into Syria with the connivance of bribed customs officials. NARA, RG84, UD2752, Box 8. 'Report on Economic and Financial Developments'. American Legation at Baghdad, 6 August 1942.

accounted for their deficient monitoring; notably, that the Free French forces lacked human and material resources to chase smugglers and 'fraudsters' who, at times, were even better equipped than the French soldiers themselves.

In reference to the *méharistes* regiments – mounted army units (horse or camel) – serving in the semi-desert areas, the author of the report considered that their role had become irrelevant: 'the era of the horse is over, the car has replaced the animal, and yet we don't have any vehicles'.[3] In sum, without the necessary material, the halting of the ongoing contraband was impossible:

> Currently more than 400 Iraqi camels round up the wheat produced in my district and they even reach Derbessia [nearby the Syrian-Turkish border]. The Iraqis are armed. The fraudsters, having seen me during the day, work now at night. Our Syrian tribes [the Shammar] take advantage of this activity and provide their Iraqi fellows with shelter. There is no time for further hesitation; we need one to two lorries to carry up to ten men. I shall manage to get some mobile units here.[4]

Twenty years after the official establishment of the French Mandate in Syria, the Free French position ironically resembled that of the early 1920s, following the occupation of the country, a likeness that is, nevertheless, misleading. A view from the borderlands reveals that by 1941, the French foothold in the Levant was weaker than ever before. While the French never thoroughly succeeded in controlling Syria's borders– nor wanted to do so, as we have seen earlier in this book – by the late 1930s, border agreements and cooperation with neighbouring countries worked relatively well. The situation had radically changed, as the Free French troops struggled to regain the Levant from the Vichy government and keep it away from intruding German influence. Although they eventually re-conquered the Levant in July 1941, the troops loyal to General de Gaulle were feeble because of their small numbers and the lack of financial and military support from Paris. Against this backdrop, the Free French administration had no other choice but to rely upon British military backing to impose a semblance of authority over Syria and Lebanon.

British involvement in the Levant's affairs, though, did not wind up all prevailing uncertainties around border control in the area. While the

---

[3] SHAT, 4H 297–2. Tel Kotchek Section, 18 August 1941.
[4] Ibid.

Franco-British military intervention helped to sever Syria's links with Nazi Germany, it also presented both opportunities and risks. For one, British presence in Syria brought its forces into touch with Turkey, a neutral country that Britain had constantly attempted to attract towards its sphere of influence since the late 1930s. Sharing now two borders with Turkey after the British re-occupation of Iraq the same year and the Franco-British campaign in Syria, officials in London saw in it a favourable context to exert further pressure on the Ankara government to make Turkey a de facto ally of the British Empire. Nonetheless, if Turkey remained neutral, the Syrian–Turkish border would become an issue of concern within the framework of the Allies' wartime strategy. Indeed, given the mountainous geography of the northern Iraqi districts, the most important flows of 'undesirable' individuals (spies, Axis agents, saboteurs), commodities, propaganda and military materials against the Allies' interests would certainly trespass the Syrian–Turkish border rather than the former. Critically, since it was impossible for the British to stop Syria trade with Turkey, Iran, Iraq and Transjordan,[5] commerce with Turkey meant the possibility to exchange with the Balkans and Germany;[6] that is, the Axis powers and their allies in the Eastern Mediterranean.[7]

As Syria was removed from the 'Navicert' area (Navigational Certificate) in the summer of 1941,[8] in the sense that export licences were required only for goods exported to Syria via Basra, it was decided to rely on the export control system together with military control of the frontiers, as an interim measure to ensure that no export to unwanted destinations could take place.[9]

---

[5] Transjordan became during the war an *entrepôt* for contraband of goods from Egypt and Palestine into Syria.

[6] TNA, FO 371/24595. Damascus, 7 December 1940.

[7] TNA, FO 371/27282. Ministry of Economic Warfare. London, 17 February 1941.

[8] Possession of a 'Navicert' proved that a shipment had already been cleared as non-contraband by the British Ambassadors in the country of origin and allowed the vessel to pass Contraband Control patrols and ports without being searched again.

[9] Before the Franco-British campaign, the British had imposed a tight commercial blockade upon Syria and Lebanon. Yet, fearing that this strict control would ultimately bring the pro-Vichy government in Syria closer to Germany, the former allowed Syria and the US to trade goods of harmless nature, i.e. those unlikely to be sent on to the enemy. TNA, FO 371/27282. Ministry of Economic Warfare. London, 17 February 1941. Despite this relaxation, German encroachment in the Levant increased in spring 1941, leading the War Office to launch, together with the Free French, the 'Operation Exporter' – military occupation – in the Levant.

In the short term, however, it was necessary to coordinate this control system with that which prevailed in British territories and, equally importantly, it required that the Free French as well as the new Syrian government participate in all fields of economic warfare.[10]

British management of external Allied-occupied states or countries under British influence had further effects, however. In the early phases of the Second World War, the British Middle Eastern Command established a small office in Cairo to assist the military chiefs in the solution of a worrying shipping bottleneck: a large flow of goods for the civilian population was arriving at the Eastern Mediterranean ports, averting vessels needed by the military and thus congesting the limited delivering, storage and forwarding facilities aground. Thus the Middle East Supply Centre (MESC), established in April 1941, was given the task of selecting civilian claims on Allied shipping and of advising the Command on how to allocate maritime traffic to the Middle East in such a way as to increase the inflow of military supplies.[11] Although the MESC put in place a system to prioritise the flows of military supplies without depriving the area of the goods deemed essential to the welfare of the civilian population, in its first months MESC policies fatally combined with a series of natural disasters to make the spectre of famine in the region real.

In the spring of 1940, important floods affected many areas in Iraq, while locusts reduced the yield of wheat crops in Mosul, Arbil, Kirkuk and Sulaimaniya districts.[12] Likewise, the harvest and the quality of barley were poorer than in previous years, creating concerns among Iraqi officials about potential shortages of basic foodstuffs.[13] Officials' fears were confirmed some months later, as Iraq registered a significant decline in its harvest, with wheat dropping down to less than a half of the preceding years. More decisively, during the winter of 1941–2, Turkey, Iraq, Syria and Palestine were all affected by severe cold weather, which caused a high rate of livestock

---

[10] TNA, FO 371/27286. Ministry of Economic Warfare. London, 29 August 1941.

[11] For a comprehensive study on the origins, functions, outcomes and shortcomings of MESC, see Martin W. Wilmington, *The Middle East Supply Centre* (Albany and London: SUNY Press and University of London Press, 1971).

[12] TNA, FO 371/24556. 'Iraq: Report on Economic Conditions for May 1940'.

[13] TNA, FO 371/24556. 'Iraq: Report on Economic Conditions for June 1940'.

mortality, particularly among sheep. In Iraq, a heavy snow in the Mosul area in January 1942 covered the grazing pastures for the first time in many years, and the unprecedented cold of that month was followed by a warm, dry spring. To make things worse, winter rains were scant in central Iraq, and poorly distributed in the northern districts.[14] Meanwhile, Iran was reported to face a situation of near famine.

As the agricultural and livestock context in the Middle East seriously deteriorated between 1940 and 1942, smuggling and speculation on wheat further exacerbated the dire economic conditions persisting in the region. Admittedly, contraband was not unheard of in the region. Yet, within the context of the Second World War marked by the blockade of the Mediterranean, controlling the movements of goods and commodities across the overland borders became a key issue, with local, regional and global repercussions. As we have seen in the previous chapter, the Taurus express train was one of the most conspicuous means by which various goods and materials between Syria, Iraq and Turkey were exchanged. Besides the railway, the most important outlet for the passage of smuggled goods between Iraq and Turkey was the Zakho connector, via the village of Fishkhabour. Elsewhere, the main hotbeds of wheat contraband were Tel Abyad, Ras al-Ayn, Derbessia, Qamishli and Tel Ziwan, on the Turkish–Syrian border, and the area stretching between Andiwar and Al Hol, and between Mayadin and Abu Kamal, on the Syrian–Iraqi border.[15]

Owing to the length of land boundaries, however, it was not possible to entirely prevent smuggling. Moreover, wartime conditions required the opening of certain borders to ease the inflows of essential goods and commodities. In other words, through MESC's mechanisms the British encouraged two apparently opposite processes at once: re-bordering the Middle East in the face of Axis allies and neutrals' challenges, on the one hand, while facilitating the circulation of troops, civil and military experts, war materials and basic foodstuffs between British-controlled territories, on the

---

[14] The estimates ranged from 20% in the south to 50% in the north, an average of 35% for the whole country. NARA, RG84, UD 2752. Box 8. 'Background Report on Economic and Financial Developments'. American Legation. Baghdad, 27 May 1942.
[15] SHAT, 4H 297–2. Contraband to abroad. Beirut, 14 May 1941.

other, thereby bolstering regional interdependency – that is, the process of de-bordering.

These parallel yet connected dynamics did not go without creating tensions and contradictions, nor were they the result of an exclusively British agenda; rather, they were shaped by the evolution of the war as well as by local states and borderlanders' strategies. Hence, this chapter makes the case for combining three sub-fields of inquiry to better apprehend how the Second World War impacted upon the Middle East and its borders from a socio-economic viewpoint and the role played by the Turkish–Syrian–Iraqi borderlands and their inhabitants within these major transformations.

First, borrowing from the sociological and historical scholarship that have explored the entanglements between war, state-making, and 'society making', this chapter explores more specifically how the Second World War affected the processes of border-making – here the management of borders – and territorialisation.[16] Indeed, hagiographic studies about MESC underscore the role of this new institution in securing the flows of commodities and goods for both civilians and Allied forces.[17] Meanwhile, Robert Vitalis and Steven Heydemann contend that statistics, census and calculations about consumption habits, for instance, became important tools for making Middle Eastern societies more decipherable.[18] Similarly, E. M. H. Lloyd – the economic advisor to the British Minister of State in Cairo – argued that one of the most important forces driving MESC was the forging of the Middle East 'as a single economic unit'. In that regard, MESC attempted to forge economic coherence through the production and distribution of numerical indicators.[19]

---

[16] Charles Tilly (ed.), *The Formation of National States in Western Europe* (Princeton, NJ: Princeton University Press, 1975); Victor L. Burke, *The Clash of Civilizations: War-Making and State Formation in Europe* (Cambridge, MA: Blackwell, 1997); Steven Heydemann, *War, Institutions, and Social Change in the Middle East* (Berkeley, CA: University of California Press, 2000).

[17] Another British wartime institution dealing with international trade was the United Kingdom Commercial Corporation (UKCC). The UKCC was formed to stop Germany buying essential commodities on the open market by buying them first.

[18] Robert Vitalis and Steven Heydemann, 'War, Keynesianism, and Colonialism: Explaining State-market Relations in the Postwar Middle East' in Steven Heydemann (ed.), *War, Institutions, and Social Change in the Middle East*, pp. 100–45.

[19] E. M. H. Lloyd, *Food and Inflation in the Middle East, 1940–5* (Stanford, CA: Stanford University Press, 1956), pp. 84–5.

Even more so, the activities of the MESC not only set a standard for state-led economic development during the war, but also provided the developmental blueprint for post-war governments to follow.[20] By managing scarcity and encouraging agricultural – and in some cases industrial – growth, MESC helped with the complicity of local states to territorialise the economy, nationally; after all, a necessary development for the consolidation of the state formation process.[21] Critically, state and mandatory authorities sought to increase 'the saturation of space inside the frontier' through the extension of rail and motor roads and the expansion of agricultural production.[22]

These contributions, as valuable as they are, tend to neglect pre-war conditions in the Middle East – i.e. the extant international cooperation, regional trade and mobility regimes – as well as local agency. In that regard, scholars such as Elizabeth Thompson and Sherene Seikaly remind us that both numerical and territorial configurations of the economy were already in play before the war.[23] In addition, the latter highlights that 'the attempts to territorialize the economy as a discrete entity were not born of a managerial imperative to rationalize the colonies and organize the colonized'. Rather, 'it was a result, at least in Palestine, [but Thompson also claims in Syria and Lebanon] of the exigencies of war and political discontent'.[24] In other words, the British had to manage the socio-economic crisis provoked by the war through a delicate balance between austerity and new conceptions of development, health and productivity, which were, at least in part, the result of constant readjustments in the face of failures and (re)negotiations with local actors.

---

[20] James Gelvin, 'Developmentalism, Revolution, and Freedom in the Arab East: The Cases of Egypt, Syria, and Iraq', in Robert H. Taylor (ed.), *The Idea of Freedom in Asia and Africa* (Stanford: Stanford University Press, 2002), p. 76.

[21] Charles Maier, 'Transformations of Territoriality, 1600–2000', in Gunilla Budde et al. (eds), *Transnationale Geschichte* (Göttingen: Vandenhoeck & Ruprecht, 2006), pp. 32–55.

[22] Charles Maier, 'Consigning the Twentieth Century to History: Alternative Narratives for the Modern Era', *American Historical Review*, Vol. 105, No. 3 (2000), pp. 807–31 (here p. 819).

[23] Elizabeth Thompson, 'The Climax and Crisis of the Colonial Welfare State in Syria and Lebanon during World War II', in Steven Heydemann (ed.), *War, Institutions, and Social Change in the Middle East*, pp. 59–99; Sherene Seikaly, *Men of Capital: Scarcity and Economy in Mandate Palestine* (Stanford, CA: Stanford University Press, 2016).

[24] Sherene Seikaly, *Men of Capital*, p. 78.

Moreover, territorialisation and border-making processes in the Middle East, as elsewhere, were also not linear. In that regard, Turkey provides a telling example. As Cyrus Schayegh puts it, Turkey, 'under tremendous economic pressure because of the war, joined the MESC trade exchange and production region and opened up its southern border'.[25] As a result, Aleppo became once again a trade centre for Turkey, Iraq and even Iran. Hence, after two decades of Turkey's political, military and economic efforts to make the Turkish–Syrian border thicker and thus replace Aleppo by Turkish city markets as new regional economic hubs for Southern Anatolia, the impact of the Second World War was reversing this trend to Ankara's dismay.

Second, and related to this last point, drawing from both the works of social historians interested in how the war was experienced 'at home' and the field of borderland studies, the chapter argues in its second section for a reassessment of the 'peripheral' status of Middle Eastern borderlands during the conflict.[26] After all, much like during the interwar years, borderlanders were testing the limits of the state and Western powers in the region by way of pursuing their interests, which, at times, intersected with those of the states, and at times, collided with them. Thus, during the Second World War the diversion of global and regional flows of goods and commodities towards overland routes – railways and roads – together with the role played by local populations in either speeding it up or, on the contrary, slowing it down, led to the growing entanglement of local, regional and global economies as well as increased contacts between borderland dwellers with a variety of state and imperial actors. The chapter will thus problematise in its last section the very notion of contraband to define the most prominent forms of international trade that unfolded across the Turkish–Syrian–Iraqi borderlands outside formal channels. For one, 'informal trade' came to be normalised by the British as

---

[25] Cyrus Schayegh, *The Middle East and the Making of the Modern World* (Cambridge, MA: Harvard University Press, 2017), p. 307.

[26] Harold L. Smith (ed.), *War and Social Change. British Society in the Second World War* (Manchester: Manchester University Press, 1990). On everyday conditions in Turkey during the Second World War, see Murat Metinsoy, *İkinci Dünya Savaşında Türkiye: Savaş ve Gündelik Yaşam* (Istanbul: Homer Kitabevi, 2007); Sabit Dokuyan, 'İkinci Dünya Savaşı Sırasında Yaşanan Gıda Sıkıntısı ve Ekmek Karnesi Uygulaması', *Turkish Studies*, Vol. 8, No. 5 (2013), pp. 193–210.

well as local state authorities to either compensate for the shortage of material and foodstuff supplies – for the former – or avoid the MESC export-import system to boost their respective national economies – for the latter – at times with the connivance of smugglers at work in the border zones.

According to Thomas Cantens, Robert Ireland and Gaël Raballand, even though informal trade is a 'sibling of smuggling', the former includes a series of exchanges that do not comply with current border rules for a variety of motives – absence of border control, avoiding corruption or excessive taxes, among others –, which can be more 'nuanced or benign' than in the case of smuggling activities that merely seek to increase the profit of illicit trade.[27] Precisely because the boundaries between informal trade and contraband are rather ambiguous and fluctuating, Middle Eastern border zones provide a remarkable site to investigate the co-production of the rules adopted by civil servants from different institutions (MESC, state and local authorities), merchants, tribesmen and smugglers during the war.

Blockade in the Mediterranean and its Effects

The first eight months of war did not radically affect the Middle East. The Mediterranean was still open, trade continued to flow from Southern Europe, Britain and America. Eastwards, India could still produce her textiles, rice, tea and spices for consumption by the Middle East. Yet Italy's declaration of war in June 1940, followed by the loss of the French Mediterranean fleet, meant that sooner or later the Mediterranean would be closed as a working trade route: 'at one blow the Middle East became one of the most distant areas of the world to supply from Britain'.[28]

In Egypt, which was a central hub for the distribution of goods and commodities throughout the region, instead of supplies arriving in Alexandria and being distributed by rail to the front, ships coming around the Cape had to discharge at the southern extremity of the Suez Canal in the Red Sea where port and rail facilities were extremely limited.[29] Likewise, one of the

---

[27] Thomas Cantens, Robert Ireland, and Gaël Raballand, 'Introduction: Borders, Informality, International Trade and Customs', *Journal of Borderlands Studies*, Vol. 30, No. 3 (2015), pp. 365–80 (here p. 367).
[28] George Kirk, *The Middle East in the War* (London: Oxford University Press, 1952), pp. 168–9.
[29] E. M. H. Lloyd, *Food and Inflation in the Middle East, 1940–45*, p. 75.

most important economic sectors in the Iraqi borderlands suffered from the spread of the war to the Mediterranean. Indeed, sheep producers and wool merchants from Mosul Province saw how the important French market was closed to them and now they could no longer ship to the United States via the Mediterranean, the cheapest route. As a result, when thousands of bales of Iraqi wool were brought by train to Basra for shipment, local wool prices fell by nearly 50%.[30]

Despite these early worrying symptoms, at first officials in Baghdad saw a window of opportunity in this new context to transform Iraqi overland and sea routes into alternative trade circuits for regional and global trade. Although the export and import of Iraqi as well as Iranian goods via Mediterranean ports had almost ceased due to the interruption of shipping services in the Mediterranean, an internal survey considered that the freight lost on this account could 'be more than compensated by inward and outward traffic to Turkey, Egypt and Palestine' which had been diverted to Basra. Such optimistic prospects were supported by the increase of goods carried by trains from Basra to Turkey in both directions. By early 1941, the Iraqi State Railways were handling nearly 1,000 tons daily and the volume of goods intended for Turkey was so great that all available space on Iraqi railways had been reserved for the following few months. The expansion was overshadowed only by the shortage of rolling stock,[31] which impeded the full exploitation of Iraq's position as an outlet and inlet for ocean-borne traffic to and from Turkey.[32]

Regardless of the flaws of the railway system, total Iraqi trade (in and out) with Turkey increased from 80,000 dinars in 1940 to 4,540,000 dinars in 1941.[33] Therefore, before the establishment of the MESC, Middle Eastern states and local actors had already developed strategies to compensate for the shortages of supply as well as the diversion of prevailing commercial routes. Significantly, in October 1940, Turkey appointed a Commercial Attaché to Baghdad, alongside a trade mission, and established Turkish consulates in

---

[30] TNA, FO 371/24556. 'Iraq. Report on Economic Conditions for June 1940'.
[31] TNA, FO 371/27109/E3025/3025/93. 'Report on the Administration of the Iraqi State Railways'. British Embassy (Ankara) to Foreign Office. Ankara, 16 April 1941.
[32] BCA.030.10.152.77.17. Ankara, 7 June 1941.
[33] *Foreign Commerce Weekly*, 20 February 1943, p. 9.

Basra and Mosul.[34] Two months later, the scarcity of rainfall in Iraq led cattle producers to approach the Baghdad government to arrange pastures for Iraqi cattle with Turkey and Iran across the respective border areas in these neighbouring countries.[35] Likewise, Baghdadi newspapers underlined that not only had Iraq become an essential transit link in Turkey's foreign trade routes, but that Turkey had also begun to purchase large quantities of goods from Iraq itself – owing to the maritime blockade – such as skins, wool, gunny-sacks and petroleum. Meanwhile, rumours conveyed the idea that Iraq would shortly open a consulate in Mardin to boost economic relations between the Turkish–Iraqi borderlands.[36] Within this favourable context, nationalist papers in Baghdad also expressed their desire to foster cultural and diplomatic relations between the two countries.[37]

Moreover, during the first months of the war, the connection Turkey–Iraq via Syria not only secured regional, but also global trade, to a certain extent. Thus, for instance, by December 1940, 3,000 tons of American-owned tobacco were shipped from Turkey by rail and were stored in Iraq. Subsequently, the shipping company arranged for four vessels (Norwegian and Swedish) to load this tobacco at Basra for the United States. While this route was not an ideal solution for it entailed a slower pace when exporting Turkish tobacco overseas, it allowed the United States to keep purchasing oriental leaf tobacco and thus become the second most important customer for Turkish products, right after Germany.[38] Every month, five to eight ships from American ports called at Basra, as well as numerous Japanese, Dutch, British, Greek and British Indian steamers. In the opposite direction, American moving picture films were being imported for distribution to all parts of the Balkans and Middle East, alongside automobile parts, tires, optical instruments, cotton and woollen cloth, chemicals, coffee and tea.[39]

---

[34] *al-Zaman*, 29 October 1940.
[35] *al-Bilad*, 18 December 1940.
[36] *al-Bilad*, 5 December 1940.
[37] *al-Istiqlal*, December 18, 1940; *al-Istiqlal*, December 20, 1940. Quoted in NARA, RG87, Reel 16, 'Current Events'. American Legation at Baghdad, 10 January 1941, pp. 7–8.
[38] The other Turkish agricultural exports to the United States were dried figs, hides and skins, filberts and opium.
[39] Philip Willard Ireland, 'Berlin to Baghdad Up-to-Date', *Foreign Affairs*, Vol. 19, No. 3 (1941), pp. 667–9.

By early 1941, however, the repercussions of trade embargoes and restrictions started to be felt in the Middle East. The context was particularly gloomy in Syria, where the British had imposed a commercial blockade as soon as the pro-Vichy General Henri Dentz took office as High Commissioner in Beirut. The blockade of Syria, however, had unintended consequences for the countries under British influence. Critically, the economic cordon established around Syria and Lebanon deprived Palestine of essential supplies from Syria, causing a rise in the cost of living.[40] In addition to this, the blockade did not succeed in its main objective, which was to better control Syria's commercial relations with a view to bringing them over the British Empire. As it happened, these measures 'while causing hardship and annoyance' to many elements in Syria favourable to Britain were 'in practice being mitigated by smuggling on a large scale across semi-desert frontiers difficult to control'.[41]

Against this background, a relaxation of the blockade was seriously considered by British officials in London in order to divert French Syria commercial relations from Germany, on the one hand, and alleviate the shortage of Syrian supplies to Palestine, on the other.[42] In April 1941, pro-Vichy French authorities seemed prepared to export to Palestine and neighbouring countries 1,000 mules, 10,000 tons of barley, 30,000 tons of wheat, 50,000 sheep and goats and other foodstuff amounting to an aggregate value of £550,000.[43] Eventually, however, there was no deal with Syria, as the Minister of State in Cairo pondered that General Dentz 'does not honour his promises'.[44] By mid-1941, the invasion of Syria seemed all the more necessary, both from military and economic viewpoints.

The main military land operations launched from British-controlled Palestine and Iraq were supported by British and Australian attacks from the air, hitting strategic infrastructures, such as airports and ports in Lebanon.[45]

---

[40] TNA, FO 371/27283/E955/11/89. 'Blockade of Syria'. Minister of State in Cairo, 15 March 1941.
[41] Ibid.
[42] TNA, FO 371/27283. Foreign Office to Beirut, 20 March 1941.
[43] TNA, FO 371/27283. British High Commission (Jerusalem) to Secretary of State for the Colonies (London), 12 April 1941.
[44] TNA, FO 371/27283. Minister of State (Cairo) to Foreign Office, 18 April 1941.
[45] For a detailed description, see Robert Lyman, *First Victory: Britain's Forgotten Struggle in the Middle East, 1941* (Constable: London, 2006), pp. 147–238.

The five-week Franco–British war in the Levant provoked between 10,000 and 15,000 casualties in total; from a strategic perspective, the departure of pro-Vichy officials meant that almost the entire Middle Eastern region was now under virtual British influence. Some weeks later, the Free French accepted the authority in the Levant of the British Middle East Command for all military matters in the region. In return, the former were recognised as the civil power in Syria and Lebanon. Notwithstanding this, the British military command in the Levant had far-reaching consequences.

First, although Free French General Catroux replaced General Dentz, his control of Syrian and Lebanese affairs rapidly looked 'more like a legal fiction than a political reality'.[46] Under pressure from both the British and Syrian nationalists', Catroux recognised the independence of Syria and Lebanon in November 1941. Officials in London made it clear to De Gaulle that the French could not pretend to manage Syrian affairs as they had done before the Second World War. Remarkably, Franco–British tension increased as Major General Sir Edward L. Spears was appointed British Minister to Syria and Lebanon in January 1942. Officially, Spears was entrusted with the mission of serving as liaison between the Free French forces on the one hand, and the British Ninth Army Command and the Minister of State in Cairo, on the other. In reality, however, the so-called 'Spears mission' assumed executive functions which went beyond the limited liaison role originally intended for it.[47]

According to Ariel Roshwald, Spears established a British shadow administration in Syria and Lebanon, and opposed some French civil initiatives that were central within the wartime context. In particular, when General Catroux proposed to set up a wheat office (Office des céréales panifiables or OCP) in spring 1942, which would monopolise the wholesale purchase of grain in Syria, Spears collaborated with the opposition in the Syrian Cabinet in order not to grant any power to Catroux. This was not completely surprising to the French. The first proposal for a centralised supply of cereals for the Middle East had come from London in August 1941. This initiative was

---

[46] Aviel Roshwald, 'The Spears Mission in the Levant: 1941–4', *The Historical Journal*, Vol. 29, No. 4 (1986), pp. 897–919 (here p. 901).
[47] Ibid.

supported by Spears, but it soundly failed.[48] Against this backdrop, Catroux saw in Spears' obstruction a mere act of revenge. In order to dispel the subsequent tension between the two men, a series of meetings were held in Cairo at which it was agreed that ultimate decision-making power was to be reserved for a two-man supervisory team consisting of Catroux and Spears themselves.[49] The role of the OCP, however, became rapidly overwhelmed by a regional agency that came to transform not only the production and distribution of foodstuffs between 1941 and 1945, but also the border regimes in the Middle East altogether: the Middle East Supply Centre or MESC.

The MESC had been set up in April 1941, with its central bureau in Cairo divided into six directorates under the Director General and his deputy: Food, Materials, Medical, Transportation, Programmes, and Administration.[50] The three main functions of MESC as defined in conjunction with London and Cairo were: a) to examine and coordinate the joint resources and civilian requirements in essential commodities of MESC territories, in order to make them as self-sufficient as possible; b) to make recommendations accordingly to the authorities concerned in regard to local production, stocks and distribution; c) to facilitate the transportation of essential supplies within and between the territories.[51] In sum, the MESC licence became the essential condition for any import to any Middle Eastern country that made any demand on the shipping and resources directly controlled by the Allies.

MESC's territorial mandate covered Aden, British Somaliland, Cyprus, Cyrenaica, Egypt, Eritrea, Ethiopia, ex-Italian Somaliland, Iraq, Iran, Lebanon, Malta, Palestine, Saudi Arabia, the Sudan, Syria, Transjordan, Tripolitania, Yemen and the sheikdoms of the Persian Gulf. In other words, MESC dealt with over twenty different governments or administrations and separate fiscal and monetary systems. Although Turkey was not included at first within the MESC scheme, Ankara eventually joined the group of states under British and,

---

[48] Ashley Jackson, *The British Empire and the Second World War* (London: Hambledon Continuum, 2006), p. 166.

[49] Aviel Roshwald, 'The Spears Mission in the Levant', p. 902.

[50] George Kirk, *The Middle East in the War*, p. 174.

[51] E. M. H. Lloyd, *Food and Inflation in the Middle East*, pp. 80–1.

from May 1942 onwards, American regulatory command for two reasons.[52] Firstly, Ankara's trade relations were increasingly affected by British measures and pressures as a result of the consolidation of the British presence in Syria and Iraq. From a British standpoint, the southern borders of Turkey were bound to play an important role as filters in the economic warfare that Allied forces displayed at the borders with enemy-occupied territories or neutral countries, such as Turkey, to avoid that certain goods and materials reached the enemy.[53] Secondly, Turkey's full-scale mobilisation removed large numbers of workers from the farms of Anatolia, thereby reducing cereal productivity. Consequently, Turkey, which until then had been nearly self-sufficient in grains, became an importer and had to look for suppliers in the Middle East, Europe and overseas; scarcity thus paved the way for the rapprochement between Turkey and the Anglo-American agency.[54]

The MESC's endeavours geared towards making local states almost self-sufficient as far as foodstuffs were concerned, eventually entailed expanding its original mission in the Middle East. Crucially, in 1942, there were indications of an outbreak of desert locusts in East Africa, threatening the food and fodder supplies needed by both the East African and Middle Eastern Command. Against this backdrop, the British established the Middle East Anti-Locust Unit, which was attached to the MESC, and started its mission a year later. Areas covered by this unit included the mountains of Persia, Northern Iraq and the borders of Palestine, the remote interior of Saudi Arabia, Yemen, Eritrea, Tripolitania and the Sudan.[55] Troops were provided from India and other countries to lay poison bait. In addition, Russian and British aircraft and personnel were also procured.[56] On top of that, governments and local administrations intensified their normal control measures and exchanged technical information on locusts. Finally, reports about the appearance of swarms and the discovery of

---

[52] To Ashley Jackson, the main reason for America's involvement in the MESC was its growing significance as a provider of civilian and military exports. Ashley Jackson, *The British Empire and the Second World War*, pp. 168–9.

[53] TNA, FO 371/27282/E188/11/89. Ministry of Economic Warfare to Foreign Office. London, 4 January 1941; SHAT, 4H–430/2. 'Economic Warfare: Turkish Borders'. 12 July 1944

[54] Martin W. Wilmington, *The Middle East Supply Centre*, p. 24.

[55] George Kirk, *The Middle East in the War*, p. 184.

[56] TNA, FO 922/107. Draft Telegram. No specific date (1943).

breeding areas were centralised fortnightly at the Anti-Locust Research Centre in London.[57]

As the numbers of Allied troops in the Middle East and social discontent increased, the fight against locusts became a top priority during the war. At his address to the 1942 anti-locust international conference in Cairo, Britain's Deputy Resident Minister of State for the Middle East considered that the threat of a locust plague was the 'gravest concern' in the region:

> [I]n the locust we have an enemy as ruthless as Gengis Khan or Hitler with the same indifference to human rights, equally willing to bring the horrors of famine to men, women and children. Like Hitler, the locust respects no rule of warfare and observers no national frontier.[58]

Likewise, in an RAF planning document, combating locusts was regarded 'as second only in importance to operations against the enemy'.[59] Critically, warfare discourse around locust pests served to justify the widespread use of poison – i.e. sodium arsenate – to destroy the 'enemy'.[60] For many years, the main large-scale method used for controlling locust plagues had been 'trenching'. This involved digging trenches into which the insects would crawl or be driven and then burying them, sometimes after burning them. A variation on trenching was to use barriers of sheets of zinc or tin. By 1942, sheeting was still used on grazing areas where Bedouins objected to the use of poison bait, as they believed it would kill their cattle.[61] In the face of local reticence about the widespread use of poison, the Middle East Anti-Locust Unit developed important means of propaganda for convincing the Bedouins and reluctant state officials to abandon outdated methods in favour of 'modern' means.

---

[57] E. M. H. Lloyd, Food and Inflation in the Middle East, pp. 289–91.

[58] Quoted in Athol Yates, 'The British Military and the Anti-locust Campaign across the Arabian Peninsula, including the Emirates, 1942–5', *The Journal of the Emirates Natural history Group*, Vol. 27 (2019), pp. 22–7 (here p. 24).

[59] TNA, CO 852/400/6. MESC, 'Proceedings of the Conference on Locust Control held in Cairo', 2–3 July 1943.

[60] TNA, FO 370/951/L4220/2/405. 'Locust Poisons'. From International Departmental Committee on Locust Control to Foreign Office, 15 September 1944.

[61] Athol Yates, 'The British Military and the Anti-locust Campaign across the Arabian Peninsula, Including the Emirates, 1942–5', p. 24.

Even though sodium arsenate was indeed a very dangerous poison, Allied experts argued that if the bait was handled correctly, it was quite 'safe'.[62]

It is nonetheless understood that the regional framework imposed by the MESC did not expunge other layers of local cooperation nor was it exempt from flaws and unintended results.[63]

The MESC's Achievements Seen from the Borderlands

According to Robert Vitalis and Steven Heydemann, the assessment of the MESC's main achievements varies depending on the field of intervention under consideration. Thus, while the MESC's policies largely succeeded in restructuring the organisation of agricultural production and food supply during the Second World War, it had 'more limited but still considerable success in shaping the management of foreign trade and promoting the development of import-substituting local industries'.[64] Finally, MESC officials had little fortune in persuading Middle Eastern governments 'to shift from indirect to direct forms of taxation as a response to the dramatic increases in money supply (and inflation) that followed the war-driven influx of Allied resources'.[65]

More importantly, for Robert Vitalis and Steven Heydemann the MESC initiatives were limited by the lack of British resources. As a consequence, the MESC regulatory regime implemented during the Second World War did not correspond entirely with British projects; rather,

> it was the imperative of responding to war-induced shortages, the result of a near total shipping embargo, that created a new demand for domestic regulatory capacity, a demand that originated not with local actors, but among Western forces operating in the Middle East.[66]

---

[62] TNA, FO 370/951/L4220/2/405. 'Locust Poisons'. From International Departmental Committee on Locust Control to Foreign Office, 15 September 1944.

[63] Bilateral meetings between, for instance, Syria and Iraq were maintained in order to coordinate joint campaigns to prevent insects from entering into their respective territories. See TNA, FO 922/241. 'Minutes of Syrian-Iraqi Meeting on the Moroccan Locust held at Damascus'. MESC. Cairo, 2 August 1944.

[64] Robert Vitalis and Steven Heydemann, 'War, Keynesianism, and Colonialism: Explaining State-market Relations in the Postwar Middle East', p. 103.

[65] Ibid. p. 104.

[66] Ibid.

Nonetheless, as Elizabeth Thompson argues, the MESC's policies were not exclusively the result of full-fledged top-down plans. After all, officials had to bargain with local politicians to construct a distinctive mix of state regulatory capacities to ensure an adequate supply of food and to cope with the effects of wartime inflation.[67] This was not only the case in the main urban centres like Damascus or Beirut, but also in the periphery.

In the Turkish–Syrian–Iraqi borderlands, the area that was the most affected by Allied plans was the Syrian Jazira. Taking its cue from previous French endeavours intended to transform the Jazira into a fertile region throughout the 1920s and 1930s, by 1942 the MESC and the OCP made the joint decision to introduce significant amounts of machinery for cultivation of the rain-fed areas of the Jazira, as one of the means of helping alleviate the food shortages in the Middle East that the war had broughy about. Plans to increase agricultural production were accompanied by projects to improve and expand roads and transportation infrastructures. The expected results of such investments were both a speeding-up of transportation and a considerable financial saving.[68] Importantly, the expansion of agriculture in the Jazira alongside the development of infrastructures contributed to fostering the integration of this area into Syrian the economy as well as reaching its national threshold: statistics and reports about Jazira's production, situation of the anti-locust campaigns, evolution of prices, among others, rendered the Jazira a constitutive part of the Syrian territory, after almost two decades of unfinished national integration.[69]

Both agencies acted through the channels of the national and local governments as well as of the large landowners of the Jazira who, conscious of the prevailing high prices of food and thus seeing the possibilities of large revenues, were by and large cooperative:[70]

---

[67] Steven Heydemann (ed.), *War, Institutions, and Social Change in the Middle East*, p. 11.
[68] TNA, FO 371/31447/E5513/207/89. Weekly Political Summary, No. 24, 16 September 1942.
[69] Jordi Tejel, 'Les territoires de marge de la Syrie mandataire: le mouvement autonomiste de la Haute Jazîra, paradoxes et ambiguïtés d'une intégration nationale inachevée (1936–9)', *Revue des mondes musulmans et de la Méditerranée*, Vol. 126 (2009), pp. 205–22.
[70] Elizabeth Thompson, 'The Climax and Crisis of the Colonial Welfare State in Syria and Lebanon during World War II', in Steven Heydemann (ed.), *War, Institutions, and Social Change in the Middle East*, pp. 75–6.

Syria was the first country in the Middle East to import agricultural machinery by lend-lease channels. The machinery itself was leased out to carefully chosen farmers and the Tractor Section itself operated on the advice of an Advisory Farm Machine Board, consisting of French, British, American, Syrian and Lebanese Representatives.[71]

While before the outbreak of the Second World War, the quantity of agricultural machinery in Syria was negligible, by the late 1949 there were 600–700 tractors and 350 combine harvesters in the Jazira, mostly imported during the war. Statistics are also available for the cultivated acreage of the Jazira in 1943 (543,600) and 1946 (783,000), respectively.[72] The pro-French newspaper *Le Matin* enthusiastically reported in 1943 that, according to local authorities in Aleppo, the wheat crop outlook was bright and made public statistics showing that the following areas would be able to supply the following quantities to the OCP: Jazira 100,000 tons, the Euphrates Valley 200,000, Aleppo area 50,000, other Syrian districts 100,000. Those quantities were stated to be more than enough for the needs of Syrian and the Lebanon for the ensuing year.[73]

Landholders' close relations with Allies and state authorities, however, could at times provoke competition between local leaders. By 1942, for instance, as the Syrian Prime Minister initiated his 'wheat tour', accompanied by British and French representatives, it became obvious that an uneasy situation had arisen in the Arab Pounar area amongst the Barazi tribal confederation, where the high-handed methods of the Basrowi family, who had been given a virtual monopoly for the collection of wheat, had brought them into conflict with their rivals, the Shahin, and intensified the animosity between the two clans. After a series of negotiations between the British and the local notables, measures were suggested for securing the loytalty of the Shahin family.[74]

---

[71] TNA, FO 922/187. 'Increased Cereal Production in Northern Syria'. Spears Mission. Beirut, December 1944; TNA, FO 922/187. Section 'Machines'. Qamishli, 8 December 1944.

[72] Hedley V. Cooke, *Challenge and Response in the Middle East: The Quest for Prosperity* (New York: Harper & Brothers, 1951), pp. 167–8.

[73] *Le Matin*, 13 May 1943.

[74] The nominal leader of the influential Barazi Confederation around Maqtele and Arab Pounar railway station was the head of the Alaudin sub-tribe, Mustapha ibn Shahin. Yet, the Shahins had a blood feud with another sub-tribe within the Barazi, the Kitkan, whose

The expansion of cultivated lands in the Syrian Jazira had other unintended effects: namely, an important wave of immigration which originated not only from nearby Syrian villages and towns, but also from south-eastern Anatolia. Indeed, as Şevket Pamuk points out, Turkey, while remaining neutral until 1945, pursued a policy of full-scale mobilisation during the Second World War.[75] If neutrality avoided the devastation of the country and its occupation by either of the two camps, full-scale mobilisation had profound effects on its economy between 1942–5. Even though the conscription of men was partly compensated by women in the agricultural sector, wartime mobilisation had an adverse effect on harvests, especially of cereals: 'Turkey, which does not normally import grains, needs barley urgently for bread adulteration. Turkey's own production will be poor because of the million men she has under permanent mobilization'.[76]

As in Syria and Iraq, the price of foodstuffs climbed rapidly and the provisioning of the urban areas emerged as a major problem for the government. As shortages in the large urban centres became more severe, the government allowed for the market sale of wheat by those producing above certain limit. As in Syria and Iraq, the new policy also mostly benefited the medium-sized farmers and large landowners, as well as those who could evade government demands. Although Pamuk considers that 'small, subsistence-oriented producers, who could not take advantage of higher market prices assumed the heaviest burden of government policies', he also contends that the rural poor were better off than their urban counterparts, because basic foodstuffs were readily accessible to them.[77]

Shaykh was Mazraat Sufi. When the British first reached this district in 1918, they favoured the Basrowi over the Shahin. After the arrival of the French in the Jazira, however, the latter leaned towards the Shahin. When the British were deployed in the area in 1941, the Kitkan seemed to regain influence owing to British support. TNA, FO 371/31447/E5513/207/89. Weekly Political Summary, No. 24, 16 September 1942.

[75] Şevket Pamuk, *Uneven Centuries: Economic Development of Turkey since 1820* (Princeton, NJ: Princeton University Press, 2018), pp. 181–2.

[76] NARA, RG84, UD2752, Box 8. 'Report on Economic and Financial Developments'. American Legation at Baghdad, 6 August 1942.

[77] Şevket Pamuk, *Uneven Centuries*, p. 182.

Reasonable as it might sound, a closer look at borderlands dynamics suggests a different view of the wartime experience in these rural areas. While important numbers of peasants travelled to the urban areas for temporary, seasonal work, the rural poor populating Turkey's southern borderlands, mainly Kurds, looked towards Syria as an alternative to hardship. In that regard, the spring of 1943 seems to have been a particular turning point, as thousands of Kurds entered illegally into the Upper Jazira. In most cases, these migrants were depicted as 'miserable individuals', hoping to find a better life in the Jazira region or 'at least some bread'.[78] Among these clandestine migrants, there were groups of 'helpless' women and children wandering unaccompanied along the border area.[79] Meanwhile, local informants reported that dozens of people at Savur (north of Mardin) had died after having eaten grass, exclusively, for a long period of time.[80]

Although the majority of Kurdish migrants aimed at permanently settling in the border zone under the protection of Syrian local tribes, others moved southwards.[81] Admittedly, 'Turkish' migration into Syria took on such proportions that the authorities of the Mardin Vilayet organised a population census to evaluate the number of individuals having left the region since January 1943. According to this census, about 18,000 people had migrated in only three months.[82] The increase of Kurdish migrants attracted by Jazira's 'prosperity' inevitably had an effect on the Syrian side of the border. On the one hand, some of these migrants provided an unexpected (and cheap) labour force that could play a significant role in the development of Jazira's agriculture production as well as in the road construction plans. On the other hand, the settlement of further Kurdish elements in the Jazira entailed some risks for the French: the dramatic increase of Muslim (Kurdish and Arab) elements in the border zone to Christians' detriment. For the Free French, this

---

[78] CADN, 1SL/1/V/2202. Special Services at Deir ez-Zor to General Delegate to the Syrian Government (Damascus), 8 April 1943.
[79] CADN, 1SL/1/V/2202. Special Services at Qamishli, 26 March 1943.
[80] CADN, 1SL/1/V/2202. Special Services at Qamishli, 1 April 1943.
[81] CADN, 1SL/1/V/2202. Special Services at Deir ez-Zor, 25 March 1943.
[82] CADN, 1SL/1/V/2202. Special Services (Deir ez-Zor) to General Delegate to the Syrian Government (Damascus), 8 April 1943.

state of affairs raised the question of deciding what to do with these newcomers: should they facilitate or impede this migration?[83]

The answer to this question became a sensitive issue, since some French officials suspected the Turkish authorities of purposively expelling poor people and even prisoners into Syria.[84] Moreover, even though the Syrian gendarmes captured illegal migrants and brought them to the Turkish border, most of them returned to Syria either voluntary or on the encouragement of the Turkish authorities.[85] Therefore, some French officials came to the conclusion that the aim of this policy was twofold: diminishing the burden of poor rural populations in Turkey, on the one hand, and increasing the numbers of Turkish citizens in the Upper Jazira in the event of a territorial annexation there, on the other. Such concerns were also shared by certain Arab nationalists in Damascus, who considered that the already settled Kurdish populations living in northern Syria were generally 'hostile' to the Syrian government.[86]

Despite the suspicions of the French and Syrian nationalists, it seems clear that poverty was the main driver accounting for this sudden migratory movement. In his ethnographic study of the Turkish–Syrian border zone, Ramazan Aras also supports this view: 'Contrary to the devastating desperation in Turkish side, people remembered the other side, the French Mandate Syria as prosperous one'.[87] Thus, according to narratives and stories gathered in the borderlands, in those years 'thousands of people living in the border regions and near cities were traveling and visiting their relatives and friends in the Syrian side in order to receive financial aid (food, grains, and other livelihoods) to survive'. Throughout his interviews, 'the repeated narrative of *nanê ceyî jî tunebû* (there was not even bread made of barley) to survive indicates the level of scarcity in the region'. Against this backdrop, many interviewees explained how 'many girls were married to a relative or someone

---

[83] Ibid.
[84] CADN, 1SL/1/V/2202. Special Services at Qamishli, 13 March 1943.
[85] CADN, 1SL/1/V/2202. Special Services at Qamishli, 26 March 1943.
[86] CADN, 1SL/1/V/2202. Sûreté aux Armées at Qamishli, 20 April 1944.
[87] Ramazan Aras, *The Wall: The Making and Unmaking of the Turkish–Syrian Border* (London: Palgrave Macmillan, 2020), p. 70.

from the Syrian side'.[88] Furthermore, the intensifying relations and kinship in those years would also play an immense role in increasing the number of legal and mostly illegal border crossings and diverse forms of other relations between people dwelling on both sides of the border. Crucially thus, cross-border mobility and the preservation of cross-border kinship networks during the Second World War decisively contributed to the de-bordering process of the Syrian–Turkish border from the bottom.

Another major impact of the war in the Middle East was the presence of very large numbers of Allied troops and the demands they placed upon local economies for accommodation, labour, food, and in the case of Palestine, the production of essential military supplies. While Palestine became the most important training ground for British and Allied forces during the war in the Middle East, the mounting foreign military presence was also felt, for better or for worse, in the Syrian–Iraqi borderlands.[89] Like in Palestine, the deployment of British forces in the northern districts of Iraq stimulated business, and large engineering contracts related to the construction of fortifications, roads and bridges attracted labour from the most remote villages. Only a few months after the re-occupation of Iraq, there were up to 20,000 labourers engaged in road and excavation works in the northern borderlands. The British army's presence also demanded compensation and rent for lands occupied around Kirkuk and Arbil.[90] Hiring local inhabitants within the war context enabled, in fact, several objectives to be met, from the strictly defensive to the propagandistic:

> The proposed field fortifications would provide employment where it was most needed, and there was no propaganda better than a full belly. Moreover, if suitably handled, these same people might afterwards prove most useful in providing shelter for the Special Officers leading guerrilla forces in the event of a withdrawal ... It was the first chance the Kurds had of full employment at a time when the cost of living was rising fast. It was also sound propaganda for the Allied cause.[91]

---

[88] Ibid. pp. 70–1.
[89] Daphna Sharfman, *Palestine in the Second World War: Strategic Plans and Political Dilemmas* (Eastbourne: Sussex Academic Press, 2014), p. 49.
[90] TNA, FO 624/25/507–1. Political Adviser. Mosul, 8 December 1941.
[91] Fieldhouse (ed.), *Kurds, Arabs, and Britons: The Memoir of Wallace Lyon in Iraq, 1918–44* (London: I. B. Tauris, 2002), pp. 222–3.

This quote points nevertheless to an undesirable effect resulting from massive Allied presence across the region: a significant expansion in the money supply and the very high rates of inflation that persisted throughout the war. Indeed, a memorandum on the economic situation in Iraq elaborated in 1942 reported that prices of essential commodities had risen on average by 200% to 300% since 1939.[92] Although the decline in goods in circulation had a significant impact on inflationist tendencies, British expenditures occupied a central position in accounting for the high inflation in Iraq: between 1941 and 1943 alone, the British spent £61.5 million on military tasks.[93] In addition, the potential positive impact of 'British Keynesianism' was unevenly experienced in the borderlands. While Kirkuk and Arbil benefited from Allied forces' presence, more peripheral districts remained aloof to this fragile economic take-off. Furthermore, the overwhelming escalation of cereal prices throughout the region encouraged landlords and merchants to profit from the export opportunities this offered, thus contributing not only to the inflationary pressures within Iraq by creating scarcity, but in the northern borderlands, 'creating real hardship, amounting to starvation'.[94]

The same ambivalent impact of Allied troops' presence could be observed in the Syrian Upper Jazira, and its main economic hub: Qamishli. Despite not being the administrative centre of the Upper Jazira, warehouses, customs houses and other official buildings had by the late 1930s already bestowed an urban semblance upon Qamishli. Subsequently, the British occupation of the Levant in 1941 opened the door to the deployment of hundreds of British soldiers and Transjordanian forces in northern Syria to monitor the Turkish–Syrian border. Besides these troops, Free French officers as well as the Syrian Gendarmerie, who increasingly took on the responsibility for internal affairs in the Jazira, were also present in the border zone.

As a result, new recreation venues, such as hotels, cafés, bars and a casino, attracted not only military personnel, but also merchants and local notables from the surrounding small towns. As in Palestine, the sudden increase of

---

[92] TNA, FO 624/28. 'The Economic Situation in Iraq'. British Embassy. Baghdad, 1942.
[93] Ashley Jackson, *Persian Gulf Command: A History of the Second World War in Iran and Iraq* (New Haven and London: Yale University Press, 2018), pp. 238–9.
[94] Charles Tripp, *A History of Iraq* (Cambridge: Cambridge University Press, 2007), p. 116.

foreign soldiers led to some public order issues, such as frequent quarrels between drunken soldiers, and a previously unknown phenomenon in the area, such as prostitution. Most prostitutes arrived, however, in Qamishli as 'artists' (foreign female performers), taking advantage of new transport facilities such as the Baghdad Railway. The category of 'artist' was nevertheless contested among local officials, and it seems that there were some ambiguities in certain instances.[95] To British officer Richard Pearse, however, there was no doubt about their 'real' status. While describing the presence of foreign women on the Taurus Express, he argued that they were essentially 'prostitutes' who travelled to the 'brothels on Syria's New Jerusalem, the thriving steppe town of Qamishli, managed to move about the train and get into the first-class compartments, to book future business'.[96]

Finally, the renewed interest of Allied and state authorities for border and customs control to establish an efficient regulatory regime that would guarantee sufficient food supplies for military personnel and civilians, posed new challenges to all parties as the evolution of the war brought together a variety of state actors (local and Western) into the border zones with, at times, conflicting interests.[97] Indeed, on a diplomatic level, after the British occupation of Iraq and the Levant, tensions flared up between Turkey and the Free French, on the one hand, and the British and the Free French, on the other, regarding the recognition of precisely who the legitimate authorities were at the Syrian borders adjacent to Turkey and Iraq, respectively, and thus the validity of pre-war border regimes.

While Great Britain recognised the Free French and extended de jure recognition to Syria and Lebanon, Turkey and the neighbouring Arab states were slow in acknowledging the new reality as well as Syrian and Lebanese independence. In July 1941, Ankara informed London that the Turkish

---

[95] On the ambiguous status of foreign female performers in Syria and Lebanon, see Camila Pastor De Maria Campos, 'Performers or Prostitutes? Artists during the French Mandate over Syria and Lebanon, 1921–46', *Journal of Middle East Women's Studies*, Vol. 13, No. 2 (2017), pp. 287–311.

[96] Richard Pearse, *Three Years in the Levant* (London: Macmillan & Co. Ltd, 1949), p. 109.

[97] TNA, FO 371/27286. 'Suggestions for Organising Economic Warfare'. Ministry of Economic Warfare. London, 8 September 1941.

government could not deal with the Free French because Turkey was still in official relations with Vichy. Officials in Ankara reckoned that if they dealt locally with any Free French authorities, they would lay themselves open to converse demands on the part of Germany that they should deal with Vichy and other puppet governments in the occupied territory since they were still in official relations with their real government.[98] Consequently, the Turkish government refused to recognise the validity of any passports or other documents issued by the Free French.[99]

Turkish reluctance to recognise the new French authorities in Syria also had an impact on warfare demands. Thus, for instance, when Turkey requested up to 1,000 mules from the British in 1942, after various efforts to obtain these elsewhere, the latter discovered that they could be provided from Syria. A difficulty then arose as the Free French wanted to barter the mules for sheep. Yet, since the Turks did not recognise the Free French, it was necessary to come up with some informal provisions: the mules were furnished by the British by way of an 'armament credit' provided by the Middle East Command, thus bypassing the Free French authorities.[100] Informality also worked in the opposite direction. Even though Turkey did not recognise Syria for the duration of the war, as Turkey integrated the MESC scheme and thus opened its southern borders to meet Allied forces' needs, de facto Turkish recognition of the Free French authorities became a reality.

Similar problems appeared between occupied Syria and Iraq, at first, as the Iraqi government found it embarrassing to even receive a Free French Liaison Mission, since they feared that by doing so, they were committing themselves publicly to some measure of recognition of the Free French position in Syria. The Iraqi government thus enquired about which authorities the frontier officials should communicate with, in accordance with the Iraqi-Syrian 'Bon Voisinage Agreement' of 1937.[101] British representatives in

---

[98] TNA, FO 371/27332/E3884/241/89. 'Turco-Syrian Relations'. British Embassy (Ankara) to Foreign Office, 15 July 1941.

[99] TNA, FO 371/27332/E4270/241/89. 'Turco-Syrian Frontier'. Minister of State (Cairo) to Foreign Office, 30 July 1941.

[100] TNA, FO 371/33284/R2179/2/44. War Office to Foreign Office, 2 April 1942.

[101] TNA, FO 371/27359. Minister of State (Cairo) to Foreign Office, 19 August 1941.

Baghdad suggested using pre-war 'machinery' for routine matters and settlement of tribal cases involving both countries, rather than going through diplomatic channels. As far as any military issues were concerned, British military commanders on the Iraq–Syria frontier could settle directly with Turkish and Iraqi authorities.[102]

The British advice to Turkish and Iraqi governments making the case for the 'normalisation' of relations with Syria through informal arrangements was not completely selfless. The War Office and the Middle East Command had pushed for the re-admission of Syria and Lebanon to the sterling area for pragmatic reasons: that is, enlisting the complete cooperation of Syria in the economic war waged by the Allies. For one thing, Syria produced commodities of high importance in economic war and her geographical position, particularly her long land frontier with Turkey, presented the constant danger of these commodities reaching the enemy.

Free French recognition of Syrian independence added a new layer to the conundrum of border control along the Turkish–Syrian–Iraqi borderlands. Critically, the Syrian government also wished to have a say in the protection of Syria's borders and customs control issues, as a way of exerting its sovereignty throughout the entire Syrian territory. After some negotiations, Syrian gendarmes were allowed to participate in the surveillance of the Taurus Express and the management of the customs offices. Yet, the diversity of authorities, together with the persistent mistrust among them, provoked flaws in combatting contraband and prevention of the passage of Axis agents across the shared borders.[103] The resulting shortcomings in border control were nevertheless part of a wider dynamic imposed by wartime constraints: namely, the increasing entanglement between formal and informal international trade.

Between Formal and Informal International Trade

Borderlanders did not develop a single or definite strategy in the face of the MESC and state officials' interventions in the Turkish–Syrian–Iraqi border zones intended to cope with the shortages of food supplies with the outbreak of the Second World War. Like in the interwar period, many along the border

---

[102] TNA, FO 371/27359. Baghdad to Foreign Office, 6 September 1941
[103] CADN, 1SL/1/V/33. Border post at Ras al-Ayn, 29 August 1944.

alternatively engaged with and evaded the state as well as wartime agencies, such as the MESC, in order to pursue their personal and financial interests. By and large, big landowners saw in MESC policies an opportunity to gain social and economic centrality in the periphery. Similarly, cross-border traders, including smugglers and merchants, also adjusted their practices to new conditions. After all, if the MESC's experts and state officials gathered data, elaborated statistics and suggested policies for diminishing economic and social risks both regionally and globally, borderland dwellers proved to be equally aware of regional and globalisation dynamics by comparing the benefits of national and international trade policies. Arguably, informal traders and their intermediaries were 'just as anxious to anticipate their lives as the other who [were] formal and [had] formalized their risks into their accountabilities'.[104]

Indeed, shifting conditions along the shared borders, together with the evolution of the conflict prompted necessary adjustments of borderlanders' strategies. In the early 1930s, the town of Ayn Diwar, for instance, had largely benefited from legal trade and contraband activities as well as the presence of French soldiers. However, the economic development of Qamishli thanks to its closeness to the Turkish town of Nusaybin and the presence of the Baghdad Railway had slowly relegated Ayn Diwar as a commercial hub in the tri-border area. During the war, the removal of the French troops from Ayn Diwar, and the strengthening of customs control in the caza of Tigris by the Syrian authorities made 'merchants and smugglers leave the area and settle either in Qamishli, Amuda or Derbessia'. Although cross-border trade did not fade away completely, the variety of smuggled goods through this border town was much more limited than in the past.[105]

Smuggling between Syria and Iraq also increased to a considerable extent during the Second World War. For the most part, the traffic along the Syrian–Iraqi border consisted of gold and sheep. While the latter was closely related to the rise of meat consumption across the region during the war, the former was due to a greater demand for gold in Syria than in other Middle

---

[104] Thomas Cantens, Robert Ireland, and Gaël Raballand, 'Introduction: Borders, Informality, International Trade and Customs', *Journal of Borderlands Studies*, p. 374.

[105] CADN, 1SL/1/V/33. Border post at Ayn Diwar, 28 July 1944.

Eastern countries, owing to the lack of confidence in the local currency and the changing political conditions in that country.[106] On the Turkish–Iraqi border, random checks on the Mosul–Zakho and Mosul–Dohuk roads only confirmed that smuggling between Turkey and Iraq was extensive. Moreover, British officers considered that to make a satisfactory check on the Turkish frontier was in fact impossible as there were hundreds of crossing points, and, more importantly, smugglers adapted their practices to the changing conditions. In that sense, the use of local knowledge vis-à-vis geography allowed smugglers to avoid 'any patrol which [was] known to be on the frontier'.[107] That was the case not only in the rugged mountains separating Turkey and Iraq, but also at Faysh Khabur, where the borders of Turkey, Syria and Iraq meet. Here, traffickers used the waters of the Tigris to cross the border and smuggle their goods without being hassled.[108] While these policy failures questioned the efficiency of borders as a monitoring institution, smuggling and the informal movement of commodities along the Turkish–Syrian–Iraqi borderlands were not limited to state-defined contraband.

First, as in the past, these two phenomena were entangled with what Eric Tagliacozzo frames as the 'political economy of corruption'.[109] The new regional political economy in the Middle East created and enhanced opportunities for smuggling, channelling such flows in new directions. Indeed, Turkish archival sources reveal that the contraband, cross-border raids and informal cross-border flows along the Turkish–Iraqi border were partly facilitated by the connivance of border and local authorities on the Turkish side. As we have seen in an earlier chapter, poverty, isolation and the difficult climatic conditions made the Eastern provinces the least popular places of appointment for Turkish state employees. As the consequences of the Second World War were increasingly felt in southern Anatolia, gendarmes' dysfunctional behaviour

---

[106] TNA, FO 922/317. 'Smuggling from and to Syria'. Controller of Foreign Exchange. 31 January 1945.
[107] TNA, FO 624/27. 'Iraq Censorship'. Deputy Controller. Baghdad, 4 November 1942.
[108] TNA, WO 201/1423. Couldrey to General Staff Intelligence, 9 December 1943.
[109] Eric Tagliacozzo, 'Smuggling in the Southeast: History and its Contemporary Vectors in an Unbounded Region', *Critical Asian Studies*, Vol. 34, No. 2 (2002), pp. 193–220 (here p. 194).

became the main subject of complaints among the borderland dwellers in the Hakkari and Mardin provinces.¹¹⁰ Against this backdrop, some officials suggested certain measures to reverse the situation. In 1943, the First Inspector General Avni Doğan wrote a long and detailed report where he underscored the corruption and ill treatment of local populations. Concretely, Doğan asked the government to appoint honest and capable people to the Eastern provinces, as well as to improve their salaries in order to eradicate 'bad practices' such as theft and accepting bribes from smugglers.¹¹¹

Such 'bad practices' did not solely affect Turkish citizens inhabiting the borderlands. According to French records, Turkish soldiers took advantage of the fluid context created by the lack of a clear border authority in Syria to steal important numbers of cattle on the Syrian side of the border, too. On 23 November 1941, for instance, three soldiers serving at the border post of Nusaybin entered into Syria and seized a herd of 190 sheep from the villagers of Hilalie (3km west of Qamishli). Only four days later, another group of Turkish soldiers stole 100 oxen, 150 goats and 100 sheep from local farmers at Tel Abyad. In December of the same year, Turkish regulars attempted to seize some flocks of sheep from villages near Derik. The subsequent inquiry revealed that, in addition to these raids, Turkish soldiers also troubled border dwellers with threats and bribes. As these episodes were recurrent, French officials considered that these acts could only be perpetrated with the complicity of their superiors, who, most likely, would 'get some benefit, too'. French suspicions were supported by evidence: while in some instances the stolen cattle were effectively returned to their Syrian owners, the numbers of recovered animals were 'always' inferior.¹¹²

Official corruption was mirrored on the other side of the Turkish border. In a secret note drafted by Lieutenant General Holmes from the Ninth Army

---

¹¹⁰ Respectively, BCA, 490.01.998.856.1, p. 51; BCA, 490.01.512.2005.1, 14 February 1944, p. 4.

¹¹¹ Mehmet Bayrak, *Açık-Gizli/Resmi-Gayrıresmi Kürdoloji Belgeleri* (Ankara: Öz-Ge Yayınları, 1994), p. 253.

¹¹² CADN, 1SL/1/V/2131. 'Border Incidents Involving Turkish Soldiers'. Border post at Qamishli, 1 March 1942; CADN, 1SL/1/V/2131. 'Border Relations'. Special Services at Qamishli, 16 February 1942.

to the Free French, the British official lamented that the latter showed little concern in the face of the widespread phenomenon of corruption among French, Syrian and British personnel serving in the border area:

> You consider that corruption and contraband are a sort of local hobby and that it is worthless for us to attempt to end with local customs and traditions. I will not debate on this . . . Nevertheless, I consider that corruption among officials who facilitate the contraband of drugs and arms should be addressed . . . Our soldiers are threatened by either the inaction of the Syrian Gendarmerie or the light punishments inflicted to our soldiers: sabotage, theft of arms or military material, corruption of English officials. It is not a matter of isolated instances, but rather frequent cases in all our sub-sections.[113]

The situation was similar in northern Iraq, where some names of British officials were 'on the lips of many' because they were said to be corrupt and were 'getting bribes on a very large scale, on dealing with contractors'.[114]

Second, the MESC's mission and wartime constraints also favoured, directly and indirectly, practices from a variety of state (government officials and Allied staff) and non-state actors (individuals, merchants and tribesmen) that revolve around the notion of 'informal trade', as suggested in the introduction to this chapter. Crucially, international 'informal trade' is what inevitably led to a both top-down and bottom-up process of de-territorialisation in the Turkish–Syrian–Iraqi borderlands. This was especially the case during the general shortage of meat from 1942 onwards. Indeed, the arrival of thousands of soldiers in the Middle East during the Second World War had a tremendous economic and environmental effect on the region. According to a British report, by 1943, the average daily army ration was from eight to ten ounces according to category and there were well over 1,000,000 soldiers in the Middle East. As a result, the extra consumption of meat was enormous.[115] After two years of the massive slaughtering of cattle, the majority of the territories which were self-supporting before the war were now obliged to

---

[113] SHAT, 4H 311–4. 'Very Secret', 4 July 1943
[114] TNA, FO 624/27. Political Adviser (Mosul), 1 July 1942.
[115] TNA, FO 922/50. 'Livestock'. MESC, Paiforce, 17 March 1943.

resort to meatless days in order to avoid seriously affecting the cattle population in the region.[116] Thus, despite the important flows of cattle from Iraq and Syria toward other members of the MESC area, very quickly the surpluses of sheep and goat could not satisfy the insatiable demand for fresh meat, thereby creating anxiety among British officials in London and Cairo.[117]

Within this context, all eyes turned towards Iraq. Prior to the war, Iraq was an important factor in the livestock trade not only in the Middle East, but also as an essential provider of skins, hides and wool for the global market. The average official exports of Iraqi cattle to neighbouring territories between 1935 and 1940 numbered 280,000 sheep and goat. In 1941 alone, Iraq exported 370,000, of which three per cent were goat.[118] According to a British survey, it was estimated that in the autumn of 1941 Iraq had the following: sheep (7,500,000), goats (2,800,000), cattle (800,000), buffaloes (90,000), horses (80,000), mules (20,000) and donkeys (300,000).[119] As the British re-occupied Iraq in May 1941, this country and in particular the Mosul Province were expected to play an important mission:

> The Iraq government has been repeatedly told by the British and American representatives at Baghdad that its greatest contribution to the Allied war effort would be to set its own economic house in order, keeping its own populace decently fed, housed and clothed, and giving its surplus supplies to its less fortunate neighbours. Iran, Turkey, Syria, the Lebanon, and the Persian Gulf states all are suffering severe shortages of foodstuffs which should be in oversupply in Iraq; by making available its surpluses in these foods to its hungry neighbours Iraq could make its best contribution to the war effort.[120]

---

[116] Ibid.
[117] During the Second World War, the USSR greatly increased the quantity of livestock it was taking from the northern districts of these countries, thereby amplifying the problem provoked by the shortage of meat, regionally. TNA, FO 922/50. 'Livestock Population of the Middle East Territories'. MESC. Cairo, 10 August 1942.
[118] TNA, FO 922/199. British Embassy (Baghdad) to MESC (Cairo), 25 November 1943.
[119] TNA, FO 922/74. 'Livestock Survey–Iraq'. British Embassy (Baghdad) to MESC (Cairo), 16 October 1943.
[120] NARA, RG84, UD2752, Box 10. American Legation (Baghdad), 26 April 1943.

Notwithstanding this, Iraqi authorities proved to be less co-operative than expected. As the demand for meat increased in Palestine and other Middle Eastern countries, British pressure on the Iraqi government, mutton merchants and pastoralist tribes also intensified. Yet, in the face of the high death rate among Iraqi livestock during the winter of 1941–2 and the large demand occasioned by the presence of the British forces, the Iraqi government prohibited the export of sheep and cattle from Iraq, as well as meat, including poultry and fish.[121] While at first the Central Supply Committee accepted Iraqi's decision, the arrival of additional troops into Palestine and the Levant strained Allied relations with Baghdad.

Tensions also arose over the policies to fight against the 'true' reasons leading to unstoppable inflation and shortages of livestock in Iraq. While the Iraqi authorities contended that the British army demands were the main factor that affected the market price of mutton for the civil population, MESC officials considered that the spiralling inflation was out of proportion to the livestock prices. For the British, there were other reasons to account for this phenomenon: 'since the butchers and Army contractors buy on the same market, it would appear that the butchers are making more than a reasonable profit'.[122] In other words, Iraqi butchers bought fresh meat at low rates – as the British did – to sell it at a higher price afterwards. At the same time, the whole question of prices was further complicated by speculative buying on the part of people who hoped to participate in the very profitable smuggling trade as well as other channels to avoid Allied regulatory measures.

Traditionally, scholarship has defined border-adjacent economic activities as 'a highly organized system of income-generating activities that deprive the state of taxation and foreign exchange'.[123] While the contraband geared towards increasing the profit from illicit trade was indeed a feature of the border zones economy during the war, some nuances seem to be necessary. According to Thomas Cantens, Robert Ireland and Gaël Raballand,

---

[121] NARA, RG84, UD2752, Box 8. 'Report on Economic and Financial Developments'. American Legation at Baghdad, 27 May 1942.

[122] TNA, FO 922/50. 'Livestock'. MESC, Paiforce, 17 March 1943.

[123] J. Mac Gaffey, *Entrepreneurs and Parasites: The Struggle for Indigenous Capitalism in Zaire* (Cambridge: Cambridge University Press, 1987).

the characterisation of informal trade as non-compliant with border agency requirements can only be made after the delineation of boundaries, the implementation of border controls, and the enactment of laws on taxation and cross-border trade.[124] In the absence of border control, cross-border activities can hardly be defined as contraband. Interestingly, even though borders had been demarcated and taxes upon sheep had been levied for many years, views about the exact nature of flows of sheep and cattle in the Syrian–Iraqi border differed among bureaucrats themselves in the 1940s. After all, what some officials referred to as 'meat smuggling' was often simply herds and herdsmen following familiar historical tracks, and was thus seen as legitimate:

> Meat smuggling in these adjacent territories has always been a source of trouble since shortages commenced and it is actually incorrect to call the practice smuggling in the true sense where Iraq and Syria are concerned as flock movements appear to have been normal practice for generations and frontiers are not drawn up to allow for these natural moves.[125]

Moreover, a significant number of sheep and goat were smuggled not in order to avoid taxation, but owing to Allied pressures and demands, which were considered as excessive by many in the borderlands. Finally, the shortage of meat at a regional level opened the door to the emergence of an informal trade in which borderland merchants, tribes, local governments and MESC staff were involved, at times, in rather intricate and unexpected ways.

At first, the Baghdad government saw in Iraq's special position in the Middle Eastern livestock market an opportunity to obtain additional economic resources. Very soon, however, sheep rearers and Iraqi authorities became disenchanted. Although the MESC managed the Middle Eastern region as a whole, contracts and prices were negotiated nationally. This uneven treatment of local producers and suppliers sowed dissatisfaction and, more importantly, paved the way for informal practices to either scape from imposed regulations or take advantage of them.

---

[124] Thomas Cantens, Robert Ireland, and Gaël Raballand, 'Introduction: Borders, Informality, International Trade and Customs', *Journal of Borderlands Studies*, p. 366.
[125] TNA, FO 922/199. Spears Mission. Beirut, 8 February 1944.

By 1942, as the embargo on cattle exports was maintained, Iraqi tribes smuggled hundreds of sheep 'every month' into Syria where prices in the black market were higher.[126] Likewise, the tribesmen drove their sheep across for shearing, in order to take advantage of the pre-emptive prices for wool paid there by the United Kingdom Commercial Corporation (UKCC).[127] The difference between prices offered in Syria and Iraq affected other smuggled animals, such as mules, which were mainly used for military operational purposes.[128] Some months later, however, the British forced the Iraqi government to resume its exports of cattle to the neighbouring countries, particularly Palestine, Syria and Lebanon.[129]

Since pre-emptive prices offered by Allied institutions in Syria were still higher, Iraqi merchants, tribesmen and Syrian authorities put in place an informal system to avoid the MESC's norms. According to British reports, several hundred head of cattle were being loaded almost weekly 'by the Syrian Railways at a station only 20 kilometres from the Iraqi frontier'.[130] Importantly, in order to obtain advantageous prices, the smuggled cattle were covered by Syrian certificates of origin. It also became obvious that such informal trade could only be carried out with the complicity of the Iraqi customs officials. Importantly, the loss of thousands of sheep for military needs over the months imposed an urgent renegotiation of terms and conditions around the Iraqi embargo upon the export of cattle.

The task was not an easy one, for the de-territorialisation of the Turkish–Syrian–Iraqi borderlands prompted a spill-over effect. While the British assumed that the Iraqi government was not completely opposed to allow the export of cattle, the former were aware that officials in Baghdad were reluctant to authorise substantial exports when it was publicly known that

---

[126] NARA, RG84, UD2752, Box 8. 'Report on Economic and Financial Developments'. American Legation at Baghdad, 27 May 1942.

[127] NARA, RG84, UD2752, Box 8. 'Report on Economic and Financial Developments'. American Legation at Baghdad, 6 August 1942.

[128] TNA, FO 624/27. Political Advisor at Mosul, 1 July 1942; TNA, FO 624/38. 'British Forces: Mules'. Baghdad, 25 March 1944.

[129] TNA, FO 922/74. MESC (Cairo) to British Embassy (Baghdad), 19 October 1943.

[130] TNA, FO 922/199. British Embassy (Baghdad) to MESC (Cairo), 25 November 1943.

considerable quantities were being smuggled out of the country with the connivance of the Syrian authorities.[131] Indeed, as Turkey opened up its southern borders owing to British pressure, Aleppo recovered its centrality as a regional market for cattle distribution in which both formal and informal trade were equally important. For one, the incessant demand of meat from the MESC countries led to an indiscriminate slaughter of cattle and the rise of contraband exportation of sheep to adjacent countries, particularly Syria. Such a dynamic could not leave Turkey immune, though. Predictably, the output of raw wool, which was one of the backbones of the economy for sheep producers in the Turkish southern borderlands, steadily dropped between 1943 and 1945.[132]

To make things even more complicated, MESC officials also favoured informal trade across Middle Eastern borders due to the shortage of meat for soldiers' consumption. Indeed, the main destination of fresh meat circulating through Aleppo's livestock market was British Palestine. In that regard, although the Syrian authorities could be approached to stop the illegal importation of cattle from Turkey, British bureaucrats in Beirut considered that given that 'the War Department openly connives at illegal importation from Turkey it is difficult to convince them that what is good for the War Department is wicked when practised by themselves'.[133] In other words, by 1943 the British Army, which was the main buyer of meat in Aleppo's market, turned a blind-eye to the informal trade that had emerged along the Turkish–Syrian–Iraqi borderlands simply because it secured the necessary supplies of foodstuff for Palestine and the Allied forces across the region. At the same time, the Syrian authorities favoured informal trade of sheep to make sure that enough fresh meat was available in the black market, while officially the government introduced three meatless days.[134] Local butchers, speculators and hoarders, as in Iraq, were the main winners of a system that maintained high prices forced by the creation of artificial scarcities. The British conundrum regarding formal

---

[131] Ibid.
[132] NARA, RG84, Reel 12, 867.50/3–446. 'Annual Economic Review'. American Embassy (Ankara), 4 March 1946.
[133] TNA, FO 922/199. Spears Mission. Beirut, 8 February 1944.
[134] TNA, FO 922/50. 'Livestock'. MESC, Paiforce, 17 March 1943.

or informal trade, as with so many other issues in the Middle East, could only be sorted it out at the end of the war.

This chapter has addressed the central position of the Turkish–Syrian–Iraqi borderlands within the context of the Allied operations in the Middle East. By observing the efforts deployed by the MESC geared towards boosting wheat and meat production and their distribution across the region, it has underscored that Great Britain at once bolstered cross-border connectivity and dependency between Middle Eastern states during the conflict, while also attempting to make regional borders thicker; that is, processes of both *de*-bordering and *re*-bordering. If the latter was the natural outcome of the wartime context, the former can be seen as a structural pattern prefigured by pre-war British and French efforts to create dense economic interactions in the region.[135] The Second World War only furthered an ongoing process under nevertheless exceptional conditions.

Although Turkey was not under direct Britain's influence, unlike most of the Arab countries during the Second World War, she de facto joined the MESC trade exchange and production region, and more importantly opened up her southern borders to facilitate the circulations of goods and livestock across Turkish territory. Incidentally, the Baghdad Railway and motor roads secured not only the stability of regional supplies but also served as doorways for global markets to compensate for the insecurity of the traditional maritime routes.

Departing from hagiographic studies on the MESC and other Allied agencies established during the Second World War, this chapter has underscored three often-neglected issues. First, this chapter has shown that British interventions in Iraq and Syria in 1941 disrupted early local war arrangements to cope with the impacts of the second world conflict, especially between Turkey and Iraq. Second, MESC intervention in the Middle East as a whole, and in the borderlands in particular, had significant side effects (inflation, competition, massive slaughtering of cattle) that scholars should not underestimate. Finally, because the British lack of resources and the contingent developments

---

[135] Cyrus Schayegh, *The Middle East and the Making of the Modern World*, p. 159.

of the war imposed some constraints on the Middle East Command, Allied staff were obliged to adjust their policies to local conditions and at times turn a blind eye on activities often deemed 'illegal'.

In that regard, borderlands and informal traders were far from being marginal spaces or actors who contributed little to national and regional wealth during the war, as has generally been assumed. Rather, this chapter has highlighted the necessary conceptualisation of borderlands as spaces and places that are at once marginal and integral to the processes of globalisation that took place during the first half of the twentieth century.[136] Similarly, by both defying international borders – migration, fostering cross-border kinship networks, contraband, informal trade – and participating to the expansion of agriculture in the peripheral regions, borderlanders contributed to parallel, yet at times, embedded processes of territorialisation and de-territorialisation.

---

[136] Victor Konrad, 'New Directions at the Post-Globalization Border', *Journal of Borderlands Studies*, Vol. 36, No. 5 (2021), pp. 716–7.

CONCLUSION

The borderlands that are central to this book have been the focus of dramatic shifts throughout the last decade. Of note is the popular Syrian revolt which began in March 2011 against the regime of Bashar al-Assad. While largely peaceful at its beginning, the regime's harsh response to this revolt paved the way for the initial stages of an armed insurgency a year later. In turn, the regime decided to pull out the Syrian Army from several towns in northern Syria in July 2012 to protect Damascus and other key economic and strategic centres. As a result, the Democratic Union Party (PYD) – a Syrian offshoot of the Kurdistan Worker's Party (PKK) – and its military force, the People's Defence Units (YPG), were able to exercise sovereign powers in all Kurdish districts until 2018. Freed from any significant opposition, the PYD alone promoted the declaration of a local administration in the cantons of Jazira, Kobane and Afrin in January 2014. This local administration laid the foundations of a political system guided by PYD's principles of 'democratic autonomy' and 'democratic confederalism', as formulated by PKK's imprisoned leader, Abdullah Öcalan.[1] This de facto autonomy was, in the eyes of the Ankara government, nothing more than a 'terror corridor'.

---

[1] Jordi Tejel, 'The Kurdish Question in Syria', in Hamit Bozarslan, Cengiz Gunes, and Veli Yadirgi (eds), *The Cambridge History of the Kurds* (Cambridge: Cambridge University Press, 2021), pp. 436–57. See also Harriet Allsopp and Wladimir van Wilgenburg, *The Kurds of Northern Syria: Governance, Diversity and Conflicts* (London: I. B. Tauris, 2019).

In the meantime, sectarian tensions in Iraq, alongside the transformation of the Syrian uprising into an open civil war, had regional consequences: massive population displacements internally and across borders, thousands of casualties as well as a power vacuum in the Syrian–Iraqi borderlands that was filled by another emerging non-state actor – the Islamic State of Iraq and Syria (ISIS), which established a trans-border 'Caliphate' in 2014, with two capitals: namely, Raqqa (Syria) and Mosul (Iraq). Subsequently, reports on burnt churches and villages as well as the mass kidnappings of Yazidi sex slaves in Sinjar evoked memories about past massacres and genocides committed in the Turkish–Syrian–Iraqi borderlands among local Armenians, Assyrians and Yazidis.[2]

Even though ISIS' siege of Kobane between 2014 and 2015 seemed at first to weaken the PYD's position to Turkey's satisfaction, the subsequent 'liberation' of this border town and the consolidation of the Kurdish *de facto* autonomy in northern Syria led to the definitive collapse of the 'Kurdish opening' – supposed to bring a peaceful resolution to the long-lasting Kurdish issue in Turkey – launched by the Turkish President Recep Tayyip Erdoğan five years earlier. Moreover, the Ankara government embarked on the construction of a 764km-long, high-tech concrete wall along the 911km Turkish–Syrian border, which was completed by June 2018.[3] Turkey's victorious military campaign in Afrin between January and March 2018 as well as the US-Turkish agreement to expel Kurdish forces from Manbij exposed the dramatic shift in power relations in the border zone. Boldened by these encouraging developments, Ankara launched Operation Peace Spring in October 2019 against the Syrian Democratic Forces (SDF), an Arab-Kurdish militia guided nonetheless by YPG cadres. As a result, Ras al-Ayn or Serê Kaniyê fell under Turkish control, too.

---

[2] Brenda Stoter, 'Suicide Rates Increase Within Iraq's Yazidi community', *Al Monitor*, 8 May 2020, https://www.al-monitor.com/originals/2020/05/iraq-minorities-yazidis-suicide.html (last accessed 9 February 2022); Marcello Mollica and Arsen Hakobyan (eds), *Syrian Armenians and the Turkish Factor: Kesab, Aleppo and Deir ez-Zor in the Syrian War* (London: Palgrave Macmillan, 2021).

[3] Cemal Özkahraman, 'Kurdish Cross-border Trade between Syria and Turkey: The Sociopolitical Trajectories of Syrian Kurds', *Middle Eastern Studies*, Vol. 57, No. 4 (2021), pp. 567–80 (here p. 576).

Furthermore, Ankara's plans in the border region seem to suggest that Turkey intends to keep a political, military and cultural influence over the area in the post-war era. Thus, for example, Turkey has opened four universities in the northern Syrian territory it controls, and Turkey's postal service opened branches in Jarablus, al-Bab and çobanbey, all located in Syria.[4] Critically, almost a quarter of Syria's population is under Turkish control directly or indirectly, including 3.6 million refugees in Turkey. Plans to resettle thousands of Syrian refugees in northern Syria have prompted alarming reports regarding Turkey's long-term goals in the area; namely, a strategy of demographic change or 'Arabisation' of the border zone at the expense of Kurdish and Armenian populations.

Further east, despite initial tensions between Turkey and the Kurdistan Regional Government (KRG), which emerged as the consequence of the Gulf War in 1991, and the subsequent establishment of a safe haven in the Kurdish provinces of Iraq a year later, by 2007, Ankara accepted making the Erbil administration a regional partner to facilitate the export of KRG oil through the Kirkuk–Ceyhan pipeline.[5] In addition, since the 1990s, the Ibrahim Khalil border gate has constituted the main corridor for overland trade between Turkey and Iraq. Notwithstanding the increasing economic interconnectedness between the two countries, Turkey has launched no less than forty military operations into northern Iraq to eliminate PKK guerrilla fighters and destroy PKK headquarters which have been situated in the border zone since the 1990s. Those operations often entail casualties among civilians and the destruction of flocks and houses, thereby straining relations between Ankara and Erbil, on the one hand, and between Erbil and borderlanders, on the other. In parallel, by August 2017, Turkish authorities began the construction of another wall, this time along the Turkish–Iranian border, in order to prevent PKK fighters, smugglers and since 2021, refugees from crossing the borderline.[6]

---

[4] Fehim Tastekin, 'Turkey Cultivating Ever-deeper Roots in Syrian Territory', *Al Monitor*, 14 June 2018, https://www.al-monitor.com/originals/2018/06/turkey-syria-turkish-university-in-al-bab.html (last accessed 9 February 2022).

[5] Robert Olson, *The Goat and the Butcher: Nationalism and State Formation on Kurdistan-Iraq since the Iraqi War* (Costa Mesa: Mazda, 2005).

[6] 'Turkey Extends Security Wall Along Iranian Border', *Hürriyet*, 15 September 2021, https://www.hurriyetdailynews.com/turkey-extends-security-wall-along-iran-border-interior-minister-167897 (last accessed 9 February 2022).

Last but not least, Erdoğan's neo-Ottomanist discourse and policy have brought about a series of new developments among which the denunciation of the post-First World War agreements by pro-government media outlets and think tanks. Thus, while the Treaty of Lausanne has been traditionally celebrated in Turkey as a diplomatic victory, in the last few years nationalist and Islamist political currents have suggested a different reading of this agreement; the latter is now seen as a political failure of the Kemalist elites, and therefore some voices even ask for the termination of the treaty, which would ultimately open the door to the re-drawing of (maritime and overland) Turkey's international borders. In sum, Turkey has the 'right' to demand the return to the national borders envisioned by the 'Mîsak-ı Millî' plan or the National Pact of 1920.[7]

Although not exhaustive, this overview of the prevailing situation in the Turkish–Syrian–Iraqi borderlands seems to suggest several similarities with the interwar developments examined throughout this book: a state of widespread violence involving state and non-state actors, the elusive presence of the Syrian and Iraqi state authorities in the northern borderlands, competing ideological projects, porous borders, significant flows of refugees and smuggled goods across the region, Ankara's discourses on external threats coming from Turkey's southern borders and thus the 'right' of Turkey to have a say in Syrian and Iraqi internal affairs, among many other factors. Obviously, today's context and actors are not the same and some dynamics are actually new. Admittedly, from a historical viewpoint, some strips of the international borders drawn in the Middle East in the interwar era have recently become 'thicker' than ever before. In addition, refugee flows have taken a reverse direction. While in the 1920s and 1930s, thousands of refugees originating from Turkey and Iraq sought protection in the Syrian lands, nowadays, millions of Syrians of all ethnic and religious backgrounds have become either internally displaced people (IDPs) or refugees in neighbouring countries – Lebanon, Jordan, Iraq and, more significantly, Turkey.[8] Taken together, however, these similarities

---

[7] Marwa Maziad and Jake Sotiriadis, 'Turkey's Dangerous New Exports: Islamist, Neo-Ottoman Visions and Regional Instability', *Middle East Institute*, 21 April 2020, https://www.mei.edu/publications/turkeys-dangerous-new-exports-pan-islamist-neo-ottoman-visions-and-regional (last accessed 9 February 2022).

[8] Dawn Chatty, 'Special Issue Introduction', *International Journal of Middle East Studies*, Vol 49, No. 4 (2017), pp. 577–82.

and discrepancies allow us to draw some general conclusions about state- and border-making processes in the post-Ottoman Middle East, topics which are at the heart of this book.

First, past and present dynamics in the Turkish–Syrian–Iraqi borderlands confirm the pertinence of adopting a borderland perspective to study the two above-mentioned processes. For one, as Mohammad-Mahmoud Ould Mohamedou aptly points out, a non-Western state cannot replicate a Western state because the latter is not a model but an instance of historical experience that displayed 'specific geographies, spaces, choices and ideologies'.[9] In that regard, states in the post-Ottoman Middle East are instances of a specific historical configuration marked by three 'related-but-inherently-distinct developments'; namely, 'the slow end of the Ottoman Empire, the violent encounter with the European colonial powers and the gradual rise of the local nationalistic and religious emancipation movements'.[10] The result of this complex and tortuous path is the difficulty for scholars to chart the very nature of the state in the Middle East after more than a century of existence, for it is at once 'strong' and 'weak', 'present' and 'absent', 'visible' and 'invisible'.[11]

Even though Turkey has been an internationally recognised independent state since 1922–23 and therefore it did not experience the same path as the majority of other Arab states in the region, as some scholars have shown, the 'Ottoman twilight' and 'Ottoman ghost' in the early republican years were still a reality in social, political and economic terms.[12] Likewise, because

---

[9] Mohammad-Mahmoud Ould Mohamedou, 'In Search of the Non-Western State: Historicising and De-Westphalianising Statehood', in Bertrand Badie, Dirk Berg-Scholsser and Leonardo Morlino (eds), *The SAGE Handbook of Political Science: A Global Perspective* (London: Sage, 2020), pp. 1335–48 (here p. 1346).

[10] Mohammad-Mahmoud Ould Mohamedou, 'A Century of Elusive State-Building in the Middle East and North Africa', in Mohammad-Mahmoud Ould Mohamedou (ed.), *State Building in the Middle East and North Africa: One Hundred Years of Nationalism, Religion and Politics* (I. B. Tauris: London, 2021), pp. 3–24 (here p. 5.)

[11] Ibid. p. 13.

[12] Cyrus Schayegh, *The Middle East and the Making of the Modern World* (Cambridge, MA: Harvard University Press, 2017), pp. 132–99; Aline Schlaepfer, Philippe Bourmaud and Iyas Hassa, 'Ghosts of Empire: Persistence and Claims of Ottomanity(ies) in Post-Ottoman Spaces', *Revue des Mondes Musulmans et de la Méditerranée*, Vol. 148 (2020), pp. 33–56.

Turkey had to collaborate on regular basis with British Iraq and French Syria to implement effective border governance, the state- and border-making processes in Turkey were not immune to the effects of inter-state cooperation as well as to socio-cultural, political and economic developments unfolding in neighbouring countries.[13]

While historians and social scientists have analysed these three developments through the observation of what happened in the respective political centres and diplomatic meetings, this book has instead suggested we recognise borders and borderlands as suitable sites for exploring the co-production and renegotiation of power, territorial, political and social loyalties in the modern Middle East. Crucially, looking at how statehood was designed and practised in the Turkish–Syrian–Iraqi borderlands allows scholars to avoid a political history that is exclusively 'associated with the history of the West and confined to the Westphalian model'.[14] Furthermore, the 'strength' and the 'weakness', the 'visibility' and the 'elusiveness', the 'presence' and the 'absence' are features of the state that are even more heightened in borderland regions.

As we have seen, the emergence of new boundaries and nation states in the post-Ottoman Middle East proved to be a complex and contentious process, including a series of multilateral negotiations as well as multiple foci of violence in which a variety of state, transnational and local actors became involved. Despite the de facto recognition of the Ankara government by the French in 1921, and the delimitation of a provisional frontier between Turkey and French Syria, the ideas of self-determination and territorial sovereignty that had become central in the conferences following the First World War continued to nourish previous tensions, while providing borderlanders with a new range of discourses and opportunities. Thus, throughout the border disputes between Turkey and French Syria, on the one hand, and between Turkey and Britain, on the other, borderland representatives advanced different claims and aspirations depending on the context and the targeted audience, allowing them to play off Turkish, French and British agents against each other and,

---

[13] See various contributions in Jordi Tejel and Ramazan Hakkı Öztan (eds), *Regimes of Mobility: Borders and State Formation in the Middle East, 1918–46* (Edinburgh: Edinburgh University Press, 2022).

[14] Mohammad-Mahmoud Ould Mohamedou, 'In Search of the Non-Western State', p. 1337.

by doing so, gain brokerage. Whether they were opportunistic or full-hearted anti-imperialists or both, local actors, through their shifting alliances, pushed British, French and Turkish authorities to the conclusion that separate permanent agreements on their respective common boundaries were the best solution for all parties.

Epistemologically, a history of border-making that pays attention to how borderlanders played off state powers and developed trans-border networks of violence and exchange also allows us to combine diplomatic, local and transnational approaches. After all, these frontier disputes were intertwined, not only because the resistance movements against Western occupation performed regionally, but also because the evolution of boundary negotiations in one instance had immediate consequences on the other. Thus, as the League of Nations granted the Mosul Vilayet to British Mandate Iraq, Turkey and France re-opened direct negotiations to clear up the uncertainties left by the messy initial territorial settlements reached in 1921. In that sense, in a key contribution to the sociology of the state, Charles Tilly suggested that not only do states make war but 'war makes states', including the process of defining their boundaries.[15] Yet, a borderlands perspective reminds us that local communities and non-state actors, often in tandem with states or fragments of it, do play a relevant role in warfare dynamics that lead to boundary-making processes, too.

Notwithstanding this, the three borders did not develop synchronously from that moment on. Independent Turkey pushed for an earlier demarcation of her southern borders, whereas Britain and France procrastinated about the precise limits of the Syrian–Iraqi border for almost two decades. Likewise, the material and discursive dimensions around them were not the same in each country. While the Ankara government perceived certain cross-border practices as a violation of their national borders and honour (*namus*), British and French Mandate authorities viewed Syrian and Iraqi (temporary) boundaries as *frontiers*; namely, a 'remote, sparsely populated, and vaguely defined territory lying beyond the periphery of two or more core powers' that

---

[15] Charles Tilly, 'War Making and State Making as Organized Crime', in Peter Evan et al. (eds), *Bringing the State Back in* (Cambridge: Cambridge University Press, 1985), pp. 169–91.

is often contested by 'rivalling imperial powers and local populations, and characterised by permanent negotiations and compromise'.[16]

This book has thus suggested moving beyond the analysis of international agreements and protocols to better understand how border regimes actually unfolded in the interwar era as well as the different relations Middle Eastern states developed with their respective borders. In that regard, border governance provides an interesting insight into how new states actually expanded their authority in the borderlands. While border governance led to a thrust of standardisation of practices aiming at making the boundary a physical reality and facilitating extradition of outlaws (smugglers, thieves, 'undesirable agents', etc.), the lack of human and material resources and local resistance, along with the primacy of different legal systems in the adjacent countries, led Turkey, France and Britain to accompany such international practices by using older legal systems – i.e. *diya* – as well as informal arrangements in the border zones. A view from the borderlands showcases the legacies of the imperial legal order and the hybridisation of different legal traditions throughout the interwar period, on the one hand, and the importance of informality in state- and border-making processes, on the other. All in all, features that were by no means either new or unique to Middle Eastern states.[17]

As Jonathan Obert has pointed out, though, creating interstate boundaries garnered with a series of formal and informal arrangements that were part of new boundary regimes was less a definite proof of the state's capacity to impose its presence in the borderlands than the mutual construction of a 'legal fiction'. Against normative Weberian understandings of state-formation processes, a borderlands' perspective thus suggests that 'border-making matters, not because the dividing lines themselves actually map on to local forms of identity and belonging, but because they create legal fictions that seem to call for organized policing on the part of the administrative state'.[18] The coherence

---

[16] Sören Urbansky, *Beyond the Steppe Frontier: A History of the Sino-Russian Border* (Princeton, NJ: Princeton University Press, 2020), p. 4.

[17] Benton, Lauren, *Law and Colonial Cultures: Legal Regimes in World History, 1400–1900* (Cambridge: Cambridge University Press, 2002); Scott Radnitz, 'Review: Informal Politics and the State', *Comparative Politics*, Vol. 43, No. 3 (2011), pp. 351–71.

[18] Jonathan Obert, 'Policing the Boundary and Bounding the Police: Fictious Borders and the Making of Gendarmeries in North America', *Journal of Borderlands Studies*, Vol. 36, No. 2 (2021), pp. 301–18 (here p. 314).

of borders' legal fictions was nevertheless hindered by states themselves, as they proved to be extremely fragmented. The situation of the Turkish–Syrian border during the Second World War is perhaps the most paradigmatic example of this; borderlanders and trespassers had to deal with representatives from no less than four different states and thus national interests – Turkey, Syria, France and Britain – in addition to diverse security apparatus, at times operating in contradictory directions.

More broadly, state- and border-making processes are never a done deal.[19] Because borders are always in motion and it is at borderlands that 'governance, inter-state relations, and development become most agile and fragile', borders and borderlands are constantly being re-imagined, contested and reconstructed through discourses as well as legal and material measures to better monitor border-crossing and mobility.[20] Ultimately, as Cyrus Schayegh puts it, the new borders created in the interwar Middle East did not simply generate more contacts between state and non-state actors; rather, they paved the way for 'new informal deals in which the very nature of what and who the state and social groups were, and how they interacted, was partially negotiated'.[21]

In that sense, the book has also demonstrated that state- and border-formation processes were not solely a top-down development. For one thing, the interactions between borderlanders and new national and Mandate authorities did not end as border agreements were sealed. In fact, as the latter attempted to implement the new international borders – i.e. demarcating the boundary and establishing a viable and lasting border governance around them – these interactions grew further. Human and non-human mobility (pests and diseases), together with borderlanders' acts and strategies became significant drivers for states to expand their (uneven) presence in the borderlands and reformulate official discourses about the Self (and the Other). Hence, refugees, Bedouins, smugglers, merchants, transnational Sufi orders and landowners possessing

---

[19] Alexander Wendt, *Social Theory of International Politics* (Cambridge: Cambridge University Press, 1999), p. 213.

[20] Yuk Wah Chan and Brantly Womack, 'Not Merely a Border: Borderland Governance, Development and Transborder Relations in Asia', *Asian Anthropology*, Vol. 15, No. 2 (2016), pp. 95–103 (here p. 98).

[21] Cyrus Schayegh, 'Afterword', in Jordi Tejel and Ramazan Hakkı Öztan (eds), *Regimes of Mobility*, pp. 355–6.

plots of land in the border zone contributed to shape both the process of implementation of international borders and territorialisation in the post-Ottoman Middle East, by either resisting or coping with this new reality. Against this backdrop, the book calls for surpassing the traditional binary of nation-state versus borderlands-based history and adopting, instead, a historical narrative that views states and borderlands – including human and non-human actors – as a part of a dialectic relationship.

Yet, because borderlands are transnational spaces, the observation of interactions unfolding in these areas cannot be limited to the traditional centre-periphery binary. Indeed, the demarcation of the three borders throughout the 1920s and 1930s was accompanied by the emergence of a new 'regime of mobility' along Middle Eastern borders that was part of an entangled global history as well as the result of socio-political contestations and negotiations between various states and multiple non-state actors, including border dwellers, travellers, and private car and train companies. Against this backdrop, borderlands and borderlanders 'became both connectors of, and active participants in, new mobility strategies that emerged from the early 1920s onwards' that surpassed the limits of each nation-state.[22] Furthermore, as we have seen, identity control of travellers using the Taurus Express in non-border towns and cities such as Aleppo or on the train reminds us that borders are not only territorial borderlines; yesterday, like today, they can be mobile and be administered on different spatial scales.[23]

Much as in other parts of the world, however, the emerging regime of mobility in the region was contingent on international events. After all, the Great Depression, the continuation of the Baghdad Railway project and the Second World War all had consequences on mobility flows that historians cannot overlook. Even though the first wave of globalisation was coming to an end by the late 1930s, growing economic relations between cities and border regions helped create real state territoriality in the so-called peripheries of Middle Eastern states; that is, the imposition of a political boundary on the populations

---

[22] Jordi Tejel and Ramazan Hakkı Öztan, 'Introduction', in Jordi Tejel and Ramazan Hakkı Öztan (eds), *Regimes of Mobility*, p. 15.

[23] Victor Konrad, 'Toward a Theory of Borders in Motion', *Journal of Borderlands Studies*, Vol. 30, No. 1 (2015), pp. 1–17.

CONCLUSION | 325

regardless of their social structure[24] was enacted by building infrastructures and by increasing the presence of state institutions in order to channel these flows. At the same time, these very same global and regional developments brought about significant challenges to the prevailing boundary regimes as well as the nascent nation-state system in the region; namely, the continuous re-negotiation regarding which people, goods and commodities could or could not circulate across the international borders. In that regard, borders and border zones are precious sites to consider together flux and fixity, as well as power relations, especially in historical moments marked by uncertainty.[25]

The double movement involving processes of re-bordering and de-bordering in the Middle East was amplified during the Second World War. Interestingly, and contrary to general assumptions, secessionist movements, informal traders and trespassers are not the only actors that may contribute to the dynamics of de-bordering and de-territorialisation. After all, territoriality is not a given: it is a set of relationships that evolves over time and does not avert reverse processes, namely, the de-territorialisation of nation states, encouraged at times by state and non-state actors, depending on the context and interests.

This was the case for the British who, through new institutions such as the Middle East Supply Centre (MESC), sought to define the Middle East as a regional economic and territorial entity bestowed with thicker external borders, while actively pushing for the blurring of the internal ones to compensate for the dramatic shortages of foodstuffs and other essential materials deemed necessary for Allies' war efforts. This was also true for the Ankara political elites who, while giving up the territorial projections envisioned by the National Pact of 1920, always considered that the Turkish–Syrian border was not a natural one. Consequently, from the onset, the Turkish Republic exploited all border-related issues – the settlement of Armenian and Kurdish refugees in the Syrian border zone, the protection of the Turkish minority rights in Alexandretta, the struggle against diseases and pests, and

---

[24] I. William Zartman, 'Identity, Movement, and Response' in I. William Zartman (ed.), *Understanding Life in the Borderlands: Boundaries in Depth and in Motion* (Athens and London: The University of Georgia Press, 2010), p. 3.

[25] On Barak and Haggai Ram, 'Beyond Connectivity: The Middle East in Global History', *Journal of Levantine Studies*, Vol. 10, No. 1 (2020), pp. 5–9 (here p. 6).

contraband, among many other issues – to gain political and military leverage along the border zone, influence neighbours' policies and, if conditions were favourable, ask for modifications of this boundary. As it turns out, the world conflict provided just such an opportunity: through border securing practices – additional mobile border units, expansion of intelligence services along the border –, on the one hand, and interventionism in Syria – propaganda, support of anti-French Syrian tribes and leaders, and to a lesser extent, Iraqi affairs –, on the other, the Ankara government contributed to the two apparently contradictory processes of bordering and de-bordering in Turkey's southern borderlands.

Border dwellers were not mere witnesses to the Second World War's dynamics, though. As in the early 1920s, borderlanders developed multiple strategies with regard to different state actors, depending on their interests and the evolution of the conflict, including competitors' alliances. The fate of the MESC's policies, in particular, was not exclusively the result of British decision-making power. They were partly implemented thanks to the involvement of borderlanders and readjusted in the face of local and global constraints. Therefore, the book highlights the necessary conceptualisation of borderlands as spaces and places that were at once marginal and integral to the processes of globalisation and state-formation that took place during the first half of the twentieth century. In other words, scholars need to acknowledge that, far from being peripheral by definition, the 'centrality' or 'de-centrality' of borderlands in the Middle East, as elsewhere, is context-specific rather than geographical.

Finally, some considerations about a notion that has been central throughout the different chapters of this book; the agency of borderlanders. Historians of borderlands have by and large postulated that borderlands are organic spaces that constitute relatively independent social units, thereby maintaining their own dynamics and identities. Although this is accurate to a certain extent, borderlands are 'never really independent from the making of state and nation.'[26] In addition, because borders meant different things at different places, at different times and to different individuals and social groups in the post-Ottoman

---

[26] Nianshen Song, *Making Borders in Modern Asia: The Tumen River Demarcation, 1881–1919* (Cambridge: Cambridge University Press, 2018), p. 11.

Middle East, borderlanders made different choices to engage with government policies and global dynamics – nationalism as a lingua franca, the making of the modern refugee, new mobility regimes, etc. – accordingly resulting in different outcomes.

Crucially, it has been argued in this book that far from being a sign of their incapacity to adapt to the new world order, borderlanders' plural and, apparently, contradictory attitudes during these critical years were a striking example of the capacity of local agency; that is, the capacity of individuals and groups to develop strategies for pursuing or safeguarding their own interests. Yet, agency does not mean complete empowerment or guaranteed success. On the contrary, as different chapters have shown, at times borderlanders' choices could lead to a backlash; tribes could thus be forcibly displaced from the border zone, refugees become the targets of nationalistic attacks, and smugglers be severely punished. Seemingly, borderlanders' agency could also have ambivalent impacts. In the end, each time those criminalised by one border authority found refuge across a border, their crossings and related social relations – informal trade, kinship groups, transnational religious and political networks, to mention a few – encouraged states to further consolidate the institutionalisation of the border,[27] thereby inadvertently contributing to the continuous reshuffling of the emerging boundary regimes in the Turkish–Syrian–Iraqi borderlands.

All in all, the book invites scholars to explore a different understanding of borderlanders' agency – one that underlines 'interdependence' instead of 'claiming independence and autonomy';[28] paradox, rather than linear and teleological accounts based on presumptions about borderland dwellers' identities and interests. To put it differently, any historical narrative of borderlands needs to be open-ended, freed of presuppositions about the aims of local actors as well as the strength of states and their official ideologies in order to capture how structure and individual and/or collective agency intertwine, affect each other and, at times, generate unforeseen consequences.

---

[27] Peter Sahlins, *Boundaries: The Making of France and Spain in the Pyrenees* (Berkeley, CA: University of California Press, 1989), p. 8.

[28] Lynn M. Thomas, 'Historicising Agency', *Gender and History*, Vol. 28, No. 2 (2016), p. 326. See also Walter Johnson, 'On Agency', *Journal of Social History*, Vol. 37, No. 1 (2003), pp. 113–24.

BIBLIOGRAPHY

Archives

Archives Dominicaines (SAULCHOIR), Paris
Başbakanlık Cumhuriyet Arşivi (BCA), Ankara
Başbakanlık Osmanlı Arşivi (BOA), Istanbul
Centre des Archives diplomatiques de la Courneuve (CADC), Paris
Centre des Archives diplomatiques de Nantes (CADN), Nantes
Centre des Hautes Etudes Administratives sur l'Afrique et l'Asie Modernes (CHEAM), Paris
Institut kurde de Paris (FONDS RONDOT), Paris
League of Nations (LON), Geneva
Middle East Centre (MEC), Oxford
Service historique de l'Armée de terre (SHAT), Paris
Stiftung Rheinisch-Westfälisches Wirtschaftsarchiv zu Köln (SRWK), Köln
The National Archives (TNA), Kew, London
The National Archives and Records Administration (NARA), College Park, Maryland
Türkiye Büyük Millet Meclisi Zabıt Ceridesi (TBMMZC), Ankara

Books and articles

Ababsa, Myriam, 'Mise en valeur agricole et contrôle politique de la vallée de l'Euphrate (1865–1946): Etude des relations Etat, nomades et citadins dans le caza de Raqqa', *Bulletin d'études orientales*, Vol. 53/54 (2001–2), pp. 459–88.
Abdallah, Stéphanie Latte and Cédric Parizot (eds), *A l'ombre du mur: Israéliens et palestiniens entre séparation et occupation* (Arlès: Actes Sud/MMSH, 2011).

Abou-El-Haj, Rifa'at 'Ali, *Formation of the Modern State: The Ottoman Empire, Sixteenth to Eighteenth Centuries* (Albany: SUNY Press, 1991).

Abou-Hodeib, Toufoul, 'Involuntary History: Writing Levantines into the Nation', *Contemporary Levant*, Vol. 5, No. 1 (2020), pp. 44–53.

Abou-Hodeib, Toufoul, 'Sanctity across the Border: Pilgrimage Routes and State Control in Mandate Lebanon and Palestine', in Cyrus Schayegh and Andrew Arsan (eds), *The Routledge Handbook of the History of the Middle East Mandates* (London: Routledge, 2015), pp. 383–94.

Aboul-Enein, Youssef and Basil Aboul-Enein, *The Secret War for the Middle East: The Influence of Axis and Allied Intelligence Operations during World War II* (Annapolis: Naval Institute Press, 2013).

Abrahamyan, Victoria, 'Citizen Strangers: Identity Labelling and Discourse in the French Mandatory Syria, 1920–1932', *Journal of Migration History*, Vol. 6, No. 1 (2020), pp. 40–61.

Abrams, Philip, 'Notes on the Difficulty of Studying the State', *Journal of Historical Sociology*, Vol. 1, No. 1 (1988), pp. 58–89.

Acara, Eda, 'From Imperial Frontier to National Heartland: Environmental History of Turkey's Nation-Building in its European Province of Thrace, 1920–40', in Onur Inal and Ethemcan Turhan (eds), *Transforming Socio-Natures in Turkey: Landscapes, State and Environmental Movements* (London and New York: Routledge, 2020), pp. 52–70.

Açıkyıldız, Birgül, *The Yezidis: The History of a Community, Culture and Religion* (London: I. B. Tauris, 2014).

Adelman, Jeremy and Stephen Aron, 'From Borderlands to Borders: Empires, Nation-States, and the Peoples in between in North American History', *The American Historical Review*, Vol. 104, No. 3 (1999), pp. 814–41.

Ahmad, Feroz, *Turkey: The Quest for Identity* (Oxford: Oneworld, 2003).

Ahmadi, Shaherzad R., 'Local Ambivalence in the Arabistan-Basra Frontier, 1881–1925', *British Journal of Middle Eastern Studies*, Vol. 48, No. 3 (2021), pp. 436–54.

Ahram, Ariel I., *Break all the Borders: Separatism and the Reshaping of the Middle East* (Oxford: Oxford University Press, 2020).

Akalın, Müslüm, *Cumhuriyet Halk Fırkası Urfa Heyet-i Ideresi Mukarrerat Defteri, 1924–6* (Urfa: Şurkav, 1999).

Akandere, Osman, *Milli Şef Dönemi, 1938–45* (Istanbul: İz Yayınları, 1998).

Akin, Yigit, *When the War Came Home: The Ottoman's Great War and the Devastation of an Empire* (Stanford, CA: Stanford University Press, 2018).

Aksakal, Mustafa, *The Ottoman Road to War in 1914: The Ottoman Empire and the First World War* (Cambridge: Cambridge University Press, 2008).
Akşin, Sina, 'Turkish–Syrian relations in the Time of Faisal, 1918–20', *The Turkish Yearbook of International Relations*, Vol. 20, No. 1 (1980), pp. 1–17.
Akyürekli, Mahmut, *Şark İstiklal Mahkemesi, 1925–7* (Istanbul: Tarih Kulübü Yayınları, 2013).
Akyüz, Kutbeddin, *Ahmed el-Haznevî ve Haznevîyye Tarikatı* (MA Thesis, Yalova: Yalova Üniversitesi, 2015).
Ali, Azad A., 'Le rôle politique des tribus kurdes Milli et de la famille d'Ibrahim Pacha à l'ouest du Kurdistan et au nord du Bilad al-Cham (1878–1908)', in Jean-Claude David and Thierry Boissière (eds), *Alep et ses territoires: Fabrique et politique d'une ville, 1868–2011* (Beirut/Damascus: Ifpo, 2014), pp. 67–79.
Ali, Othman, 'The Kurdish factor in the Struggle for Vilayet Mosul, 1921–5', *Journal of Kurdish Studies*, Vol. 4 (2001–2), pp. 31–48.
Ali, Othman, 'The Career of Ozdemir: A Turkish Bid for Northern Iraq, 1921–3', *Middle Eastern Studies*, Vol. 53, No. 6 (2017), pp. 966–85.
Allsopp, Harriet and Wladimir van Wilgenburg, *The Kurds of Northern Syria: Governance, Diversity and Conflicts* (London: I. B. Tauris, 2019).
Alon, Yoav, *The Making of Jordan: Tribes, Colonialism and the Modern* State (London: I. B. Tauris, 2007).
Altuğ, Seda and Benjamin T. White, 'Frontière et pouvoir d'Etat: La frontière turco-syrienne dans les années 1920 et 1930', *Vingtième Siècle. Revue d'histoire*, Vol. 103 (2009), pp. 91–104.
Altuğ, Seda, 'Sectarianism in the Syrian Jazira: Community, Land and Violence in the Memories of World War I and the French Mandate, 1915–39' (PhD dissertation, Utrecht: University of Utrecht, 2011).
Altuğ, Seda, 'Syrian-Armenian Memory and the Refugee Issue in Syria under the French Mandate, 1921–46', *The Armenian Weekly*, 2012, <armenianweekly.com/2012/07/05/syrian-armenian-memory-and-the-refugee-issue-in-syria-under-the-french-mandate-1921-46> (accessed 1 March 2022).
Altuğ, Seda, 'The Turkish–Syrian Border and Politics of Difference in Turkey and Syria, 1921–39' in Matthieu Cimino (ed.), *Syria: Borders, Boundaries, and the State* (London: Palgrave Macmillan, 2020), pp. 47–73.
Amilhat Szary, Anne-Laure and Frédéric Giraut, *Borderities and the Politics of Contemporary Mobile Borders* (London: Palgrave Macmillan, 2015).
Anastassiadis, Tassos and Nathalie Clayer, 'Beyond the Incomplete or Failed Modernization Paradigm', in Tassos Anastassiadis and Nathalie Clayer (eds),

Society, Politics and State Formation in Southeastern Europe during the 19th Century (Athens: Alpha Bank, 2011), pp. 11–32.

Anderson, James and Liam O'Dowd, 'Borders, Border Regions and Territoriality: Contradictory Meanings, Changing Significance', *Regional Studies*, Vol. 33, No. 7 (1999), pp. 593–604.

Andurain, Julie de and Cloé Drieu, 'Introduction: Par-delà le théâtre européen de 14–18. L'autre Grande Guerre dans le monde musulman', *Revue des Mondes Musulmans et de la Méditerranée*, Vol. 141 (2017), pp. 11–33.

Anzaldúa, Gloria, *Borderlands/La Frontera: The New Mestiza* (San Francisco, CA: Aunt Lute Books, 1987).

Aras, Ramazan, 'Naqshandi Sufis and Their Conception of Place, Time and Fear on the Turkish–Syrian Border and Borderland', *Middle Eastern Studies*, Vol. 34, No. 4 (2018), pp. 44–66.

Aras, Ramazan, *The Wall: The Making and Unmaking of the Turkish–Syrian Border* (London: Palgrave Macmillan, 2020).

Armiero, Marco and Richard Tucker (eds), *Environmental History of Modern Migrations* (London and New York: Routledge, 2017).

Arsan, Andrew, *Interlopers of Empire: The Lebanese Diaspora in Colonial French West Africa* (London: Hurst, 2014).

al-Askari, Jafar Pasha, *A Soldier's Story: From Ottoman Rule to Independent Iraq: The Memoirs of Jafar Pasha al-Askari*, trans. by Mustafa Tariq al-Askari (London: Arabian Publishing, 2003).

Aslan, Senem, 'Everyday Forms of State Power and the Kurds in the Early Turkish Republic', *International Journal of Middle East Studies*, Vol. 43, No. 1 (2011), pp. 75–93.

Atabaki, Touraj and Erik J. Zürcher (eds), *Men of Order: Authoritarian Modernization under Atatürk and Reza Shah* (London: I. B. Tauris, 2004).

Atatürk, *Atatürk'ün Söylev ve Demeçleri, V* (Ankara: Türk İnkilap Tarihi Enstitüsü, 1972).

Atatürk, *Atatürk'ün Söylev ve Demeçleri, I–III* (Ankara: Atatürk Araştırma Merkezi, 1997).

Ateş, Sabri, 'Bones of Contention: Corpse Traffic and Ottoman-Iranian Rivalry in Nineteenth-Century Iraq', *Comparative Studies of South Asia, Africa and the Middle East*, Vol. 30, No. 3 (2010), pp. 512–32.

Ateş, Sabri, *The Ottoman-Iranian Borderlands. Making a Boundary, 1843–1914* (Cambridge: Cambridge University Press, 2013).

Atmaca, Metin, 'Fragile Frontiers: Sayyid Taha II and the Role of Kurdish Religio-Political Leadership in the Ottoman East during the First World War', *Middle Eastern Studies*, Vol. 54, No. 3 (2018), pp. 361–81.

Aybars, Ergün, *İstiklal Mahkemleri, 1920–7* (Izmir: Eylül University, 1988).

Ayberk, Nuri Fehmi, 'Türkiye Trahom Mücadelesi Tarihçesine ait Hatıralarım', *Göz Kliniği*, Vol. 10 (1961), pp. 127–34.

Ayberk, Nuri Fehmi. 'Dünya Trahom Mücadelesi', *Türk Oftalmoloji Gazetesi*, Vol. 1, No. 11–12 (1931), pp. 688–710.

Aydın, Mustafa, 'Turkish Foreign Policy in the Chaos of War, 1939–45', *Journal of Balkan and Near East Studies*, Vol. 23, No. 6 (2021), pp. 854–71.

Badie, Bertrand, *La fin des territoires. Essai sur le désordre international et sur l'utilité sociale du respect* (Paris: Fayard, 1995).

Balandier, Georges, *Anthropologie politique* (Paris: PUF, 1967).

Balistreri, Alexander E., 'Revisiting Millî: Borders and the Making of the Turkish Nation State', in Jordi Tejel and Ramazan Hakkı Öztan (eds), *Regimes of Mobility: Borders and State Formation in the Middle East, 1918–46* (Edinburgh: Edinburgh University Press, 2022), pp. 29–58.

Banko, Lauren, 'Refugees, Displaced Migrants, and Territorialization in Interwar Palestine', *Mashriq & Mahjar*, Vol. 5, No. 2 (2018), pp. 19–48.

Banko, Lauren, 'Border Transgressions, Border Controls: Mobility along Palestine's Northern Frontier, 1930–46', in Jordi Tejel and Ramazan Hakkı Öztan (eds), *Regimes of Mobility: Borders and State Formation in the Middle East, 1918–46* (Edinburgh: Edinburgh University Press, 2022), pp. 256–85.

Baraç, Sema Yasar, 'Nestorians, Kurds, and the State: The Struggle to Survive in the Frontier in the Late Ottoman Period, 1839–1908' (MA Thesis, Istanbul: Bogaziçi University, 2015).

Barak, On and Haggai Ram, 'Beyond Connectivity: The Middle East in Global History', *Journal of Levantine Studies*, Vol. 10, No. 1 (2020), pp. 5–9.

Barak, On, *Powering Empire: How Coal Made the Middle East and Sparked Global Carbonization* (Berkeley, CA: University of California Press, 2020).

Barakat, Nora, 'An Empty Land? Nomads and Property Administration in Hamidian Syria' (PhD dissertation, Berkeley, CA: University of California, 2015).

Barkey, Karen, *Bandits and Bureaucrats: The Ottoman Route to State Centralization* (Ithaca: Cornell University Press, 1994).

Barkey, Karen, *Empire of Difference: The Ottomans in Comparative Perspective* (Cambridge: Cambridge University Press, 2008).

Barlas, Dilek, *Etatism and Diplomacy in Turkey: Economic and Foreign Policy Strategies in an Uncertain World, 1929–39* (Leiden: Brill, 1998).

Barlas, Dilek, 'Friends or Foes? Diplomatic Relations between Italy and Turkey, 1923–36', *International Journal of Middle East Studies*, Vol. 36, No. 2 (2004), pp. 231–52.

Barlas, Dilek and Seçkin Barış Gülmez, 'Turkish-British Relations in the 1930s: From Ambivalence to Partnership', *Middle Eastern Studies*, Vol. 54, No. 5 (2018), pp. 827–40.

Barr, James, *A Line in the Sand: Britain, France and the Struggle that Shaped the Middle East* (London: Simon and Schuster, 2011).

Bartov, Omer and Eric D. Weitz (eds), *Shatterzone of Empires: Coexistence and Violence in the German, Habsburg, Russian, and Ottoman Borderlands* (Bloomington: Indiana University Press, 2013).

Bashford, Alison, 'Global Biopolitics and the History of World Health', *History of the Human Sciences*, Vol. 19, No. 1 (2006), pp. 67–88.

Bashkin, Orit, *The Other Iraq: Pluralism and Culture in Hashemite Iraq* (Stanford, CA: Stanford University Press, 2008).

Bashkin, Orit, *New Babylonians: A History of Jews in Modern Iraq* (Stanford, CA: Stanford University Press, 2012).

Baud, Michiel and Willem van Schendel, 'Toward a Comparative History of Borderlands', *Journal of World History*, Vol. 8, No. 2 (1997), pp. 211–42.

Bauman, Zygmunt, 'Reconnaissance Wars of the Planetary Frontierland', *Theory, Culture and Society*, Vol. 19, No. 4 (2002), pp. 82–90.

Bayar, Yeşim, 'The League of Nations, Minorities, and Post-Imperial Turkey', *Journal of Historical Sociology*, Vol. 33, No. 1 (2020), pp. 172–83.

Bayat, Asef, *Life as Politics: How Ordinary People Change the Middle East* (Stanford, CA: Stanford University Press, 2010).

Bayrak, Mehmet, *Açık-Gizli/Resmi-Gayrıresmi Kürdoloji Belgeleri* (Ankara: Öz-Ge Yayınları, 1994).

Bayraktaroğlu, Sena, 'Development of Railways in the Ottoman Empire and Turkey' (MA Thesis, Istanbul: Boğaziçi University, 1995).

Behr, Hartmut, 'Deterritorialisation and the Transformation of Statehood: The Paradox of Globalisation', *Geopolitics*, Vol. 13, No. 2 (2008), pp. 359–82.

Bein, Amit, *Kemalist Turkey and the Middle East: International Relations in the Interwar Period* (Cambridge: Cambridge University Press, 2017).

Benton, Lauren, *Law and Colonial Cultures: Legal Regimes in World History, 1400–1900* (Cambridge: Cambridge University Press, 2002).

Berberian, Houri, *Roving Revolutionaries: Armenians and the Connected Revolutions in the Russian, Iranian, and Ottoman Worlds* (Oakland, CA: University of California Press, 2019).

Berdine, Michael D., *Redrawing the Middle East: Sir Mark Sykes, Imperialism and the Sykes-Picot Agreement* (London: I. B. Tauris, 2018).

Berman, Marshall, *All That is Solid Melts Into Air: The Experience of Modernity* (London: Verso, 1983).

Beverley, Eric L., 'Frontier as Resource: Law, Crime, and Sovereignty on the Margins of Empire', *Comparative Studies in Society and History*, Vol. 55, No. 2 (2013), pp. 241–72.

Bhabha, Homi, *The Location of Culture* (London and New York: Routledge, 1994).

Blecher, Robert, 'Desert Medicine, Ethnography, and the Colonial Encounter in Mandatory Syria', in Nadine Méouchy and Peter Sluglett (eds), *The British and French Mandates in Comparative Perspectives* (Leiden: Brill, 2004), pp. 249–68.

Bloxham, Donald, *The Great Game of Genocide: Imperialism, Nationalism, and the Destruction of the Ottoman Armenians* (Oxford: Oxford University Press, 2005).

Blumi, Isa, 'Illicit Trade and the Emergence of Albania and Yemen', in I. William Zartman (ed.), *Understanding Life in the Borderland: Boundaries in Depth and in Motion* (Athens, GA: University of Georgia Press, 2010), pp. 58–84.

Blumi, Isa, 'Agents of Post-Ottoman States: The Precariousness of the Berlin Congress Boundaries of Montenegro and How to Define/Confine People', in Hakan Yavuz and Peter Sluglett (eds), *War and Diplomacy: The Russo-Turkish War of 1877–1878 and the Treaty of Berlin* (Salt Lake City: University of Utah, 2011), pp. 194–231.

Blumi, Isa, *Foundations of Modernity: Human Agency and the Imperial State* (London: Routledge, 2012).

Blunt, Alison, 'Cultural Geographies of Migration: Mobility, Transnationalism and Diaspora', *Progress in Human Geography*, Vol. 31, No. 5 (2007), pp. 684–94.

Bocco, Riccardo, 'Asabiyât tribales et Etats au Moyen-Orient: Confrontations et connivences', *Maghreb-Machrek*, No. 147 (1995), pp. 3–12.

Bolaños, Isacar A., 'The Ottomans during the Global Crises of Cholera and Plague: The View from Iraq and the Gulf', *International Journal of Middle East Studies*, Vol. 51, No. 4 (2019), pp. 603–20.

Bolton, Herbert E., *The Spanish Borderlands: A Chronicle of Old Florida and the Southwest* (New Haven: Yale University Press, 1921).

Bonin, Hubert et al. (eds), *L'esprit économique impérial (1830–1970): Groupes de pression et réseaux du patronat colonial en France et dans l'Empire* (Paris: Publications de la SFHOM, 2008).

Bonnardi, Pierre, *L'Imbroglio syrien* (Paris: Rieder, 1927).

Bou-Nacklie, N. E., 'Les Troupes Spéciales: Religious and Ethnic Recruitment, 1916–46', *International Journal of Middle East Studies*, Vol. 25, No. 4 (1993), pp. 645–60.

Bourmaud, Philippe, 'Internationalizing Perspectives: Re-Reading Mandate History through a Health Policy Lens', *Canadian Bulletin of Medical History*, Vol. 30, No. 2 (2013), pp. 9–21.

Boyar, Ebru, 'Taking Health to the Village: Early Turkish Republican Health Propaganda in the Countryside', in Ebru Boyar and Kate Fleet (eds), *Middle Eastern and North African Societies in the Interwar Period* (Leiden: Brill, 2019), pp. 164–211.

Bozan, Oktay, *Millî Mücadele Döneminde Diyarbakır, 1918–23* (Konya: Çizgi Kitabevi, 2016).

Brandell, Inga (ed.), *State Frontiers: Borders and Boundaries in the Middle East* (London and New York: I. B. Tauris, 2006).

Brehony, Noel, *Yemen divided: The Story of a Failed State in South Arabia* (London: I. B. Tauris, 2013).

Brenner, Neil, 'Beyond State-Centrism? Space, Territoriality, and Geographical Scale in Globalization Studies', *Theory and Society*, Vol. 28 (1999), pp. 39–78.

Brockett, Gavin D., *How Happy to Call Oneself a Turk: Provincial Newspapers and the Negotiation of a Muslim National Identity* (Austin: University of Texas Press, 2011).

Bruinessen, Martin van, *Agha, Shaikh and the State: The Social and Political Structures of Kurdistan* (London: Zed Books, 1992).

Burke, Victor L., *The Clash of Civilizations: War-Making and State Formation in Europe* (Cambridge, MA: Blackwell, 1997).

Burns, Norman, *The Tariff of Syria, 1919–1932* (Beirut: American Press, 1933).

Büyüksaraç, Güldem B., 'Trans-Border Minority Activism and Kin-State Politics: The Case of Iraqi Turkmen and Turkish Interventionism', *Anthropological Quarterly*, Vol. 90, No. 1 (2017), pp. 17–54.

Cagaptay, Soner, *Islam, Secularism and Nationalism in Modern Turkey: Who is a Turk?* (London and New York: Routledge, 2006).

Çağlayan, Ercan, *Cumhuriyet'in Diyarbakır'da Kimlik İnşası* (Istanbul: İletişim, 2014).

Cantens, Thomas, Robert Ireland and Gaël Raballand, 'Introduction: Borders, Informality, International Trade and Customs', *Journal of Borderlands Studies*, Vol. 30, No. 3 (2015), pp. 365–80.

Casey, Edward S., 'Border Versus Boundary at La Frontera', *Environment and Planning D: Society and Space*, Vol. 29 (2011), pp. 384–98.

Casey, James, 'Sacred Surveillance: Indian Muslims, Waqf, and the Evolution of State Power in French Mandate Syria', in James R. Fichter (ed.), *British and French Colonialism in Africa, Asia and the Middle East: Connected Empires across the Eighteenth to the Twentieth Centuries* (London: Palgrave Macmillan, 2019), pp. 89–110.

Çelik, Adnan, 'Challenging State Borders: Smuggling as Kurdish Infra-Politics during "The Years of Silence"', in Lucie Drechselova and Adnan Çelik (eds), *Kurds in Turkey: Ethnographies of Heterogeneous Experiences* (Lanham: Lexington Books, 2019), pp. 159–84.

Cemil Paşa, Ekrem, *Muhtasar Hayatım* (Brussels: Kurdish Institute of Brussels, 1991).

Cemil Paşa, Kadri, *Doza Kurdistan. Kürdistan Davası. Kürt Milletinin 60 Yıllık Esaretten Kurtuluş Savaşı Hatıraları* (Ankara: Öz-Ge Yayınları, 1991).

Cerbus, Cameron A., 'The Legacy of Air Control: A Reassessment of the "Splendid Training Ground" of Mandate Iraq' (MA Thesis, Beirut: American University of Beirut, 2021).

Certeau, Michel de, *L'invention du quotidien Vol. I* (Paris: Gallimard, 1990).

Çetinsaya, Gökhan, 'Challenges of a Frontier Region: The Case of Ottoman Iraq in the Nineteenth Century', in A. C. S. Peacock (ed.), *The Frontiers of the Ottoman World* (Oxford: Oxford University Press, 2009), pp. 271–87.

Chan, Yuk Wah and Womack, Brantly, 'Not Merely a Border: Borderland Governance, Development and Transborder Relations in Asia', *Asian Anthropology*, Vol. 15, No. 2 (2016), pp. 95–103.

Chantre, Luc, *Pèlerinages d'empire: Une histoire européenne du pèlerinage à La Mecque* (Paris: Editions de la Sorbonne, 2018).

Chatty, Dawn, 'The Bedouin in Contemporary Syria: The Persistence of Tribal authority and Control', *Middle East Journal*, Vol. 64, No. 1 (2010), pp. 29–49.

Chatty, Dawn, 'Refugees, Exiles, and Other Forced Migrants in the Late Ottoman Empire', *Refugee Survey Quarterly*, Vol. 32, No. 2 (2013), pp. 35–52.

Chatty, Dawn, 'Special Issue Introduction', *International Journal of Middle East Studies*, Vol. 49, No. 4 (2017), pp. 577–82.

Chevallier, Dominique, 'Lyon et la Syrie en 1919: Les bases d'une intervention', *Revue historique*, No. 1 (1960), pp. 275–320.

Chiffoleau, Sylvia, *Genèse de la santé publique internationale: De la peste d'Orient à l'OMS* (Rennes: Presses Universitaires de Rennes, 2012).

Chiffoleau, Sylvia, 'Entre bienfaisance, contrôle des populations et agenda international: La politique sanitaire du mandat français en Syrie et au Liban', *Canadian Bulletin of Medical History*, Vol. 30, No. 2 (2013), pp. 91–111.

Christie, Agatha, *Murder on the Orient Express* (London: Collins Crime Club, 1934).

Cigerli, Sabri and Didier Le Saout, *Les Kurdes: L'émergence du nationalisme kurde (1874–1945) dans les archives diplomatiques françaises* (Paris: L'Harmattan, 2019).

Cigerwxîn, *Jînenîgariya min* (Spanga: Apec, 1995).

Cimino, Matthieu (ed.), *Syria: Borders, Boundaries, and the State* (London: Palgrave Macmillan, 2020).

Clyne, Anthony, 'Man's Immemorial Enemy: New Anti-Locust Campaign in Africa and the Middle East', *The African World*, 1943, p. 97.

Cole, Simon A., *Suspect Identities: A History of Fingerprinting and Criminal Identification* (Cambridge, MA: Harvard University Press, 2002).

Cooke, Hedley V., *Challenge and Response in the Middle East: The Quest for Prosperity* (New York: Harper & Brothers, 1951).

Cox, Jafna L., 'A Splendid Training Ground: The Importance of the Royal Air Force in its Role in Iraq, 1919–32', *Journal of Imperial and Commonwealth History*, Vol. 13 (1985), pp. 157–84.

Cuthell, David, 'The Muhacirin Komisyonu: An Agent in the Transformation of Ottoman Anatolia, 1860–6' (PhD dissertation, New York: Columbia University, 2005).

Danforth, Nicholas, 'Nomads, No Problem: Rethinking Border Regimes in the Post-Ottoman Middle East', www.midafternoonmap.com/2017/01/the-myth-of-myth-of-borders.html (last accessed 2 March 2018).

Davis, Diane K., *The Arid Lands: History, Power, Knowledge* (Cambridge, MA: MIT Press, 2016).

Davis, Eric, *Memories of State: Politics, History, and Collective Identity in Modern Iraq* (Berkeley, CA: University of California Press, 2005).

Dawisha, Adeed and I. William Zartman (eds), *Beyond Coercion: The Durability of the Arab State* (London: Croom Helm, 1988).

Delay, Brian (ed.), *North American Borderlands* (London: Routledge, 2013).

Demir, Enes, *Yeni Belgeler Işığında. Vazgeçilmeyen Topraklar Mîsak-ı Millî* (Istanbul: Post, 2017).

Demirci, Sevtap, 'Turco-British Diplomatic Manoeuvres on the Mosul Question in the Lausanne Conference, 1922–3', *British Journal of Middle Eastern Studies*, Vol. 3, No. 1 (2010), pp. 57–71.

Deringil, Selim, *Turkish Foreign Policy during the Second World War: An 'Active' Neutrality* (Cambridge: Cambridge University Press, 1989).

Destremau, Christian, *Le Moyen-Orient pendant la seconde guerre mondiale* (Paris: Perrin, 2011).

Dewachi, Omar, *Ungovernable Life: Mandatory Medicine and Statecraft in Iraq* (Stanford, CA: Stanford University Press, 2017).

Dijkink, Gertjan, *National Identity and Geopolitical Visions: Maps of Pride and Pain* (London: Routledge, 1996).

Dillemann, Louis, 'Les Français en Haute Djézireh', *Revue Française d'Histoire d'Outre-Mer*, t. LXVI (1979), pp. 33–58.

Dodge, Toby, *Inventing Iraq: The Failure of Nation Building and a History Denied* (New York: Columbia University Press, 2003).

Dokuyan, Sabit, 'İkinci Dünya Savaşı Sırasında Yaşanan Gıda Sıkıntısı ve Ekmek Karnesi Uygulaması', *Turkish Studies*, Vol. 8, No. 5 (2013), pp. 193–210.

Dolbee, Samuel, 'The Locust and the Starling: People, Insects, and Disease in the Late Ottoman Jazira and After, 1860–1940' (PhD dissertation, New York: New York University, 2017).

Dolbee, Samuel, "The Desert at the End of Empire: An Environmental History of the Armenian Genocide', *Past and Present*, Vol. 247, No. 1 (2020), pp. 197–233.

Dolbee, Samuel, 'Borders, Disease, and Territoriality in the Post-Ottoman Middle East', in Jordi Tejel and Ramazan Hakkı Öztan (eds), *Regimes of Mobility: Borders and State Formation in the Middle East, 1918–46* (Edinburgh: Edinburgh University Press, 2022), pp. 205–27.

Donnan, Hastings and Thomas M. Wilson (eds), *Borderlands: Ethnographic Approaches to Security, Power, and Identity* (London and New York: University Press of America, 2010).

Douki, Caroline and Philippe Minard, 'Histoire globale, histoires connectées: Un changement d'échelle historiographique ?', *Revue d'histoire moderne contemporaine*, Vol. 54–5, No. 5 (2007), pp. 7–21.

Driver, Felix and Raphael Samuel, 'Re-Thinking the Idea of Place', *History Workshop Journal*, Vol. 39, No. 1 (1995), pp. v–vii.

Duffy, Andrea E., 'Civilizing through Cork: Conservationism and *la Mission Civilisatrice* in French Colonial Algeria', *Environmental History*, Vol. 23 (2018), pp. 270–92.

Dullin, Sabine, 'L'invention d'une frontière de guerre froide à l'ouest de l'Union soviétique (1945–9)', *Vingtième Siècle Revue d'histoire*, No. 102 (2009), pp. 49–61.

Dumont, Paul, *Mustafa Kemal invente la Turquie moderne* (Brussels: Complexe, 1997).

Dündar, Fuat, 'Statisquo: British Use of Statistics in the Iraqi Question, 1919–32', Crown Paper (Brandeis University), No. 7 (2012), pp. 1–63.

Dunn, Joe P., 'A Death in Dohuk: Roger C. Cumberland, Mission and Politics among the Kurds in Northern Iraq, 1923–38', *Journal of Third World Studies*, Vol. 32, No. 1 (2015), pp. 245–71.

al-Durah, Mahmud, *al-Harb al-Iraqiyya al-Britaniyya 1941* (Beirut: Dar al-Taliah, 1973).

Eagleton, William, *The Kurdish Republic of 1946* (London: Oxford University Press, 1963).

Ediger, Volkan S. and John V. Bowlus, 'Greasing the Wheels: The Berlin-Baghdad Railways and Ottoman Oil, 1888–1907', *Middle Eastern Studies*, Vol. 56, No. 2 (2020), pp. 193–206.

Edmonds, Cecil J., *Kurds, Turks and Arabs* (London: Oxford University Press, 1957).

Efrati, Noga, *Women in Iraq: Past Meets Present* (New York: Columbia University Press, 2012).

Efrati, Noga, 'The First World War and its Legacy for Women in Iraq', in T. G. Fraser (ed.), *The First World War and its Aftermath: The Shaping of the Middle East* (London: Cingko, 2015), pp. 77–89.

Ekmekçioğlu, Lerna, 'Republic of Paradox: The League of Nations Minority Protection Regime and the New Turkey's Step-Citizens', *International Journal of Middle East Studies*, Vol. 46, No. 4 (2014), pp. 657–79,

Eleftériadès, Eleuthère, *Les chemins de fer en Syrie et au Liban: Etude historique, financière et économique* (Beirut: Impr. Catholique, 1944).

Ellis, Matthew, 'Over the Borderline? Rethinking Territoriality at the Margins of Empire and Nation in the Modern Middle East (Part I)', *History Compass*, Vol. 13, No. 8 (2015), pp. 411–22.

Ellis, Matthew H., *Desert Borderland: The Making of Modern Egypt and Libya* (Stanford, CA: Stanford University Press, 2018).

Erdoğan, Bariş, 'L'Etat, la presse et la violence déployée contre les Kurdes de Turquie', *The Journal of Kurdish Studies*, Vol. IV (2001–2002), pp. 49–56.

Ersoy, Nermin, Yuksel Gungor and Alishan Akpinar, 'International Sanitary Conferences from the Ottoman Perspective, 1851–1938', *Hygiea Internationalis: An Interdisciplinary Journal for the History of Public Health*, Vol. 10, No. 1 (2011), pp. 53–79.

Eskander, Saad, 'Southern Kurdistan under Britain's Mesopotamian Mandate: From Separation to Incorporation, 1920–3', *Middle Eastern Studies*, Vol. 37, No. 2 (2001), pp. 153–80.

Evans, Peter B., Dietrich Rueschemeyer and Theda Skocpol (eds), *Bringing the State Back In* (Cambridge: Cambridge University Press, 1985).

Evered, Kyle T. and Emine Ö. Evered, 'State, Peasant, Mosquito: The Biopolitics of Public Health Education and Malaria in Early Republican Turkey', *Political Geography*, Vol. 31 (2012), pp. 311–23.

Fahrenthold, Stacy, *Between the Ottomans and the Entente: The First World War in the Syrian and Lebanese Diaspora, 1908–25* (Oxford: Oxford University Press, 2019).

Fattah, Hala, *The Politics of Regional Trade* (Albany: SUNY Press, 1997).

Fawaz, Leila T., *A Land of Aching Hearts: The Middle East in the Great War* (Cambridge, MA: Harvard University Press, 2014).

Fawcett, Louise, 'States and Sovereignty in the Middle East: Myths and Realities', *International Affairs*, Vol. 93, No. 4 (2017), pp. 789–807.

Fethi, Rükneddin, *Doğu Köylerinde* (Istanbul: Çığır Kitabevi, 1938).

Fieldhouse, D. K. (ed.), *Kurds, Arabs and Britons: The Memoir of Wallace Lyon in Iraq, 1918–44* (London: I. B. Tauris, 2002).

Fiey, J. M., 'The Iraqi Section of the Abbasid Road Mosul-Nisibin', *Iraq*, Vol. 26, No. 2 (1964), pp. 106–17.

Fink, Carole, 'The League of Nations and the Minority Question', *World Affairs*, Vol. 157, No. 4 (1995), pp. 197–205.

Flateau, Cosima, 'La sortie de guerre de l'Empire ottoman: Grande Guerre, guerre nationale, guerre coloniale à la frontière syro-turque, 1918–23', *Les Cahiers Sirice*, Vol. 17, No. 3 (2016), pp. 29–45.

Fletcher, Robert S., 'Running the Corridor: Nomadic Societies and Imperial Rule in the Inter-War Syrian desert', *Past and Present*, Vol. 220, No. 1 (2013), pp. 185–215.

Fletcher, Robert S., *British Imperialism and the Tribal Question* (Oxford: Oxford University Press, 2015).

Fletcher, Robert S., 'Decolonization and the Arid World', in Martin Thomas and Andrew S. Thompson (eds), *The Oxford Handbook of the Ends of Empire* (Oxford: online publication, 2018): DOI:10.1093/oxfordhb/9780198713197.013.22 (accessed 1 March 2022).

Fletcher, Robert S., 'When Nomads Flee: 'Raider', 'Rebel' and 'Refugee' in Southern Iraq, 1917–30' in Jordi Tejel and Ramazan Hakkı Öztan (eds), *Regimes of Mobility: Borders and State Formation in the Middle East, 1918–46* (Edinburgh: Edinburgh University Press, 2022), pp. 286–318.

Foliard, Daniel, *Dislocating the Orient: British Maps and the Making of the Middle East* (Chicago: University of Chicago Press, 2017).

Forestier-Peyrat, Etienne, 'Fighting Locusts Together: Pest Control and the Birth of Soviet Development Aid, 1920–1939', *Global Environment*, Vol. 7, No. 2 (2014), pp. 536–71.

Foster, Zachary J., 'The 1915 Locust Attack in Syria and Palestine and its Role in the Famine during the First World War', *Middle Eastern Studies*, Vol. 51, No. 3 (2015), pp. 370–94.

Foucher, Michel, *Fronts et frontières: Un tour du monde géopolitique* (Paris: Fayard, 1991).

Fraser, T. G., Andrew Mango and Robert McNamara, *The Makers of the Modern Middle East* (London: Gingko Library, 2011).

Fratantuono, Ella, 'Producing Ottomans: Internal Colonization and Social Engineering in Ottoman Immigrant Settlement', *Journal of Genocide Research*, Vol. 21, No. 1 (2019), pp. 1–24.

Fromkin, David, *A Peace to End all Peace: The Fall of the Ottoman Empire and the Creation of the Modern Middle East*, rev. ed. (New York: Henry Holt and Company, 2009, 1st version 1989).

Fuccaro, Nelida, *The Other Kurds: Yazidis in Colonial Iraq* (London: I. B. Tauris, 1998).

Fuccaro, Nelida, 'Minorities and Ethnic Mobilization: The Kurds in Northern Iraq and Syria', in Nadine Méouchy and Peter Sluglett (eds), *The British and French Mandates in Comparative Perspectives* (Leiden: Brill, 2004), pp. 579–95.

Galbraith, Peter, *The End of Iraq: How American Incompetence Created a War Without End* (New York: Simon and Schuster, 2006).

Gatrell, Peter, *The Making of the Modern Refugee* (Oxford: Oxford University Press, 2013).

Gatrell, Peter et al. 'Reckoning with Refugeedom: Refugee Voices in Modern History', *Social History*, Vol. 46, No. 1 (2021), pp. 70–95.

Gaulle, Charles de, *Mémoires de guerre* (Paris: Plon, 1999).

Gavrilis, George, *The Dynamics of Interstate Boundaries* (Cambridge: Cambridge University Press, 2008).

Gellner, David N. (ed.), *Borderland Lives in Northern South Asia* (London: Rowman & Littlefield, 2013).

Gellner, Ernest, 'Tribalism and State in the Middle East', in Philip S. Khoury and Joseph Kostiner (eds), *Tribes and State Formation in the Middle East* (London: I. B. Tauris, 1990), pp. 109–26.

Gelvin, James L., *Divided Loyalties: Nationalism and Mass Politics in Syria at the Close of Empire* (Berkeley, CA: University of California Press, 1998).

Gelvin, James L., 'Developmentalism, Revolution, and Freedom in the Arab East: The Cases of Egypt, Syria, and Iraq', in Robert H. Taylor (ed.), *The Idea of Freedom in Asia and Africa* (Stanford, CA: Stanford University Press, 2002), pp. 62–96.

Gelvin, James L. and Nile Green (eds), *Global Muslims in the Age of Steam and Print* (Oakland, CA: University of California Press, 2014).

Genelkurmay belgelerinde Kürt Isyanları, Vol. I (Ankara: Kaynak Yayınları, 1992).

Gerwarth, Robert and John Horne (eds), *War in Peace: Paramilitary Violence in Europe after the Great War* (Oxford: Oxford University Press, 2012).

Gerwarth, Robert and Erez Manela (eds), *Empires at War, 1911–23* (Oxford: Oxford University Press, 2014).

Giddens, Anthony, *The Nation-State and Violence* (Cambridge: Cambridge University Press, 1985).

Gil-Har, Yitzhak, 'French Policy in Syria and Zionism: Proposal for a Zionist Settlement', *Middle Eastern Studies*, Vol. 30, No. 1 (1994), pp. 155–65.

Gilad, Efrat, 'Meat in the Heat: A History of Tel Aviv under the British Mandate for Palestine, 1920s–40s' (PhD dissertation, Geneva: The Graduate Institute of International and Development Studies, 2021).

Gingeras, Ryan, *Sorrowful Shores: Violence, Ethnicity, and the End of the Ottoman Empire, 1912–1923* (Oxford: Oxford University Press, 2009).

Gingeras, Ryan, *Fall of the Sultanate: The Great War and the End of the Ottoman Empire, 1908–1922* (Oxford: Oxford University Press, 2016).

Ginio, Eyal, *Ottoman Culture of Defeat: The Balkan Wars and their Aftermath* (Oxford: Oxford University Press, 2015).

Glick Schiller, Nina and Noel B. Salazar, 'Regimes of Mobility across the Globe', *Journal of Ethnic and Migration Studies*, Vol. 39, No. 2 (2013), pp. 183–200.

Göç, Eray, 'Türk İstihbaratının Tarihsel Gelişimi', *Çankırı Karatekin Üniversitesi İktisadi ve İdari Bilimler Fakültesi Dergisi*, Vol. 3, No. 2 (2013), pp. 85–111.

Gökmen, Ertan, 'Batı Anadolu'da çekirge felâketi, 1850–1915', *Belleten. Türk Tarihi Kurumu*, Vol. 74/269 (2010), pp. 127–80.

Goodhand, Jonathan, 'Epilogue: The View from the Border', in Benedikt Korf and Timothy Raeymaekers (eds), *Violence on the Margins: States, Conflict, and Borderlands* (New York: Palgrave Macmillan, 2013), pp. 247–64.

Gossman, Lionel, *The Passion of Max von Oppenheim: Archaeology and Intrigue in the Middle East from Wilhelm II to Hitler* (Cambridge: Open Book Publishers, 2013).

Grant, Christina Phelps, *The Syrian Desert: Caravans, Travel and Exploration* (New York: Macmillan, 1936).

Gratien, Chris, *The Unsettled Plain: An Environmental History of the Late Ottoman Frontier* (Stanford, CA: Stanford University Press, 2022).

Green, Nile, 'Fordist Connections: The Automotive Integration of the United States and Iran', *Comparative Studies in Society and History*, Vol. 58, No. 2 (2016), pp. 290–321.

Güçlü, Yücel, 'The Controversy over the Delimitation of the Turco-Syrian Frontier in the Period between the two World Wars', *Middle Eastern Studies*, Vol. 42, No. 4 (2006), pp. 641–57.

Güngör, Evren, 'Les transports en Turquie: Problèmes et points de vue sur les solutions', *Anatolia moderna*, T. 5 (1994), pp. 155–61.

Gupta, Akhil, 'Blurred Boundaries: The Discourse of Corruption, the Culture of Politics, and the Imagined State', in Aradhana Sharma and Akhil Gupta (eds), *The Anthropology of the State: A Reader* (Malden, MA: Wiley–Blackwell, 2005), pp. 211–41.

Gurani, Ali Saydu, *Min Amman Ila al-Imadiyya Aw Jawla fi Kurdistan al-Janubiyya* (Cairo: al-Sa'adaa, 1939).

Gutman, David, 'Travel Documents, Mobility Control, and the Ottoman State in the Age of Global Migration, 1880–1915', *Journal of Ottoman and Turkish Studies Association*, Vol. 3, No. 2 (2016), pp. 347–68.

Güztoklusu, Murat, *Elcezire ve Özdemir Harekatı* (Istanbul: Ümit Yayınları, 2006).

Hämäläinen, Pekka and Samuel Truett, 'On Borderlands', *Journal of American History*, Vol. 98, No. 2 (2011), pp. 338–61.

Hämäläinen, Pekka, *The Comanche Empire* (New Haven and London: Yale University Press, 2011).

Hamed-Troyansky, Vladimir, 'Circassian Refugees and the Making of Amman, 1878–1914', *International Journal of Middle East Studies*, Vol. 49, No. 4 (2017), pp. 605–23.

Hamelink, Wendelmoet and Hanifi Baris, 'Dengbêjs on Borderlands: Borders and the State as Seen through the Eyes of Kurdish Singer-Poets', *Kurdish Studies*, Vol. 2, No. 1 (2014), pp. 34–60.

Hansen, Randall, 'State Controls: Borders, Refugees, and Citizenship', in Elena Fiddina Qasmiyeh et al. (eds), *The Oxford Handbook of Refugee and Forced Migration Studies* (Oxford: Oxford University Press, 2014), pp. 1–14.

Haznevî, Şeyh Alâaddin, *Hazret ve Şah-ı Hazne*, ed. by Abdullah Demiray (Istanbul: Semerkand Yayınları, 2012).

Heper, Metin, *The State Tradition in Turkey* (Hull: Eothen Press, 1985).

Heydemann, Steven, *War, Institutions, and Social Change in the Middle East* (Berkeley, CA: University of California Press, 2000).

Hilmi, Rafiq, *Yaddaşt* (London: New Hope, 2007).

Hopkins, Benjamin D., 'The Bounds of Identity: The Goldsmith Mission and the Delineation of the Perso-Afghan border in the Nineteenth Century', *Journal of Global History*, Vol. 2, No. 2 (2007), pp. 233–54.

Hopkins, Benjamin D. and Magnus Marsden, *Fragments of the Afghan Frontier* (London: Hurst, 2011).

Houtum, Henk van and Ton van Naerssen, 'Bordering, Ordering and Othering', *Tijdschrift voor Economische en Sociale Geografie*, Vol. 93, No. 2 (2002), pp. 125–36.

Huber, Valeska, 'The Unification of the Globe by Disease? The International Sanitary Conferences on Cholera, 1851–94', *The Historical Journal*, Vol. 49, No. 2 (2006), pp. 453–76.

Huber, Valeska, *Channelling Mobilities: Migration and Globalisation in the Suez Canal Region and Beyond, 1869–1914* (Cambridge: Cambridge University Press, 2013).

Huber, Valeska, 'International Bodies: The Pilgrimage to Mecca and International Health Regulation', in Eric Tagliacozzo and Shawkat M. Toorawa (eds), *The Hajj: Pilgrimage in Islam* (Cambridge: Cambridge University Press, 2015), pp. 175–95.

Huis, Arnold van, Keith Cressman and Joyce I. Magor, 'Preventing Desert Locust Plagues: Optimizing Management Interventions', *Entomologia Experimentalis et Applicata*, Vol. 122, No. 3 (2007), pp. 191–214.

Huvelin, Paul, *Que vaut la Syrie?* (Marseille: Chambre de Commerce de Marseille, 1919).

Ilkin, Selim, *A Foreign Capital Investment Enterprise in Turkey in the Years 1922–3: The Chester Railway Project* (Istanbul: Türkiye İş Bankası, 1981).

İnönü, İsmet, *Defterler (1919–73) Vol. I*, ed. by Ahmet Demirel (Istanbul: YKY, 2008).

İnönü, İsmet, *Hatıralar* (Ankara: Bilgi Yayınevi, 2014).

Ireland, Philip Willard, 'Berlin to Baghdad Up-to-Date', *Foreign Affairs*, Vol. 19, No. 3 (1941), pp. 665–9.

Irvine, Rebecca, 'Anticolonial Resistance in the Post-Ottoman Mashriq: Examining the Iraqi Jazirah' (MA Thesis, Lund: Lund University, 2018).

Isçi, Onur, *Turkey and the Soviet Union during World War II* (London: I. B. Tauris, 2019).

Isenberg, Andrew C. (ed.), *The Oxford Handbook of Environmental History* (Oxford: Oxford University Press, 2014).

Jackson, Ashley, *The British Empire and the Second World War* (London: Hambledon Continuum, 2006).

Jackson, Ashley, *Persian Gulf Command: A History of the Second World War in Iran and Iraq* (New Haven and London: Yale University Press, 2018).

Jackson, Simon, 'What is Syria Worth? The Huvelin Mission, Economic Expertise and the French Project in the Eastern Mediterranean, 1918–22', *Monde(s)*, No. 4 (2013), pp. 83–103.

Jáquez Martínez, Oscar, *Border People: Life and Society in the US-Mexico Borderlands* (Tucson: University of Arizona Press, 1994).

Jaquier, César, 'Motor Cars and Transdesert Traffic: Channelling Mobilities between Iraq and Syria, 1923–30', in Jordi Tejel and Ramazan Hakkı Öztan (eds), *Regimes of Mobility: Borders and State Formation in the Middle East, 1918–46* (Edinburgh: Edinburgh University Press, 2022), pp. 228–55.

Johnson, Rob, *The Great War and the Middle East* (Oxford: Oxford University Press, 2016).

Johnson, Walter, 'On Agency', *Journal of Social History*, Vol. 37, No. 1 (2003), pp. 113–24.

Jones, Reece, 'Spaces of Refusal: Rethinking Sovereign Power and Resistance at the Border', *Annals of the Association of American Geographers*, Vol. 102, No. 3 (2012), pp. 685–99.

Jones, Reece, *Violent Borders: Refugees and the Right to Move* (London: Verso, 2016).

Joseph, John, *The Modern Assyrians of the Middle East: Encounters with Christian Missions, Archeologists, and Colonial Powers* (Leiden: Brill, 2000).

Josselin, Daphné and William Wallace, 'Non-State Actors in World Politics: A Framework', in Daphné Josselin and William Wallace (eds), *Non-State Actors in World Politics* (New York: Palgrave/Macmillan, 2002), pp. 1–20.

al-Jumaily, Izzet, *Irak ve Kemalizm Hareketi, 1919–23* (Ankara: Atatürk Araştırma Merkezi, 1999).

Jwaideh, Wadie, *The Kurdish Nationalist Movement: Its Origins and Development* (Syracuse, NY: Syracuse University Press, 2006).

Kadhim, Abbas, *Reclaiming Iraq: The 1920 Revolution and the Founding of the Modern State* (Austin: University of Texas Press, 2012).

Kadıoğlu, Ayşe, 'The Twin Motives of Turkish Nationalism', in Ayşe Kadıoğlu and E. Fuat Keyman (eds), *Symbiotic Antagonisms: Competing Nationalisms in Turkey* (Salt Lake City: University of Utah Press, 2011), pp. 33–56.

Kale, Başak, 'Transforming an Empire: The Ottoman Empire's Immigration and Settlement Policies in the Nineteenth and Early Twentieth Centuries', *Middle Eastern Studies*, Vol. 50, No. 2 (2014), pp. 252–71.

Kamal Nuri, Maruf, *Yaddaştakanî Sheikh Latif-i Hafid Lasar Şoreşakanî Sheikh Mahmud-i Hafid* (Pirmam: Cultural Centre of Kurdistan Democratic Party, 1995).

Kamel, Lorenzo, *The Middle East from Empire to Sealed Identities* (Edinburgh: Edinburgh University Press, 2019).

Kasaba, Reşat, *A Moveable Empire: Ottomans, Nomads, Migrants, and Refugees* (Seattle and London: University of Washington Press, 2009).

Kaufman, Asher, *Reviving Phoenicia: The Search for Identity in Lebanon* (London: I. B. Tauris, 2004).

Kaufman, Asher, *Contested Frontiers in the Syria-Lebanon-Israel Region: Cartography, Sovereignty, and Conflict* (Washington, DC: Woodrow Wilson Centre Press, 2014).

Kaya, Ugur, 'Frontière et territorialité dans la perception selon l'Etat turc', *Confluence Méditerranée*, Vol. 101, No. 2 (2017), pp. 13–25.

Kazancıgil, Ali and Ergun Özbudun (eds), *Atatürk: Founder of a Modern State* (London: Hurst, 1981).

Khairallah, Shereen, *Railways in the Middle East, 1856–1948* (Beirut: Libraire du Liban, 1991).

Khairallah, Shereen, 'Railway Networks of the Middle East to 1948', in Thomas Philipp and Birgit Schaebler (eds), *The Syrian Land: Processes of Integration and Fragmentation* (Stuttgart: Franz Steiner Verlag, 1998), pp. 77–93.

Khawaja, Ahmed, *Çim Dît: Şoreşakanî Sheikh Mahmud-i Mezin* (Erbil: Dar Aras, 2013).

Khoury, Dina R., *State and Provincial Society in the Ottoman Empire: Mosul, 1540–1834* (Cambridge: Cambridge University Press, 1997).

Khoury, Philip S., 'The Tribal Shaykh, French Tribal Policy, and the Nationalist Movement in Syria between Two World Wars', *Middle Eastern Studies*, Vol. 18, No. 2 (1982), pp. 180–93.

Khoury, Philip S., *Syria and the French Mandate: The Politics of Arab Nationalism, 1920–45* (Princeton, NJ: Princeton University Press, 1987).

Kieser, Hans-Lukas, *Talaat Pasha: Father of Modern Turkey, Architect of Genocide* (Princeton, NJ: Princeton University Press, 2018).

Kirk, George, *The Middle East in the War* (London: Oxford University Press, 1952).

Klein, Janet, *The Margins of Empire: Kurdish Militias in the Ottoman Tribal Zone* (Stanford, CA: Stanford University Press, 2011).

Knatchbull-Hugessen, Sir Hughe, *Diplomat in Peace and War* (London: John Murray, 1949).

Knox, Macgregor, *Mussolini Unleashed, 1939–41: Politics and Strategy in Fascist Italy's Last War* (Cambridge: Cambridge University Press, 1982).

Koçak, Cemil, *Türkiye'de Millî Şef Dönemi, 1938–45* (Istanbul: İletişim Yayınları, 1996).

Koçak, Celim, *Umumî Müfettişlikler, 1927–52* (Istanbul: İletişim, 2010).

Konrad, Victor, 'Toward a Theory of Borders in Motion', *Journal of Borderlands Studies*, Vol. 30, No. 1 (2015), pp. 1–17.

Konrad, Victor, 'New Directions at the Post-Globalization Border', *Journal of Borderlands Studies*, Vol. 36, No. 5 (2021), pp. 713–43.

Korkusuz, M. Şerif, *Nehri'den Hazne'ye Meşayih-i Nakşibendî* (Istanbul: Kilim Matbaacılık, 2010).

Kozma, Liat, Cyrus Schayegh and Avner Wishnitzer (eds), *A Global Middle East: Mobility, Materiality and Culture in the Modern Age, 1880–1940* (London: I. B. Tauris, 2015).

Kozma, Liat, *Global Women, Colonial Ports: Prostitution in the Interwar Middle East* (Albany: SUNY Press, 2017).

Kozma, Liat, 'Doctors Crossing Borders: The Formation of a Regional Profession in the Interwar Middle East', in Ebru Boyar and Kate Fleet (eds), *Middle Eastern and North African Societies in the Interwar Period* (Leiden: Brill, 2018), pp. 123–43.

Kratochwil, Friedrich, 'Of Systems, Boundaries, and Territoriality: An Inquiry into the Formation of the State System', *World Politics*, Vol. 39, No. 1 (1986), pp. 27–52.

Kurd Ali, Muhammad, *Al-Mudhakkirat, Vol. II* (Riyadh: Adwa al-Salaf, 2010), <www.dimoqrati.info/?p=52101> (accessed 17 February 2021).

Kurt, Ümit, 'Revising the Legal Infrastructure for the Confiscation of Armenian and Greek Wealth: An Analysis of the CUP Years and the Early Modern Republic', *Middle Eastern Studies*, Vol. 53, No. 5 (2017), pp. 700–23.

Kütük, Ahmet, 'Tairihi Süreç İçerisinde Nusaybin Yahudileri', *Islâmî Ilimler Dergisi*, Vol. 10, No. 2 (2015), pp. 93–115.

Lagroye, Jacques (ed.), *La politisation* (Paris: Belin, 2003).

Laine, Jussi P., 'The Multiscalar Production of Borders', *Geopolitics*, Vol. 21, No. 3 (2016), pp. 465–82.

Lamprou, Alexandros, *Nation-Building in Modern Turkey: The People's Houses, the State and the Citizen* (London: I. B. Tauris, 2015).

Lange, Katharina, 'Peripheral Experiences: Everyday Life in the Kurd Dagh during the Allied Occupation in the Second World War' in Heike Liebau et al. (eds), *World in World Wars* (Leiden: Brill, 2010), pp. 401–28.

Laskier, Michael M., 'Syria and Lebanon', in Reeva Spector Simon, Michale Menachem Laskier and Sara Reguer (eds), *The Jews of the Middle East and North Africa in Modern Times* (New York: Columbia University Press, 2002), pp. 316–34.

Lawson, Fred H., 'The Northern Syrian Revolts of 1919–21 and the Sharifian Regime: Congruence or Conflict of Interests and Ideologies?', in Thomas Philipp and Christof Schumann (eds), *From the Syrian Land to the States of Syria and Lebanon* (Beirut: Orient-Institut der DMG Beirut, 2004), pp. 257–74.

Lee, Lloyd E., *The War Years: A Global History of the Second World War* (London: Routledge, 1989).

Lefebvre, Camille, 'We have Tailored Africa: French Colonialism and the "Artificiality" of Africa's Borders in the Interwar Period', *Journal of Historical Geography*, Vol. 37, No. 2 (2011), pp. 191–202.

Lefebvre, Henri, *The Production of Space*, trans. by D. Nicholson-Smith (Oxford: Blackwell, 1991).

Lenczowski, George, *The Middle East in World Affairs* (Ithaca: Cornell University Press, 1952).

Lerner, Daniel, *The Passing of Traditional Society: Modernizing the Middle East* (Glencoe, IL: Free Press, 1958).

Levene, Mark, 'Creating a Modern Zone of Genocide: The Impact of Nation- and State-Formation on Eastern Anatolia, 1878–1923', *Holocaust and Genocide Studies*, Vol. 12, No. 3 (1998), pp. 393–433.

Levi, Giovanni, 'Frail Frontiers?', *Past and Present*, Vol. 242, Supplement 14 (2019), pp. 37–49.

Lewis, Bernard, *The Emergence of Modern Turkey* (London: Oxford University Press, 1962).

Lewis, Norman N., *Nomads and Settlers in Syria and Jordan, 1800–1980* (Cambridge: Cambridge University Press, 1987).

Liebisch-Gümüş, Carolin, 'Embedded Turkification: Nation Building and Violence within the Framework of the League of Nations, 1919–37', *International Journal of Middle East Studies*, Vol. 52, No. 2 (2020), pp. 229–44.

Lipsky, Michael, *Street-Level Bureaucracy: Dilemmas of the Individual in Public Services* (New York: Russel Sage Foundation, 1980).

Little, Adrian, 'The Complex Temporality of Borders: Contingency and Normativity', *European Journal of Political Theory*, Vol. 14, No. 4 (2015), pp. 429–47.

Lloyd, E. M. H., *Food and Inflation in the Middle East, 1940–5* (Stanford, CA: Stanford University Press, 1956).

Longrigg, Stephen H., *Iraq, 1900 to 1950: A Political, Social and Economic History* (Oxford: Oxford University Press, 1953).

Low, Michael C., 'Empire and the Hajj: Pilgrims, Plagues, and Pan-Islam under British Surveillance, 1865–1908', *International Journal of Middle East Studies*, Vol. 40, No. 2 (2008), pp. 269–90.

Lukitz, Liora, *A Quest in the Middle East: Gertrude Bell and the Making of Modern Iraq* (London: I. B. Tauris, 2006).

Lyman, Robert, *First Victory: Britain's Forgotten Struggle in the Middle East, 1941* (London: Little Brown, 2006).

MacArthur-Seal, Daniel-Joseph, 'Resurrecting Legal Extraterritoriality in Occupied Istanbul, 1918–23', *Middle Eastern Studies*, Vol. 54, No. 5 (2018), pp. 769–87.

Mac Gaffey, Janet, *Entrepreneurs and Parasites: The Struggle for Indigenous Capitalism in Zaire* (Cambridge: Cambridge University Press, 1987).

Macfie, A. L., 'British Intelligence and the Causes of Unrest in Mesopotamia, 1919–21', *Middle Eastern Studies*, Vol. 35, No. 1 (1999), pp. 165–77.

Maier, Charles, 'Consigning the Twentieth Century to History: Alternative Narratives for the Modern Era', *American Historical Review*, Vol. 105, No. 3 (2000), pp. 807–31.

Maier, Charles, 'Transformations of Territoriality, 1600–2000', in Gunilla Budde et al. (eds), *Transnationale Geschichte* (Göttingen: Vandenhoeck & Ruprecht, 2006), pp. 32–55.

Maisel, Sebastian, *Yezidis in Syria: Identity Building among a Double Minority* (Lanham: Lexington Books, 2016).

Malley, Shawn, 'Layard Enterprise: Victorian Archaeology and Informal Imperialism in Mesopotamia', *International Journal of Middle East Studies*, Vol. 40, No. 4 (2008), pp. 623–46.

Mameli-Ghaderi, Soheila, 'Le tracé de la frontière entre la Syrie et la Turquie (1921–1929)', *Guerres mondiales et conflits contemporains*, Vol. 207, No. 3 (2002), pp. 125–38.

Manela, Erez, *The Wilsonian Moment: Self-Determination and the International Origins of Anticolonial Nationalism* (Oxford: Oxford University Press, 2007).

Massicard, Elise, *Street-Level Governing: Negotiating the State in Urban Turkey* (Stanford, CA: Stanford University Press, 2022).

Matsuda, Hiroko, *Liminality of the Japanese Empire: Border Crossings from Okinawa to Colonial Taiwan* (Honolulu: University of Hawaii Press, 2018).

Maziad, Marwa and Jake Sotiriadis, 'Turkey's Dangerous New Exports: Islamist, Neo-Ottoman Visions and Regional Instability', *Middle East Institute*, 21 April 2020, www.mei.edu/publications/turkeys-dangerous-new-exports-pan-islamist-neo-ottoman-visions-and-regional (Accessed 9 February 2022).

Mazower, Mark, *No Enchanted Palace: The End of Empire and the Ideological Origins of the United Nations* (Princeton, NJ: Princeton University Press, 2009).

Mazower, Mark, *Governing the World: The History of an Idea* (London: Penguin Books, 2012).

McDowall, David, *A Modern History of the Kurds* (London: I. B. Tauris, 1996).

McMeekin, Sean, *The Berlin-Baghdad Express: The Ottoman Empire and Germany's Bid for World Power* (Cambridge, MA: Harvard University Press, 2010).

McNeill, John R., José Augusto Padua and Mahesh Rangarajan (eds), *Environmental History as if Nature Existed* (Oxford: Oxford University Press, 2010).

Meier, Daniel, *Shaping Lebanon's Borderlands* (London: I. B. Tauris, 2016).

Meier, Daniel, 'Introduction to the Special Issue: Bordering the Middle East', *Geopolitics*, Vol. 23, No. 3 (2018), pp. 495–504.

Melka, R. L., 'Max Freiherr von Oppenheim: Sixty Years of Scholarship and Political Intrigue in the Middle East', *Middle Eastern Studies*, Vol. 9, No. 1 (1973), pp. 81–93.

Mentzel, Peter, *Transportation Technology and Imperialism in the Ottoman Empire, 1800–1923* (Washington, DC: American Historical Association, 2006).

Méouchy, Nadine (ed.), *France, Syrie et Liban, 1918–1946: Les ambiguïtés et les dynamiques de la relation mandataire* (Damascus: IFEAD, 2002).

Méouchy, Nadine and Peter Sluglett (eds), *The British and French Mandates in Comparative Perspectives* (Leiden: Brill, 2004).

Méouchy, Nadine, 'Rural Resistance and the Introduction of Modern Forms of Consciousness in the Syrian Countryside, 1918–1926', in Thomas Philipp and Christof Schumann (eds), *From the Syrian Land to the States of Syria and Lebanon* (Beirut: Ergon Verlag, 2004), pp. 275–89.

Meray, Seha L., *Lozan Barış Konferansı, Tutanaklar, Belgeler*, Vol. 2 (Istanbul: Yapı Kredi Yayınları, 2011).

Metinsoy, Murat, *İkinci Dünya Savaşında Türkiye: Savaş ve Gündelik Yaşam* (Istanbul: Homer Kitabevi, 2007).

Metinsoy, Murat, 'Rural Crimes as Everyday Peasant Politics: Tax Delinquency, Smuggling, Theft and Banditry in Modern Turkey', in Stephanie Cronin (ed.), *Crime, Poverty and Survival in the Middle East and North Africa: The 'Dangerous Classes' since 1800* (London: I. B. Tauris, 2019), pp. 135–54.

Migdal, Joel S., *State in Society: Studying How States and Societies Transform and Constitute One Another* (Cambridge: Cambridge University Press, 2001).

Migdal, Joel S. (ed.), *Boundaries and Belonging: States and Societies in the Struggle to Shape Identities and Local Practices* (Cambridge: Cambridge University Press, 2004).

Mikhail, Alan, *Under Ottoman's Tree: The Ottoman Empire, Egypt, and Environmental History* (Chicago: University of Chicago Press, 2017).

Miller, Bradley, *Borderline Crime: Fugitive Criminals and the Challenge of the Border, 1819–1914* (Toronto: University of Toronto Press, 2016).

Miller, Michael B., 'Pilgrims' Progress: The Business of the Hajj', *Past and Present*, Vol. 191, No. 1 (2006), pp. 189–228.

Miller, Ruth A., *Legislating Authority: Sin and Crime in the Ottoman Empire and Turkey* (New York and London: Routledge, 2005).
Misra, Sanghamitra, *Becoming a Borderland: The Politics of Space and Identity in Colonial Northeastern India* (New Delhi: Routledge, 2011).
Mitchell, Timothy, 'The Limits of the State: Beyond Statist Approaches and their Critics', *American Political Science Review*, Vol. 85, No. 1 (1991), pp. 77–96.
Mitchell, Timothy, *Rule of Experts: Egypt, Techno-Politics, Modernity* (Berkeley, CA: University of California Press, 2002).
Mizrahi, Jean-David, 'La répression du banditisme sur les confins de la Syrie mandataire: Nouveaux Etats et nouvelles frontières dans le Moyen-Orient des années 1920', *Relations Internationales*, No. 114 (2003), pp. 173–87.
Mizrahi, Jean-David, 'Le nationalisme de la frontière turco-syrienne au début des années 1920', *Vingtième siècle. Revue d'histoire*, No. 78 (2003), pp. 19–34.
Mizrahi, Jean-David, *Genèse de l'Etat mandataire: Service des renseignements et bandes armées en Syrie et au Liban dans les années 1920* (Paris: Publications de la Sorbonne, 2003).
Mohamedou, Mohammad-Mahmoud Ould, 'In Search of the Non-Western State: Historicising and De-Westphalianising Statehood', in Bertrand Badie, Dirk Berg-Scholsser and Leonardo Morlino (eds), *The SAGE Handbook of Political Science: A Global Perspective* (London: SAGE, 2020), pp. 1335–48.
Mohamedou, Mohammad-Mahmoud Ould, 'A Century of Elusive State-Building in the Middle East and North Africa', in Mohammad-Mahmoud Ould Mohamedou (ed.), *State Building in the Middle East and North Africa: One Hundred Years of Nationalism, Religion and Politics* (London: I. B. Tauris, 2021), pp. 3–24.
Mollica, Marcello and Arsen Hakobyan (eds), *Syrian Armenians and the Turkish Factor: Kesab, Aleppo and Deir ez-Zor in the Syrian War* (London: Palgrave Macmillan, 2021).
Motadel, David, *Islam and Nazi Germany's War* (Cambridge, MA: Harvard University Press, 2014).
Moubayed, Sami M., *The Politics of Damascus, 1920–46: Urban Notables and the French Mandate* (Damascus: Tlass House, 1999).
Müge Göçek, Fatma, *The Transformation of Turkey: Redefining State and Society from the Ottoman Empire to the Modern Era* (London: I. B. Tauris, 2011).
Munro, John M., *The Nairn Way: Desert Bus to Baghdad* (Delmar, NY: Caravan Books, 1980).
Murton, Galen, 'Nobody Stops and Stays Anymore: Motor Roads, Uneven Mobilities, and Conceptualizing Borderland Modernity in Highland Nepal', in Alexander

Horstmann, Martin Saxer, and Alessandro Rippa (eds), *Routledge Handbook of Asian Borderlands* (London and New York: Routledge, 2018), pp. 315–24.

Mylonas, Harris, *The Politics of Nation-Building: Making Co-Nationals, Refugees, and Minorities* (Cambridge: Cambridge University Press, 2012).

Nafiz, Dr. Ehmed, 'Ta, Tawî û Tabir', *Hawar*, No. 2 (1932), pp. 3–4.

Neep, Daniel, 'Policing the Desert: Coercion, Consent and the Colonial Order', in Laleh Khalili and Jillian Schwedler (eds), *Policing and Prisons in the Middle East: Formations of Coercion* (London: Hurst, 2010), pp. 41–56.

Newman, David, 'On Borders and Power: A Theoretical Framework', *Journal of Borderlands Studies*, Vol. 18, No. 1 (2003), pp. 13–25.

Noiriel, Gérard, *La tyrannie du National: Le droit d'asile en Europe, 1793–1993* (Paris, Calmann-Lévy, 1991).

Nordman, Daniel, *Frontières de France: De l'espace au territoire XVIe–XIXe siècles* (Paris: Gallimard, 1999).

Norwegian Institute for International Affairs Report, 'How a Post-Sectarian Strategy Can Change the Logic and Facilitate Sustainable Political Reform in Iraq', February 2009. Available at: english.nupi.no/content/download/8891/91333/file/Iraq%20 Report%20%284%29.pdf (last accessed 3 March 2020).

Novak, Paolo, 'The Flexible Territoriality of Borders', *Geopolitics*, Vol. 16, No. 4 (2011), pp. 741–67.

Nugent, Paul and Asiwaju, A.I. (eds), *African Boundaries: Barriers, Conduits and Opportunities* (London: Cassell/Pinter, 1996).

Nugent, Paul, *Smugglers, Secessionists and Loyal Citizens: The Life of the Borderlands since 1914* (Oxford: James Currey, 2002).

O'Shea, Maria, *Trapped between the Map and Reality: Geography and Perceptions of Kurdistan* (London: Routledge, 2004).

O'Sullivan, Adrian, *The Baghdad Set: Iraq through the Eyes of British Intelligence, 1941–5* (London: Palgrave Macmillan, 2019).

Obert, Jonathan, 'Policing the Boundary and Bounding the Police: Fictitious Borders and the Making of Gendarmeries in North America', *Journal of Borderlands Studies*, Vol. 36, No. 2 (2021), pp. 301–18.

Ögut, Tahir and Akkaş, Erhan, 'Suriye Toprak Reformunun Türkiye'ye Yansımaları: Pasavan Rejimi Krizi', *Journal of Social Policy Conferences*, Vol. 71, No. 2 (2016), pp. 127–63.

Ohmae, Kenichi, *The Borderless World: Power and Strategy in the Interlinked Economy* (New York: Harper Business, 1990).

Olson, Robert, *The Emergence of Kurdish Nationalism and the Sheikh Said Rebellion, 1880–1925* (Austin: University of Texas Press, 1989).

Olson, Robert, *The Goat and the Butcher: Nationalism and State Formation in Kurdistan-Iraq since the Iraqi War* (Costa Mesa: Mazda, 2005).

Omissi, David E., *Air Power and Colonial Control: The Royal Air Force 1919–39* (Manchester: Manchester University Press, 1990).

Omissi, David, 'Britain, the Assyrians and the Iraq Levies, 1919–32', *The Journal of Imperial and Commonwealth History*, Vol. 17, No. 3 (1989), pp. 301–22.

Onley, James, 'The Raj Reconsidered: British India's Informal Empire and Spheres of Influence in Asia and Africa', *Asian Affairs*, Vol. 40, No. 1 (2009), pp. 44–62.

Oualdi, Mohammad, 'Nationality in the Arab World, 1830–1960: Negotiating Belonging and the Law', *Revue des Mondes Musulmans et de la Méditerranée*, No. 137 (2015), <journals.openedition.org/remmm/9108> (Accessed 9 October 2022).

Owen, Roger and Pamuk, Şevket, *A History of Middle East Economies in the Twentieth Century* (London: I. B. Tauris, 1999).

Özbek, Nadir, 'Policing the Countryside: Gendarmes of the Late 19th-Century Ottoman Empire (1876–1908)', *International Journal of Middle East Studies*, Vol. 40, No. 1 (2008), pp. 47–67.

Özbek, Nadir, 'The Politics of Taxation and the "Armenian Question" during the Late Ottoman Empire, 1876–1908', *Comparative Studies in Society and History*, Vol. 54, No. 4 (2012), pp. 770–97.

Özbilge, Nevcihan, *Çekirgeler, Kürtler ve Devlet: Erken Cumhuriyet Dönemine Yeniden Bakmak* (Istanbul: Tarih Vakfı Yurt Yayınları, 2020).

Özer, Sevilay, 'Türkiye'de Trahomla Mücadele, 1925–45', *Ankara Üniversitesi Türk İnkılâp Tarihi Enstitüsü Atatürk Yolu Dergisi*, No. 54 (2014), pp. 121–52.

Özer, Sevilay, *Anadolu'da Görülen Çekirge İstilaları ve Halk Üzerindendeki Etkisi, 1914–45* (Ankara: Türk Tarih Kurumu Yayınları, 2016).

Özkahraman, Cemal, 'Kurdish Cross-Border Trade between Syria and Turkey: The Socio-Political Trajectories of Syrian Kurds', *Middle Eastern Studies*, Vol. 57, No. 4 (2021), pp. 567–80.

Özkan, Behlül, *From the Abode of Islam to the Turkish Vatan: The Search for a National Homeland in Turkey* (New Haven, CT: Yale University Press, 2012).

Özkan, Fulya, 'Gravediggers of the Modern State: Highway Robbers on the Trabzon-Bayezid Road, 1850–1910s' *Journal of Persianate Studies*, Vol. 7, No. 2 (2014), pp. 219–50.

Özmen, Abidin, 'Genel Müfettişlikler Hakkında Bir Düşünce', *Idâre Dergisi*, Vol. 184 (1947), pp. 237–45.

Özoğlu, Hakan, 'Exaggerating and Exploiting the Sheikh Said Rebellion of 1925 for Political Gains', *New Perspectives on Turkey*, Vol. 41 (2009), pp. 181–210.

Öztan, Ramazan Hakkı, 'Tools of Revolution: Global Military Surplus, Arms Dealers and Smugglers in the Late Ottoman Balkans, 1878–1908', *Past & Present*, Vol. 237, No.1 (2017), pp. 167–95.

Öztan, Ramazan Hakkı, 'The Great Depression and the Making of Turkish–Syrian Border, 1921–39', *International Journal of Middle East Studies*, Vol. 52, No. 2 (2020), pp. 311–26.

Öztan, Ramazan Hakkı, 'Republic of Conspiracies: Cross-Border Plots and the Making of Modern Turkey, 1919–39,' *Journal of Contemporary History*, Vol. 56, No. 1 (2021), pp. 55–76.

Öztan, Ramazan Hakkı and Yenen, Alp, 'Age of Rogues: Transgressive Politics at the Frontiers of the Ottoman Empire', in Ramazan Hakkı Öztan and Alp Yenen (eds), *Age of Rogues: Revolutionaries and Racketeers at the Frontiers of Empires* (Edinburgh: Edinburgh University Press, 2021), pp. 3–52.

Öztan, Ramazan Hakkı, 'The Last Ottoman Merchants: Regional Trade and Politics of Tariffs in Aleppo's Hinterland, 1921–9' in Jordi Tejel and Ramazan Hakkı Öztan (eds), *Regimes of Mobility: Borders and State Formation in the Middle East, 1918–46* (Edinburgh: Edinburgh University Press, 2022), pp. 80–108.

Öztürk, Saygı, *İsmet Paşa'nın Kürt Raporu* (Istanbul: Doğan Kitap, 2007).

Özyüksel, Murat, *The Berlin-Baghdad Railway and the Ottoman Empire: Industrialization, Imperial Germany and the Middle East* (London: I. B. Tauris, 2016).

Özyürek, Mustafa, *Akşam Gazetesi Basyazarı Necmeddin Sadık Bey'in Lozan Mektupları* (Ankara: Gece Akademi, 2019).

Pamuk, Şevket, *Uneven Centuries: Economic Development of Turkey Since 1820* (Princeton, NJ: Princeton University Press, 2018).

Panzac, Daniel, 'Politique sanitaire et fixation des frontières: L'exemple ottoman (XVIIIe–XIXe siècles)', *Turcica*, No. 31 (1999), pp. 87–108.

Parsons, Laila, *The Commander: Fawzi Al-Qawuqji and the Fight for Arab Independence, 1914–48* (London: Saqi, 2018).

Parsons, Talcot, *The Social System* (Glencoe, IL: Free Press, 1951).

Pastor De Maria Campos, Camila, 'Performers or Prostitutes? Artistes during the French Mandate over Syria and Lebanon, 1921–46', *Journal of Middle East Women's Studies*, Vol. 13, No. 2 (2017), pp. 287–311.

Peacock, A. C. S (ed.), *The Frontiers of the Ottoman World* (Oxford: Oxford University Press, 2009).

Pearse, Richard, *Three Years in the Levant* (London: Macmillan & Co. Ltd, 1949).

Pedersen, Susan, *The Guardians: The League of Nations and the Crisis of Empire* (Oxford: Oxford University Press, 2015).

Peirce, Leslie P., *Morality Tales: Law and Gender in the Ottoman Court of Aintab* (Berkeley, CA: University of California Press, 2003).

Pétriat, Philippe, 'Caravan Trade in the late Ottoman Empire: The Aqil Network and the Institutionalization of Overland Trade', *Journal of Economic and Social History of the Orient*, Vol. 63, No. 1–2 (2019), pp. 38–72.

Pétriat, Philippe, 'The Uneven Age of Speed: Caravans, Technology, and Mobility in the Late Ottoman and Post-Ottoman Middle East', *International Journal of Middle East Studies*, Vol. 53, No. 2 (2021), pp. 273–90.

Piazza, Pierre, *Un œil sur le crime. Naissance de la police scientifique. Alphonse Bertillon de A à Z* (Bayeux: Orep Editions, 2016).

Polat, Zöhre, 'The Presidents Perspective on Landscape: Sample of the First President Mustafa Kemal Atatürk in Turkey', *Türk Bilimsel Derlemeler Dergisi*, Vol. 6, No. 2 (2013), pp. 158–62.

Popescu, Gabriel, *Bordering and Ordering the Twenty-first Century* (Lanham: Rowman & Littlefield Publishers, 2011).

Poulleau, Alice, *À Damas sous les bombes: Journal d'une Française pendant la révolution syrienne, 1924–6* (Yvetot: Imprimerie Bretteville, s.d.).

Prescott, John R. V., *The Geography of Frontiers and Boundaries* (Chicago: Aldine Publishing Company, 1965).

Provence, Michael, *The Great Syrian Revolt and the Rise of Arab Nationalism* (Austin: University of Texas Press, 2005).

Provence, Michael, *The Last Ottoman Generation and the Making of the Modern Middle East* (Cambridge: Cambridge University Press, 2017).

Pursley, Sara, 'Lines Drawn on an Empty Map: Iraq's Borders and the Legend of the Artificial state (Part I and II)', *Jadaliyya*, 2 June 2015, <www.jadaliyya.com/Details/32140> and <www.jadaliyya.com/Details/32153> (Accessed 9 October 2022).

Pursley, Sara, *Familiar Futures: Time, Selfhood, and Sovereignty in Iraq* (Stanford, CA: Stanford University Press, 2019).

Pusterla, Elia and Francesca Piccin, 'The Loss of Sovereignty and the Illusion of Building Walls', *Journal of Borderlands Studies*, Vol. 27, No. 2 (2012), pp. 121–38.

Qarqut, Dhuqan, *Tatawor al-Haraka al-Wataniyya fi Suriyya, 1920–39* (Beirut: Dar al-Taliah, 1975).

Radnitz, Scott, 'Review: Informal Politics and the State', *Comparative Politics*, Vol. 43, No. 3 (2011), pp. 351–71.

Rafeq, Abdul-Karim, 'Arabism, Society and Economy in Syria, 1918–20', in Youssef M. Choueiri (ed.), *State and Society in Syria and Lebanon* (Exeter: University of Exeter Press, 1993), pp. 1–27.

Rawilson, Alfred, *Adventures in the Near East, 1918–22* (London: Jonathan Cape, 1923).
Reş, Konê, 'Doktor û welatparêzê ku nayê ji bîrkirin Dr. Ehmed Nafiz Zaza', *Armanc*, No. 148 (1994), p. 5.
Rey, Matthieu, 'Drawing a Line on the Sand? Another (Hi)story of Borders', in Matthieu Cimino (ed.), *Syria: Borders, Boundaries, and the State* (London: Palgrave Macmillan, 2020), pp. 27–46.
Reynolds, Michael, *Shattering Empires: The Clash and Collapse of the Ottoman and Russian Empires, 1908–18* (Cambridge: Cambridge University Press, 2011).
Rieber, Alfred J., *The Struggle for the Eurasian Borderlands: From the Rise of Early Modern Empires to the End of the First World War* (Cambridge: Cambridge University Press, 2014).
Robertson, Scot, *The Development of RAF Strategic Bombing Doctrine, 1919–39* (Westport, CT: Praeger, 1995).
Robson, Laura, 'Peripheries of Belonging: Military Recruitment and the Making of a "Minority" in Wartime Iraq', *First World War Studies*, Vol. 7, No. 1 (2016), pp. 23–42.
Robson, Laura, 'Refugee Camps and the Spatialization of Assyrian Nationalism in Iraq', in Sasha R. Goldstein-Sabbah and Heleen L. Murre-van den Berg (eds), *Modernity, Minority, and the Public Sphere: Jews and Christians in the Middle East* (Leiden: Brill, 2016), pp. 237–56.
Robson, Laura, *States of Separation: Transfer, Partition, and the Making of the Modern Middle East* (Oakland, CA: University of California Press, 2017).
Robson, Laura, *The Politics of Mass Violence in the Middle East* (Oxford: Oxford University Press, 2020).
Rodogno, Davide, *Against Massacre: Humanitarian Interventions in the Ottoman Empire, 1815–1914* (Princeton, NJ: Princeton University Press, 2011).
Rodogno, Davide, Bernhard Struck and Jakob Vogel (eds), *Shaping the Transnational Sphere: Experts, Networks and Issues from the 1840s to the 1930s* (New York: Berghahn, 2014).
Rodogno, Davide, 'Non-State Actors' Humanitarian Operations in the Aftermath of the First World War: The Case of the Near East Relief', in Fabian Klose (ed.), *The Emergence of Humanitarian Intervention: Ideas and Practice from the Nineteenth Century to the Present* (Cambridge: Cambridge University Press, 2015), pp. 185–207.
Rodriguez Garcia, Magaly, Davide Rodogno and Liat Kozma, 'Introduction', in Magaly Rodriguez Garcia, Davide Rodogno, and Liat Kozma (eds), *The League of Nations: Work on Social Issues* (Geneva: UN Publications, 2016), pp. 13–28.

Rogan, Eugene, *The Fall of the Ottomans: The Great War in the Middle East* (New York: Basic Books, 2015).
Rogers, John, 'The Foreign Policy of Small States: Sweden and the Mosul Crisis, 1924–5', *Contemporary European History*, Vol. 16, No. 3 (2007), pp. 349–69.
Roitman, Janet, 'The Garrison-Entrepôt: A Mode of Governing in the Chad Bassin', in Aihwa Ong and Stephen J. Collier (eds), *Global Assemblages: Technology, Politics and Ethics as Anthropological Problems* (London: Blackwell, 2005), pp. 417–36.
Roitman, Janet, 'A Successful Life in the Illegal Realm', in Peter Geschiere, Birgit Meyer and Peter Pels (eds), *Readings in Modernity in Africa* (Bloomington: Indiana University Press, 2008), pp. 214–20.
Roosevelt Jr, Archie, 'The Kurdish Republic of Mahabad', *Middle East Journal*, Vol. 1, No. 3 (1947), pp. 247–69.
Rosati, Massimo, *The Making of a Postsecular Society: A Durkheimian Approach to Memory, Pluralism and Religion in Turkey* (Farnham: Ashgate, 2015).
Roshwald, Aviel, 'The Spears Mission in the Levant 1941–4', *The Historical Journal*, Vol. 29, No. 4 (1986), pp. 897–919.
Russell, Edmund, *War and Nature: Fighting Humans and Insects with Chemicals from World War I to Silent Spring* (Cambridge: Cambridge University Press, 2001).
Rutledge, Ian, *Enemy on the Euphrates: The Battle for Iraq, 1914–21* (London: Saqi Books, 2014).
Sack, Robert D., *Human Territoriality: Its Theory and History* (Cambridge: Cambridge University Press, 1986).
Sadan, Mandy, *Being and Becoming Kachin: Histories Beyond the State in the Borderworlds of Burma* (Oxford: Oxford University Press, 2013).
Sahlins, Peter, *Boundaries: The Making of France and Spain in the Pyrenees* (Berkeley, CA: University of California Press, 1989).
Sakatni, Mehdi, 'From Camel to Truck? Automobiles and the Pastoralist Nomadism of Syrian Tribes during the French Mandate (1920–46)', *Comparative Studies of South Asia, Africa and the Middle East*, Vol. 39, No. 1 (2019), pp. 159–69.
Saral, Ahmet H., *Türk İstiklal Harbi cilt IV: Güney Cephesi: İngiliz ve Fransızların Güney-Doğu Anadolu'yu işgal etmeleri Milli Mücadele hareketleri, bu bölgede yapılan muharebeler ve Revandiz Harekatı* (Ankara: Genelkurmay Başkanlığı Harp Tarihi Dairesi, 1966).
Satia, Priya, *Spies in Arabia: The Great War and the Foundations of Britain's Covert Empire in the Middle East* (Oxford: Oxford University Press, 2008).
Satia, Priya, 'A Rebellion of Technology: Development, Policing, and the British Arabian Imaginary', in Diana K. Davis and Edmund Burke III (eds), *Environmental*

Imaginaries of the Middle East and North Africa (Athens, OH: Ohio University Press, 2011), pp. 23–59.

Schayegh, Cyrus, 'The Many Worlds of 'Abud Yasin; or, What Narcotics Trafficking in the Interwar Middle East Can Tell Us about Territorialization', *The American Historical Review*, Vol. 116, No. 2 (2011), pp. 273–306.

Schayegh, Cyrus and Andrew Arsan (eds), *The Routledge Handbook of the History of the Middle East Mandates* (London: Routledge, 2015).

Schayegh, Cyrus, *The Middle East and the Making of the Modern World* (Cambridge, MA: Harvard University Press, 2017).

Schayegh, Cyrus, 'Afterword', in Jordi Tejel and Ramazan Hakkı Öztan (eds), *Regimes of Mobility: Borders and State Formation in the Middle East, 1918–46* (Edinburgh: Edinburgh University Press, 2022), pp. 351–62.

Schelle, Judith, *Smugglers and Saints of the Sahara: Regional Connectivity in the Twentieth Century* (Cambridge: Cambridge University Press, 2012).

Schiller, Nina Glick and Noel B. Salazar, 'Regimes of Mobility across the Globe', *Journal of Ethnic and Migration Studies*, Vol. 39, No. 2 (2013), pp. 183–200.

Schlaepfer, Aline, Philippe Bourmaud and Iyas Hassa, 'Ghosts of Empire: Persistence and Claims of Ottomanity(ies) in Post-Ottoman Spaces', *Revue des Mondes Musulmans et de la Méditerranée*, Vol. 148 (2020), pp. 33–56.

Schlosser, Katherine, *Trachoma through History* (New York: International Trachoma Initiative, 2020).

Schofield, Clive H., 'Elusive Security: The Military and Political Geography of South Lebanon', *GeoJournal*, Vol. 31, No. 2 (1993), pp. 149–61.

Schofield, Clive H. (ed.), *Global Boundaries: World Boundaries, Vol. I* (London and New York: Routledge, 1994).

Schofield, Richard (ed.), *Arabian Boundary Disputes* (Farnham Common: Archive Editions, 1992).

Schofield, Richard, 'Laying it Down in Stone: Delimiting and Demarcating Iraq's Boundaries by Mixed International Commission', *Journal of Historical Geography*, Vol. 34, No. 3 (2008), pp. 397–421.

Schofield, Richard, 'Foreword', in Gilbert E. Hubbard, *From the Gulf to Ararat: Imperial Boundary Making in the Late Ottoman Empire* (London: I. B. Tauris, 2016), pp. xii–xxiii.

Schofield, Richard, 'International Boundaries and Borderlands in the Middle East: Balancing Context, Exceptionalism and Representation', *Geopolitics*, Vol. 23, No. 3 (2017), pp. 608–31.

Scott, James C., *The Art of Not Being Governed: An Anarchist History of Upland Southeast Asia* (New Haven and London: Yale University Press, 2009).

Seikaly, Sherene, *Men of Capital: Scarcity and Economy in Mandate Palestine* (Stanford, CA: Stanford University Press, 2016).

Semerdjian, Elyse, *'Off the Straight Path': Illicit Sex, Community and Law in Ottoman Aleppo* (Syracuse, NY: Syracuse University Press, 2008).

Şenoğuz, Pınar, *Community, Change and Border Towns* (London: Routledge, 2018).

Shamir, Ronen, 'Without Borders? Notes on Globalization as a Mobility Regime', *Sociological Theory*, Vol. 23, No. 2 (2005), pp. 197–217.

Shapiro, Michael and Hayward Alker (eds), *Challenging Boundaries: Global Flows, Territorial Identities* (Minneapolis: University of Minnesota Press, 1996).

Sharfman, Daphna, *Palestine in the Second World War: Strategies and Dilemmas* (Eastbourne: Sussex Academic Press, 2014).

Shields, Sarah D., *Mosul before Iraq: Like Bees Making Five-Sided Cells* (Albany: SUNY Press, 2000).

Shields, Sarah D., 'Mosul, the Ottoman legacy and the League of Nations', *International Journal of Contemporary Iraqi Studies*, Vol. 3, No. 2 (2009), pp. 217–30.

Shields, Sarah D., *Fezzes in the River: Identity Politics and European Diplomacy in the Middle East on the Eve of World War II* (Oxford: Oxford University Press, 2011).

Shils, Edward, *Center and Periphery: Essays in Macrosociology* (Chicago: University of Chicago Press, 1975).

Shorrock, William I., 'The Origin of the French Mandate in Syria and Lebanon: The Railroad Question, 1901–14', *International Journal of Middle East Studies*, Vol. 1, No. 2 (1970), pp. 133–53.

Şimşir, Bilal, *Lozan Telgrafları I* (Ankara: Atatürk Kültür Dil ve Tarih Yüksek Kurumu, 1990).

Skran, Claudena, *Refugees in Interwar Europe: The Emergence of a Regime* (Oxford: Clarendon Press, 1995).

Slight, John, *The British Empire and the Hajj, 1865–1956* (Cambridge, MA: Harvard University Press, 2015).

Sluga, Glenda, *Internationalism in the Age of Nationalism* (Philadelphia: University of Pennsylvania Press, 2013).

Sluglett, Peter, *Britain in Iraq: Contriving King and Country* (New York: Columbia University Press, 2007).

Smiley, Will, 'The Burdens of Subjecthood: The Ottoman state, Russian Fugitives, and Interimperial Law, 1774–1869', *International Journal of Middle East Studies*, Vol. 46, No. 1 (2014), pp. 73–93.

Smith, Harold L. (ed.), *War and Social Change: British Society in the Second World War* (Manchester: Manchester University Press, 1990).

Soane, Lindfield, 'A Recent Journey in Kurdistan', *Journal of the Royal Central Asian Society*, Vol. 22, No. 3 (1935), pp. 403–17.

Solomon, Solomon (Sawa), *The Assyrian Levies* (Chicago: Atour, 2006).

Song, Nianshen, *Making Borders in Modern Asia: The Tumen River Demarcation, 1881–1919* (Cambridge: Cambridge University Press, 2018).

Sonyel, Salahi R., 'Mustafa Kemal and Enver in Conflict, 1919–22', *Middle Eastern Studies*, Vol. 25, No. 4 (1989), pp. 506–15.

Steen, Eveline van der, *Near Eastern Tribal Societies during the Nineteenth Century: Economy, Society and Politics between the Tent and Town* (London: Routledge, 2014).

Stocker, Laura, 'The Camel Dispute: Cross-Border Mobility and Tribal Conflicts in the Northern Badiya, 1929–34', in Jordi Tejel and Ramazan Hakkı Öztan (eds), *Regimes of Mobility: Borders and State Formation in the Middle East, 1918–46* (Edinburgh: Edinburgh University Press, 2022), pp. 319–50.

Stoler, Ann Laura, 'Colonial Archives and the Arts of Governance', *Archival Science*, Vol. 2, No. 1-2 (2002), pp. 87–109.

Stoter, Brenda, 'Suicide rates increase within Iraq's Yazidi community', *Al Monitor*, 8 May 2020, <https://www.al-monitor.com/originals/2020/05/iraq-minorities-yazidis-suicide.html> (Accessed 9 February 2022).

Stratton, Morton B., 'British Railways and Motor Roads in the Middle East, 1930–40', *Economic Geography*, Vol. 20, No. 3 (1944), pp. 189–203.

Suny, Ronald G., *Looking Toward Ararat: Armenia in Modern History* (Bloomington: Indiana University Press, 1993).

Suny, Ronald G., *'They Can Live in the Desert but Nowhere Else': A History of the Armenian Genocide* (Princeton, NJ: Princeton University Press, 2015).

Sykes, Mark, 'Kurdish Tribes of the Ottoman Empire', *The Journal of the Royal Anthropological Institute of Great Britain and Ireland*, Vol. 38 (1908), pp. 451–86.

Tagliacozzo, Eric, 'Smuggling in the Southeast: History and its Contemporary Vectors in an Unbounded Region', *Critical Asian Studies*, Vol. 34, No. 2 (2002), pp. 193–220.

Tagliacozzo, Eric, *The Longest Journey: Southeast Asians and the Pilgrimage to Mecca* (Oxford: Oxford University Press, 2013).

Tagliacozzo, Eric and Shawkat M. Toorawa, 'Introduction', in Eric Tagliacozzo and Shawkat M. Toorawa (eds), *The Hajj: Pilgrimage in Islam* (Cambridge: Cambridge University Press, 2015), pp. 1–9.

Tastekin, Fehim, 'Turkey cultivating ever-deeper roots in Syrian territory', *Al Monitor*, 14 June 2018, <https://www.al-monitor.com/originals/2018/06/turkey-syria-turkish-university-in-al-bab.html> (last accessed 9 February 2022).

Tatchijan, Vahé, *La France en Cilicie et en Haute-Mésopotamie: Aux confins de la Turquie, de la Syrie et de l'Irak* (Paris: Karthala, 2004).

Tatchjian, Vahé, 'Des camps de réfugiés aux quartiers urbains: Processus et enjeux', in Reymond Kévorkian et al. (eds), *Les Arméniens, 1917–39: La quête d'un refuge* (Beirut: Presses de l'Université Saint-Joseph, 2006), pp. 112–45.

Tauber, Eliezer, 'The struggle for Dayr al-Zur: The Determination of Borders between Syria and Iraq', *International Journal of Middle East Studies*, Vol. 23, No. 3 (1991), pp. 361–85.

Tejel, Jordi, *Le mouvement kurde de Turquie en exil: Continuités et discontinuités du nationalisme kurde sous le mandat français en Syrie et au Liban, 1925–46* (Bern: Peter Lang, 2007).

Tejel, Jordi, 'Urban Mobilization in Iraqi Kurdistan during the British Mandate: Sulaimaniya, 1918–30', *Middle Eastern Studies*, Vol. 44, No. 4 (2008), pp. 537–52.

Tejel, Jordi, 'Les territoires de marge de la Syrie mandataire: Le mouvement autonomiste de la Haute Jazîra, paradoxes et ambiguïtés d'une integration nationale inachevée (1936–9)', *Revue des mondes musulmans et de la Méditerranée*, Vol. 126 (2009), pp. 205–22.

Tejel, Jordi, 'The Shared Political Construction of the East as a Resistant Territory and Cultural Sphere in the Kemalist Era, 1923–38', *European Journal of Turkish Studies*, No. 10 (2009), <http://ejts.revues.org/index4064.html> (Accessed 9 October 2022).

Tejel, Jordi, 'Un territoire de marge en Haute Djézireh syrienne (1921–40), *Etudes rurales*, No. 186 (2010), pp. 61–76.

Tejel, Jordi, 'Making Borders from Below: The Emergence of the Turkish-Iraqi Frontier, 1918–25', *Middle Eastern Studies*, Vol. 54, No. 5 (2018), pp. 811–26.

Tejel, Jordi and Ramazan Hakkı Öztan, 'Towards Connected Histories of Refugeedom in the Middle East', *Journal of Migration History*, Vol. 6, No. 1 (2020), pp. 1–15.

Tejel, Jordi, 'Des femmes contre des moutons: Franchissements féminins de la frontière turco-syrienne (1929–44)', *20 & 21. Revue d'histoire*, Vol. 145 (2020), pp. 35–48.

Tejel, Jordi, 'The Kurdish Question in Syria', in Hamit Bozarslan, Cengiz Gunes and Veli Yadirgi (eds), *The Cambridge History of the Kurds* (Cambridge: Cambridge University Press, 2021), pp. 436–57.

Tejel, Jordi, 'The Last Ottoman Rogues: The Kurdish-Armenian Alliance in Syria and the New State System in the Interwar Middle East', in Ramazan Hakkı Öztan and Alp Yenen (eds), *Age of Rogues: Rebels, Revolutionaries and Racketeers at the Frontiers of Empires* (Edinburgh: Edinburgh University Press, 2021), pp. 355–82.

Tejel, Jordi, 'States of Rumors: Politics of Information along the Turkish–Syrian Border, 1925–45', *Journal of Borderlands Studies*, Vol. 37, No. 1 (2022), pp. 95–113.

Tejel, Jordi and Ramazan Hakkı Öztan, 'Introduction', in Jordi Tejel and Ramazan Hakkı Öztan (eds), *Regimes of Mobility: Borders and State Formation in the Middle East, 1918–46* (Edinburgh: Edinburgh University Press, 2022), pp. 1–25.

Tejel, Jordi and Ramazan Hakkı Öztan, 'Borders of Mobility? Crime and Punishment along the Syrian-Turkish Border, 1921–39', in Kate Fleet and Ebru Boyar (eds), *Borders, Boundaries and Belonging in Post-Ottoman Space in the Interwar Period* (Leiden: Brill, 2023), pp. 204–24.

Tekeli, Ilhan and Selim Ilkin, 'Cumhuriyetin Demiryolu Politikalarının Olusumu ve Uygulanması', *Cumhuriyetin Harcı Modernitenin Altyapısı*, Vol. III (Istanbul: Bilgi Üniversitesi Yayınları, 2010), pp. 271–324.

Ter Minassian, Taline, *Colporteurs du Komintern: L'Union Soviétique et les minorités au Moyen-Orient* (Paris: Sciences Po, 1997).

Ter-Matevosyan, Vahram, *Turkey, Kemalism and the Soviet Union* (London: Palgrave Macmillan, 2019).

Thomas, Lynn M., 'Historicising Agency', *Gender and History*, Vol. 28, No. 2 (2016), pp. 324–39.

Thomas, Martin, 'Bedouin Tribes and the Imperial Intelligence Services in Syria, Iraq and Transjordan in the 1920s', *Journal of Contemporary History*, Vol. 38, No. 4 (2003), pp. 539–61.

Thomas, Martin, *Empires of Intelligence: Security Services and Colonial Disorder after 1914* (Berkeley, CA: University of California Press, 2007).

Thompson, Elizabeth, *Colonial Citizens: Republican Rights, Paternal Privilege, and Gender in French Syria and Lebanon* (New York: Columbia University Press, 1999).

Thompson, Elizabeth, 'The Climax and Crisis of the Colonial Welfare State in Syria and Lebanon during World War II', in Steven Heydemann (ed.), *War, Institutions, and Social Change in the Middle East* (Berkeley, CA: University of California Press, 2000), pp. 59–99.

Thompson, Elizabeth F., *How the West Stole Democracy from the Arabs: The Syrian Arab Congress of 1920 and the Destruction of its Historic Liberal-Islamic Alliance* (New York: Atlantic Monthly Press, 2020).

Tilly, Charles (ed.), *The Formation of National States in Western Europe* (Princeton, NJ: Princeton University Press, 1975).

Tilly, Charles, 'War Making and State Making as Organized Crime', in Peter Evan et al. (eds), *Bringing the State Back in* (Cambridge: Cambridge University Press, 1985), pp. 169–91.

Tilly, Charles, *Coercion, Capital and European States, AD 990–1990* (Cambridge: Blackwell, 1990).

Toktamis, Kumru, 'Yashar Khanum: The Woman for Whom the War Never Ended', in Tomasz Pudlocki and Kamil Ruszala (eds), *Intellectuals and World War I: A Central European Perspective* (Krakow: Jagiellonian University Press, 2018), pp. 283–306.

Torpey, John, *The Invention of the Passport: Surveillance, Citizenship and the State* (Cambridge: Cambridge University Press, 1999).

Toth, Anthony B., 'The Transformation of a Pastoral Economy: Bedouin and States in Northern Arabia, 1850–1950' (PhD dissertation, Oxford: Oxford University, 2000).

Toth, Anthony B., 'Tribes and Tribulations: Bedouin Losses in the Saudi and Iraqi Struggles Over Kuwait's Frontiers, 1921–43', *British Journal of Middle Eastern Studies*, Vol. 32, No. 2 (2005), pp. 145–67.

Tripp, Charles, *A History of Iraq* (Cambridge: Cambridge University Press, 2000).

Turnaoğlu, Burna, *The Formation of Turkish Republicanism* (Princeton, NJ: Princeton University Press, 2017).

Tyner, Judith, 'Persuasive Cartography', *Journal of Geography*, Vol. 81, No. 4 (1982), pp. 140–44.

Tyner, Judith, *Principles of Map Design* (New York: The Guilford Press, 2010).

Ulrichsen, Kristian Coaster, *The First World War in the Middle East* (London: Hurst, 2014).

Umar, Ömer O., *Türkiye-Suriye İlişkileri, 1918–40* (Elazığ: Ortadoğu Araştırmaları Yayınaları, 2003).

Üngör, Uğur Ü., *The Making of Modern Turkey: Nation and State in Eastern Anatolia, 1913–50* (Oxford: Oxford University Press, 2011).

Üngör, Uğur Ü., 'Rethinking the Violence of Pacification: State Formation and Bandits in the Young Turk Era, 1914–37', *Comparative Studies in Society and History*, Vol. 54, No. 4 (2012), pp. 746–69.

Urbansky, Sören, *Beyond the Steppe Frontier: A History of the Sino-Russian Border* (Princeton, NJ: Princeton University Press, 2020).

Uvarov, Boris P., *Locusts and Grasshoppers: A Handbook for their Study and Control* (London: The Imperial Bureau of Entomology, 1928).

Uvarov, Boris P., 'Ecological Studies on the Moroccan Locust in Western Anatolia', *Bulletin of Entomological Research*, Vol. 23, No. 2 (1932), pp. 273–87.

Uvarov, Boris P., 'Ecology of the Moroccan Locust in Iraq and Syria and the Prevention of its Outbreaks', *Bulletin of Entomological Research*, Vol. 24, No. 3 (1933), pp. 407–18.

Vallet, Elisabeth (ed.), *Borders, Fences and Walls: State of Insecurity?* (Farnham: Ashgate, 2014).

Varlık, Bülent, *Umumî Müfettişler Toplantı Tutanakları, 1936* (Ankara: Dipnot Yayınları, 2010).

Varlık, Nükhet, 'Oriental Plague or Epidemiological Orientalism?' in Nükhet Varlık (ed.), *Plague and Contagion in the Islamic Mediterranean* (Kalamazoo, MI: Arc Humanities Press, 2017), pp. 57–87.

Velud, Christian, 'L'émergence et l'organisation sociales des petites villes de Jézireh, en Syrie, sous le mandat français', *URBAMA*, No. 16–17 (1986), pp. 85–103.

Velud, Christian, 'La politique mandataire française à l'égard des tribus et des zones de steppe en Syrie: L'exemple de la Djézireh', in Riccardo Bocco, Ronald Jaubert and Françoise Métral (eds), *Steppes d'Arabie. Etats, pasteurs, agriculteurs et commerçants: le devenir des zones sèches* (Paris: PUF, 1993), pp. 61–86.

Vignal, Leïla (ed.), *The Transnational Middle East: People, Places, Borders* (London and New York: Routledge, 2017).

Vigneswaran, Darshan and Joel Quirk (eds), *Mobility Makes States: Migration and Power in Africa* (Philadelphia: University of Pennsylvania Press, 2015).

Visser, Reida, 'Introduction', in Reida Visser and Gareth Stansfield (eds), *An Iraq of Its Regions: Cornerstones of a Federal Democracy?* (New York: Columbia University Press, 2008), pp. 1–26.

Vitalis, Robert and Steven Heydemann, 'War, Keynesianism, and Colonialism: Explaining State-Market Relations in the Postwar Middle East' in Steven Heydemann (ed.), *War, Institutions, and Social Change in the Middle East* (Berkeley, CA: University of California Press, 2000), pp. 100–45.

Vito, Christian G. De, 'History without Scale: The Micro-Spatial Perspective', *Past and Present*, Vol. 242, Supplement 14 (2019), pp. 348–72.

Vollaard, Hans, 'The Logic of Political Territoriality', *Geopolitics*, Vol. 14, No. 4 (2009), pp. 687–706.

Warf, Barney and Arias Santa (eds), *The Spatial Turn: Interdisciplinary Perspectives* (London: Routledge, 2008).

Watenpaugh, Keith D., 'Towards a New Category of Colonial Theory: Colonial Cooperation and the Survivors' Bargain – The case of the Post-Genocide Armenian Community of Syria under French Mandate', in Nadine Méouchy and Peter Sluglett (eds), *The British and French Mandates in Comparative Perspectives* (Leiden: Brill, 2004), pp. 597–622.

Watenpaugh, Keith D., *Being Modern in the Middle East: Revolution, Nationalism, Colonialism and the Arab Middle Class* (Princeton, NJ: Princeton University Press, 2006).

Watenpaugh, Keith D., 'The League of Nations' Rescue of Armenian Genocide Survivors and the Making of Modern Humanitarianism, 1920–7', *American Historical Review*, Vol. 115, No. 5 (2010), pp. 1315–39.

Watenpaugh, Keith D., *Bread from Stones: The Middle East and the Making of Modern Humanitarianism* (Oakland, CA: University of California Press, 2015).

Weber, David J., 'Turner, the Boltonians, and the Borderlands', *American Historical Review*, Vol. 91, No. 1 (1986), pp. 66–81.

Wendt, Alexander, *Social Theory of International Politics* (Cambridge: Cambridge University Press, 1999).

Wenzlhuemer, Roland, *Connecting the Nineteenth-Century World: The Telegraph and Globalization* (Cambridge: Cambridge University Press, 2015).

White, Benjamin T., *The Emergence of Minorities in the Middle East: The Politics of Community in French Mandate Syria* (Edinburgh: Edinburgh University Press, 2011).

White, Benjamin T., 'Refugees and the Definition of Syria, 1920–39', *Past & Present*, Vol. 235, No. 1 (2017), pp. 141–78.

White, Richard, 'What is Spatial History?', *Stanford University Spatial History Lab Working Paper*, 1 February 2010, pp. 1–6.

Wichhart, Stefanie K., 'A New Deal for the Kurds: Britain's Policy in Iraq, 1941–5', *The Journal of Imperial and Commonwealth History*, Vol. 39, No. 5 (2011), pp. 815–31.

Wichhart, Stefanie K., 'Selling Democracy during the Second British Occupation of Iraq, 1941–5', *Journal of Contemporary History*, Vol. 48, No. 3 (2013), pp. 509–36.

Widdis, Randy, 'Migration, Borderlands, and National Identity', in John J. Bukowczy (ed.), *Permeable Border: The Great Lakes Basin as Transnational Region* (Pittsburgh: University of Pittsburgh Press, 2005), pp. 152–74.

Widdis, Randy, 'Looking through the Mirror: A historical Geographical View of the Canadian-American Borderlands', *Journal of Borderlands Studies*, Vol. 30, No. 2 (2015), pp. 175–88.

Widdis, Randy, 'New Directions at the Border: A Historical Geographical Perspective', *Journal of Borderlands Studies*, Vol. 36, No. 5 (2021), pp. 853–71.

Wien, Peter, *Iraqi Arab Nationalism: Authoritarian, Totalitarian, and pro-Fascist Inclinations, 1932–41* (London: Routledge, 2006).

Wigglesworth, Vincent B., 'Boris Petrovitch Uvarov', *Biographical Memoirs of Fellows of the Royal Society*, Vol. 17 (1971), pp. 713–40.

Wilmington, Martin W., *The Middle East Supply Centre* (Albany, NY and London: SUNY Press and University of London Press, 1971).

Wilson, Thomas M. and Hastings Donnan (eds), *Border Identities: Nation and State at International Frontiers* (Cambridge: Cambridge University Press, 1998).

Wilson, Thomas M. and Hastings Donnan, 'Border and Border Studies', in Thomas M. Wilson and Hastings Donnan (eds), *A Companion to Border Studies* (London: Wiley–Blackwell, 2012), pp. 1–25.

Winter, Stefan, 'Les Kurdes du Nord-Ouest syrien et l'Etat ottoman, 1690–1750', in Mohammad Afifi et al. (eds), *La société rurale à l'époque ottomane* (Cairo: IFAO, 2005), pp. 243–58.

Winter, Stefan, 'The Other Nahdah: The Bedirxan, the Millis and the Tribal Roots of Kurdish Nationalism in Syria', *Oriente Moderno*, Vol. 86, No. 3 (2006), pp. 461–74.

Winter, Stefan, *A History of the Alawis: From Medieval Aleppo to the Turkish Republic* (Princeton, NJ and Oxford: Princeton University Press, 2016).

Wyrtzen, Jonathan, *Worldmaking in the Long Great War: How Local and Colonial Struggles Shaped the Modern Middle East* (New York: Columbia University Press, 2022).

Yadirgi, Veli, *The Political Economy of the Kurds of Turkey: From the Ottoman Empire to the Turkish Republic* (Cambridge: Cambridge University Press, 2017).

Yalçin-Heckmann, Lale, *Tribe and Kinship among the Kurds* (Frankfurt: Peter Lang, 1991).

Yamaç, Müzehher, 'Fransız Diplomatik Belgerinde Türkiye-Suriye Sınır Sorunu, 1918–40', *Belleten*, Vol. 82 (2018), pp. 1153–74.

Yanikdağ, Yücel, *Healing the Nation: Prisoners of War, Medicine and Nationalism in Turkey* (Edinburgh: Edinburgh University Press, 2013).

Yates, Athol, 'The British Military and the Anti-Locust Campaign across the Arabian Peninsula, including the Emirates, 1942–5', *The Journal of the Emirates Natural History Group*, Vol. 27 (2019), pp. 22–7.

Yaycioglu, Ali, *Partners of the Empire: The Crisis of the Ottoman Order in the Age of Revolutions* (Stanford, CA: Stanford University Press, 2016).

Yeğen, Mesut, 'The Turkish State Discourse and the Exclusion of Kurdish identity', *Middle Eastern Studies*, Vol. 32, No. 2 (1996), pp. 216–29.

Yelbasi, Caner, *The Circassians of Turkey: War, Violence and Nationalism from the Ottomans to Atatürk* (London: I. B. Tauris, 2019).

Yenen, Alp, 'Elusive Forces in Illusive Eyes: British Officialdom's Perception of the Anatolian Resistance Movement', *Middle Eastern Studies*, Vol. 54, No. 5 (2018), pp. 788–810.

Yıldırım, Ismail, 'Atatürk Dönemi Demiryolu Politikasına Bir Bakış', *Atatürk Araştırma Merkezi Dergisi*, Vol. 12, No. 35 (1996), pp. 387–96.

Yıldırım, Onur, *Diplomacy and Displacement: Reconsidering the Turco-Greek Exchange of Populations, 1922–34* (New York: Routledge, 2006).

Yılmaz, Hale, *Becoming Turkish: Nationalist Reforms and Cultural Negotiations in Early Republican Turkey 1923–45* (Syracuse, NY: Syracuse University Press, 2016).

Zartman, I. William, 'Identity, Movement, and Response' in I. William Zartman (ed.), *Understanding Life in the Borderlands: Boundaries in Depth and in Motion* (Athens, GA and London: University of Georgia Press, 2010), pp. 1–18.

Zartman, I. William (ed.), *Understanding Life in the Borderlands: Boundaries in Depth and in Motion* (Athens, GA and London: University of Georgia Press, 2010).

Zaza, Noureddine, *Ma vie de Kurde* (Lausanne: Les éditions du Tigre, 2021).

Zolberg, Aristide et al., 'International Factors in the Formation of Refugee Movements', *International Migration Review*, Vol. 20, No. 2 (1986), pp. 151–69.

Zubaida, Sami, 'Contested Nations: Iraq and the Assyrians', *Nations and Nationalism*, Vol. 6, No. 3 (2000), pp. 363–82.

Zürcher, Erik J., *The Unionist Factor: The Role of the Committee of Union and Progress in the Turkish National Movement, 1905–26* (Leiden: Brill, 1984).

Zürcher, Erik J., 'The Vocabulary of Muslim Nationalism', *International Journal of the Sociology of Language*, Vol. 137 (1999), pp. 81–92.

Zürcher, Erik J., 'Afterword', in Ramazan Hakkı Öztan and Alp Yenen (eds), *Age of Rogues: Revolutionaries and Racketeers at the Frontiers of Empires* (Edinburgh: Edinburgh University Press, 2021), pp. 383–9.

Zylberman, Patrick, 'Civilizing the State: Borders, Weak States and International Health in Modern Europe', in Alison Bashford (ed.), *Medicine at the Border: Disease, Globalization and Security, 1850 to the Present* (New York: Palgrave Macmillan, 2007), pp. 21–40.

INDEX

Note: **bold** indicates figures

Abrahamyan, Victoria, 116
Abu Kemal, 87, 89, 92
Adana, 142, 232
Adıyaman, 176
Afrin, 254
agency, 9, 71, 283
    and border-making, 5, 66, 68, 69–71
    of borderlanders, 68, 69–70, 71, 326–7
    and railroads, 220–9
    of refugees, 106, 113–22
Agha Petros (General), 109
Aintab, 142
al-Qaida, 9
Alawites, 99
Aleppo, 36, 99, 100, 141, 149, 159, 163, 170–1, 205, 210, 221, 249, 260, 284, 312
Alexandretta, 3, 4, 36, 83, 149, 214, 216, 220, 236, 246, 257–8
Ali Fuad Pasha, 42
Alliance Israélite School, Damascus, 72–3, 74
Altuğ, Seda, 115, 119–20

Amadiya, 60, 73
Amasya Protocol, 43
American Consulate, Beirut, 113
Amuda, 104, 144, 225, 272
Anastassiadis, Tassos, 15
Anatolia, 3, 40, 41, 42, 52, 53, 80–1, 95, 171, 190, 240, 296
Anderson, James, 22
Ankara Accord, 83, 171
Ankara Agreement, 3, 45–6
Ankara, Treaty of, 83, 134–5, 210, 214
Antep, 52, 149, 172
Aqra, 60, 73
Aras, Ramazan, 298
Arbil, 61, 66, 299, 300
archaeology, 108–9
armed bands, 40, 45, 50, 75, 133, 148, 211
Armenia, 18, 41, 42
Armenians, 94, 96, 121, 241, 265
    irredentism, 273–4
    nationalism, 243–4
    othering of, 116
    refugees, 100, 102, 113
    and smuggling, 145

Armistice of Mudros, 41, 42
al-Assad, Bashar, 315
Assyrians, 60–1, 68, 81, 94, 101, 104–5, 121
   and the British, 108–11
   in Iraq, 74–5, 108–9, 113–14
   massacres, 68–9, 75, 114, 117–18, 123
Atlantic Charter (1941), 272, 273
Ayn Diwar, 104, 136, 144, 187, 304

Baiji, 218, 220
Balfour Declaration, 10–11
Balistreri, Alexander E., 44
bandits and brigands, 53, 58, 191, 202, 236
Baqubah, 74, 109
Barazi (tribe), 151, 295
Barkey, Karen, 18
Barzani, Mustafa, 242, 269–70
Basra, 14, 80, 286
Bedouins, 57, 102, 108, 134, 193, 196, 200–1, 262–3, 292
   arms distribution to, 251
   attacks on roads, 201–2
   cross-border mobility, 25
   desert medicine, 188
   as disease carriers, 166
   railroads, use of, 235–6
   viewed as a problem, 183–4
Beirut, 100, 149, 172, 177
Berlin–Baghdad Railway *see* railroads
Bey, Esat Mahmut, 191
Bilad al-Sham, 13–14, 170
Bingöl, 144
Bitlis, 144
Blecher, Robert, 188
blockades, 170, 218, 220, 281, 285–93
Blumi, Isa, 18
Bolton, Herbert E., 22

borderlanders, 79, 137
   agency, 68, 69–70, 71, 326–7
   and ant-locust policies, 196
   bi-nationals, 150
   contradictory strategies and attitudes, 70–1
   identities, 70–1
   interactions with states' discourses and strategies, 64–71
   multiple strategies for different state actors, 274–5
   networks, 70, 128–30
   and pests/diseases, 167
   political resistance, 126–7
   post-Ottoman borders, negative effects of, 125–6
   resistance to modern health notions, 192–3
   and resolution of crime, 153–4
   and smuggling, 146–7, 160
   space of refusal notion, 126
   trade strategies, 303–4
   and transport developments, 205–6, 229–38
borders and borderlands
   agency, 5, 66, 68, 69–71
   artificiality, 11–12
   border governance consolidation and smuggling, 137–48
   border passes, 131–3, **132**, 135, 214
   border posts, 72, 82, 92, 134, 144, 274
   border zones, 20–2, 81–2
   centrality in Middle Eastern history, 4–5
   changing nature of, 26
   commissions, 65–6, **67**, 68–9, 70–1, 79, 80, 81–2, 83, 85–6, 89–91, 106, 119, 134, 149
   cross-border mobility, 5–6, 92–3, 122, 166–7, 203–4, 235, 324
   current situation, 316–19

borders and borderlands (*cont.*)
  definitions of, 20–5, 53–4
  delimitation procedures, 80–7, **82**, 89–92, 106, 131
  formation, 14, 39
  historiography, 5, 7, 9, 10–19
  identity and territoriality along borderlands, discourses on, 51–9
  infrastructure, 82, 144
  infringements and illicit/illegal border crossings, 21, 24, 50, 119–20, 123–60, 191, 193–4
  interactions between borderlanders and states' discourses and strategies, 64–71
  legal fictions, 322–3
  Middle East bordering, 78–100
  ordering and othering, 93–100, 121
  police, 74–5
  post-Ottoman borders, negative effects of, 125–6
  post Second World War, 2–3
  Second World War, effects of, 250–7
  as social constructs, 19, 21
  and state formation, 19–26
  state weaknesses, 101–2
  studies, 22–5
  tensions, 79
  Turkish–Syrian–Iraqi borderlands, map of, **8**
  see also de-bordering and re-bordering
boundaries
  boundary pillars, 81–2, **82**, 86, 92, 119
  delimitation procedures, 4, 80–7, **82**, 89–92, 90–2, 106, 131
  identity boundaries, 99–100
  management of, in the tri-border area, 130–6

Boyar, Ebru, 197
Britain, 35, 38, 275
  and the Assyrians, 108–11
  and France, 3, 52, 179–81, 214–16, 249–50, 278–9, 289–90
  imperial interests, 80–1, 85, 87, 89–90, 99–100, 120, 121–2, 214–16
  and Iraq, 47, 48, 49, 60–1, 74, 110–11
  Kurdish policy, 59–60, 64–5, 268–70, 274
  mandates of, 41, 46–7, 48, 66, 74, 86–7, 90–2, 94–5, 107, 110–11, 163
  Middle East policy, 46–8
  Second World War role in the Middle East, 248–50
  and Turkey, 46–51, 247, 259–62, 275, 279
Brussels Line, 49–50, 81
Bunsen Committee, 80

Cairo Conference (1921), 46–7
Cantens, Thomas, 285, 309–10
Catroux, Georges, 289–90
Chan, Yuk Wah, 137
Chicago Tribune, 68
cholera, 167–8, 169, 173
Cilicia, 42, 52, 59
citizenship, 6, 97, 115, 151
  women, 158
Clayer, Nathalie, 15
Çobanbey, 83, 84, 86, 210, 211, 220
colonialism, 7, 12–13, 15, 38, 120
  and refugees, 100–12
  resistance to, 40
Committee of Union and Progress (CUP), 35, 42
Constantinople Conference (1866), 168
Conventions of Friendship and Good Neighbourly Relations, 84, 92, 131, 131–3, 134–5, 149, 150

corruption, 305–7
Cox, Percy, 86–7
crime/criminals, 129, 134, 135, 322
    attacks on roads, 201–2
    collaboration between authorities, 149–50
    connivance of authorities, 151
    cross-border raids, 151, 153–4
    diya/diyet (compensation), 154–5, 322
    drug trafficking, 27
    investigation methods, 150
    and legal pluralism, 148–55
    and local traditions, 153–6
    and women, 155–9
Cumberland, Roger C., 123–5, 128, 129, 145
Cumhuriyet, 118
customs policies/posts, 4, 92, 135, 138, 236, 301, 303, 304
    customs union, 140
    duties and tariffs, 140–1, 213
    Navicert (Navigational Certificate), 279–80
    Syrian–Turkish Customs Agreement, 221

Damascus, 52, 53, 99, 100, 115, 163, 177–8, 185, 220, 298, 315
Dashnak (Armenian party), 118–19, 241, 265, 266–7, 273
de-bordering and re-bordering, 277–314, 325, 326
    formal and informal international trade, 303–13
    Mediterranean blockade and its effects, 285–93
    Middle East Supply Centre (MESC), achievements in the borderlands, 293–303

de Gaulle, Charles, 248–9, 272, 278, 289
Defence of National Right Societies, 42
Deir ez-Zor, 1, 136, 149, 225, 259
Demir Kapu, 85–6
Democratic Union Party (PYD), 315, 316
Denaturalisation Law 1927 (Turkey), 97
Dentz, Henri, 288, 289
Derbessia, 104, 187, 281
Derik, 104, 144
deserters, 6, 253
Destremeau, Christian, 244
diseases and pests, 27, 28–9, 33, 131, 161–99, 192, 291–3, 325–6
    and Anglo-French rivalries, 179–81
    attitudes to, 168–9
    bogus doctors, 197–8
    border inspections, 198
    British and French health policies, 186–9
    child mortality, 192
    drug shortages, 188, 197
    education, 181–2
    experts in the sanitary transnational networks, role of, 175–81
    financial constraints, 196–7
    hygiene, 181–2
    interstate and transnational cooperation, 165–6, 167–75
    pesticides, 195–6, 292–3
    quarantine measures, 168, 169, 198
    and railroads, 227–8
    sanitary conditions, 170–1, 172
    sanitary policies, 182
    socioeconomic factors, 193
    state flaws and local attitudes, 192–9
    and stigmatisation, 166
    Turkish health policies, 189–92
    vaccination, 173, 197, 198
    veterinary convention, 173–4

displacement, 24, 65, 71, 95–6, 98
Diyarbakır, 73, 87, 102, 141, 144, 221, 242
Dodge, Toby, 186
Doğan, Avni, 306
Dohuk, 123, 189
Dolbee, Samuel, 172, 185, 195, 227
Druzes, 99
Duck's Bill (Bed de Canard), 50, 79, 85, 91, 111

Eastern Pact of Saadabad (1937), 265
economic development, 282–4
Edmonds, Cecil J., 268, 269
Egypt, 244–5, 285
Egyptian Medical Association, 177
Elazığ, 144
Enver Pasha, 42, 43
environmental history, 28–9
Erzincan, 144
Erzurum, 43, 144
etatism (*devletçilik*), 138–9, 213
extradition procedures, 32, 124, 125, 129, 130, 133, 134, 135, 148–9, 152–3, 157, 322

Fata al-Arab, 224
Fata al-Iraq, 222–3
Faysal, King of Iraq, 47, 53, 55, 86–7
Faysh Khabur, 91, 92
Fidan Wuld (tribe), 55–6, 57
First World War, 9, 37, 38, 60, 109, 170, 174–5, 222
France, 83
  and Britain, 3, 52, 179–81, 214–16, 289–90
  Free French, 1, 248–50, 252, 253, 260, 268–9, 277–8, 280, 297–8, 301–3
  health policies in Lebanon and Syria, 170, 186–7
  imperial interests, 85–6, 87, 89–90, 99–100, 101–2, 111, 120, 121–2, 214–16
  mandates of, 41, 45, 50, 87, 90–2, 94–5, 101, 107, 112, 139, 163, 170, 183–4, 252
  policies for nomads, 184–5
  rejection of Assyrians, 75
  Services Spéciaux (SS), 112, 136, 200, 201
  Syrian economic programme, 101–4
  and Turkey, 1, 3, 38, 45–6, 56–7, 70, 82–4, 301–2
  and the Turkish–Syrian border, 50
  Vichy government, 248, 249, 288
Franco-British Convention (1920), 87–9, **88**
Franco-Syrian Treaty (1936), 4, 247, 257
Franco-Turkish Agreement *see* Ankara Agreement
Franco-Turkish Protocol (1929), 134
Franklin-Bouillon, Henry, 83
Fromkin, David, 11–12
Frontier Protocol (1929), 173, 214
fugitives, 32, 123–5, 133, 148
  women, 155–9

Gatrell, Peter, 120
al-Gaylani, Rashid Ali, 247–8
General Inspectorate for the Eastern Provinces, 98–9
Geneva *see* League of Nations
German–Soviet Nonaggression Pact (1939), 245
Germany, 240–1
  intelligence services, 256
  and Muslim groups, 248, 256, 266–7
  propaganda, 248, 266–7
globalisation, 9, 10, 33, 203–5, 237, 324, 326
governance, 12–13, 29, 32–3, 154, 188, 320, 322, 323
  and smuggling, 137–48
  transnational governance, 159–60

Goyan, 35–6
Grand National Assembly (Turkey), 44, 46, 49
Great Depression, 138, 139, 141, 159–60, 213, 222, 324
Great Syrian Revolt, 84
Greater Syria, 4, 52
Greeks, 95–6
Gutani, Ali Saydu, 117

al-Hadi, Daham, 202–3
Haifa, 215
Hajim, Shaykh, 56–8, 59
Hajj, 163–5, 175
Hajo Agha (Heverkan), 111–12, 118–19
Hakkari, 109, 124, 306
Hakkı Öztan, Ramazan, 141
Hämäläinen, Pekka, 7, 28
Hananu, Ibrahim, 53
Hasaka, 5, 104, 112, 136, 147, 188, 196, 225, 259
Hatay, 264
Hentig, Werner Otto von, 240–1, 266
Heverkan (tribe), 111–12
Heydemann, Steven, 282, 293
Hilmi, Rafiq, 61
historiography
  of borders/borderlands, 5, 7, 9, 10–19, 26–9
  combining micro- and global history, 27
  Ottoman Empire, 18
  Turkey, 44
Hizan, 161
homogenisation, 95–6
Houtum, Henk van, 93
Huber, Valeska, 169
Hulaiman, Hikmat, 218
human trafficking, 234–5
humanitarianism, 100, 103, 120–1
Husayn, Sharif of Mecca, 56
Al-Husseini, Amin, 247–8

ibn Muhayd, Hajim, 55–6
Ibrahim Pasha, 58, 240–1, 266
identities, 5, 7, 12, 93, 115, 121
  borderlanders, 70–1
  communal identification, promotion of, 106–7
  identification documents, 131–3, **132**, 198–9, 235
  identity boundaries, 99–100
  Kurds, 190
  national identities, 52
  and patriotism, 13–14
  and territoriality along borderlands, discourses on, 51–9
Idlib, 254
information, exchange of, 135–6, 232–3
infringements and illicit/illegal border crossings *see* borders and borderlands
Inönü, Ismet, 83, 142, 213
International Locust Bureau, 177–81
International Sanitary Convention, 169
Iran, 11, 60, 216, 242, 243, 244–5, 249, 250, 252–3, 270, 272, 281
Iraq, 3, 4, 41, 44, 74, 84, 105, 172, 173, 218, 247–8
  anti-Britishness, 247–8
  anti-refugee discourses, 115–17
  border delimitation, 80–3, **82**, 85–7, 89–92
  borders with Turkey and Syria, **8**, 29, 47, 49–50, 51, 78–84, **82**, 86–7, 89–93, 96, 119–21, 302–3
  British policy, 47, 48, 49, 60–1, 110–11, 244–5
  health policies, 188–9
  inflation, 300, 309
  Kurds, 64–6
  livestock exports, 308–9, 311–12
  locust eradication, 195
  Mediterranean blockade and its effects, 285–6

Iraq (cont.)
   and smuggling, 144–7
   trade with Turkey, 286–7
   urban–rural divide, 185–6
   and Yazidis, 90–1
Ireland, Robert, 285, 309–10
irredentism, 2, 4, 34, 239–76
   mounting instability in the Middle East, 246–50
   Second World War and the borderlands, 250–7
   small nation revisionism, 265–76
   Turkish irredentism, 257–64
Iselin, Frédéric, 91
al-Islah, 223
Islam, 38, 54–5, 61–2, 64
Islamic State of Iraq and Syria (ISIS), 9, 316
Ismet Pasha, 48
Italy, 4, 218, 246–7, 249, 257, 266, 285

Jackson, Ashley, 244–5
Jaquier, César, 92
Jarablus, 144, 146, 254
Jazira, 40, 50, 55–6, 57–8, 72, 74, 75–6, 104, 112, 184–5, 258
   agricultural production, 294–6
   Kurdish immigration, 297–8
   refugees, 101–3, 115–17
   Turkish migrations to, 263
Jazirat ibn Umar, 35, 36, 42, 83, 84, 85, 87, 134
Jess (tribe), 151
Jews, 72–4, 76, 234–5
Jones, Reece, 126

Karabekir, Kazim, 42
Karbala, 169
Kasaba, Reşat, 18
Kaya, Şükrü, 141

Kemal, Mustafa, 3, 18–19, 36, 42, 44, 46, 184, 213, 220, 246
   and armed groups, 45, 53
   and Raqqa, 56
   and religion, 54–5
   and Vilayet, 49
Khan Maysalun, Battle of, 53
Khanum, Yashar, 230
Khazna, 161
Khaznawi, Shaykh Ahmad, 161–5, 166, 167, 193
Khoury, Philip S., 247
Khoybun League, 112, 118–19, 241, 265, 266, 270
Kilis, 83
Kirkuk, 44, 60, 61, 66, 299, 300
Klein, Janet, 18
Kozma, Liat, 177
Kurd Ali, Muhammad, 118
Kurdish League, 272
Kurdistan Worker's Party (PKK), 315
Kurds, 18, 35–6, 41, 47, 48, 50–1, 72, 117–18, 252, 259
   Agri-Dagh (Ararat) revolt (1927–31), 105, 190, 191
   Barzan Amnesty Law, 270
   British policy, 59–60, 64–5, 268–70, 274
   cultural activities, 265, 269
   dehumanisation, 191–2
   flag, 63
   Free French policies, 268–70, 274
   identities, 190
   independence, 241–2, 243
   in Iraq, 64–6, 270
   Kurdistan (Southern), 59–64
   language, 269
   memorandums to Allied forces, 272–4
   migrations, 235, 297–8
   minority rights, 121

nationalism, 47, 62–4, 112, 265–7, 271–3
rebellion (1925), 65, 84, 97, 98, 99, 102, 190, 212
refugees, 84, 97–8, 101, 102–3
self-determination, 62–3
and smuggling, 145
and the Soviet Union, 271–2
threats to, 66, 68
Turkish amnesty, 103
Turkish–Kurdish unity notion, 64

La Syrie, 224
Latakia, 149
Lausanne Peace Conference (1922), 47–8, 64, 83
Lausanne, Treaty of, 3, 47–8, 83, 96–7, 138, 171, 212–13, 318
Le Matin, 295
Le Monde, 242
Leachman Accord, 86–7
League of Nations, 3, 4, 11, 32, 38, 48, 49, 51, 65–6, 79, 89, 94, 94–5, 106, 110–11, 321
communal identification, promotion of, 106–7
and the Mosul Affair, 65–6, 68–9, 70–1, 82
nationality and sovereignty principles, 97
refugees, 76–7, 78, 96, 100, 107–8, 114–15
role in disease control, 170–1
Lebanon, 3, 41, 99, 100, 170
legal pluralism, 129
dynamics of, and criminals, 148–55
gender contours of, 155–9
Levi, Giovanni, 29
Lewis, Norman N., 57
Lice, 144
liminality, 7–8, 22–3, 70

livestock, 68, 131, 148, 151, 169, 183, 193, 194, 221, 280–1
diseases, 171–4, 198
exports, 308–9
losses to pesticides, 196
Mediterranean blockade and its effects, 285–6, 288
shortages, 307–8, 309
smuggling, 304–5, 310–12
theft of, 306
transportation of, 230, 236
Lloyd, E. M. H., 282
locusts, 28–9, 33, 165, 169, 170, 177–81, 190, 191, 192, 193, 194–6, 227–8, 280, 291–3

Mahabad, 242, 272
Mahmud Beg ibn Ibrahim Pasha, 58–9
Mahmud Berzinji, Shaykh, 60
Mahmud Bey, 103, 140
Mahmud Khan Dizli, 62–4
malaria, 170–1, 177, 186, 188, 192
Malatya, 144
Manela, Erez, 51, 106
Maraş, 52, 53
Mardin, 98, 111, 145, 149, 172, 191, 306
marriage, 155–9, 193, 298–9
Marxism, 16
Mecca, 163–5, 168, 169, 174
Méouchy, Nadine, 55
Mesopotamia, 2, 46, 87, 182
Meydan Ekbez, 45, 210–11, 254–5
Middle East Supply Centre (MESC), 34, 280, 281, 282–3, 284–5, 303–4, 306–7, 309, 310, 312, 313, 325, 326
achievements in the borderlands, 293–303
functions of, 290
territorial mandate, 290–1

Migdal, Joel S., 17
migration, 19, 235, 263, 296, 297–8
millî (national), 53–4
Milli tribal confederation, 58–9
Milliyet, 103, 118
Minassian, Taline Ter, 270–1
minority rights, 64, 83, 96–7, 106, 107, 115, 121, 325–6
Mitchell, Timothy, 17, 199
Mohamedou, Mohammad-Mahmoud Ould, 15, 319
Molotov, Vyacheslav, 240, 271
Mosul, 3, 40, 41, 46, 47–8, 49–51, 60, 65–6, 69–70, 87, 205, 206–7, 208, 216–17, 221–3, 316
Mosul Affair, 46–7, 48, 61, 64, 65–71, **67**, 82, 131
Mosul Chamber of Commerce, 221–2
Mosul Province, 36, 46, 60, 64, 82, 84, 147
Motadel, David, 248
Muş, 144
Mussolini, Benito, 246–7, 258
Mutasarrif of Mosul, 222
Mutual Life Insurance Company, 170–1
Mydiat, 144

Naerssen, Tonk Van, 93
Nafiz, Ahmad, 187
Najaf, 169
Naqshbandi, 161
National Bloc (Syrian), 92, 220, 247
National Pact (Ottoman), 36, 43–4, 46, 53–4, 257, 318, 325
nationalism, 7, 11, 12, 38, 39, 51–2, 56, 64
  Kurds, 47, 62–4
  Turkey, 54–5
Nazism, 240–1, 268
Nejd, 3–4

networks, 167
  borderlanders, 70
  of motor companies, 225
  nomads, 193
  sanitary transnational networks, 175–81
  smuggling, 142, 144
  solidarity networks, 70, 128–30
  trans-border networks, 128–9
  of trust, 156–7
Nimet, Lt Col Şamir, 53
Noel, Maj Edward W.C., 60, 63
nomads, 102, 135
  and animals, 171–3, 183, 194, 196, 236
  cross-border movement of, 171–3
  networks, 193
  railroads, use of, 235–6
  resistance to modern health notions, 192–3, 199
  Turkish attitudes to, 171–3
  viewed as a problem, 183–4
Norshin, 161
Novak, Paolo, 93
Nugent, Paul, 128
Nusaybin, 72, 73, 83, 84, 85, 134, 209, 210, 211, 214, 220–1, 304

Obert, Jonathan, 322
OCP (wheat office), 289–90, 294–5
O'Dowd, Liam, 22
open-door policy, 139
Oppenheim, Max von, 231, 240
O'Shea, Maria, 274
Ottoman Empire, 11, 109, 204
  disease management, 168–70
  disintegration of, 2–3, 5, 16, 38, 41, 95
  historiography, 18
  refugees, 77
Owen, Roger, 138
Özdemir Pasha, 61, 64, 65

Palestine, 3, 73–4, 87, 122, 172, 180–1, 234–5, 245, 283, 288, 299
Palu, 144
Pamuk, Şevket, 138, 296
Paris International Sanitary Conference (1851), 168
Paris Peace Conference (1919), 160
Parsons, Talcot, 16
passavant regime, 132, **132**, 133–4
passports, 134, 151, 198–9, 214, 255, 302
pastoralism, 25, 37, 184, 193
Payas, 83, 84
Pearse, Richard, 230–1, 231–2, 234, 301
Persian Gulf, 80, 209, 215, 216, 308
pilgrimages, 73, 90, 163–5, 193
  as disease carriers, 166, 168, 169, 174–5
Pizhdar (tribe), 241
poverty, 298–9
propaganda, 35, 49, 54, 61, 64, 103, 240, 248, 259, 266–7, 326
  Germany, 248, 266–7
  Soviet Union, 271, 272
prostitution, 301
Pursley, Sara, 12

Qamishli, 72–3, 76, 104, 112, 144, 187–8, 200, 225, 226–7, 229, 259, 281, 300–1, 304
Qazi, Muhammad, 242
quinine, 187, 188, 197

Raballand, Gaël, 285, 309–10
railroads, 33, 141, 200–38, 210–11
  Aleppo–Nusaybin, 223–5
  attacks on, 200–1, 236
  Baghdad–Haifa, 215, 217, 222
  Berlin–Baghdad Railway, 33, 45–6, 83, 200–1, 204, 205, 206–20, **219**, 221, 222, 225, 226–7, 229–38, 245–6, 253–6, 264, 274, 304, 313, 324
  and border town development, 226–7
  and borders, 210–11, 212, 214, 215, 217–18, 220–1, 229–38, 239–40
  as a cause of fires, 228–9
  companies, 210–11, 212
  complementarity of railroad and motor facilities, 225–6
  demand for, 208–9
  Franco-British rivalries, 214–16
  gauge differences, 210
  human trafficking, 234–5
  Iraq Railway, 221, 286
  local agency and its repercussions, 220–9
  local appropriations of the Baghdad railway, 229–38
  merchandise and luggage checks, 255
  and nomads, 235–6
  passenger and staff control, 254–6, 324
  passenger identities, 230–3, **233**, 235
  Railway Agreement (1936), 218
  and the Second World War, 245–6, 249, 253–5, 274, 286
  and smuggling, 233–4, 236
  and space reorganisation, 227
  Taurus Express, 207, 211, 214, 218, 229, 230–2, 234, 239, 245–6, 254, 255–6, 274, 281, 303, 324
  and territoriality, 227
  Turco-Syrian railroad, 263–4
  Turkey to Iraq, 261–2
  Turkish priorities, 212–14
Raqqa, 55–6, 316
Ras al-Ayn, 59, 104, 144, 187, 281, 316
Rauf Pasha, 42
re-bordering *see* de-bordering and re-bordering
rebels and rebellions, 35–6, 52, 53–5, 65, 84, 97–9, 105, 111, 190, 212, 242, 243, 315

refugees, 4, 6, 19, 27, 32, 60, 68, 71, 72–122, 227, 317, 325–6
  agency, 106, 113–22
  anti-refugee discourses, 115–17
  Armenians, 100–1
  bordering the Middle East, 78–100
  camps, 74, 109
  Christian, 72
  diplomatic and public pressure on, 118
  and economic development, 101–4, 107–8
  forced emigrations, 95–6, 98, 114–15
  Jewish, 72
  Kurds, 84
  land distribution, 102, 107–8
  and the League of Nations, 76–7, 78, 96, 100, 107–8
  Migrants Commission (Ottoman), 77
  othering and borderland ordering, 78, 93–100, 116, 121
  post-WWI policies, 77–8
  protection of, 99–100
  recruitment into supplementary forces, 35, 60–1n, 74–5, 81, 104–5, 109
  and relief and colonialism, 100–12
religion, 3–4, 12, 13, 17, 54–5, 61–2, 64, 90, 108–10, 161–5, 227
  ethno-religious division policies, 120
revisionism, 240, 247, 257
  small nation revisionism, 265–76
Reynolds, Michael, 51
rinderpest, 171–4
Roshwald, Ariel, 289
routes
  Aleppo–Deir ez-Zor, 225–6
  Aleppo–Mosul, 216
  Baghdad–Damascus, 164, 201–2
  bandits and brigands, 201–3
  Nusaybin–Mosul trail, 220–1
  old Roman road, 220
  for pilgrimage, 163–5, 221

Rowanduz, 36, 49, 60, 61, 226
Royal Air Force, 47, 81, 195
Russia, 48; *see also* Soviet Union

Sack, Robert, 93
Sahlins, Peter, 6
Said, Nuri, 105, 113–14, 247
Said, Shaykh, 65, 84, 97, 98, 99, 102, 190, 212
Sami, Bakir, 46
San Remo conference, 11, 14
Saraçoğlu, Şükrü, 249, 261, 264
Sasoon, 144
Satia, Priya, 186
Schayegh, Cyrus, 26, 136, 244, 284, 323
Schofield, Clive, 136
Schofield, Richard, 80
Scott, James C., 126
Second World War, 26, 34, 150–1, 187–8, 197, 207, 208, 220, 224, 225, 227, 230–1, 240, 243, 324, 325–6
  allied invasion of Syria, June 1941, 249, 288–9
  in the borderlands, 250–7
  and economic development, 282–4
  illegal arms distribution, 250–3
  impact on regulatory and surveillance administration, 274–5
  Mediterranean blockade and its effects, 170, 218, 220, 281, 285–93
  Middle East as a peripheral theatre, 244–5
  Middle Eastern instability, 246–50
  military presence, economic effects of, 299–301, 307–9, 312–13
  railroads, use of, 245–6, 249, 253–5, 274, 286
  Turkish army deserters, 253
Seikaly, Sherene, 283
self-determination, 9, 41, 51–2, 55, 62–3, 70, 106, 109–10, 272, 320

Sèvres, Treaty of, 3, 41–2, 48–9, 59, 240, 273
Shahin (tribe), 295
Shammar (tribe), 202–3
Shia Muslims, 99
Shils, Edward, 16
Sidqi, Bakr, 114, 218
Siirt, 144
Silvan, 144, 161
Simele, 114
Sinjar (Jabal), 74, 79, 87, 89–92, 111, 112, 136, 146–7
Şırnak, 144
Sivas Congress, 43, 52
Siverek, 144
Sluglett, Peter, 49
smallpox, 191, 192, 197
smuggling and contraband, 6, 7, 21, 25, 126–7, 128, 130, 134, 193, 304, 325–6
  arrested, wounded and killed, numbers of, 145
  and border governance consolidation, 137–48
  collusion of borderlanders, 146–7
  compared with informal trade, 285
  contraband routes, 142–4, **143**
  and corruption, 305–7
  effects on Turkey, 141–2, 144–7
  food supplies, 277, 281
  gold, 304–5
  livestock, 304–5, 310–12
  networks, 142, 144
  punishments for, 142, 145
  railroads, use of, 233–4, 236
  special courts, 142
  of weapons, 252–3
Soane, E. B., 63
sovereignty, 6, 21, 22, 25, 70, 97, 160
  territorial sovereignty, 10, 11, 320
  see also territoriality

Soviet Union, 240, 242–4, 270–1, 273, 274
Spears, Edward, 250, 289–90
state formation, 5, 6, 7, 283, 326
  and borders/borderlands, 19–26
  in the Middle East, 9–19
state-social relations, 16–19, 23, 26
structuralism, 7, 16
Suez Canal, 222, 245, 285
Sufism, 162, 166, 167, 193
Sulaimaniya, 44, 60, 61, 63–4, 99, 269
Sunni Muslims, 99
Süreyya Bey, Mehmet, 180
surveillance, 133, 134, 145, 233, 254, 274–5, 303
Sykes-Picot Agreement, 9, 10
Syria, 1–2, 3, 4, 41, 44, 45, 55–6, 72, 141, 218, 220, 224, 247, 249, 254, 270
  agricultural production, 294–6
  allied invasion of, June 1941, 249, 288–9
  and animal diseases, 171–2
  borders with Turkey and Iraq, **8**, 29, 51, 57, 70, 78–9, 84, 89–93, 96, 119–21, 134, 302–3
  delimitation procedures, 86–7
  French divisions, 99
  French economic programme, 101–4, 139
  health policies, 170
  Kurdish immigration, 297–8
  national identity, 116
  and nomads, 183–5
  public health, 186–7
  refugees, 100–3, 115, 116, 227
  revolt of 2011, 315
  rumours of Turkish annexation of northern Syria, 239
  and smuggling, 147–8
  and Turkey, 84, 139
  see also Greater Syria

Syrian–Arab Congress, 13
Syrian Desert, 182–4

Tainsh, Ramsay, 216–17
Tajer, Nassim, 75–6
Talat Pasha, 42
tariffs *see* customs policies/posts
Tauber, Eliezer, 52
Tel Abyad, 281
Tel Afar, 136
Tel Kotchek, 200–1, 203, 208–9, 210, 217, 218, 220, 223, 224, 232, **233**, 249, 252, 254, 277
Tel Rumailan, 89
Tel Ziwan, 208, 214, 217–18, 223, 254, 281
territoriality, 10, 23, 39, 40–1, 115, 122, 128, 166, 284, 324–5
  and identity along borderlands, discourses on, 51–9
  and railroads, 227
  see also sovereignty
Thompson, Elizabeth, 283, 294
Thrace, 44, 95
Tilly, Charles, 39, 321
tourism, 226
Trabzon, 144
trachoma, 162, 171, 176–7, 190, 192
trade, 27, 69, 90, 126, 128, 138, 216, 221–2, 223, 284
  formal and informal international trade, 303–13
  free trade, 141
  informal trade, 284–5
  Mediterranean blockade and its effects, 170, 218, 220, 281, 285–93
  monopolies, 140
  between Turkey and Iraq, 286–7
Transjordan, 3, 4, 172, 180–1
transportation
  complementarity of railroad and motor facilities, 225–6
  of goods, 221–2, 223–5
  of livestock, 230, 236
  motor companies, 225
  motor roads, 207–8, 221–2, 225–6
  wartime lack of, 211, 225
  see also railroads; routes
Truett, Samuel, 7, 28
Tur Abdin, 111
Turkey, 11, 18–19, 118, 270, 316
  and Anatolia, 95
  army deserters, 253
  border delimitation, 80–6, **82**
  borders and borderlands, 44
  borders with Syria and Iraq, **8**, 29, 47, 49–50, 51, 57, 59, 70, 78–87, **82**, 96, 119–21, 134, 257–63, 279
  and Britain, 46–51, 247, 259–62, 275, 279
  citizenship, 97
  Constitution, 97
  distrust of southern neighbours, 79
  economic challenges and policies, 137–8, 213, 284
  exploitation of health issues, 166, 171–2, 189–90, 192
  forced emigrations, 95–6, 98
  and France, 1, 3, 45–6, 56–7, 70, 82–4, 247, 257–8, 301–2
  health policies, 176–7, 178–9, 189–92
  historiography, 44
  homogenisation, 95–7, 190
  irredentism, 257–64
  and Italy, 246–7, 257
  Kurdish amnesty, 103
  and the MESC, 290–1
  military operations in Iraq, 317
  mobilisation, 296
  nationalism, 44, 54–5, 189
  neutrality, 259, 270, 279, 296
  and nomads, 171–3
  protectionism, 141

railroad priorities, 212–14
Republic of, 54
smuggling, effects of, 141–2, 144–7
and the Soviet Union, 240, 242–3, 270, 274
and Syria, 1–2, 4, 84, 257–63
trade with Iraq, 286–7
Turkish–Kurdish unity notion, 64
Village Laws, 189
Turner, Frederick J., 22

United States, 113, 273, 274, 287
Urfa, 52, 56, 57, 59, 96, 144, 149, 172, 176
Uvarov, Boris P., 179–80, 195

Van, 61, 144
Versailles, Treaty of, 209–10
violence, 6–7, 17, 35–71, 41–51, 59–64, 113, 117–18, 320
  challenging post-war settlements, 41–51
  forced emigrations, 95–6, 98, 99
  identity and territoriality along borderlands, discourses on, 51–9
  interactions between borderlanders and states' discourses and strategies, 64–71

massacres, 35–6, 60, 68–9, 75, 114, 117–18, 123
murders, 123–5, 128, 129
Southern Kurdistan, 59–64
Viranşehir, 144
Vitalis, Robert, 282, 293

Wahhabism, 3–4
Watenpaugh, Keith D., 100, 106
Weber, David J., 22
Weberianism, 16, 17, 322
White, Benjamin T., 115, 136
Wilson, Woodrow, 51–2, 55, 106, 273
women, 155–9, 230, 232, 298–9, 301

Yamurk Valley, 89
Yazidis, 74, 90–1, 98, 111, 316

Zakho, 35, 60, 68, 82, 136, 281
Zaza, Noureddine, 198, 232
Zionism, 117
  immigration, 75–6
Zürcher, Erik J., 54

EU representative:
Easy Access System Europe
Mustamäe tee 50, 10621 Tallinn, Estonia
Gpsr.requests@easproject.com

www.ingramcontent.com/pod-product-compliance
Lightning Source LLC
Chambersburg PA
CBHW050159240426
43671CB00013B/2178